Law of Defamation

(Release #3, 2/90)

The Clark Boardman
Entertainment & Communications Law Library

Lindey on Entertainment, Publishing and the Arts
by Alexander Lindey and various contributors

Entertainment, Publishing and the Arts Handbook
by various contributors

Cable Television and Other Nonbroadcast Video: Law and Policy
by Daniel L. Brenner and Monroe E. Price

The Rights of Publicity and Privacy
by J. Thomas McCarthy

Law of Defamation
by Rodney A. Smolla

Law of Defamation

by Rodney A. Smolla

Clark Boardman Company, Ltd.
New York, New York

(Release #3, 2/90)

Library of Congress Cataloging-in-Publication Data
Smolla, Rodney A.
Law of defamation.
Includes index.
1. Libel and slander—United States. I. Title.
KF1266.S56 1986 346.7303'4 86-14687
347.30634
ISBN 0-87632-512-6

About the Author

Rodney A. Smolla is the James G. Cutler Professor of Constitutional Law and Director of the Institute of Bill of Rights Law at the College of William and Mary, Marshall-Wythe School of Law. He holds a B.A. degree from Yale and a J.D. degree from Duke University. Author of *Suing the Press,* a highly acclaimed 1986 publication, Professor Smolla has also published numerous articles on constitutional law topics in general and libel, media, and first amendment issues in particular. He lectures extensively and has sat on panels and delivered papers before such institutions as the U.S. Civil Rights Commission, the United States Senate Judiciary Committee Subcommittee on the Constitution, the Practising Law Institute, and the Institute for the Study of Bill of Rights Law, at the College of William and Mary. During 1988 he served as Project Director of the Libel Reform Project of the Annenberg Washington Program for Communications Policy Studies, of Northwestern University, and he has continued his affiliation as a Fellow of the Annenberg Washington Program. In 1989, he was appointed by former Chief Justice Warren Burger to the position of Reporter to the Bill of Rights Advisory Committee to the Commission on the Bicentennial of the United States Constitution.

Preface

In the very last paragraph of *The Adventures of Huckleberry Finn,* Huck reflects on his literary travails, saying: "[T]here ain't nothing more to write about, and I am rotten glad of it, because if I'd a knowed what a trouble it was to make a book I wouldn't a tackled it and ain't agoing to no more." Huck surely spoke for all authors at the final stage of a project; as the last infinitives are united, cites rechecked, and proofs proofed, the prospect that finally "there ain't nothing more to write about" will make anyone "rotten glad." Huck got a little help of course, from "Mr. Mark Twain," who could not keep Huck's vow, and kept on writing until he died. And Huck paid his own tribute to Twain in the very first paragraph of the *Adventures,* describing Twain as an author who "told the truth, mainly."

In this treatise on the law of defamation, I have also tried to tell the truth, mainly. The task is not easy, for the "truth" about this extraordinarily complex subject is very often elusive, and is always changing. The cut-off date for research was September 1, 1985. A brief discussion of one very recent 1986 Supreme Court case, *Philadelphia Newspapers, Inc. v. Hepps,* dealing with the plaintiff's burden of proof on the falsity issue, was inserted in Chapter 5 just as the book was going to press. I have tried to project some of what the future may hold, emphasizing, for example, the implications of the Supreme Court's 1985 decision in *Dun & Bradstreet, Inc. v. Greenmoss Builders, Inc.*, and discussing the growing interest in alternate remedies. Nonetheless, the law of defamation has been volatile ever since *New York Times Co. v. Sullivan,* and will remain so for the foreseeable future, insuring that no treatise will ever do much more than tell the truth, "mainly."

For an author, the life of a book may often be more wrapped up in the story of the people who provided support during the process than in the finished product. That, at any rate, is true for me: this book is dedicated to the family and friends who really made it possible, most specially my wife Linda A. Malone, and my parents Richard and Harriet Smolla.

Rodney A. Smolla

Summary of Contents

Table of Contents

PART I
Defamation

CHAPTER 1
Overview

CHAPTER 2
The Public Figure/Private Figure Dichotomy

CHAPTER 3
Fault Requirements for Defamation

CHAPTER 4
Defamatory Meaning

CHAPTER 5
Truth as a Constitutional Defense

CHAPTER 6
Opinion and Fair Comment

CHAPTER 7

Special Harm—Libel and Slander Per Se Rules

CHAPTER 8
Common Law Privileges

CHAPTER 9
Damages and Other Remedies

PART II
Invasion of Privacy and Related Torts

CHAPTER 10
Invasion of Privacy

CHAPTER 11
Emotional Distress, Injurious Falsehood, and Negligent Publication

PART III
Litigation, Counseling, and Strategy

CHAPTER 12
Litigation

CHAPTER 13
Counseling and Strategy

CHAPTER 14
Insurance

PART I

Defamation

CHAPTER 1

Overview

§ 1.01 Introduction

The Book of Proverbs states: "A good name is rather to be chosen than great riches."[1] Moral injunctions as old as the Ten Commandments pronounce "Thou shalt not bear false witness against thy neighbour."[2] Shakespeare wrote:

> Good name in man and woman, dear my lord,
> Is the immediate jewel of their souls:
> Who steals my purse steals trash; tis something, nothing,
> 'Twas mine, 'tis his, and has been slave to thousands;
> But he that filches from me my good name
> Robs me of that which not enriches him,
> And makes me poor indeed.[3]

In the words of Supreme Court Justice Potter Stewart, words that continue to be cited with approval by the Supreme Court, the individual's right to protection of his own good name "reflects no more than our basic concept of the essential dignity and worth of every human being — a concept at the root of any decent system of ordered liberty. The protection of private personality, like the protection of life itself, is left primarily to the individual States under the Ninth and Tenth Amendments. But this does not mean that the right is entitled to any less recognition by this Court as a basic of our constitutional system."[4]

This great tradition of reverence for reputation, however, has never been matched with consistency or clarity in the legal system's protection of reputation. The words of Baron Pollock still apply: "No branch of the law has been more fertile of litigation than this (whether plaintiffs

---

1 Prov. 22:1.

2 Exod. 20:16.

3 *Othello,* act III, scene iii, lines 158-64, in Complete Works of William Shakespeare: The Cambridge Text 955, 971 (1980). It is worth pointing out, however, that Iago, the character who utters these famous words, speaks of reputation elsewhere in the play in less reverent terms:

> As I am an honest man, I thought you had received
> some bodily wound; there is more sense in that than
> in reputation. Reputation is an idle and most
> false imposition; oft got without merit and lost
> without deserving. You have lost no reputation at
> all, unless you repute yourself such a loser.

Id. at act II, scene iii, lines 261-66.

4 Rosenblatt v. Baer, 383 U.S. 75, 92 (1966)(Stewart, J., concurring). Justice Stewart's words were quoted with approval in the Court's landmark decision in Gertz v. Robert Welch, Inc., 418 U.S. 323, 341 (1974), and most recently in the Court's reinterpretation of *Gertz,* in Dun & Bradstreet, Inc. v. Greenmoss Builders, Inc., 105 S. Ct. 2939 (1985).

be more moved by a keen sense of honor, or by the delight of carrying on personal controversies under the protection and with the solemnities of civil justice), nor has any been more perplexed with minute and barren distinctions."[5] As the Prosser treatise on torts explains, "[i]t must be confessed at the beginning that there is a great deal in the law of defamation which makes no sense."[6]

For the practitioner attempting to make sense of the modern law of defamation, two dominant historical facts are essential to know. First, much of the law of defamation today remains the creature of state tort law,[7] and much of that state tort law is in turn the descendant of centuries of haphazard, byzantine, and often baffling evolution, "developed according to no particular aim or plan."[8] This common law evolutionary process continues in each state, constantly making adjustments to the basic tort rules governing defamation. Second, beginning with the 1964 decision in *New York Times Co. v. Sullivan,*[9] the Supreme Court "constitutionalized" a substantial portion of the law of defamation, holding that the first amendment places limitations on the defamation rules created by the states. In the two decades since *New York Times,* the first amendment rules governing defamation have undergone a number of drastic changes,[10] the most recent of which have tended to relax somewhat the constitutional restrictions on the states, permitting them greater freedom to return to pre-*New York Times* common law rules.

The common law and constitutional law development of defamation rules thus continue side by side. Throughout this volume, common law and constitutional law principles are thus compared, contrasted, and where possible, integrated and reconciled.

---

[5] Pollock, Law of Torts 243 (13th ed. 1929).

[6] W. Keeton, D. Dobbs, R. Keeton & D. Owen, Prosser and Keeton on Torts § 111, at 771 (5th ed. 1984).

[7] *See, e.g.,* Dun & Bradstreet, Inc. v. Greenmoss Builders, Inc., 105 S. Ct. 2939 (1985); Gertz v. Robert Welch, Inc., 418 U.S. 323, 341 (1974).

[8] Prosser and Keeton, *supra* note 6, § 111, at 772.

[9] 376 U.S. 254 (1964).

[10] *See, infra* §§ 2.01-2.04 and 3.01-3.05.

§ 1.02 History

[1] Origins of Defamation Law

Centuries ago the remedy for defamation was to cut out the offender's tongue.[11] This barbaric pre-thirteenth century remedy gave way to the jurisdition of the ecclesiastical courts, which treated slander as a spiritual offense, punishing the sin with appropriate penance.[12] The sinner would be wrapped in a white shroud and required to kneel in public, holding a lighted candle and acknowledging his false witness before the priest and parish wardens, begging the pardon of God and the injured party.[13] By the late sixteenth century the common law courts had begun to assert jurisdiction for defamation, and by the seventeenth century the notorious Court of Star Chamber, in a separate strain of development, began to punish the offense of political libel.[14] The Star Chamber's prosecutions originated to suppress political sedition, but were later extended to encompass libels of a nonpolitical nature.[15] When the Star Chamber was, happily, abolished, jurisdiction for all defamation passed in turn to the common law courts. But by this time the die was cast: The law of defamation would forever be "a forest of complexities, overgrown with anomalies, inconsistencies, and perverse regidities,"[16] a veritable "fog of fictions, inferences, and presumptions."[17]

[2] Ambivalence Toward Defamation

In America, the history of illogical common law rules was further complicated by the differences between American and English cul-

---

11 *See* Lovell, *The "Reception" of Defamation by the Common Law,* 15 Vand. L. Rev. 1051, 1053 (1962)(citing a passage from the Laws of Alfred the Great, compiled in about 880 A.D.: "If anyone is guilty of public slander, and it is proved against him, it is to be compensated with no lighter penalty than the cutting off of his tongue.").

12 *See* Eaton, *The American Law of Defamation Through* Gertz v. Robert Welch, Inc. *and Beyond: An Analytical Primer,* 61 U. Va. L. Rev. 1349, 1350 (1975).

13 *See* L. Eldredge, *The Law of Defamation* § 3, at 5 (1978); Lovell, *supra* note 11, at 1055.

14 *See generally* Veeder, *The History and Theory of the Law of Defamation* (parts 1 & 2), 3 Colum. L. Rev. 546 (1903), 4 Colum L. Rev. 33 (1904).

15 *See* Prosser and Keeton, *supra* note 6, § 111, at 772; Eaton, *supra* note 12, at 1350.

16 Eaton, *supra* note 12, at 1350.

17 Coleman v. MacLennan, 78 Kan. 711, 740, 98 P. 281, 291 (1908).

ture.[18] The American solicitude for freedom of speech and the press, even before the United States Supreme Court intervened to constitutionalize much of the field, left many American courts wary of the memory of the Star Chamber, timid in dealing with defamation.[19] Libel litigation was perceived by many as almost un-American.[20] "A libeled American," Zechariah Chafee once wrote, "prefers to vindicate himself by steadily pushing forward his career and not by hiring a lawyer to talk in a courtroom."[21] Perhaps the American ambivalence towards defamation was related in part to a larger theme in earlier American tort law that looked askance at attempts to compensate persons for what was essentially "psychic" injury. Calvert Magruder, for example, writing in 1936, noted that "the common law has been reluctant to recognize the interest in one's peace of mind as deserving of general and independent legal protection."[22] Magruder approved of this reluctance, arguing that it would be quixotic for the law to pursue the general securing of peace of mind: "Against a large part of the frictions and irritations and clashing of temperaments incident to participation in a community life, a certain toughening of the mental hide is a better protection than the law could ever be."[23] Writing in 1942, David Reisman again seemed to suggest that there was something almost un-American about pursuing a libel suit. He argued that protection of reputation is intrinsically unimportant in American captialist culture:

> [T]he American attitude towards reputation is unique. In Europe, where pre-capitalist concepts of honor, family, and privacy survive, reputation is a weighty matter not only for the remnants of the nobility who still fight duels to protect it, but for all the middle groups who flood the courts with petty slander litigations as we flood ours with automobile and other negligence actions. But where tradition is capitalistic rather than feudalistic, reputation is only an asset, "good will," not an attribute to be sought after for its intrinsic value. And in the United States these business attitudes

---

[18] *See* Reisman, *Democracy and Defamation: Control of Group Libel,* 42 Colum. L. Rev. 727, 730 (1942).

[19] *See generally* Prosser and Keeton, *supra* note 6, §111, at 772; Leflar, *Legal Liability for the the Exercise of Free Speech,* 10 Ark. L. Rev. 155 (1956); Pound, *Equitable Relief Against Defamation and Injuries to Personality,* 29 Harv. L. Rev. 640 (1916); Shientag, *From Seditious Libel to Freedom of the Press,* 11 Brooklyn L. Rev. 125 (1942).

[20] *See* Smolla, *Let the Author Beware: The Rejuvenation of the American Law of Libel,* 132 U. Pa. L. Rev. 1, 17 (1983).

[21] Z. Chafee, Government and Mass Communications, 106-07 (1947).

[22] Magruder, *Mental and Emotional Disturbance in the Law of Torts,* 49 Harv. L. Rev. 1033, 1035 (1936).

[23] *Id.*

have colored social relations. The law of libel is consequently unimportant.[24]

The irony of this attitude was that while as a culture America did not seem particularly disposed toward the aggressive use of defamation litigation, as a strict matter of legal doctrine the law of defamation during this period was quite inviting to the plaintiff, for it was essentially a strict liability tort with most rules stacked in the plaintiff's favor.[25]

[3] The Modern Defamation Explosion

However much Americans once seemed reluctant to pursue defamation suits, the landscape in recent years has changed dramatically. Despite the imposition of new first amendment barriers to recovery, the American law of defamation has exploded in the last decade. America has developed a new fascination with defamation: More suits are brought and American juries, the legal system's most reliable barometer of changing attitudes, have on the whole proved extremely sympathetic to plaintiffs both in terms of the propensity to decide in their favor and in the size of damages awards.[26] These changes, which have been monitored by the Libel Defense Resource Center,[27] indicate that the law of defamation is and probably will remain an area of substantial litigation activity.[28]

---

24 Reisman, *supra* note 18, at 730.

25 *See infra* § 1.03[1].

26 *See generally* Franklin, *Suing the Media for Libel: A Litigation Study,* 1981 Am. B. Found. Research J. 795; Franklin, *Winners and Losers and Why: A Study of Defamation Litigation,* 1980 Am. B. Found. Research J. 455; Smolla, *supra* note 20, at 1-11.

27 The Libel Defense Resource Center (LDRC), a New York based information clearinghouse organized by media groups to monitor developments in defamation and invasion of privacy law, is the best source for up-to-date statistical data on the current state of such litigation, which is available through periodic bulletins and surveys. The LDRC is located at 708 Third Ave., 32d Floor, New York, New York 10017.

28 The most recent LDRC data as of this writing is summarized very cogently by James C. Goodale in "Survey of Recent Media Verdicts, Their Disposition on Appeal, and Media Defense Costs," in Media Insurance and Risk Management 1985 (J. Lankenau, ed.)(Practising Law Institute 1985).

§ 1.03 Cause of Action Prior to the *New York Times* Decision

[1] Strict Liability Tort

Prior to the intervention of the Supreme Court in *New York Times Co. v. Sullivan*,[29] the American common law of defamation was a strict liability tort.[30] American law and English law were still essentially identical; in the words of Justice Holmes: "Whatever a man publishes, he publishes at his peril."[31]

[2] Basic Elements

The original *Restatement of Torts* characterized the basic cause of action for defamation with deceptive simplicity:

> To create liability for defamation there must be an unprivileged publication of false and defamatory matter of another which
> (a) is actionable irrespective of special harm, or
> (b) if not so actionable, is the legal cause of special harm to the other.[32]

The first *Restatement* defined as defamatory any statement that "tends so to harm the reputation of another as to lower him in the estimation of the community or to deter third persons from associating or dealing with him."[33] Damages at common law were "presumed;" no "actual harm" to reputation was needed to support a prima facie case: "To be defamatory, it is not necessary that the communication actually cause harm to another's reputation or deter third persons from associat-

---

[29] 376 U.S. 254 (1964).

[30] *See* Eldredge, *supra* note 13, § 5, at 15.

[31] Peck v. Tribune Co., 214 U.S. 185, 189 (1909) (quoting from Lord Mansfield, in Rex v. Woodfall, Lofft 776, 781, 98 Eng. Rep. 914, 916 (1774)). *See also* Washington Post v. Chaloner, 250 U.S. 290, 294 (1919)("Considering the wide circulation of present-day newspapers and their power for doing injury to reputation, it is highly important that the ancient doctrine 'Whatever a man publishes, he publishes at his peril' should be strictly enforced.").

[32] Restatement of Torts § 558 (1938). It is worth noting that Robert Sack has quite legitimately made the same accusation of deceptive simplicity concerning the summary of the elements of the defamation cause of action in the second *Restatment*, Restatement (Second) of Torts § 558 (1977). *See* R. Sack, Libel, Slander, and Related Problems § II.1., at 40 (1980).

[33] Restatement of Torts § 559 (1938).

ing or dealing with him. Its character depends on its general tendency to have such an effect."[34]

Once the plaintiff demonstrated the defamatory character of the speech, and that the defendant published it, the plaintiff's job of putting forth a prima facie case was essentially over. The plaintiff was not required to show that the statement was false. The plaintiff had to plead falsity, but not prove it; truth was an affirmative defense which the defendant bore the burden of pleading and proving.[35] No fault or "malice" of any kind was required. Although malice, in the sense of spite or ill will, was required in defamation actions prior to 1825, in that year, in *Bromage v. Prosser*,[36] the common law rule was established that from the mere publishing of the defamatory statement malice "is conclusively implied and the defendant cannot rebut it."[37]

Once the defendant established a prima facie case, the defendant could avoid liability by proving either substantial truth, or that the statement fell within one of a number of absolute or conditional privileges under common law.[38] A conditional privilege was lost if the defendant published with malice, or if the defendant either knew the statement was false or acted unreasonably in believing it to be true.[39]

§ 1.04 The Common Law Libel/Slander Distinction

[1] In General

Defamation actually consists of the twin torts of "libel" and "slander." The short and simple distinction between the terms is that libel is defamation by written or printed words, or by the embodiment of the communication in some tangible or physical form,[40] while slander con-

---

34 *Id.*, comment d.

35 *See* Eldredge, *supra* note 13, § 6, at 26; Eaton, *supra* note 12, at 1353. Truth was recognized as a "complete defense." Restatement of Torts § 582 (1938).

36 107 Eng. Rep. 1051 (K.B. 1825).

37 *Id.* at 1055.

38 *See* Restatement of Torts §§ 582-598 (1938).

39 *Id.*, §§ 600, 601; Eaton, *supra* note 12, at 1354.

40 *See, e.g.*, Burton v. Crowell Publishing Co., 82 F.2d 154 (2d Cir. 1936); Ilitzky v. Goodman, 57 Ariz. 216, 112 P.2d 860, 862 (1941); Spence v. Funk, 396 A.2d 967, 970 (Del. 1978); Ostrowe v. Lee, 175 N.E. 505, 256 N.Y. 36 (1931); Merle v. Sociological Research Film Corp., 166 A.D. 376, 152 N.Y.S. 829 (1915).

sists of communication of a defamatory statement by spoken words, or by transitory gestures.[41]

[2] Special Problems in Applying the Distinction

The distinction between libel and slander is often difficult to apply, resulting in a series of specialized (and often arbitrary) rules. The oral reading of a defamatory statement that is written down is treated as libel rather than slander, even if a third party only hears and does not see the writing, or does not know that the writing is being read.[42] If the defendant makes an oral statement that is intended to be and is reduced to writing—e.g., dictation to a stenographer or a telephone call to a news reporter in the expectation that what is said on the phone will be published in the paper—the defamation is libel, not slander.[43] Libel has been held to include such tangible embodiments as pictures, signs, statutes, and motion pictures,[44] "and even conduct carrying a defamatory imputation, such as hanging the plaintiff in effigy [or] erecting gallows before his door."[45] On the other hand, transitory gestures, such as the signals of the deaf, or the act of a storekeeper publicly stopping a customer to search a shopping bag, are treated as slander.[46]

[3] Policies Underlying the Distinction

The original common law position was to treat libels as more serious torts than slanders. As Professor Marc Franklin has observed, the "distinction arose when relatively few people could read and the written word was awesome and thus more credible."[47] The written word was thought to leave a more indelible blot on the plaintiff's reputation, was likely to reach a larger audience, and arguably evidenced greater delib-

---

[41] *See, e.g.*, Simpson v. Oil Transfer Corp., 75 F. Supp. 819, 822 (D.N.Y. 1948); Aiken v. May, 73 Ga. App. 502, 37 S.E.2d 225, 226 (1946); Foley v. Hoffman, 188 Md. 273, 52 A.2d 476, 481 (1947); Woodruff v. Woodruff, 72 N.Y.S. 39, 40, 36 Misc. 15 (1901); Reiman v. Pacific Development Soc., 132 Or. 82, 284 P. 575, 577 (1930).

[42] *See, e.g.*, Bander v. Metropolitan Life Ins. Co., 313 Mass. 337, 47 N.E.2d 595 (1943); Ohio Public Serv. Co. v. Myers, 54 Ohio App. 40, 6 N.E.2d 29 (1934).

[43] *See* Ostrowe v. Lee, 256 N.Y. 36, 175 N.E. 505 (1931); Valentine v. Gonzalez, 190 A.D. 490, 179 N.Y.S. 711 (1920); Christy v. Staufer Publications, Inc., 437 S.W.2d 814 (Tex. Civ. App. 1969).

[44] *See, e.g.*, Thayer v. Worcester Post Co., 284 Mass. 160, 187 N.E. 292 (1933); Merle v. Sociological Research Film Corp., 166 A.D. 376, 152 N.Y.S. 829 (1915).

[45] Prosser and Keeton, *supra* note 6, § 112, at 786.

[46] *See* Bennett v. Norban, 396 Pa. 94, 151 A.2d 476 (1959).

[47] M. Franklin & R. Rabin, Tort Law and Alternatives 874 (3d ed. 1983).

eration and premeditation by the defendant.[48] These policy rationales, however suitable they may once have been, today present more problems than they solve, because modern forms of communication often present as much or more potential for harm when "oral" as when "written."

The *Restatement (Second)*, sensitive to these policies, has broadened the definition of libel to embrace any "form of communication that has the potentially harmful qualities characteristic of written or printed words,"[49] specifying that the factors to be considered in classifying the defamatory speech are "the area of dissemination," the "deliberate and premeditated character of its publication," and the "persistence of the defamation."[50]

[4] Special Definitional Problems

Radio, television, and other forms of computerized or electronic communication may be difficult to categorize under the traditional dichotomy between oral and written communication. Imagine a television or radio broadcast in which a reporter makes a defamatory statement. The communication is "oral," but it may have been heard by 50 million viewers or listeners and may thus be as damaging as a written libel could ever be. Some jurisdictions treat offending radio and television broadcasts as slander[51] and some treat them as libel.[52] Some decisions have held that a statement read from a script and broadcast is libel.[53] Some distinguish between a statement made extemporaneously and one read from a prepared script, calling the defamation slander

---

48 *See* Spence v. Funk, 396 A.2d 967, 970 (Del. 1978).

49 Restatement (Second) of Torts § 568(1)(1977).

50 *Id.*, § 568(3).

51 *See* Arno v. Stewart, 245 Cal. App. 2d 955, 54 Cal. Rptr. 392 (1966). *See generally* Donnelly, *Defamation by Radio: A Reconsideration*, 34 Iowa L. Rev. 12 (1948); Graham, *Defamation and Radio*, 12 Wash. L. Rev. 282 (1937); Remmers, *Recent Legislative Trends in Defamation by Radio*, 64 Harv. L. Rev. 727 (1951).

52 *See* Shor v. Billingsley, 4 Misc. 2d 857, 158 N.Y.S.2d 476 (N.Y. Sup. 1956), *aff'd without opinion*, 4 A.D.2d 1017, 169 N.Y.S.2d 416 (1st Dept. 1957).

53 *See* Charles Parker Co. v. Silver City Crystal Co., 142 Conn. 605, 610-12, 116 A.2d 440 (1955); Sorenson v. Wood, 123 Neb. 348, 353, 243 N.W.82, *appeal dismissed*, 290 U.S. 599 (1932); Landau v. Columbia Broadcasting System, 205 Misc. 357, 128 N.Y.S.2d 254, *aff'd without opinion*, 1 A.D.2d 660, 147 N.Y.S.2d 687 (1954); Hartmann v. Winchell, 296 N.Y. 296, 73 N.E.2d 30 (1947).

when no script exists.[54] (Arguably, even a statement made extemporaneously has been reduced to "tangible form" if it is recorded on tape, either in the studio or by the recipient of the broadcast.) One decision has even adopted a special label, the "defamacast," to describe broadcast defamation, though the case appears to treat such defamation as libel.[55]

The better view, in light of the policies undergirding the common law distinction, is to treat all broadcasts as libel. As the court observed in *Shor v. Billingsley*:[56]

> When account is taken of the vast and far-flung audience reached by radio today—often far greater in number than the readers of the largest metropolitan newspaper, it is evident that the broadcast of scandalous utterances is in general as potentially harmful to the defamed person's reputation as a publication by writing. That defamation by radio, in the absence of a script or transcription, lacks the measure of durability possessed by written libel in no wise lessens its capacity for harm.[57]

The *Restatement (Second) of Torts* follows this more reasonable position, flatly declaring that defamation broadcast on radio or television is libel, whether read from a manuscript or not.[58] The wide dissemination that results from such a broadcast, and the power and impact of the electronic media in contempory American life, makes this position the most logical in light of the policy underlying the libel/slander distinction, which is to treat as libel those communications more likely to be seriously harmful.[59]

Some states have resolved the matter by statute, and the statutory resolutions go both ways. Illinios, for example, treats all defamatory broadcasts as libel.[60] California, on the other hand, in legislation that is

---

[54] *See* Remington v. Bentley, 88 F. Supp. 166 (S.D.N.Y. 1949). The first *Restatement* took the position that: "A libel may be published by broadcasting over the air by means of the radio, if the speaker reads from a prepared manuscript or speaks from written or printed notes on memoranda." Restatement of Torts § 568 comment f (1938).

[55] American Broadcasting-Paramount Theatres, Inc. v. Simpson, 106 Ga. App. 230, 126 S.E.2d 873 (1962).

[56] 4 Misc. 2d 857, 158 N.Y.S.2d 476 (N.Y. Sup. 1956), *aff'd without opinion*, 4 A.D.2d 1017, 169 N.Y.S.2d 416 (1st Dept. 1957).

[57] *Id.*, 158 N.Y.S.2d at 484.

[58] Restatement (Second) of Torts §568A (1977).

[59] *Id.*, comment a.

[60] Ill. Ann. Stat. ch. 38, § 27-1 (1964). The English Defamation Act of 1952 treats broadcasts as libel. 15 & 16 Geo. VI and Eliz. II, c. 66 § 1 (1952).

designedly intended to be protective of the media, treats defamatory broadcasts as slander.[61]

[5] The Special Harm Requirement

The distinction between libel and slander would be nothing more than a quaint vestige of old common law vocabulary if the elements of both torts were identical. In modern defamation law the significance of the libel/slander dichotomy rests in the relevance of that dichotomy to one issue: the requirement that is sometimes imposed that a plaintiff plead and prove "special damages" or "special harm." Special harm is a term of art in defamation law that refers to actual pecuniary loss.[62] (The meaning of special harm and its relation to the libel and slander distinction is discussed in greater detail in Chapter 7 of this volume.)[63] In a nutshell, the prevailing common law position (as discussed *infra*, there are a number of confusing variations among the states) is that the plaintiff in an action for slander must prove special damages, unless the defamation falls within four special categories of "slander per se:"[64] (1) imputation of a serious crime involving moral turpitude;[65] (2) possession of a loathsome disease;[66] (3) an attack on the plaintiff's competency in his business, trade, or profession;[67] or (4) unchastity in a woman.[68] Slanders not falling within these four categories (slanders "per quod") required special damages. Originally all libels were actionable without proof of special harm, but gradually the rule developed that libels in which the defamatory meaning was clear from the face of the words were actionable "per se" without proof of special damages, while libels requiring proof of extrinsic facts to support their defamatory meaning

---

61 Cal. Civ. Code §§ 46, 48.5 (West 1954).

62 *See* Restatement (Second) of Torts § 575 comment b (1977).

63 *See infra* §§ 7.02[1], 7.06-7.07.

64 Prosser and Keeton, *supra* note 6, § 112, at 788.

65 *See* Morris v. Evans, 22 Ga. App. 11, 95 S.E. 385 (1918); Walker v. Tucker, 220 Ky. 363, 295 S.W,138 (1927); Restatement (Second) of Torts § 571 (1977). *See infra* § 7.05[2].

66 There is essentially no modern case law to support this category, and the law would do well to discard it altogether. *See infra* § 7.05[4].

67 *See, e.g.*, Nolan v. Standard Publishing Co., 67 Mont. 212, 216 P. 571 (1923); Dietrich v. Hauser, 45 Misc. 2d 805, 257 N.Y.S.2d 716 (1965); Restatement (Second) of Torts § 573 (1977).

68 *See* Hollman v. Brady, 233 F.2d 877 (9th Cir. 1956); Gnapinsky v. Goldyn, 23 N.J. 243, 128 A.2d 697 (1957).

were considered "per quod," and did require proof of special damages.[69]

These confusing and crude rules operated generally to make libel suits easier to bring than slander suits. Their significance has to some degree been muted by constitutional developments, but the rules—with many further confusing variations—remain operative in most jurisdictions, and are given substantial coverage later in this volume.[70] For overview purposes it is enough to note that the significance of the libel/slander distinction rests in the necessity for proving special harm, and that, broadly speaking, proof of special harm is more often required for slanders than for libels.

§ 1.05 The Constitutionalization of Modern Defamation Law

To complete the overview of contemporary defamation law, it is necessary to outline the major first amendment developements in the field in the last 20 years. Since these developments play a dominant role in modern defamation litigation, they occupy a substantial portion of the material in this book, and are merely summarized briefly in this section. The evolution of first amendment restraints on defamation essentially consists of four stages of evolution, each represented by a landmark Supreme Court decision.

[1] *New York Times Co. v. Sullivan*

New York Times Co. v. Sullivan[71] first brought the first amendment to bear on the law of libel. The decision held that actions by public official plaintiffs must be supported by "actual malice," a constitutional term of art defined as publishing a statement "with knowledge that it was false or with reckless disregard of whether it was false or not."[72]

[2] *Walker* and *Butts*

In the companion cases *Curtis Publishing Co. v. Butts*[73] and *Associated Press v. Walker*[74] the Supreme court extended the actual malice

---

69 *See* Franklin & Rabin, *supra* note 47, at 874-76; Eaton, *supra* note 12, at 1354-55.
70 *See infra* §§7.01-7.08.
71 376 U.S. 254 (1964).
72 *Id.* at 279-80. The *Times* case is discussed at length in § 2.01, *infra*.
73 388 U.S. 130 (1967).
74 388 U.S. 130 (1967).

requirement to plaintiffs who were "public figures."[75]

[3] *Gertz v. Robert Welch, Inc.*

Most of the framework for the modern law of defamation emanates from *Gertz v. Robert Welch, Inc.*,[76] which established the principal dichotomy of contemporary defamation law, the distinction between public official and public figure plaintiffs on the one hand, and private figure plaintiffs on the other.[77] *Gertz* reaffirmed *New York Times, Butts,* and *Walker,* by holding that actual malice was required for public figures and public officials. *Gertz* held, however, that for private figures, states could establish their own standard of liability, so long as they did not impose liability without fault, effectively requiring negligence in all actions.[78] *Gertz* also held that states could not permit recovery of "presumed" or "punitive" damages without proof of actual malice, and that in cases in which actual malice was not demonstrated, proof of "actual harm" (a term not limited to "special" or pecuniary loss, but including general damage to reputation and personal anguish, humiliation, and suffering) was required.[79]

[4] *Dun & Bradstreet, Inc. v. Greenmoss Builders, Inc.*

In a dramatic recent cutback on *Gertz,* the Supreme Court in *Dun & Bradstreet, Inc. v Greenmoss Builders, Inc.*,[80] ruled that the *Gertz* rule restricting awards of presumed and punitive damages to cases in which actual malice is shown does not apply to defamatory statements which "do not involve matters of public concern."[81] In a somewhat opaque and splintered 5 - 4 decision,[82] the Court thus created a major

---

75 *Butts* and *Walker* are discussed in § 2.02, *infra.*

76 418 U.S. 323 (1974).

77 *Gertz* rejected the standard that had been proposed three years earlier by a plurality of the Court in Rosenbloom v. Metromedia, Inc., 403 U.S. 29 (1971), which would have placed the applicability of the actual malice standard on whether the defamatory speech involved matters of "public or general interest," as opposed to whether it was directed toward a private or public person. For a discussion of *Rosenbloom, see infra* § 2.03.

78 418 U.S. at 348.

79 *Id.* at 349-50.

80 105 S. Ct. 2939 (1985). The *Dun & Bradstreet* decision is discussed at length *infra* §§3.01-3.05.

81 105 S. Ct. at 2941, 2946.

82 The judgment of the Court was announced by Justice Powell, in an opinion in which Justices Rehnquist and O'Connor joined. Chief Justice Burger and Justice White each wrote opinions concurring in the judgment. Justice Brennan, joined by Justices Marshall, Blackmun, and Stevens, dissented.

revision of *Gertz*, returning at least a portion of the law of defamation that had apparently been "constitutionalized" back to its common law status. Two Justices in the majority, Chief Justice Burger and Justice White, even went so far as to suggest reexamining and overruling *New York Times Co. v. Sullivan.*[83] The precise scope of *Dun & Bradstreet* remains unclear; it will take years for its implications to evolve fully. As discussed subsequently, the two principal questions it poses are (1) whether *all* the *Gertz* rules, including the no liability without fault rule, are completely outside of first amendment restrictions when the speech is not of "public concern," or whether the case is limited to the presumed and punitive damages issues; and (2) how courts are to define what types of speech fall within the definition of "matters of public concern."[84]

§ 1.06 Protection of Reputation—Purposes

The general regard in Anglo-American culture for "reputation" was discussed in the opening section. It is possible, however, to identify a number of "subcomponents" to the functions served by legal protection for defamation, and it is useful to summarize those subcomponents for the purpose of helping to think more clearly about the constant trade-offs between reputational and free expression interests that this area poses.

[1] Protection of Relational Interests

"Society has a pervasive and strong interest in preventing and redressing attacks upon reputation."[85] The law of defamation is largely aimed at preventing wrongful disruption of the "relational interest" that an individual has in maintaining personal esteem in the eyes of others.[86] Professor David Anderson had recognized four distinct types of relational interests protected by defamation:

(1) the protection of existing relations with third persons;
(2) protection of future relations with third persons;

---

[83] *See* 105 S. Ct. at 2948 (Burger, C.J., concurring), and 105 S. Ct. at 2950-53 (White, J., concurring).

[84] *See infra* §§ 3.02-3.05.

[85] Rosenblatt v. Baer, 383 U.S. 75, 86 (1966).

[86] *See* Green, *Relational Interests*, 31 Ill. L. Rev. 35, 36 (1936).

(3) protection of an existing general "public image"; and
(4) prevention of a negative public image for one with no previous public image.[87]

[2] Compensation for Economic Injury

Some defamation produces tangible pecuniary injury, such as lost employment or diminished business. In such instances the law of defamation performs a compensation function indistinguishable from that of any other tort.

[3] Compensation for Emotional Injury

The orthodoxy has always been that the primary function of the law of defamation is to protect the relational interest in loss of reputation, rather than to compensate for the emotional disturbance caused by the defamation,[88] which was left primarily to the law of privacy and infliction of emotional distress.[89] Nevertheless, compensation for embarrassment, mental anguish, or humilation is permitted, either as a form of "parasitic" recovery after reputational damage is shown,[90] or as a free-standing basis of recovery in its own right.[91] In at least a subsidiary sense, therefore, the modern law of defamation serves as an adjunct to the privacy and emotional distress torts in compensating for psychic injury.[92]

[4] Promotion of Human Dignity

One of the major functions of modern tort law is the promotion of human dignity "by discouraging the violation of an individual's personal or psychological integrity."[93] As the Supreme Court has several times

---

87 Anderson, *Reputation, Compensation, and Proof,* 25 Wm. & Mary L. Rev. 747, 764-66 (1984). Professor Anderson's categories are discussed later in connection with proving reputational damage. *See generally* Chapter 9, *infra.*

88 *See* Smolla, *supra* note 20, at 18; Wade, *Defamation and the Right of Privacy,* 15 Vand. L. Rev. 1093, 1094 (1962).

89 *See infra* §§ 10.01, 12.01.

90 *See* Gobin v. Globe Publishing Co., 232 Kan. 1, 649 P.2d 1239 (1982).

91 *See* Time, Inc. v. Firestone, 424 U.S. 448 (1976).

92 *See* Probert, *Defamation, A Camouflage of Psychic Interests: The Beginning of a Behavioral Analysis,* 15 Vand. L. Rev. 1173 (1962).

93 Ingber, *Defamation: A Conflict Between Reason and Decency,* 65 Va. L. Rev. 785, 791 (1979).

emphasized,[94] the law of defamation is designed to protect human dignity, a purpose it accomplishes by providing a civilized forum for an official declaration that the attack on the victim was undeserved, by imposing an economic penalty on the wrongdoer, and by providing compensation for loss.[95]

[5] The Deterrent Function

The law of defamation serves an important social interest as a deterrent on the publication of false and injurious speech.[96] This deterrent function is best exemplified in cases involving the award of punitive damages. Of all the functions served by the law of defamation, this is perhaps the most controversial and problematic, for it tends to conflict directly with free expression values, particularly because of the danger that juries may exact such punishment primarily against unpopular causes and ideas, punishing the speaker more for what he stands for than for the real harm in what he said.[97]

[6] The Check and Balance Function

In the context of media speech, the law of defamation serves one final social function: it provides a check and balance on the media's great power by opening up the media's news-gathering and decision-making processes to public scrutiny and accountability. Although the best cure for "bad" speech is counterspeech, contemporary American society is simply not willing to let corrective speech act as the only restraint on media power; the law of defamation is one of the few tether lines on the press, which has emerged as an American institution with enormous influence. This function of the law of defamation was given its greatest impetus by *Herbert v. Lando*,[98] in which the Supreme Court held that plaintiffs could use discovery to explore directly the editorial

---

[94] *See* Rosenblatt v. Baer, 383 U.S. 75, 92 (1966) (Stewart, J., concurring)(defamation protects "essential dignity and worth of every human being"), *quoted with approval in* Dun & Bradstreet, Inc. v. Greenmoss Builders, Inc., 105 S. Ct. 2939, 2945 (1985); Gertz v. Robert Welch, Inc., 418 U.S. 323, 341 (1974).

[95] *See* Ingber, *supra* note 93, at 791-92.

[96] Eldredge, *supra* note 13, § 3, at 6.

[97] *See* Van Alstyne, *First Amendment Limitations on Recovery from the Press—An Extended Comment on "The Anderson Solution,"* 25 Wm. & Mary L. Rev. 793, 801-09 (1984). This problem is futher discussed in the context of punitive damages. *See infra* § 9.04.

[98] 441 U.S. 153 (1979).

process, in order to attempt to establish the existence of actual malice.[99] The practical effect of *Herbert* was to open up the inner sanctums of the press to greater public scrutiny.

§ 1.07 Countervailing Functions of Free Speech

[1] In General

Zechariah Chafee identified two distinct interests protected by the first amendment:[100] "There is an individual interest, the need of many men to express their opinions on matters vital to them if life is to be worth living, and a social interest in the attainment of truth, so that the country may not only adopt the wisest course of action but carry it out in the wisest way."[101] Chafee thus identified two quite different purposes for promoting freedom of speech, one concerned primarily with the speaker's own self-realization or self-fulfillment, the other concerned primarily with society's interest in enlightenment. The "enlightenment" function of free speech can in turn be subdivided into two different first amendment conceptualizations: the first, and narrower, defining "enlightenment" in the limited sense of political self-governance, and the second, broader, approach treating the enlightenment function as designed to explore truths across a much wider spectrum of ideas and topics, both political and nonpolitical.

Both the self-fulfillment and the enlightenment functions have often been recognized by the Supreme Court. In a 1984 libel decision, *Bose Corp. v. Consumers Union of United States,*[102] the Court stated that "the First Amendment presupposes that the freedom to speak one's mind is not only an aspect of individual liberty—and thus a good unto itself—but also is essential to the common quest for truth and the vitality of society as a whole."[103] The Court has tended to emphasize the social interest in free speech more heavily, however, as seen in statements that the first amendment "rests on the assumption that the widest possible dissemination of information from diverse and antagonistic

[99] *See generally* Chapter 13, *infra.*

[100] Free Speech in the United States 31-35.

[101] *Id.* For an outstanding recent treatment of first amendment theory, including an excellent discussion of the functions of free speech, *see* M. Nimmer, Nimmer on Freedom of Speech (1984).

[102] 104 S. Ct. 1949 (1984).

[103] *Id.* at 1961.

sources is essential to the welfare of the public."[104]

[2] The Self-Fulfillment Function

As Professor Melville Nimmer has put it, "[t]he nature of man is such that he can realize the fulfillment of self only if he is able to speak without restraint."[105] In Justice Thurgood Marshall's words: "The First Amendment serves not only the needs of the polity but also those of the human spirit—a spirit that demands self-expression."[106] This "achievement of self-realization" makes free expression valuable even when the speaker has no realistic hope that the audience will be persuaded to his or her viewpoint, for it nonetheless provides the speaker with an inner satisfaction and realization of self-identity essential to individual human autonomy and dignity.[107] In the context of the law of libel, as Professor Hill has noted, the value of the first amendment "is not merely the cultivation of uninhibited expression with a view to the potential contribution of such expression to the common good, but more fundamentally the protection of the speaker from governmental restraint—a sense that the speaker has a right to be let alone in the absence of a compelling reason to the contrary."[108]

[3] The Political Self-Governance Function

The function of free speech as an aid to societal self-governance has repeatedly been emphasized by the Supreme Court and by first amendment theorists. Justice Brandeis stated that "freedom to think as you will and to speak as you think are means indispensible to the discovery and spread of political truth."[109] The court has stated that "Whatever differences may exist about interpretations of the First Amendment, there is practically universal agreement that a major purpose of that

---

[104] Citizen Publishing Co. v. United States, 394 U.S. 131, 139-40 (1969).

[105] Nimmer, *supra* note 101, § 1.03, at 1-49.

[106] Procunier v. Martinez, 416 U.S. 396, 427 (1974).

[107] *See* Cohen v. California, 403 U.S. 15, 24 (1971); T. Emerson, The System of Self-Expression 6 (1970); L. Tribe, American Constitutional Law 578 (1978).

[108] Hill, *Defamation and Privacy Under the First Amendment,* 76 Colum. L. Rev. 1205, 1208 (1976). *See also* Bose Corp. v. Consumers Union of United States, 104 S. Ct. 1949, 1961 (1984); Daniels, *Public Figures Revisited,* 25 Wm. & Mary L. Rev. 957, 962-67 (1984).

[109] Whitney v. California, 274 U.S. 354, 375 (1927) (Brandeis, J., concurring).

Amendment was to protect the free discussion of governmental affairs."[110]

Perhaps the most famous exponent of the view that the primary purpose of free speech is political self-governance was Dr. Alexander Meiklejohn.[111] In Meiklejohn's words, "[w]hat is essential is not that everyone shall speak, but that everything worth saying shall be said." The essential purpose of freedom of speech "is to give every voting member of the body politic the fullest possible participation in the understanding of these problems with which the citizens of a self-governing society must deal." For Meiklejohn, it is the "mutilation of the thinking process of the community" against which the first amendment is directed; the "principle of the freedom of speech springs from the necessities of the program of self-government."[112]

[4] The Broader Enlightenment Function

In his later writing Alexander Meiklejohn departed from his original emphasis on the political function of free speech, acknowledging that free expression served social interests in enlightenment that went beyond the purely political.[113] Although still giving primacy to political speech, he recognized that "there are many forms of thought and expression within the range of human communications from which the voter derives knowledge, intelligence, sensitivity to human values: the capacity for sane and objective judgment which, so far as possible, a

---

110 Landmark Communications, Inc. v. Virginia, 435 U.S. 829, 838 (1978).

See also Brown v. Hartlage, 456 U.S. 45, 52 (1982)(political speech "[a]t the core of the First Amendment"); In re Primus, 436 U.S. 412, 437-38 (1978)(state must regulate with "significantly greater precision" in the "context of political expression and association"); First National Bank of Boston v. Bellotti, 435 U.S. 765, 786 (1978)(where "the speech is intimately related to the process of governing, 'the State may prevail only upon showing a subordinating interest which is compelling' "); Buckley v. Valeo, 424 U.S. 1, 14 (1976)("there is practically universal agreement that a major purpose of the Amendment was to protect the free discussion of governmental affairs"); City of Chicago v. Mosley, 408 U.S. 92, 95 (1972)(purpose of first amendment "[T]o permit the continued building of our politics"); Red Lion Broadcasting Co. v. FCC, 395 U.S. 367, 390 (1969)(free speech " 'the essence of self-government' "); Mills v. Alabama, 384 U.S. 214, 218 (1966)(a major purpose of first amendment "was to protect the free discussion of governmental affairs.")

111 *See* A. Meiklejohn, Free Speech and Its Relation to Self-Government (1948).

112 *Id.* at 27. *See also* Bork, *Neutral Principles and Some First Amendment Problems,* 47 Ind. L.J. 1, 20 (1971). Professor Vincent Blasi has articulated as a value of free speech the power it has to "serve in checking the abuse of power by public officials." Blasi, *The Checking Value in First Amendment Theory,* 1977 Am. B. Found. Res. J. 521, 527.

113 *See* Meiklejohn, *The First Amendment Is an Absolute,* 1961 Sup. Ct. Rev. 245, 255-57.

ballot should express."[114] Meiklejohn then listed four such forms of speech: (1) "[e]ducation, in all its phases," (2) the "achievements of philosophy and the sciences in creating knowledge and understanding of men," (3) "[l]iterature and the arts," and (4) "[p]ublic discussions of public issues."[115]

Although there is no question that political speech is well within the core of the first amendment's protection,[116] it is equally clear that the Supreme Court squarely rejects the suggestion that the amendment's protection is limited to speech related to self-government: Nonpolitical speech covering an almost infinite variety of issues and topics also falls within the ambit of first amendment protection.[117] In *Time, Inc. v. Hill,*[118] for example, an important invasion of privacy case decided under the *New York Times* standard, the Court stated that "guarantees for speech and press are not the preserve of political expression or comment upon public affairs, essential as those are to healthy government."[119] The first amendment confers a "right of the public to receive suitable access to social, political, esthetic, moral, and other ideas and experiences."[120] The free speech and free press guarantees "are not confined to any field of human interest,"[121] and it is "immaterial whether the beliefs sought to be advanced by association pertain to political, economic, religious or cultural matters."[122] As the Court put it in *West Virginia State Board of Education v. Barnette,*[123] "If there is any fixed star in our constitutional constellation, it is that no official, high or petty, can prescribe what shall be orthodox in politics, nationalism, religion, or other matters of opinion."[124]

The great debates over the function of the first amendment never go away. Easily the most controversial case of the Supreme Court's 1989 Term, for example, was the Supreme Court's flag-burning decision,

---

114 *Id.* at 256-57.

115 *Id.*

116 *See* cases cited in note 110, *supra.*

117 Nimmer, *supra* note 101, § 3.01, at 3-3.

118 385 U.S. 374 (1967).

119 *Id.* at 388.

120 Red Lion Broadcasting Co. v. FCC, 395 U.S. 367, 390 (1969).

121 United Mine Workers v. Illinois Bar Ass'n, 389 U.S. 217, 223 (1967).

122 NAACP v. Alabama, 357 U.S. 449, 460 (1958). *See also* Abood v. Detroit Board of Educ., 431 U.S. 209, 323 (1977).

123 319 U.S. 624 (1943).

124 *Id.* at 642.

Texas v. Johnson.[124.1] The case is worth examining in some detail for what it reveals about the current state of freedom of speech in the United States.

Gregory Lee Johnson was in Dallas in the summer of 1984 to protest against the Republican National Convention, which was about to renominate Ronald Reagan for four more years as President of the United States. Johnson was part of the "Republican War Chest Tour," a group organized to demonstrate against the policies of the Reagan/Bush administration and a number of Dallas-based corporations. Johnson and about 100 fellow demonstrators made speeches remonstrating Reagan, the military, and corporate America, distributed protest literature, and staged "die-ins" intended to dramatize the effects of nuclear war. Against President Reagan they shouted, "Ronald Reagan, killer of the hour, Perfect example of U.S. power." Betraying the bipartisan nature of their cynical disgust, they also screamed, "Reagan, Mondale, which will it be? Either one means World War III." Some of the protestors went beyond this vocal but peaceful dissent, spray-painting the walls of buildings and overturning potted plants. Gregory Johnson did not participate in those acts of destruction.[124.2]

One of the protestors took down an American flag from a pole outside a downtown office building, and handed it to Johnson. Johnson accepted it, and as the marchers reached the front of the Dallas City Hall, he unfurled the flag, doused it with kerosene, and set it on fire. While the flag burned, the demonstrators chanted, "America, the red, white, and blue, we spit on you, you stand for plunder, you will go under."

Many onlookers to the flag-burning episode were deeply offended by the incident. When the marchers dispersed, one of the witnesses solemnly collected the flag's charred remains, and took the burned remnants home to his backyard for a respectful burial.

Gregory Johnson was the only one of the 100 demonstrators to be arrested. Johnson was charged with violation of a Texas criminal statute, entitled "Desecration of a Venerated Object." The Texas law declared that it is a criminal offense if one "intentionally or knowingly desecrates" a "public monument," a "place of worship or burial," or a "state or national flag." The statute states that " 'desecrate' means deface, damage, or otherwise physically mistreat in a way that the actor knows

124.1 109 S. Ct. 2533 (1989).

124.2 *Id.* at 2536-37.

will seriously offend one or more persons likely to observe or discover his action."[124.3]

Johnson went to trial, was convicted, and sentenced to one year in prison and a fine of $2,000. A first Texas appellate court affirmed his conviction, but a higher Texas court reversed, holding that the first amendment barred Texas from prosecuting Johnson for the flag-burning. The United States Supreme Court then granted review.

In a 5–4 decision, the Supreme Court affirmed, holding that Johnson's conviction was inconsistent with the first amendment.[124.4] Justice Brennan's opinion for the majority was a ringing celebration of freedom of speech, reminiscent of his famous opinion in *New York Times Co. v. Sullivan.*[124.5] The Court stressed that when "overtly political" expression, such as burning an American flag in protest against the policies of the Reagan Administration, is "restricted because of the content of the message . . . conveyed," the restriction will be subject to " 'the most exacting scrutiny.' "[124.6]

The Court found that the flag burning conviction was not content-neutral because it was *directly* related to the message conveyed. The Texas statute singled out "only those severe acts of physical abuse of the flag carried out in a way likely to be offensive." Because the conviction rested on "the likely communicative impact of [the] expressive conduct" the Court reasoned that the state was regulating "emotive impact." The conviction was inconsistent with "a bedrock principle underlying the First Amendment . . . that the Government may not prohibit the expression of an idea simply because society finds the idea itself offensive or disagreeable."[124.7]

The alignment of Justices in *Texas v. Johnson* was fascinating. That the opinion of the Court was written by Justice Brennan was no surprise, for he had long been a staunch defender of expansive protection for free expression, and Brennan predictably was joined by Justices Marshall and Blackmun; what *was* surprising was that Justices Scalia and Kennedy also joined the Brennan opinion. Chief Justice Rehnquist and Justices White, O'Connor, and Stevens all dissented. It was thus the stalwart liberal wing of the Court plus the two relatively recent conservative appointees of President Reagan, Scalia and Kennedy, that car-

---

124.3 Tex. Penal Code Ann. § 42.09(a)(3) (1989).

124.4 Texas v. Johnson, 109 S. Ct. 2533 (1989).

124.5 376 U.S. 254 (1964).

124.6 109 S. Ct. at 2543.

124.7 *Id.* at 2544.

ried the day. Justice Rehnquist's impassioned dissent quoted everything from the National Anthem to John Greenleaf Whittier, conjured up images from Iwo Jima, Korea, and Vietnam, and argued vehemently that the Constitution did not proscribe protection of our national symbol.[124.8] Yet all these emotional stops could not pull out a fifth vote.

Despite the close vote in the case, and the political firestorm that has followed it, *Texas v. Johnson* underscored the basic abiding strength of the principle that speech may not be proscribed merely because it is offensive to mainstream sensibilities. If anything, the surprise in the case was that the vote was as close as it was, suggesting that it was driven as much as anything by the unique emotive power of the flag. Only a few days following *Johnson,* for example, the Supreme Court decided a case involving "dial-a-porn," and was unanimous in upholding the free speech claim.[124.9] And even Chief Justice Rehnquist, notwithstanding his vigorous dissent in *Johnson,* would not appear to reject the general principle that "offensiveness" is not enough, standing alone, to sustain restrictions on speech.

It is instructive, for example, to compare his dissent in *Johnson* with his opinion for a unanimous Court the term before in *Hustler Magazine v. Falwell,*[124.10] in which he denied recovery for Reverend Jerry Falwell for intentional infliction of emotional distress for a paraody that some might regard as more offensive than even the act of flag-burning at issue in *Johnson.*[124.11]

[5] First Amendment Functions

In some areas of modern defamation law, such as the absolute constitutional protection against liability for expression of opinion,[125] one can see all of the various functions in first amendment theory at work. An expression of opinion is at once an act of self-fulfillment and a contribution to the free trade in ideas that is essential to political and nonpolitical enlightenment.[126] But for the most part the Supreme Court's intervention into the defamation field has been dominated by emphasis on the enlightenment function.

124.8 *Id.* at 2548-57 (Rehnquist, J., concurring).

124.9 Sable Communications, Inc. v. FCC, 109 S. Ct. 2829 (1989).

124.10 485 U.S. 46 (1988).

124.11 The *Falwell* case is discussed in detail *infra* Chapter 11. *See also* R. Smolla, Jerry Falwell v. Larry Flynt: The First Amendment on Trial (1988).

125 *See* Chapter 6, *supra.*

126 *See generally,* J.S. Mill, On Liberty 490-94 (Dolphin ed. 1961).

The *New York Times*[127] decision, imposing the actual malice standard on defamation suits by public officials, seemed based primarily on the narrow politically centered version of the enlightenment function popularized in the early writings of Alexander Meiklejohn.[128] As the Court extended the actual malice standard to public figures,[129] however, it quite clearly moved to a wider theoretical base—to the broader formulation of the enlightenment function, the formulation that spans the whole spectrum of philosophic, literary, scientific, religious, and cultural speech. The Court's most recent innovation in the defamation area, its decision in *Dun & Bradstreet*[130] restricting the application of certain of the *Gertz*[131] rules to speech involving matters of "public concern," seems virtually to abandon the self-fulfillment rationale, placing the first amendment restrictions on defamation solely on enlightenment function grounds. Furthermore, at least the tone of the opinion, if not its holding, seems strongly to emphasize the more restrictive political formulation of enlightenment over the broader nonpolitical formulation.[132]

As the long-term reconciliation of the competing reputational and free expression interests implicated by the law of defamation continues, perhaps no underlying policy issues will be more significant than whether the "public figure" formulation in *Gertz* and the "public inter-

(*Text continued on page 1-23*)

---

127 376 U.S. 254 (1964).

128 *See* Sunstein, *Hard Defamation Cases,* 25 Wm. & Mary L. Rev. 891, 897 (1984). *See also* Justige Goldberg's concurring opinion in the *Times* case, 376 U.S. 254, 301 ("Purely private defamation has little to do with the political ends of a self-governing society. The imposition of liability for private defamation does not abridge the freedom of public speech.")

129 *See* Curtis Publishing Co, v. Butts, 388 U.S. 130 (1967); Associated Press v. Walker, 388 U.S. 130 (1967). *See infra* § 2.02.

130 Dun & Bradstreet, Inc. v. Greenmoss Builders, Inc., 105 S. Ct. 2939 (1985).

131 Gertz v. Robert Welch, Inc., 418 U.S. 323 (1974).

132 *See infra* §§ 3.02-3.04.

est" formulation in *Dun & Bradstreet* are given broad or narrow interpretations.

§ 1.08 Elements of the Modern Cause of Action

There is simply no way succinctly to state the elements of a modern cause of action for defamation, because the constitutional minimums that apply to the tort differ depending on the public or private status of the plaintiff and the public or private status of the speech. Individual states, furthermore, are free to establish fault levels above minimum constitutional requirements. Finally, states follow many different approaches as to when they impose the requirement of special harm. The following list contains all the principal elements that are possible in a modern cause of action for defamation. There are notations, where appropriate, indicating situations in which an element may be unnecessary. Depending on the circumstances and jurisdiction, the modern action for defamation includes some or all of the following elements:

(1) a statement of fact (opinion is never actionable);
(2) that is false;
(3) and defamatory;
(4) of and concerning the plaintiff;
(5) that is published to a third party (other than the plaintiff and defendant);
(6) not absolutely or conditionally privileged;
(7) that causes actual injury (this requirement is sometimes obviated by the device known as presumed harm, which remains available in certain cases);
(8) that is the result of fault by the defendant (this requirement is also waived in certain cases, which may be governed by strict liability; when "fault" is required it may range from "actual malice" to ordinary negligence, depending on the circumstances and jurisdiction);
(9) that causes special (pecuniary) harm in addition to generalized reputational injury (this requirement is often excused, if under the law of the state the defamation involved is categoried as "libel per se" or "slander per se").

The interrelationships among the elements are such that they are not necessarily best explained in the order in which they appear on the list above. Some of these elements are common law requirements; others are imposed (depending on the circumstances) by the Constitution. Because the application of the common law rules is no longer intelligible without a thorough understanding of constitutional requirements, Chapters 2 and 3 begin by establishing the basic constitutional fault rules in the modern law of defamation, discussing the critical public figure/private figure dichotomy and the problems of proving the existence of actual malice and negligence. (Because of the exceptional importance of the principal Supreme Court decisions in this area, the first 9 sections of Chapter 2 cover the primary Supreme Court cases in substantial detail.) Chapter 4 encompasses the technical common law requirements of the cause of action: defamatory meaning, the "of and concerning" the plaintiff requirement, and publication. Chapters 5 and 6 deal with the related issues of truth and the fault/opinion distinction, respectively, and Chapter 7 covers the confusing special harm rules. The many absolute and conditional common law privileges are discussed in Chapter 8, and the coverage of defamation is concluded in Chapter 9 with an explanation of modern rules governing damages and other remedies.

CHAPTER 2

The Public Figure/Private Figure Dichotomy

§ 2.01 The Starting Point: *New York Times Co. v. Sullivan*

[1] Background

New York Times Co. v. Sullivan[1] is the starting point for all modern discussion concerning the American law of defamation.[2] The case revolutionalized the law of defamation by holding for the first time that the traditional tort rules governing the law of libel were subject to the overriding constraints of the first amendment. In the years since the historical 1964 decision in the *New York Times* case, courts from the Supreme Court down have repeatedly been put to the task of working out step by step the full ramifications of the *Times* ruling. Debate over the "central meaning" of the decision continues to be of practical relevance to lawyers engaged in defamation litigation. Since the "constitutionalization" of the law of defamation in 1964, it has been impossible to separate pragmatic legal advice and strategy in the defamation area from a sound understanding of the theoretical first amendment underpinnings of the *Times* ruling.[3]

---

1 376 U.S. 254 (1964).

2 *See generally* Berney, *Libel and the First Amendment—A New Constitutional Privilege,* 51 Va. L. Rev. 1 (1965); Bertelsman, *The First Amendment and Protection of Reputation and Privacy*—New York Times Co. v. Sullivan *and How it Grew,* 56 Ky. L.J. 718 (1967); Bertelsman, *Libel and Public Men,* 52 A.B.A. J. 657 (1966); Brennan, *The Supreme Court and the Meiklejohn Interpretation of the First Amendment,* 79 Harv. L. Rev. 1 (1965); Carter, *Right of Reply Versus the* Sullivan *Rule: Time for a Second Look,* 27 Loy. L. Rev. 41 (1981); Green, *The* New York Times *Rule: Judicial Overkill,* 12 Vill. L. Rev. 730 (1967); Kalven, *The* New York Times *Case: A Note on "The Central Meaning of the First Amendment,"* 1964 Sup. Ct. Rev. 191; Lewis, New York Times v. Sullivan *Reconsidered: Time to Return to "The Central Meaning of the First Amendment,"* 83 Colum. L. Rev. 603 (1983); Merin, *Libel and the Supreme Court,* 11 Wm. & Mary L. Rev. 371 (1969); Nelson, *Newsmen and the* Times *Doctrine,* 12 Vill. L. Rev. 738 (1967); Ottley, Bruce & Ottley, New York Times v. Sullivan: *A Retrospective Examination,* 33 De Paul L. Rev. 741 (1984); Pedrick, *Freedom of the Press and the Law of Libel: The Modern Revised Translation,* 49 Corn. L.Q. 581 (1964); Pierce, *The Anatomy of an Historic Decision,* New York Times Co. v. Sullivan, 43 N.C. L. Rev. 315 (1965); Smolla, *Let the Author Beware: The Rejuvenation of the American Law of Libel,* 132 U. Pa. L. Rev. 1 (1983).

3 Litigation and counseling related to media are, in this respect, unique. Although at times representation of media clients resembles any other form of sophisticated corporate defense practice, such representation remains to a substantial degree the practice of constitutional law. The same is true from the plaintiff's side; one simply cannot navigate the waters of a modern defamation case without a solid understanding of the constitutional values that emanate from the *Times* decision and its progeny. Unlike a products liability or a medical malpractice case, a tort suit for defamation today routinely implicates fundamental philosophical conflicts and elusive conceptual abstractions. Because understanding the *New York Times* decision is essential to sound practice in this field, this case is the only one in this volume in which the facts and holding are described at length.

The *New York Times* case arose out of the struggle for racial equality in the South.[4] On February 29, 1960, Dr. Martin Luther King, Jr., was arrested on trumped-up charges involving two counts of perjury in connection with the filing of his Alabama state income tax return.[5] On March 19, 1960, three weeks after King's arrest, the *New York Times* ran an editorial in support of King's efforts; the *Times* praised the efforts of blacks in the South to resist racism, and admonished Congress to "heed their rising voices, for they will be heard."[6] The editorial phrase would later be picked up by a newly formed "Committee to Defend Martin Luther King," which on March 29, 1960, published a full page advertisement entitled "Heed Their Rising Voices."[7] At the bottom of the ad were the names of a number of prominent Americans compris-

---

[4] *See, e.g.*, A. Bickel, The Least Dangerous Branch 267 (1962); Kalven, *supra* note 2, at 197-99; Lewis, *supra* note 2, at 604; Pierce, *supra* note 2, at 316-23.

[5] King was ultimately acquitted on the charges, which were rather transparently motivated by a desire to punish King for his civil rights activities in Alabama. Pierce, *supra* note 2, at 318 n.17.

[6] N.Y. Times, March 29, 1960, p.25, col. 1-8 (a copy of the advertisement is attached as an appendix to the Supreme Court's opinion). New York Times Co. v. Sullivan, 376 U.S. 254, 292 (1964).

[7] The ad began by proclaiming, "As the whole world knows [black students in the South are] engaged in wide-spread non-violent demonstrations in positive affirmation of the right to live in human dignity as guaranteed by the United States Constitution and the Bill of Rights," and the efforts of those students are "being met by an unprecedented wave of terror."

The ad claimed that 400 students had been ejected from lunch counters in South Carolina, teargassed, soaked to the skin with fire hoses in freezing weather, and arrested en masse. According to the ad, after students in Montgomery, Alabama, sang "My Country, 'Tis of Thee" on the State Capitol steps, "their leaders were expelled from school, and truckloads of police armed with shotguns and tear gas ringed the Alabama State College Campus." When the student body at Alabama State protested to state authorities by refusing to re-register, the ad alleged, their dining hall "was padlocked in an attempt to starve them into submission." The ad lauded the efforts of the students, praising them as "rising to glory," and stated that certain "Southern violators" had repeatedly answered Dr. King's peaceful protests with intimidation and violence. "They have bombed his home almost killing his wife and child," it stated. "They have assaulted his person. They have arrested him seven times—for speeding, loitering, and similar offenses." The ad then alleged that "now they have charged him with perjury—a *felony* under which they could imprison him for *ten years.*" According to the advertisement, it was obvious "that their real purpose is to remove him physically as the leader to whom the students and millions of others look for guidance and support, and thereby to intimidate *all* leaders who may rise in the South." The ad ended with a plea for funds to assist in the civil rights struggle and the defense of Dr. King, stating that "[W]e urge you to join hands with our fellow Americans in the South by supporting, with your dollars, the combined appeal for all three needs—the defense of Martin Luther King—the support of the embattled students—and the struggle for the right-to-vote." 376 U.S. at 292.

ing "The Committee to Defend Martin Luther King and the Struggle for Freedom in the South."[8]

The *New York Times* was paid a little over $4,800 for running the advertisement. The total circulation of the issue was about 650,000, but only 394 copies of the *Times* were sent to Alabama newsdealers and only 35 copies found their way into Montgomery County, Alabama.[9] The *Times* ad stirred up a whirlwind of bitter reaction in Alabama, and soon after its publication a number of Alabama politicians commenced libel suits, including separate suits by John Patterson, the Governor of Alabama, one former Montgomery city commissioner, and three incumbent Montgomery commissioners.[10]

A similar demand for a retraction was also made by one of the incumbent Montgomery city commissioners, L.B. Sullivan, who as Commissioner of Public Affairs was supervisor of the Montgomery departments of scales, cemeteries, fire, and police. The *Times* wrote back to Sullivan and told him it had investigated the matter and was "somewhat puzzled as to how you think the statements in any way reflect on you." Without answering the letter, Sullivan sued the *Times* for libel in Montgomery County, seeking $500,000 in damages.[11] The *Times* advertisement did not actually mention Sullivan by name, and much of the ad referred to events entirely outside of Alabama.[12] Some of the statements in the

[8] *Id.*

[9] Pierce, *supra* note 2, at 321.

[10] Governor Patterson sent a letter to the *Times* claiming that the paper had charged him with "grave misconduct and of improper actions as Governor of Alabama," and demanding a retraction to mollify the Governor. The *Times* did print a retraction in response to Patterson's letter. *Id.* at 322 n.34.

[11] Sullivan also sued four Alabama Ministers connected with the ad, the Reverends Fred Shuttlesworth, S.S. Seay, Sr., J.E. Lowrey, and Ralph D. Abernathy. *Id.*

[12] Sullivan's theory was that the word "police" in the paragraph concerning Montgomery would be understood as referring to Sullivan, because Sullivan was the Montgomery Commissioner who supervised the Police Department. He thus argued that the ad imputed to him the "ringing" of the Alabama State campus with police and the padlocking of the dining hall to starve students into submission. Sullivan further reasoned that since arrests are ordinarily made by the police, the statement "They have arrested [Dr. King] seven times" would be read as referring to Sullivan, and that the "they" who did the arresting would be equated with the "they" who committed the other described acts of the "Southern violators," thereby effectively accusing Sullivan himself of complicity in bombing Martin Luther King's home, assaulting his person, and charging him with perjury. New York Times Co. v. Sullivan, 376 U.S. 254, 258-59 (1964).

advertisement were false, but those errors were largely technical and insubstantial.[13]

After a trial that lasted only three days, the jury returned a verdict of $500,000 against the *Times* and four individual black ministers. The Supreme Court of Alabama affirmed the award.[14] In affirming the judgment, the Supreme Court of Alabama held that "[w]here the words published tend to injure a person libeled by them in his reputation, profession, trade or business, or charge him with an indictable offense, or tend to bring the individual into public contempt," they are "libelous per se;" "the matter complained of is, under the above doctrine, libelous per se, if it was published of and concerning the plaintiff;" and that it was actionable without "proof of pecuniary injury . . . , such injury being implied."[15] Approving the trial court's ruling that the jury could find the statements to have been made "of and concerning" Commissioner Sullivan, the Alabama Supreme Court stated: "We think it common knowledge that the average person knows that municipal agents, such as police and firemen, and others, are under the control and direction of the city governing body, and more particularly under the direction and control of a single commissioner. In measuring the performance or deficiencies of such groups, praise or criticism is usually

[13] Although black students in Montgomery did stage a demonstration on the Capitol steps, the song they sang was not "My Country, 'Tis of Thee," it was the national anthem. Although nine black students had been expelled from college, they were not expelled for leading the demonstration on the statehouse steps, but rather for demanding service at a lunch counter inside the Montgomery County Courthouse. Not the entire student body, only most of it, had protested the expulsions, and not by refusing to register for classes, but by boycotting classes on a single day. The dining hall was never literally padlocked, although some students who had neither registered nor obtained temporary meal tickets were barred from entering. Although police were called to the Alabama State campus in large numbers because of race related protests on three occasions, the police never physically "ringed" the campus, and they were never actually deployed in connection with the State Capitol demonstration. Dr. King had not been arrested seven times, only four; and although King claimed to have been physically assaulted by a Montgomery police officer in connection with an arrest for loitering outside a classroom, one of the arresting officers denied that an assault had occurred. Dr. King's home was in fact bombed twice when his wife and child were there, but both bombings took place prior to Commissioner Sullivan's tenure. The police were never implicated in the bombings, and had actually made efforts to apprehend those who were. Three of King's four arrests antedated Sullivan's period as Commissioner; and Sullivan was not personally involved in procuring the perjury indictments brought against King. *See* Kalven, *supra* note 2, at 198-99.

[14] New York Times Co. v. Sullivan, 273 Ala. 656, 144 So. 2d 25 (1962).

[15] *Id.* at 673, 144 So. 2d at 37.

attached to the official in complete control of the body."[16] In sustaining the trial court's determination that the verdict was not excessive, the Alabama Supreme Court said that malice could be inferred from a number of factors: (1) the *Times's* "irresponsibility" in printing the advertisement while the *Times* had in its files articles already published which would have demonstrated the "falsity" of the allegations in the ad; (2) from the *Times's* failure to retract as to Commissioner Sullivan while retracting as to Governor Patterson, even though "the matter contained in the advertisement was equally false as to both parties;" and (3) from the testimony of the *Times* secretary that, apart from the statement that the dining hall was padlocked, he thought the two paragraphs were "substantially correct."[17] The Alabama Supreme Court summarily rejected the *Times's* constitutional objections with brief statements that "The First Amendment of the U.S. Constitution does not protect libelous publications" and "The Fourteenth Amendment is directed against State action and not private action."[18]

The threat to the *Times* posed by the Alabama Supreme Court's affirmance went well beyond the $500,000 verdict in Sullivan's case. A string of other libel suits against the *Times* had risen in Alabama in connection with its reporting on racial matters;[19] in one of those suits another $500,000 verdict had already been returned,[20] and the total potential liability from the various suits filed was $5,600,000.[21] After some internal debate within the corporate hierarchy at the *Times*, the decision was made to pursue review in the United States Supreme Court.[22]

[2] The Holding and Rationale

The opinion by Justice Brennan began by disposing of two preliminary contentions. First, the Court stated that although the case was a civil tort suit between private litigants, the state rules of tort law applied by the Alabama court system imposed restrictions on the free-

16 *Id.* at 674-75, 144 So. 2d at 39.

17 *Id.* at 686-87, 144 So. 2d at 50-51.

18 *Id.* at 676, 144 So. 2d at 40.

19 *See* Parks v. New York Times Co., 195 F. Supp. 919 (M.D. Ala. 1961), *rev'd*, 308 F.2d 474 (5th Cir. 1962).

20 New York Times Co. v. Sullivan, 376 U.S. 254, 278 n.18 (1964).

21 *See* Lewis, *Annals of Law, The Sullivan Case*, New Yorker, Nov. 5, 1984, at 52, 61, col. 3.

22 *See* Anthony Lewis's account of this discussion in Lewis, *supra* note 21, at 56-61.

doms of speech and press, and that application of state power, even if it was effectuated through mere common law rules, was subject to the restrictions of the first amendment.[23] Second, the Court held that the first amendent was not rendered inapplicable merely because the allegedly libelous statements were part of a paid "commercial" advertisement.[24] The Court stated that the *Times* ad was not a "commercial" advertisement in the sense that the Court had previously defined "commercial speech."[25] The ad communicated information, expressed opinions, recited grievances, protested claimed abuses, and "sought financial support on behalf of a movement whose existence and objectives are matters of the highest public interest and concern."[26]

The Supreme Court then summarized applicable Alabama law, which faithfully tracked the majority rules in existence across the United States at the time. Under Alabama libel law, a publication was "libelous per se" if the words tended to injure a person in his reputation or to bring him into "public contempt."[27] The standard was met if the words were such as to "injure him in his public office, or impute misconduct to him in his office, or want of official integrity, or want of fidelity to a public trust."[28] The words were required to be "of and concerning" the plaintiff, but where the plaintiff was a public official, his place in the government heirarchy was sufficient evidence to support a finding that his reputation had been affected by statements that reflect upon the agency of which he is in charge.[29] Once "libel per se" had been established the defendant had no defense as to stated facts unless he could persuade the jury that those facts were true in all their particulars.[30] This privilege of "fair comment" for expressions of opinion depended on the truth of the facts upon which the comment was based.[31] Unless the defendant could discharge the burden of proving truth, general

[23] New York Times Co. v. Sullivan, 776 U.S. 254, 265 (1964). The test, the Court stated, "is not the form in which state power has been applied but, whatever the form, whether such power has in fact been exercized." *Id.* (citing Ex parte Virginia, 100 U.S. 339 (1879); American Federation of Labor v. Swing, 312 U.S. 321 (1941)).

[24] 376 U.S. at 265.

[25] *Id.* (citing Valentine v. Chrestensen, 316 U.S. 52 (1942)).

[26] 376 U.S. at 266 (citing NAACP v. Button, 371 U.S. 415 (1963)).

[27] 376 U.S. at 267.

[28] *Id.*

[29] *Id.*

[30] Johnson Publishing Co. v. Davis, 271 Ala. 474, 494-95, 124 So. 2d 441, 457-58 (1960); Alabama Ride Co. v. Vance, 235 Ala. 263, 178 So. 438 (1938).

[31] Parsons v. Age-Herald Publishing Co., 181 Ala. 439, 450, 61 So. 345, 350 (1913).

damages were presumed and could be awarded without proof of pecuniary injury.[32] A showing of actual malice was a prerequisite to recovery of punitive damages, and the defendant could in any event forestall a punitive award by a retraction meeting certain statutory requirements.[33] Good motives and belief in the truthfulness of the statements did not negate an inference of malice but were relevant only in mitigation of punitive damages if the jury chose to accord them weight.[34]

The Court then turned to the question of whether these Alabama rules were consistent with the first amendment. In deciding the question, the Court said that the analysis should not be linked to "mere labels," for the mere epithet "libel" did not render the speech unprotected.[35] The Court then emphasized the "marketplace of ideas" theory of the first amendment and the significance of the unfettered interchange of ideas.[36] " 'The maintenance of the opportunity for free political discussion,' " the Court stated, " 'to the end that government may be responsive to the will of the people and that changes may be obtained by lawful means, an opportunity essential to the security of the Republic, is a fundamental principle of our constitutional system.' "[37] And then, in the most famous line of Justice Brennan's opinion, he stated that the Court thus considered the case "against the background of a profound national commitment to the principle that debate on public issues should be uninhibited, robust, and wide-open, and that it may well include vehement, caustic, and sometimes unpleasantly sharp attacks on government and public officals."[38] Criticism of offical conduct does not lose its constitutional protection, Justice Brennan argued, merely because it is effective criticism and hence diminishes the reputations of the officials involved. Justice Brennan then spoke of the lessons to be drawn from the great controversy over the Sedition Act of 1798, which first crystallized a national awareness of the "central mean-

---

32 New York Times Co. v. Sullivan, 376 U.S. 254, 267 (1964).

33 *Id.*

34 Johnson Publishing Co. v. Davis, 271 Ala. 474, 495, 124 So. 2d 441, 458 (1960).

35 376 U.S. at 269.

36 *Id.* (citing Roth v. United States, 354 U.S. 476, 484 (1957)).

37 376 U.S. at 269 (quoting Stromberg v. California, 283 U.S. 359, 369 (1931)).

38 376 U.S. at 270 (citing Terminello v. Chicago, 337 U.S. 1, 4 (1949); DeJonge v. Oregon, 299 U.S. 353, 365 (1937)).

ing" of the first amendment.[39] That statute made it a crime, punishable by a $5,000 fine and five years in prison, "if any person shall write, print, utter or publish . . . any false, scandalous and malicious writing or writings against the government of the United States, or either house of the Congress . . . , or the President . . . , with intent to defame . . . or to bring them, or either of them, into contempt or disrepute; or to excite against them, or either of any of them, the hatred of the good people of the United States."[40] The Act, an Americanized "improvement" on the old English crime of seditious libel, required the jury to be judges both of law and of fact.[41] Despite these qualifications, the Act was vigorously condemned as unconstitutional in an attack joined by both Thomas Jefferson and James Madison.[42] Although no case challenging the validity of the Sedition Act ever reached the Supreme Court,[43] Justice Brennan noted (as had Justice Holmes several decades earlier)[44] that "the attack upon its validity had carried the day in the court of history."[45]

Turning to the heart of the opinion's analysis, Justice Brennan then spoke of the necessity of fashioning libel rules that do not chill the free exercise of public criticism. The traditional common law tort rule that compels the critic of official conduct to guarantee the truth of all his factual assertions—and to do so on pain of libel judgments virtually unlimited in amount—leads, the Court held, to intolerable self-censorship.[46] But why isn't the danger of self-censorship alleviated by the common law defense of truth? The answer, Justice Brennan reasoned, is that allowance of the defense of truth, with the burden of proving it on the defendant, does not mean that only false speech will be deterred.

---

[39] *See generally* L. Levy, Legacy of Suppression 258 (1960); Mayton, *Seditious Libel and the Lost Guarantee of a Freedom of Expression*, 84 Colum. L. Rev. 91, 121-30 (1984).

[40] 1 Stat. 596 (1798).

[41] *See* H. Kalven, The Negro and the First Amendment 20 (1965).

[42] Madison's attacks were contained in the famous Virginia Resolutions of 1798. *See* J. Madison, "Report Accompanying the Virginia Resolution," reprinted in 4 *The Debates in the Several State Conventions on the Adoption of the Federal Constitution* 553-54 (1876). The Supreme Court quoted extensively from Madison's report. New York Times Co. v. Sullivan, 376 U.S. 254, 274 (1964).

[43] The Act expired by its own terms two years after enactment, and was never reinstated. When Thomas Jefferson came to the presidency in 1800 he pardoned all violators of the Act, and Congress eventually made reparations for the fines enacted under it. *See* Kalven, *supra* note 41, at 18.

[44] *See* Abrams v. United States, 250 U.S. 616, 630 (Holmes, J., dissenting).

[45] New York Times Co. v. Sullivan, 376 U.S. 254, 276 (1964).

[46] *Id.* at 279.

It is often too difficult to produce legal proofs that the alleged libel was true in all its factual particulars.[47] "Under such a rule, would-be critics of official conduct may be deterred from voicing their criticism, even though it is believed to be true and even though it is in fact true, because of doubt whether it can be proved in court or fear of the expense of having to do so."[48] This leads to an unhealthy timidity in which people tend to make statements steering wide of the danger zone. The traditional defamation rule "dampens the vigor and limits the variety of public debate."[49] Justice Brennan then stated the holding that would launch an entirely new era for the law of libel: "The constitutional guarantees require, we think, a federal rule that prohibits a public official from recovering damages for a defamatory falsehood relating to his official conduct *unless he proves that the statement was made with actual malice—that is, with knowledge that it was false or with reckless disregard of whether it was false or not.*"[50]

After announcing the new constitutional rule, the Court, "in the interest of effective judicial administration,"[51] undertook a review of the record to determine whether it could constitutionally support a judgment for Sullivan. In undertaking that review, a series of important subsidiary principles emerged from the Court's opinion, all of which would in later cases surface as important components of the constitutional picture. First, because the constitutional guarantees the Court had fashioned would be inextricably bound up with questions of fact, the Court engaged in "an independent examination of the whole record" to determine if the evidence would support a finding of actual malice.[52] Second, in undertaking the review of the evidence the Court

---

47 *Id.* (citing Post Publishing Co. v. Hallam, 59 F. 530, 540 (6th Cir. 1893); Noel, *Defamation of Public Officers and Candidates,* 49 Col. L. Rev. 875, 892 (1949)).

48 376 U.S. at 279.

49 *Id.*

50 *Id.* at 279-80 (emphasis added). A similar rule had previously been adopted by a number of state courts. *See* Phoenix Newspapers v. Choisser, 82 Ariz. 271, 276-77, 312 P.2d 150, 154 (1957); Snively v. Record Publishing Co., 185 Cal. 565, 571-76, 198 P. 1 (1921); Salinger v. Cowles, 195 Iowa 873, 889. 191 N.W. 167, 174 (1922); Stice v. Beacon Newspaper Corp., 185 Kan. 61, 65-67, 340 P.2d 396, 400-01 (1959); Coleman v. MacLennan, 78 Kan. 711, 98 P. 281 (1908); Lawrence v. Fox, 357 Mich. 134, 146, 97 N.W.2d 719, 725 (1959); Ponder v. Cobb, 257 N.C. 281, 299, 126 S.E.2d 67, 80 (1962).

51 376 U.S. at 284.

52 *Id.* at 285. This principle of "independent" appellate review was recently reconfirmed by the Court. *See* Bose Corp. v. Consumers Union of United States, Inc., 104 S. Ct. 1949 (1984). The principle is a cornerstone of modern defamation practice. *See generally* Chapter 13, *infra.*

stated that the proof of actual malice must be of "convincing clarity," a standard distinctly more rigorous than the preponderance of the evidence standard of proof that normally applies to civil actions.[53] Third, neither the *Times*'s failure to retract nor its failure to check the facts in the ad against its own files constituted "actual malice."[54] Finally, the statements in the ad were too far removed from a personalized attack on Commissioner Sullivan constitutionally to support a finding that the libelous material was "of and concerning" Sullivan.[55]

The *Times* decision profoundly changed the American law of defamation; it has proved to be a case of enduring vitality, a case that continues to foster intense debate and continues to be drawn upon by courts charged with the task of reconciling the strong societal interest in protecting reputation with the "central meaning" of the first amendment.

§ 2.02 Extension of *New York Times* to Public Figures

[1] The Harlan Opinion

Three years after the *New York Times* decision, the Supreme Court dramatically extended the coverage of the actual malice standard in the companion cases *Curtis Publishing Co. v. Butts*[56] and *Associated Press v. Walker*,[57] to include "public figures" not occupying governmental office. The *Butts* case involved an ariticle in the *Saturday Evening Post* that accused University of Georgia football coach Wally Butts of fixing a football game between Georgia and Alabama.[58] Although Georgia is a state university, Butts was actually employed by a private corporation that administered the university's athletic activities.[59] *Associated Press v. Walker* involved a suit by Edwin Walker, a retired army general

[53] 376 U.S. at 285-86. *See infra* § 3.08.

[54] 376 U.S. at 286-88.

[55] *Id.* at 288-91.

[56] 388 U.S. 130 (1967).

[57] 388 U.S. 130 (1967).

[58] *Id.* at 135.

[59] Arguably, Butts was technically a public official, considering his intimate connection to a major state institution. The Supreme Court had in a prior case characterized the athletic association as a body carrying on "a business comparable in all essentials to those usually conducted by private owners." Allen v. Regents of the University System of Georgia, 304 U.S. 439, 451 (1938). Georgia law, however, specifically stated that athletic associations were not to be considered agencies of the State. *See* Curtis Publishing Co. v. Butts, 388 U.S. 130, 135-36 n.2 (1967).

accused of taking command of a violent crowd and personally leading a charge against federal marshals who were attempting to enforce a federal court decree permitting the enrollment of a black student, James Meredith, at the University of Mississippi.[60] The article portrayed Walker as encouraging violence on the racially charged campus. Walker, a private citizen at the time of the riot at the University of Mississippi, had pursued a long and successful military career, and had actually been in command of federal troops sent to Little Rock, Arkansas, in 1957 to assist in the desegregation of Little Rock Central High School.[61] Walker had resigned from the military to engage in political activity and was strongly opposed to federal intervention in desegregation efforts.[62]

Justice Harlan wrote an opinion for a plurality of four Justices in the *Butts* and *Walker* decisions. Justice Harlan noted that neither Butts nor Walker held any position in government at the time of the alleged libels, and therefore the "seditious libel" considerations of *New York Times* did not apply.[63] However, Justice Harlan stated, "the public interest in the circulation of the materials involved, and the publisher's interest in circulating them, is not less than that involved in *New York Times*."[64]

After declaring that Butts and Walker were both "public figures,"[65] Justice Harlan went on to write that unlike public officials, public figures should be able to recover on a showing of less than "actual malice."[66] A mere public figure, Harlan reasoned, should be able to recover "on a showing of highly unreasonable conduct constituting an extreme departure from the standards of investigation and reporting ordinarily adhered to by responsible publishers."[67] (Justice Harlan's opinion held that the *Saturday Evening Post* had been guilty of such conduct in the

---

60 388 U.S. at 140.

61 *See generally* Cooper v. Aaron, 358 U.S. 1 (1958); E. Huckaby, Crisis at Central High (1980); Farber, *The Supreme Court and the Rule of Law:* Cooper v. Aaron *Revisited*, 1982 Ill. L. Rev. 387, 290-96.

62 388 U.S. at 140.

63 *Id.* at 153.

64 *Id.* at 154.

65 *Id.* (citing Spahn v. Julian Messner, Inc., 18 N.Y.2d 324, 274 N.Y.S.2d 877, 221 N.E.2d 543 (1966), *judgment vacated*, 387 U.S. 239 (1967), *aff'd later proceedings*, 21 N.Y.2d 124, 233 N.E.2d 840, 286 N.Y.S.2d 832 (1967), *appeal dismissed*, 393 U.S. 1046 (1969)).

66 388 U.S. at 155.

67 *Id.*

Butts case, but the Associated Press in the *Walker* case had not.)[68] Contrary to apparent misconceptions in several lower court decisions following *Butts* and *Walker,*[69] Justice Harlan's opinion did not and never has commanded a majority of the court.

[2] The Warren Opinion

The critical opinion in the two cases was actually authored by Chief Justice Earl Warren, who concurred in the result reached by the plurality, but on the grounds that the *New York Times* knowing or reckless disregard of the truth formulation of "actual malice" should apply to public figures just as it applied to public officials.[70] To Chief Justice Warren, "differentiation between public figures and public officials and adoption of separate standards of proof for each have no basis in law, logic or First Amendment policy."[71] Warren reasoned that in contemporary America power and influence over the course of public events are often originated and orchestrated by an array of corporations, commissions, associations, boards and committees loosely associated with more formal political institutions. Many individuals who do not hold governmental office are nonetheless intimately involved in the resolution of public issues, using their fame and power to shape events in areas of concern to society at large.[72] Justices Brennan and White agreed with Chief Justice Warren that the *Times* actual malice standard should govern both cases, but they voted to remand the *Butts* case for a fresh jury determination on the issue of actual malice.[73]

[3] The Absolutists—Black and Douglas

Justices Black and Douglas took an "absolutist" position, arguing that under the first amendment the press should be totally immune from

---

[68] *Id.* at 156-59.

[69] *See* Oliver v. Village Voice, Inc., 417 F. Supp. 235, 238 (S.D.N.Y. 1976); Cohn v. National Broadcasting Co., 67 A.D.2d 140, 414 N.Y.S.2d 906 (1st Dept. 1979); Weaver v. Pryor Jeffersonian, 569 P.2d 967 (Okla. 1977).

[70] 388 U.S. at 162. *See generally* Kalven, *The Reasonable Man and the First Amendment,* Hill, Butts, *and* Walker, 1967 Sup. Ct. Rev. 267; Schauer, *Public Figures,* 25 Wm. & Mary L. Rev. 905 (1984); Note, *The Constitutional Law of Defamation and Privacy:* Butts *and* Walker, 53 Corn. L. Rev. 649 (1968); Note, *Extension of* Sullivan's *Actual Malice Standard to Defamation of Public Figures,* 2 Ga. L. Rev. 393 (1968).

[71] 388 U.S. at 163. (Warren, C.J., concurring in the result).

[72] *Id.* at 163-64 (Warren, C.J., concurring in the result).

[73] *Id.* at 172-74 (Brennan, J., concurring in *Walker* and dissenting in *Butts*).

libel judgments.[74] Justices Black and Douglas thus concurred in the result in *Butts*, but dissented in *Walker*. (Since the retirement of Justices Black and Douglas, the absolutist approach has had no active supporters on the Court.)[75]

[4] The "Box Score"

The box score of the *Butts* and *Walker* decisions was thus a 5-4 victory for Wally Butts (with the result arguably even more one-sided, since two of the four minority votes were for remand, rather than victory for the *Post*) and a 9-0 defeat for Walker. The box score on the legal standard applicable to public figures was a splintered 4-3-2 configuration, however, with four votes for "unreasonable conduct constituting an extreme departure" from ordinary journalistic standards, three votes for "actual malice," and two votes for "absolute" press protection. Because five of the nine members of the Court required "actual malice or better," the *Butts* and *Walker* decisions came to be applied by lower courts as requiring *New York Times* actual malice in public figure cases.[76] (In reviewing this bottom line, Harry Kalven, Jr., remarked, "You can't tell the players without a score card."[77]) In a number of subsequent cases the Supreme Court explicitly endorsed this interpretation, with solid majorities of five or more Justices adopting the actual malice standard in public figure cases.[78]

§ 2.03 The Short-Lived "Public Interest" Approach

The expansion of the coverage of the *New York Times* standard continued after *Butts* and *Walker*, reaching its highwater mark in 1971 with the short-lived adoption of a "public interest" test. In *Rosenbloom*

---

[74] *Id.* at 170-72 (Black, J., concurring in the result in *Walker* and dissenting in *Butts*).

[75] *See generally* Reich, *Mr. Justice Black and the Living Constitution*, 76 Harv. L. Rev. 673 (1963).

[76] *See, e.g.*, Cepeda v. Cowles Magazines and Broadcasting, Inc., 392 F.2d 417 (9th Cir.), *cert. denied*, 393 U.S. 840 (1968); News-Journal Co. v. Gallagher, 233 A.2d 166 (Del. 1967); Grayson v. Curtis Publishing Co., 72 Wash. 2d 999, 436 P.2d 756 (1967); Kalven, *supra* note 70, at 275; Schauer, *supra* note 70, at 907.

[77] Kalven, *supra* note 70, at 275.

[78] *See, e.g.*, Bose Corp. v. Consumers Union of United States, Inc., 104 S. Ct. 1949, 1954 (1984); Gertz v. Robert Welch, Inc., 418 U.S. 323, 336 n.7 (1974); Monintor Patriot Co. v. Roy, 401 U.S. 265 (1971); Greenbelt Cooperative Publishing Ass'n v. Bresler, 398 U.S. 6 (1971).

v. Metromedia, Inc.,[79] a suit for libel was brought by George Rosenbloom, an alleged distributor of nudist magazines in the Philadelphia area, against the operators of radio station WIP in Philadelphia. Following Rosenbloom's arrest during a police crackdown on the distribtution of allegedly obscene books and newspapers, WIP broadcast a series of news stories describing Rosenbloom's arrest and the seizure of pornographic books and magazines from both his home and a local warehouse. Rosenbloom sued the radio station because of certain factual errors in the broadcasts. The station claimed that it was entitled to invoke the *New York Times* actual malice standard as a defense. The judgment of the Supreme Court was announced in a plurality opinion written by Justice Brennan, who phrased the issue before the court as:

> whether the *New York Times'* knowing-or-reckless-falsity standard applies in a state civil libel action brought not by a "public official" or a "public figure" but by a private individual for a defamatory falsehood uttered in a news broadcast by a radio station about the individual's involvement in an event of public or general interest.[80]

Using an analysis heavily solicitous of press freedom, the plurality opinion of Justice Brennan held that the *New York Times* standard applied to any defamatory speech involving matters of "public or general interest."[81] Justice Brennan's analysis shifted the focus of the *New York Times* standard from the status of the defamation victim to the status of the speech itself. "If a matter is a subject of public or general interest," Justice Brennan wrote, "it cannot suddenly become less so merely because a private individual is involved, or because in some sense the individual did not 'voluntarily' choose to become involved."[82] Rather, Brennan reasoned, the public's primary interest is in the event; the public's natural attention is on the participants in newsworthy events, not the participants' prior anonymity, notoriety, or fame. The Court thus extended the coverage of *New York cimes* "to all discussion and communication involving matters of public or general concern, without regard to whether the persons involved are famous or anonymous."[83]

---

[79] 403 U.S. 29 (1971).

[80] *Id.* at 31-32.

[81] *Id.* at 52. The phrase "public or general interest" was derived from the seminal article on the right to privacy, Warren & Brandeis, *The Right to Privacy*, 4 Harv. L. Rev. 193, 214 (1890).

[82] Rosenbloom v. Metromedia, Inc., 403 U.S. 29, 43 (1971).

[83] *Id.* at 44.

§ 2.04 The Modern Approach

[1] Background

The *Rosenbloom* experiment, such as it was, lasted only three years. In 1974, the Supreme Court retreated from *Rosenbloom* and settled on a compromise approach, establishing a matrix of guidelines grounded in a dichotomy between public and private figures. In *Gertz v. Robert Welch, Inc.*,[84] the Supreme Court repudiated *Rosenbloom's* preoccupation with whether the defamatory speech involved subjects of public interest and concern. *Gertz* involved a libel action brought by Elmer Gertz, a well-known Chicago attorney and law professor, against Robert Welch, Inc., the publisher of the monthly magazine *American Opinion*, an organ of the John Birch Society.[85] (The late Robert Welch was the founder of the John Birch Society, and was, to say the least, an avid "communist hunter.")[86] Gertz had been retained as co-counsel by the family of 17-year-old Ronald Nelson to pursue civil remedies against Richard Nuccio, a Chicago police officer who had killed Nelson.[87] Nuccio was convicted of Nelson's murder, but Gertz played no role in Nuccio's criminal prosecution and made no public statements or comments concerning the civil or criminal actions. Shortly after Nuccio's conviction, an article appeared in *American Opinion* entitled "Frame-Up—Richard Nuccio and the War on Police."[88] The article alleged that Nuccio was being "railroaded" as part of a communist conspiracy to undermine local police so as to pave the way for a national police force which would support and enforce a communist dictatorship.[89] The article named Elmer Gertz as one of the members of this conspiracy. He was identified as the lawyer for the Nelson family and one of the leaders of the attack on Nuccio. Gertz was further described, among other

---

[84] 418 U.S. 323 (1974).

[85] In the early 1960's the publication *American Opinion* began to sound warnings of a nationwide conspiracy to discredit local police forces and establish in their stead a national law enforcement agency capable of supporting a communist dictatorship. *Id.* at 325.

[86] *See* Anderson, *Reputation, Compensation, and Proof*, 25 Wm. & Mary L. Rev. 747, 755 (1984).

[87] 418 U.S. at 326.

[88] *Id.*

[89] *Id.*

things, as a "Communist-fronter," a "Leninist" and a "Marxist."[90] Virtually everything of significance in the *American Opinion* article was false.[91]

American Opinion claimed that Gertz was a public figure and that the magazine was thus entitled to the protection of the *New York Times* actual malice standard. In a pretrial ruling the district court held that the words published by the magazine constituted libel per se.[92] Due to this ruling, injury was presumed under Illinois law and only the issue of damages was submitted to the jury.[93] The district court, however, having second thoughts, granted a judgment notwithstanding the verdict on the grounds that the subject matter of the article was of "public interest," and therefore required the plaintiff to prove actual malice as defined in *New York Times.*[94] The decision was affirmed by the United States Court of Appeals for the Seventh Circuit,[95] whereupon the Supreme Court granted certiorari and reversed.[96]

---

[90] *Id.*

[91] Eight years after the historic decision in *Gertz,* Elmer Gertz finally prevailed in the litigation, with the Seventh Circuit Court of Appeals affirming the plaintiff's judgment in the district court, which had followed the Supreme Court's remand. Gertz v. Robert Welch, Inc., 680 F.2d 527 (7th Cir. 1982), *cert. denied,* 103 S. Ct. 1233 (1983). Gertz was able to establish both negligence and actual malice, and the Court of Appeals affirmed an award of $100,000 in compensatory damages and $300,000 in punitive damages. The decision is discussed later in this volume in connection with the problem of preconceived story lines and unreasonable reliance on sources. *See infra* § 3.02[5].

[92] Gertz v. Robert Welch, Inc., 306 F. Supp. 310, 311 (N.D. Ill. 1969).

[93] *Id.*

[94] Gertz v. Robert Welch, Inc., 322 F. Supp. 997, 1000 (N.D. Ill. 1979).

[95] 471 F.2d 801 (7th Cir. 1972).

[96] 418 U.S. 323 (1974). The commentary on the case is expansive. *See, e.g.,* Anderson, *Libel and Press Self-Censorship,* 53 Tex. L. Rev. 422 (1975); Ashdown, Gertz *and* Firestone: *A Study in Constitutional Policy Making,* 61 Minn. L. Rev. 645 (1977); Brosnahan, *From* Times v. Sullivan *to* Gertz v. Robert Welch: *Ten Years of Balancing Libel Law and the First Amendment,* 26 Hast. L.J. 777 (1975); Christie, *Underlying Contradictions in the Supreme Court's Classification of Defamation,* 1981 Duke L.J. 811; Eaton, *The American Law of Defamation Through* Gertz v. Robert Welch, Inc. *and Beyond: An Analytic Primer,* 61 Va. L. Rev. 1349 (1975); Frakt, *The Evolving Law of Defamation:* New York Times Co. v. Sullivan *to* Gertz v. Robert Welch, Inc. *and Beyond,* 6 Rut. Cam. L.J. 471 (1975); Gutman, *The Attempt to Develop an Appropriate Standard of Liability for the Defamation of Public and Private People: The Supreme Court and the Federalization of Libel Law,* 10 N.C. Cent. L.J. 201 (1979); LaRue, *Living With* Gertz: *A Practical Look at Constitutional Libel Standards,* 67 Va. 1. Rev. 287 (1981); Phillips, *Defamation, Invasion of Privacy, and The Contitutional Standard of Care,* 16 Santa Clara L. Rev. 77 (1976); Robertson, *Defamation and the First Amendment: In Praise of* Gertz v. Robert Welch, Inc., 54 Tex L. Rev. 199 (1976); Smith, *The Rising Tide of Libel Litigation: Implications of the* Gertz *Negligence Rule,* 44 Mont. L. Rev. 71 (1983); Watkins & Schwartz, Gertz *and the Common Law of Defamation: Of Fault, Nonmedia Defendants, and Conditional Privileges,* 15 Tex. Tech. L. Rev. 823 (1984).

[2] An Overview of *Gertz v. Robert Welch, Inc.*

In *Gertz,* the Supreme Court established a series of guidelines to govern the interplay between the first amendment principles articulated in *New York Times* and the traditional solicitude for interests in reputation evidenced by the common law. *Gertz* represented a judicial compromise that attempted to accommodate the competing values of "uninhibited, robust, and wide open" debate on public issues with society's need to protect reputation. The *Gertz* court reiterated the unsuitability in a free society of the traditional rule of strict liability for defamation, since compelling a speaker to "guarantee the accuracy of his factual assertions may lead to intolerable self-censorship."[97] The need to avoid self-censorship, however, was not the only societal value recognized by the Court; to give absolute protection to the news media would completely dissolve the competing social concerns underlying the law of defamation.[98] *Gertz* attempted to resolve the inherent friction between freedom of speech and protection of reputation by announcing a grouping of rules (each of these *Gertz* rules is given substantial individual attention elsewhere in this volume) setting forth the minimum constitutional requirements for compensating injury to reputation:

(1) Suits brought by public officials and public figures (at least involving speech of "public concern."[99]), must always meet the *New York Times* actual malice test.[100]

(2) Defamation suits brought by private individuals (at least those concerning public issues) must at the minimum be based upon proof of "fault," which has come to be understood as requiring a minimum of "negligence" in all such cases.[101]

(3) "Presumed damages" would no longer be permitted unless the

---

[97] Gertz v. Robert Welch, Inc., 418 U.S. 323, 340 (1974).

[98] *Id.* at 341 (quoting Rosenblatt v. Baer, 383 U.S. 75, 92 (1966)(Stewart, J., concurring)) (The individual's right to protect his or her own name "reflects no more than our basic concept of the essential dignity and worth of every human being—a concept at the root of any decent system of ordered liberty.")

[99] *Gertz* by its own terms referred only to media defendants. The Supreme Court recently eschewed any distinction between media and nonmedia defendants, instead limiting the applicability of *Gertz* to speech involving matters of "public concern." Dun & Bradstreet, Inc. v. Greenmoss Builders, Inc., 105 S. Ct. 2939 (1985). *See infra* §§ 3.02-3.05.

[100] 418 U.S. at 343.

[101] *Id.* at 347. *See infra* § 3.24.

plaintiff met the actual malice test; in the absence of actual malice, damages could not be awarded without proof of "actual injury," though the scope of "actual injury" and the nature of the evidence required remained broad. (This element of *Gertz* was narrowed significantly by the 1985 decision in *Dun & Bradstreet.*)[102]

(4) Any award of punitive damages would always require a showing of actual malice. (This rule also was altered by *Dun & Bradstreet.*)[103]

(5) *Gertz* appeared to establish absolute protection for the expression of opinion, raising to constitutional status the common law fact/opinion distinction.[104]

Although the *Gertz* opinion stated that it was unwise for the Supreme Court to proceed on a case-by-case basis in attempting to balance the constitutional claims of the press against individual claims for compensation, the Court invited the state courts to develop for themselves the proper standard of liability in suits brought by private plaintiffs.[105] Thus, the Court stated that as long as the states did not dip below the negligence standard, they should "retain substantial latitude in their efforts to enforce a legal remedy for defamatory falsehood injuries to the reputation of a private individual."[106]

§ 2.05 The "Access to the Media" Rationale

The *Gertz* compromise was grounded in two rationales reflecting the Supreme Court's perceptions about the differences between public and private figures. The first of these rationales is the "access to the media" argument. Public officials and figures, the Court reasoned, are more likely to have effective opportunities for self-help when they are defamed. Given the fact that, generally, public officials and public figures enjoy significantly greater access to channels of effective communication, the Court assumed that they have, as a class, a more realis-

---

102 418 U.S. at 349-50. On the definition of actual harm, *see infra* § 7.01[2]. For a discussion of the impact of *Dun & Bradstreet, see infra* § 3.02.

103 418 U.S. at 350. *See also infra* § 3.02.

104 418 U.S. at 339-40. *See infra* § 6.03[3]

105 418 U.S. at 345-46. The various state responses to *Gertz* are discussed in §§ 3.09-3.12, *infra.*

106 418 U.S. at 345-46.

tic opportunity to contradict the lie or correct the error than do private individuals.[107]

§ 2.06 The "Assumption of Risk" Rationale

The second rationale of the Court in *Gertz* was more normative, largely reflecting the homespun moral that one who seeks the public arena must accept the heat of the fire as part of the price of entering the kitchen. People who voluntarily attain public figure status often have assumed roles of special prominence in social affairs, and in all fairness they can be required to accept greater public scrutiny and greater exposure to defamation as part of the cost of such fame.[108]

§ 2.07 Subcategories of Public Figures

The Court in *Gertz* subdivided its discussion of public figures into two categories, "limited" (or "vortex") public figures, and "universal" (or "unlimited" or "pervasive") public figures. Some public figures occupy positions of such great power and influence that they are public figures for all purposes.[109] A sports star like Mohammed Ali, or an entertainer like Johnny Carson, might be considered such an "unlimited" public figure.[110] Most public figures, however, are "limited" public figures, persons who have "thrust themselves to the forefront of particular controversies in order to influence the resolution of the issues involved."[111] Such limited public figures are subject to the *New York Times* standard when they are defamed in connection with issues about which they have invited attention, but in all other aspects of their lives they remain private figures, for whom states are free to create compensation on a lesser showing of simple negligence.[112] Litigation involving "limited" public figures has produced the greater volume of cases and involves more problematic judgment calls than litigation involving the rarer "all purpose" public figure. The sections that follow elaborate on

---

107 *Id.* at 344.
108 *Id.* at 345.
109 *Id.*
110 *See infra* § 2.22.
111 *See infra* § 2.21.
112 418 U.S. at 349.

the factors and tests that have emerged to define limited public figures.[113]

§ 2.08 "Vortex" or "Limited Purpose" Concept

In the aftermath of *Gertz,* the Supreme Court undertook a series of refinements of the "limited" public figure, consistently giving the term an application more restricted in scope than the simple word "public" might suggest as a matter of popular colloquial usage.

[1] The *Firestone* Case

Time, Inc. v. Firestone[114] involved a defamation action brought by Mary Alice Firestone, wife of Russell Firestone, a member of the wealthy Firestone family. In 1964, the Firestones became embroiled in a vigorously contested divorce proceeding in Palm Beach County, Florida. Mary Alice Firestone had filed a complaint seeking separate maintenance and Russell Firestone had counterclaimed for divorce on grounds of "extreme cruelty and adultery."[115] The circuit court granted the divorce.[116] Through a wire service report and an account in a New

[113] *See infra* §§ 2.08-2.20.

[114] 424 U.S. 448 (1976).

[115] *Id.* at 450.

[116] The court included, in the final judgment, the following language:

> According to certain testimony in behalf of the defendant, extramarital escapades of the plaintiff were bizarre and of an amatory nature which would have made Dr. Freud's hair curl. Other testimony, in plaintiff's behalf, would indicate that defendant was guilty of bounding from one bedpartner to another with the erotic zest of a satyr. The court is inclined to discount much of this testimony as unreliable. Nevertheless, it is the conclusion and finding of the court that neither party is domesticated within the meaning of that term as used by the Supreme Court of Florida. . . .
>
> In the present case, it is abundantly clear from the evidence of marital discord that neither of the parties has shown the least susceptibility to domestication, and that the marriage should be dissolved. The premises considered, it is thereupon ORDERED AND ADJUDGED as follows:
>
> 1. That the equities in this cause are with the defendant; that defendant's counterclaim for divorce be and the same is hereby granted, and the bonds of matrimony which have heretofore existed between the parties are hereby forever dissolved.
>
> . . . .
>
> 4. That the defendant shall pay unto the plaintiff the sum of $3,000 per month as alimony beginning January 1, 1968, and a like sum on the first day of each and every month thereafter until the death or remarriage of the plaintiff.

Id. at 450-51 (quoting from trial court decree).

York newspaper,[117] *Time's* editorial staff, headquartered in New York, was alerted to the fact that a judgment had been rendered in the Firestone divorce proceeding. The staff subsequently received further information regarding the Florida decision from *Time's* Miami bureau chief and from a "stringer" working on special assignment in the Palm Beach area.[118] On the basis of these four sources, *Time's* staff composed an item, which appeared in the magazine's "Milestones" section the following week.[119]

Mary Alice Firestone sued *Time* for defamation and won a jury verdict of $100,000, a decision that was affirmed by the Florida Supreme Court.[120] On appeal to the United States Supreme Court, *Time* argued that the actual malice standard should have applied because the Firestone divorce was a "cause celebre" and Mary Alice Firestone was a "limited public figure" with regard to the divorce proceedings.[121] *Time* pointed out that Mrs. Firestone subscribed to a press clipping service that chronicled her media exposure, and that she held several press conferences during the divorce proceeding in which she answered press questions regarding the divorce litigation. *Time* proffered this evidence to demonstrate that Mrs. Firestone had voluntarily injected herself into a matter of public interest, thereby rendering her a "limited purpose" public figure with regard to coverage of the divorce litigation.[122]

The Supreme Court held that Mrs. Firestone was not a public figure and that the defendant was not entitled to the protection of the *New York Times* standard with regard to her claim. Mary Alice Firestone's prominence in what Justice Marshall depicted as "the sporting set" did not qualify her as a person of "especial prominence in the affairs of

---

117 *Id.* at 448, 451.

118 *Id.*

119 The item read:

> DIVORCED. By Russell A. Firestone, Jr., 41, heir to the tire fortune: Mary Alice Sullivan Firestone, 32, his third wife; a onetime Palm Beach schoolteacher; on grounds of extreme cruelty and adultery; after six years of marriage, one son; in West Palm Beach, Fla. The 17-month intermittent trial produced enough testimony of extramarital adventures on both sides, said the judge, "to make Dr. Freud's hair curl."

Id.

120 Firestone v. Time, Inc., 305 So. 2d 172 (Fla. 1974).

121 Time, Inc. v. Firestone, 424 U.S. 448, 454 (1976).

122 *Id.* at 448, 454 n.3.

society."[123] Even though Mrs. Firestone initiated litigation in a public court of law, the Court held that her action was not a purposeful insertion into a matter of public controversy, since state law compelled her to resort to legal process in order to obtain lawful release from the bonds of matrimony.[124] Furthermore, the Court refused to extend *New York Times* protection to all reports of judicial proceedings. Even if narrowed to reports of what actually transpires in a courtroom, the Court held, application of the *New York Times* privilege would sweep too broadly, because "the details of many, if not most, courtroom battles would add almost nothing towards advancing the uninhibited debate on public issues."[125] Although the Court conceded that some participants in some litigation may be legitimate public figures, either generally or for the limited purpose of press coverage concerning the litigation, the majority will resemble Mary Alice Firestone, "drawn into a public forum largely against their will in order to attempt to obtain the only redress available to them or to defend themselves against actions brought by the State or by others."[126]

[2] The *Wolston* Case

Wolston v. Reader's Digest Association, Inc.,[127] involved a book entitled *KGB, The Secret Work of Soviet Agents,* written by John Barron and published by the Reader's Digest Corporation. The book described Soviet espionage efforts since World War II. One segment chronicled a 1957-58 New York City grand jury investigation into Soviet intelligence activities in the United States. Wolston was subpoenaed by the grand jury after his aunt and uncle pleaded guilty to charges of espionage.[128] After appearing before the grand jury on several occasions, Wolston ignored a subpoena requiring him to appear before the grand jury in 1958, and subsequently pleaded guilty to a charge of criminal contempt.[129] Wolston's episode with the grand jury investigation and his subsequent conviction for criminal contempt resulted in 15 newspa-

---

123 *Id.* at 453.

124 *Id.* at 454.

125 *Id.* at 457. On the question of attorneys involved in litigation as public or private figures, *see infra* § 2.21[9][a].

126 *Id.*

127 443 U.S. 157 (1979).

128 *Id.* at 161-62.

129 *Id.* at 162-63.

per articles in New York and Washington, D.C.[130] Furthermore, Wolston was mentioned in two publications concerning Soviet espionage activities prior to the KGB book.[131] Wolston was also classified in a published FBI report as among those whom "the F.B.I. investigation . . . identified as Soviet intelligence agents."[132]

Sixteen years after the grand jury probe into Soviet intelligence activities, Mr. Barron's book was published by the defendant. The KGB book listed the plaintiff as being among a group of "Soviet agents identified in the United States," and further stated that those on the list were "Soviet agents who were convicted of espionage or falsifying information or perjury and/or contempt charges following espionage indictments, or who fled to the Soviet bloc to avoid prosecution."[133] Wolston sued Reader's Digest Corporation for defamation, and the lower courts held that Wolston was a "public figure" and that the actual malice standard of *New York Times* therefore applied.[134] The Court of Appeals further held that although the book erroneously implied that Wolston had been indicted for espionage, there was, nonetheless, "no genuine issue with respect to the existence of actual malice" on the part of the defendants.[135]

The United States Supreme Court reversed, holding that Wolston was not a public figure within the meaning of *Gertz* and that it was therefore wrong to apply the actual malice standard to Wolston's claim.[136] Wolston, the Court noted, was clearly not a "general public figure" under *Gertz,* because he had achieved no general fame or notoriety and had assumed no role of special prominence in the affairs of society as a result of his contempt citation or his connection with the grand jury investigation into Soviet spy activity.[137] Moreover, the Supreme Court explicitly rejected the lower courts' holdings that Wolston was a "limited public figure" to whom the *New York Times* test would apply for the limited purpose of comment regarding his connection to

130 *Id.* at 163.

131 *Id.* at 163 n.6.

132 *Id.* (quoting S. Doc. No. 114, 86th Cong., 2d Sess. 24, 26-27 (1960)).

133 443 U.S. at 159.

134 Wolston v Reader's Digest Ass'n, 429 F. Supp. 167, 176 (D.D.C. 1977), *aff'd,* 578 F.2d 427, 429-31 (D.C. Cir. 1978), *rev'd,* 443 U.S. 157 (1979).

135 578 F.2d at 434.

136 443 U.S. at 163-69.

137 *Id.* at 165.

or involvement with the Soviet espionage world.[138] This holding by the Court constricted the public figure concept substantially, for it might well have been argued that Wolston had in fact voluntarily entered the controversy by not appearing before the grand jury. That same nonappearance had already resulted in Wolston's being mentioned in 15 newspaper articles, one other book, and an official public FBI report. At the very least, it seems that Wolston's refusal to appear before the grand jury and his subsequent plea of guilty to contempt charges qualified him as having involved himself purposefully in a matter of legitimate public interest concerning the espionage investigation that formed the subject matter of the grand jury's work.

The Supreme Court's refusal to accept this argument demonstrates how truly "limited" the Court's view of the limited public figure may be.[139] The Court heavily emphasized the fact that Wolston had been "dragged unwillingly" into the controversy surrounding the KGB's presence in the United States, rather than having "voluntarily thrust" or "injected himself into the forefront" of public attention.[140] There was no "controversy" about espionage into which Wolston could have thrust himself, the Court noted, "because all responsible United States citizens understandably were and are opposed to" espionage.[141] As will be discussed subsequently, lower courts have not wholeheartedly embraced *Wolston's* sharply constricted definition of what qualifies as a public controversy, and it would be a fair summary of the trend of lower court decisions to say that they have not, on the whole, applied Wolston with the rigidity that the Supreme Court's analysis in the case might suggest.

---

138 *Id.* at 166.

139 *See generally* Rosen, *Media Lament—The Rise and Fall of Involuntary Public Figures,* 54 St. John's L. Rev. 487 (1980); Watkins, *The Demise of the Public Figure Doctrine,* 27 J. Comm. 47 (1977); Watkins & Schwartz, *supra* note 96, at 830; Note, *The Supreme Court Places Further Limitations on Designation as "Public Figure" in Libel Actions,* 1980 B.Y.U. L. Rev. 450; Note, *Whither the Limited Purpose Public Figure?* 8 Hofstra L. Rev. 403 (1980); Note, *Libel—Creation and Resurrection of a Limited-Purpose Public Figure as a Prerequisite to the Application of the* New York Times *Actual Malice Standard,* 8 N. Ky. L. Rev. 647 (1981); Note, *Libel Becomes Viable: The Narrow Application of Limited Public Figure Status in Current Defamation Law,* 7 Ohio N.U. L. Rev. 125 (1980); Note, *Constitutional Protection of Critical Speech and the Public Figure Doctrine: Retreat by Reaffirmation,* 1980 Wis. L. Rev. 568.

See also infra § 2.16.

140 443 U.S. at 166.

141 *Id.* at 166 n.8.

[3] The *Hutchinson* Case

Hutchinson v. Proxmire[142] involved a suit brought by Ronald Hutchinson, an adjunct professor at Western Michigan University and the Director of Research at Kalamazoo State Mental Hospital, in Michigan, against William Proxmire, a United States Senator from Wisconsin, and Proxmire's legislative aide. In 1975, Proxmire invented a mock prize that he termed the "Golden Fleece of the Month Award." Proxmire would present the award periodically to point out those examples of waste the Senator perceived as particularly egregious.[143] In April 1975, the Golden Fleece was awarded jointly to the National Science Foundation, the National Aeronautics and Space Administration, and the Office of Naval Research, for spending more than $500,000 during a seven-year period to fund Dr. Hutchinson's research.[144] Hutchinson's research involved the examination of patterns of emotional behavior of certain animals, e.g., the clenching of jaws of primates when exposed to irritating or stressful stimuli. Proxmire ridiculed federal spending on such research in a speech and press release that sarcastically belittled Hutchinson's work.[145]

Most of the Supreme Court's opinion involved the determination that Proxmire was not absolutely shielded from liability under the speech or debate clause of the United States Constitution[146] (an issue discussed *infra* under the heading of absolute immunity).[147] The Supreme Court did, however, deal secondarily with Proxmire's argument that he was entitled to the benefit of the *New York Times* actual malice standard because Hutchinson was a "limited public figure" for the purpose of commentary on his publicly funded research.[148] Hutchinson had "voluntarily" applied for federal funds, and reports of his successes in obtaining federal grants appeared in local newspapers and scientific journals.[149] Furthermore, Hutchinson was not without access to the media; some newspapers and wire services reported Hutchinson's re-

---

142 443 U.S. 111 (1979).

143 *Id.* at 114.

144 *Id.*

145 121 Cong. Rec. 10, 803 (1975).

146 U.S. Const. art. I, § 6, cl. 1. *See* Hutchinson v Proxmire, 443 U.S. 111, 123-33 (1979).

147 *See infra* § 8.03.

148 433 U.S. at 133-36.

149 *Id.* at 115 n.119.

sponse to the Golden Fleece Award.[150]

The Supreme Court found, however, that Hutchinson was not a public figure within the narrowed meaning of that term after *Firestone* and *Wolston*. The Court stated that Proxmire could not turn Hutchinson into a public figure by virture of Proxmire's own allegations, because that would permit a defendant to create a public figure defense through the defendant's own conduct.[151] Pointing to *Wolston's* emphasis on the term "public controversy" as limited to matters of public debate, the Court noted that Hutchinson did not thrust himself into the public eye "to influence others."[152] General concern about public expenditures, even large ones, was not enough, in the Court's view, to activate the *New York Times* test, because that would implicate the discredited *Rosenbloom* approach of subject matter classification[153] and ignore the public figure/private figure compromise struck in *Gertz*.[154]

§ 2.09 Practical Application of the Limited Public Figure Standard

[1] The Elusive Classification Problem

The practical task of classifying particular plaintiffs as public or private figures has been left primarily to lower court judges, and the task has proved difficult. In *Rosanova v. Playboy Enterprises, Inc.*,[155] the court encapsulated the frustration with which lower courts have grappled with the public figure/private figure dichotomy: Demarcating between public and private figures "is much like trying to nail a jelly fish to the wall."[156] In struggling with the problem, the lower courts have realized that the Supreme Court "has not fleshed out the skeletal descriptions of public figures and private persons enunciated in *Gertz*."[157]

---

150 *Id.* at 134.

151 *Id.* at 135-36. This "bootstrap" problem is discussed in § 2.10, *infra*.

152 *Id.*

153 *See supra* § 2.03.

154 *See supra* § 2.04.

155 411 F. Supp. 440 (S.D. Ga. 1976), *aff'd*, 580 F.2d 859 (5th Cir. 1978).

156 411 F. Supp. at 443.

157 Waldbaum v. Fairchild Publications, Inc., 627 F.2d 1287, 1292 (D.C. Cir.), *cert. denied*, 449 U.S. 898 (1980). The secondary problem of defining "public controversy" has proved equally difficult. *See, e.g.*, Street v. National Broadcasting Co., 645 F.2d 1227, 1234 (6th Cir.), *cert. denied*, 454 U.S. 815, *cert. dismissed*, 454 U.S. 1095 (1981) (noting that it "is evident that it is not simply any controversy of general or public interest").

One of the common denominators running through *Gertz, Firestone, Wolston,* and *Hutchinson* is the requirement that the plaintiff, to be classified as a limited public figure, must have voluntarily injected himself into a matter of "public controversy."[158] This requirement obviously puts great definitional pressure on the term "public controversy," and explication of that term has proved to be central to the efforts of lower courts to apply the public figure/private figure distinction.[159]

[2] "Public Controversy" and "Plaintiff Involvement"

Virtually all the approaches adopted by lower courts to define "public figure" status involve two basic subcomponents:

(1) A "public controversy" of some kind must exist.
(2) There must be "involvement" by the plaintiff in that public controversy.

To recognize those two basic subcomponents is one thing,[160] to apply them is quite another. Within the general parameters of these two components the methodology employed by lower courts in defining the public figure concept has varied considerably, and in general has not been as stringently limited as the Supreme Court precedent might, standing alone, indicate. A number of lower court decisions have simply not accepted the narrow language of cases such as *Firestone, Wolston,* and *Hutchinson* literally, and have employed more creative and subtle standards for determining the existence of a public figure status.[161]

---

158 *See* Wolston v. Reader's Digest Ass'n, 443 U.S. 157, 167-68 (1979); Hutchinson v. Proxmire, 443 U.S. 111, 134-36 (1979); Time, Inc. v. Firestone, 424 U.S. 448, 454 (1976); Gertz v. Robert Welch, Inc., 418 U.S. 323, 346 (1974).

159 *See generally* Note, *Defining a Public Controversy in the Constitutional Law of Defamation,* 69 Va. L. Rev. 931 (1983).

160 *See* Clark v. American Broadcasting Companies, 684 F.2d 1208, 1218 (6th Cir. 1982), *cert. denied,* 460 U.S. 1040 (1983) ("a public controversy must exist" and "the nature and extent of the individual's participation in the particular controversy must be ascertained").

161 *See, e.g.,* Marcone v. Penthouse International, Ltd., 11 Med. L. Rep. (BNA) 1577, 1582-85 (3d Cir. 1985); Rebozo v. Washington Post Co., 637 F.2d 375 (5th Cir.), *cert. denied,* 454 U.S. 964 (1981); Waldbaum v. Fairchild Publications, 627 F.2d 1287 (D.C. Cir.), *cert. denied,* 449 U.S. 898 (1980); Brewer v. Memphis Publishing Co., 626 F.2d 1238 (5th Cir. 1980), *cert. denied,* 452 U.S. 962 (1981); Chuy v. Philadelphia Eagles Football Club, 595 F.2d 1265 (3d Cir. 1979)(en banc); Harris v. Tomczak, 94 F.R.D. 687 (E.D. Cal. 1982); McManus v. Doubleday & Co., 513 F. Supp. 1383 (S.D.N.Y. 1981); Vitale v. National Lampoon, Inc., 449 F. Supp. 442 (E.D. Pa. 1978); Rosanova v. Playboy Enterprises, 411 F. Supp. 440 (S.D. Ga. 1976), *aff'd,* 580 F.2d 859 (5th Cir. 1978); Sewell v. Brookbank,

Some courts essentially define the limited public figure through an ad hoc judgment approach. The Fifth Circuit stated in *Rosanova v. Playboy Enterprises,*[162] for example, "[a]lthough the public figure concept has evolved a truly working definition, it falls within that class of legal abstractions where 'I know it when I see it,' in Mr. Justice Stewart's words." [163] Most courts, however, have embarked on more elaborate definitions.

[3] Multifactor Tests

The ad hoc approach appears gradually to be giving way to a sensitivity to more sharply refined assessments of factors relevant to the classification issue. In recent years, a number of lower courts have attempted to fashion more detailed formulations of the public figure requirement. In *Waldbaum v. Fairchild Publications,*[164] for example, the court emphasized an objective three part test. The *Waldbaum* court stated that a person has become a public figure for limited purposes if he:

(1) is attempting to have, or realistically can be expected to have, a major impact on the resolution of a specific public dispute

(2) that has foreseeable and substantial ramifications for persons beyond its immediate participants.

(3) In making a determination, the court has to look through the eyes of a reasonable person at the facts taken as a whole.[165]

---

119 Ariz. 422, 581 P.2d 267 (Ct. App. 1978); Byers v. Southeastern Newspaper Corp., 161 Ga. App. 717, 288 S.E.2d 698 (1982); Colson v. Steig, 89 Ill. 2d 205, 433 N.E.2d 246 (1982); Kobar v. Hite, 43 Ill. App. 3d 636, 357 N.E.2d 135 (1976); State v. Defley, 395 So. 2d 759 (La. 1981); Johnston v. Corinthian Television Corp., 583 P.2d 1101 (Okla. 1978); Press, Inc. v. Verran, 569 S.W.2d 435 (Tenn. 1978). *See also* Ashdown, *Of Public Figures and Public Interest—The Libel Law Conundrum,* 25 Wm. & Mary L. Rev. 937 (1984); Daniels, *Public Figures Revisited,* 25 Wm. & Mary L. Rev. 957 (1984).

[162] 580 F.2d 859 (5th Cir. 1978). One commentator has estimated that "[a]pproximately four-fifths of the decided cases may properly be classified as ad hoc because they fail to articulate any rule of decision applicable to future public controversy questions." Note, *Defining a Public Controversy, supra* note 159, at 944 n.77.

[163] 580 F.2d at 861 (quoting Jacobellis v. Ohio, 378 U.S. 184, 197 (1964)(Stewart, J., concurring)).

[164] 627 F.2d 1287 (D.C. Cir.), *cert. denied,* 449 U.S. 898 (1980).

[165] *Id.* at 1292.

Another multifactor test was articulated by the district court in *Fitzgerald v. Penthouse International, Ltd.*[166] To determine whether the plaintiff is a limited purpose public figure the court must assess:

(1) the plaintiff's access to effective channels of communication;
(2) the extent to which the plaintiff voluntarily assumed a role of special prominence in regard to a public controversy;
(3) the extent to which the plaintiff sought to influence the outcome of the controversy;
(4) whether the controversy predated the publication of the allegedly defamatory communication; and
(5) whether the plaintiff's public figure status was retained at the time of the publication.[167]

A three factor test was announced by the Sixth Circuit in *Clark v. American Broadcasting Companies:*[168]

(1) the extent to which the plaintiff's participation in the controversy is voluntary;
(2) the extent to which the plaintiff has access to channels of effective communications to counter the false defamatory statements;
(3) the prominence of the role played by the plaintiff.[169]

The Second Circuit in *Lerman v. Flynt Distributing Company*[170] phrased the analysis of the public figure/private figure in terms of a four part test. A defendant must show the plaintiff has:

(1) successfully invited public attention to his views in an effort to influence others prior to the incident that is the subject of the litigation;
(2) voluntarily injected himself into a public controversy related to the subject of the litigation;
(3) assumed a position of prominence in the public controversy; and

---

166 525 F. Supp. 585 (D. Md. 1981), *aff'd in part and rev'd in part,* 691 F.2d 666 (4th Cir. 1982), *cert. denied,* 460 U.S. 1024 (1983).

167 525 F. Supp. at 592.

168 684 F.2d 1208 (6th Cir. 1982), *cert. denied,* 460 U.S. 1040 (1983).

169 *Id.* at 1218.

170 745 F.2d 123 (2d Cir. 1984), *cert. denied,* 105 S. Ct. 2114 (1985).

(4) maintained regular and continuing access to the media.[171]

[4] Relevant Factors

The factors in the following list (each factor is given individual attention in subsequent sections)[172] are the ones that courts have in many different combinations found influential in individual public figure/private figure determinations:

(1) The extent to which the "controversy" preexisted the defamatory speech (the "bootstrap" problem);
(2) The effect of the "controversy" on the interests of nonparticipants;
(3) The level of voluntariness in the plaintiff's involvement in the controversy;
(4) The plaintiff's access to channels of communication for counterspeech;
(5) The degree of public divisiveness concerning the controversy;
(6) The extent of the plaintiff's prominence in the controversy;
(7) The extent of the plaintiff's efforts to attempt to influence resolution of the controversy;
(8) The extent to which the plaintiff's public figure status continued to exist at the time of publication;
(9) The extent to which the allegedly defamatory speech is geographically or institutionally limited to the area in which the plaintiff had achieved public figure status.

Not all of the factors will be relevant in every defamation suit, and indeed the strong presence or absence of just one or two of the factors listed might in any given situation tip the determination in favor of or against classification as a public figure. At times individual factors may cut against each other, making the decision particularly difficult. For example, the public controversy may be extremely visible and divisive, it may predate the defamatory speech, it may have a major impact on nonparticipants, and the plaintiff may play a prominent role within it—all factors pointing toward classification as a public figure. The same plaintiff, however, may have had his role in the controversy thrust upon him, may have only modest access to channels of communication, and may have been out of the public eye at the time the defamatory speech

---

[171] *Id.* at 136-37.

[172] *See infra* §§ 2.10-2.20.

was published—all factors cutting against public figure status. The usefulness of this list is that it focuses attention on the wide variety of circumstances that may legitimately bear on the classification, circumstances that are necessarily as various as the myriad contexts in which the public figure/private figure question can arise. An excellent example of sensitivity to the sifting and weighing of multiple factors is the discussion in *Marcone v. Penthouse International, Ltd.*,[173] in which the court admitted candidly that:

> This is a close case, and if each element of the equation is taken separately it may be argued that no one aspect may be sufficient to create public figure status. Nevertheless, *when all the relevant factors are considered in context as a whole*, we believe that [the plaintiff] has crossed the line from private to limited purpose public figure.[174]

§ 2.10 The Bootstrap Problem

In *Hutchinson v. Proxmire*,[175] the Supreme Court addressed in passing an issue that had always been a problem in application of the public figure/private figure dichotomy: the media's potential for "bootstrapping" itself into the protection of the actual malice standard by pointing to its own coverage of the plaintiff as evidence that the plaintiff is a public figure. The Court stated that "[c]learly, those charged with defamation cannot, by their own conduct, create their own defense by making the claimant a public figure."[176] Responding to this bootstrap problem and to the language of *Hutchinson*, a number of courts have emphasized that the public controversy must "preexist" the speech giving rise to the defamation suit.[177]

---

173 754 F.2d 1072 (3d Cir.), *cert. denied*, 474 U.S. 864, *reh'g denied*, 474 U.S. 1014 (1985).

174 *Id.* at 1086 (emphasis supplied).

175 443 U.S. 111 (1979). *See supra* § 2.08[3].

176 *Id.* at 135.

177 *See, e.g.*, Kassel v. Gannett Co., 875 F.2d 935 (1st Cir. 1989); Marcone v. Penthouse International, Ltd., 754 F.2d 1072 (3d Cir.), *cert. denied*, 474 U.S. 864, *reh'g denied*, 474 U.S. 1014 (1985); Lerman v. Flynt Distributing Co., 745 F.2d 123 (2d Cir. 1984), *cert. denied*, 471 U.S. 1054, 105 S. Ct. 2114 (1985); Fitzgerald v. Penthouse, International Ltd., 691 F.2d 666, 668-69 (4th Cir. 1982), *cert. denied*, 460 U.S. 1024 (1983); Bruno & Stillman, Inc. v. Globe Newspaper Co., 633 F.2d 583, 591 (1st Cir. 1980); Waldbaum v. Fairchild Publications, Inc., 627 F.2d 1287, 1297, 1299 (D.C. Cir.), *cert. denied*, 449 U.S. 898 (1980); Schultz v. Reader's Digest Ass'n, 468 F. Supp. 551 (E.D. Mich. 1979); Fairley v. Peekskill Star Corp., 83 A.D.2d 294, 445 N.Y.S.2d 156 (2d Dept. 1981); Greenberg v. CBS, Inc., 69 A.D.2d 693, 419 N.Y.S.2d 988, 993-94 (2d Dept. 1979).

§ 2.11 Preexisting Controversy Requirement

[1] Problems Attending Investigative Reporting

In some cases there is no preexisting public controversy in a literal sense, because the issue giving rise to the defamatory speech has not yet been "uncovered."[178] The public may be deeply interested in the "problem" in a general sense, but have no specific knowledge of the specific events involved in the defamatory speech until that speech is published. The public may have a general interest in organized crime,[179] political corruption,[180] attorney misconduct,[181] or consumer protection,[182] for example, but not yet be aware that a specific individu-

---

178 *See, e.g.*, Lawrence v. Moss, 639 F.2d 634 (10th Cir.), *cert. denied*, 451 U.S. 1031 (1981)(plaintiff alleged to be a "bagman" for former Vice-President Spiro Agnew); Rosanova v. Playboy Enterprises, 580 F.2d 859 (5th Cir. 1978)(involving alleged organized crime connection); Schultz v. Reader's Digest Ass'n, 468 F. Supp. 551 (E.D. Mich. 1979)(involving Jimmy Hoffa's disappearance); Logan v. District of Columbia, 447 F. Supp. 1328 (D.D.C. 1978)(police "sting" operation); Rancho La Costa, Inc. v. Superior Court, 106 Cal. App. 3d 646, 165 Cal. Rptr. 347 (1980), *appeal dismissed*, 450 U.S. 902 (1981)(resort and its officers alleged to have connections to organized crime); Marchiondo v. Brown, 98 N.M. 394, 649 P.2d 462 (1982)(alleged connections to organized crime); Burns v. Times Argus Ass'n, 139 Vt. 381, 430 A.2d 773 (1981)(alleged misuse of state funds by wife of lieutenant governor).

179 *See* Rosanova v. Playboy Enterprises, 580 F.2d 859 (5th Cir. 1978); Rancho La Costa v. Superior Court, 106 Cal. App. 3d 646, 165 Cal. Rptr. 347 (1980), *appeal dismissed*, 450 U.S. 902 (1981); Marchiondo v. Brown, 98 N.M. 394, 649 P.2d 462 (1982).

180 Lawrence v. Moss, 639 F.2d 634 (10th Cir.), *cert. denied*, 451 U.S. 1031 (1981); Clyburn v. News World Communication, 705 F. Supp. 635 (D.D.C. 1989); Buchanan v. Associated Press, 398 F. Supp. 1196 (D.D.C. 1975); Burns v. Times Argus Ass'n, 139 Vt. 381, 430 A.2d 773 (1981).

181 Littlefield v. Fort Dodge Messenger, 614 F.2d 581 (8th Cir.), *cert. denied*, 445 U.S. 945 (1980)(attorney's guilty plea in a disciplinary action); Dodrill v. Arkansas Democrat Co., 265 Ark. 628, 590 S.W.2d 840 (1979), *cert. denied*, 444 U.S. 1076 (1980)(false statement that attorney suspended for unethical conduct and had failed state bar exam); Bandelin v. Pietsch, 98 Idaho 337, 563 P.2d 395, *cert. denied*, 434 U.S. 891 (1977)(attorney's alleged mishandling of an estate); Steere v. Cupp, 226 Kan. 566, 602 P.2d 1267 (1979)(attorney's fee contract in a murder trial); Hayes v. Booth Newspapers, Inc., 97 Mich. App. 758, 295 N.W.2d 858 (1980)(attorney's behavior in trying a murder case); Peisner v. Detroit Free Press, Inc., 82 Mich. App. 153, 266 N.W.2d 693 (1978)(attorney's defense of an indigent criminal defendant).

182 *See* Steaks Unlimited, Inc. v. Deaner, 623 F.2d 264 (3d Cir. 1980)(involving meat sale); Yiamouyiannis v. Consumers Union of the United States, Inc., 619 F.2d 932 (2d Cir.), *cert. denied*, 449 U.S. 839 (1980)(water flouridation); General Products Co. v. Meredeth Corp., 526 F. Supp. 546 (E.D. Va. 1981)(manufacturer of chimneys); American Benefit Life Ins. Co. v. McIntyre, 375 So. 2d 239 (Ala. 1979)(insurance company operations); Antwerp Diamond Exchange v. Better Business Bureau, 130 Ariz. 523, 637 P.2d 733 (1981)(diamond seller); Commercial Programming Unlimited v. CBS, Inc., 81 Misc. 2d 678, 367 N.Y.S.2d 986 (Sup. Ct. 1975)(computer training schools); Wright v. Haas, 586

al has a crime connection, or is guilty of political abuse, or is involved in attorney misconduct, or has perpetrated consumer fraud. Courts faced with this sort of situation sometimes decide that the public controversy requirement has been satisfied,[183] and sometimes decide that it has not.[184]

Courts that rigidly apply the preexisting controversy requirement may improperly penalize investigative reporting that uncovers the plaintiff's alleged involvement in a given activity by citing the principle that the defendant cannot create his own defense by focusing attention on the plaintiff. The temptation to rigidly apply the preexisting controversy requirement is an outgrowth of the repudiation of the "public interest" test from *Rosenbloom*,[185] for if one emphasizes only the preexisting public concern with the general issue rather than the more specific events giving rise to the defamation, one seems to allow the public figure analysis to slide into the discredited public interest approach.[186]

P.2d 1093 (Okla. 1978)(utility rates); Martin v. Griffin Television, Inc., 549 P.2d 85 (Okla. 1976) (conditions in a pet shop); Exner v. American Medical Ass'n, 12 Wash. App. 215, 529 P.2d 863 (1974)(water treatment).

183 *See, e.g.*, Steaks Unlimited, Inc. v. Deaner, 623 F.2d 264 (3d Cir. 1980); Yiamouyiannis v. Consumers Union of the United States, Inc., 619 F.2d 932 (2d Cir.), *cert. denied*, 449 U.S. 839 (1980); Rosanova v. Playboy Enterprises, 580 F.2d 859 (5th Cir. 1978); Bandelin v. Pietsch, 98 Idaho 337, 563 P.2d 395, *cert. denied*, 434 U.S. 1891 (1977); Marchiondo v. Brown, 98 N.M. 394, 649 P.2d 462 (1982).

184 *See, e.g.*, Wolston v. Reader's Digest Ass'n, 443 U.S. 157 (1979); Jenoff v. Hearst Corp., 644 F.2d 1004 (4th Cir. 1981); Dodrill v. Arkansas Democrat Co., 265 Ark. 628, 590 S.W.2d 840 (1979), *cert. denied*, 444 U.S. 1076 (1980); Rancho La Costa, Inc. v. Superior Court, 106 Cal. App. 3d 646, 165 Cal. Rptr. 347 (1980), *appeal denied*, 450 U.S. 902 (1981); Vegod Corp. v. American Broadcasting Co., 25 Cal. 3d 763, 603 P.2d 14, 160 Cal. Rptr. 97 (1979), *cert. denied*, 449 U.S. 886 (1980).

185 Rosenbloom v. Metromedia, Inc., 403 U.S. 29 (1971). As Professor Tribe has put it, "[N]ow judges are asked to determine whether a controversy is 'public,' . . . a determination indistinguishable to the naked eye from whether the subject matter is of public or general concern." L. Tribe, American Constitutional Law, 644 (1978). *See supra* § 2.03.

186 For an excellent discussion of this problem, *see* Bruno & Stillman, Inc. v. Globe Newspaper Co., 633 F.2d 583, 591 (1st Cir. 1980), *See also* Franklin v. Lodge 1108, Benevolent & Protective Order of Elks, 97 Cal. App. 3d 915, 930-31, 159 Cal. Rptr. 131, 140 (1979); James v. Gannett Co., 40 N.Y.2d 415, 422, 353 N.E.2d 834, 839-40, 386 N.Y.S.2d 871, 876 (1976). The problem, of course, is now further complicated by the resurrection of the "public concern" test to determine whether *Gertz* applies at all in private figure plaintiff cases, in light of the Supreme Court's holding in Dun & Bradstreet, Inc. v. Greenmoss Builders, Inc., 472 U.S. 749, 105 S. Ct. 2939 (1985). *See infra* §§ 3.02-3.05.

[2] A Flexible Solution

It is possible, however, to apply the preexisting controversy requirement with sufficient flexibility to avoid penalizing investigative journal-

(*Text continued on page 2-37*)

ism, at the same time steering clear of the public interest approach of *Rosenbloom.* When the plaintiff is allegedly involved in a blameworthy activity and has engaged in efforts to conceal that involvement, the court in its determination of the public figure issue may legitimately treat the blameworthy activity and the acts of concealment as surrogates for the more traditional form of open public controversy.[187] The public interest in hidden corruption is every bit as strong as in open corruption—it would be illogical to say that the first newspaper story uncovering facts about the Watergate break-in is to be treated as having less first amendment protection than subsequent stories. The controversy can, in a sense, be said to "pre-exist" the story; it merely remained "latent" until exposed. Although some recent opinions appear to evince a general hostility toward aggressive investigative reporting,[188] some decisions indicate a willingness on the part of some courts to treat the preexisting controversy requirement more flexibly, finding public figure status when other factors point strongly in that direction.[189]

§ 2.12 Interests of Nonparticipants

One relatively reliable indicator that a public controversy exists is that the issues being debated have an impact beyond the immediate parochial interests of the participants in the debate. To the extent that one of the primary first amendment values protected by *Gertz* is the allowance of breathing space for speech directed at the resolution of issues of social concern,[190] it makes sense to inquire whether persons other than the immediate participants in the controversy are affected by it. The District of Columbia Court of Appeals has thus spoken of the

---

[187] *See* Rosanova v. Playboy Enterprises, 580 F.2d 859, 861 (5th Cir. 1978)(plaintiff's voluntary association with organized crime figures "was bound to attract attention and comment" and rendered plaintiff a public figure); Logan v. District of Columbia, 447 F. Supp. 1328 (D.D.C. 1978)(plaintiff who obtained position in fencing operation was public figure for purposes of report on use of illicit drugs by those involved in the operation).

[188] *See generally* Tavoulareas v. Washington Post Co., 759 F.2d 90 (D.C. Cir. 1985), *vacated,* 817 F.2d 762 (D.C. Cir.)(en banc), *cert. denied,* 108 S. Ct. 200 (1987). *See infra* § 3.20[5].

[189] *See, e.g.,* Marcone v. Penthouse International, Ltd., 754 F.2d 1072, 1080-82 (3d Cir.), *cert. denied,* 474 U.S. 864, *reh'g denied,* 474 U.S. 1014 (1985); Rosanova v. Playboy Enterprises, 580 F.2d 859 (5th Cir. 1978); Rancho La Costa v. Superior Court, 106 Cal. App. 3d 646, 165 Cal. Rptr. 347 (1980), *appeal dismissed,* 450 U.S. 902 (1981); Marchiondo v. Brown, 98 N.M. 394, 649 P.2d 462 (1982).

[190] *See* Dun & Bradstreet, Inc. v. Greenmoss Builders, Inc., 472 U.S. 749, 105 S. Ct. 2939 (1985).

"impact on the resolution of a specific public dispute that has foreseeable and substantial ramifications *for persons beyond its immediate participants*"[191] as one of the factors to be weighed in determining public figure status. A number of other courts have similarly discussed the impact on nonparticipants, in cases that have found that a public controversy does exist[192] as well as cases finding that one does not.[193] Speech involving collective action such as the activity of labor unions, publicly held corporations, political activity, or consumer boycotts, because it tends intrinsically to be linked to interests beyond those of the immediate participants, is more likely to be classified as pertinent to a public controversy.[194]

§ 2.13 Plaintiff's Voluntary Involvement

[1] In General

There is little question that the extent to which the plaintiff *voluntarily* injects himself or herself into a particular public controversy is one of the single most important factors in determining public figure status. The Supreme Court in *Gertz* stated that in each case the question is "the nature and extent of an individual's participation in the particular controversy giving rise to the defamation."[195] The "assumption of risk" rationale—that those who enter the kitchen must accept the heat[196]—is one of the two essential underpinnings of *Gertz,*[197] and it makes very little sense to speak of assumption of risk as a justifying rationale unless that assumption is voluntary.

---

191 Waldbaum v. Fairchild Publications, 627 F.2d 1287, 1292 (D.C. Cir.), *cert. denied,* 449 U.S. 898 (1980)(emphasis supplied).

192 *See* Avins v. White, 627 F.2d 637 (3d cir.), *cert. denied,* 449 U.S. 982 (1980)(public controversy existed over accreditation of law school); Fitzgerald v. Penthouse International, Ltd., 525 F. Supp. 585 (D. Md. 1981), *aff'd in part and rev'd in part on other grounds,* 691 F.2d 666 (4th Cir. 1982), *cert. denied,* 460 U.S. 1024 (1983)(public controversy existed regarding use of dolphins for military and intelligence purposes); Bose Corp. v. Consumers Union of the United States, 508 F. Supp. 1249 (D. Mass. 1981), *rev'd on other grounds,* 692 F.2d 189 (1st Cir. 1982), *aff'd,* 466 U.S. 485, 104 S. Ct. 1949 (1984)(public controversy found to exist over quality of plaintiff manufacturer's speaker systems).

193 *See* Denny v. Mertz, 100 Wis. 2d 332, 302 N.W.2d 503 (1981), *aff'd,* 106 Wis. 2d 636, 318 N.W.2d 141, *cert. denied,* 459 U.S. 883 (1982)(no public controversy existed over internal dispute concerning corporate management).

194 *See* Note, *Defining a Public Controversy, supra* note 159, at 962-63.

195 Gertz v. Robert Welch, Inc., 418 U.S. 323, 352 (1974).

196 *See supra* § 2.05.

197 *See* 418 U.S. at 344, 351-52.

Supreme Court cases subsequent to *Gertz* seem to have given the voluntariness requirement even greater emphasis. In *Firestone,*[198] the Court emphasized that Mary Alice Firestone had not "thrust herself to the forefront of any particular public controversy in order to influence the resolution of the issues involved in it."[199] That Mrs. Firestone sought a divorce did not constitute a voluntary act or an assumption of risk sufficient to render her a public figure, since she had no choice but to commence litigation if she was to obtain legal dissolution of her marriage.[200] Similarly, in *Wolston,*[201] the Court held that plaintiff Wolston had not voluntarily entered the controversy surrounding investigation into Soviet espionage, but had been dragged unwillingly into the controversy.[202] And in *Hutchinson,*[203] the Court noted that although Hutchinson had been a writer for professional journals, he had not thrust himself or his views into the public eye.[204]

Virtually every lower court discussion of the public figure/private figure dichotomy since *Wolston* and *Hutchinson* has treated the voluntariness requirement as central to the determination, and it is probably the most firmly entrenched of all the factors courts consider.[205] Volun-

---

198 Time, Inc. v. Firestone, 424 U.S. 448, 454.

199 *Id.* at 453.

200 *Id.* at 454-55.

201 Wolston v. Reader's Digest Ass'n, 443 U.S. 157 (1979).

202 *Id.* at 166.

203 Hutchinson v. Proxmire, 443 U.S. 111 (1979).

204 *Id.* at 135-36.

205 The voluntariness element is truly an example of the existence of authorities "too numerous to mention," for almost no case dealing with the public figure classification problem fails to discuss it. *See, e.g.,* Marcone v. Penthouse International, Ltd., 754 F.2d 1072 (3d Cir.), *cert. denied,* 474 U.S. 864, *reh'g denied,* 474 U.S. 1014 (1985); Lerman v. Flynt Distributing Co., 745 F.2d 123 (2d Cir. 1984), *cert. denied,* 471 U.S. 1054, 105 S. Ct. 2114 (1985); National Foundation for Cancer Research v. Council of Better Business Bureaus, 705 F.2d 98, 101-02 (4th Cir.), *cert. denied,* 464 U.S. 830, 104 S. Ct. 108 (1983); Clark v. American Broadcasting Co., 684 F.2d 1208, 1218 (6th Cir. 1982), *cert. denied,* 460 U.S. 1040 (1983); Brewer v. Memphis Publishing Co., 626 F.2d 1238 (5th Cir. 1980), *cert. denied,* 452 U.S. 962 (1981); Steaks Unlimited, Inc. v. Deaner, 623 F.2d 264, 273-74 (3d Cir. 1980); Littlefield v. Fort Dodge Messenger, 614 F.2d 581 (8th Cir.), *cert. denied,* 445 U.S. 945 (1980); Chuy v. Philadelphia Eagles Football Club, 595 F.2d 1265 (3d Cir. 1979)(en banc); Fitzgerald v. Penthouse International, Ltd., 525 F. Supp. 585, 592 (D. Md. 1981), *aff'd in part and rev'd in part on other grounds,* 691 F.2d 666 (4th Cir. 1982), *cert. denied,* 460 U.S. 1024 (1983); Schultz v. Reader's Digest Ass'n, 468 F. Supp. 551 (E.D. Mich. 1979); Rosanova v. Playboy Enterprises, Inc., 411 F. Supp. 440 (S.D. Ga. 1976), *aff'd,* 580 F.2d 859 (5th Cir. 1978); Greenberg v. CBS, Inc., 69 A.D.2d 693, 419 N.Y.S.2d 988 (2d Dept. 1979).

tariness in fact appears to be almost the exclusive preoccupation in some decisions.[206]

[2] "Voluntary" Participation vs. Voluntary Acceptance of Media Attention

Plaintiffs sometimes advance the argument that they cannot properly be classified as public figures because they did not "voluntarily" invite media attention, even though they may have voluntarily engaged in the activity out of which the media attention arose. Based on a popular misconception surrounding the public figure issue, this is an altogether spurious defense. Of course many plaintiffs find media attention undesirable, particularly unflattering attention, and do not volunteer for it. But just as the media is not permitted to bootstrap itself into creating its own defense by focusing attention on the plaintiff through the very speech alleged to be defamatory, the plaintiff is not permitted to avoid the strictures of the actual malice standard by protesting, "I didn't want the attention." The proper question is not whether the plaintiff volunteered for the publicity but whether the plaintiff volunteered for an activity out of which publicity would foreseeably arise.[207]

In *Marcone v. Penthouse,*[208] for example, *Penthouse* had published an article entitled "The Stoning of America" that depicted the emergence of marijuana trade as a multibillion dollar agribusiness. Frank Marcone, a Philadelphia attorney, was claimed to be an example of the "criminal attorneys and attorney criminals" who surround the drug industry. Marcone had previously been indicted along with 24 others for conspiring "knowingly, intentionally and unlawfully [to] possess with intent to distribute, and to distribute" marijuana, in violation of federal

---

[206] *See* Brewer v. Memphis Publishing Co., 626 F.2d 1238 (5th Cir. 1980), *cert. denied,* 452 U.S. 962 (1981); Chuy v. Philadelphia Eagles Football Club, 595 F.2d 1265 (3d Cir. 1979) (en banc).

[207] *See* Marcone v. Penthouse International, Ltd., 754 F.2d 1072, 1083 (3d Cir.)(citing Smolla, *supra* note 2, at 68-71), *cert. denied,* 474 U.S. 864, *reh'g denied,* 474 U.S. 1014 (1985); Rosanova v. Playboy Enterprises, Inc., 580 F.2d 859, 861 (5th Cir. 1978); Barger v. Playboy Enterprises, Inc., 564 F. Supp. 1151, 1156 (N.D. Cal. 1983), *aff'd,* 732 F.2d 163 (9th Cir.)(unpublished opinion), *cert. denied,* 469 U.S. 853, 105 S. Ct. 175 (1984); Chuy v. Philadelphia Eagles Football Club, 431 F. Supp. 254, 267 (E.D. Pa. 1977), *aff'd,* 593 F.2d 1265 (3d Cir. 1979)(en banc).

[208] Marcone v. Penthouse International, Ltd., 754 F.2d 1072 (3d Cir.), *cert. denied,* 474 U.S. 864, *reh'g denied,* 474 U.S. 1014 (1985).

law.[209] Because of the "legal technicalities" involved in tying Marcone to a larger conspiracy, however, the government withdrew that charge, which had been filed in Detroit, without prejudice to Marcone's being reindicted in Philadelphia.[210] Marcone was not subsequently reindicted.[211] Marcone had also gained notoriety through his legal representation of two motorcycle gangs, and through certain other contacts with the gangs outside of his professional duties—he made visits to gang headquarters and occasionally accompanied the gang on weekend trips.[212] The Third Circuit ruled that Marcone was a public figure, despite the fact that he had not intended for his activities to attract attention.[213] The court held, very astutely, that it was "of no moment that Marcone did not desire such status," for the "purpose of the first amendment would be frustrated if those persons and activities that most require public scrutiny could wrap themselves in a veil of secrecy and thus remain beyond the reach of public knowledge."[214] The court recognized the difficult conflict between some plaintiffs' claim of secrecy and the countervailing danger of the media bootstrap:

> We recognize that there are countervailing dangers from a media that has untrammeled freedom to publish inaccurate and damaging statements with impunity. Moreover, when a sensational story by one news organization is picked up by many, the snowballing of media attention may transform an unknown individual into a virtual celebrity almost overnight. The possibility therefore exists that by relying on this snowballing of attention a media defendant might be able to bootstrap itself into first amendment protection. Such a sequence of events might concededly defeat public figure status in an appropriate case, but plaintiff's situation is not such a case.[215]

A similar analysis was employed by the Fifth Circuit in *Rosanova v. Playboy Enterprises, Inc.*,[216] a case involving a reputed underworld personality. The plaintiff vigorously argued that he could not be a public figure, because he had not sought publicity concerning his alleged underworld activities. The court held that it was enough to satisfy the re-

---

209 21 U.S.C. §§ 841(a)(1), 846 (1982).

210 Marcone v. Penthouse International, Ltd., 754 F.2d 1072, 1076 (3d Cir.), *cert. denied,* 474 U.S. 864, *reh'g denied,* 474 U.S. 1014 (1985).

211 *Id.*

212 *Id.*

213 *Id.* at 1086.

214 *Id.* (citing Medico v. Time, Inc., 643 F.2d 134, 142 (3d Cir.), *cert. denied,* 454 U.S. 836 (1981)(discussing the difficulty and the importance of reporting on organized crime)).

215 754 F.2d at 1086.

216 580 F.2d 859 (5th Cir. 1978).

quirements for public figure status that the plaintiff voluntary engaged in a course of activity that was bound to invite attention and comment.[217] The court reasoned that the plaintiff could not himself be in control of the first amendment standard:

> In our view of the law resulting from the inevitable collision between First Amendment freedoms and the right of privacy, the status of public figure *vel non* does not depend upon the desires of an individual. The purpose served by limited protection to the publisher of comment upon a public figure would often be frustrated if the subject of the publication could choose whether or not he would be a public figure. *Comment upon people and activities of legitimate public concern often illuminates that which yearns for shadow. It is no answer to the assertion that one is a public figure to say, truthfully, that one doesn't choose to be.* It is sufficient, as the district court found, that "Mr. Rosanova voluntarily engaged in a course that was bound to invite attention and comment."[218]

Similarly, in *Chuy v. Philadelphia Eagles Football Club,*[219] the district court held that plaintiff, a professional football player, was a public figure with regard to a defamation action resulting from an inaccurate report by the Philadelphia Eagles club that he had a fatal disease. The court held that where a person has "chosen to engage in a profession which draws him regularly into regional and national view and leads to fame and notoriety in the community, even if he has no ideological thesis to promulgate, he invites general public discussion."[220] Voluntary entry into such a sphere of activity, the court reasoned, was sufficient to satisfy the voluntariness element of the public figure inquiry: "If society chooses to direct massive public attention to a particular sphere of activity, those who enter that sphere inviting such attention overcome the *Times* standard."[221]

§ 2.14 Can "Involuntary" Vortex Public Figures Exist?

[1] Involuntary Status

In *Gertz,*[222] the Supreme Court raised the possibility that in exceptional cases a plaintiff might achieve public figure status for a limited purpose through no voluntary action on the plaintiff's part: "Hypotheti-

---

217 *Id.* at 861.

218 *Id.* at 861 (emphasis added)(citing 411 F. Supp. at 445 (district court opinion)).

219 431 F. Supp. 254 (E.D. Pa. 1977), *aff'd,* 595 F.2d 1265 (3d Cir. 1979) (en banc).

220 431 F. Supp. at 267.

221 *Id.*

222 Gertz v. Robert Welch, Inc., 418 U.S. 323 (1974).

cally, it may be possible for someone to become a public figure through no purposeful action of his own, but the instances of truly involuntary public figures must be exceedingly rare."[223]

The heavy emphasis on voluntariness in the Supreme Court's opinions in *Firestone, Wolston,* and *Hutchinson,*[224] however, has cast some doubt on the continued vitality of such a classification.[225] Several lower courts have discussed the possible existence of the involuntary public figure class.[226] If such a classification does still survive, its most likely application would be for relatives of persons who have achieved public figure status involving an extremely high level of fame or notoriety. In *Carson v. Allied News Co.,*[227] for example, it was held that the wife of Johnny Carson (himself an "all purpose" public figure) was a vortex public figure. Similarly, in *Meeropol v. Nizer,*[228] it was held that the children of Julius and Ethel Rosenberg were public figures.[229] Since both *Firestone* and *Wolston* involved plaintiffs who were at least to some degree the focus of attention because of relatives,[230] however, the use of public figure classifications in such cases is likely to remain extremely rare, limited to persons associated with the exceptionally famous.

[a] The *Dameron* Decision

A potentially significant subcategory within the involuntary public figure classification was framed by the D.C. Circuit Court of Appeals

---

223 *Id.* at 345.

224 *See supra* § 2.14[1].

225 *See generally* Schultz v. Reader's Digest Ass'n, 468 F. Supp. 551, 559-60 (E.D. Mich. 1979); Rosen, *supra* note 139; Note, *The Involuntary Public Figure Class of* Gertz v. Robert Welch: *Dead or Merely Dormant?* 14 U. Mich. J.L. Ref. 71 (1980).

226 *See* Waldbaum v. Fairchild Publications, 627 F.2d 1287, 1295 n.18 (D.C. Cir.), *cert. denied,* 449 U.S. 898 (1980); Steaks Unlimited, Inc. v. Deaner, 623 F.2d 264, 272-73 (3d Cir. 1980); Schultz v. Reader's Digest Ass'n, 468 F. Supp. 551, 559-60 (E.D. Mich. 1979).

227 529 F.2d 206, 210 (7th Cir. 1976).

228 381 F. Supp. 29 (S.D.N.Y. 1974), *aff'd in relevant part,* 560 F.2d 1061 (2d Cir. 1977), *cert. denied,* 434 U.S. 1013 (1978).

229 *See generally* Note, *An Analysis of the Distinction Between Public Figures and Private Defamation Plaintiffs Applied to Relatives of Public Persons,* 49 S. Cal. L. Rev. 1131 (1976).

230 Mary Alice Firestone was the wife of an heir to the Firestone family fortune. Time, Inc. v. Firestone, 424 U.S. 448, 450-51 (1976). *See supra* § 2.08[1]. Ilya Wolston's aunt and uncle, Myra and Jack Soble, were arrested and charged with espionage, to which they pleaded guilty; on the day of their arrest Wolston was interviewed by the FBI, which resulted in subsequent interviews and grand jury subpoenas. Wolston v. Reader's Digest Ass'n, 443 U.S. 157, 162-66 (1979). *See supra* § 2.08[2].

in *Dameron v. Washington Magazine, Inc.*[230.1] Applying a modified version of the three-prong test set forth in *Waldbaum,* the court found that an individual could be thrust into a matter of public controversy not merely by familial relation to a major actor in the controversy or through his own voluntary actions, but also through "sheer bad luck."

The plaintiff, Merle Dameron, was "the sole air traffic controller on duty" at Washington, D.C.'s Dulles Airport on the day that a TWA 727 crashed into Mt. Weather, Virginia, killing ninety-two people. Eight years after that disaster, following the crash of an Air Florida jetliner at Washington's National Airport, *The Washingtonian* magazine published an article entitled "The Inside Story of the Crash of Air Florida's Flight 90: A False Feeling of Security." In addition to providing readers with a dramatic account of that tragedy, the article focused on the general issue of air traffic safety in several sidebars, one of which addressed the specific question of safety at National Airport. Putting National's safety record in context, part of this section explained that the air traffic control system has rarely been faulted in major airline accidents.

Dameron claimed that this story libeled him, even though his name was not used, because through prior publicity his name had become linked to the tragedy in the public mind. In spite of that fact, he claimed to be a private figure for purposes of the determination of liability. He maintained that the statement regarding controller error was false because he was not found blameworthy in the accident, a federal district court having dismissed claims brought against the government on the theory of controller negligence under the Federal Tort Claims Act.

On appeal, the Court of Appeals determined that a clear public controversy existed surrounding the accident and that the allegedly defamatory article focused on issues germane to that controversy. It was also found apparent that flight controller Dameron had played a central role in the controversy under the second prong of *Waldbaum,* yet his involvement lacked the usual elements of "activity and injection." Here, the Court of Appeals modified the test and, citing the *Gertz* Court's dicta that it is "possible to become a public figure through no purposeful action of [one's] own," declared that Dameron had become an involuntary, limited purpose public figure in connection with the Mt. Weather crash.

Even though Dameron had not sought the public eye, his involvement in the air crash investigation was so central that he became closely

230.1 779 F.2d 736 (D.C. Cir. 1985).

identified with the case. Indeed, a principal element of the defamation claim was that he was identifiable from the oblique reference in the magazine article, a situation that would not have existed were it not for the plaintiff's notoriety.

[2] The "All Purpose" Classification

Courts are more likely to resort to the all purpose public figure classification whenever position and status are more significant than voluntariness,[231] as in the classification of former President Richard Nixon's close friend Charles ("Bebe") Rebozo as an all purpose public figure.[232] And as discussed in the previous section,[233] courts may also avoid the involuntary public figure classification where the plaintiff's actions are voluntary even though his or her media attention is not, by recognizing that the requirement of voluntariness may at times speak to the underlying endeavor, not to the attention it draws.[233.1] In the end, however, the admonition of *Gertz* continues to be apt: "the instances of truly involuntary public figures must be exceedingly rare."[234]

§ 2.15 Access to Counterspeech

Access to the media for corrective speech was, as previously discussed,[235] one of the two central underpinnings of *Gertz*.[236] To the extent that the individual harmed by a defamatory story has the ability to rebut the defamation by counterspeech, first amendment interests are better served by encouraging the remedy of self-help than by en-

---

231 *See* Marcone v. Penthouse International, Ltd., 754 F.2d 1072, 1084 n.9 (3d Cir.), *cert. denied*, 474 U.S. 864, *reh'g denied*, 474 U.S. 1014 (1985)(in lieu of creating a separate category for involuntary public figures, it may be preferable to "view such a description as merely one way an individual may come to be considered a general or limited purpose public figure. Thus, to the extent a person attains public figure status by position, status, or notorious act he might be considered an involuntary public figure.").

232 *See* Rebozo v. Washington Post, 637 F.2d 375 (5th Cir.), *cert. denied*, 454 U.S. 964 (1981).

233 *See supra* § 2.13[2].

233.1 *See* McDowell v. Paiwonsky, 769 F.2d 942 (3d Cir. 1985)(architect/engineer found to be voluntary limited purpose public figure, despite a sincere desire to remain out of the public eye, in connection with his acceptance of the difficult task of redesigning a controversial public school project).

234 Gertz v. Robert Welch, Inc., 418 U.S. 323, 345 (1974). *See also* Marcone v. Penthouse International, Ltd., 754 F.2d 1072, 1084 n.9 (3d Cir.), *cert. denied*, 474 U.S. 864, *reh'g denied*, 474 U.S. 1014 (1985).

235 *See supra* § 2.05.

236 Gertz v. Robert Welch, Inc., 418 U.S. 323, 344 (1974).

couraging commencement of litigation. The use of the actual malice standard for those with effective access to the media serves to funnel remedies toward counterspeech, enhancing the first amendment values recognized in *Gertz.* Not suprisingly, lower courts have consistently emphasized the maintenance of access to channels of effective counterspeech in making the public figure/private figure determination.[237] In one such instance, an inventor who solicited media attention for a demonstration of an air powered vehicle was held to be a nonpublic figure with respect to a later report on the success of that demonstration. The publicity arising from the demonstration was limited to the single press conference, and therefore did not establish the plaintiff's regular and continuing access to the press.[237.1]

It is worth noting, however, that access to media channels alone will normally not suffice to create public figure status. The Supreme Court, at least, appears to treat the voluntariness element as more significant than access to the media. Elmer Gertz, for example, was a prominent lawyer who had written four books and had substantial media access, but the Supreme Court emphasized the absence of voluntariness on Gertz's part in the particular controversy that gave rise to the defamation.[238] Similarly, in *Time, Inc. v. Firestone,*[239] Mary Alice Firestone, a member of what Justice Marshall called "the sporting set,"[240] subscribed to a press clipping service to monitor her media exposure, and held several press conferences during the course of her divorce litigation in order to answer questions regarding the case.[241] Despite this ample access to the media, the Supreme Court held that Mrs. Firestone was not a public figure, emphasizing that she had been drawn into the public forum largely against her will.[242]

---

237 *See, e.g.,* Lerman v. Flynt Distributing Co., 745 F.2d 123 (2d Cir. 1984), *cert. denied,* 471 U.S. 1054, 105 S. Ct. 2114 (1985); Clark v. American Broadcasting Companies, 684 F.2d 1208, 1218 (6th Cir. 1982), *cert. denied,* 460 U.S. 1040 (1983); Bruno & Stillman, Inc. v. Globe Newspaper Co., 633 F.2d 583 (1st Cir. 1980); Fitzgerald v. Penthouse International, Ltd., 525 F. Supp. 585 (D. Md. 1981), *aff'd in relevant part and rev'd in part,* 691 F.2d 666 (4th Cir. 1982), *cert. denied,* 460 U.S. 1024 (1983). *But see* Reliance Insurance Co. v. Barron's, 442 F. Supp. 1341, 1348 (S.D.N.Y. 1977)("The access to the media argument is no more than a makeweight.").

237.1 Re v. Gannett, 480 A.2d 662, 666 (Del. Super. Ct. 1984), *aff'd,* 496 A.2d 553 (Del. 1985). The court also held that neither the demonstration or the larger public issue to which it responded (the energy crisis) was a matter of "public dispute." *See infra* § 2.16.

238 Gertz v. Robert Welch, Inc., 418 U.S. 323, 344-53 (1974).

239 424 U.S. 448 (1976).

240 *Id.* at 486 (Marshall, J., dissenting).

241 *Id.* at 450-54.

242 *Id.* at 457.

§ 2.16 Public Divisiveness

[1] In General

There is a certain amount of confusion concerning the extent to which the public controversy requirement is limited to issues of public debate or disputes—issues, that is, over which people are divided—or whether it encompasses "controversies" in a broader sense—significant problems or events about which the public is concerned.[243] (A parallel formulation of much the same issue is treated in the following section: the extent to which the achievement of public figure status must involve some attempt to *influence the resolution* of controversies, as opposed to simply "being a part of" some social problem or significant event.[244]

[2] The *Wolston* Dicta

In *Wolston v. Reader's Digest Association,*[245] the Supreme Court, in a loose and ill-considered bit of dicta contained in a footnote,[246] appeared to endorse the much narrower view of "public controversy." Ilya Wolston did have some connection to a problem that was arguably a matter of "public controversy," the presence of Soviet spies in the United States. His aunt and uncle were convicted of espionage and Wolston himself was interviewed by the FBI and subpoenaed by a grand jury in connection with an investigation into espionage.[247] Most of the Supreme Court's analysis centered on Wolston's lack of voluntariness concerning these events,[248] but in a footnote the Court went a step further, challenging the defendant's claim that a "public controversy" existed in the first place. There was no "controversy" about espionage that Wolston could have thrust himself into, the Court maintained, "because all responsible United States citizens understandably were and are opposed to it."[249]

This statement was dicta, for the Court's analysis of Wolston's lack of voluntariness made it unnecessary to determine whether Soviet espionage qualified as a matter of public controversy. Although the state-

243 *See* Smolla, *supra* note 2, at 56.

244 *See supra* § 2.17.

245 443 U.S. 157 (1979).

246 *Id.* at 166 n.8.

247 *Id.* at 162-66.

248 *Id.*

249 *Id.* at 166 n.8.

ment has been picked up and incorporated in at least one subsequent formulation of the public figure test,[250] it has also been severely criticized by commentators[251] and flatly rejected by at least one court of appeals.[252] The *Wolston* footnote has been labeled a "bizarre bit of illogic,"[253] an "irrationality" that must be stopped,[254] and "a facially spurious argument."[255]

[3] A Critique of *Wolston*

The illogic of the *Wolston* dicta is easily demonstrable. Imagine an issue about which there can be no "debate," the propriety of attempting to assassinate a President, for example. In the language of *Wolston,* "all responsible United States citizens understandably were and are opposed to" presidential assassination. But can there be any doubt that presidential assassination attempts ought to be treated as matters of public controversy and individuals connected to such events as vortex public figures? Under the *Wolston* formulation, John Hinckley, Jr. might not qualify as a vortex public figure merely for having shot President Ronald Reagan, because the assassination attempt was not a matter of "public controversy," that is, all responsible Americans would be opposed to it.[256] Hinckley would become a public figure after his acquittal on attempted murder charges by reason of insanity, however, because the insanity defense is an issue over which Americans are divided.[257] This distinction is indefensible; it rests on a hypertechnical construction of the term "controversy" that treats only *debate* as a matter of first amendment concern, eliminating a plethora of issues and events such as crime, violence, and disease which are obviously subjects

---

250 *See* Rancho La Costa, Inc. v. Superior Court, 106 Cal. App. 3d 646, 658, 165 Cal. Rptr. 347, 354 (1980).

251 *See* Smolla, *supra* note 2, at 56-57; Note, *Defining A Public Controversy, supra* note 159, at 942 n.66, 947 n.91.

252 Marcone v. Penthouse International, Ltd., 754 F.2d 1072, 1083 n.8 (3d Cir.)(citing Smolla, *supra* note 2, at 56-57), *cert. denied,* 474 U.S. 864, *reh'g denied,* 474 U.S. 1014 (1985).

253 Note, *Defining a Public Controversy, supra* note 159, at 942 n.66.

254 *Id.* at 947 n.91.

255 Smolla, *supra* note 2, at 56.

256 In this particular example, of course, someone like Hinckley might be classified an all purpose public figure merely on the basis of his notorious act, obviating the need to undertake the public controversy inquiry. Others engaged in criminal activity, however, might not have achieved Hinckley's notoriety, and thus the *Wolston* narrowing of the public controversy concept would remain a problem.

257 Smolla, *supra* note 2, at 57.

of profound concern, and for which full first amendment protection for speech is vital, whether or not "all responsible citizens" are opposed to them.[258]

Presumably, all responsible citizens are opposed to organized crime, but that has not stopped courts from quite properly declaring certain plaintiffs purportedly connected to organized crime activity to be public figures.[259] Similarly, all responsible Americans are presumed to be opposed to illegal trafficking in drugs, but as the Third Circuit stated in *Marcone v. Penthouse International, Ltd.*,[260] we should "reject the notion that merely because most people would agree that drug trafficking is undesirable, there is no 'controversy' regarding the matter."[261]

§ 2.17 Plaintiff's Efforts to Influence

Decisions sometimes speak of the plaintiff attempting to influence the outcome of a public controversy as one of the prerequisites to public figure status.[262] In *Fitzgerald v. Penthouse International, Ltd.*,[263] for example, the court listed as part of the test for public figure status "whether the plaintiff sought to influence the resolution of the controversy."[264] And in *Lerman v. Flynt Distributing Co.*,[265] the court stated that to establish public figure status the defendant must show, among other things, that the plaintiff has "successfully invited public attention to his

---

[258] *Id.*

[259] *See* Rosanova v. Playboy Enterprises, 580 F.2d 859 (5th Cir. 1978). *Cf.* Schultz v. Reader's Digest Ass'n, 468 F. Supp. 551 (E.D. Mich. 1979)(disappearance of Jimmy Hoffa was a "public controversy" but plaintiff was not a public figure as he lacked voluntary association with that controversy). *But see* Rancho La Costa, Inc. v. Superior Court, 106 Cal. App. 3d 646, 165 Cal. Rptr. 347 (1980); Marchiondo v. Brown, 98 N.M. 394, P.2d 462 (1982).

[260] 754 F.2d 1072 (3d Cir.), *cert. denied,* 474 U.S. 864, *reh'g denied,* 474 U.S. 1014 (1985).

[261] *Id.* at 1083 n.8.

[262] *See* Hutchinson v. Proxmire, 443 U.S. 111, 135 (1979); Time, Inc. v. Firestone, 424 U.S. 448, 455 n.3 (1976); Gertz v. Robert Welch, Inc., 418 U.S. 323, 351 (1974); Lerman v. Flynt Distributing Co., 745 F.2d 123 (2d Cir. 1984), *cert. denied,* 471 U.S. 1054, 105 S. Ct. 2114 (1985); Bruno & Stillman, Inc. v. Globe Newspaper Co., 633 F.2d 583 (1st Cir. 1980); Littlefield v. Fort Dodge Messenger, 614 F.2d 581, 584 (8th Cir.), *cert. denied,* 445 U.S. 945 (1980); Howard v. Buffalo Evening News, 89 A.D.2d 793, 453 N.Y.S.2d 516 (4th Dept. 1982).

[263] 525 F. Supp. 585 (D. Md. 1981), *aff'd in relevant part and rev'd in part,* 691 F.2d 666 (4th Cir. 1982), *cert. denied,* 460 U.S. 1024 (1983).

[264] 525 F. Supp. at 592.

[265] 745 F.2d 123 (2d Cir. 1984), *cert. denied,* 471 U.S. 1054, 105 S. Ct. 2114 (1985).

views in an effort to influence others prior to the incident that is the subject of litigation."[266]

These statements are defensible to the extent that they purport to define the "effort to influence others" element as a factor to be weighed in making the public figure determination. The statements are less defensible if they are meant to insist on "attempts to influence" as an absolute requirement.

There are two reasons that efforts to influence others should not be treated as the sine qua non to public figure status. First, as argued in the previous section,[267] not all public controversies involve debates and not all public figures assume ideological positions in debates.[268] An organized crime figure[269] or a drug trafficker[270] may legitimately be deemed a public figure even though it would be hard to characterize their activity as attempting to "influence the outcome" of a public issue. Second, innumerable holdings quite properly list prominent social "personalities" as public figures, because those persons have voluntarily entered a public "controversy" in the broad sense of "sphere of public concern," even though their prominence is not of an "influencing" nature.[271] These persons may not always be famous enough to qualify as all purpose public figures, but they clearly are appropriate persons for public figure status concerning the particular activity in which they have voluntarily participated. Professional athletes such as Warren Spahn[272] or

---

266 *Id.* at 316.

267 *See supra* § 2.16.

268 *See* Chuy v. Philadelphia Eagles Football Club, 431 F. Supp. 254, 267 (E.D. Pa. 1977), *aff'd,* 595 F.2d 1265 (3d Cir. 1979)(en banc)("even if he had no ideological thesis to promulgate, he invites general public discussion"). *See also* Marcone v. Penthouse International, Ltd., 754 F.2d 1072, 1080-84 (3d Cir.), *cert. denied,* 474 U.S. 864, *reh'g denied,* 474 U.S. 1014 (1985).

269 *See* Rosanova v. Playboy Enterprises, Inc., 580 F.2d 859 (5th Cir. 1978).

270 *See* Marcone v. Penthouse International, Ltd., 754 F.2d 1072 (3d Cir.), *cert. denied,* 474 U.S. 864, *reh'g denied,* 474 U.S. 1014 (1985).

271 *See, e.g.,* Curtis Publishing Co. v. Butts, 388 U.S. 155 (1967); Brewer v. Memphis Publishing Co., 626 F.2d 1238 (5th Cir. 1980), *cert. denied,* 452 U.S. 962 (1981); Chuy v. Philadelphia Eagles Football Club, 595 F.2d 1265, 1280 (3d Cir. 1979)(en banc); Cepeda v. Cowles Magazines, 392 F.2d 417 (9th Cir. 1968); Barry v. Time, Inc., 584 F. Supp. 1110, 1113 (N.D. Cal. 1984); Bell v. Associated Press, 584 F. Supp. 128 (D.D.C. 1984); Burnett v. National Enquirer, Inc., 144 Cal. App. 3d 991, 193 Cal. Rptr. 206 (1983), *appeal dismissed,* 104 S. Ct. 1260 (1984); James v. Gannett Co., 40 N.Y.2d 415, 353 N.E.2d 834, 386 N.Y.S.2d 871 (1976).

272 *See* Spahn v. Julian Messner, Inc., 18 N.Y.2d 324, 274 N.Y.S.2d 877 (1966), *vacated and remanded,* 387 U.S. 239, *aff'd in later proceedings,* 21 N.Y.2d 124, 233 N.E.2d 840, 286 N.Y.S.2d 832 (1967), *appeal dismissed,* 393 U.S. 1046 (1969)(pre-*Gertz* privacy case holding baseball star Warren Spahn to be "public personality").

Orlando Cepeda,[273] or entertainers such as Anita Brewer[274] or Carol Burnett,[275] have quite properly been classified as public figures even though one would not describe their activity in terms of attempting to influence others on a matter under debate.

This is not to say that efforts to influence others are irrelevant to public figure status. Quite the contrary, such efforts are a factor which invokes the self-governance[276] and broader enlightenment functions[277] of the first amendment, and which adds to the strength of the assumption of risk rationale.[278] The essential point is that efforts to influence should not be treated as an absolute requirement—the absence of any effort to influence the resolution of a controversy should not disqualify the plaintiff from being designated a vortex public figure.

§ 2.18 Plaintiff's Prominence in the Controversy

In weighing the factors that go into the mix of determining whether the plaintiff is a public figure, it is appropriate to adjust the balance upward or downward in accordance with the level of prominence of the plaintiff in the public controversy. The more peripheral the role played by the plaintiff in the controversy, the less likely the plaintiff is to be deemed a public figure. Courts frequently use the term "prominence" in discussing the public figure determination;[279] like the other considerations relevant to public figure status, however, it should be treated as a factor to be weighed and not as an absolute prerequisite to public figure status.

---

[273] *See* Cepeda v. Cowles Magazines, 392 F.2d 417 (9th Cir. 1968).

[274] *See* Brewer v. Memphis Publishing Co., 626 F.2d 1238 (5th Cir. 1980), *cert. denied,* 452 U.S. 962 (1981).

[275] *See* Burnett v. National Enquirer, Inc., 144 Cal. App. 3d 991, 193 Cal. Rptr. 206 (1983), *appeal dismissed,* 104 S. Ct. 1260 (1984).

[276] *See supra* § 1.07[3].

[277] *See supra* § 1.07[4].

[278] *See supra* § 2.06.

[279] *See, e.g.,* Lerman v. Flynt Distributing Co., 745 F.2d 123 (2d Cir. 1984), *cert. denied,* 471 U.S. 1054, 105 S. Ct. 2114 (1985) (discussing whether plaintiff has "assumed a position of a prominence in the public controversy"); Clark v. American Broadcasting Companies, 684 F.2d 1208, 1218 (6th Cir. 1982), *cert. denied,* 460 U.S. 1040 (1983)(discussing "the prominence of the role played in the public controversy"); Fitzgerald v. Penthouse International, Ltd., 525 F. Supp. 585, 592 (D. Md. 1981), *aff'd in relevant part and rev'd in part,* 691 F.2d 666 (4th Cir. 1982), *cert. denied,* 460 U.S. 1024 (1983) (discussing whether the plaintiff voluntarily "assumed a role of special prominence in a public controversy").

§ 2.19 The Effect of Passage of Time on Public Figure Status

[1] In General

The passage of time might theoretically permit some persons who were once public figures to regain private figure status, even for speech connected to the original public controversy out of which the earlier public figure status arose.[280] This proposition must be hedged with the word "theoretically" because, although the problem has attracted substantial attention from commentators,[281] actual court decisions have

(*Text continued on page 2-51*)

---

280 *See* Wolston v. Reader's Digest Ass'n, 443 U.S. 157, 171 (Blackmun, J., concurring); Marcone v. Penthouse International, Ltd., 754 F.2d 1072, 1087 n.10 (3d Cir.), *cert. denied,* 474 U.S. 864, *reh'g denied,* 474 U.S. 1014 (1985)("We note that theoretically the passage of time might permit a public figure to retain private status, but such was not the case here.").

281 *See* Note, *Defamation Law: Once a Public Figure Always a Public Figure?* 10 Hofstra L. Rev. 803-30 (1982); Note, *Public Status Over Time: A Single Approach to the Retention Problem in Defamation and Privacy Law,* 1982 U. Ill. L. Rev. 951 (1982); Note, *Libel—Creation and Resurrection of a Limited Purpose Public Figure as a Prerequisite to the Application of the* New York Times *Actual Malice Standard,* 8 N. Ky. L. Rev. 647

thus far remained relatively hostile to attempts by plaintiffs to fade back from public to private figure status.[282] At least in the cases to date, public figure status is a door that swings only one way.

The Supreme Court has said very little on the issue. In *Rosenblatt v. Baer,*[283] the Court held that the actual malice standard could apply to a former county employee who sued for libel resulting from reports critical of his official conduct, published six months after his discharge. His conduct was still a matter of lively interest at the time of the discharge. The Court did note, however, that there may be cases in which a person is so far removed from a former position of authority that comment on the manner in which he performed his office may no longer command the interest required to justify application of the actual malice standard.[284]

[2] Historical Reporting vs. Contemporaneous Reporting

In *Wolston v. Reader's Digest Association,*[285] the Court expressly reserved judgment on whether the lapse of time between the original public controversy and subsequent defamatory statements could affect public figure status.[286] As previously discussed, the Court held for other

---

(1981); Note, *Public Figures and the Passage of Time: Scottsboro Revisited in* Street v. National Broadcasting Co., 34 Stan. L. Rev. 901 (1982); Note, *Public Figures and the Passage of Time,* 39 Wash. & Lee L. Rev. 1327 (1982).

282 *See* Street v. National Broadcasting Co., 645 F.2d 1227, 1235 (6th Cir.), *cert. granted* 454 U.S. 815, *cert. dismissed,* 454 U.S. 1095 (1981); Brewer v. Memphis Publishing Co., 626 F.2d 1238 (5th Cir. 1980), *cert. denied,* 452 U.S. 962 (1981); Time, Inc. v. Johnston, 448 F.2d 378 (4th Cir. 1971); Holt v. Cox Enterprises, 590 F. Supp. 408 (N.D. Ga. 1984); Underwood v. First National Bank, 8 Med. L. Rep. (BNA) 1278 (Minn. Dist. Ct. 1982); Mobile Press Register v. Faulkner, 372 So. 2d 1282, 1286 (Ala. 1979); Newson v. Henry, 443 So. 2d 817 (Miss. 1983). *See also* Meeropol v. Nizer, 560 F.2d 1061 (2d Cir. 1977), *cert. denied,* 434 U.S. 1013 (1978) (passim); Perry v. Columbia Broadcasting Systems, Inc., 499 F.2d 797 (7th Cir.), *cert. denied,* 419 U.S. 883 (1974) (privacy case); Sidis v. F-R Publishing Corp., 113 F.2d 806 (2d Cir.), *cert. denied,* 311 U.S. 711 (1940)(privacy case); Bernstein v. National Broadcasting Co., 129 F. Supp. 817 (D.D.C. 1955), *aff'd,* 232 F.2d 369 (D.C. Cir.), *cert. denied,* 352 U.S. 945 (1956)(privacy case); Cohen v. Marx, 94 Cal. App. 2d 704, 211 P.2d 320 (1949)(privacy case); Leopold v. Levin, 45 Ill. 2d 434, 259 N.E.2d 250 (1970)(privacy case). For discussion of the analogous problems in the invasion of privacy area, *see* Chapter 10, *infra.*

283 383 U.S. 75 (1966).

284 *Id.* at 87 n.14.

285 443 U.S. 157 (1979).

286 *Id.* at 166 n.7.

reasons that the plaintiff Wolston was not a public figure.[287] In a concurring opinion joined by Justice Marshall, Justice Blackmun did directly address the issue, arguing that the passage of time could sufficiently attenuate public interest in the original controversy to eliminate public figure status.[288] Justice Blackmun maintained that the elements of access to the media and assumption of risk may be dispelled by the passage of time, and that a plaintiff's efforts to regain anonymity may in some cases be sufficient to negate prior public figure status.[289] Justice Blackmun then focused on a distinction between historical writing and contemporaneous reportage:

> While historical analysis is no less vital to the marketplace of ideas than reporting current events, historians work under different conditions than do their media counterparts. A reporter trying to meet a deadline may find it totally impossible to check thoroughly the accuracy of his sources. A historian writing *sub specie aeternitatis* has both the time for reflection and the opportunity to investigate the veracity of the pronouncements he makes.[290]

In a dissenting opinion in *Wolston,* Justice Brennan also addressed the lapse of time issue, disagreeing somewhat with Justice Blackmun's analysis.[291] Although Justice Brennan did not discount altogether the possibility that time might eventually cause public figure status to lapse, he argued that it could not be a determinative factor, and should give way to the continued public interest in the controversy.[292]

[3] A Critique of the Distinction

The distinction between historical and contemporaneous reportage suggested by Justice Blackmun is subject to a number of criticisms. First, it simply is not true that historians necessarily have an "accuracy advantage" over contemporaneous observers of events. While the historian has the advantages of an absence of "hot news" deadline pressure and the wider perspective that history brings, the historian is correspondingly disadvantaged by the corrosive features of time: lapses in memory, the deaths of witnesses and participants, loss of documents, and similar problems that accompany evidence grown stale. Second,

287 *See supra* §§ 2.08[2], 2.16.
288 443 U.S. at 170 (Blackmun, J., concurring).
289 *Id.* at 170-71.
290 *Id.* at 171.
291 *Id.* at 172 (Brennan, J., dissenting).
292 *Id.*

the whole focus of Justice Blackmun on the purported ability of the historian to be more accurate is arguably misplaced. That issue is relevant only to the historian's level of *fault* if the story turns out wrong—the absence of deadline pressure, for example, might bear in some cases on the existence of actual malice, but it has nothing to do with the plaintiff's *status.*[293]

[4] Lower Court Treatment of the Time Issue

Recent lower court decisions have not found Justice Blackmun's passage of time argument persuasive. In *Street v. National Broadcasting Co.,*[294] NBC televised a "docudrama" depicting events surrounding the controversial 1931 Scottsboro trials, in which nine black youths were accused of raping two white women on a freight train in Alabama. The NBC show portrayed one of the alleged victims, Victoria Price Street, as a prostitute and perjurer. The Sixth Circuit held that Victoria Price Street remained a public figure 40 years after the original Scottsboro trials placed her in the public eye. "[O]nce a person becomes a public figure in connection with a particular controversy," the court stated, "that person remains a public figure thereafter for purposes of later commentary or treatment of that controversy."[295]

In *Brewer v. Memphis Publishing Co.,*[296] the plaintiff, singer Anita Brewer, was alleged to have been romantically involved with Elvis Presley during the period 1955-1961. Her husband, John Brewer, also a plaintiff, retired in 1970 after a successful career as a professional football player and then entered the restaurant business in New Orleans. A 1972 article stated that the Brewers were divorced and intimated that Anita Brewer was reviving her relationship with Presley. The Fifth Circuit reiterated Justice Blackmun's analysis in *Wolston,* but held that on the facts before it both Brewers remained public figures despite the passage of time.[297] The court noted that although Anita Brewer had sought anonymity in the eight years before the publication of the article, her name continued to appear in connection with books

[293] *See* R. Sack, *Libel, Slander, and Related Problems,* § V.6.3, at 237 (1980)(citing Curtis Publishing Co. v. Butts, 388 U.S. 130, 157-58 (1967)).

[294] 645 F.2d 1227 (6th Cir.), *cert. granted,* 454 U.S. 815, *cert. dismissed,* 454 U.S. 1095 (1981).

[295] *Id.* at 1235.

[296] 626 F.2d 1238 (1980), *cert. denied,* 452 U.S. 962 (1981).

[297] *Id.* at 1257.

and articles about Elvis Presley and she remained a public figure with regard to stories about Presley.[298] The court's analysis of John Brewer's plight was more interesting, for the court essentially held that the "fading public figure" device could not be implemented indirectly by the husband when it was barred directly for the wife: "[T]o hold that he might recover on a showing of negligence would, however, strip the required protection from the press to write about" his wife.[299]

In *Time, Inc. v. Johnston,*[300] the plaintiff Johnston, a former professional basketball player, brought a libel action against the publisher of *Sports Illustrated.* The suit arose out of an article discussing the career of the great Boston Celtics basketball star and coach Bill Russell, who was alleged to have "destroyed" Johnston on the court. Johnston, who had retired nine years earlier, alleged that the article damaged his reputation as a coach (he was an assistant coach at Wake Forest University) and that the passage of time had rendered him a private figure. The Fourth Circuit held that since public interest in events between Johnston and Russell remained alive, Johnston was still a public figure.[301]

[5] Can Public Figure Status Fade Away?

Although plaintiffs have thus far been relatively unsuccessful in asserting the passage of time argument, the principle is certainly not buried, and some public figures may, like old soldiers, "just fade away." To revert back to private figure status, however, the likelihood is that the plaintiff will need to demonstrate that the plaintiff's *original* status as a public figure was not connected to events or controversies that have become part of the permanent historical consciousness of the nation. Some stories involve "not merely fleeting news, but sensational events of deep and lasting public interest."[302] The trial and execution of Julius and Ethel Rosenberg,[303] the murder perpetrated by Leopold

---

298 *Id.*

299 *Id.*

300 448 F.2d 378 (4th Cir. 1971).

301 *Id.* at 300-01.

302 Man v. Warner Bros., 317 F. Supp. 50, 53 (S.D.N.Y. 1970).

303 *See* Meeropol v. Nizer, 560 F.2d 1061 (2d Cir. 1977), *cert. denied,* 434 U.S. 1013 (1978). In the *Meeropol* case, the natural children of Julius and Ethel Rosenberg sued the defendants for libel arising from an account of the Rosenberg trial published in 1974. The children were held to be public figures.

and Loeb,[304] the persecution of the Scottsboro boys,[305] the romances of Elvis Presley[306] become part of the folklore and consciousness of the culture. These events take on meanings larger than the original stories, and time does not wash away those meanings. To relive in 1976 the 1931 trial of nine blacks in Alabama is not merely to revive a controversial trial, it is to examine the history of the South and southern racism. There are times "when an event involving private citizens may be so unique as to capture the imagination of all. In such cases—*e.g.*, the behavior of the passengers on the sinking Titantic, the heroism of Nathan Hale, the horror of the Saint Valentine's Day Massacre—purely private individuals may by accident of history lose their privacy regarding that incident for all time. There need be no 'reattraction' of the public eye because the public interest never waivered."[307] To quote Faulkner's *Requiem for a Nun,* "The past is never dead. It isn't even past."

§ 2.20 Extent of Publication

[1] The "Context Public Figure"

One of the traditional factors used in the application of conditional common law privileges long before *New York Times Co. v. Sullivan*[308] was ever decided was the extent of publication.[309] Conditional common law privileges were normally lost if the speaker published speech beyond the audience to whom the particular common law privilege was relevant.[310] The privilege to speak in self-defense, for example, was lost if the speech was published beyond the group of persons to whom self-defensive action was useful.[311] This common law conditional privilege concept can be borrowed for the purpose of applying the constitu-

---

304 *See* Leopold v. Levin, 45 Ill. 2d 434, 259 N.E.2d 250 (1970).

305 Street v. National Broadcasting Co., 645 F.2d 1227, 1235 (6th Cir.), *cert. granted,* 454 U.S. 815, *cert. dismissed,* 454 U.S. 1095 (1981).

306 Brewer v. Memphis Publishing Co., 626 F.2d 1238 (1980), *cert. denied,* 452 U.S. 962 (1981).

307 Briscoe v. Reader's Digest Ass'n, 4 Cal. 3d 529, 538, 93 Cal. Rptr. 866, 872, 483 P.2d 34, 40 (1971).

308 376 U.S. 254 (1964).

309 For discussion of the restrictions governing common law privileges, *see* Chapter 8, *infra.*

310 *See* Restatement (Second) of Torts § 604 (1977).

311 *See* W. Prosser, Handbook on the Law of Torts § 115, at 787 (4th ed. 1971).

tional public figure principle, not to limit application of the public figure doctrine, but to extend it. The extension may occur by recognizing that courts should be more willing to declare persons public figures when the defamatory speech is limited in its publication to an audience in which the plaintiff is well known. (It should be pointed out here that the Supreme Court has never endorsed such a view, and if anything, the philosophical underpinnings of the majority opinions in the latest Supreme Court defamation case, *Dun & Bradstreet*,[312] appear somewhat antithetical to the suggestions contained in this section.)[313]

It may well be worthwhile in analyzing the question of who is a public figure to take into account the total context in which the particular speech is uttered. We tend to think of public figures in terms of national archetypes,[314] people like Reverend Jerry Falwell[315] or Ralph Nader[316] or William F. Buckley[317] or Dan Rather.[318] But for most people, speech that takes place in the neighborhood, the workplace, and other institutions in which they operate daily is more immediately vital than the speech that appears in the *Washington Post* or *Harper's* or on the "CBS Evening News."[319] There are, in short, national marketplaces of ideas and local marketplaces of ideas, and for many citizens the local marketplaces are every bit as important as speech in a national context. The values of wide open, robust, and uninhibited discussion are just as relevant in a local context as in the national context. Very few people purposefully inject themselves into an arena of national attention. But many people involve themselves in events and controversies in their neighborhoods, in their children's schools, and in their workplaces. A professor at a law school, for example, is not likely to be a public figure as defined in *Gertz* with regard to an article in *Newsweek*,[320] but might

---

312 Dun & Bradstreet, Inc. v. Greenmoss Builders, Inc., 105 S. Ct. 2939, 2947 (1985)(emphasizing the limited extent of publication in holding that speech did not involve matters of "public concern").

313 *See infra* § 3.02.

314 *See* Schauer, *supra* note 70, at 914.

315 *See* Falwell v. Penthouse, 521 F. Supp. 1204 (D. W. Va. 1981).

316 *See* Nader v. de Toledano, 408 A.2d 31 (D.C. 1979), *cert. denied*, 444 U.S. 1078 (1980).

317 *See* Buckley v. Littell, 539 F.2d 882 (2d Cir. 1976), *cert. denied*, 429 U.S. 1062 (1977).

318 *See* Schauer, *supra* note 70, at 908, 916.

319 *See* Smolla, *supra* note 2, at 68.

320 *Cf.* Kaplan v. Newsweek, 10 Med. L. Rep. (BNA) 2142 (N.D. Cal. 1984)(without reaching public figure/private figure issue, court holds that magazine article describing John Kaplan, Jackson Eli Reynolds Professor of Law at Stanford Law School, not defamatory).

very well be a public figure for the purposes of more localized discussions concerning that professor's teaching, scholarship, or public service.[321] A letter to the editor of a student newspaper involving allegations of a professor's arbitrary grading arguably deserves the protection of the actual malice standard even though one might not treat the same sorts of allegations in a national magazine under that standard.[322]

[2] The Local All Purpose Public Figure

In an innovative application of this sort of analysis in the context of "all purpose public figures," the Montana Supreme Court in *Williams v. Pasma*[323] adopted the principle that a plaintiff might be a general public figure within a geographically limited area. The plaintiff had been a candidate for a United States Senate seat and he was former chairman of the Montana Republican Party, as well as the author of books on business topics and the subject of a number of articles in business publications. The Montana Supreme Court, in an exceptionally astute analysis, stated that while "[s]ome courts have hinted that national notoriety is necessary to attain general public figure status," the court could find no United States or state Supreme Court authority for that proposition.[324] In fact, the court argued, "the language 'in the community' appears to require only local notoriety."[325] The court found that the plaintiff "had general fame or notoriety in the community (Montana) and exhibited pervasive involvement in the affairs of society and thus was a public figure as a matter of law."[326]

A somewhat similar analysis appears to have been undertaken by the Alabama Supreme Court in *Mobile Press Register v. Faulkner*,[327] in which the court held that Jimmy Faulkner, who had served as mayor and Alabama state senator, had run unsuccessfully for governor, and

---

321 *See* Avins v. White, 627 F.2d 637 (3d Cir.), *cert. denied*, 449 U.S. 982 (1980)(former dean and law professor held to be public figure for purpose of statements related to process of obtaining accreditation for the law school); Torgeson v. Minneapolis Star & Tribune, 7 Med. L. Rep. (BNA) 1805 (D. Minn. 1981)(dean of law school held to be a public figure); Gallman v. Carnes, 254 Ark. 987, 497 S.W.2d 47 (1973)(assistant dean and professor at law school held to be public official).

322 *See* Smolla, *supra* note 2, at 68.

323 656 P.2d 212 (Mont. 1982).

324 *Id.* at 216.

325 *Id.*

326 *Id.*

327 372 So. 2d 1282 (Ala. 1979).

who was active in business, political, and civic affairs, was "a famed figure *throughout Alabama*"[328] who occupied "a position of such power and influence that he must be deemed a public figure for *all* purposes."[329]

[3] The Local Vortex Public Figure

The second useful application of the context public figure concept concerns plaintiffs who voluntarily inject themselves into a localized controversy, and are then allegedly defamed by speech published only within that locale. One example of this sort of thought process about vortex public figures comes from a recent Illinois Supreme Court case. In *Colson v. Stieg,*[330] the plaintiff Colson, an assistant professor in the Department of Library Science at Northern Illinois University, brought suit against Stieg, the chairman of the school's Library Science Department. Colson had accepted the position at Northern Illinois with the expectation that he would ultimately be granted tenure. Colson's expectations were never realized, however, and it was the University's denial of Colson's request for promotion and tenure that precipitated the suit against Stieg. Stieg had on two occasions stated to review committees that he had information which he could not divulge that reflected adversely on Colson's performance as a teacher. Colson learned of these statements and sued Stieg for defamation.

The Illinois Supreme Court held that Colson was a public figure. The court's opinion in *Colson* strongly emphasized the importance of avoiding self-censorship on controversial subjects. In order to accord the "breathing space" essential to the exercise of first amendment rights, the court observed, the actual malice standard is imposed.[331] In reaching an accommodation between the competing concerns of the first amendment and the state's interest in protecting reputation, the *Col-*

---

328 *Id.* at 1286 (emphasis added).

329 *Id.* (emphasis in original). *See also* Whitaker v. Denver Post, Inc., 401 F. Supp. 60 (D. Wyo. 1975), *rev'd on other grounds sub nom.* Anselmi v. Denver Post, Inc., 552 F.2d 316 (10th Cir.), *cert denied,* 432 U.S. 911 (1977) (holding that a participant in Wyoming politics "stands in Wyoming as a legitimate subject of comment and reporting.").

330 89 Ill. 2d 205, 433 N.E.2d 246, 60 Ill. Dec. 449 (1982). *See generally* Smolla & Malone, *The Future of Defamation in Illinois After* Colson v. Steig *and* Chapski v. Copley Press, Inc., 32 De Paul L. Rev. 219 (1983); Kendall, *Torts/Defamation: Defamatory Statements Concerning Subjects of Public Interest are Constitutionally Protected Under the First Amendment if Publication is Limited to Persons with a Legitimate Interest and Concern in the Subject,* 71 Ill. Bar. J. 438 (1983).

331 89 Ill. 2d at 212-13, 433 N.E.2d at 249.

son court held, *"the challenged statement must be assessed in the context in which it was published."*[332] Rather than focus exclusively on the private or public status of the person defamed, the *Colson* court focused on the statement, the audience, and the functional relationship between the two. Thus, the court emphasized that "whether or not one is defamed depends upon the effect the publication had upon those who received it," and that "[t]he focus therefore must be upon the statement and its predictable effect upon those who received the publication."[333]

This functional relationship analysis led to the invocation of the actual malice privilege. The publication of Stieg's comments concerning Colson was made not to the general public but to a small specialized group of committee members. The audience apparently consisted of four state employees charged with the duty of evaluating the academic performance of another state employee.[334] This departmental personnel committee was thus involved in a matter of central importance to the functioning of Northern Illinois University, a public institution. It is certainly understandable that the Supreme Court of Illinois would treat speech concerning the teaching ability of a professor at a state university as a matter important enough to require breathing space for free and uninhibited discussion. In the court's words, "[t]he need for the free flow of information and for vigorous and uninhibited discussion in a situation [involving tenure and promotion decisions] is such that the first amendment privilege in *New York Times* must apply to the publication of statements to this committee."[335] Whether one accepts the first amendment pedigree of these concerns, the court's worries about self-censorship intuitively ring true. Most of us are not heroic. Without some degree of enhanced protection frank appraisals of teachers would often not be forwarded to personnel committees. People are likely to accept the institutional risk of allowing persons they deem unqualified to be considered for promotion if in speaking up they must run the personal risk of a suit for defamation.[336]

The Illinois court's rethinking of the public figure concept is persuasive because it is fully consistent with the two policy considerations articulated in *Gertz,* the normative judgment about the types of persons

---

332 *Id.* at 212, 443 N.E.2d at 249 (emphasis added).

333 *Id.*

334 *Id.*

335 *Id.* at 213, 433 N.E.2d at 249.

336 *See* Smolla, *supra* note 2, at 75-76.

who may properly be held to have assumed the risk of heightened public scrutiny,[337] and a more pragmatic judgment concerning the types of persons best equipped to counter defamatory statements through their own access to the media.[338] *Colson* applied these two concepts in a manner that made them more relevant to the communications of everyday life. Critiques of one's job performance are certainly within the normal risks assumed in accepting any job. And Professor Colson, as the court noted, had ample opportunity to present his own case before the very persons to whom the allegedly defamatory remarks were made.[339] Whatever effect Stieg's remarks may have had on those charged with evaluating Colson's career, the remarks were not spoken in a vacuum: Colson could both offer his own counterspeech and appeal the initial decision of the department's personnel committee to a universitywide forum.[340]

[4] Litigation Strategy

Decisions such as *Williams v. Pasma*[341] and *Colson v. Stieg*[342] evidence a laudable flexibility in the application of public figure doctrine. As a matter of litigation strategy, however, defense counsel must judge whether to ground this sort of argument in the first amendment or in state common law. Although many might applaud the incorporation of the context public figure notion into the set of first amendment rules set forth in *Gertz,* as a litigation strategy defendants may, depending on the jurisdiction, prefer to frame the context public figure approach either solely in common law terms or in both constitutional and common law terms. In light of the Supreme Court's current conservatism in its formulation of the public figure doctrine—as exemplified by cases such as *Firestone,*[343] *Wolston,*[344] and *Hutchinson*[345]—as well as the expression of doubt by some Justices as to the soundness of the whole *New York Times* line of precedent—as exemplified by several opinions in

337 *See supra* § 2.06.

338 Gertz v. Robert Welch, Inc., 418 U.S. 323, 344 (1974). *See supra* § 2.05.

339 Colson v. Steig, 89 Ill. 2d 205, 214, 433 N.E.2d 246, 250 (1982).

340 *Id.*

341 656 P.2d 212 (Mont. 1982), *cert. denied,* 103 S. Ct. 2122. *See supra* § 2.20[2].

342 89 Ill. 2d 205, 433 N.E.2d 246 (1982).

343 Time, Inc. v. Firestone, 424 U.S. 448 (1976). *See supra* § 2.07[1].

344 Wolston v. Reader's Digest Ass'n, 443 U.S. 157 (1979). *See supra* § 2.07[2].

345 Hutchinson v. Proxmire, 443 U.S. 1ll (1979). *See supra* § 2.07[3].

Dun & Bradstreet[346]—there is a danger that any lower court adopting a more flexible approach to the public figure definition will be reversed on appeal. To the extent that the context public figure concept is treated as an elaboration on common law conditional privileges, however, this danger may be substantially diminished. As discussed subsequently, this is one of many examples in current defamation law in which the lawyer must decide whether to rely on state common law or federal constitutional law grounds, or on both.[347]

§ 2.21 Examples of Limited Public Figures

[1] A Cautionary Note

It is misleading to rely mechanically on lists of particular types of persons who qualify as limited public figures. Individuals from any walk of life may thrust themselves into the forefront of a particular controversy and become subject to the *New York Times* standard with regard to that controversy. Each holding in the list that follows obviously turns on its own peculiar facts; similar persons who occupy similar positions might in other contexts be held not to be public figures. Courts have found persons to be public figures in an almost infinite variety of circumstances. Courts have found public figure status for a student class president,[348] school officials and teachers at all levels,[349] the head of an agricultural cooperative,[350] a reputed mobster,[351] an undercover police officer,[352] law school deans,[353] a Roman Catholic priest,[354] a doctor,[355] a

---

346 Dun & Bradstreet, Inc. v. Greenmoss Builders, Inc., 105 S. Ct. 2939, 2948 (opinions of Burger, C.J., and White, J.). *See infra* § 3.02.

347 For a discussion of the risks and benefits incident to this judgment, *see* Chapter 13, *infra.*

348 *See* Henderson v. Kaulitz, 644 F.2d 885 (6th Cir. 1981).

349 *See, e.g.,* Sewell v. Brookbank, 119 Ariz. 422, 581 P.2d 267 (1978); Byers v. Southeastern Newspaper Corp., 161 Ga. App. 717, 288 S.E.2d 698 (1982); Johnson v. Board of Junior College Dist. No. 508, 31 Ill. App. 3d 270, 334 N.E.2d 442 (1975); State v. Defley, 395 So. 2d 759 (La. 1981); Kapiloff v. Dunn, 27 Md. App. 514, 343 A.2d 251 (1975); Reaves v. Foster, 200 So. 2d 453 (Miss. 1967).

350 Waldbaum v. Fairchild Publications, Inc., 627 F.2d 1287 (D.C. Cir.), *cert. denied,* 449 U.S. 898 (1980).

351 Rosanova v. Playboy Enterprises, 580 F.2d 859 (5th Cir. 1978).

352 Ethridge v. North Miss. Communications, Inc., 460 F. Supp. 347, 350 (N.D. Miss. 1978); Cassidy v. American Broadcasting Co., 60 Ill. App. 3d 831, 377 N.E.2d 126 (1978).

353 Avins v. White, 627 F.2d 637 (3d Cir.), *cert. denied,* 449 U.S. 982 (1980); Torgeson v. Minneapolis Star & Tribune, 7 Med. L. Rep. (BNA) 1805 (D. Minn. 1981). *See also* Gallman v. Carnes, 254 Ark. 987, 497 S.W.2d 47 (1973) (assistant dean at state law school held to be a public official).

lawyer,[356] an author of pop psychology books,[357] a football player,[358] a basketball player,[359] a social worker,[360] an official of a credit union,[361] a former president's personal confidant and advisor,[362] a woman who posed for a *Playboy* centerfold,[363] a belly dancer,[364] a seminude dancer,[365] the winner of a Nobel Prize,[366] business operations of all sorts,[367] the convicted murderer of a civil rights leader,[368] candidates for public office,[369] a biographer,[370] a sports writer,[371] a well-known political commentator and writer,[372] the author of a letter to the editor,[373] a sociology professor,[374] officers in a taxpayers' association,[375] a prisoner active in correctional system protests and reform,[376] a chiropractor,[377] a consum-

---

354 McManus v. Doubleday & Co., 513 F. Supp. 1383 (S.D.N.Y. 1981).

355 Farnsworth v. Chicago Tribune Co., 43 Ill. 2d 286, 253 N.E.2d 408 (1969).

356 Orr v. Argus-Press Co., 586 F.2d 1108 (6th Cir. 1978), *cert. denied*, 440 U.S. 960 (1979); Weingarten v. Block, 102 Cal. App. 3d 129, 162 Cal. Rptr. 701, *cert. denied*, 449 U.S. 899 (1980).

357 Harris v. Tomczak, 94 F.R.D. 687 (E.D. Cal. 1982).

358 Chuy v. Philadelphia Eagles Football Club, 595 F.2d 1265, 1280 (3d Cir. 1979)(en banc).

359 Time, Inc. v. Johnston, 448 F.2d 378 (4th Cir. 1971).

360 Press, Inc. v. Verran, 569 S.W.2d 435 (Tenn. 1978).

361 Korbar v. Hite, 43 Ill. App. 3d 636, 357 N.E.2d 135 (1976), *cert. denied*, 434 U.S. 837 (1977).

362 Rebozo v. Washington Post Co., 637 F.2d 375 (5th Cir.), *cert. denied*, 454 U.S. 964 (1981).

363 Vitale v. National Lampoon, Inc., 449 F. Supp. 442 (E.D. Pa. 1978).

364 James v. Gannett Co., 40 N.Y.2d 415, 353 N.E.2d 834, 386 N.Y.S.2d 871 (1976).

365 Griffin v. Kentucky Post, 10 Med. L. Rep. (BNA) 1159 (Ky. Cir. Ct. 1983).

366 Pauling v. National Review, Inc., 22 N.Y.2d 818, 292 N.Y.S.2d 913, 239 N.E.2d 654 (1968).

367 *See, e.g.*, Steaks Unlimited v. Deaner, 623 F.2d 264 (3d Cir. 1980); Reliance Insurance Co. v. Barron's, 442 F. Supp. 1341, 1346-48 (S.D.N.Y. 1977); Mashburn v. Collin, 355 So. 2d 879 (La. 1977).

368 Ray v. Time, Inc., 452 F. Supp. 618 (W.D. Tenn. 1976), *aff'd without opinion*, 582 F.2d 1280 (6th Cir. 1978).

369 *See, e.g.*, Sigman v. Gove, 169 Ga. App. 580, 314 S.E.2d 238 (1984); Guthrie v. Annabel, 50 Ill. App. 3d 969, 365 N.E.2d 1367 (1977); Weaver v. Pryor Jeffersonian, 569 P.2d 967 (Okla. 1977).

370 Hotchner v. Castillo-Puche, 551 F.2d 910 (2d Cir.), *cert. denied*, 434 U.S. 834 (1977).

371 Maule v. NYM Corporation, 76 A.D.2d 58, 62, 429 N.Y.S.2d 891 (1st Dept. 1980), *rev'd on other grounds*, 54 N.Y.2d 880, 444 N.Y.S.2d 909, 429 N.E.2d 416 (1981).

372 Buckley v. Littell, 539 F.2d 882 (2d Cir. 1976), *cert. denied*, 429 U.S. 1062 (1977).

373 Wright v. Haas, 586 P.2d 1043 (Okla. 1978).

374 Rose v. Koch, 278 Minn. 235, 154 N.W.2d 409 (1967).

375 Lawrence v. Bauer Publishing, 89 N.J. 451, 446 A.2d 469 (1982).

376 Ali v. Daily News Publishing Co., 540 F. Supp. 142 (D.V.I. 1982).

377 Cera v. Gannett Co., 47 A.D.2d 797, 365 N.Y.S.2d 99 (4th Dept. 1975).

er advocate,[378] a nutrition expert,[379] the president of a major oil corporation,[380] the producer of a documentary on nuclear power,[381] a labor and civil rights activist,[382] and many others.

As one court put the matter: " 'Public figures' are those persons who, though not public officials, are 'involved in issues in which the public has a justified and important interest.' Such figures are, of course, numerous and include artists, athletes, business people, dilettantes, anyone who is famous or infamous because of who he is or what he has done."[383]

[2] Differentiating Limited Purpose and All Purpose Public Figures

In many of the following examples of persons held to be public figures, the opinion rendered by the court discusses both the "limited" and "all purpose" public figure concepts, and then goes on to classify the plaintiff as a public figure without explicitly stating whether it based the decision on a "limited" or "all purpose" analysis. Some of the cases discussed below under the limited purpose category also contain overtones of "all purpose" analysis in the court's decision, and thus are also subsequently discussed within that framework.[384] The examples below are far from exhaustive; they involve public figure classifications that present recurring problems.

[3] Candidates for Public Office

A candidate for public office is always a public figure, at least with regard to stories about the candidate's suitability for public office and

---

378 Nader v. deToledano, 408 A.2d 31 (D.C. 1979), *cert. denied,* 444 U.S. 1078 (1980)(Ralph Nader conceded public figure status in this litigation).

379 Hoffman v. Washington Post Co., 433 F. Supp. 600 (D.C. Cir. 1977), *aff'd without opinion,* 188 U.S. App. D.C. 200, 578 F.2d 442 (D.C. Cir. 1978).

380 Tavoulareas v. Washington Post Co., 567 F. Supp. 651 (D.D.C. 1983), *rev'd on other grounds,* 759 F.2d 90 (D.C. Cir. 1985), *vacated,* 817 F.2d 762 (D.C. Cir.) (en banc), *cert. denied,* 108 S. Ct. 200 (1987). The Court of Appeals decision did not reach the issue of whether Mobil Oil President William Tavoulareas was a public figure, but did state that the issue "would not be free from difficulty." *Id.* at 103 n.12.

381 Widener v. Pacific Gas & Elec., 75 Cal. App. 3d 415, 142 Cal. Rptr. 304 (1977), *cert. denied,* 436 U.S. 918 (1978).

382 Williams v. Trust Co. of Georgia, 140 Ga. App. 49, 230 S.E.2d 45 (1976).

383 Cepeda v. Cowles Magazines, 392 F.2d 417 (9th Cir. 1968).

384 *See infra* § 2.22.

other matters relating to the campaign.[385] Since it is just as important to judge suitability for office and uncover skeletons in the closet before an election or appointment as after, the scope of actual malice coverage for candidates is commensurate with the broad scope permitted for public officials.[386] Some more visibile candidates for public office go beyond the limited public figure category and enter the all purpose category.[387]

[4] Entertainers and Other "Personalities"

[a] Famous Entertainers

Entertainers and other cultural "personalities" are routinely classified as public figures.[388] In most defamation litigation involving entertainers, in fact, public figure status is simply conceded by the plaintiff. Johnny Carson or Carol Burnett simply cannot avoid the public figure classification.[389] Entertainers at this level are peculiarly susceptible to stories about their personal lives—particularly their marriages, romances, health, and alcohol or drug habits. Courts generally have con-

---

385 *See, e.g.,* Brown v. Herald Co., 698 F.2d 949, 951 (8th Cir. 1983); Goldwater v. Ginzburg, 414 F.2d 324 (2d Cir. 1969), *cert. denied,* 396 U.S. 1049 (1970); Sigman v. Gove, 169 Ga. App. 580, 314 S.E.2d 238 (1984); Guthrie v. Annabel, 50 Ill. App. 3d 969, 365 N.E.2d 1367 (1977); Williams v. Pasma, 656 P.2d 212 (Mont. 1982); Clements v. Gannett Co., 5 Med. L. Rep. (BNA) 1567 (N.Y. Sup. Ct., Monroe County, 1979); Weaver v. Pryor Jeffersonian, 569 P.2d 967 (Okla. 1977).

386 *See infra* § 2.27. Although candidates who run for office are always public figures, those who advise them "from the wings" may retain private figure status in some circumstances. In Lawrence v. Moss, 639 F.2d 634 (10th Cir.), *cert. denied,* 451 U.S. 1031 (1981), the court reached the somewhat troubling conclusion that a plaintiff who had served on the staff of Vice-President Spiro Agnew in a decision making capacity, who had been a Deputy Director of CREEP in President Richard Nixon's reelection campaign, and who had served as an advisor and consultant to several conservative political action committees remained a private figure for the purposes of remarks made in the course of a senate campaign in Utah.

387 *See* Goldwater v. Ginzburg, 414 F.2d 324 (2d Cir. 1969), *cert. denied,* 396 U.S. 1049 (1970). *See infra* § 2.22[2].

388 *See, e.g.,* Brewer v. Memphis Publishing Co., 626 F.2d 1238 (5th Cir. 1980), *cert. denied,* 452 U.S. 962 (1981); Carson v. Allied News Co., 529 F.2d 209, 209-10 (7th Cir. 1976); Vitale v. National Lampoon, Inc., 449 F. Supp. 442 (E.D. Pa. 1978); Eastwood v. Superior Court, 149 Cal. App. 3d 409, 198 Cal. Rptr. 342 (1983); Burnett v. National Enquirer, Inc., 144 Cal. App. 3d 991, 193 Cal. Rptr, 206 (1983), *appeal dismissed,* 104 S. Ct. 1260 (1984); Griffin v. Kentucky Post, 10 Med. L. Rep. (BNA) 1159 (Ky. Cir. Ct. 1983); James v. Gannett Co., 40 N.Y.2d 415, 386 N.Y.S.2d 871, 353 N.E.2d 834 (1976).

389 *See* Carson v. Allied News Co., 529 F.2d 209, 209-10 (7th Cir. 1976); Burnett v. National Enquirer, Inc., 144 Cal. App. 3d 991, 193 Cal. Rptr. 206 (1983), *appeal dismissed,* 104 S. Ct. 1260 (1984).

sidered such inquiries within the scope of the actual malice standard's coverage for entertainers and personalities, which means that such persons are among the most common examples of the all purpose, as opposed to limited, public figure.[390]

[b] Less Famous Entertainers

For less famous "lower echelon" entertainers and personalities, courts are more likely to require some nexus between the entertainer's voluntary entry into a controversy and the defamatory communication. This nexus, however, may in some instances be supplied by the entertainer's entertainment act itself. In *Griffin v. Kentucky Post,*[391] for example, it was held that a nude or seminude dancer is a public figure for purposes relating to the legality of the dancer's performance. In *Braun v. Flynt,*[392] on the other hand, it was held that a plaintiff who obtained limited public exposure because of her job, which involved working in an amusement park novelty act, but who was involved in no public controversy and had no hand in determining the outcome of any important public issue, was a private figure.

[5] Sports Figures

[a] In General

A number of cases involving sports figures, including players, coaches, owners, managers, agents, and athletic directors, have held the persons involved to be public figures.[393] In *Barry v. Time, Inc.,*[394] for

---

390 *See infra* § 3.22.

391 10 Med. L. Rep. (BNA) 1159 (Ky. Cir. Ct. 1983). *See also* James v. Gannett Co., 40 N.Y.2d 415, 386 N.Y.S.2d 871, 353 N.E.2d 834 (1976)(holding that cabaret performances of a belly dancer placed plaintiff in public spotlight).

392 726 F.2d 245 (5th Cir. 1984).

393 *See, e.g.,* Curtis Publishing Co. v. Butts, 388 U.S. 130 (1967)(college football coach); Silvester v. American Broadcasting Cos., 839 F.2d 1491 (11th Cir. 1988) (owner of jai alai fronton); Chuy v. Philadelphia Eagles Football Club, 595 F.2d 1265, 1280 (3d Cir. 1979)(en banc)(professional football player); Time, Inc. v. Johnston, 448 F.2d 378 (4th Cir. 1971)(professional basketball player); Cepeda v. Cowles Magazines, 392 F.2d 417 (9th Cir. 1968)(professional baseball player); Holt v. Cox Enterprises, 590 F. Supp. 408 (N.D. Ga. 1984)(former college football star); Barry v. Time, Inc., 584 F. Supp. 1110 (N.D. Cal. 1984)(head college basketball coach); Bell v. Associated Press, 584 F. Supp. 128, 130-31 (D.D.C. 1984)(professional football player); Woy v. Turner, 573 F. Supp. 35, 38 (N.D. Ga. 1983)(agent for baseball player); Rood v. Finney, 418 So. 2d 1 (La. Ct. App.), *cert. denied,* 420 So. 2d 979 (La. 1982), *cert. denied,* 460 U.S. 1013 (1983)(professional golfer); Nussbaumer v. Time, 13 Med. L. Rep. (BNA) 1753 (Ohio App. 1986)(player personnel director

example, it was held that by accepting a position as a head basketball coach at a university which was under investigation for recruiting violations, the plaintiff thrust himself into the forefront of a public controversy involving recruiting and the proper role of athletics at a university. The coach was thus a limited purpose public figure with regard to a magazine article reporting on a basketball player's accusation that he had received illegal payments from that coach.

[b] Figures from the Past

In *Holt v. Cox Enterprises,*[395] it was held that a former star player on a 1961 University of Alabama football team had voluntarily assumed the risk of public comment on his manner of play. The plaintiff, during a highly publicized game with Georgia Tech, was involved in an altercation with the captain of the Georgia Tech team. The incident, which may have lead to Georgia Tech's decision to stop playing against Alabama, and which precipitated a public controversy concerning the purpose of college football, caused the plaintiff to remain a public figure in his libel action against a newspaper. In 1979, the newspaper ran articles reporting on the resumption of games between Alabama and Georgia Tech;[396] the resumption of the games between the two schools naturally revived interest in the 1961 incident and in effect rewarmed the controversy in which the plaintiff had been involved.[397]

[c] Scope of Comment

As with entertainers, the scope of the actual malice standard for sports figures frequently shades towards the all purpose category, encompassing inquiry into matters such as drug use, romantic involvements, or criminal activity. The leading sports figure case, of course,

---

for professional football team); Winter v. Northern Tier Publishing Co., 4 Med. L. Rep. (BNA) 1348 (N.Y. Sup. Ct. 1978)(high school football coach); Milkovich v. Lorain Journal, 65 Ohio App. 2d 143, 416 N.E.2d 662 (1979), *cert denied,* 449 U.S. 966 (1980)(high school wrestling coach); Johnston v. Corinthian Television Corp., 583 P.2d 1101 (Okla. 1978)(grade school wrestling coach); Grayson v. Curtis Publishing Co., 72 Wash. 2d 999, 436 P.2d 756 (1967)(college basketball coach). *But see* Andreescu v. Lane, 5 Med. L. Rep. (BNA) 1290 (Colo. Dist. 1979)(famous racer held to be private figure in story about race fixing).

394 584 F. Supp. 1110 (N.D. Cal. 1984).

395 590 F. Supp. 408 (N.D. Ga. 1984).

396 *Id.* at 412.

397 *Id.*

is *Curtis Publishing Co. v. Butts,*[398] in which University of Georgia head coach Wally Butts was declared by the Supreme Court to be a public figure with regard to a *Saturday Evening Post* story alleging that Butts had conspired to fix a college football game. Similarly, Theo Bell, a professional football player whose athletic career received substantial press coverage and who was subjected to considerable press attention concerning his activities off the field, was held in *Bell v. Associated Press*[399] to be a limited public figure for the purposes of certain alleged criminal misconduct. And, In *Rood v. Finney,*[400] Floyd Rood, a professional golfer, had devoted a substantial portion of his time to an activity he coined "highway golf," a cross-country golfing tour aimed at raising money to combat drug abuse by young people. A *Houston Chronicle* story erroneously reported that Rood's highway golf tour was aimed at raising money to "help solve *his* drug addiction problem,"[401] rather than to help solve *the* drug addiction problem—thus erroneously turning Rood from a hero into a drug addict. Rood was held to be a public figure, and consequently he lost his libel suit at the summary judgment stage.[402]

[6] Writers, Artists, Critics

Writers, artists, and critics of all kind are usually held to be public figures, at least with regard to critiques of their literary or artistic endeavors.[403] One of the few aberrations from the pattern is *Hellman v.*

---

398 388 U.S. 130 (1967). *See supra* § 2.02[1].

399 584 F. Supp. 128, 130-31 (D.D.C. 1984).

400 418 So. 2d 1 (La. Ct. App), *cert. denied,* 420 So. 2d 979 (La. 1982), *cert. denied,* 460 U.S. 1013 (1983).

401 418 So. 2d at 2.

402 *Id.* at 2-3.

403 *See, e.g.* Lerman v. Flynt Distributing Co., 745 F.2d 123, 137-38 (2d Cir. 1984), *cert. denied,* 471 U.S. 1054, 105 S. Ct. 2114 (1985)(well-known author); Hotchner v. Castillo-Puche, 551 F.2d 910 (2d Cir.), *cert. denied,* 429 U.S. 1062 (1977)(well-known writer, editor, talk-show host, and critic); Falls v. Sporting News Publishing Co., 714 F. Supp. 843 (E.D. Mich. 1989), *rev'd on other grounds,* 834 F.2d 611 (6th Cir. 1989); Montandon v. Triangle Publications, 45 Cal. App. 3d 938, 120 Cal. Rptr. 186, *cert. denied,* 423 U.S. 893 (1975)(author of book *How to Be a Party Girl*); Rose v. Koch, 278 Minn. 235, 154 N.W.2d 409, 426 (1967)(well-known author); Maule v. NYM Corp., 76 A.D.2d 58, 62, 429 N.Y.S.2d 891 (1st Dept. 1980), *rev'd on other grounds,* 54 N.Y.2d 880, 444 N.Y.S.2d 909, 429 N.E.2d 416 (1981)(author and writer for *Sports Illustrated*); Atkins v. Friedman, 49 A.D.2d 852, 374 N.Y.S.2d 11 (1st Dept. 1975)(physician who wrote books on dieting). *But see* Hellman v. McCarthy, 10 Med. L. Rep. (BNA) 1789, 1792 (N.Y. Sup. Ct. 1984)(on defendant's motion for summary judgment, court would not hold writer Lillian Hellman to be a public figure as a matter of law).

McCarthy.[404] Lillian Hellman, one of the more famous American writers of this century, was allegedly libeled by a statement made by another well-known writer, Mary McCarthy, on the "Dick Cavett Show," by McCarthy's statements that Hellman was "a dishonest writer" and that "every word she writes is a lie," including " 'and' and 'the.' " The court held on the defendant's motion for summary judgment that Hellman could not be deemed as a matter of law to be a public figure, since public figure status not only involves general fame or notoriety but requires the plaintiff's participation in a public issue, question, or controversy. The court held that Lillian Hellman arguably had not voluntarily participated in any such controversy.[405]

While it is of course true that Lillian Hellman did not invite Mary McCarthy to appear on television and label Hellman a dishonest writer, Hellman did write and have published a great many plays and books, and by that voluntary activity did in fact thrust herself into the arena of literary criticism. The better view, and the view certainly more in line with the mainstream of authority, is that any writer, artist, or critic of Hellman's stature is a public figure as a matter of law in connection with any statements concerning his or her creative efforts.[406]

[7] Religious Figures and Organizations

A number of cases involving priests, ministers, and religious organizations have held the plaintiffs to be public figures.[407] In *McManus v. Doubleday & Co.,*[408] the plaintiff, a Roman Catholic priest actively involved in the controversy over the independence of Northern Ireland, was held to be a public figure. Reverend Jerry Falwell conceded public

---

[404] 10 Med. L. Rep. (BNA) 1789 (N.Y. Sup. Ct. 1984).

[405] *Id.* at 1792.

[406] *See, e.g.*, Lerman v. Flynt Distributing Co., 745 F.2d 123, 137-38 (2d Cir. 1984), *cert. denied,* 471 U.S. 1054, 105 S. Ct. 2114 (1985); Hotchner v. Castillo-Puche, 551 F.2d 910 (2d Cir.), *cert. denied,* 434 U.S. 834 (1977); Buckley v. Littell, 539 F.2d 882 (2d Cir. 1976), *cert. denied,* 429 U.S. 1062 (1977).

[407] *See, e.g.*, Falwell v. Penthouse, 521 F. Supp. 1204 (D. W.Va. 1981); McManus v. Doubleday & Co., 513 F. Supp 1383 (S.D.N.Y. 1981); Church of Scientology v. Siegelman, 475 F. Supp. 950 (S.D.N.Y. 1979); Holy Spirit Ass'n v. Sequoia Elsevier, 4 Med. L. Rep. (BNA) 1744 (N.Y. Sup. Ct. 1978), *modified on other grounds,* 75 A.D.2d 523, 426 N.Y.S.2d 759 (1980). Plaintiffs in cases involving religious figures such as Rev. Falwell often simply concede public figure status.

[408] 513 F. Supp. 1383 (S.D.N.Y. 1981).

figure status in a suit against *Penthouse.*[409] Public figure status was accorded the Church of Scientology, a church with over 5 million members,[410] as well as the Holy Spirit Association for the Unification of World Christianity, better known as the Unification Church.[411] In *Haan v. Board of Publications,*[412] however, it was held that a plaintiff who was the pastor of a church, and who was the president of two corporations associated with his church, was a private figure with regard to a church magazine article from his former affiliated denomination concerning the financial difficulties of the split-away church and corporation.[413]

[8] Corporate Executives, Business Leaders, Entrepreneurs, and Inventors

[a] In General

Corporate executives, business leaders, entrepreneurs, and inventors may at times qualify as public figures,[414] but mere prominence in business activity standing alone is usually not enough to trigger the public figure classification.[414.1] From a sheerly numerical perspective, there appear to be more cases holding such persons to be private figures than

---

409 Falwell v. Penthouse International, Ltd., 521 F. Supp. 1204, 1208 (D. W.Va. 1981).

410 Church of Scientology v. Siegelman, 475 F. Supp. 950 (S.D.N.Y. 1979).

411 Holy Spirit Ass'n v. Sequoia Elsevier, 4 Med. L. Rep. (BNA) 1744 (N.Y. Sup. Ct. 1978), *modified on other grounds,* 75 A.D.2d 523, 426 N.Y.S.2d 759 (1980).

412 10 Med. L. Rep. (BNA) 1671 (Colo. Dist. Ct. 1984).

413 *Id.* at 1672.

414 *See* Tavoulareas v. Washington Post Co., 8 Med. L. Rep. 2262 (D.D.C. 1982)(memorandum opinion ruling plaintiff William Tavoulareas, President of Mobil Oil Corporation, to be a public figure), *subsequent opinion,* 567 F. Supp. 651 (D.D.C. 1983)(post-trial opinion granting defendant's motion for judgment n.o.v.), *rev'd,* 759 F.2d 90 (D.C. Cir. 1985)(reversing grant of judgment n.o.v. and reinstating plaintiff's jury verdict), *vacated,* 817 F.2d 762 (D.C. Cir.)(en banc)(vacating plaintiff's judgment on grounds of failure to prove actual malice with convincing clarity), *cert. denied,* 108 S. Ct. 200 (1987); Wiegel v. Capital Times Co., 426 N.W.2d 43 (Wis. App. 1988)(wealthy farmer held to be vortex public figure in controversy resulting from pesticide and fertilizer pollution of a public lake); Mobile Press Register v. Faulkner, 372 So. 2d 1282 (Ala. 1979)(prominent Alabama businessman also active in civic and political affairs held to be a public figure); Kobar v. Hite, 43 Ill. App. 3d 636, 357 N.E.2d 135 (Ct. App. 1976), *cert. denied,* 434 U.S. 837 (1977). *See also* Miller v. Transamerican Press, Inc., 621 F.2d 721 (5th Cir.), *as modified in denial of rehearing,* 628 F.2d 932 (5th Cir. 1980), *cert. denied,* 450 U.S. 1041 (1981)(secretary-treasurer of Teamsters Union was a public figure with regard to his official duties).

414.1 The Court of Appeals for the D.C. Circuit has recently reaffirmed that "[b]eing an executive within a prominent and influential company does not by itself make one a [limited purpose] public figure." Tavoulareas v. Piro, 817 F.2d 762, 773 (D.C. Cir.), *cert. denied,* 108 S. Ct. 200 (1987)(quoting Waldbaum v. Fairchild Publications, Inc., 627 F.2d 1287, 1299 (D.C. Cir.), *cert. denied,* 449 U.S. 898 (1980)).

public figures,[415] and this is clearly an area where each case turns on its own facts.

[b] The *Tavoulareas* Holding

Probably the most celebrated case brought by a corporate executive is *Tavoulareas v. Washington Post,*[416] in which William P. Tavoulareas, the President and Chief Executive Officer of Mobil Oil Corporation, sued the *Washington Post* for libel arising from a *Post* story implying that Tavoulareas had used his influence to "set up" his son Peter in an oil shipping venture involving Saudi Arabian oil, and then diverted some of Mobil's shipping business to him.

The district court in the *Tavoulareas* litigation ruled that William Tavoulareas did not qualify as an all purpose public figure merely by virtue of being president of Mobil Oil, for that would render virtually all major corporate leaders all purpose public figures.[417] Despite Tavou-

---

415 A substantial number of cases involving plaintiffs engaged in various levels of business activity have declared the plaintiffs to be private figures. *See, e.g.,* Wilson v. Scripps-Howard Broadcasting Co., 642 F.2d 371 (6th Cir.), *cert. granted,* 454 U.S. 962, *cert. dismissed,* 454 U.S. 1130 (1981)(cattleman held private figure); Dixson v. Newsweek, 562 F.2d 626 (10th Cir. 1977)(former airline vice-president private figure); Mead Corporation v. Hicks, 448 So. 2d 308, 311 (Ala. 1983)(plaintiff businessman involved in garbage collection, waste disposal for nuclear power plant, landfill, grocery, farming, and cattle operations a private figure); Peagler v. Phoenix Newspapers, 114 Ariz. 304, 560 P.2d 1216 (1977), *verdict for defendants aff'd after remand,* 640 P.2d 1110 (Ariz. Ct. App. 1981)(president of used car business against whom alleged consumer complaints were lodged a private figure); Rancho La Costa v. Superior Court, 106 Cal. App. 3d 646, 165 Cal. Rptr. 347 (1980), *cert. denied,* 450 U.S. 902 (1981)(officers of exclusive California resort alleged to be "hangout" for underworld figures held to be private figures); Forrest v. Lynch, 347 So. 2d 1255 (La. App. 1977), *cert. denied sub nom.* Times-Picayune v. Forrest, 435 U.S. 971 (1978)(consulting engineer on public project held to be private figure); Zetes v. Richamn, 336 N.Y.S.2d 778, 86 A.D.2d 746 (4th Dept. 1982)(seller of Olympic souvenirs a private figure); Grobe v. Three Village Herald, 420 N.Y.S.2d 3, 69 A.D.2d 175 (2d Dept. 1979), *aff'd mem.,* 49 N.Y.2d 932 (1980)(owner of shopping center private figure); Martin v. Griffin Television, 549 P.2d 85 (Okla. 1976)(owner of pet store accused of poor care of pets a private figure); Taskett v. KING Broadcasting Co., 86 Wash. 2d 439, 546 P.2d 81 (1976)(advertising agency head alleged to have appropriated clients' money a private figure).

416 759 F.2d 90 (D.C. Cir. 1985), *vacated,* 817 F.2d 762 (D.C. Cir.)(en banc), *cert. denied,* 108 S. Ct. 200 (1987).

417 Tavoulareas v. Washington Post Co., 8 Med. L. Rep. 2262 (D.D.C. 1982)(memorandum order on public figure issue), *subsequent opinion,* 567 F. Supp. 651 (D.D.C. 1983)(post-trial opinion granting defendant's judgment n.o.v.), *rev'd,* 759 F.2d 90 (D.C. Cir. 1985)(reversing grant of judgment n.o.v. and reinstating plaintiff's verdict), *vacated,* 817 F.2d 762 (D.C. Cir.)(en banc)(vacating plaintiff's judgment on grounds of failure to prove actual malice), *cert. denied,* 108 S. Ct. 200 (1987).

lareas' "conceded prominence as a businessman," the court could not find that "his name is a household word or that he is a celebrity in society at large."[418] (It is worth noting that Tavoulareas in this respect is probably different from a corporate leader like Chrysler President Lee Iaccoca, who's name probably is a household word and who quite probably has achieved "at large" celebrity status.)

The district court did hold, however, that Tavoulareas was a limited purpose public figure in connection with the material contained in the *Post* article.[419] In reaching this decision the court ruled that *prior to* publication of the *Post* article on the shipping business deal involving William Tavoulareas' son Peter, a public controversy concerning the propriety of that deal existed.[420] The court noted that Mobil was an innovative company and that the particular business deal in question involved pioneering efforts on Mobil's part to structure new and controversial relationships with Saudi Arabia following the 1973 oil embargo. William Tavoulareas was the major architect of Mobil's new policy, and the arrangements that were put together involving his son were part of the structure he created.[421] The court then turned to analyze Tavoulareas' access to the media:

> The court's conclusion is buttressed by William Tavoulareas' access to the media—primarily through Mobil's public affairs department—and his ability to respond with his version of the facts depicted in the two articles in question. As one of the most dynamic and successful businessmen in the nation, and as President of Mobil, he has far more access to the press than the vast majority of citizens in this country. . . . Mr. Tavoulareas' access to the media is especially great when the subject matter concerns the affairs of Mobil or of the oil industry. In short, he commands the attention of the press when he comments on the oil industry's relationship with the Arab world, in general, or on Mobil's relationship with Saudi Arabia, in particular. Mr. Tavoulareas' access to the media on these subjects is confirmed by his ability to command coverage of his side of the facts in this very case.[422]

The *Tavoulareas* case was thus tried under the premise that Tavoulareas was a public figure. The jury returned an award of $250,000 in

---

[418] 8 Med. L. Rep. (BNA) at 2264.

[419] *Id.* at 2264-66.

[420] *Id.* at 2265. In this respect the court was applying the preexisting controversy requirement adhered to in the District of Columbia Circuit. *See* Waldbaum v. Fairchild Publications, Inc., 627 F.2d 1287 (D.C. Cir), *cert. denied,* 449 U.S. 898 (1980). *See also supra* § 2.10.

[421] 8 Med. L. Rep. (BNA) at 2264.

[422] *Id.* at 2265.

compensatory damages and $1.8 million in punitive damages against the *Post.* The district court erased the jury award on the defendant *Post*'s motion for judgment notwithstanding the verdict,[423] but the Court of Appeals for the District of Columbia reversed the district court's grant of judgment n.o.v., reinstating the jury award.[424] The Court of Appeals found that there was sufficient evidence of actual malice to support the jury verdict against the *Post,* and so the Court of Appeals did not find it necessary to review the issue of whether Tavoulareas was a public figure.[425] The Court of Appeals stated in a footnote, however, that "the public figure determination in this case would not be free from difficulty."[426] In further discussing the "difficulty" that might exist, the Court of Appeals cast doubt on whether the public controversy concerning the business dealings of Mobil, Saudi Arabia, and Tavoulareas' son preexisted the *Post*'s first article on the subject.[427]

On rehearing before the Court of Appeals sitting en banc, the panel's decision was vacated.[427.1] Using the three step analysis set forth in *Waldbaum v. Fairchild Publications, Inc.,*[427.2] the Court of Appeals concluded that Tavoulareas had thrust himself into the national controversy surrounding the oil industry by "spearheading a public counterattack on the movement for reform" in the industry,[427.3] thereby qualifying himself as a public figure for the purposes of that debate. The nepotism alleged in the *Post* article was found germane to this controversy because "the credibility and integrity of representatives of the oil industry had become an issue."[427.4]

In addition, the Court of Appeals agreed with the district court's determination that Tavoulareas was a public figure in connection with the more narrowly defined controversy concerning the particular business deals involving Mobil, Saudi Arabia, and Tavoulareas' son.[427.5] Although the *Post* was the first general circulation newspaper to discuss the in-

---

423 *See* 567 F. Supp. 651 (D.D.C. 1983).

424 759 F.2d 90 (D.C. Cir. 1985), *vacated,* 817 F.2d 762 (D.C. Cir.)(en banc), *cert. denied,* 108 S. Ct. 200 (1987).

425 759 F.2d at 103.

426 *Id.* at 103 n.12.

427 *Id.*

427.1 Tavoulareas v. Piro, 817 F.2d 762 (D.C. Cir.), *cert. denied,* 108 S Ct. 200 (1987).

427.2 627 F.2d 1287, 1297 (D.C. Cir.), *cert. denied,* 449 U.S. 898 (1980). *See supra* § 2.09[3].

427.3 Tavoulareas v. Piro, 817 F.2d 762, 773 (D.C. Cir.), *cert. denied,* 108 S. Ct. 200 (1987).

427.4 *Id.* at 774.

427.5 *Id.*

volvement of Peter Tavoulareas in the venture,[427.6] other journalists inquired about the arrangement long before the *Post* article appeared.[427.7] Furthermore, Tavoulareas and Mobil had publicly acknowledged Peter's participation through a "widely read oil industry periodical"[427.8] and via a mailing to shareholders.[427.9] Finally, the arrangement had been subject to criticism by outside members of Mobil's board of directors[427.10] and had been investigated by the Securities Exchange Commission.[427.11] These facts were sufficient to establish a preexisting public controversy.

[c] Summary

In sum, although it is quite clear that business leaders may in proper circumstances qualify as public figures, defendants frequently have an uphill battle convincing courts to so classify them, and at present mere entry into business dealings that are not independently part of a "public controversy" of some kind is usually not enough to trigger public figure status.[428]

[9] Professionals

[a] Attorneys

It is clear from the *Gertz*[429] decision itself that an attorney does not become elevated to public figure status merely by virtue of representing clients in litigation that attracts media attention. Elmer Gertz was in fact a reasonably prominent attorney; he had written four books, had represented a number of famous and infamous clients, and had been involved in a number of civil rights and other cases that attracted media attention. None of these activities, however, was sufficient to render

---

427.6 *Id.* at 775 n.13.

427.7 *Id.* at 774.

427.8 *Id.*

427.9 *Id.*

427.10 *Id.* at 775.

427.11 *Id.*

428 For discussion of the special problems of corporations (as opposed to individual business persons) as public or private figure defamation plaintiffs, *see supra* §2.23. *See also* Healy v. New England Newspapers, 555 A.2d 321 (R.I. 1989) (a physician who was also president of an organization involved in a public controversy is a private figure in his libel action against the newspaper based on an article about his role as a physician and his failure to act in response to a medical emergency during a meeting of the organization, because the article referred to the physician's private life, not his public life).

429 Gertz v. Robert Welch, Inc., 418 U.S. 323 (1974).

Gertz an all purpose public figure,[430] and the Supreme Court held that Gertz's agreeing to act as the attorney for the family of a boy shot by a Chicago policeman in a civil action against the policeman did not qualify as thrusting himself into the vortex of a public issue.[431]

[b] Ethical or Disciplinary Matters

Following the lead of *Gertz,* several decisions have held lawyers not to be public figures.[432] Two of the cases holding attorneys to be private figures involved newspaper articles that discussed matters relating to alleged professional misconduct or discipline. In *Littlefield v. Fort Dodge Messenger,*[433] the court held that an attorney did not become a public figure despite the fact that he was practicing law in violation of criminal probation, an admittedly voluntary activity of substantial public interest. Similarly, in *Dodrill v. Arkansas Democrat Co.,*[434] the plaintiff, a lawyer who had been suspended from practice for a year for breach of the public trust and was reinstated only upon retaking and passing the bar exam, was erroneously reported to have failed the exam. The Arkansas Supreme Court held that he had not voluntarily thrust himself into a public controversy and was not a public figure.[435]

These decisions construe *Gertz* and the public controversy requirement far too mechanically, for of course no attorney guilty of misconduct literally volunteers for the glare of public scrutiny.[436] As Arkansas Supreme Court Justice Darrell Hickman cogently observed in a dissenting opinion in *Dodrill,* the plaintiff was "in the public eye because of his breach of a public trust."[437] Justice Hickman then remarked:

> Would a physician, seeking return of his license after losing it for improperly authorizing drugs, become a public figure? Would a druggist become a public figure under the same circumstances? Such individuals, like Dodrill, would not be ordinary professional people minding their own business, practicing their trade, unwittingly subject to the glare of publici-

---

430 *Id.* at 351-52.

431 *Id.*

432 *See* Littlefied v. Fort Dodge Messenger, 614 F.2d 581 (8th Cir.), *cert. denied,* 445 U.S. 945 (1980); Dodrill v. Arkansas Democrat Co., 265 Ark. 628, 590 S.W.2d 840 (1979), *cert. denied,* 444 U.S. 1076 (1980); Peisner v. Detroit Free Press, 82 Mich. App. 153, 266 N.W.2d 693 (1978), *subsequent appeal,* 104 Mich. App. 59, 304 N.W.2d 814 (1981).

433 614 F.2d 581 (8th Cir.), *cert. denied,* 445 U.S. 945 (1980).

434 265 Ark. 628, 590 S.W.2d 840 (1979), *cert. denied,* 444 U.S. 1076 (1980).

435 *Id.* at 636-37.

436 *See supra* §§ 2.13-2.14.

437 Dodrill v. Arkansas Democrat Co., 265 Ark. 628, 640-41, 590 S.W.2d 840, 846. (Hickman, J., dissenting), *cert. denied,* 444 U.S. 1076 (1979).

ty. They would be individuals who had violated their public trust because of their own misdeeds and were, for good or ill, about to resume their

(*Text continued on page 2-75*)

roles as individuals having a public trust. The public in every such instance has a right to know about such a situation and that is a consideration that must be given when deciding such cases.[438]

[c] Going Beyond Mere Legal Representation

Despite the authority of *Gertz,* courts more often than not have held that attorneys are public figures when they become defamation plaintiffs.[439] If an attorney does no more than represent a client in a strictly legal context, he or she will not through that representation alone become a public figure, for that would place an undue burden on attorneys who represent famous or notorious clients.[440] But if an attorney goes beyond legal representation and thrusts himself or herself into a public controversy connected to the litigation—such as conducting news conferences to affirmatively make the case a public issue—"then those voluntary activities may be counted in the public figure calculus."[441] Second, if an attorney has contacts with a client that rise to the level of thrusting himself or herself into a public controversy outside of the attorney's actual legal work, such contacts may be counted quite strongly in favor of public figure status. In *Marcone v. Penthouse International, Ltd.,*[442] for example, the plaintiff was an attorney who represented motorcycle gangs. The Court of Appeals for the Third Circuit, ruling that the plaintiff was a public figure, found it important, in what was concededly a "close case,"[443] that the plaintiff had previously attracted media attention by visiting gang headquarters and taking week-

---

438 *Id. See also* Orr v. Argus-Press Co., 586 F.2d 1108 (6th Cir. 1978), *cert. denied,* 440 U.S. 960 (1979)(attorney charged with securities law violations held to be public figure).

439 *See, e.g.,* Marcone v. Penthouse International, Ltd., 754 F.2d 1072 (3d Cir.), *cert. denied,* 474 U.S. 864, *reh'g denied,* 474 U.S. 1014 (1985); Orr v. Argus-Press Co., 586 F.2d 1108 (6th Cir. 1978), *cert. denied,* 440 U.S. 960 (1979); Ratner v. Young, 465 F. Supp. 386 (D.V.I. 1978); Weingarten v. Block, 102 Cal. App. 3d 129, 162 Cal. Rptr. 701, *cert. denied,* 449 U.S. 899 (1980); Steere v. Cupp, 226 Kan. 566, 602 P.2d 1267 (1979); Miller v. Charleston Gazette, 9 Med. L. Rep. (BNA) 2540 (W. Va. Cir. Ct. 1983).

440 *See* Gertz v. Robert Welch, Inc., 418 U.S. 323, 352 (1974); Marcone v. Penthouse International, Ltd., 754 F.2d 1072, 1085-86 (3d Cir.), *cert. denied,* 474 U.S. 864, *reh'g denied,* 474 U.S. 1014 (1985); Steere v. Cupp, 226 Kan. 566, 571, 602 P.2d 1267, 1273-74 (1979).

441 Marcone v. Penthouse International, Ltd., 754 F.2d 1072, 1086 (3d Cir.), *cert. denied,* 474 U.S. 864, *reh'g denied,* 474 U.S. 1014 (1985)(citing Ratner v. Young, 465 F. Supp. 386, 399-400 (D.V.I. 1979)(defense attorneys in widely publicized trial held to be public figures because of their out of court activities).

442 754 F.2d 1072 (3d Cir.), *cert. denied,* 474 U.S. 864, *reh'g denied,* 474 U.S. 1014 (1985).

443 *Id.* at 1086.

end trips with one of the gangs.[444]

[d] Other Professionals

In addition to lawyers, courts have found doctors, priests, and other "professionals" to be public figures in some contexts.[445] Following the pattern established in the attorney cases, the decisions seem to require more than merely engaging in professional activity that happens to catch the public eye; the professional must usually go beyond mere service to the client and affirmatively inject himself or herself into a public controversy. It is worth noting, however, that at times the professional's voluntary use of innovative or controversial professional methods may be enough to confer public figure status. An architect who proposes a radically unorthodox design for the new city hall or the heart surgeon who pioneers a new artificial heart may be public figures, particularly if they mount the rostrum to announce or defend their professional innovations. Similarly, a professional who takes a strong stand on a public health issue, e.g., flouridation,[446] or who, on the other side of the coin, engages in treatment methods that appear to be unsound or deceptive,[447] may be classified as a public figure.

---

444 *Id.*

445 *See, e.g.,* McDowell v. Paiwonsky, 769 F.2d 942 (3d Cir. 1985)(architect/civil engineer found to be public figure in controversy surrounding trouble-plagued public buildings that he designed); Avins v. White, 627 F.2d 637 (3d Cir.), *cert. denied,* 449 U.S. 982 (1980)(law professor and dean held to be public figure for purposes of controversy surrounding law school accreditation); Yiamouyiannis v. Consumers Union of the United States, Inc., 619 F.2d 932 (2d Cir.), *cert. denied,* 449 U.S. 839 (1980)(plaintiff, a Ph.D. and employee of National Health Federation and active opponent of flouridation of public water supplies, held to be public figure); Harris v. Tomczak, 94 F.R.D. 687 (E.D. Cal. 1982)(plaintiff, Dr. Thomas Harris, M.D., co-author of book *I'm Okay—You're Okay,* and his wife/co-author both public figures); Farnsworth v. Chicago Tribune Co., 43 Ill. 2d 286, 253 N.E.2d 408 (1969)(osteopathic physician held to be public figure in pre-*Gertz* case that heavily emphasized "public interest" approach). *But see* Franklin v. Lodge 1108, Benevolent & Protective Order of Elks, 97 Cal. App. 3d 915, 159 Cal. Rptr. 131 (1979)(teacher held to be private figure); Forrest v. Lynch, 347 So. 2d 1255 (La. App. 1977), *cert. denied sub nom.* Times-Picayune v. Forrest, 435 U.S. 971 (1978)(consulting engineer held to be private figure); Greenberg v. CBS, Inc., 69 A.D.2d 693, 419 N.Y.S.2d 988 (2d Dept. 1979)(physician who had written scientific articles but not invited public attention held to be private figure).

446 *See* Yiamouyiannis v. Consumers Union of the United States, Inc., 619 F.2d 932 (2d Cir.), *cert. denied,* 449 U.S. 839 (1980).

447 *See* Farnsworth v. Chicago Tribune, Co., 43 Ill. 2d 286, 253 N.E.2d 408 (1969)(plaintiff, an osteopathic physician labeled as a "quack" in a *Chicago Tribune* article, held subject to actual malice standard in a pre-*Gertz* case). For a discussion of *Farnsworth, see* Smolla & Malone, *supra* note 330, at 229-32.

§ 2.22 Defining the "All Purpose" Public Figure

[1] Significance of the Category

The second type of public figure recognized in *Gertz*[448] is the far rarer bird known variously as the "general" or "all purpose" or "pervasive" or "unlimited" public figure.[449] The same actual malice test applies to all public figures, without regard to whether they fall within the limited or all purpose subcategory.[450] The only difference between the two subcategories is that the actual malice test applies to limited public figures only with regard to speech connected to the public controversy out of which the public figure status arises, whereas the pervasive public figure is subject to the actual malice test in all defamation actions. Thus, the Court in *Gertz* stated that "[s]ome occupy positions of *such pervasive power and influence that they are deemed public figures for all purposes.*"[451]

[2] Rarity of the Category

Near the end of the *Gertz* opinion, the Court made two additional points concerning the all purpose public figure. First, examples of such figures are rare, and the all purpose status should not be conferred lightly:

> We would not lightly assume that a citizen's participation in community and professional affairs rendered him a public figure for all purposes. Absent clear evidence of general fame or notoriety in the community, and pervasive involvement in the affairs of society, an individual should not be deemed a public personality for all aspects of his life.[452]

Second, the Court admonished lower courts to resort to the narrower limited public figure approach whenever possible:

> It is preferable to reduce the public figure question to a more meaningful context by looking to the nature and extent of an individual's participation in the particular controversy giving rise to the defamation.[453]

(*Text continued on page 2-77*)

---

448 Gertz v. Robert Welch, Inc., 418 U.S. 323 (1974).

449 *See generally* Note, *General Public Figures Since* Gertz v. Robert Welch, Inc., 58 St. John's L. Rev. 355 (1984).

450 Gertz v. Robert Welch, Inc., 418 U.S. 323, 344-46 (1974).

451 *Id.* at 345 (emphasis added).

452 *Id.* at 352.

453 *Id.*

§ 2.23 Examples of All Purpose Public Figures

[1] In General

Although at times decisions utilizing the all purpose public figure category explicitly adopt the classification, some decisions are somewhat less precise, typically discussing both the all purpose and vortex categories of *Gertz* and then declaring the plaintiff to be a public figure, without explicitly designating which variety. When this somewhat fuzzy methodology is used, the clue that the court was in fact using the all purpose category will usually be the failure to mention or emphasize the "public controversy" requirement, since the existence of a public controversy as such is not a prerequisite to all purpose public figure status. What follows is a nonexhaustive index of the types of persons that have been explicitly or implicitly designated as all purpose public figures.

[2] Political Candidates

Political candidates frequently achieve pervasive fame or notoriety, and thereby often open themselves up to all purpose public figure status.[454] In *Goldwater v. Ginzburg,*[455] for example, the Second Circuit held that "[b]y seeking election to the office of President of the United States, Senator Goldwater invited the press and public to scrutinize *every aspect of his life,* public and private alike. His mental and physical health were proper targets for investigation and for adverse comment."[456] Utilizing the "local all purpose public figure"[457] notion, similar logic can be applied to candidates for state and local office.[458]

---

454 *See, e.g.,* Goldwater v. Ginzburg, 414 F.2d 324 (2d Cir. 1969), *cert. denied,* 396 U.S. 1049 (1970); Sigman v. Gove, 169 Ga. App. 580, 314 S.E.2d 238 (1984); Guthrie v. Annabel, 50 Ill. App. 3d 969, 365 N.E.2d 1367 (1977); Williams v. Pasma, 656 P.2d 212 (Mont. 1982); Clements v. Gannett Co., 5 Med. L. Rep. (BNA) 1657 (N.Y. Sup. Monroe County 1979); Weaver v. Pryor Jeffersonian, 569 P.2d 967 (Okla. 1977).

455 414 F.2d 324 (2d Cir. 1969), *cert. denied,* 396 U.S. 1049 (1970).

456 *Id.* at 335 (emphasis added).

457 *See supra* §2.20 [2].

458 *See* Williams v. Pasma, 656 P.2d 212 (Mont. 1982), *cert. denied,* 103 S. Ct. 2122 (1983). *See also* Guthrie v. Annabel, 50 Ill. App. 3d 969, 365 N.E.2d 1367 (1977)(local candidate for sheriff who had also been chairman for central committee of political party).

[3] Entertainers and Other "Personalities"

Entertainers and other prominent "personalities" are perhaps the best examples of individuals who achieve public figure status less from voluntary entry into a controversy and more by sheer fame and position —the hallmarks of the all purpose public figure. In the United States entertainers such as Johnny Carson,[459] Carol Burnett,[460] and Clint Eastwood[461] must simply accept that as a quid pro quo for their success their lives will be subject to pervasive scrutiny, a scrutiny that goes beyond their roles strictly as entertainers and extends to inquiry into matters as "private" as their marriages,[462] social habits,[463] and romantic liaisons.[464] Such entertainers, and even their spouses,[465] often become public figures for all purposes, no matter how unwelcome that status may be.[466]

[4] Political, Social, and Consumer Activists

All purpose public figure status may be granted to persons who become prominent advocates of social, political, or consumer causes. Such figures essentially take on many of the functional attributes of policy-influencing public officials. Figures like Reverend Jerry Falwell,[467] Jane Fonda, Ralph Nader,[468] and Reverend Jesse Jackson[469] may by their prominence and position achieve such pervasive public attention and influence that they become all purpose public figures.

---

459 Carson v. Allied News Co., 529 F.2d 209, 209-10 (7th Cir. 1976).

460 Burnett v. National Enquirer, Inc., 144 Cal. App. 3d, 997, 193 Cal. Rptr. 206, 216 (1983), *appeal dismissed,* 104 S. Ct. 1260 (1984).

461 Eastwood v. Superior Court, 149 Cal. App. 3d 409, 198 Cal. Rptr. 342 (1983).

462 *See* Carson v. Allied News Co., 529 F.2d 209, 209-10 (7th Cir. 1976).

463 *See* Burnett v. National Enquirer, Inc., 144 Cal. App. 3d, 193 Cal. Rptr. 206, 216 (1983), *appeal dismissed,* 104 S. Ct. 1260 (1984).

464 *See* Eastwood v. Superior Court, 149 Cal. App. 3d 409, 198 Cal. Rptr. 342 (1983).

465 *See* Carson v. Allied News Co., 529 F.2d 209, 210 (7th Cir. 1976)("the wife of a public figure such as Carson more or less automatically becomes at least a part-time public figure herself").

466 *Id.*

467 *Cf.* Falwell v. Penthouse, 521 F. Supp. 1204 (D. W. Va. 1981)(plaintiff Jerry Falwell admitted to being a public figure from the outset of this litigation).

468 *Cf.* Nader v. de Toledano, 408 A.2d 31 (D.C. 1979), *cert. denied,* 444 U.S. 1078 (1980)(plaintiff Ralph Nader concedes public figure status in libel suit arising from Nader's crusade against the safety of General Motors' Corvair).

469 *Cf.* Williams v. Trust Co. of Georgia, 140 Ga. App. 49, 230 S.E.2d 45, 48-50 (1976)(civil rights and labor activist Hosea Williams, "whether deemed a dissident of notoriety or considered a champion for civil rights," is a public figure).

[5] Business and Community Leaders; Major Corporations

Reflecting to a degree the "flip side" of the "activist" as all purpose public figure, several opinions have found business, civic, and political party leaders to be pervasive public figures.[470] Similarly, in *Reliance Insurance Co. v. Barron's*,[471] it was held that a billion dollar corporation's role in society was sufficiently pervasive to create all purpose public figure status.[472]

[6] Political Confidants and Advisors

All purpose public figure status may at times be achieved on the coattails of another all purpose public figure or public official, if the plaintiff has achieved special prominence and influence through his or her connection to the principal public figure or official. This is particularly apt for advisors to the politically powerful. In *Rebozo v. Washington Post*,[473] for example, it was held that Charles ("Bebe") Rebozo, President Nixon's closest friend and confidant, was a public figure even for purposes of inquiry into Rebozo's own business and personal affairs.

[7] Writers, Critics, and Columnists

Writers, critics, and columnists may achieve sufficiently pervasive fame and influence to achieve all purpose public figure status. Courts have found such status, for example, for political writers and commentators such as William F. Buckley,[474] well-known authors,[475] and prominent sports writers.[476]

---

[470] *See, e.g.*, Whitaker v. Denver Post, Inc., 401 F. Supp. 60 (D. Wyo. 1975), *rev'd on other grounds sub nom.* Anselmi v. Denver Post, Inc., 552 F.2d 316 (10th Cir.), *cert. denied*, 432 U.S. 911 (1977); Mobile Press Register v. Faulkner, 372 So. 2d 1282 (Ala. 1979); News Journal Co. v. Gallagher, 233 A.2d 166 (Del. 1967); Guthrie v. Annabel, 50 Ill. App. 3d 969, 365 N.E.2d 1367 (1977); A.S. Asbell Co. v. Barnes, 258 Md. 56, 265 A.2d 207 (1970), *cert. denied*, 403 U.S. 921 (1971); Perkins v. Mississippi Publishing Corp., 241 So. 2d 139 (Miss. 1970); Williams v. Pasma, 656 P.2d 212 (Mont. 1982); Adams v. Frontier Broadcasting Co., 555 P.2d 556 (Wyo. 1976).

[471] 442 F. Supp. 1341 (S.D.N.Y. 1977).

[472] *Id.* at 1348. In somewhat the same vein, a college or university may achieve all purpose public figure status. *See* Ithaca College v. Yale Daily News Publishing Co., 105 Misc. 2d 793, 433 N.Y.S.2d 530 (N.Y. Sup. 1980), *aff'd on other grounds*, 85 A.D.2d 817, 445 N.Y.S.2d 621 (3d Dept. 1981).

[473] 637 F.2d 375 (5th Cir.), *cert. denied*, 454 U.S. 964 (1981).

[474] Buckley v. Littell, 539 F.2d 882 (2d Cir. 1976), *cert. denied*, 429 U.S. 1062 (1977).

[475] Montandon v. Triangle Publications, 45 Cal. App. 2d 938, 120 Cal. Rptr. 186, *cert. denied*, 423 U.S. 893 (1975)(Pat Montandon, author of *How to Be a Party Girl*, conceded public figure status).

[476] Maule v. NYM Corporation, 76 A.D.2d 58, 62, 429 N.Y.S.2d 891 (1st Dept. 1980),

[8] Religious Figures and Organizations

Religious leaders and religious organizations may achieve all purpose public figure status because of their prominence and influence.[477] Religious leaders often become enormously influential on matters covering a broad spectrum of social issues.[478] Religious organizations often actively solicit new members and contributions,[479] becoming highly visible and controversial.[480]

[9] Attorneys

Attorneys may run the full gamut from private figures such as Elmer Gertz,[481] to vortex public figures,[482] to all purpose public figures.[483] The lesson of *Gertz* is that for an attorney to be a public figure at all, let alone a pervasive public figure, his or her prominence must normally transcend simple involvement in a single case that happens to attract media attention. In *Steere v. Cupp,*[484] for example, the plaintiff, classified as an all purpose public figure, had been involved for many years in a number of major social disputes and activities. Similarly, in *Ratner v. Young,*[485] the all purpose public figure plaintiff was an attorney who had become nationally controversial for representing unpopular causes in litigation. An attorney recommended for public office should also normally be subject to public figure status, for a range of criticism that would be commensurate with the broad range of inquiry permitted for actual

---

rev'd on other grounds, 429 N.E.2d 416, 54 N.Y.2d 880, 444 N.Y.S.2d 909 (1981).

477 *See* Church of Scientology v. Siegelman, 475 F. Supp. 950, *rehearing denied,* 481 F. Supp. 866 (S.D.N.Y. 1979); Holy Spirit Ass'n v. Sequoia Elsevier Pub. Co., 75 A.D.2d 523, 426 N.Y.S.2d 759 (1980).

478 *Cf.* Falwell v. Penthouse, 521 F. Supp. 1204 (D. W. Va. 1981).

479 *See* Church of Scientology v. Siegelman, 475 F. Supp. 950, *rehearing denied,* 481 F. Supp. 866 (S.D.N.Y. 1979).

480 *See* Holy Spirit Ass'n v. Sequoia Elsevier Pub. Co., 75 A.D.2d 523, 426 N.Y.S.2d 759 (1980).

481 Gertz v. Robert Welch, Inc., 418 U.S. 423 (1974).

482 *See* Orr v. Argus-Press Co., 586 F.2d 1108 (6th Cir. 1978), *cert. denied,* 440 U.S. 960 (1979).

483 *See* Steere v. Cupp, 226 Kan. 566, 602 P.2d 1267 (1979).

484 *Id.*

485 465 F. Supp. 386 (D.V.I. 1978).

public officials or candidates for elective public office.[486]

[10] Persons Associated with Criminal Activity

Pervasive public figure status may attach to participants in particularly heinous crimes,[487] or persons related to those participants,[488] or persons allegedly associated with organized underworld activity.[489]

[11] Publishers and Major Media Outlets

It is only proper that media outlets that benefit from the public figure rules as defendants should be subjected to the public figure standard when they sue as plaintiffs. It would be hard to imagine a more pervasive public figure in today's media than major media outlets such as the *New York Times* or CBS. Individual publishers such as the *Manchester Union Leader*'s William Loeb may similarly reach sufficient prominence and influence to warrant all purpose public figure status.[490]

§ 2.24 Corporate Plaintiffs and the Public Figure/Private Figure Dichotomy

[1] In General

When corporations sue as defamation plaintiffs, a number of special problems are created, including the issue of whether to classify the corporation as a public or private figure.[491] The special problems exist

---

486 *See* Miller v. Charleston Gazette, 9 Med. L. Rep. (BNA) 2540 (W. Va. Cir. 1983).

487 *See* Ray v. Time, Inc., 452 F. Supp. 618 (W.D. Tenn. 1978)(involving James Earl Ray, convicted assassin of Dr. Martin Luther King).

488 *See* Meeropol v. Nizer, 560 F.2d 1061 (2d Cir. 1977), *cert. denied*, 434 U.S. 1013 (1978)(children of Ethel and Julius Rosenberg).

489 *See* Rosanova v. Playboy Enterprises, Inc., 580 F.2d 859 (5th Cir. 1978).

490 *See* Loeb v. Globe Newspaper Co., 489 F. Supp. 481 (D. Mass. 1980)(newspaper owner); Tait v. King Broadcasting Co., 1 Wash. App. 250, 460 P.2d 307 (1969)(newspaper editor).

491 *See generally* Fetzer, *The Corporate Defamation Plaintiff as First Amendment "Public Figure": Nailing the Jellyfish*, 68 Iowa L. Rev. 35 (1982); Stevens, *Private Enterprise and Public Reputation: Defamation and the Corporate Plaintiff*, 12 Am. Bus. L.J. 281 (1974); Note, *Defamation and the First Amendment in the Corporate Context*, 46 Alb. L. Rev. 603 (1982); Note, *Corporate Defamation and Product Disparagement: Narrowing the Analogy to Personal Defamation*, 75 Colum. L. Rev. 963 (1975); Note, *Libel and the Corporate Plaintiff*, 69 Colum. L. Rev. 1496 (1969); Note, *In Search of the Corporate Private Figure: Defamation of the Corporation*, 6 Hofstra L. Rev. 339 (1978); Note, *A Criticism of the* Gertz *Public Figure/Private Figure Test in the Context of the Corporate Defamation Plaintiff*, 18 San Diego L. Rev. 721 (1982).

because of the interplay of three factors: (1) corporations are fictional legal entities and thus do not have "feelings" or a "reputational interest" in quite the same sense as a natural individual; (2) most corporate defamation cases involve some form of discussion of the corporation's business or commercial conduct, and "commercial speech" in general tends to receive somewhat less first amendment protection than do other forms of speech; and (3) corporations are often pervasively visible and powerful economic, political, and social forces in American life.

[2] The Diminished Corporate Interest in Reputation

In the words of Chief Justice John Marshall in the *Dartmouth College*[492] case, a corporation is "an artificial being" that exists "only in contemplation of law," and "[b]eing the mere creature of law, it possesses only those properties which the charter of its creation confers upon it, either expressly, or as incidental to its very existence."[493] Consequently, long before *New York Times Co. v. Sullivan,*[494] courts placed special disabilities on the corporate defamation plaintiff, recognizing that the defamed corporation has no "character" that can be damaged in the human sense.[495] The impersonal nature of a corporation is thus a factor militating in favor of treating corporations as public figures, since corporate reputation is arguably of less significant importance than the interests in human dignity protected by defamation rules for natural individuals.[496]

[3] *Dun & Bradstreet* and Commercial Speech Doctrines

By the same token, however, the lesser quantum of protection that the first amendment accords "commercial speech" often means that

---

492 Dartmouth College v. Woodward, 17 U.S. (4 Wheat) 518, 536 (1819).

493 *Id.*

494 376 U.S. 254 (1964).

495 *See* Dupont Engineering Co. v. Nashville Banner Pub. Co., 13 F.2d 186, 193-96 (D. Tenn. 1925)(a corporation, as it lacks a personal reputation, cannot sustain injury from defamation after it has ceased to do business); Reporters' Ass'n of America v. Sun Printing & Publishing Ass'n, 186 N.Y. 437, 440, 79 N.E. 710, 711 (1906)(unlike a natural person, a corporation has no personal reputation that can be injured by a libel, but it can be libeled in a business capacity). Corporations have historically been denied equal footing with natural persons in the enjoyment of rights to privacy and other purely personal constitutional guarantees. *See* California Bankers Ass'n v. Shultz, 416 U.S. 21, 65-67 (1974); United States v. White, 322 U.S. 694, 698-701 (1944).

496 *See* Fetzer, *supra* note 491, at 54.

speech concerning corporate affairs is arguably of less vital first amendment concern, a factor that tends to militate toward treating corporations as private figures. Although the Supreme Court has abandoned the early position of *Valentine v. Chrestensen*[497]—that "commercial speech" was not protected by the first amendment—[498] in favor of what is essentially an uncharted ad hoc approach,[499] it is a fair characterization of the Court's current disposition to state that "the Court has granted only limited protection to commercial speech."[500]

In the specific context of libel this position was reinforced by the Supreme Court in *Dun & Bradstreet*,[501] in which the Court held that a credit report concerning a corporation was not a matter of "public concern" and not entitled to the special first amendment protections of *Gertz*. There is a strong possibility that one of the incidental effects of *Dun & Bradstreet* will be an inclination by lower courts to treat those corporations that do fall within the *Gertz* coverage as private figures.

[4] The Pervasive Influence of Corporations

Perhaps because the diminished importance of corporate reputation and the diminished level of first amendment protection for commercial speech roughly balance each other out, the vast majority of courts, cognizant of the central role of the modern corporation in contemporary life, have chosen to apply the *Gertz* public figure/private figure

[497] 316 U.S. 52 (1942).

[498] *See generally* J. Nowak, R. Rotunda & J. Young, Constitutional Law, 923-43 (2d ed. 1983); Farber, *Commercial Speech and First Amendment Theory*, 74 Nw. U. L. Rev. 372 (1979); Rotunda, *The Commercial Speech Doctrine in the Supreme Court*, 1976 U. Ill. L. Forum 1080.

[499] *See, e.g.*, Bolger v. Youngs Drug Products Corp., 463 U.S. 60 (1983); Los Angeles City Council v. Taxpayers for Vincent, 104 S. Ct. 2118 (1984); Matter of R.M.J., 455 U.S. 191 (1982); Metromedia, Inc. v. City of San Diego, 433 U.S. 490 (1981); Central Hudson Gas & Elec. Corp. v. Public Service Comm'n, 447 U.S. 557 (1980); Consolidated Edison Co. of New York, Inc. v. Public Service Comm'n, 447 U.S. 530 (1980); Friedman v. Rogers, 440 U.S. 1 (1979); Ohralik v. Ohio State Bar Ass'n, 436 U.S. 447 (1978); In re Primus, 436 U.S. 412 (1978); First National Bank v. Bellotti, 435 U.S. 765 (1978); Bates v. State Bar of Arizona, 433 U.S. 350 (1977); Carey v. Population Services, Internat'l, 431 U.S. 678 (1977); Virginia State Bd. of Pharmacy v. Virginia Citizens Consumer Council, 425 U.S. 748 (1976); Pittsburg Press Co. v. Pittsburg Comm'n on Human Relations, 413 U.S. 376 (1973).

[500] J. Nowak, et. al, *supra* note 498, at 942. *See also* Watkins & Schwartz, *supra* note 96, at 858 (noting that "[n]o clear definition of commercial speech has emerged").

[501] Dun & Bradstreet, Inc. v. Greenmoss Builders, Inc., 105 S. Ct. 2939 (1985). *See generally infra* §§3.02-3.05.

distinction to corporations in a manner that resembles as much as possible the application of *Gertz* to natural individuals.

[5] The Minority "Public Interest" Approach

In *Martin Marietta Corp. v. Evening Star Newspaper Co.*,[502] the court eschewed the public figure/private figure methodology of *Gertz* for the purposes of corporate defamation plaintiffs, holding instead that the "public interest" standard of *Rosenbloom v. Metrodmedia, Inc.*[503] should be resurrected in the corporate plaintiff situation. The *Martin Marietta* court reasoned "that the values considered important enough to merit accommodation with interests protected by the first amendment are associated solely with natural persons and that corporations, while legal persons for some purposes, possess none of the attributes the court [in *Gertz*] sought to protect."[504] The *Martin Marietta* court conceded that states do have *some* interest in protecting corporations from defamation, but that interest is sufficiently accommodated by applying the actual malice standard to all corporate plaintiff cases arising from issues concerning matters of legitimate public interest.[505]

In *Jadwin v. Minneapolis Star*,[506] the Minnesota Supreme Court endorsed the *Martin Marietta* analysis, adopting a somewhat more detailed version of the "public interest" approach for corporate plaintiffs:

> We hold, therefore, that corporate plaintiffs in defamation actions must prove actual malice by media defendants when the defendants establish that the defamatory material concerns matters of legitimate public interest in the geographic area in which the defamatory material is published, either because of the nature of the business conducted or because the

---

502 417 F. Supp. 947 (D.D.C. 1976).

503 403 U.S. 29 (1971). *See supra* §2.03.

504 Martin Marietta Corp. v. Evening Star Newspaper Co., 417 F. Supp. 947, 955 (D.D.C. 1976).

505 *Id.* at 956. In Colorado, the *Rosenbloom* plurality approach has been adopted, imposing the actual malice standard in cases involving private figures when the allegedly defamatory matters of legitimate public interest. *See* Diversified Management v. Denver Post, Inc., 653 P.2d 1103 (Colo. 1982); Walker v. Colorado Springs Sun, Inc., 188 Colo. 86, 538 P.2d 450 (1975). In the *Diversified Management* case, the *Rosenbloom* analysis was applied to a corporate plaintiff and the actual malice test was deemed appropriate, resulting in an application in Colorado of what is essentially the *Martin Marietta* approach to corporate plaintiffs, but through a different series of steps. Diversified Management v. Denver Post, Inc., 653 P.2d at 1106-08.

506 11 Med. L. Rep. (BNA) 1905 (Minn. Sup. Ct. 1985).

public has an especially strong interest in the investigation or disclosure of the commercial information at issue.[507]

The court in *Jadwin* grounded its decision in the enormously strong interest in a free enterprise economy of intelligent and well-informed decisions about economic matters, rendering indispensible the free flow of commercial information.

Similarly, in *Dairy Stores, Inc. v. Sentinel Publishing Co.*,[508] the court rejected the public figure/private figure dichotomy for cases involving "news stories about the quality or contents of products and services," stating that the actual malice standard should apply in all such cases because of an independent first amendment right to convey and receive commercial and consumer information.[509]

[6] The Majority "Particularized" Approach

Most courts that have dealt with corporate defamation plaintiffs have not followed the *Rosenbloom* approach of *Martin Marietta, Jadwin,* and *Dairy Stores;* they have instead used what has been called a "particularized" case-by-case methodology in classifying the particular corporation as either a public or private figure, thus adhering to the *Gertz* guidelines in corporate cases.[510] The Supreme Court has yet to deal squarely with the application of the public figure test in a corporate plaintiff case. In *Bose Corp. v. Consumers Union of the United States, Inc.*[511] the district court held that the plaintiff Bose Corporation was a public figure, and on appeal Bose chose not to contest that determina-

---

[507] *Id.* at 1913 (quoting Virginia State Bd. of Pharmacy v. Virginia Citizens Consumer Council, Inc., 425 U.S. 748 (1976)).

[508] 191 N.J. Super. 202, 465 A.2d 953, 960 (1983).

[509] *Id.*

[510] *See, e.g.,* National Foundation for Cancer Research v. Council of Better Business Bureaus, 705 F.2d 98 (4th Cir.), *cert. denied,* 104 S. Ct. 108 (1983); Bruno & Stillman, Inc. v. Globe Newspaper Co., 633 F.2d 583 (1st Cir. 1980); Arctic Co., Ltd. v. Loudoun Times Mirror, 624 F.2d 518 (4th Cir. 1980), *cert. denied,* 449 U.S. 1102 (1981); Steaks Unlimited, Inc. v. Deaner, 623 F.2d 264 (3d Cir. 1980); Trans World Accounts, Inc. v. Associated Press, 425 F. Supp. 814 (N.D. Cal. 1977); American Benefit Life Insurance Co. v. McIntyre, 375 So. 2d 239 (Ala. 1979); Vegod Corp. v. American Broadcasting Companies, 25 Cal. 3d 763, 603 P.2d 14, 160 Cal. Rptr. 97 (1979), *cert. denied,* 449 U.S. 886 (1980). *See also* Fetzer, *supra* note 491, at 74-81.

[511] 508 F. Supp. 1249, 1274 (D. Mass. 1981), *rev'd on other grounds,* 692 F.2d 189 (1st Cir. 1982), *aff'd,* 104 S. Ct. 1949 (1984).

tion; both the Court of Appeals[512] and the U.S. Supreme Court[513] explicitly declined to pass on the question.

In applying the particularized *Gertz* approach to corporate plaintiffs, courts have tended to distinguish between routine corporate activity involving the ordinary incidents of manufacturing and selling,[514] and corporate activity that rises above the commonplace to inject the corporation into a public controversy. In *Bank of Oregon v. Independent News, Inc.*,[515] for example, the court held that "[m]erely opening one's doors to the public, offering stock for public sale, advertising, etc., even if considered a thrusting of one's self into matters of public interest, is not sufficient to establish that a corporation is a public figure."[516] On the other hand, corporations engaging in highly regulated activities,[517] or subjected to special scrutiny or investigation by official agencies,[518] or engaged in unusually agressive or controversial advertising,[519] are

---

512 692 F.2d at 197.

513 104 S. Ct. at 1955 n.8.

514 In Golden Bear Distributing Sys. v. Chase Revel, Inc., 708 F.2d 944 (5th Cir. 1983), for example, the court held that the corporate plaintiff did not become a public figure sheerly by virtue of advertising for its services, because such normal advertising had not thrust itself into a public controversy. *See also* Bruno & Stillman, Inc. v. Globe Newspaper Co., 633 F.2d 583 (1st Cir. 1980); Arctic Co., Inc. v. Loudoun Times Mirror, 624 F.2d 518 (4th Cir 1980), *cert. denied*, 449 U.S. 1102 (1981); Vegod Corp. v. American Broadcasting Companies, 25 Cal. 3d 763, 160 Cal. Rptr. 97, 603 P.2d 14 (1979), *cert. denied*, 449 U.S. 886 (1980); Tribune Co. v. Levin, 426 So. 2d 45 (Fla. Ct. App. 1982); Bank of Oregon v. Independent News, Inc., 298 Or. 434, 693 P.2d 35, 42, *cert. denied*, 474 U.S. 826 (1985).

515 298 Or. 434, 693 P.2d 35, 42, *rehearing denied*, 11 Med. L. Rep. (BNA) 1903 (1985).

516 *Id.*

517 *See* Beech Aircraft Corp. v. National Aviation Underwriters, 11 Med. L. Rep. (BNA) 1401 (D. Kan. 1984)(heavily regulated aircraft manufacturer a public figure); American Benefit Life Insurance Co. v. McIntyre, 375 So. 2d 239, 242 (Ala. 1979)(insurance company a public figure); Coronado Credit Union v. KOAT Television, 99 N.M. 233, 656 P.2d 896 (Ct. App. 1982)(heavily regulated financial institution a public figure). *But see* Blue Ridge Bank v. Veribank, Inc., 866 F.2d 681 (4th Cir. 1989) (bank's participation in a government regulated industry of national economic importance does not elevate it or every member of its class to public figure status); Bank of Oregon v. Independent News, 298 Or. 434, 693 P.2d 35, *cert. denied*, 474 U.S. 826 (1985) (bank is not a public figure without a preexisting controversy).

518 *See* Reliance Insurance Co. v. Barron's, 442 F. Supp. 1341 (S.D.N.Y. 1977)(corporation a public figure in connection with story concerning stock offering); Trans World Accounts, Inc. v. Associated Press, 425 F. Supp. 814 (N.D. Cal. 1977)(corporation a public figure in connection with story concerning proposed administrative complaint by Federal Trade Commission).

519 *See* Steaks Unlimited, Inc. v. Deaner, 623 F.2d 264 (3d Cir. 1980)(beef retailer a public figure by virtue of widespread advertising campaign with story concerning quality of retailer's product); Economy Carpets Manufacturers & Distributors, Inc. v. Better Business Bureau, Inc., 361 So. 2d 234 (La. Ct. App. 1978), *cert. denied*, 440 U.S. 915 (1979)(corporate plaintiff rendered public figure because of advertising).

more likely to be deemed public figures. The reported cases involving corporate plaintiffs appear to have proliferated in very recent years and the aggregate outcomes are roughly evenly divided between decisions holding corporations to be public figures[520] and decisions holding them to be private figures.[521]

§ 2.25 Definition of Public Official

[1] Not All Public Employees Covered

In *Hutchinson v. Proxmire*,[522] Chief Justice Burger stated that "[t]he Court has not provided precise boundaries for the category of 'public official,' it cannot be thought to include all public employees, however." Despite the Chief Justice's cautionary note, there are relatively few ex-

520 *See, e.g.*, National Foundation for Cancer Research v. Council of Better Business Bureaus, 705 F.2d 98, 101-02 (4th Cir), *cert. denied*, 104 S. Ct. 108 (1983); Steaks Unlimited, Inc. v. Deaner, 623 F.2d 264 (3d Cir. 1980); Beech Aircraft Corp. v. National Aviation Underwriters, 11 Med. L. Rep. (BNA) 1401 (D. Kan. 1984); Bose Corp. v. Consumers Union of the United States, Inc., 508 F. Supp. 1249, 1274 (D. Mass. 1981), *rev'd on other grounds*, 692 F.2d 189 (1st Cir. 1982), *aff'd*, 104 S. Ct. 1949 (1984); Adams v. Maas, 7 Med. L. Rep. (BNA) 1188 (S.D. Tex 1977); Reliance Insurance Co. v. Barron's, 442 F. Supp. 1341, 1348 (S.D.N.Y. 1977); Trans World Accounts, Inc. v. Associated Press, 425 F. Supp. 814 (N.D. Cal. 1977); Martin Marietta Corp. v. Evening Star Newspaper Co., 417 F. Supp. 947, 955-56 (D.D.C. 1976)(applying actual malice through public interest approach); American Benefit Life Insurance Co. v. McIntyre, 375 So. 2d 239, 242 (Ala. 1979); Economy Carpets Manufacturers & Distributors, Inc. v. Better Business Bureau, Inc., 361 So. 2d 234 (La. Ct. App. 1978)*cert. denied*, 440 U.S. 915 (1979); Jadwin v. Minneapolis Star and Tribune Co., 11 Med. L. Rep. (BNA) 1905, 1913 (Minn. Sup. Ct. 1985)(applying actual malice through public interest approach); Dairy Stores, Inc. v. Sentinel Pub. Co., 191 N.J. Super. 202, 465 A.2d 953 (1983)(applying actual malice through public interest approach); Coronado Credit Union v. KOAT Television, 99 N.M. 233, 656 P.2d 896 (Ct. App. 1982); Ithaca College v. Yale Daily News Publishing Co., 105 Misc. 2d 793, 433 N.Y.S.2d 530 (Sup. Ct. 1980); Autobuses Internationales & De R. L., Ltd. v. El Continental Publishing Co., 483 S.W.2d 506, 508 (Tex. Civ. App. 1972).

521 *See, e.g.*, Golden Bear Distributing Sys. v. Chase Revel, Inc., 708 F.2d 944 (5th Cir. 1983); Bruno & Stillman, Inc. v. Globe Newspaper Co., 633 F.2d 583 (1st Cir. 1980); Arctic Co. v. Loudoun Times Mirror, 624 F.2d 518 (4th Cir. 1980), *cert. denied*, 449 U.S. 1102 (1981); Protzmanns v. McGraw-Hill, 500 F.2d 830 (8th Cir. 1974); Eastern Milk Producers v. Milkweed, 8 Med. L. Rep. (BNA) 2100 (N.D.N.Y. 1982); Peagler v. Phoeniz Newspapers, 144 Ariz. 309, 560 P.2d 1216 (1977), *subsequent appeal after remand*, 640 P.2d 1110 (Ariz. Ct. App. 1981); Rancho La Costa v. Superior Court, 106 Cal. App. 3d 646, 165 Cal. Rptr. 347 (1980), *appeal dismissed*, 450 U.S. 902 (1981); Vegod Corp. v. American Broadcasting Co., 25 Cal. 3d 763, 160 Cal. Rptr. 97, 603 P.2d 14 (1979), *cert. denied*, 449 U.S. 886 (1980); Carlucci v. Poughkeepsie Newspapers, 88 A.D.2d 608, 450 N.Y.S.2d 54 (2d Dept.), *aff'd*, 57 N.Y.2d 803, 442 N.E.2d 442 (1982); Bank of Oregon v. Independent News, 298 Or. 434, 693 P.2d 35, *cert. denied* 474 U.S. 826 (1985).

522 443 U.S. 111 (1979).

amples of government-related defamation plaintiffs who are held *not* to be public officials subject to the *New York Times* standard. Those government-related plaintiffs held not to be public officials usually have a peripheral or transient connection to governmental activity, or are extremely low in the organizational heirarchy.[523] Furthermore, although it is true that precise boundaries for determining public official status do not exist, courts have actually had very little difficulty applying the public official concept, and have remarked that it is substantially easier to apply than the elusive public figure/private figure dichotomy.[524] The definition of public official is, in fact, one of the few areas of modern defamation law marked by relative stability and certainty.

One of the few cases to classify someone affiliated with government as outside the scope of the public official definition was *Jones v. Palmer Communications, Inc.*[524.1] The case involved a Des Moines firefighter who sued for libel and false light invasion of privacy stemming from a news broadcast concerning his termination with the fire department. The Iowa Supreme Court noted that some courts "have adopted an expansive view" of the public official test, under which virtually all government employees will be classified as public officials if they demonstrate a "government affiliation."[524.2]

The Iowa Supreme Court rejected this expansive view, stating that it "strains credibility to say that Jones, as a low-ranking fire fighter, had

---

[523] *See* Jenoff v. Hearst Corp., 644 F.2d 1004 (4th Cir. 1981)(undercover police informant not a public official); Franklin v. Lodge 1108, Benevolent & Protective Order of Elks, 97 Cal. App. 3d 915, 159 Cal. Rptr. 131 (1979) (teacher who had not actively sought to influence policy issues not a public official); Steere v. Cupp, 226 Kan. 566, 602 P.2d 1267 (1979)(private criminal defense lawyer who was appointed by the court and paid with state funds not a public official); Madison v. Yunker, 589 P.2d 126 (Mont. 1978)(state university print shop director not a public official); De Luca v. New York News, 438 N.Y.S.2d 199 (1981) (teacher not public official for purposes of article on health benefits); Zeck v. Spiro, 52 Misc. 2d 629, 276 N.Y.S.2d 395 (N.Y. Sup. 1966)(attorney in private practice appointed to represent municipal sewer district not a public official); Foster v. Laredo Newspapers, Inc., 541 S.W.2d 809 (1976), *cert. denied*, 429 U.S. 1123 (Tex. 1977)(part-time civil engineer not a public official); Himango v. Prime Time Broadcasting, Inc., 37 Wash. App. 259, 680 P.2d 430 (1984)(police officer who did not exercise general policy influence not a public official). *See generally* Elder, *Defamation, Public Officialdom, and the* Rosenblatt v. Baer *Criteria—A Proposal for Revivification Two Decades After* New York Times Co. v. Sullivan, 33 Buf. L. Rev. 579 (1985).

[524] *See* Harris v. Tomczak, 94 F.R.D. 687 (E.D. Cal. 1982).

[524.1] 16 Med. L. Rep. (BNA) 2137 (Iowa 1989).

[524.2] *Id.* at 2143.

substantial responsibility over the conduct of governmental affairs."[524.3] The court distinguished a prior decision,[524.4] in which it had held that a police captain was a public figure, by noting that the fireman "did not have responsibility or influence comparable to that of a captain of a police force."[524.5]

[2] Definition Is Broad

The definition of public officials is not limited to those policy-making roles at the very top of the governmental structure. *Rosenblatt v. Baer*[525] was a case arising from a verdict in favor of a former public recreation area supervisor against a columnist for a local New Hampshire newspaper. The Court in this case indicated that for constitutional purposes the definition of public figure would not be tied to state standards that evolved prior to the *New York Times* cases, but would be an extremely expansive first amendment standard. The Court stated that "the public official designation applies at the very least to those among the hierarchy of government employees who have, or appear to the public to have, substantial responsibility for or control over the conduct of governmental affairs."[526] In order to give the public official designation the latitude envisioned by this formulation, the Court held,

(*Text continued on page 2-89*)

524.3 *Id.*

524.4 McCarney v. Des Moines Register & Tribune Co., 329 N.W.2d 152 (Iowa 1976).

524.5 16 Med. L. Rep. (BNA) at 2143.

525 383 U.S. 75 (1966).

526 *Id.* at 85.

it is for the trial judge to determine in the first instance whether the proofs show that a plaintiff is a public official. The Court embarked on this course "to lessen the possibility that a jury will use the cloak of the general verdict to punish unpopular ideas or speakers and assure an appellate court the record of findings for review of constitutional decisions."[527]

[3] After the Official Leaves Office

A person remains a public official, the *Rosenblatt* Court stated, for the purposes of the *New York Times* actual malice standard even after he or she has left office, at least with regard to stories that refer to that person's conduct while he or she was in office.[528] In a significant caveat, however, the Court stated that the passage of time eventually may so erode public interest in the official's conduct during office that application of the *New York Times* rule would no longer be justified. There may be cases, the Court said, "where a person is so far removed from a former position of authority that comment on the manner in which he performed his responsibilities no longer has the interest necessary to justify the *New York Times* rule."[529]

Despite this caveat in *Rosenblatt,* the instances in which the passage of time will be held to eliminate the actual malice standard are so rare as to be virtually nonexistent: lower courts have consistently refused to permit the passage of time to destroy public official status for speech relating to the activities of the official while in office.[530]

§ 2.26 Examples of Public Officials

[1] Law Enforcement Personnel

Police and other law enforcement personnel are almost always classified as public officials.[531] It is hard to conceive of speech more vital to

---

[527] *Id.*

[528] *Id.* at 87 n.14.

[529] *Id.*

[530] *See, e.g.,* Gray v. Udevitz, 656 F.2d 588 (10th Cir. 1981); Stripling v. Literary Guild, 5 Med. L. Rep. (BNA) 1958 (W.D. Tex. 1979); Hart v. Playboy Enterprises, 5 Med. L. Rep. (BNA) 1811 (D. Kan. 1979); Johnson v. Capital City Press, 346 So. 2d 819 (La. Ct. App. 1977), *writ denied,* 350 So. 2d 677 (1977).

[531] *See, e.g.,* Time, Inc. v. Pape, 401 U.S. 279, 291-92 (1971)(deputy chief of detectives); St. Amant v. Thompson, 390 U.S. 727, 730 (1968)(deputy sheriff); Henry v. Collins, 380

a free and democratic society than speech concerning police officials, for the police are the embodiment of the government's maintenance of social order. It was, it should be remembered, Commissioner Sullivan's role as the commissioner in charge of police in Montgomery, Alabama, that precipitated his lawsuit in *New York Times Co. v. Sullivan.*[532] The case authority holding that law enforcement personnel are public figures is so overwhelming,[533] in fact, that in 1981 the Maine Supreme Court declared that "[o]ur research has disclosed that every court that has faced the issue has decided that an officer of law enforcement, from ordinary patrolman to Chief of Police, is a 'public official' within the meaning of federal constitutional law."[534] The Maine court's statement, however, no longer remains completely true. In *Himango v. Prime Time Broadcasting, Inc.,*[535] it was held that a police patrolman who served on a vice gambling unit but did not exercise any general influence over public affairs was not a public official. In *Jenoff v. Hearst Corp.,*[536] it was held that an undercover police *informant* was not a

---

U.S. 356, 357 (1965)(per curiam)(city police chief and county attorney); Gray v. Udevitz, 656 F.2d 588 (10th Cir. 1981)(ex-patrolman); Meiners v. Moriarity, 563 F.2d 343, 352 (7th Cir. 1977)(federal DEA agent); Ethridge v. North Mississippi Communications, 460 F. Supp. 347 (N.D. Miss. 1978)(undercover narcotics agent); Thuma v. Hearst Corp., 340 F. Supp. 867, 869 (D. Md. 1972)(police captain); Rosales v. City of Eloy, 122 Ariz. 134, 135, 593 P.2d 688, 689 (1979)(police sergeant); Willis v. Perry, 677 P.2d 961 (Colo. App. 1983)(police officers); Moriarity v. Lippe, 162 Conn. 371, 294 A.2d 326 (1972)(patrolman); Hines v. Florida Publishing Co., 7 Med. L. Rep. (BNA) 2605 (Fla. Cir. Ct. 1982)("moonlighting" policeman); Bishop v. Wometco Enterprises, Inc., 235 So. 2d 759 (Fla. App.), *cert. denied,* 240 So. 2d 813 (Fla. 1970)(investigator); Whitfield v. Southeastern Newspapers, 10 Med. L. Rep. (BNA) 1771 (Ga. Super. 1984)(county sheriff); Coursey v. Greater Niles Township Publishing Co., 40 Ill. 2d 257, 264-65, 239 N.E.2d 837, 841 (1968)(patrolman); McCarney v. Des Moines Register & Tribune Co., 239 N.W.2d 152 (Iowa 1976)(police captain); Rawlins v. Hutchinson Publishing Co., 218 Kan. 295, 543 P.2d 988, 992 (1975)(patrolman); Kidder v. Anderson, 354 So. 2d 1306 (La. 1978)(police chief); Roche v. Egan, 433 A.2d 757, 762 (Me. 1981)(all law enforcement personnel); Ammerman v. Hubbard Broadcasting, 91 N.M. 250, 572 P.2d 1258 (N.M. App. 1977)(deputy sheriff); La Rocca v. New York News, Inc., 156 N.J. Super. 59, 383 A.2d 451 (1978)(patrolman); Orr v. Lynch, 60 A.D.2d 949, 401 N.Y.S.2d 897 (3d Dept.), *aff'd,* 45 N.Y.2d 903, 411 N.Y.S.2d 10, 383 N.E.2d 562 (1978)(patrolman); Graham v. New York News, Inc., 2 Med. L. Rep. (BNA) 2356 (N.Y. Sup. 1977)(police lieutenant); Frankhouser v. Findlay Publishing Co., 4 Med. L. Rep. (BNA) 2437 (Ohio Ct. Comm. Pleas 1979)(chief of police and lieutenant); Akins v. Altus Newspapers, Inc., 3 Med. L. Rep. (BNA) 1449 (Okla. 1977)(patrolman); McNabb v. Oregonian Publishing Co., 69 Ore. App. 136, 685 P.2d 458 (1984)(police officer); Colombo v. Times-Argus Ass'n, 135 Vt. 454, 380 A.2d 80 (1977)(patrolman).

532 376 U.S. 254 (1964). *See supra* §2.01.

533 *See* cases cited *supra* note 531.

534 Roche v. Egan, 433 A.2d 757, 762 (Me. 1981).

535 37 Wash. App. 259, 680 P.2d 432 (1984).

536 644 F.2d 1004 (4th Cir. 1981).

public official. Nevertheless, the authority for the proposition that police and law enforcement personnel at all levels will virtually always be classified as public officials remains impressive.[537]

[2] Elected Officials

Elected officials are always public officials, since they openly and voluntarily place their character and conduct before the public.[538]

[3] Judicial, Administrative, and Military Personnel

Judicial, administrative, and military personnel, both elected and nonelected, are routinely classified as public officials, particularly when they exercise some degree of policy-making authority.[539] Although the

---

[537] *See supra* note 531.

[538] *See, e.g.*, Garrison v. Louisiana, 379 U.S. 64 (1964); Alioto v. Cowles Communications, 430 F. Supp. 1363 (N.D. Cal. 1977), *aff'd*, 623 F.2d 616 (9th Cir. 1980), *cert. denied*, 449 U.S. 1102 (1981)(mayor of San Francisco); Pierce v. Capital Cities Communications, 427 F. Supp. 180 (E.D. Pa. 1977), *aff'd*, 576 F.2d 495 (3d Cir.), *cert. denied*, 439 U.S. 861 (1978)(mayor and port authority commissioner); Glover v. Herald Co., 549 S.W.2d 858 (Mo.), *cert. denied*, 434 U.S. 965 (1977)(alderwoman).

[539] *See, e.g.*, Rosenblatt v. Baer, 383 U.S. 75 (1966)(county recreation area supervisor); Garrison v. Louisiana, 379 U.S. 64 (1964)(district attorney); Arnheiter v. Random House, 578 F.2d 804 (9th Cir. 1978), *cert. denied*, 444 U.S. 931 (1979)(commander of United States Navy vessel); Grzelak v. Calumet Publishing Co., 543 F.2d 579 (7th Cir. 1975) (employee in public works department); Bellamy v. Arno Press, 8 Med. L. Rep. (BNA) 1920 (E.D.N.C. 1982)(court clerk); Fadell v. Minneapolis Star & Tribune Co., 425 F. Supp. 1075 (N.D. Ind. 1976), *aff'd*, 557 F.2d 107 (7th Cir.), *cert. denied*, 434 U.S. 966 (1977)(tax assessor); Klahr v. Winterble, 4 Ariz. App. 158, 418 P.2d 404 (1966)(student member of university senate); Weingarten v. Block, 102 Cal. App. 3d 129, 162 Cal. Rptr. 701, *cert. denied*, 449 U.S. 899 (1980)(counsel to city's redevelopment agency); Tague v. Citizens for Law & Order, 75 Cal. App. 3d Supp. 16, 142 Cal. Rptr. 689 (1977)(assistant public defender); Manuel v. Fort Collins Newspapers, Inc., 42 Colo. App. 324, 599 P.2d 931 (1979)(county computer services director); Gadd v. News Press Publishing Co., 10 Med. L. Rep. (BNA) 2362 (Fla. Cir. Ct. 1984)(administrator of large public hospital); Walker v. Southeastern Newspapers, 9 Med. L. Rep. (BNA) 1516 (Ga. 1982)(executive director of State Human Relations Commission); Tagawa v. Maui Publishing Co., 49 Hawaii 675, 427 P.2d 79 (1967), *subsequent appeal*, 50 Hawaii 648, 448 P.2d 337 (1968), *cert. denied*, 396 U.S. 822 (1969)(member of county board of supervisors); Cooper v. Rockford Newspapers, Inc., 50 Ill. App. 3d 247, 365 N.E.2d 744 (1977)(chief deputy clerk of circuit court); Fopay v. Noveroske, 31 Ill. App. 3d 182, 334 N.E.2d 79 (1975)(county hospital chief x-ray technician); Doctor's Convalescent Center, Inc. v. East Shore Newspapers, Inc., 104 Ill. App. 2d 271, 244 N.E.2d 373 (1968)(privately owned nursing home licensed and regulated by the state); Guzzardo v. Adams, 411 So. 2d 1148 (La. App.), *cert. denied*, 415 So. 2d 942 (La. 1982)(parish court clerk coordinator of personnel); Callahan v. Westinghouse Broadcasting Co., 363 N.E.2d 240 (Mass. 1977)(local licensing board member); Hall v.

fact that the official is appointed rather than elected may in some cases be a factor militating somewhat against a finding of public official status, at least one court has remarked that "[t]he fact that the public official is appointed, rather then elected, has no bearing upon his status as a public official."[540]

[4] School Personnel

Public school and state university officials including teachers, coaches, professors, administrators, and board members have been held to be public officials.[541]

[5] Policy-Making Authority and Access to the Press

In close cases, courts have begun to emphasize the degree of policy-making authority wielded by the plaintiff in his or her official position, as well as the plaintiff's level of access to the media, as factors to be weighed in making the public official determination. In *Arctic v. Loudoun Times Mirror*,[542] for example, it was held that a company hired as

---

Piedmont Publishing Co., 46 N.C. App. 760, 266 S.E.2d 397 (1980) (county medical examiner); Rinaldi v. Holt, Rinehart & Winston, Inc., 42 N.Y.2d 369, 397 N.Y.S.2d 943, 336 N.E.2d 1299, *cert. denied*, 434 U.S. 969 (1977) (judge); Sibowitz v. Lipper, 32 A.D.2d 520, 299 N.Y.S.2d 564 (1st Dept. 1969)(post office supervisor); Hodges v. Oklahoma Journal Publishing Co., 617 P.2d 191 (Okla. 1980)(tag agent in vehicle licensing bureau); Press, Inc. v. Verran, 569 S.W.2d 435 (Tenn. 1978)(county social worker); Van Dyke v. KUTV, 663 P.2d 52 (Utah 1983)(director of financial aid at state college); Rye v. Seattle Times, 7 Med. L. Rep. 2267 (Wash. App. 1981), *rev'd on other grounds*, 37 Wash. App. 45, 678 P.2d 1282, *cert. denied*, 102 Wash. 2d 1004 (1984)(executive director of anti-poverty agency); Martonik v. Durban, 23 Wash. App. 47, 596 P.2d 1054 (1979)(clerk of state senate); Clawson v. Longview Publishing Co., 91 Wash. 2d 408, 589 P.2d 1223 (1979)(administrator of county motor pool).

540 Walker v. Southeastern Newspapers, 9 Med. L. Rep. (BNA) 1516, 1518 (Ga. 1982) (citing Time, Inc. v. Pape, 401 U.S. 279 (1971)).

541 Cone v. John H. Phipps Broadcasting Stations, 5 Med. L. Rep. (BNA) 1972 (N.D. Ga. 1979)(school superintendent); Gallman v. Carnes, 254 Ark. 987, 497 S.W.2d 47 (1973)(law professor and assistant dean); Basarich v. Rodeghero, 24 Ill. App. 3d 889, 321 N.E.2d 739 (1974)(teacher); Kapiloff v. Dunn, 27 Md. 514, 343 A.2d 251 (1975), *cert. denied*, 426 U.S. 907 (1976)(high school principal); Reaves v. Foster, 200 So. 2d 453 (Miss. 1967)(school principal); Cabin v. Community Newspapers, Inc., 27 A.D.2d 543, 275 N.Y.S.2d 396 (2d Dept. 1966)(school board member); Johnston v. Corinthian Television Corp., 583 P.2d 1101 (Okla. 1978)(teacher). *But see* Franklin v. Lodge 1108, Benevolent & Protective Order of Elks, 97 Cal. App. 3d 915, 159 Cal. Rptr. 131 (1979)(public school teacher not a public official).

542 624 F.2d 518 (4th Cir. 1980), *cert. denied*, 449 U.S. 1102 (1982).

research consultant to a local government was not a public official, with the court emphasizing that:

> It [the consultant] had no control over the conduct of government affairs. It made no recommendations, participated in no policy determinations, and exercised no discretion. Its position was not of such apparent importance that the public has an independent interest in its qualifications beyond the general interests in the qualifications and performance of all government employees or consultants.[543]

The exercise of policy-making authority, however, may exist at the lowest echelons of a particular governmental agency, rendering even employees at the lowest rungs of authority public officials. This is particularly true of police officers. In *Coursey v. Greater Niles Township Publishing Corp.*,[544] for example, the court stated:

> It is our opinion that the plaintiff is within the "public official" classification. Although as a patrolman he is "the lowest rank of police officials" and would have slight voice in setting department policies, his duties are peculiarly "governmental" in character and highly charged with the public interest.[545]

And in *Gray v. Udevitz*,[546] the Tenth Circuit Court of Appeals noted:

> The cop on the beat is the member of the department who is most visible to the public. He possesses both the authority and the ability to exercise force. Misuse of his authority can result in significant deprivation of constitutional rights and personal freedoms, not to mention bodily injury and financial loss. The strong public interest in ensuring open discussion and criticism of his qualifications and job performance warrant the conclusion that he is a public official.[547]

---

[543] *Id.* at 522. *See also* Rosenblatt v. Baer, 383 U.S. 75, 87 n.13 (1966)("The employee's position must be one which would invite public scrutiny and discussion of the person holding it, entirely apart from the scrutiny and discussion occasioned by the particular charges in controversy."); Kassel v. Gannett Co., 875 F.2d 935 (1st Cir. 1989) (a Veterans Administration psychologist who did not routinely supervise, manage, or direct government operations, who did not formulate policy, who had no access to media for self-help, and who did not assume the risk of media coverage was not a public official for purposes of his libel action, even though he was a public employee); Sellers v. Stauffer Communications, 10 Med. L. Rep. (BNA) 2081 (Kan. Ct. App. 1984)(CETA file clerk who "exercised no sovereign power or control over the exercise of governmental affairs" not a public official). *Accord,* Steere v. Cupp, 226 Kan. 566, 572, 602 P.2d 1267 (1979).

[544] 40 Ill. 2d 257, 264-65, 239 N.E.2d 837, 841 (1968).

[545] 239 N.E.2d at 841.

[546] 656 F.2d 588 (10th Cir. 1981).

[547] *Id.* at 591.

§ 2.27 Scope of Comment on Public Officials

[1] Application of the Actual Malice Standard

When a person is a public official, does that mean that the person's entire life is open to media scrutiny and that any story about any aspect of the person's life becomes subject to the *New York Times* actual malice standard? No Supreme Court decision has ever indicated that the scope of the actual malice standard for public officials is unlimited. Nonetheless, just as the Supreme Court has been expansive in defining who is a public official, the Court has been expansive in defining the scope of comment to which the *New York Times* standard for public officials applies. In *Garrison v. Louisiana*,[548] a case decided the same year as *New York Times*, the court held that statements about the influence on local judges by racketeers, and allegations of other abuses by local judges, did not involve purely private matters but were well within the *New York Times* actual malice protection. The Court stated the *New York Times* rule is not rendered inapplicable merely because an official's private reputation as well as his public reputation is harmed, for it is often impossible to separate the two.[549] The public official rule protects the paramount public interest in a free and open flow of information to the people concerning their public servants. To this end, "anything which might touch on an official's fitness for office" is relevant.[550] Few personal attributes are more relevant to fitness for office than dishonesty, malfeasance, or improper motivation, even though these characteristics may also affect the official's private character. Similarly, it is well established that allegations concerning prior criminal misconduct on the part of an official in office or on the part of a candidate for office, even when those allegations are extremely remote in time, fall as a matter of constitutional law within the *New York Times* actual malice standard.[551]

[2] A Framework for Analysis

At least three approaches might be employed to determine the "scope" of the applicability of the actual malice standard to public officials. One approach would be to subdivide public officials into the same two "all purpose" and "limited" categories used for public figures in

548 379 U.S. 64 (1964).
549 *Id.* at 77.
550 *Id.*
551 *See* Monitor Patriot Co. v. Roy, 401 U.S. 265, 277 (1971).

Gertz.[552] Some public officials, a state Governor or the President of the United States, for example, would be deemed subject to the actual malice privilege for all purposes. Other sorts of public officials lower in the governmental hierarchy would be subject to the actual malice standard only with regard to statements that contain a nexus to the particular official's job performance, or the official's voluntary involvement in a matter of public controversy.

A second approach would be to eschew any importation of the *Gertz* public figure subclasses into public official analysis, and simply to declare all persons designated as public officials to be of the "all purpose" variety, subject to the actual malice privilege for any defamatory communications concerning them.

The third approach, and the approach that seems actually to be applied by the courts, is a cross between the two extremes set out above: Public officials are subject to the actual malice standard with regard to any speech connected to the official's performance in or fitness for office.[553] This nexus requirement is construed extremely broadly, however. There is a continuum applicable to the public official category, with the scope of comment at the higher ends of the hierarchy so broad that it is equivalent to the all purpose public figure, and at the lowest end of the hierarchy narrowing to encompass comment more concretely and directly related to the official's job performance or fitness for office.

§ 2.28 Absolute Immunity for Criticism of a Public Official

[1] The *New York Times* Holding Revisited

One of the central but often overlooked components in *New York Times Co. v. Sullivan*[554] is the principle that a public official must establish that the allegedly defamatory statement was directed at the official personally and not merely at the governmental unit to which the offi-

---

[552] *See supra* § 2.04.

[553] *See, e.g.*, Monitor Patriot Co. v. Roy, 401 U.S. 265, 273-75 (1971); Garrison v. Louisiana, 379 U.S. 64, 76-77 (1964); New York Times Co. v. Sullivan, 376 U.S. 254, 283 n.23 (1964); Gray v. Udevitz, 656 F.2d 588 (10th Cir. 1981); Guinn v. Texas Newspapers, 738 S.W.2d 303 (1987), *cert. denied*, 109 S. Ct. 864 (1989).

[554] 376 U.S. 254 (1964).

cial belongs.[555] This element of the *New York Times* decision is profoundly important, for it reaffirms one of the cornerstones of first amendment jurisprudence, that under our Constitution there is no such thing as libel against the government. As Harry Kalven has so eloquently explained, the *Times* decision drew on the essential repugnance of the concept of seditious libel to first amendment values.[556]

[2] Other Interpretations of *New York Times*

It is one thing to state the proposition that "there is no libel against the government," and another to apply it. The problem is that most criticism of govermental action is couched in personal terms against particular officials: Americans are more apt to criticize the President than the presidency, the Senator than the Senate. There are alternative interpretations of the rule that there is no libel against the government. The first is that the proposition adds nothing to the law of defamation that is not already encompassed by other existing common law and constitutional requirements, such as the requirement that defamatory speech be "of and concerning" the plaintiff,[557] the *New York Times* actual malice standard,[558] the absolute constitutional protection for opinion,[559] the neutral reportage privilege,[560] and the privilege of fair report of official proceedings.[561] Under this view the statement that there is no libel against the government is merely a shorthand compilation of the other rules of modern defamation law that work to block liability for speech aimed at governmental units rather than individual governmental officers.

A second interpretation of the proposition that there is no libel against the government, however, adds an extra, independently standing defense to the law of defamation which goes beyond the collection of common law and constitutional defenses that already exist. Under the second view defamatory speech directed against *individual officials* concerning their official conduct at the very highest echelons of

---

555 *Id.* at 292. *See also* Rosenblatt v. Baer, 383 U.S. 75 (1966); L. Tribe, American Constitutional Law § 12-12 at 633-34 (1978).

556 *See* H. Kalven, The Negro and the First Amendment (1964); Kalven, *supra* note 2.

557 *See infra* §4.09.

558 *See supra* §2.01.

559 *See infra* §6.03.

560 *See infra* §4.15.

561 *See infra* Chapter 8.

government is absolutely privileged, on the theory that at the top levels of government it is impossible to separate the person from the governmental unit itself. If individual identity and governmental identity merge at the top of the governmental pyramid, then to criticize the individual is to criticize the government, and such criticism, even if false and defamatory, is absolutely protected under the first amendment. Under this view, people like Richard Nixon, Ronald Reagan, William Westmoreland, or Ariel Sharon in a sense *are* the government, and they may never sue for defamatory speech arising out of their "governmental conduct."

[3] The Assertions of Absolute Immunity in the *Westmoreland* and *Sharon* Cases

In both *Westmoreland v. CBS*[562] and *Sharon v. Time, Inc.*,[563] the second of the two interpretations was advanced by the media defendants. CBS in *Westmoreland* urged the district court to recognize absolute protection for defamation of high-ranking officials. CBS's allegations against General Westmoreland were, the network argued, essentially criticisms of the United States and its conduct of the Vietnam war.[564] Similarly, *Time* magazine in the *Sharon* litigation argued that it should receive absolute protection for speech concerning Israeli Defense Minister Ariel Sharon's responsibility for the Christian Phalangist massacres at the Palestinian refugee camps at Sabra and Shatilla in Lebanon.[565] *Time* argued that the absolute protection was appropriate

---

562 596 F. Supp. 170 (S.D.N.Y. 1984).

563 599 F. Supp. 538 (S.D.N.Y. 1984).

564 The *Westmoreland* case arose from a documentary broadcast by CBS on January 23, 1982, entitled "The Uncounted Enemy: A Vietnam Deception." General William Westmoreland alleged that the central theme of the broadcast was that he participated in a conspiracy to suppress and distort intelligence estimates regarding the size and strength of enemy forces prior to the Tet Offensive of 1968.

565 The *Sharon* case arose out of an article by *Time* magazine concerning an Israeli government commission's report on massacres at refugee camps in Lebanon. During Ariel Sharon's tenure as Defense Minister of Israel, the Israeli army invaded Lebanon. While Israel occupied West Beiruit, certain Christian Phalangist militia were permitted to enter two Palestinian refugee camps at Sabra and Shatilla. The massacre that ensued included the brutal slaughter of many hundreds of women and children. In response to the tragedy, Israel established a Commission of Inquiry, popularly known as the Kahan Commission, to investigate the events surrounding the massacres. The Kahan Commission issued a final report in February 1983, and in *Time*'s next issue the results of that report were extensively examined in the magazine's cover article. Sharon sued *Time* for defamation allegedly arising from one paragraph of the article, which stated, among other

for four reasons: (1) it would encourage free discussion of critical issues such as responsibility for the massacres; (2) high public officials have absolute immunity for their own statements made in the course of their public duties; (3) such officials enjoy sufficient access to the press to rebut charges made against them; and (4) prosecution of civil actions for defamation by high public officials is tantamount to prosecution for seditious libel.[566]

The district court in the *Westmoreland* case refused to rule at the summary judgment stage on CBS's claim of absolute privilege to defame high officials. Judge Pierre Leval noted that CBS conceded that "there is no precedent giving direct support to its contentions," but also noted that "[t]he libel action by very high public officials is an unusual phenomenon."[567] Judge Leval decided, however, that it would be more appropriate to rule on CBS's novel argument after the development of a full trial record.[568]

In the *Sharon* case, District Judge Abraham Sofaer did rule directly on *Time*'s claim of absolute immunity for high public officials, rejecting *Time*'s argument.

Judge Sofaer, in a scholarly and closely reasoned opinion, ruled that *Time*'s claim of absolute immunity would be inconsistent with the balance between interests in free expression and interests in reputation struck in *New York Times*.[569] In the *New York Times* litigation, the Supreme Court had directly considered the arguments for absolute immunity—arguments essentially identical to those advanced by *Time* in the *Sharon* case—and rejected them. A distinction exists, Judge Sofaer argued, between seditious libel, which is a government's effort to punish speech critical of official policy or acts, and a defamation suit brought by an individual official arising from allegations that he acted contrary to official policy and human decency. Judge Sofaer noted that the statement that formed the basis of Ariel Sharon's suit "names him

---

things, "*Time* has learned" that a secret special appendix to the Kahan Commission report contained details about a meeting between Sharon and the family of the slain Christian Lebanese leader Bashir Gemayel, in which, in *Time's* words, Sharon "reportedly discussed with the Gemayels the need for the Phalangists to take revenge for the assassination of Bashir." Sharon v. Time, Inc., 599 F. Supp. 538 (S.D.N.Y. 1984).

566 *Id.* at 553-54.

567 Westmoreland v. CBS, Inc., 596 F. Supp. 1170 (S.D.N.Y. 1984).

568 *Id.* at 1171.

569 Sharon v. Time, Inc., 599 F. Supp. 538 (S.D.N.Y. 1984).

personally, without attributing his alleged discussion about revenge to his government."[570]

In Judge Sofaer's view, the law of defamation at both the common law and constitutional law levels already contains built-in safeguards adequate to protect the press against the use of the libel suit as a weapon for political persecution. The actual malice standard, the plaintiff's burden of proving falsity, the absolute privilege for opinion, the doctrines of neutral reportage and fair report of official proceedings, all combine to create a balance amply protective of free expression. If *Time* had simply stated that Israel's Commission of Inquiry concerning the massacres *should* have held Sharon directly responsible, Judge Sofaer argued, absolute immunity would arguably be appropriate even if such a statement would not be construed strictly as "opinion"—for such a statement would in fact be a form of criticism of governmental rather than mere individual conduct.[571] But *Time* went further, stating that "*Time* has learned" of secret evidence implicating Sharon directly, and Judge Sofaer concluded that "however much value *Time*'s arguments may have in the abstract, this is not a case in which those arguments would justify immunity."[572]

Judge Sofaer's opinion in the *Sharon* litigation will undoubtedly be highly influential precedent in cases involving assertions of an absolute privilege for defamation of high public officials. Even if courts are unwilling to recognize an absolute privilege as such, however, they should nonetheless be exceptionally vigilant in applying *other* defamation defenses liberally in cases involving high public officials. Perhaps that is the best encapsulation of the contemporary meaning of the *New York Times* prohibition on libel against the government: At every step of the way in libel litigation brought by officials at the pinnacle of power, courts should apply common law and constitutional law rules in a manner giving free speech values maximum breathing space. In a close case on the issue of whether the defamatory speech is "of and concerning" an individual or the government itself, it should be construed as of and concerning the government. In a close case as to whether the speech is fact or opinion, it should be construed as opinion. In a close case as to whether the evidence will support a finding of actual malice, the evidence should be construed against such a finding. In short, although no absolute immunity in cases involving high officials

570 *Id.* at 555.
571 *Id.* at 555-56.
572 *Id.*

should exist, the normal rules of defamation under *New York Times* and the common law should be applied with a special sensitivity to first amendment values in such cases. To avoid shading into the dangers of seditious libel, in high official cases courts should on all close questions prefer to risk error in favor of the defendants rather than risk the error of punishing speech aimed primarily against the government itself.

§ 2.29 The Role of Judge and Jury in Classifying Plaintiffs

[1] Public Officials

The Supreme Court declared in *Rosenblatt v. Baer*[573] that "as is the case with questions of privilege generally, it is for the trial judge in the first instance to determine whether the proofs show respondent to be a 'public official.' "[574] In treating the public official designation as an issue for the trial judge to resolve "in the first instance," with review by the appellate court, the Supreme Court was clearly concerned with the dangers of jury nullification, for it stated that "[s]uch a course will both lessen the possibility that a jury will use the cloak of a general verdict to punish unpopular ideas or speakers, and assure an appellate court the record and findings required for review of constitutional decisions."[575]

The designation of an individual as a public official is thus exclusively an issue for the court, and it is universally recognized as such in lower court decisions, without significant discussion or comment.[576] Although a jurisprudence expert would describe the public official classification as a "mixed question of law and fact," courts routinely refer to the issue simply as "a question of law," which conveniently indicates that the jury has no role in the determination.[577]

[2] Public Figures and Private Figures

Although the Supreme Court has never explicitly stated that the question of the plaintiff's status as a public figure is, like the public

573 383 U.S. 75 (1966).

574 *Id.* at 88.

575 *Id.* at 88 n.15.

576 *See, e.g.*, Rebozo v. Washington Post Co., 637 F.2d 375, 379 (5th Cir.), *cert. denied*, 454 U.S. 964 (1981); Harris v. Tomczak, 94 F.R.D. 687 (E.D. Cal. 1982).

577 *See* Rebozo v. Washington Post Co., 637 F.2d 375, 379 (5th Cir.), *cert. denied*, 454 U.S. 964 (1981).

official determination in *Rosenblatt,* a question of law for the court to decide, the Supreme Court has in a number of cases implicitly *treated* the question as an issue of law.[578] There are, arguably, differences between the procedural treatment that should be accorded the public official and the public figure questions, because in most cases it is much simpler to determine public official status than it is to determine public figure status.[579] Nevertheless, lower court decisions that have dealt with the issue have quite wisely equated the public figure question with the public official question, treating both as questions of law to be determined initially by the trial judge and then scrutinized by the appellate court, with no role for the jury.[580] The risk of jury nullification is just as severe in public figure cases as in public official cases. The jury's task in defamation cases is extremely complex as it stands; to give the jury the additional function of determining which of two standards of liability to apply would, at least in general verdict situations, turn the law of defamation into high stakes roulette with first amendment values constantly at risk.

---

[578] *See, e.g.,* Wolston v. Reader's Digest Ass'n, 443 U.S. 157 (1979); Hutchinson v. Proxmire, 443 U.S. 111 (1979); Time, Inc. v. Firestone, 424 U.S. 448 (1976); Gertz v. Robert Welch, Inc., 418 U.S. 323 (1974).

[579] *See* Belli v. Orlando Daily Newspapers, Inc., 389 F.2d 579, 588 (5th Cir. 1967), *cert. denied,* 393 U.S. 825 (1968)("In most cases it is a relatively simple matter to determine whether the plaintiff is a public official."); Harris v. Tomczak, 94 F.R.D. 687 (E.D. Cal. 1982)("Because of the nature of the definition of a public official, however, it is unlikely that there will arise disputed issues of fact material to the ultimate determination.").

[580] *See, e.g.,* Tavoulareas v. Piro, 817 F.2d 762, 772 (D.C. Cir.), *cert. denied,* 108 S. Ct. 200 (1987); Marcone v. Penthouse International, Ltd., 754 F.2d 1072, 1081 n.4 (3d Cir.), *cert. denied,* 474 U.S. 864, *reg'h denied,* 474 U.S. 1014 (1985); Rebozo v. Washington Post Co., 637 F.2d 375, 379 (5th Cir.), *cert. denied,* 454 U.S. 964 (1981); Waldbaum v. Fairchild Publications, Inc., 627 F.2d 1287, 1293 n.12 (D.C. Cir.), *cert. denied,* 449 U.S. 898 (1980); Brewer v. Memphis Publishing Co., 626 F.2d 1238, 1247 (5th Cir. 1980), *cert. denied,* 452 U.S. 962 (1981); Virgil v. Time, Inc., 527 F.2d 1122, 1130 n.13 (9th Cir. 1975), *cert. denied,* 425 U.S. 998 (1976); Harris v. Tomczak, 94 F.R.D. 687 (E.D. Cal. 1982); Velle Transcendental Research Ass'n v. Sanders, 518 F. Supp. 512, 515 (C.D. Cal. 1981); Hoffman v. Washington Post Co., 433 F. Supp. 600, 604 (D.D.C. 1977), *aff'd,* 578 F.2d 442 (D.C. Cir. 1978); Rosanova v. Playboy Enterprises, Inc., 411 F. Supp. 440, 444 (S.D. Ga. 1976), *aff'd,* 580 F.2d 859 (5th Cir. 1978); Weingarten v. Block, 102 Cal. App. 3d 129, 134 (1980), 162 Cal. Rptr. 701, *cert. denied,* 449 U.S. 899 (1980).

§ 2.30 Determining Status on Motions for Summary Judgment

[1] In General

Although there is overwhelming precedent in support of the position that the status of the plaintiff as a public official, public figure, or private figure is an issue for the court and not for the jury,[581] there appears to be some confusion over the approach to be taken by the trial court when the question arises on a motion for summary judgment.[582] The most sensible approach is that suggested by two Fifth Circuit cases. The classification of the plaintiff's status is nominally always "a matter of law," in the sense that it is *never* appropriate to submit the issue to a jury.[583] When the trial judge makes the determination, however, he or she is clearly dealing with a mixed question of law and fact. And at times, the facts relevant to the plaintiff's status will be in dispute. To properly rule on the plaintiff's status, the trial court must have an adequately developed factual record, and that factual record may not always be generated by the evidentiary materials submitted to the court in support of or opposition to a motion for summary judgment. The Fifth Circuit's response to the problem is quite sensible: Although the public figure determination is for the trial court in the first instance, the trial court should not rule on the issue at the summary judgment stage if there is a genuine dispute as to material facts relevant to the determination.[584]

[2] The "Evidentiary Hearing" Alternative

When a trial judge believes that the paper record available at the summary judgment stage is inadequate to make the public figure determination, must the judge automatically carry the issue forward for development at trial, or is some intermediate step available? In some cases it may be the judge's conviction that a relatively brief evidentiary hearing may be sufficient to clarify any ambiguities in the paper record, permitting the trial judge to rule on the public figure issue in advance

581 *See supra* notes 573-580.

582 *See* Harris v. Tomczak, 94 F.R.D. 687 (E.D. Cal. 1982).

583 *See* Brewer v. Memphis Publishing Co., Inc., 626 F.2d 1238, 1247 (5th Cir.), *cert. denied,* 449 U.S. 898 (1980).

584 Rebozo v. Washington Post Co., 637 F.2d 375, 379 (5th Cir.), *cert. denied,* 454 U.S. 964 (1981).

of the trial. Such an advance evidentiary hearing may substantially streamline the actual trial by narrowing the focus to either the negligence or actual malice standard; it may also permit the judge to dispose of the entire case at the summary judgment stage.

Imagine, for example, that the plaintiff simply has not alleged the existence of actual malice, because there are no reasonable grounds for belief that actual malice existed. Imagine further, however, that the plaintiffs have alleged a very strong case of negligence, so strong, in fact, that the defense simply concedes that negligence existed. Assuming that all the other elements of the cause of action are present, the liability side of such a case turns solely on whether the plaintiff is a public figure or a private figure. If the plaintiff is a public figure, the plaintiff loses; if a private figure, the plaintiff wins. Imagine that on cross-motions for summary judgment, the trial court decides that the public figure determination in the case hinges on whether the plaintiff was voluntarily part of a public controversy that preexisted the defamatory communication, or whether the controversy was actually created by that communication. The judge may feel that the depositions generated by discovery do not adequately clarify the issue, but that direct and cross-examination of one or two key witnesses in open court might well resolve the question one way or the other. In this setting it would be sound judicial administration to hold the summary judgment ruling in abeyance while a brief evidentiary hearing is conducted. If the plaintiff is then determined to be a public figure, summary judgment would be appropriate. If the plaintiff is a private figure, the case would proceed to trial on damages. The advantage of the evidentiary hearing alternative in this situation is that it carries the potential of saved court time and litigation expense, since without the hearing both sides will be forced to fully prepare for the trial, which would be litigated on both the public figure and damages issues. Even if the court were to hear the public figure evidence at the trial stage first, the clients for both sides would necessarily incur the expense of attorney preparation time on the damages issue, preparation time that will be a total waste if the court rules in favor of the defendant on the public figure issue. The District of Columbia Court of Appeals has made reference to this sort of evidentiary hearing, "analogous to a court's ruling on the question of probable cause for search and seizure."[585] At other times, of course, the

---

585 Wolston v. Reader's Digest Ass'n, 578 F.2d 427, 429 (D.C. Cir. 1978), *rev'd on other grounds*, 443 U.S. 157 (1979). *See also* Waldbaum v. Fairchild Publications, Inc., 627 F.2d

circumstances may be such that nothing at all will be saved by such a hearing, in which case, if material issues of fact are in dispute, the public figure issue must simply be carried forward with the trial.[586]

1287, 1292 (D.C. Cir.), *cert. denied*, 449 U.S. 898 (1980). For an excellent discussion of the problem, *see generally* Harris v. Tomczak, 94 F.R.D. 687 (E.D. Cal. 1982).

586 *See* Taggart v. Wadleigh-Maurice Ltd., 489 F.2d 434, 439 (3d Cir. 1973), *cert. denied*, 417 U.S. 937 (1974)("Just as disputed facts in a non-jury case are determined by trial and not on summary judgment motion, a trial judge's decision to instruct the jury with the *New York Times* standard . . . [i]s made after a full trial on the contested issues."). *See also* Gordon v. Random House, Inc., 486 F.2d 1356 (3d Cir. 1973), *vacated and remanded for reconsideration in light of Gertz v. Robert Welch, Inc.*, 419 U.S. 812 (1974).

CHAPTER 3

Fault Requirements for Defamation

§ 3.01 Constitutional Fault Standards

[1] Dichotomy Between Public Official/Public Figures and Private Figures

As explained in Chapter 2, the central distinction governing the modern law of defamation ever since *Gertz v. Robert Welch, Inc.*[1] is the division between public officials and public figures on the one hand, and private figures on the other.

[1] 418 U.S. 323 (1974).

[2] Actual Malice

Public official and public figure plaintiffs must, as a matter of federal constitutional law, establish the existence of "actual malice" in order to recover in an action for defamation.[2] In *New York Times* the Supreme Court defined a statement made with "actual malice" as one made "with knowledge that it was false or with reckless disregard of whether it was false or not."[3]

[3] Negligence

Under *Gertz*, private figure plaintiffs must establish "fault" on the part of the defendant as a prerequisite for recovery,[4] and as explained subsequently in this chapter, the term "fault" has been interpreted as requiring, as a constitutional minimum, the existence of negligence.[5]

[4] Strict Liability

The Supreme Court's opinion in the *Dun & Bradstreet*[6] case is subject to the possible interpretation that none of the first amendment fault level restrictions in *Gertz* are operable when the plaintiff is a private figure and the defamatory speech does not concern matters of public interest. If this interpretation of *Dun & Bradstreet* is followed, then the states may be free to return a substantial portion of their defamation actions—those involving no public issues and private figure plaintiffs—to pre-*Gertz* strict liability standards.

---

[2] *See* Gertz v. Robert Welch, Inc., 418 U.S. 323 (1974); Curtis Publishing Co. v. Butts, 388 U.S. 130 (1967); New York Times Co. v. Sullivan, 376 U.S. 254 (1964). *See supra* §§ 2.01-2.04.

[3] 376 U.S. at 280.

[4] Gertz v. Robert Welch, Inc., 418 U.S. 323, 347 (1974).

[5] As explained in subsequent sections in this chapter, there are variations among the states as to precisely how the negligence standard is to be interpreted and applied. *See infra* §§ 3.24-3.26.

[6] Dun & Bradstreet, Inc. v. Greenmoss Builders, Inc., 105 S. Ct. 2939 (1985), discussed *infra* § 3.02.

§ 3.02 Strict Liability in Suits Not Involving Matters of Public Concern

[1] *Dun & Bradstreet*

In *Dun & Bradstreet, Inc. v. Greenmoss Builders, Inc.*,[7] the credit reporting agency Dun & Bradstreet issued an inaccurate credit report about the plaintiff Greenmoss Builders, a residential and commercial building contractor. Greenmoss's president was meeting with the company's principal creditor, a bank, to discuss future financing, when he was told by the bank's representative that the bank had just received a credit report from Dun & Bradstreet indicating that Greenmoss had recently filed a voluntary petition in bankruptcy. In fact Greenmoss was in healthy financial condition and had filed no such petition. Although the bank's representative never actually believed the report, the bank did put off any consideration of future financing until the discrepancy was cleared up. The bank later terminated Greenmoss's credit, for reasons allegedly unrelated to the report.

Dun & Bradstreet committed the error because one of its employees, a 17-year-old high school student paid $200 a year to review Vermont bankruptcy petitions, had inadvertently attributed a bankruptcy petition of a former Greenmoss employee to Greenmoss itself. Dun & Bradstreet's routine practice was first to corroborate the accuracy of such a report with a business concern before publishing this sort of information, but no prepublication verification was ever attempted in the Greenmoss episode.

Dun & Bradstreet's business is to send factual and financial reports about individual business enterprises exclusively to paid subscribers to its service. Five subscribers received the erroneous Greenmoss report. In response to Greenmoss's complaint, Dun & Bradstreet issued a corrective notice to those five subscribers indicating the error and stating that Greenmoss "continued in business as usual." Greenmoss was dissatisfied with the correction because it implied that the initial mistake had been caused by Greenmoss, not Dun & Bradstreet, and ultimately commenced an action against Dun & Bradstreet for defamation.

After a trial by jury, a verdict was returned in favor of the plaintiff Greenmoss for $50,000 in compensatory damages and $300,000 in punitive damages. The trial court told the jury that because the report

---

[7] 105 S. Ct. 2939 (1985).

was libelous per se,[8] the plaintiff was not required "to prove actual damages . . . . since damage and loss [are] conclusively presumed."[9] The jury was also told that it could award punitive damages only if it found "actual malice," but the court failed to define actual malice in the terms required by *New York Times*[10] and its progeny, instead defining simple "malice" in terms that included such concepts as "bad faith."[11] The trial court also stated that liability could not be established unless the plaintiff showed "malice or lack of good faith on the part of the defendant."[12]

The trial court later realized that its instructions on liability and damages were inconsistent with the requirements of *Gertz v. Robert Welch, Inc.*[13]—if the case should have been governed by *Gertz*, that is. For *Gertz* prohibits any award of "presumed"[14] or "punitive"[15] damages in the absence of actual malice—knowledge of falsity or reckless disregard for the truth—a standard not properly articulated to the jury. The trial court accordingly granted the defendant's motion for a new trial.

The Vermont Supreme Court reversed, holding that Dun & Bradstreet was not a member of the "media," and "as a matter of federal constitutional law the media protections outlined in *Gertz* are inapplicable to nonmedia defamation actions."[16] Vermont, following decisions in several other states,[17] thus held *Gertz* inapplicable to nonmedia defendants.[18]

---

8 On common law libel per se rules, *see* Chapter 7, *infra*.

9 105 S. Ct. at 2943.

10 *See infra* § 3.13.

11 105 S. Ct. at 2943.

12 *Id.*

13 418 U.S. 323 (1974).—

14 For a discussion of presumed damages, *see infra* § 7.02[3], and Chapter 9.

15 For a discussion of punitive damages, *see infra* § 7.03[3].

16 Greenmoss Builders, Inc. v. Dun & Bradstreet, Inc., 143 Vt. 66, 75, 461 A.2d 414, 418 (1983), *aff'd on other grounds*, 105 S. Ct. 2939 (1985).

17 *See* Rowe v. Metz, 195 Colo. 424, 579 P.2d 83 (1978); Stuempages v. Park, Davis & Co., 297 N.W.2d 252 (Minn. 1980); Harley-Davidson Motorsports, Inc., v. Markley, 279 Or. 361, 568 P.2d 1359 (1977); Denny v. Mertz, 106 Wis. 2d 636, 318 N.W.2d 141, *cert. denied*, 459 U.S. 883 (1982); Calero v. Del Chemical Corp., 68 Wis. 2d 487, 228 N.W.2d 737 (1975). *But see* Antwerp Diamond Exchange v. Better Business Bureau, 130 Ariz. 523, 637 P.2d 733 (1981); Rodriguez v. Nishiki, 653 P.2d 1145, 1150 (Hawaii 1982); Anderson v. Low Rent Hous. Comm'n, 304 N.W.2d 239, 247 (Iowa), *cert. denied*, 454 U.S. 1086 (1981); Michaud v. Inhabitants of Livermore Falls, 381 A.2d 1110, 1113 (Me. 1978); De Carvalho v. Da Silva, 414 A.2d 806, 813 (R.I. 1980).

18 For an excellent review of the decisions on this problem prior to Dun & Bradstreet, *see* Watkins & Schwartz, Gertz *and the Common Law of Defamation: Of Fault, Nonmedia Defendants, and Conditional Privileges*, 15 Tex. Tech. L. Rev. 823 (1984).

The United States Supreme Court affirmed in a 5-4 ruling, but on grounds other than the media/nonmedia distinction cited by the Vermont Supreme Court. The Supreme Court's decision in *Dun & Bradstreet* is somewhat opaque, partly because the five-Justice majority was formed by a three-Justice plurality opinion written by Justice Powell (joined by Justices Rehnquist and O'Connor), and individual concurring opinions by Chief Justice Burger and Justice White. Further confusion is created by the fact that Justice Powell's opinion is relatively short, with very little elaboration on a number of crucial points, and at places seems almost purposely ambiguous. Justice Powell framed the issue relatively narrowly:

> In *Gertz v. Robert Welch, Inc.*, . . . we held that the First Amendment restricted the damages that a private individual could obtain from a publisher for a libel that involved a matter of public concern. More specifically, we held that in these circumstances the First Amendment prohibited awards of presumed and punitive damages unless the plaintiff shows "actual malice," that is, knowledge of falsity or reckless disregard for the truth. The question presented in this case is whether the rule of *Gertz* applies when the false and defamatory statements do not involve matters of public concern.[19]

After reviewing the history of constitutional developments from *New York Times* through *Gertz*, Powell stated that the Court had "never considered whether the *Gertz* balance obtains when the defamatory statements involve no issue of public concern."[20] In weighing the balance between the individual interest in reputation and free speech in the case before it, Justice Powell heavily emphasized the enlightenment function of the first amendment, particularly speech directed toward self-governance.[21] Writing that "[w]e have long recognized that not all speech is of equal First Amendment importance,"[22] Powell stated that speech "on matters of public concern" is at the heart of the first amendment, which "was fashioned to assure unfettered interchange of ideas for the bringing about of political and social change."[23]

---

19 105 S. Ct. at 2941.

20 *Id.* at 2944.

21 *Id.* at 2945-46. *See supra* § 1.07[3].

22 105 S. Ct. at 2945.

23 *Id.* (quoting Roth v. United States, 354 U.S. 476, 484 (1957)). Justice Powell cited and quoted from a number of cases that emphasized the enlightenment function of the first amendment, particularly the self-governance rationale. *See* 105 S. Ct. at 2945-46 (citing First National Bank of Boston v. Bellotti, 435 U.S. 765, 776 (1978); Thornhill v. Alabama, 310 U.S. 88, 101 (1940); Connick v. Myers, 461 U.S. 138, 145 (1983); New York

"Speech on matters of purely private concern," Justice Powell wrote, "is of less First Amendment concern." Endorsing the common law rule of presumed damages, Powell noted that the "rationale of the common law rules has been the experience and judgment of history that 'proof of actual damages will be impossible in a great many cases where, from the character of the defamatory words and the circumstances of the publication, it is all but certain that serious harm has resulted in fact.' "[24] As a result, "courts for centuries have allowed juries to presume some damage occurred from many defamatory utterances and publications," a rule that "furthers the state interest in providing remedies for defamation by ensuring that those remedies are effective."[25] Powell then announced the central holding of the case: "In light of the reduced constitutional value of speech involving no matters of public concern, we hold that the state interest adequately supports awards of presumed and punitive damages—even absent a showing of 'actual malice.' "[26]

[2] Rejection of the Media/Nonmedia Distinction

In the aftermath of *Gertz* there was considerable debate over whether the holding ought to be applied to media and nonmedia speakers alike.[27] Several states specifically held *Gertz* inapplicable to nonmedia

---

Times Co. v. Sullivan, 376 U.S. 254, 269 (1964); Garrison v. Louisiana, 379 U.S. 64, 74-75 (1964); NAACP v. Clairborne Hardware Co., 458 U.S. 886, 913 (1982); Carey v. Brown, 447 U.S. 455, 467 (1980)).

24 105 S. Ct. at 2946 (quoting W. Prosser, Law of Torts § 112, at 765 (4th ed. 1971), and citing Rowe v. Metz, 195 Colo. 424, 425-26, 579 P.2d 83, 84 (1978), and Note, *Developments in the Law—Defamation*, 69 Harv. L. Rev. 875, 891-92 (1956)).

25 105 S. Ct. at 2946 (citing Restatement of Torts § 568, comment b, at 162 (1938)).

26 *Id.* In a footnote to this statement, Justice Powell directly challenged Justice Brennan's dissenting opinion, which he characterized as out to "constitutionalize the entire common law of libel," by stating that Justice Brennan's position "would lead to the protection of all libels—no matter how attenuated their constitutional interest. If the dissent were the law, a woman of impeccable character who was branded a 'whore' by a jealous neighbor would have no effective recourse unless she could prove 'actual malice' by clear and convincing evidence." *Id.* at 2946-47 n.7.

27 *See generally* Brosnahan, *From* Times v. Sullivan *to* Gertz v. Welch: *Ten Years of Balancing Libel Law and the First Amendment*, 26 Hastings L.J. 777 (1975); Christie, *Injury to Reputation and the Constitution: Confusion Amid Conflicting Approaches*, 75 Mich. L. Rev. 43, 50 (1976); Lange, *The Speech and Press Clauses*, 23 U.C.L.A. L. Rev. 77 (1975); Nimmer, *Is Freedom of the Press a Redundancy: What Does It Add to Freedom of Speech?* 26 Hastings L.J. 639, 649 (1975); Shiffrin, *The First Amendment and Economic Regulation: Away From a General Theory of the First Amendment*, 78 Va. L. Rev. 1212, 1268 (1983); Shiffrin, *Defamatory Non-Media Speech and First Amendment Methodology*, 25 U.C.L.A. L. Rev. 915 (1978); Smolla, *Let the Author Beware: The Rejuvenation of*

defendants when the plaintiff was a private figure.[28] When the plaintiff was a public official or public figure, however, decisions generally held that the actual malice standard governed even against nonmedia defendants.[29]

Rejecting the media/nonmedia distinction altogether, some decisions found *Gertz* applicable even to cases involving private figure plaintiffs and nonmedia defendants.[30] The Supreme Court, in *Hutchinson v. Proxmire,* [31] stated in a footnote that the applicability of the actual malice standard of *New York Times* in the nonmedia context remained an open issue.[32]

All of this debate has apparently been rendered obsolete, for all the Justices in *Dun & Bradstreet* either explicitly or implicitly rejected the media/nonmedia distinction. The plurality opinion of Justice Powell rests on the "public concern" test rather than the media/nonmedia

---

the American Law of Libel, 132 U. Pa. L. Rev. 1, 29-33, 90 (1983); Stewart, *"Or of the Press,"* 26 Hastings L.J. 631 (1975); Watkins & Schwartz, *supra* note 18, at 831-63; Note, *Mediaocracy and Mistrust: Extending* New York Times *Defamation Protection to Non-Media Defendants,* 95 Harv. L. Rev. 1876, 1877 n.9 (1982); Note, *First Amendment Protection Against Libel Actions: Distinguishing Media and Non-Media Defendants,* 47 S. Cal. L. Rev. 902 (1974).

28 *See* Rowe v. Metz, 195 Colo. 424, 579 P.2d 83 (1978); Stuempages v. Park, Davis & Co., 297 N.W.2d 252 (Minn. 1980); Wheeler v. Green, 286 Or. 99, 593 P.2d 777 (1979); Harley-Davidson Motorsports, Inc. v. Markley, 279 Or. 361, 568 P.2d 1359 (1977); Greenmoss Builders, Inc. v. Dun & Bradstreet, Inc., 143 Vt. 66, 461 A.2d 414 (1983), *aff'd on other grounds,* 105 S. Ct. 2939 (1985); Denny v. Mertz, 106 Wis. 2d 636, 318 N.W.2d 141, *cert. denied,* 459 U.S. 883 (1982); Calero v. Del Chemical Corp., 68 Wis. 2d 487, 228 N.W.2d 737 (1975).

29 *See* Avins v. White, 627 F.2d 637, 649 (3d Cir.), *cert. denied,* 449 U.S. 982 (1980); Davis v. Schuchat, 510 F.2d 731, 734 n.3 (D.C. Cir. 1975); Woy v. Turner, 533 F. Supp. 102, 104 (N.D. Ga. 1981); Antwerp Diamond Exchange v. Better Business Bureau, 130 Ariz. 523, 637 P.2d 733, 737 (1981); Rodriguez v. Nishiki, 653 P.2d 1145, 1150 (Hawaii 1982); Anderson v. Low Rent Hous. Comm'n, 304 N.W.2d 239, 247 (Iowa), *cert. denied,* 454 U.S. 1086 (1981); Michaud v. Inhabitants of Livermore Falls, 381 A.2d 1110, 1113 (Me. 1978); Williams v. Pasma, 656 P.2d 212, 215 (Mont. 1982), *cert. denied,* 103 S. Ct. 2122 (1983); De Carvalho v. Da Silva, 414 A.2d 806, 813 (R.I. 1980).

30 The lead case on the issue was Jacron Sales Co. v. Sindorf, 276 Md. 580, 350 A.2d 688 (1976). *See also* Maheu v. Hughes Tool Co., 569 F.2d 459, 478-79 (9th Cir. 1977); Rimmer v. Colt Industries Operating Corp., 495 F. Supp. 1217 (W.D. Mo. 1980), *rev'd on other grounds,* 656 F.2d 323 (8th Cir. 1981); Handley v. May, 588 S.W.2d 772, 776 (Tenn. App. 1979); Ryder Truck Rentals, Inc. v. Latham, 593 S.W.2d 334 (Tex. Civ. App. 1979); Fleming v. Moore, 221 Va. 884, 275 S.E.2d 532 (1981).

31 431 U.S. 111 (1979).

32 *Id.* at 133 n.16.

distinction,[33] and at one point in the Powell opinion it is stated that the *Gertz* protections "were not 'justified solely by reference to the interest of the press and broadcast media in immunity from liability.' "[34] Although the issue was not specifically addressed, it thus seems clear that Justice Powell, joined by Justices Rehnquist and O'Connor, eschewed the media/nonmedia approach. Chief Justice Burger similarly failed to mention the media/nonmedia distinction by name. He would overrule *Gertz* entirely, but until that happens he would follow Justice Powell's public interest approach.[35] Again, one can safely assume that the Chief Justice does not accept any division between media and nonmedia defendants.

Justice White was more direct, stating that the plurality had wisely avoided the media/nonmedia distinction and that no such distinction should ever be accepted:

> Wisely, in my view, Justice Powell does not rest his application of a different rule here on a distinction drawn between media and nonmedia defendants. On that issue, I agree with Justice Brennan that the First Amendment gives no more protection to the press in defamation suits than it does to others exercising their freedom of speech. None of our cases affords such a distinction; to the contrary, the Court has rejected it at every turn. It should be rejected again, particularly in this context, since it makes no sense to give the most protection to those publishers who reach the most readers and therefore pollute the channels of communication with the most misinformation and do the most damage to private reputation. If *Gertz* is to be distinguished from this case, on the ground that it applies only where the allegedly false publication deals with a matter of general or public importance, then where the false publication does not deal with such a matter, the common-law rules would apply whether the defendant is a member of the media or other public disseminator or a nonmedia individual publishing privately.[36]

Similarly, Justice Brennan, joined by Justices Marshall, Blackmun, and Stevens, explicitly rejected the media/nonmedia dichotomy, stating that "[s]uch a distinction is irreconcilable with the fundamental First Amendment principle that '[t]he inherent worth of . . . speech in terms of its capacity for informing the public does not depend upon the

---

33 *See supra* § 3.03.

34 105 S. Ct. at 2945 (quoting Gertz v. Robert Welch, Inc., 418 U.S. 323, 343 (1974)).

35 105 S. Ct. at 2948 (Burger, C.J., concurring).

36 *Id.* at 2953 (White, J., concurring).

identity of its source.' "[37] Justice Brennan noted the extreme difficulty in determining what is and what is not "media" speech,[38] and stated that the first amendment case law emanating from *New York Times* "implies no endorsement of the principle that speakers other than the press deserve lesser First Amendment protection."[39]

The Supreme Court's 1986 decision in *Philadelphia Newspapers, Inc. v. Hepps*[39.1] has thrown the apparent rejection of the media/nonmedia distinction in *Dun & Bradstreet* into a handbasket. The majority opinion by Justice O'Connor in *Hepps* expressly treated the issue as open, conspicuously framing the issue before the Court as a case involving a private figure plaintiff, public speech, and a *media* defendant.[39.2] Only Justice Brennan, in a brief concurrence joined by Justice Blackmun, pressed the point, arguing as he had in *Dun & Bradstreet* that maintenance of a media/nonmedia distinction is irreconcilable with the first amendment principle that the value of speech does not depend on the identity of the speaker.[39.3]

The best educated guess, however, is that the media/nonmedia distinction will ultimately be rejected by the Court. Had the Court been inclined to proceed along the media/nonmedia path, *Dun & Bradstreet* was its chance. The doctrinal course embarked upon in *Dun & Bradstreet,* which superimposes the "matters of public concern" analysis upon the public figure/private figure dichotomy, was the Court's substitute for a media/nonmedia distinction. To add, at this juncture, a media/nonmedia distinction would simply complicate matters beyond all plausible manageability. Significantly, the distinction has several vocal and vigorous opponents on the Court, but no openly professed defenders—at most a majority seems disinclined to face the issue.

[3] Does *Dun & Bradstreet* Open the Door to Strict Liability in Private Figure Cases Not Involving Issues of Public Concern?

As Justice Powell was careful to emphasize in the opening paragraph of his opinion, only the *Gertz* presumed and punitive damages rules

[37] *Id.* at 2957 (Brennan, J., dissenting) (quoting First National Bank of Boston v. Bellotti, 435 U.S. 765, 777 (1978)).

[38] 105 S. Ct. at 2958 n.7 (Brennan, J., dissenting).

[39] *Id.* (Brennan, J., dissenting).

[39.1] 106 S. Ct. 1558 (1986).

[39.2] *Id.* at 1565 n.4.

[39.3] *Id.* at 1565-66 (Brennan, J., concurring).

were technically before the Supreme Court in *Dun & Bradstreet.* The question of whether the *Gertz* liability rules are also swept away in cases not involving matters of public importance thus remains open. More specifically, *Dun & Bradstreet* fails to answer this question conclusively: May a state impose common law strict liability standards in cases involving private figure plaintiffs and defamatory speech not involving matters of public concern, or does the *Gertz* prohibition on liability without fault continue to apply to all private figure cases?

Justice Brennan was careful to point out in his dissent that the parties in *Dun & Bradstreet* did not "question the requirement of *Gertz* that respondent must show fault to obtain a judgment and actual damages."[40] It is equally clear that both Justice White and Chief Justice Burger would return to common law strict liability in such cases, and Justice White interpreted the plurality opinion as necessarily carrying that same implication, stating that: "Although Justice Powell speaks only of the inapplicability of the *Gertz* rule with respect to presumed and punitive damages, it must be that the *Gertz* requirement of some kind of fault on the part of the defendant is also inapplicable in cases such as this."[41]

A careful reading of the plurality opinion supplies a number of clues indicating that the plurality would probably endorse a return to strict liability in private figure cases not involving speech of public concern. First, throughout the opinion Justice Powell's language slipped from the narrow formulation of the issue before the Court to a broader phrasing of the question in terms of "whether *Gertz* applies to the case before us,"[42] phraseology suggesting that Powell would abandon all of *Gertz,* not just the damages rules, in such cases. Second, Justice Powell's opinion conspicuously quoted with approval language from the Oregon Supreme Court's decision in *Harley-Davidson Motorsports, Inc. v. Markley*[43] that in such a case:

> [t]here is no threat to the free and robust debate of public issues; there is no potential interference with a meaningful dialogue of ideas concerning self-government; and threat of liability causing a reaction of self-censorship by the press. The facts of the present case are wholly without

40 *Id.* at 2957 (Brennan, J., dissenting).

41 *Id.* at 2953 (White, J., concurring).

42 *Id.* at 2943. *See also id.* at 2944 ("We have never considered whether the *Gertz* balance obtains when the defamatory statements involve no issue of public concern.").

43 279 Or. 361, 568 P.2d 1359 (1977).

> the First Amendment concerns with which the Supreme Court of the United States has been struggling.[44]

This quotation from *Harley-Davidson*, placed at the centerpoint of Justice Powell's analysis, is an important signal, for *Harley-Davidson* was the leading state court decision applying strict liability in a private figure nonmedia situation. The Court similarly cited with approval *Denny v. Mertz*,[45] a Wisconsin Supreme Court decision that held all the *Gertz* protections inapplicable in a private figure vs. nonmedia situation.[46]

Finally, if one applies the analytic structure adopted by Justice Powell on the damages issues to the strict liability question, it is difficult to conclude anything other than that Justice Powell would permit strict liability in such cases. Justice Powell's methodology was simply to balance the importance of the type of speech involved against the state's interest in applying the common law rule. Justice Powell strongly downgraded the constitutional significance of speech not involving matters of public concern. *That half of Justice Powell's balance would not change at all when the focus shifts from damages to liability rules, for the type of speech involved would remain the same.* Applying Justice Powell's balance, therefore, the only significant question left is whether the state's interest in applying its common law strict liability

(*Text continued on page 3-13*)

---

[44] *Id.* at 366, 568 P.2d at 1363, *quoted at* 105 S. Ct. at 2946.

[45] 106 Wis. 2d 636, 661, 318 N.W.2d 141, 153, *cert. denied*, 459 U.S. 883 (1982).

[46] The Court also cited with approval Rowe v. Metz, 195 Colo. 424, 426, 579 P.2d 83, 84 (1978), which held that *Gertz* did not bar presumed damages in a private figure nonmedia case.

rule is as strong as its interest in applying its common law presumed and punitive damages rules.

Justice Powell's opinion actually did not discuss *at all* the state's interest in awarding punitive damages on a showing of something less than actual malice. Justice Powell did, however, list two rationales for the common law presumed damages rule. First, the rule captures the "experience and judgment of history" that actual damage is often impossible to prove even though it is all but certain that it exists. Second, the rule "furthers the state interest in providing remedies for defamation by ensuring that those remedies are effective."

How would the state's interest in applying strict liability compare with this analysis? In comparison to the state's interest in awarding punitive damages on something less than actual malice, it would seem that the state interest in its strict liability rule is actually much stronger. The strict liability principle goes to the very heart of the tort at common law, representing the state's interest in protecting the defamed individual's dignity and easing the path to compensation. The punitive damages rule, by contrast, has only the argument of punishment and deterrence to support it. From a plaintiff's perspective, in short, the strict liability standard is probably of greater aid in vindicating reputation than the common law punitive damages rule (which still, after all, requires proof of common law malice).

When the state's interest in permitting presumed damages is compared to its interest in applying strict liability, the analysis is somewhat more difficult. Both rules clearly further the state's general interest in providing remedies for defamation "by ensuring that those remedies are effective." The two rules complement each other at common law, working hand in hand to facilitate a plaintiff's recovery.

The presumed damages rule arguably has an additional ground to support it that the strict liability rule does not: the difficulty of proof. While there is some common sense to the notion that harm to reputation is often there but can't be seen or proved, there seems to be less difficulty in proving the existence or nonexistence of negligence, which is a routine problem typical of tort cases.

This potential distinction, however, appears too thin to justify any difference in the treatment of the two rules. On the one hand, given the already broad constitutional definition of "actual harm," the additional bonus given a plaintiff through the presumed harm rules may be overrated—few plaintiffs have found the actual harm requirement a complete barrier to recovery, if a barrier at all. The requirement of proving negligence, on the other hand, may at times be a substantial impediment. Defendants often have a monopoly on the information necessary to establish fault, so a plaintiff's efforts to prove negligence may be frustrating and costly. Strict liability is thus a powerful plaintiff's weapon that in many cases serves the state's interests as much or more than do presumed harm rules. The most logical reading of *Dun & Bradstreet* is, therefore, that it opens the door to a return by states (if they wish) to strict liability standards in private figure cases not involving defamatory speech related to matters of public concern.

§ 3.03 The "Matters of Public Concern" Standard

[1] *Dun & Bradstreet*

The plurality opinion in *Dun & Bradstreet* did little to define the phrase "matters of public concern." Quoting from *Connick v. Myers,*[47] the opinion stated that " 'whether . . . speech addresses a matter of public concern must be determined by [the expression's] content, form, and context . . . as revealed by the whole record.' "[48] This standard, which says essentially that the court is to weigh everything, is not very revealing. In deciding that the Dun & Bradstreet credit report was not speech about a matter of public concern, however, Justice Powell appeared to concentrate quite heavily on the fact that the report concerned solely the individual interests of the speaker and its audience, and on the limited dissemination of the report. Justice Powell thus characterized the speech as "solely in the individual interest of the speaker and its specific business audience," and further noted that the report "was made available to only five subscribers, who, under the terms of the subscription agreement, could not disseminate it further."[49] Thus, Justice Powell reasoned, the report did not involve any " ' strong interest in the free flow of commercial information.' "[50] Justice Powell concluded that "[t]here is simply no credible argument that this type of credit reporting requires special protection to ensure that

47 461 U.S. 138 (1983).

48 Dun & Bradstreet, Inc. v. Greenmoss Builders, Inc., 105 S. Ct. 2939, 2947 (1985) (quoting Connick v. Myers, 461 U.S. 138, 147-48 (1983)).

49 105 S. Ct. at 2947.

50 *Id.* (quoting Virginia Pharmacy Bd. v. Virginia Consumer Council, 425 U.S. 748, 764 (1976)).

'debate on public issues [will] be uninhibited, robust, and wide-open.' "[51]

[2] The *Dun & Bradstreet* Standard vs. the *Gertz* Standard

It is extremely important to keep the "matters of public concern" standard articulated in *Dun & Bradstreet* separate from the term of art "public controversy" used as part of the vortex public figure test in *Gertz.* By definition, any person who is a private figure plaintiff *has already failed to voluntarily thrust himself into a public controversy;* otherwise, that plaintiff would be deemed a public figure. If anyone who did not fall into the public figure classification could automatically claim that the speech involved did not implicate matters of public concern, then the negligence standard in *Gertz* would never apply as a constitutional minimum—the case would be either tried under the actual malice test or under common law strict liability. *Dun & Bradstreet* clearly held no such thing; it did not establish an all or nothing regime. Rather, *Dun & Bradstreet* subdivided the universe of cases involving private figures into those containing defamatory *speech* about matters of public concern, and those not containing defamatory speech about matters of public concern. This means that the "public concern" standard may include speech that is "public" even when the plaintiff is "private." The public controversy formulation is linked to the plaintiff's voluntary participation in the public arena,[52] but the public concern test looks primarily to the speech itself.

[3] The Refitting of *Rosenbloom*

Ironically, the most logical point of reference for beginning to define "matters of public concern" is *Rosenbloom v. Metromedia, Inc.,*[53] which employed essentially identical terminology. *Rosenbloom,* prior to being overruled by *Gertz,* briefly elevated all libels involving a "matter of public or general interest"[54] to the actual malice standard. (The term "public or general interest" in *Rosenbloom* came from a famous Warren

---

[51] 105 S. Ct. at 2947 (quoting New York Times v. Sullivan, 376 U.S. 254, 270 (1964)).

[52] *See supra* §§ 2.08-2.15.

[53] 403 U.S. 29 (1971).

[54] *Id.* at 44 (opinion of Brennan, J.).

and Brandeis article published in 1890.[55]) Justice Powell's *Dun & Bradstreet* opinion refitted *Rosenbloom* for a different purpose: to contract first amendment protection rather than expand it. Whereas *Rosenbloom* used the "public interest" test to trigger the application of actual malice, *Dun & Bradstreet* utilized it to delineate between the *Gertz* restrictive presumed and punitive damages rules, and probably also the *Gertz* negligence rule, and the generous pro-plaintiff rules of the common law.

Finally, as previously indicated, it is worth pointing out that the definition of "matters of public concern" in *Dun & Bradstreet* is, at least in tone, arguably narrower than the comparable "public or general interest" phraseology in *Rosenbloom,* for Justice Powell's opinion in *Dun & Bradstreet* appeared to emphasize the political self-governance aspects of the enlightenment function of the first amendment.[56] Just as the bulk of the task of defining "public figure" has devolved on lower courts, however, so will the fleshing out of *Dun & Bradstreet* be left primarily to those courts, and how they choose to define "public concern" will have a substantial effect on the future direction of the American law of defamation.

§ 3.04 Does *Dun & Bradstreet* Have Any Impact on Public Official and Public Figure Cases?

Dun & Bradstreet is a private figure plaintiff case, and arguably has no impact whatsoever on cases involving public officials and public figures. What constitutional standard now applies, however, when the plaintiff is a public official or public figure but the *speech* involves a private matter bearing no connection to the public official's performance or fitness for duty, or no connection to the plaintiff's public figure status? (Since, in the case of limited purpose public figures, the defamatory speech must be linked to a public controversy in which the plaintiff has thrust himself, this problem can arise only for all purpose public figures, and is not an issue for limited purpose public figures.)[57] This is arguably not a very significant problem, since defamatory speech about public officials or all purpose public figures almost always will qualify

---

[55] Warren & Brandeis, *The Right to Privacy,* 4 Harv. L. Rev. 193, 214 (1890).

[56] *See* 105 S. Ct. at 2945-47. *See supra* § 1.07[3].

[57] *See* chart in § 3.05, *infra.*

as a matter of public concern.[58] If, however, there are *some* topics that remain private matters for public officials and all purpose public figures and are therefore outside the ambit of the actual malice test, does *Dun & Bradstreet* authorize the "skipping over" of the negligence standard and the imposition of strict liability in such cases? The answer, arguably, would be yes: Because the speech is outside of the scope of comment on public officials or public figures to whom the actual malice test applies, those persons may essentially "revert" to private figure status, and since the speech is not about a matter of public concern, strict liability may apply. (In a public official situation, if the speech was unrelated to job qualifications but still involved an issue of public concern, the negligence standard would of course apply.)

A counterargument might be made, however, that *Dun & Bradstreet* should be limited to private figure cases, on the theory that the analysis of the case was never meant to fit (and simply does not fit) into the public official/public figure framework. Remembering that *Gertz* described all purpose public figures as plaintiffs who "occupy positions of such pervasive power and influence that they are deemed public figures *for all purposes,*"[59] there does not seem to be any room for carving out any exceptions to the actual malice standard for such plaintiffs. And if the "all purpose public figure" is *always* subject to the actual malice test, it does not seem logical that public officials would be subject to any less expansive coverage.

Nevertheless, the implications of *Dun & Bradstreet* are yet to be worked out, and it seems at least possible that for certain purely private matters, defamatory speech involving public officials and all purpose public figures could revert below the *Gertz* negligence standard all the way to strict liability.[60]

§ 3.05 Chart Summarizing Fault Standards After *Dun & Bradstreet*

On the assumption that *Dun & Bradstreet* will come to be interpreted in many jurisdictions, and ultimately by the Supreme Court itself, as

---

[58] The scope of comment on public officials for which the actual malice standard applies is, as previously discussed, extremely broad. *See supra* § 2.26.

[59] Gertz v. Robert Welch, Inc., 418 U.S. 323, 345 (1974).

[60] For an excellent review of these problems as they appeared in the aftermath of *Gertz,* see Eaton, *The American Law of Defamation Through* Gertz v. Robert Welch, Inc. *and Beyond: An Analytical Primer,* 61 U. Va. L. Rev. 1349 (1975).

permitting a return to strict liability in cases not involving issues of public concern,[61] the law of defamation today is, as far as constitutional minimums are concerned, three-tiered, embracing either actual malice, negligence or strict liability, depending on the public or private status of the plaintiff and on the speech.

Figure 3.1 below summarizes the constitutional minimum fault standards now governing the law of defamation. Some of the fault levels remain "problematic" because of ambiguities in the interplay of *New York Times, Gertz,* and *Dun & Bradstreet;*[62] in such cases reference should be had to the appropriate discussion in prior sections, as indicated in parenthesis in Figure 3.1.

Figure 3.1

Status of the Plaintiff	*Status of the Subject Matter*	*Minimum Constitutional Standard of Fault that Applies*
Public Official	Within Broadly Defined Scope of Matters Relating to Performance and Fitness for Office	Actual Malice (§ 2.27)
Public Official	Totally Irrelevant to Performance or Fitness for Office But Still of Public Concern	Problematic; Negligence at Minimum, Arguably Actual Malice (§§ 2.27; 3.04)
Public Official	Totally Irrelevant to Performance or Fitness for Office and Not of Public Concern	Problematic; May Be Strict Liability or Negligence (§§ 2.06; 3.04)

61 *See supra* § 3.02.

62 *See also* Eaton, *supra* note 60, at 1450-51.

Status of the Plaintiff	*Status of the Subject Matter*	*Minimum Constitutional Standard of Fault that Applies*
All Purpose Public Figure	Matter of Public Concern	Actual Malice (§ 2.22)
All Purpose Public Figure	Not Matter of Public Concern	Problematic; Actual Malice May Always Apply, or May Revert to Negligence or Strict Liability (§§ 2.22; 3.04)
Limited Purpose Public Figure	By Definition, Will Always Involve Speech Relevant to a "Public Controversy"	Actual Malice (§ 2.04)
Private Figure	Matter of Public Concern	Negligence (§§ 2.04; 3.02)
Private Figure	Not Matter of Public Concern	Although Not Technically Resolved by *Dun & Bradstreet,* Probably Strict Liability (§§ 3.02; 3.03)

§ 3.06 Burden of Proof in Establishing Actual Malice and Negligence

The plaintiff bears the burden of proof in establishing the required level of fault (actual malice or negligence, as the case may be), as part of his or her prima facie case.[63] The placement of the burden of proof

[63] *See* New York Times v. Sullivan, 376 U.S. 254, 279-80, 285-86 (1964); Meiners v.

on the plaintiff was implicit in *New York Times*,[64] and explicitly recognized by Justice Harlan in *Curtis Publishing Co. v. Butts*,[65] in which Justice Harlan stated that public officials could recover "only when *they prove* that the publication was deliberately falsified, or published recklessly despite the publisher's awareness of probable falsity."[66] Although the rules emanating from *New York Times* and *Gertz* are popularly described as constitutional "privileges," the term privilege is actually a misnomer, for proof of actual malice in public plaintiff cases and negligence in private plaintiff cases is now actually part of the plaintiff's prima facie case. In both public and private plaintiff cases that fall within the *Gertz* coverage, "[t]he burden of proof of showing fault is undoubtedly upon the plaintiff."[67]

§ 3.07 The Special "Convincing Clarity" Standard

In *New York Times Co. v. Sullivan*,[68] the Supreme Court stated that in the case before it "the proof presented to show actual malice lacks the convincing clarity which the constitutional standard demands, and hence . . . would not constitutionally sustain the judgment."[69] The plaintiff's burden of proof regarding actual malice, therefore, must go beyond the normal "preponderance of the evidence" standard in civil litigation and instead be made with "convincing clarity."[70] As the New York Court of Appeals has recognized, "[T]he terms 'convincing clarity' and 'clear and convincing' are used interchangeably in the case law on

---

Moriarty, 563 F.2d 343 (7th Cir. 1977); Firestone v. Time, Inc., 460 F.2d 712, 722 (5th Cir.) (Bell, J., concurring), *cert. denied*, 409 U.S. 875 (1972); Farnsworth v. Tribune Co., 43 Ill. 2d 286, 253 N.E.2d 408 (1969); Michaud v. Inhabitants of the Town of Livermore Falls, 381 A.2d 1110 (Me. 1978); Restatement (Second) of Torts, § 588 (1977).

64 *See* Firestone v. Time, Inc., 460 F.2d 712, 722 (5th Cir.) (Bell, J., concurring), *cert. denied*, 409 U.S. 875 (1972) (Judge Bell explains the implicit burden of proof shift in the *Times* decision).

65 388 U.S. 130 (1967). *See supra* § 2.02.

66 *Id.* at 153 (Harlan, J.).

67 Restatement (Second) of Torts § 580B comment j (1977). See also *id.*, § 580A, comment e ("The plaintiff has the burden of alleging and proving that the defendant had knowledge or acted in reckless disregard."). These burden of proof requirements would not, apparently, be applicable in cases now outside of *Gertz*, pursuant to *Dun & Bradstreet*. *See supra* §§ 3.02-3.03.

68 376 U.S. 254 (1964).

69 *Id.* at 285-86.

70 Restatement (Second) of Torts § 580A comment f (1977).

this subject."[71] "Clear and convincing" proof requires a higher probability than proof by a mere preponderance of the evidence—it must be strong, positive, and decisive—but it is still something less than the proof beyond a reasonable doubt required in criminal cases.[72]

§ 3.08 The Preponderance of the Evidence Standard

The "convincing clarity" requirement is invariably linked to the actual malice standard, and the assumption has been that in private plaintiff cases tried under a negligence standard the Constitution requires no more than the traditional preponderance of the evidence. Indeed, one of the grounds for Justice Brennan's dissenting opinion in *Gertz* was his view that "in contrast to proof by clear and convincing evidence required under the *New York Times* test, the burden of proof for reasonable care will doubtless be the preponderance of the evidence."[73] Justice Brennan's prediction has apparently been generally accepted, without significant debate.[74] The *Restatement* takes the position that "[t]here has been no indication that proof of fault in the ordinary defamation case must meet the unusual standard of 'clear and convincing proof' that the Supreme Court has held to be required in showing knowledge or reckless disregard as to falsity in an action by a public official or public figure. . . . It seems doubtful that this requirement will be imposed in the application of the [negligence] rule."[75]

---

[71] Rinaldi v. Viking Penguin, 52 N.Y.2d 422, 436 n.4, 438 N.Y.S.2d 496, 420 N.E.2d 377 (1981). *See also* Lent v. Huntown, 470 A.2d 1162, 1169 (Vt. 1983).

[72] *See, e.g.*, Manuel v. Ft. Collins Newspapers, 599 P.2d 931, 933 (Colo. App. 1979), *rev'd on other grounds*, 631 P.2d 1114 (Colo. 1981); Dacey v. Connecticut Bar Ass'n, 170 Conn. 520, 537, 368 A.2d 125, 134 (1976); Callahan v. Westinghouse Broadcasting Co., 372 Mass. 582, 363 N.E.2d 240, 243-44 (1977); Stone v. Essex County Newspapers, Inc., 367 Mass. 849, 330 N.E.2d 161, 175 (1975); Germann v. Mathiss, 250 A.2d 424 (N.J. Super 1969).

[73] Gertz v. Robert Welch, Inc., 418 U.S. 323, 366 (1974) (Brennan, J., dissenting).

[74] *See, e.g.*, Embers Supper Club, Inc. v. Scripps-Howard Broadcasting Co., 9 Ohio St. 3d 22, 457 N.E.2d 1164 (1984), *cert. denied*, 104 S. Ct. 2679 (1984) (describing preponderance of evidence standard as proper in negligence cases); Gazette, Inc. v. Harris, 325 S.E.2d 713 (Va. 1985) (preponderance of evidence for negligence cases).

[75] Restatment (Second) of Torts § 580B comment j (1977). *See also* Chapadeau v. Utica Observer-Dispatch, Inc., 38 N.Y.2d 196, 199, 379 N.Y.S.2d 61, 341 N.E.2d 569 (1975) (adopting preponderance of the evidence standard for New York's unique "grossly irresponsible" test for private figure plaintiffs). *See infra* § 3.12.

§ 3.09 States Are Free to Set Standards of Fault

[1] Private Figure Cases Involving Matters of Public Concern

The Supreme Court in *Gertz* stated that it did not believe that it was wise for the Court itself to proceed on a case-by-case basis in evolving the appropriate level of fault for recovery by private figure plaintiffs.[76] Instead, the Court invited states to experiment with their own standards, as long as they did not establish liability without fault.[77] Thus, the Court stated that provided they do not dip below the minimum constitutional requirement of negligence, "[s]tates should retain substantial latitude in their efforts to enforce a legal remedy for defamatory falsehood injurious to the reputation of a private individual."[78] In response to this invitation to experiment, individual states have adopted a variety of approaches including a number of differing negligence formulations,[79] the actual malice standard,[80] and an intermediate gross negligence test.[81]

[2] Private Figure Cases Not Involving Matters of Public Concern

Similarly, after *Dun & Bradstreet* states will have the freedom to choose whether to adopt strict liability or negligence (or even, conceivably, actual malice) in cases involving private figures and speech on topics not a matter of public concern.[82] Presumably, those jurisdictions that opted for strict liability in nonmedia cases under the now obsolete media/nonmedia distinction[83] will tend to opt for strict liability in the private figure/not a matter of public concern situation.

§ 3.10 States that Have Adopted Some Form of Negligence as the Standard for Private Figure Cases

The vast majority of states have chosen the "low option" under *Gertz*, opting for some form of negligence standard in defamation actions brought by private figure plaintiffs. These decisions are always

---

76 Gertz v. Robert Welch, Inc., 418 U.S. 323, 347 (1974).

77 *Id.* at 345-46.

78 *Id.*

79 *See infra* §§ 3.10, 3.25-3.26.

80 *See infra* § 3.11.

81 *See infra* § 3.12.

82 *See supra* §§ 3.02-3.05

83 *See* cases cited *supra* note 27.

matters of state law, and therefore the list is necessarily somewhat fluid—new states may be added to the negligence list, or states formerly on it may reverse themselves and adopt some higher standard. The roster below should therefore be updated carefully by any attorney researching the law of defamation for a particular jurisdiction. Cases classifying any specific jurisdiction as applying the negligence standard range from state supreme court decisions, to lower state court decisions, to federal decisions applying their best "*Erie* guess" as to what standard state courts would apply. When appropriate, these considerations are parenthetically noted in the footnotes. Similarly, some jurisdictions may apply the negligence standard in *name* for private figure plaintiffs, but then turn around and interpret the public figure/private figure dichotomy in a manner that seems to resemble the "public interest" test of *Rosenbloom v. Metromedia, Inc.*,[84] leaving that state closer as a practical matter to an actual malice standard for private figure plaintiffs than a negligence standard. As indicated below, Illinois may be in such a category.[85] Since states are free to adopt special interpretations of the negligence/actual malice division as a matter of state law,[86] attorneys researching any given jurisdiction should again be alert to such nuances. As of this writing, the following states appear to apply a negligence standard to private figure cases:

— Alabama;[87]
— Arizona;[88]
— Arkansas;[89]

---

84 403 U.S. 29 (1971). *See supra* § 2.03.

85 *See infra* note 98.

86 Montana, for example, which is not included on the list below, has spoken ambiguously about a "fault" requirement rather than an actual malice requirement in private figure cases. *See* Madison v. Yunker, 180 Mont. 54, 589 P.2d 126 (1978). The *Restatement* has adopted the negligence standard. Restatement (Second) of Torts § 580B (1977). On the problem of separating state grounds from federal grounds in state court decisions, *see* discussion in Chapter 13, *infra.* Finally, it must be remembered that *all* of the state fault rules for private figure cases are now potentially subject to modification in light of *Dun & Bradstreet, Inc. v. Greenmoss Builders, Inc.*, 105 S. Ct. 2939 (1985), which may eliminate fault as a first amendment requirement in cases not involving issues of public concern. *See supra* §§ 3.02-3.05.

87 Mead Corporation v. Hicks, 448 So. 2d 308 (Ala. 1983). *See also* Browning v. Birmingham News, 348 So. 2d 455 (Ala. 1977) (applying negligence standard without discussion).

88 Peagler v. Phoenix Newspapers, Inc., 114 Ariz. 309, 315, 560 P.2d 1216, 1222 (1977).

89 Little Rock Newspapers, Inc. v. Dodrill, 281 Ark. 25, 660 S.W.2d 933 (1983); KARK-TV v. Simon, 280 Ark. 228, 656 S.W.2d 702 (1983); Dodrill v. Arkansas Democrat, 265 Ark. 628, 637, 590 S.W.2d 840, 844 (1979), *cert. denied,* 444 U.S. 1076 (1980).

— California;[90]
— Connecticut;[91]
— Delaware;[92]
— District of Columbia;[93]

---

[90] The law in California is ambiguous. In Rollenhagen v. City of Orange, 116 Cal. App. 3d 414, 172 Cal. Rptr. 49 (1981), the court, interpreting California Civil Code §§ 47(3) and 48a(4)(d), required a private figure plaintiff to show "actual malice" as defined in Cal. Civ. Code § 48a(4)(d): "That state of mind arising from hatred or ill will toward the plaintiff; provided, however, that such a state of mind occasioned by a good faith belief on the part of the defendant in the truth of the libelous publication or broadcast at the time it is published or broadcast shall not constitute actual malice." *Rollenhagen* required a showing of malice as defined in Cal. Civ. Code § 48a(4)(d) in order to overcome the *common law* privilege of fair comment on matters of public interest codified in Cal. Civ. Code § 47(3). *Rollenhagen* discussed the fact that some states, such as Colorado and Indiana, have chosen the actual malice test of *Rosenbloom* for matters of public interest through judicial decision, and held that no such judicial innovation was necessary under California law because the statutory scheme of Cal. Civ. Code §§ 47(3) and 48a(4)(d) already provided such protection.

Rollenhagen's statutory interpretation has two possible weaknesses. First, it is not at all clear that the conditional common law privileges codified in Cal. Civ. Code § 47(3) are as expansive as *Rollenhagen* assumed, covering the whole spectrum of matters in the public interest. *See* Rancho La Costa, Inc. v. Superior Court, 106 Cal. App. 3d 646, 165 Cal. Rptr. 347 (1980), *appeal dismissed,* 450 U.S. 902 (1981)(holding that Cal. Civ. Code § 47(3) does not apply merely because the allegedly defamatory speech involves a topic of public interest). Second, it is not at all clear that "malice" as defined in Cal. Civ. Code § 48a(4)(d) is equivalent to the actual malice standard of *New York Times.* Although it uses the phrases "actual malice" and "good faith belief . . . in the truth," the Civil Code definition appears to be closer to the common law ill will formulation of malice than the knowing or reckless formulation of *New York Times.* It is well established that it is error to confuse common law malice and constitutional malice, and that common law malice is insufficient to satisfy the *New York Times* standard. *See infra* § 3.10.

Another California decision, Widener v. Pacific Gas & Electric Co., 75 Cal. App. 3d 415, 433, 142 Cal. Rptr. 304 (1977), *cert. denied,* 436 U.S. 918 (1978), stated that negligence is the proper standard for private figure plaintiffs under California law. The *Widener* statement is dictum, however, because the case was litigated under an actual malice standard pursuant to a plaintiff's stipulation. Finally, to add one more element of uncertainty to the picture, a federal district court has made the suggestion that the California Constitution may require adoption of the actual malice test in private figure cases. *See* Lewis v. Time, Inc., 83 F.R.D. 455, 464 n.8 (E.D. Cal. 1979).

Although California may provisionally be classified as a negligence state, the issue must in reality be seen as undecided until the California Supreme Court rules definitively on the question.

[91] *Cf.* Corbett v. Register Publishing Co., 33 Conn. Supp. 4, 356 A.2d 472 (1975). Connecticut is still arguably in the "undecided" category. *Corbett* applied the negligence standard without definitive discussion.

[92] Re v. Gannett, 480 A.2d 662, 10 Med. L. Rep. (BNA) 2267 (Del. Super. Ct. 1984), *aff'd,* 496 A.2d 553, 11 Med. L. Rep. (BNA) 2327 (Del. 1985).

[93] Phillips v. Evening Star Newspaper Co., 424 A.2d 78, 90 (D.C. 1980), *cert. denied,* 451 U.S. 989 (1981).

— Florida;[94]

— Georgia;[95]

— Hawaii;[96]

— Idaho;[97]

— Illinois;[98]

— Kansas;[99]

— Kentucky;[100]

— Louisiana;[101]

— Maryland;[102]

---

[94] Miami Herald Publishing Co. v. Ane, 458 So. 2d 239 (Fla. 1984); Tribune Co. v. Levin, 458 So. 2d 243 (Fla. 1984); Arnold v. Taco Properties, Inc., 427 So. 2d 216 (Fla. Dist. Ct. App.), *petition denied,* 434 So. 2d 886 (1983).

[95] Triangle Publications, Inc. v. Chumley, 317 S.E.2d 534 (Ga. 1984); Savannah News–Press Div. v. Whetsell, 149 Ga. App. 233, 254 S.E.2d 151 (1979); Williams v. Trust Co. of Ga., 140 Ga. App. 49, 230 S.E.2d 45 (1976).

[96] Cahill v. Hawaiian Paradise Park Corp., 56 Hawaii 522, 543 P.2d 1356 (1975).

[97] Idaho law is not completely clear. Although no Idaho court has considered the issue, a statute predating the *Gertz* decision and pertaining only to broadcasters adopts a general negligence standard. Idaho Code § 6-708. No court has yet considered whether this statute might be applied in private plaintiff cases, despite the fact that it is clearly unconstitutional with respect to public figures and public officials.

[98] Illinois law is particularly interesting, for it appears to contain the substance of a *Rosenbloom* public interest approach in the shell of a negligence standard. The "official" standard in Illinois for private figure plaintiffs is clearly negligence. *See* Troman v. Wood, 62 Ill. 2d 184, 340 N.E.2d 292 (1975). The Illinois Supreme Court, however, appears to define the term "public figure" much more broadly than the United States Supreme Court, as a matter of *state* law. In *Colson v. Stieg,* 89 Ill. 2d 205, 433 N.E.2d 246 (1982), the Illinois Supreme Court declared an assistant professor at a state university to be a public figure for purposes of allegedly defamatory statements made by a faculty administrator about the plaintiff professor's teaching. The remarks occurred in the course of a tenure review decision in which the plaintiff was ultimately denied tenure. The court's analysis in *Colson* heavily emphasized the public interest in the qualifications of state university teachers, and was virtually indistinguishable from *Rosenbloom. See* Smolla & Malone, *The Future of Defamation in Illinois After* Colson v. Stieg *and* Chapski v. Copley Press, Inc., 32 De Paul L. Rev. 219 (1983). *Colson* may also be an example of the "context public figure" approach. *See* Smolla, *supra* note 27, at 68-74. *See also supra* § 2.20.

[99] Gobin v. Globe Publishing Co., 216 Kan. 223, 531 P.2d 76 (1975); Sellars v. Stauffer Communications, Inc., 9 Kan. App. 2d 573, 684 P.2d 450 (Kan. App. 1984).

[100] McCall v. Courier-Journal & Louisville Times Co., 623 S.W.2d 882 (Ky. 1981), *cert. denied,* 456 U.S. 975 (1982).

[101] *See* Wilson v. Capital City Press, 315 So. 2d 393 (La. Ct. App.), *cert. denied specifically approving decision,* 320 So. 2d 203 (La. 1975). *See also* Melon v. Capital City Press, 407 So. 2d 85 (La. Ct. App.), *cert. denied,* 409 So. 2d 656 (La. 1982); Le Boeuf v. Times-Picayune Publishing Corp., 327 So. 2d 430, 431 (La. Ct. App. 1976).

[102] General Motors Corp. v. Piskor, 277 Md. 165, 171, 352 A.2d 810, 814-15 (1976); Jacron Sales Co. v. Sindorf, 276 Md. 580, 350 A.2d 688 (1976).

— Massachussets;[103]
— Michigan[103.1]
— Minnesota;[103.2]
— Mississippi;[104]
— New Hampshire;[104.1]
— New Mexico;[105]
— North Carolina;[106]
— Ohio;[107]
— Oklahoma;[108]
— Oregon;[109]
— Pennsylvania;[110]

---

103 Stone v. Essex County Newspapers, Inc., 367 Mass. 849, 856, 330 N.E.2d 161, 164 (1975).

103.1 Michigan clearly adopted the negligence standard in 1986. *See* Rouch v. Enquirer & News of Battle Creek, 427 Mich. 157, 398 N.W.2d 245 (1986). *See also* Deitz v. Wometco West Michigan TV, 160 Mich. App. 367, 407 N.W.2d 649 (1987). Prior to the *Rouch* decision other courts applying Michigan law had applied the actual malice standard in private figure cases involving issues of public concern. *See, e.g.,* Bichler v. Union Bank, 745 F.2d 1006 (6th Cir. 1984) (en banc); Clark v. American Broadcasting Cos., 684 F.2d 1208, 1216 (6th Cir. 1982), *cert. denied,* 460 U.S. 1040 (1983); Schultz v. Newsweek, Inc., 668 F.2d 911, 918 (6th Cir. 1982).

103.2 Jadwin v. Minneapolis Star & Tribune Co., 367 N.W.2d 476 (Minn. 1985).

104 *See* Brewer v. Memphis Publishing Co., 626 F.2d 1238, 1247 (5th Cir. 1980), *cert. denied,* 452 U.S. 962 (1981)(dicta in Fifth Circuit decision applying Mississippi law).

104.1 McCusker v. Valley News, 121 N.H. 258, 428 A.2d 493 (1981).

105 Marchiondo v. Brown, 98 N.M. 394, 402, 649 P.2d 462, 470 (1982).

106 Walters v. Sanford Herald, 228 S.E.2d 766, 767 (N.C. 1976).

107 Thomas H. Maloney & Sons, Inc. v. E. W. Scripps Co., 43 Ohio App. 2d 105, 110, 324 N.E.2d 494, 498 (1974), *cert. denied,* 423 U.S. 883 (1975). Embers Supper Club v. Scripps-Howard Broadcasting Co., 9 Ohio St. 3d 22, 457 N.E.2d 1164, *cert. denied,* 104 S. Ct. 2679 (1984). In 1987, the Ohio Supreme Court modified the standard of proof required to prove negligence in private-figure defamation actions, abandoning a "preponderance of the evidence" standard and adopting a requirement of proof by clear and convincing evidence. Landsdowne v. Beacon Journal Publishing Co., 512 N.E.2d 979 (Ohio 1987).

108 Martin v. Griffin Television, Inc., 549 P.2d 85, 89 (Okla. 1976).

109 Bank of Oregon v. Independent News, 298 Or. 434, 670 P.2d 616 (1985). *See also* Wheeler v. Green, 286 Or. 99, 593 P.2d 777 (1979)(applying negligence standard without discussion).

110 *See* Mathis v. Philadelphia Newspapers, 455 F. Supp. 406 (E.D. Pa. 1978)(federal district court applying Pennsylvania law). *See also* Marcone v. Penthouse International, Ltd., 533 F. Supp. 353, 360-61 (E.D. Pa. 1982), *rev'd on other grounds,* 754 F.2d 1072 (3d Cir. 1985)(applying Pennsylvania law); Medico v. Time, Inc., 509 F. Supp. 268, 277 n.7 (E.D. Pa. 1980), *aff'd on other grounds,* 643 F.2d 134 (3d Cir.), *cert. denied,* 454 U.S. 836 (1981)(applying Pennsylvania law).

- — Puerto Rico;[111]
- — Rhode Island;[112]
- — South Carolina;[112.1]
- — Tennessee;[113]

(*Text continued on page 3-27*)

---

[111] Torres-Silva v. El Mundo, 106 D.P.R. 15, 3 Med. L. Rep. (BNA) 1508 (Puerto Rico Sup. Ct. 1977). Two other island jurisdictions have also apparently adopted the negligence standard. *See* Porter v. Guam Publications, Inc., 643 F.2d 615 (9th Cir. 1981) (Guam); Ali v. Daily News Publishing Co., 540 F. Supp. 142 (D.V.I. 1982)(Virgin Islands).

[112] *See* De Carvalho v. Da Silva, 414 A.2d 806 (R.I. 1980)(applying negligence standard without discussion).

[112.1] Jones v. Sun Publishing Co., 292 S.E.2d 23 (S.C. 1982), *cert. denied,* 459 U.S. 944 (1983).

[113] Memphis Publishing Co. v. Nichols, 569 S.W.2d 412, 417 (Tenn. 1978).

— Texas;[114]
— Utah;[115]
— Vermont;[116]
— Virginia;[117]
— Washington;[118]
— West Virginia;[119]
— Wisconsin;[120]
— Wyoming.[121]

§ 3.11 States that Have Adopted Actual Malice in Private Figure Cases

A handful of states have adopted the actual malice standard in private figure cases in which the allegedly defamatory speech involves matters of public or general interest. These states have accepted as persuasive Justice Brennan's reasoning in *Rosenbloom v. Metromedia, Inc.*[122] that the public nature of the subject matter, rather than the public status of the plaintiff, should trigger the actual malice standard.[123]

The most recent development along these lines came when the New Jersey Supreme Court held in *Sisler v. Gannett Co., Inc.*[123.1] that the actual malice standard would apply against a media defendant in a private figure case focusing on "matters of legitimate public concern involving a knowledgeable individual who exposes himself to the risk

---

[114] Foster v. Laredo Newspapers, Inc., 541 S.W.2d 809, 818 (Tex. 1976), *cert. denied,* 429 U.S. 1123 (1977).

[115] *See* Miller v. KSL, Inc., 626 P.2d 968, 973 (Utah 1981).

[116] *See* Colombo v. Times-Argus Ass'n, 135 Vt. 454, 380 A.2d 80 (1977)(applying negligence standard without discussion).

[117] Gazette v. Harris, 325 S.E.2d 713 (Va. 1985). *See also* Mills v. Kingsport Times-News, 475 F. Supp. 1005 (W.D. Va. 1979)(applying Virginia law).

[118] Caruso v. Local Union No. 690, 100 Wash. 2d 343, 670 P.2d 240 (1983); Bender v. Seattle, 99 Wash. 2d 582, 664 P.2d 492 (1983); Taskett v. KING Broadcasting Co., 86 Wash. 2d 439, 455, 546 P.2d 81, 85 (1976).

[119] Crump v. Beckley Newspapers, Inc., 320 S.E.2d 70 (W. Va. Sup. Ct. App. 1984).

[120] Denny v. Mertz, 106 Wis. 2d 636, 318 N.W.2d 141,*cert. denied,* 459 U.S. 883 (1982).

[121] Adams v. Frontier Broadcasting Co., 555 P.2d 556 (Wyo. 1976)(applying negligence standard without discussion).

[122] 403 U.S. 29 (1971).

[123] *See supra* § 2.03.

[123.1] 516 A.2d 1083, 104 N.J. 256 (Sup. Ct. 1986).

of possible publicity."[123.2] As of this writing, the brief list of jurisdictions that have accepted the actual malice test for private figure cases involving speech of public or general interest includes:

— Alaska[124]
— Colorado[125]
— Indiana[126]
— New Jersey[127]

§ 3.12 The Intermediate "Gross Irresponsibility" Standard

[1] The *Chapadeau* Test

New York has chosen to go its own way in adopting a standard halfway between actual malice and negligence in private figure cases. In *Chapadeau v. Utica Observer-Dispatch, Inc.*,[128] the New York Court of Appeals held that "where the content of the article is arguably within the sphere of legitimate public concern, which is reasonably related to matters warranting public exposition," a private figure defamation plaintiff may recover only if he or she can "establish by a preponderance of the evidence that the publisher acted in a grossly irresponsible manner without due consideration for the standards of information gathering and dissemination ordinarily followed by responsible parties."[129] The *Chapadeau* test thus involves five key elements:

(1) The burden of proof is on the plaintiff.
(2) The evidentiary standard is the "preponderance of the evidence."

123.2 *Id.* at 1093.

124 *See* Gay v. Williams, 486 F. Supp. 12 (D. Alaska 1979)(federal district court applying Alaska law).

125 Diversified Management, Inc. v. Denver Post, Inc., 653 P.2d 1103, 1106 (Colo. 1982). *See also* Walker v. Colorado Spring Sun, Inc., 188 Colo. 86, 538 P.2d 450, *cert. denied*, 423 U.S. 1025 (1975); Haan v. Board of Publications of the Christian Reformed Church, Inc., 10 Med. L. Rep. (BNA) 1671, 1672 (Colo. Dist. Ct. 1984).

126 Aafco Heating & Air Conditioning Co. v. Northwest Publications, Inc., 162 Ind. App. 671, 679, 321 N.E.2d 580, 585-86 (1974), *cert. denied*, 424 U.S. 913 (1976).

127 Sisler v. Gannett Co., Inc., 516 A.2d 1083, 104 N.J. 256 (Sup. Ct. 1986).

128 38 N.Y.2d 196, 379 N.Y.S.2d 61, 341 N.E.2d 569 (1975).

129 *Id.* at 199, 379 N.Y.S.2d at 64-65, 341 N.E.2d at 571.

(3) The level of fault for speech falling within the standard is "gross irresponsibility" (which is used interchangeably with the terminology "gross negligence").

(4) The gross negligence standard is applied by comparing the defendant's conduct to the "standards of information gathering and dissemination ordinarily followed by responsible parties."

(5) To come within *Chapadeau* the defamatory speech must be "arguably within the sphere of legitimate public concern."

[2] The Meaning of "Gross Irresponsibility"

Although the *Chapadeau* test requires the trier of fact to determine the "responsible" standards for news gathering and dissemination, this does not mean that conduct falling below those standards is actionable. Mere deviation from reasonable standards amounting to nothing more than ordinary negligence is *not* gross irresponsibility. The New York courts have quite clearly emphasized that gross irresponsibility requires journalistic conduct that "grossly" deviates from reasonable standards.[130]

Mere failure to investigate the truth "does not, *ispso facto,* constitute gross irresponsibility."[131] Similarly, mere misplaced reliance on sources cannot constitute gross irresponsibility.[132] Nor can gross irresponsibility be established by a simple error in terminology in an otherwise carefully prepared and researched effort.[133] An excellent and often quoted

[130] *See, e.g.,* Gaeta v. New York News, 62 N.Y.2d 340, 477 N.Y.S.2d 82, 465 N.E.2d 802 (1984); Pollnow v. Poughkeepsie Newspapers, Inc., 11 Med. L. Rep. (BNA) 1528, 1531-33 (2d Dept. 1985); Simonsen v. Malone Evening Telegram, 98 A.D.2d 905, 470 N.Y.S.2d 898 (3d Dept. 1983); Sbarbati v. New York Post, 10 Med. L. Rep. (BNA) 2190 (N.Y. Sup. Ct. 1984); DeLuca v. New York News, Inc., 438 N.Y.S.2d 199, 7 Med. L. Rep. (BNA) 1302 (Sup. Ct. 1981), *see also earlier decision,* 109 Misc. 2d 341, 4 Med. L. Rep. (BNA) 2312 (Sup. Ct. 1978).

[131] Pollnow v. Poughkeepsie Newspapers, Inc., 11 Med. L. Rep. (BNA) 1528, 1532-33 (2d Dept. 1985).

[132] *See, e.g.,* Gaeta v. New York News, 62 N.Y.2d 340, 477 N.Y.S.2d 82, 465 N.E.2d 802 (1984); Sbarbati v. New York Post, 10 Med. L. Rep. (BNA) 2190 (N.Y. Sup. Ct. 1984); Robart v. Post-Standard, 74 A.D.2d 963, 425 N.Y.S.2d 891 (1980), *aff'd,* 52 N.Y.2d 843 (1981); Carlucci v. Poughkeepsie Newspapers, 450 N.Y.S.2d 54, *aff'd,* 57 N.Y.2d 803, 442 N.E.2d 442 (1982).

[133] DeLuca v. New York News, Inc., 438 N.Y.S.2d 199, 7 Med. L. Rep. (BNA) 1302, 1306 (Sup. Ct. 1981).

summation of the standard was offered by Justice Greenfield:

> Research can continue endlessly, but accepted standards of journalism require neither exhaustive research nor painstaking judgments. Newspapers, and reporters, have the right to be wrong so long as they are not guilty of not checking their facts at all, making gross distortions of the record or jumping to totally unwarranted conclusions. The entire purpose of affording scope and latitude in the reporting of public issues is to stimulate thought, discussion, investigation and change.[134]

[3] *Chapadeau*'s "Sphere of Legitimate Public Concern" Standard

In *Gaeta v. New York News, Inc.*,[135] the New York Court of Appeals elaborated on the scope of *Chapadeau*'s "arguably within the sphere of legitimate public concern" standard. The plaintiff in *Gaeta* was the ex-wife of a patient in a state mental hospital; she sued for allegedly defamatory statements made about her in connection with an article on the transfer of some 50,000 patients from state mental hospitals to nursing homes. The article featured the plight of the plaintiff's husband as an example of broader conditions, and in the process made allegedly false statements about the plaintiff, involving an alleged "messy divorce" and the suicide of the plaintiff's son. The plaintiff maintained that these statements fell outside of the area encompassed by *Chapadeau*, and that a standard of simple negligence therefore applied.

The Court of Appeals began its analysis of the scope of *Chapadeau* by warning that there are no "mechanical rules" for identifying matters of "genuine public concern."[136] Matters involving the business of government, the court stated, "clearly come within this category."[137] Beyond governmental matters, however, the court went on to provide an extremely wide definition of "matters of public concern," a definition that as a practical matter appears essentially to let the media decide for itself what the phrase "public concern" means:

> The *Chapadeau* standard, moreover, in describing the editorial content as to which the gross irresponsibility standard applies, recognizes the need for judgment and discretion to be exercised by the journalists, sub-

---

[134] Revici v. New York News, Inc., No. 2065/73 (Sup. Ct., N.Y. County, May 20, 1977)(unpublished opinion), *quoted with approval in* Sbarbati v. New York Post, 10 Med. L. Rep. (BNA) 2190, 2192 (N.Y. Sup. Ct. 1984); DeLuca v. New York News, Inc., 438 N.Y.S.2d 199, 7 Med. L. Rep. (BNA) 1302 (Sup. Ct. 1981).

[135] 62 N.Y.2d 340, 477 N.Y.S.2d 82, 465 N.E.2d 802 (1984).

[136] *Id.* at 350, 477 N.Y.S.2d at 85.

[137] *Id.*

> ject only to review by the courts to protect against clear abuses. *Determining what editorial content is of legitimate public interest and concern is a function for editors.* While not conclusive, "a commercial enterprise's allocation of its resources to specific matters and its editorial determination of what is 'newsworthy' may be powerful evidence of the hold those subjects have on the public's attention." [citation omitted] *The press, acting responsibly, and not the courts* must make the *ad hoc* decisions as to what are matters of genuine public concern, and while subject to review, *editorial judgments as to news content will not be second-guessed so long as they are sustainable.*[138]

Although this paragraph does not go so far as to declare that any issue focused on by the media automatically qualifies as a matter of "public concern" under *Chapadeau,* it quite forcefully establishes enormous deference to editorial judgment, subject only to highly deferential review for "clear abuse." Applying this standard to the facts before it, the court found that the subject matter of the article fell well within *Chapadeau*'s public interest requirement.[139] This expansive interpretation of *Chapadeau* puts real life into the *Chapadeau* court's use of the word "arguably." For after *Gaeta* it is clear that "arguably within the public interest" really means "arguably"—New York courts are not to painstakingly second-guess editorial judgment.

§ 3.13 The Supreme Court's Actual Malice Test

[1] Early Supreme Court Statements

The United States Supreme Court's efforts to give definition to the term "actual malice" have been relatively limited. In the *New York Times* case the Court made it clear that the mere failure of the *Times* to check the advertisement involved in that case against its own records did not satisfy the burden of proving actual malice.[140] In a subsequent case decided in 1964, *Garrison v. Louisiana,* [141] the Court said that there must be a showing that the statements were made with "a high

---

138 *Id.* (emphasis added).

139 *Id.* at 350-51, 477 N.Y.S.2d at 85-86.

140 New York Times Co. v. Sullivan, 376 U.S. 254, 287 (1964). *See generally supra* § 2.01.

141 379 U.S. 64.

degree of awareness of their probable falsity" in order to satisfy the *Times* standard.[142]

[2] The *Butts* and *Walker* Elaborations

In *Curtis Publishing Co. v. Butts,*[143] the Court again emphasized that recklessness would require publication "despite the publisher's awareness of probable falsity."[144] In the *Butts* case, Chief Justice Warren in his crucial concurring opinion found that actual malice did exist, emphasizing that the *Saturday Evening Post* writers knew that their only source for the story charging Coach Wally Butts with fixing a football game was a person who had criminal charges on his record.[145] Furthermore, the *Post* writers did not see the source's notes of what the source had told them. Other potential sources of information, Justice Warren emphasized, including sports experts, game films, and witnesses were not utilized at all in the *Post*'s investigation, even though the *Post* was aware of their existence.[146] Furthermore, the *Post* "was anxious to change its image by instituting a policy of 'sophisticated muckraking' and the pressure to produce a successful exposé may have induced a stretching of standards."[147] Before the article was published, allegations that the story was false were brought to the attention of the *Post.* Those allegations did not, however, trigger any further investigation on behalf of the *Post.* Finally, there was no time pressure to produce the story. It appeared in a weekly magazine long after the football game in question. The story was in no sense the news of the day.[148]

The finding of actual malice by Chief Justice Warren in the *Butts* case should be contrasted with Warren's decision that no such actual malice existed in the companion case to *Butts, Associated Press v. Walker.*[149] *Walker* involved a "hot news" situation requiring immediate dissemination by the news media.[150] Wire service dispatches on the story were internally consistent, emanating from a reporter who was witnessing the events firsthand and who on the surface "gave every indication of

142 *Id.* at 74.
143 388 U.S. 130 (1967). *See generally supra* § 2.02.
144 *Id.* at 153.
145 *Id.* at 170. (Warren, C.J., concurring).
146 *Id.* at 157.
147 *Id.* at 158.
148 *Id.* at 158.
149 388 U.S. 130 (1967). *See generally supra* § 2.02.
150 388 U.S. at 159.

being trustworthy and competent."[151] Furthermore, there was nothing on the face of the reports to lend them any inherent improbability. General Walker had previously taken public positions that made it at least conceiveable that he might be involved in the sorts of disruptive efforts that were apparently taking place on the University of Mississippi campus. Even though it turns out that Walker was not in fact involved in such efforts to the extent that the Associated Press reported, to those receiving the AP reporter's dispatches the reports would not have appeared patently "unreasonable" in light General Walker's prior position on the race issues involved.[152]

Although *Butts* and *Walker* were decided relatively early on in the growth period of the *New York Times* actual malice standard, they remain among the very few examples of Justices of the Supreme Court parsing through the record fact by fact to make the actual malice determination, and for that reason they remain important guides to interpreting the actual malice standard.

[3] *St. Amant v. Thompson*

By far the most important Supreme Court explication of the actual malice standard came in its 1968 decision in *St. Amant v. Thompson.*[153] To this date the *St. Amant* case remains the governing law in the area, and it is well worth parsing the opinion carefully. The case grew out of statements made by the defendant St. Amant, a candidate for political office in Louisiana; the statements concerned the plaintiff, Herman Thompson, an East Baton Rouge Parish deputy sheriff. During the course of a speech, St. Amant stated that there were certain illegalities in the sheriff's office, including corruption, and that Herman Thompson was implicated.

Purporting to apply the *New York Times* actual malice standard, the Louisiana Supreme Court ruled that St. Amant broadcast the false information about Thompson recklessly, though not knowingly. The Louisiana Supreme Court gave a number of reasons for its conclusion. St. Amant, in fact, had no personal knowledge of Mr. Thompson's activities. Rather, he relied solely on an affidavit, although the record was silent as to the affiant's reputation for veracity. Furthermore, St. Amant failed to verify the information with those who might have known the

---

151 *Id.* at 158-59.

152 *Id.*

153 390 U.S. 727 (1968).

facts. He gave no consideration to whether the statements defamed Thompson when he made the speech and he went ahead heedless of the consequences. Apparently he mistakenly believed that he had no responsibility for the broadcast, because he was merely quoting the affiant's words.[154]

The United States Supreme Court ruled that these factors fell short of proving that St. Amant had acted with reckless disregard for the truth or falsity of the statements. The Court noted that although reckless disregard cannot be fully encompassed within one infallible definition, and that, invariably, its outer limits would be marked out by a case-by-case adjudication, it was nonetheless true that cases prior to *St. Amant* had provided sufficient guidance to make it clear that St. Amant's conduct did not constitute recklessness.[155] In the most important passage in the *St. Amant* decision, the Court said that "reckless conduct is not measured by whether a reasonably prudent man would have published or would have investigated before publishing. There must be sufficient evidence to permit the conclusion that the defendant in fact entertained serious doubts as to the truth of his publication. Publishing with such doubts shows reckless disregard for truth or falsity and demonstrates actual malice."[156]

The key to the Supreme Court's formulation in *St. Amant v. Thompson* is the requirement that there be evidence that the defendant "in fact entertained serious doubts as to the truth of his publication."[157] That passage emphasizes that the actual malice standard is not an objective standard but rather a subjective one in which the state of mind of the defendant is at issue.[158] The Court acknowledged that it might be said that such a formulation puts a premium on ignorance and encourages the irresponsible publisher not to inquire, thus permitting the actual malice issue to be determined by the media defendant's testimony that it published the statement in good faith, unaware of probable falsity.[159] The Court noted, however, that although, concededly, a premium on ignorance was to some degree built in to the actual malice standard, permitting recovery in fewer situations than would be the case if an objective standard were to apply, that result was the very

[154] *Id.* at 728-30.
[155] *Id.* at 730-31.
[156] *Id.* at 731.
[157] *Id.*
[158] *See infra* § 3.09.
[159] 390 U.S. at 731.

point of the special *New York Times* protection in the first place. The whole purpose of the *New York Times* test was to emphasize the importance of free expression with regard to criticism of public officials, and the recognition that neither the defense of truth nor the standard of ordinary care could completely protect against self-censorship.[160]

In an important qualifying statement, however, the Court noted that a defendant in a defamation action brought by a public official cannot "automatically insure a favorable verdict by testifying that he published with the belief that the statements were true."[161] Mere protestations of a lack of subjective doubt do not establish that no subjective doubt existed.[162] The trier of fact must believe the defendant when the defendant claims that no doubt entered its mind. Thus, the Court wrote, "the trier of fact must determine whether the publication was indeed made in good faith."[163] In making this determination, the Court emphasized that "professions of good faith will be unlikely to prove persuasive, for example, where a story is fabricated by the defendant, is the product of his imagination, or is based wholly on an unverified anonymous telephone call."[164] The Court then, in a very important elaboration on the standard, noted that at times the allegedly defamatory allegations themselves may be evidence as to the state of mind of the defendant.[165] The Court stated that defendants will not be likely to prevail "when the publisher's allegations are so inherently improbable that only a reckless man would have put them in circulation. Likewise, recklessness may be found where there are obvious reasons to doubt the veracity of the informant or the accuracy of his reports."[166]

In applying the formulation it had just announced to the facts in the case before it, the Court held that nothing in the record indicated an awareness by St. Amant of the probable falsity of the informant's statements about Thompson. Failure to investigate does not itself establish bad faith, the Court stated.[167] The fact that St. Amant made a mistake about his probable legal liability was not evidence of a doubtful mind as to the truth or falsity of what he was saying. The evidence in the

---

160 *Id.*
161 *Id.* at 732.
162 *Id.*
163 *Id.*
164 *Id.*
165 *Id.*
166 *Id.*
167 *Id.* at 733.

record that there was no evidence of the informant's reputation for veracity, the Court said, merely underlined the failure of Thompson's evidence to demonstrate that the defendant possessed doubts that his source was reliable. The record did not demonstrate that St. Amant had any subjective reason to doubt the source's reliability. St. Amant had, in fact, known the informant for some months and he had provided reliable, verifiable information to St. Amant in the past. He had also gone to the trouble of making an affidavit which contained the libelous charges. On this record, the Court noted, no actual malice existed.[168]

§ 3.14 Actual Malice Is a Subjective Standard, Though "Objective" Evidence May Be Probative

[1] The Standard Is Subjective

In the aftermath of *St. Amant v. Thompson* the Supreme Court and the lower courts have repeatedly emphasized the subjective nature of the actual malice standard. (This issue is discussed again in the litigation and discovery context.)[169] Thus, in *Herbert v. Lando*,[170] the Supreme Court considered whether the plaintiff could use discovery to probe the editorial decision-making processes of CBS in connection with a "60 Minutes" segment portraying a Vietnam War hero's allegations concerning atrocities which supposedly took place during the war. The Supreme Court concluded that the plaintiff could inquire into the defendant's mental processes, rejecting the defendant's claim of special first amendment privilege, emphasizing that *New York Times* and its progeny require the plaintiff to focus on the defendant's subjective state of mind.[171] And in *Bose Corporation v. Consumers Union of United States*,[172] the Supreme Court, in reaffirming the principle of independent appellate review of the actual malice determination,[173] again emphasized the subjective nature of the inquiry, noting that the actual malice issue before it "rests entirely on an evaluation of [the author's]

---

168 *Id.*

169 *See* Chapter 13, *infra.*

170 441 U.S. 153 (1979).

171 *Id.* at 170.

172 104 S. Ct. 1949 (1984).

173 *See* Chapter 13, *infra.*

state of mind when he wrote his initial report, or when he checked the article against that report."[174]

Lower courts have repeatedly emphasized that the "constitutional definition of malice is . . . concerned with showing the publisher's subjective reckless disregard for accuracy."[175] The existence of " 'reckless disregard' is determined on a case-by-case basis, and it is not measured by an objective standard."[176] The focus of the actual malice inquiry "is on a defendant's attitude toward the truth or falsity of the publication," on his "subjective awareness of its probable falsity," and on his "actual doubts as to its accuracy."[177] The "inquiry in 'actual malice' focuses largely on the defendant's belief regarding truthfulness."[178]

[2] Objective Data as Probative of Subjective State of Mind

As the Supreme Court strongly emphasized in *St. Amant v. Thompson,*[179] the fact that the actual malice standard requires an inquiry into the defendant's state of mind does not mean that the trier of fact is limited to the defendant's own version of what was in his or her mind at the time of publication—mere "[p]rofessions of good faith" will not insulate a defendant from liability.[180] *St. Amant* explicitly permits, and even encourages, the introduction of objective evidence for the light it sheds on the defendant's mental state.[181] This is indeed the only con-

---

[174] 104 S. Ct. at 1956.

[175] Orr v. Argus-Press Co., 586 F.2d 1108, 1116 (6th Cir. 1978), *cert. denied,* 440 U.S. 960 (1979).

[176] Trapp v. Southeastern Newspapers Corp., 10 Med. L. Rep. (BNA) 1985, 1986 (S.D. Ga. 1984).

[177] Lawrence v. Bauer Publishing, 89 N.J. 451, 467-68 (1982). *See also* Carson v. Allied News Co., 529 F.2d 206, 209 (7th Cir. 1976)(" 'actual malice' concentrates on the defendant's attitude toward the truth or falsity of the material published").

[178] Nevada Broadcasting v. Allen, 664 P.2d 337, 344 (Nev. 1983). *See also* Brown v. Herald Co., 698 F.2d 949, 951 (8th Cir. 1983); Barry v. Time, Inc., 584 F. Supp. 1110, 1122 (N.D. Cal. 1984); Fogus v. Capital Cities Media, 111 Ill. App. 3d 1060, 1064, 555 N.E.2d 1100 (1982); Lexington Hearld-Leader v. Graves, 9 Med. L. Rep. (BNA) 1065, 1070-71 (Ky. Sup. Ct. 1982); Maine Yankee v. Maine Nuclear Referendum Committee, 9 Med. L. Rep. (BNA) 1561, 1568 (Me. Super. Ct. 1983); Phillips v. Washington, 9 Med. L. Rep. (BNA) 1601, 1604 (Md. Cir. Ct. 1983); Postill v. Booth Newspapers, 118 Mich. App. 608, 325 N.W.2d 511, 519 (1982); Doubleday v. Rogers, 674 S.W.2d 751 (Tex. Sup. Ct. 1984); Bowes v. Wisconsin Vocational, Technical & Adult Education Board, 9 Med. L. Rep. (BNA) 2372, 2379-80 (Wis. Cir. Ct. 1983). *See generally* Hill, *Defamation and Privacy Under the First Amendment,* 76 Colum. L. Rev. 1205, 1211, n.19 (1976).

[179] 390 U.S. 727 (1968). *See supra* § 3.08[3].

[180] *Id.* at 732.

[181] *Id. See supra* § 3.08[3].

ceivable rule, for defendants are not likely voluntarily to confess their own subjective recklessness.[182]

Courts thus routinely permit objective facts to be introduced to prove or disprove the existence of actual malice.[183] As the First Circuit Court of Appeals has put it:

> The subjective determination of whether [a defendant] in fact entertained serious doubts as to the truth of the statement may be proved by inference, as it would be rare for a defendant to admit such doubts. . . . A court typically will infer actual malice from objective facts. . . . These facts should provide evidence of negligence, motive, and intent such that an accumulation of the evidence and appropriate inferences supports the existence of actual malice.[184]

§ 3.15 Distinguishing Constitutional Actual Malice from Common Law "Ill Will" Malice

It is perfectly clear that it is error to confuse the constitutional malice standard required by *New York Times v. Sullivan* and the traditional common law malice usually articulated in the form of ill will, spite, or hatred.[185] A defendant may hate a plaintiff with the darkest of hearts and still subjectively believe in the truth of the statement he is making about the plaintiff. In instructing the jury in *Greenbelt Publishing Corp. v. Bresler,*[186] the trial court defined malice to include "spite, hostility or deliberate intention to harm." Additionally, the trial judge in-

---

182 *See* Stone v. Essex County Newspapers, Inc., 367 Mass. 849, 868, 330 N.E.2d 161, 173 (1975).

183 *See, e.g.*, Harte-Hanks Communications, Inc. v. Connaughton, 109 S. Ct., 2678, 2686 (1989); Tavoulareas v. Washington Post Co., 759 F.2d 90, 115 (D.C. Cir. 1985),*rehearing en banc granted*, 763 F.2d 1472 (D.C. Cir. 1985). Bose Corp. v. Consumers Credit Union of United States, 692 F.2d 189, 196 (1st Cir. 1982), *aff'd*, 104 S. Ct. 1949 (1984); Goldwater v. Ginzburg, 414 F.2d 324, 342 (2d Cir. 1969), *cert. denied*, 396 U.S. 1049 (1970); Washington Post Co. v. Keogh, 365 F.2d 965, 968 (D.C. Cir. 1966),*cert. denied*, 385 U.S. 1011 (1967). *See also* Oakes, *Proof of Actual Malice in Defamation Actions: An Unresolved Dilemma*, 7 Hofstra L. Rev. 655, 666-67 (1979).

184 Bose Corp. v. Consumers Union of United States, 692 F.2d 189, 196 (1st Cir. 1982), *aff'd*, 104 S. Ct. 1949 (1984).

185 *See, e.g.*, Dun & Bradstreet, Inc. v. Greenmoss Builders, Inc., 105 S. Ct. 2939, 2943 (1985); Greenbelt Cooperative Publishing Ass'n v. Bresler, 398 U.S. 6, 10 n.3 (1970); Garrison v. Louisiana, 379 U.S. 64, 75 (1964); Carson v. Allied News Co., 529 F.2d 206, 209 (7th Cir. 1976); Reliance Ins. Co. v. Barron's, 442 F. Supp. 1314, 1350 (S.D.N.Y. 1977); Postill v. Booth Newspapers, 118 Mich. App. 608, 626, 325 N.W.2d 511 (1982); Novi Ambulance, Inc. v. Farmington Observer, 11 Med. L. Rep. (BNA) 1644, 1646 (Mich. Cir. Ct. 1985); Nevada Broadcasting v. Allen, 664 P.2d 337, 344 (Nev. 1983).

186 398 U.S. 6 (1970).

structed the jury that malice could be found from the language of the publication itself. The Supreme Court held that this was error of constitutional magnitude. The definition of malice in these common law terms was constitutionally insufficient under *New York Times.*[187]
As one federal district court has nicely put it, "[w]hen the Supreme Court uses a word, it means what the Court wants it to mean. 'Actual malice' is now a term of art having nothing to do with actual malice."[188] In the context of a modern defamation action, actual malice is thus a constitutional term that "simply does not mean ill-will or spite" in the common law sense.[189]

§ 3.16 Common Law Malice as Probative of Constitutional Actual Malice

It is error to confuse common law "ill will" malice with constitutional "actual malice,"[190] but it is perfectly proper to permit the existence or nonexistence of common law ill will malice to be established as evidence probative of the existence or nonexistence of actual malice. Courts permit evidence of ill will, hatred, or spite to be introduced for whatever weight it deserves on the actual malice question, with the caveat that ill will, hatred, or spite *standing alone* can never establish knowing or reckless disregard for the truth.[191] Although "the concepts underlying malice and actual malice are not the same, . . . this does not preclude a relationship between them."[192] "While 'ill-will' is not an element of the legal definition of 'actual malice,' . . . it is nevertheless relevant and admissible as evidence in the determination of whether defendant possessed a state of mind highly conducive to reckless disregard of falsity."[193] Similarly, this sort of "[c]ircumstantial evidence may

---

[187] *Id.* at 10.

[188] Reliance Ins. Co. v. Barron's, 442 F. Supp. 1314, 1350 (S.D.N.Y. 1977)(Brieant, J.).

[189] *Id.* at 1349.

[190] *See supra* § 3.10.

[191] *See, e.g.*, Bose Corp. v. Consumers Union of United States, 692 F.2d 189, 196 (1st Cir. 1982), *aff'd on other grounds*, 104 S. Ct. 1949 (1984); Cochran v. Indianapolis Newspapers, 372 N.E.2d 1211, 1220 (Ind. App. 1978); DiLorenzo v. New York News, 81 A.D.2d 844, 432 N.Y.S.2d 483 (1981); Hellman v. McCarthy, 10 Med. L. Rep. (BNA) 1789, 1794 (N.Y. Sup. Ct. 1984).

[192] DiLorenzo v. New York News, 81 A.D.2d 844, 432 N.Y.S.2d 483 (1981).

[193] Cochran v. Indianapolis Newspapers, 175 Ind. App. 548, 560, 372 N.E.2d 1211, 1220 (1978).

also be relied upon to show 'high degree of awareness of probable falsity.' "[194]

Whenever evidence of ill will is admitted in a case litigated under the actual malice standard, trial judges should be enormously cautious in explaining to the jury the distinction between common law malice and constitutional malice, and should repeatedly admonish the jury that evidence of ill will is merely probative, and never conclusive, on the issue of actual malice.

§ 3.17 Failure to Investigate

[1] Lack of Journalistic Initiative Alone Not Actual Malice

The failure of a defendant to further investigate a story before publishing it can never, *standing alone,* be actual malice, because the simple failure to investigate merely establishes possible negligence—it does not establish subjective knowledge of falsity or serious doubt about the truth of the story.[195]

An overwhelming number of cases involving victories for defendants on appeal on the actual malice standard involve fact patterns in which the worst that can be said of the publisher or broadcaster is that a reporter failed to show significant initiative in corroborating, verifying, or further investigating the story.[196] These decisions repeatedly emphasize that the mere failure to investigate, even when that failure to investigate is less than reasonable or responsible journalism, does not in and of itself meet the actual malice test. There must be some evidence of subjective suspicion that further investigation is needed. That evi-

---

194 *Id.*

195 *See, e.g.,* St. Amant v. Thompson, 390 U.S. 727, 731 (1968); Harte-Hanks Communications, Inc. v. Connaughton, 109 S. Ct. 2678, 2698 (1989); Hardin v. Santa Fe Reporter, 745 F.2d 1323 (10th Cir. 1984); New York Times Co. v. Connor, 365 F.2d 567, 576 (5th Cir. 1966); Reveley v. Berg Publications, 601 F. Supp. 44 (W.D. Tex. 1984); Foodscience Corp. v. McGraw-Hill, Inc., 592 F. Supp. 362 (D. Vt. 1984); Dowd v. Calabrese, 589 F. Supp. 1206 (D.D.C. 1984); Lins v. Evening News Ass'n, 129 Mich. App. 419, 342 N.W.2d 573, 580 (1983); Postill v. Booth Newspapers, 118 Mich. App. 608, 325 N.W.2d 511, 519 (1982); Novi Ambulance, Inc. v. Farmington Observer, 11 Med. L. Rep. (BNA) 1644, 1647 (Mich. Cir. Ct. 1985); Pasculli v. Jersey Journal and Jersey Observer, 7 Med. L. Rep. (BNA) 2574 (N.J. Super. 1981), *pet. denied,* 89 N.J. 424 (1982); Bruno v. New York News, 89 A.D.2d 260, 265 (2d Dept. 1982); Miskovsky v. Oklahoma Publishing, 654 P.2d 587, 596 (Okla.), *cert. denied,* 495 U.S. 923 (1982); McNabb v. Oregonian Publishing Co., 69 Or. App. 136, 685 P.2d 458 (1984); Doubleday v. Rogers, 674 S.W.2d 751 (Tex. Sup. Ct. 1984); Burns v. The Times-Argus Ass'n, 139 Vt. 381, 389, 430 A.2d 773 (1981).

196 *See supra* note 192.

dence, of course, can be met by circumstantial data,[197] including such things as the reliability or unreliability of the source[198] or the inherent implausibility of the allegation,[199] but something other than the stark failure to pursue investigation must be established.

[2] Mere Failure to Check Story Against Information in Internal Files Not Actual Malice

The Supreme Court in the *New York Times* case held that the mere failure to check the accuracy of a story against information contained in a defendant's own internal files (or today, in an electronic data base) is not actual malice.[200] There was evidence that the *Times* published the advertisement without checking its accuracy against the news stories in the *Time's* own files. The mere presence of the stories in the files did not, the Court held, establish that the *Times* "knew" the advertisement was false, since the state of mind required for actual malice would have to be brought home to the persons in the *Times* organization having responsibility for the publication of the advertisement.[201] With respect to the failure of those persons to make the check, the record demonstrated that they relied upon their knowledge of the good reputation of many of those whose names were listed as sponsors of the advertisement, and upon the letter from A. Philip Randolph, known to them as a responsible individual, certifying that the use of the names was authorized.[202] There was testimony that the persons handling the advertisement saw nothing in it that would render it unacceptable under the *Times'* policy of rejecting advertisements containing "attacks of a personal character;" their failure to reject it was thus not unreasonable. The Court thus held that "the evidence against the *Times* supports at most a finding of negligence in failing to discover the misstatements, and is constitutionally insufficient to show the recklessness that is required for a finding of actual malice."[203]

---

[197] *See supra* § 3.09.

[198] *See infra* § 3.19.

[199] St. Amant v. Thompson, 390 U.S. 727, 732 (1968).

[200] New York Times Co. v. Sullivan, 376 U.S. 254, 287 (1964).

[201] *Id.*

[202] *Id. See also supra* § 2.01.

[203] *Id.* citing Charles Parker Co. v. Silver City Crystal Co., 142 Conn. 605, 618, 116 A.2d 440, 446 (1955); Phoenix Newspapers, Inc. v. Choisser, 82 Ariz. 271, 277-78, 312 P.2d 150, 154-55 (1957)).

§ 3.18 Failure to Check Obvious Sources as Evidence of Actual Malice

[1] In General

If, as the Supreme Court held, the failure of the staff in *New York Times v. Sullivan*[204] to check the accuracy of the information against its own files was not, standing alone, actual malice,[205] it would seem to follow inexorably that the failure to contact obvious sources or persons involved in a story to verify information would also, standing alone, never be sufficient evidence of actual malice. The issue is not quite so simple, however. For although it is absolutely clear that the mere failure to investigate can never, by itself, constitute actual malice,[206] in certain rare circumstances the failure to verify a story by checking an obvious and accessible source may be so suspicious as to create an inference that the defendant in fact entertained serious doubts and intentionally avoided verification for fear that it would contradict the story the defendant was about to publish.

The Colorado Supreme Court has thus held that "a reporter's failure to pursue the most obvious available sources of possible corroboration or refutation may clearly and convincingly evidence a reckless disregard for the truth."[207] Similarly, the Oklahoma Supreme Court has held that when a reporter neglected to make personal contact with *anyone* involved in the reported incident and did no further checking before publication, there was sufficient "evidence of heedless conduct to show wanton indifference to consequences."[208]

The proposition that the failure to verify may at times be so egregious as to constitute actual malice must be interpreted very cautiously, however. To be reconciled with Supreme Court holdings such as *New York Times* and *St. Amant*,[209] the proposition must be qualified by the statement that a failure to verify must be of such a nature as to generate suspicion that the defendant entertained serious subjective doubts

---

204 376 U.S. 254, 287 (1964).

205 *See supra* § 3.12[2].

206 *See supra* § 3.14, note 156.

207 Kuhn v. Tribune-Republican Publishing Co., 637 P.2d 315, 319 (Colo. 1981) (citing Alioto v. Cowles Communications, Inc., 519 F.2d 777 (9th Cir. 1975).

208 Akins v. Altus Newspapers, 609 P.2d 1263, 1269 (Okla. 1977), *cert. denied*, 449 U.S. 1010 (1980). *See also* Kerwick v. Orange County Publications, 53 N.Y.2d 625, 438 N.Y.S.2d 778 (1981).

209 *See supra* § 3.08.

about the truth and "did not want to know more." An alleged failure to verify must be evaluated "in light of the total information developed and used by the publisher."[210]

A failure to verify may legitimately be used to establish actual malice when a reporter, during the process of interviewing a witness or source, refrains from asking the source the "key question," even though the reporter knows what that question is, has formulated his or her own answer to it, and intends to write a story reflecting that answer. In this situation, the reporter is in effect saying "I think I know what the truth on this point is, but I am not going to ask you about it for fear that you will upset my applecart." Under these circumstances verification literally costs the defendant nothing in time or money, since the source is already at hand. Such an omission, then, is exceptionally suspicious: The failure to ask the critical question quite naturally raises the inference that the reporter, contrary to later protestations, did in fact entertain subjective doubts about the "truth" of what he or she was about to publish.[211] Two instructive examples of this phenomenon are *Sharon v. Time, Inc.*[212] and *Harte-Hanks Communications, Inc. v. Connaughton.*[212.1]

[2] *Sharon v. Time, Inc.*

The *Sharon* case arose out of a *Time* story reporting on an official Israeli Commission inquiry into the events surrounding the massacre at the Sabra and Shatilla refugee camps in Lebanon during the Israeli

---

210 Rosanova v. Playboy Enterprises, Inc., 411 F. Supp. 440, 447 (S.D. Ga. 1976), *aff'd*, 580 F.2d 859 (5th Cir. 1978).

211 This sort of pattern influenced the reasoning of the Fifth Circuit Court of Appeals in Rebozo v. Washington Post Co., 637 F.2d 375 (5th Cir.), *cert. denied*, 454 U.S. 964 (1981). The suit was brought by Charles ("Bebe") Rebozo, close friend and confidant of President Richard Nixon. The court held that a genuine issue of material fact as to the existence of actual malice was present, in part because a reporter failed to pursue a key question with a source: "In investigating the story, even though [the reporter] Kessler went to the trouble of calling [the source] Riley, he failed to review with Riley the words in Riley's earlier deposition upon which Kessler eventually based the article's lead. . . . Despite Kessler's professed belief in the veracity of Riley's deposition testimony, Kessler's resolution of the obvious ambiguity . . . in favor of the most potentially damaging alternative creates a jury question on whether the publication was indeed made with serious doubt as to its truthfulness." *Id.* at 382.

212 599 F. Supp. 538 (S.D.N.Y. 1984). *See generally Libel on Trial: The* Westmoreland *and* Sharon *Cases*, BNA Special Report (1985).

212.1 109 S. Ct. 2678 (1989).

invasion and occupation of Lebanon in 1982.[213] *Time* accurately reported that the Israeli report, known as the Kahan Commission Report, had severely criticized General Sharon, stating, for example, that his "blunders constitute non-fulfillment of the duty with which he was charged."[214] The bottom line of the Kahan Commission Report was that General Sharon bore indirect responsibility for the massacres, and *Time* accurately reported that conclusion. But *Time* took the story one step further. *Time* spoke of a part of the report that had been kept secret from the public, and then stated that it had learned what was in the secret section. *Time* thus reported:

> One section of the report, known as Appendix B, was not published at all, mainly for security reasons. That section contains the names of several intelligence agents referred to elsewhere in the report. *Time* has learned that it also contains further details about Sharon's visit to the Gemayel family on the day after Bashir Gemayel's assassination. Reportedly Sharon told the Gemayels' that the Israeli army would be moving into West Beirut and that he expected the Christian forces to go into the Palestinian refugee camps. Sharon also reportedly discussed with the Gemayels the need for the Phalangists to take revenge for the assassination of Bashir, but the details of the conversation are not known.[215]

The evidence disclosed that *Time*'s Jerusalem correspondent had filed a report with *Time* based on a "highly reliable" confidential source claiming that at a condolence meeting between Ariel Sharon and the grieving Gemayel family, Sharon "had given the Gemayels the feeling" that he understood the necessity for the Gemayels to take revenge, and that the Israeli army would not hinder them or try to stop them. Two months later, when the Kahan Commission Report was released, *Time*'s Jerusalem bureau chief wanted to know if the Secret Appendix would substantiate the Jerusalem correspondent's prior report. The Jerusalem correspondent testified that he told the bureau chief "there is a case against General Sharon or Minister Sharon between the lines" of the Kahan report and that "it is probably in Appendix B." The Jerusalem correspondent then went on to seek out his confidential source to verify his suspicion.

The testimony at the trial, however, indicated that the confidential source, named "Source C," never actually confirmed the reporter's suspicion. At the trial *Time* attempted to equate its confidential source with the famous "Deep Throat" of the Watergate scandal. But, unlike

213 *See generally* 599 F. Supp. at 560-85.

214 *Id.* at 542.

215 *Id.* at 543.

Deep Throat, Source C apparently did not actually verify the information at issue. Source C, the testimony went, told *Time* that Appendix B was a "reference book" of names, sources, and intelligence agents used by the Kahan Commission. Source C also confirmed that certain agents of the Mossad, the Israeli Secret Service, were mentioned in Appendix B, including an agent who was present at the meeting between Sharon and the Gemayels. The Jerusalem correspondent did not ask his confidential source, however, whether Appendix B literally stated that Sharon had discussed revenge with the Gemayels. As Judge Abraham Sofaer ruled in an opinion dealing with *Time*'s motion for summary judgment, a jury could find that *Time*'s Jerusalem correspondent chose not to ask Source C the ultimate question because he knew or suspected that Source C's answer would undermine the reporter's hypothesis.[216] Judge Sofaer indicated that the reporter's "decision to treat Source C as a total confirmation of his hypothesis is particularly questionable in view of his decision not to tell Source C the information that his response would be viewed as supporting;" the *Time* reporter's actions, Judge Sofaer ruled, could be read to convey his subjective awareness of probable falsity.[217]

The *Time* case, of course, ended with a victory for *Time* because the jury determined that the evidence did not satisfy the *New York Times* actual malice standard. In an extremely unusual procedure following the verdict, however, the jury foreman read a statement from the jury accompanying the verdict, which said that the jury had found that "certain *Time* employees, particularly [*Time*'s Jerusalem correspondent], acted negligently and carelessly in reporting and verifying the information which ultimately found its way into the published paragraph."[218] Although this statement by the jury obviously had no legal or precedential effect, it is highly illustrative of the dangers that exist when reporters extrapolate from the information they have received from confidential sources, or appear to intentionally avoid corroboration. Given Judge Sofaer's analysis in his summary judgment motion ruling, there was certainly a substantial possibility that if the jury had found actual malice, the court would not have overturned the finding. The perils suggested by *Sharon* lie not so much in the failure to verify as

[216] Judge Sofaer engaged in a careful and meticulous analysis of this point, distinguishing between not checking with the source at all, and checking with the source but *not* asking for a confirmation or denial of the critical issue. *Id.* at 584-85.

[217] *Id.*

[218] *See* New York Times, Jan. 25, 1985, at 1; Washington Post, Jan. 25, 1985, at Al.

in the use of "selective verification," and in extrapolation from that selective verification.

[3] *Harte-Hanks Communications, Inc. v. Connaughton*

In *Harte-Hanks Communications, Inc. v. Connaughton,*[218.1] Daniel Connaughton was an unsuccessful challenger for the position of Municipal Judge of Hamilton, Ohio, in 1983. *The Journal News,* published by petitioner, supported the incumbent in the election. About a month before the election, the incumbent's Director of Court Services resigned and was arrested on bribery charges and a grand jury investigation was initiated.

A witness for the grand jury, a Ms. Thompson, was quoted in a front page story in *The Journal News* as stating that Connaughton had used "dirty tricks" in offering her and her sister jobs, and promising a trip to Florida in appreciation for their help in the investigation.

After Ms. Thompson disclosed this information to *The Journal News,* the newspaper interviewed Connaughton. Mr. Connaughton admitted meeting with Ms. Thompson, but denied any involvement in trying to bribe her. Both Mr. Connaughton and Ms. Thompson maintained that Thompson's sister could verify their story.

A small group of reporters was instructed to interview all of the witnesses to the conversation between Connaughton and Thompson, with one exception, Ms. Thompson's sister. No one was asked to interview her and no one made any attempt to do so. Tapes of an interview between Connaughton and Ms. Thompson's sister were made available to the newspaper by Mr. Connaughton, yet no one at *The Journal News* took the initiative or the time to listen to them.

The court of appeals upheld the jury award of $200,000 to Mr. Connaughton. For the first time in more than twenty years, the U.S. Supreme Court allowed a public figure to collect a libel damage award from a member of the media.[218.2]

The Supreme Court noted that while a failure to investigate is not itself actual malice, purposefully avoiding the truth is in a different category.[218.3] Such a blatant omission is evidence that the inaction was likely a product of a deliberate decision not to acquire knowledge of facts that might confirm the probable falsity of Thompson's charge.[218.4]

218.1 109 S. Ct. 2678 (1989).

218.2 Curtis Publishing Co. v. Butts, 388 U.S. 130 (1967).

218.3 109 S. Ct. 2678, 2698.

218.4 *Id.*

The Court next compared *Connaughton* to *Curtis Publishing Co. v. Butts.*[218.5]

> Although there was reason to question the informant's veracity, just as there was reason to doubt Thompson's story, the editors did not interview a witness who had the same access to the facts as the informant and did not look at films that revealed what actually happened at the game in question. This evidence of an intent to avoid the truth was not only sufficient to convince the plurality that there had been an extreme departure from professional publishing standards, but it was also sufficient to satisfy the more demanding *New York Times* standard. . . . As in *Butts*, the evidence in the record in this case, when reviewed in its entirety, is "unmistakably" sufficient to support a finding of actual malice.[218.6]

[4] When Verification Is Impractical

In rare situations the failure to verify (or perhaps it is better to say, the use of "selective verification") may lead to a finding of actual malice. The general rule remains, however, that lack of verification is not, by itself, actual malice, particularly when caused by time or financial constraints. As stated by Judge J. Skelly Wright in *Washington Post v. Keogh*:[219]

> Verification is a time consuming process, a factor especially significant in the newspaper business when news quickly goes stale, commentary rapidly becomes irrelevant, and commercial opportunity in the form of advertisements can easily be lost. In many instances considerations of time and distance make verification impossible. Thus, the newspaper is confronted with the choice of publication without verification or suppression. Verification is also a costly process and the newspaper business is one in which economic survival has become a major problem, made increasingly grave by the implications of this fact for free debate. We should be hesitant to impose responsibilities upon newspapers which can be met only through costly procedures or self-censorship designed to avoid the risk of publishing controversial material.[220]

§ 3.19 Actual Malice and Reliance on Sources and Tips

[1] In General

One of the most often litigated issues relevant to the actual malice determination is the propriety of the defendant's reliance on informa-

---

[218.5] 388 U.S. 130 (1967).

[218.6] 109 S. Ct. 2678, 2699.

[219] 125 U.S. App. D.C. 32, 365 F.2d 965 (1966), *cert. denied*, 385 U.S. 1011 (1967).

[220] *Id.* at 39, 365 F.2d at 972.

tion from the defendant's sources. The general proposition, dating back to *St. Amant v. Thompson,*[221] is that actual malice cannot be established merely because reliance on a source's information is negligent. There must be subjective doubt in the defendant's mind as to the source's credibility.[222] "Negligent investigative reporting alone does not constitute actual malice, there must be a showing that the publisher entertained serious doubts as to the truth of the matter published."[223]

Nevertheless, as in all actual malice determinations, the subjective state of mind may be established through objective circumstantial evidence,[224] and when there are obvious objective reasons to doubt the integrity and credibility of a source, those reasons may be introduced in an attempt to prove that subjective doubt existed.[225] Thus, there is ample case authority for the rule that reliance on sources without subjective doubt is not actual malice.[226] However, there is also some sup-

---

221 390 U.S. 727, 730-33 (1968).

222 *Id.;* Brown v. Hearld Co., 698 F2d 949, 951 (9th Cir. 1983); Ryan v. Brooks, 634 F.2d 726, 734 (4th Cir. 1980); New York Times Co. v. Connor, 365 F.2d 567, 576 (5th Cir. 1966); Dupler v. Mansfield Journal Co., 64 Ohio St. 2d 115, 413 N.E.2d 1187 (1980), *cert. denied,* 452 U.S. 962 (1981); Colombo v. Times-Argus Ass'n, 135 Vt. 454, 380 A.2d 80 (1977).

223 Tucci v. Gannett Publishing Co., 464 A.2d 161, 169-70 (Me. 1983). *See also* Harte-Hanks Communications, Inc. v. Connaughton, 109 S. Ct. 2678, 2696 (1989).

224 *See supra* § 3.14.

225 *See, e.g.,* St. Amant v. Thompson, 390 U.S. 727, 733 (1968); Burnett v. National Enquirer, Inc., 144 Cal. App. 3d 991, 193 Cal. Rptr. 206, *appeal dismissed,* 104 S. Ct. 1260 (1984); Bindrim v. Mitchell, 92 Cal. App. 3d 61, 741, 155 Cal. Rptr. 29, *cert. denied,* 444 U.S. 984 (1979); Stevens v. Sun Publishing Co., 240 S.E.2d 812 (S.C. 1978), *cert. denied,* 436 U.S. 945 (1978).

226 *See, e.g.,* St. Amant v. Thompson, 390 U.S. 727, 730-33 (1968); Ryan v. Brooks, 634 F.2d 726, 734 (4th Cir. 1980); Brewer v. Memphis Publishing Co., 626 F.2d 1238 (5th Cir. 1980); Vandenburg v. Newsweek, Inc., 507 F.2d 1024, 1028 (5th Cir. 1975); New York Times Co. v. Connor, 365 F.2d 567, 576 (5th Cir. 1966); Dowd v. Calabrese, 589 F. Supp. 1206 (D.D.C. 1984); Barry v. Time, Inc., 584 F. Supp. 1110, 1122 (N.D. Cal. 1984); Loeb v. New Times Communications Corp., 497 F. Supp. 85 (S.D.N.Y. 1980); Loeb v. Globe Newspaper Co., 489 F. Supp. 481 (D. Mass. 1980); Schultz v. Newsweek, 481 F. Supp. 881 (E.D. Mich. 1979), *aff'd,* 668 F.2d 911 (6th Cir. 1982); Schultz v. Reader's Digest, 468 F. Supp. 551, 565 (E.D. Mich. 1979); Trans World Accounts, Inc. v. Associated Press, 425 F. Supp. 814, 822 (N.D. Cal. 1977); Reader's Digest v. Marin County Superior Court, 37 Cal. 3d 244, 208 Cal. Rptr. 137, 690 P.2d 610 (1984); Phillips v. Washington Post, 8 Med. L. Rep. (BNA) 1834 (D.C. Super. Ct. 1982); Fogus v. Capital Cities Media, 11 Ill. App. 3d 1060, 1064, 444 N.E.2d 1100 (1982); Tucci v. Gannett Publishing Co., 464 A.2d 161, 169-70 (Me. 1983); Maine Yankee v. Maine Nuclear Referendum Committee, 9 Med. L. Rep. (BNA) 1561, 1568 (Me. Super. Ct. 1983); Philips v. Washingtonian, 9 Med. L. Rep. (BNA) 1601 (Md. Cir. Ct. 1981); Lins v. Evening News Ass'n, 129 Mich. App. 419, 342 N.W.2d 573, 580 (1983); Pelzer v. Minneapolis Star & Tribune Co., 7 Med. L. Rep. (BNA) 2507 (Minn. Dist. 1981); Doubleday v. Rogers, 674 S.W.2d 751 (Tex. Sup. Ct. 1984); A.H. Belo Corp. v. Rayzor, 644 S.W.2d 71, 85 (Tex. App. 1982). Similar results have been

port for the proposition that "reliance on the reports of others does not automatically shield one from liability."[227] The plaintiff may attack and overcome that reliance with clear and convincing evidence that the defendant was subjectively aware of a high probability that the source's information was inaccurate.[228] In *Pep v. Newsweek*,[229] for example, the court stated that "[f]acts such as a failure to investigate, or reliance on a questionable source, are relevant to that [actual malice] determination: they may tend to show that a publisher did not care whether an article was truthful or not, or perhaps the publisher did not want to discover facts which would have contradicted his source."[230]

[2] Knowledge of a Source's Possible Bias

When a source harbors biases or hostilities against a plaintiff, and the defendant is aware of those biases or hostilities, that awareness is probative of the existence of actual malice, but is not by itself sufficient to establish actual malice with clear and convincing clarity. Standing alone, mere evidence that a "reporter knew of the hostility of his sources" is "insufficient to establish a prima facie case by evidence of convincing clarity that the reporter wrote his article with reckless disregard for its truth or falsity."[231] Nevertheless, reliance on an obviously biased source is a factor that may legitimately be included in the actual malice determination, in combination with other factors, such as con-

(*Text continued on page 3-49*)

---

reached applying New York's "gross irresponsibility" standard. *See, e.g.*, Ortiz v. Valdescastilla, 102 A.D.2d 513, 516, 478 N.Y.S.2d 895 (1st Dept. 1984); Sbarbati v. New York Post, 10 Med. L. Rep. (BNA) 2190, 2192 (N.Y. Sup. Ct. 1984); Freeze Right Refrigeration v. City of New York, 101 A.D.2d 175, 184, 475 N.Y.S.2d 383 (1st Dept. 1984); Carlucci v. Poughkeepsie Newspapers, 88 A.D.2d 608, 450 N.Y.S.2d 54 (2d Dept.), *aff'd*, 57 N.Y.2d 803, 442 N.E.2d 442 (1982); Zetes v. Richmond, 86 A.D.2d 746, 336 N.Y.S.2d 778 (4th Dept. 1982); Robart v. Post-Standard, 74 A.D.2d 963, 425 N.Y.S.2d 891 (3d Dept. 1980), *aff'd mem.*, 52 N.Y.2d 843 (1981); Karaduman v. Newsday, 51 N.Y.2d 531, 416 N.E.2d 557, 435 N.Y.S.2d 556 (1980).

[227] Schultz v. Reader's Digest, 468 F. Supp. 551, 565 (E.D. Mich. 1979).

[228] *See, e.g.*, Bindrim v. Mitchell, 92 Cal. App. 3d 61, 74, 155 Cal. Rptr. 29, *cert. denied*, 444 U.S. 984 (1979); Grebner v. Runyon, 347 N.W.2d 741 (Mich. Ct. App. 1984).

[229] 553 F. Supp. 1000 (S.D.N.Y. 1983).

[230] *Id.* at 1002-03. *See also* Harte-Hanks Communications, Inc. v. Connaughton, 109 S. Ct. 2678, 2698 (1989).

[231] Rye v. Seattle Times Co., 37 Wash. App. 45, 678 P.2d 1282, 1288, *cert. denied*, 102 Wash. 2d 1004 (1984). *See also* Trapp v. Southeastern Newspapers, 10 Med. L. Rep. (BNA) 1985 (S.D. Ga. 1984); Loeb v. New Times Communications Corp., 497 F. Supp. 85 (S.D.N.Y. 1980).

tradictory evidence, or the absence of a "hot news" deadline.[232]

[3] Reliance on Secondary Sources

Reliance on reputable secondary sources, in the absence of subjective doubt regarding the accuracy of those sources, is insufficient to raise an issue with respect to actual malice.[233]

[4] Reliance on Information Supplied by Wire Services, Free-Lance Writers, and Authors

The defendant is normally entitled to rely on information supplied by professional third party sources such as wire services, free lance writers, or authors.[234] "Absence of knowledge of the veracity of an author does not establish that the publisher should suspect the truth of an article," for "only where an author has a reputation for persistent

---

[232] *See* Tavoulareas v. Washington Post Co., 759 F.2d 90, 117-20, *rehearing en banc granted*, 763 F.2d 1472 (D.C. Cir. 1985) (personal bias of source one of many factors utilized to affirm jury finding of actual malice); Alioto v. Cowles Communications, Inc., 430 F. Supp. 1363 (N.D. Cal. 1977), *aff'd*, 623 F.2d 616 (9th Cir. 1980), *cert. denied*, 449 U.S. 1102 (1981) (finding of actual malice sustained when allegedly defamatory allegations based on hearsay evidence from source of unknown veracity sustained); Stevens v. Sun Publishing Co., 240 S.E.2d 812 (S.C.), *cert. denied*, 436 U.S. 945 (1978) (reliance on an obviously biased source, when added to evidence that the author was under no "hot news" deadline pressure, was sufficient to demonstrate actual malice); Mahnke v. Northwest Publications, Inc., 280 Minn. 328, 160 N.W.2d 1 (1968) (jury question on actual malice existed when source was priest whose information had been obtained from a distraught parishioner).

[233] *See* Ryan v. Brooks, 634 F.2d 726, 734 (4th Cir. 1980); Schultz v. Reader's Digest Ass'n, 468 F. Supp. 551, 565 (E.D. Mich. 1979).

[234] *See, e.g.*, Hotchner v. Castillo-Puche, 551 F.2d 910 (2d Cir.), *cert. denied*, 434 U.S. 834 (1977) (book publisher as matter of law not guilty of actual malice when it relied on good reputation of author); Herbert v. Lando, 596 F. Supp. 1178 (S.D.N.Y. 1984) (no actual malice when magazine relied on reputation of reputable television journalist); Nader v. de Toledano, 408 A.2d 31 (D.C. App. 1979), *cert. denied*, 444 U.S. 1078 (1980) (newspaper syndicate guilty of no actual malice in reliance on columnist); Bindrim v. Mitchell, 92 Cal. App. 3d 61, 155 Cal. Rptr. 29, *cert. denied*, 44 U.S. 984 (1979) (book publisher guilty of no actual malice in reliance on author's representations, at least prior to receipt of contradictory information from plaintiff); Mehau v. Gannett Pacific Corp., 658 P.2d 312 (Hawaii 1983) (newspaper not guilty of actual malice in reliance on reputable wire service); Rinaldi v. Holt, Rinehart & Winston, Inc., 42 N.Y.2d 369, 336 N.E.2d 1299, *cert. denied*, 434 U.S. 969 (1977) (book publisher not guilty of actual malice for reliance on journalist even though his reports were controversial when first published). *See also* Reader's Digest v. Marin County Superior Court, 37 Cal. 3d 244, 208 Cal. Rptr. 137, 690 P.2d 610 (1984) (reliance on reputations of publishers of a newspaper and a professor concerning a religious group (the Synanon Church) not actual malice).

inaccuracy can the publisher be expected to entertain such suspicion."[235] Similarly, in *Mehau v. Gannett Pacific Corp.*[236] the court remarked that the defendant newspaper, which had taken its information from United Press International, "was a subscriber to one of the leading news services in the United States; it had no reason to question the reliability of the organization as a news gatherer."[237]

[5] Anonymous Sources

Although reliance on an anonymous source does not itself establish actual malice, such reliance is admissable as evidence of actual malice. The Supreme Court in *St. Amant v. Thompson*[238] noted that a defendant's profession of belief in the accuracy of a source will not be highly persuasive when the story is "based wholly on an unverified telephone call."[239] It seems clear that both triers of fact and judges tend to look with some skepticism on anonymous sources.[240]

[6] Reckless Reliance: The Carol Burnett Litigation

Lest one get the mistaken impression that reliance on tips and sources will render a defendant immune from a finding of actual malice, it is worth looking in some detail at one of the best recent illustrations of the actual malice standard being met, in Carol Burnett's suit against the *National Enquirer*.[241] The *Enquirer* published a news item that read in its entirety:

> In a Washington restaurant, a boisterous Carol Burnett had a loud argument with another diner, Henry Kissinger. Then she traipsed around the place offering everyone a bite of her dessert. But Carol really raised eyebrows when she accidentally knocked a glass of wine over one diner and started giggling instead of apologizing. The guy wasn't amused and "accidentally" spilled a glass of water over Carol's dress.

---

235 Nader v. de Toledano, 408 A.2d 31 (D.C. App. 1979), *cert. denied*, 444 U.S. 1078 (1980).

236 658 P.2d 312 (Hawaii 1983).

237 *Id.* at 322.

238 390 U.S. 727 (1968).

239 *Id.* at 733.

240 *See, e.g.*, Holter v. WLCY-TV, Inc., 366 So. 2d 445 (Fla. App. 1978), *cert. denied*, 373 So. 2d 462 (Fla. 1979); Downing v. Monitor Publishing Co., Inc., 415 A.2d 683 (N.H. 1980); Greenberg v. CBS, Inc., 69 A.D.2d 693, 419 N.Y.S.2d 988 (2d Dept. 1979).

241 Burnett v. National Enquirer, Inc., 144 Cal. App. 3d 991, 193 Cal. Rptr. 206 (1983), *appeal dismissed*, 104 S. Ct. 1260 (1984).

At trial it was shown that the actual events out of which the *Enquirer's* story arose took place on the evening of January 29, 1976, some five weeks before the gossip column item was published. Burnett and her husband had been dining with friends at the Rive Gauche restaurant in the Georgetown section of Washington, D.C. Burnett was in Washington to perform at the White House. She had "two or three" glasses of wine but she was not inebriated. She did in fact, in a very friendly gesture, share some of her dessert with a young couple seated next to her table. The exchange, however, was made by waiters, and after Burnett's gracious offer, the young couple offered to make a similar exchange with some of their dessert. Later in the evening, as she was leaving the restaurant, she was introduced very briefly by a friend to Henry Kissinger, who also happened to be dining at the restaurant that night. After an exchange of pleasantries, Burnett and her party left the restaurant. According to the testimony of Henry Kissinger, he and Burnett were politely introduced, "exchanged a few words," spoke in a "perfectly civilized manner," and had "no commotion of any kind."

The evidence concerning the *Enquirer's* methodology is extremely important to journalists and media lawyers. The *Enquirer's* interest in the story commenced with a tip from a "free-lance tipster" who was paid by the *Enquirer* for information he supplied on an intermittent basis, if that information was ultimately published. The tip, communicated through an *Enquirer* writer, was that the tipster had been told that Burnett had taken her souffle at the restaurant and flamboyantly given bits of it to other people. The tipster also claimed to have "unverified" information about a wine spilling incident, but according to his sources Burnett was "specifically, emphatically not drunk." The tip made no mention whatsoever of any incident involving Henry Kissinger. The writer passed this information on to another *Enquirer* writer, the person under whose name the gossip column was written. The original writer expressed doubt as to whether the tipster could be trusted, and the gossip columnist concurred in those doubts. Another *Enquirer* reporter was then asked to try to verify the story. That reporter was only able to confirm that Burnett had shared some of her dessert with others. The reporter also learned that Burnett had had a conversation with Henry Kissinger.

Despite the fact that no evidence whatsoever had surfaced of any argument with Kissinger, that no verification of any wine spilling incident had been made, that no details concerning Burnett's sharing of her dessert had been obtained, and that the sources had uniformly emphasized that Burnett was not intoxicated, the writer nonetheless composed the four sentence item that appeared in the gossip column under the headline "Carol Burnett and Henry K. in Row."

Both the trial appellate courts affirmed the jury's finding that actual malice existed. The trial court, in language endorsed by the California Court of Appeals, labeled the *Enquirer's* conduct as "highly reprehensible," amounting to "fabrication and reckless disregard" of the truth.[242]

§ 3.20 Actual Malice and the Reporting and Editing Process

[1] Editorial Point of View

It is not recklessness merely for a publication to have an editorial point of view or a distinctive political slant. In fact all media outlets have points of view. Some of them are distinctive and readily identifiable. Most Americans understand, for example, that the *National Review* is "conservative" and the *Nation* "liberal." But even *Newsweek* and "CBS News" have points of view, though they tend toward relatively centrist, consensus, mainstream opinion. Whatever a publication's political point of view, however, it is irrelevant to actual malice. A conservative public figure, for example, will not be heard to assert that actual malice is established merely because the defendant is a known "liberal" magazine.[243]

[2] Lack of Balance

Actual malice is not synonymous with a lack of balance or neutrality in the gathering, reporting, or editing of news. It is not reckless disregard for the truth *as such* to "selectively" report the facts, if the defendant subjectively believes that the selection represents the truth. When the facts are ambigious, the mere selection of the most damaging inference does not, *by itself,* establish actual malice.[244] If, following research

242 Burnett v. National Enquirer, 7 Med. L. Rep. (BNA) 1321 (Cal. Super. Ct., Los Angeles County, 1981) (trial court opinion).

243 *See* Walker v. Pulitzer Publishing Co., 394 F.2d 800, 806 (8th Cir. 1968) (opinion of the Circuit Judge, later Supreme Court Justice Blackmun). *See also* McQuoid v. Springfield Newspapers, 502 F. Supp. 1050 (W.D. Mo. 1980).

244 *See* Time, Inc. v. Pape, 401 U.S. 279 (1981); Orr v. Argus-Press Co., 586 F.2d 1108 (6th Cir. 1978), *cert. denied,* 440 U.S. 960 (1979); Simmons Ford v. Consumers Union of the United States, Inc., 516 F. Supp. 742 (S.D.N.Y. 1981). Trans World Accounts, Inc. v. Associated Press, 425 F. Supp. 814 (N.D. Cal. 1977).

or investigation, a defendant is convinced that one version of events is accurate, the defendant is under no first amendment obligation to present the other side of the story.[245]

The leading Supreme Court discussion of the problem is in *Time, Inc. v. Pape.*[246] The Court held that *Time's* resolution of ambiguities in a manner adverse to the plaintiff did not constitute actual malice:

> Time's ommission of the word "alleged" amounted to the adoption of one of a number of possible rational interpretations of a document that bristled with ambiguities. The deliberate choice of such an interpretation, though arguably reflecting a misconception, was not enough to create a jury issue of "malice" under *New York Times.*[247]

The resolution of ambiguities and inferences in a manner adverse to the plaintiff is thus not, by itself, actual malice. A defendant need not believe every witness, and indeed must often make credibility choices; the failure to report contradictory evidence, particularly unexplained or self-serving denials, does not by itself establish subjective doubt as to the truth or falsity.[248] The telling of *any* news story requires some selectivity, and the judgments inherent in journalism are not rendered reckless merely because some information is discarded out of genuine disbelief in its accuracy.

[3] The Choice of Facts and Resolution of Inferences or Ambiguities May Be Probative of Actual Malice

Courts have held that the defendant's choice of which facts to report, or the defendant's resolution of inferences or ambiguities in a manner adverse to the plaintiff, while not alone constituting actual malice, may be probative of the existence of actual malice.[249]

---

[245] *See* Arnheiter v. Random House, Inc., 578 F.2d 804 (9th Cir. 1978), *cert. denied,* 444 U.S. 931 (1979); Reliance Ins. Co. v. Barron's, 442 F. Supp. 1341, 1352 (S.D.N.Y. 1977).

[246] 401 U.S. 279 (1971).

[247] *Id.* at 290.

[248] *See* Martin Marietta Corp. v. Evening Star Newspaper Co., 417 F. Supp. 947 (D.D.C. 1976); Graham v. New York Times, Inc., 2 Med. L. Rep. (BNA) 2356 (N.Y. Sup. Ct. 1977). It is worth noting, of course, that plaintiffs who have been given an opportunity to counter allegedly defamatory statements usually have a more difficult time establishing actual malice; thus, balance does have its rewards. *See* Brophy v. Philadelphia Newspapers, Inc., 281 Pa. Super. 621, 422 A.2d 625 (1980) (that article reported on a number of opinions on an issue of local interest was a factor in finding no actual malice).

[249] *See* Tavoulareas v. Washington Post Co., 759 F.2d 90, 124-25, *rehearing en banc granted,* 763 F.2d 1472 (D.C. Cir. 1985); Rebozo v. Washington Post Co., 637 F.2d 375, 382 (5th Cir.), *cert. denied,* 454 U.S. 964 (1981); Time, Inc. v. Ragano, 427 F.2d 219, 221

There is a subtle difference between the principle that a defendant may select from among various interpretations of the "truth," and conscious manipulation of the evidence at hand. At some point on the continuum of journalistic judgment "honest selectivity" gives way to distortion—the evidence is deliberately mischaracterized or edited in such a way as to create the possibility that the defendant acted with knowledge of falsity or reckless disregard for the truth. A lack of balance may, therefore, in some cases be probative of actual malice. In *Rebozo v. Washington Post Co.*,[250] for example, the court held that the resolution of uncertainty in such a way as to cast the plaintiff "in the worst possible light" and to make "a front-page story of an episode which otherwise might not have commanded any significant attention" could "amount to evidence of a reporter's reckless disregard for the truth."[251]

Similarly, in *Tavoulareas v. Washington Post Co.*,[252] the court stated that "a defendant's selection of a reasonable inference from among a number of ambiguities, whether damaging or not, may be evidence that he acted without actual malice."[253] On the other hand, the court stated, "a defendant's selection of the most damaging inference—an inference which is, in fact, false—may be probative of a determination to incorrectly describe the plaintiff, place him in the most damaging light, and thereby with other evidence demonstrate a state of mind that is probative of a reckless disregard for the truth."[254]

[4] The Issues Posed by *Westmoreland v. CBS*

In *Westmoreland v. CBS*,[255] General William Westmoreland brought suit against CBS and several individual defendants for defamation allegedly arising from a CBS broadcast entitled *"CBS Reports—The Uncounted Enemy: A Vietnam Deception."* The CBS documentary, Westmoreland claimed, defamed the General by implying his complici-

---

(5th Cir. 1970); Wasserman v. Time, Inc., 424 F.2d 920, 922 (D.C. Cir.), *cert. denied*, 398 U.S. 940 (1970); Montandon v. Triangle Publications, Inc., 45 Cal. App. 3d 938, 943-44, 120 Cal. Rptr. 186, 189, *cert. denied*, 423 U.S. 893 (1975); Indianapolis Newspapers, Inc. v. Fields, 254 Ind. 219, 259 N.E.2d 651, 662, *cert. denied*, 400 U.S. 930 (1970).

[250] 637 F.2d 375 (5th Cir.), *cert. denied*, 454 U.S. 964 (1981).

[251] *Id.* at 382.

[252] Tavoulareas v. Washington Post Co., 759 F.2d 90 (D.C. Cir. 1985), *rehearing en banc granted*, 763 F.2d 1472 (D.C. Cir. 1985).

[253] *Id.* at 122.

[254] *Id.*

[255] 596 F. Supp. 1170 (S.D.N.Y. 1984).

ty in a conspiracy to suppress and distort intelligence as to the size of enemy forces in Vietnam prior to the Tet Offensive of 1968.

Westmoreland's theory for establishing the existence of actual malice on the part of CBS raised significant new issues for journalists and media lawyers, for he attempted to predicate actual malice largely on CBS's editing techniques, relying to a great extent on what was *left out of the broadcast* to attempt to demonstrate actual malice. A substantial element of Westmoreland's case, for example, involved comparisons between "outtakes" of raw interview tapes with the edited versions of those interviews actually shown on the broadcast. The Westmoreland suit ended through settlement before it was sent to the jury, and we thus do not have the benefit of either a trier of fact's or an appellate court's assessment of this theory of actual malice. In a significant decision denying CBS's motion for summary judgment, however, District Judge Pierce Leval held that Westmoreland's theory, in light of the evidence before the court on the summary judgment motion, was sufficient to create a triable issue of fact for the jury as to actual malice.

Judge Leval noted that a reporter is not "required to accept denials of wrongdoing as conclusive, or prefer them over apparently creditable accusations."[256] If Westmoreland's position were "supported only by such contentions of insufficient thoroughness, bloodhound-determination, and bias," Judge Leval wrote, the "defendants might well be entitled to summary judgment where they could show they had relied after investigation on apparently creditable sources."[257] Judge Leval then went on, however, to endorse the position that at some point *the editing and presentation of a story may be so imbalanced as to become evidence of actual malice:*

> Plaintiff, however, also asserts contentions of dishonesty and willful falsity in the editing and presentation of evidence. These contentions concern arguable deliberate misstatements of the evidence supporting the broadcast thesis.
>
> Although a reporter may have sufficient evidence of his charge to foreclose any material issue of constitutional malice for its publication, he may nonetheless make himself liable if he knowingly or recklessly misstates that evidence to make it seem more convincing or condemnatory than it is. If, for example, a publication asserts falsely and without basis that the charge was confirmed by an eyewitness, if in the editing process it distorts statements of witnesses so that they seem to say more than in

---

256 *Id.* at 1174.

257 *Id.*

> fact was said, or if it falsely overstates a witness' basis for his accusation, these might raise triable issues of constitutional malice in spite of a sufficient foundation for the constitutionally protected publication of the basic charge.[258]

Despite its inconclusive ending, the *Westmoreland* litigation may well have broken new ground in terms of utilizing allegedly biased editing techniques as a basis for establishing actual malice.

[5] Preconceived Story Lines

Evidence that a defendant conceived a story line in *advance* of an investigation and then consciously set out to make the evidence conform to the preconceived story is evidence of actual malice, and may often prove to be quite powerful evidence. In the aftermath of the Supreme Court's decision in *Gertz v. Robert Welch, Inc.*,[259] the litigation was remanded for a new trial. The remanded case ended in a plaintiff's victory, with one of the largest damage awards ever sustained on appeal—$100,000 in compensatory damages and $300,000 in punitive damages. In affirming the award of punitive damages, the Seventh Circuit Court of Appeals found that a finding of actual malice was supported by evidence of a preconceived story line and selection of a writer with known unreasonable propensities:

> [The editor] *conceived of a story line, solicited . . . a writer with a known and unreasonable propensity to label persons or organizations as Communist,* to write the article; and after the article was submitted, made virtually no effort to check the validity of statements that were defamatory.[260]

In a somewhat related line of reasoning, courts seem increasingly willing to take into account a publication's "image" as having a predisposition toward "sensationalist," or "hard-hitting" reportage as evidence probative of actual malice. This sort of analysis actually dates back to the famous concurring opinion of Chief Justice Warren in *Curtis*

---

[258] *Id.* (citing Goldwater v. Ginzburg, 414 F.2d 324, 327 (2d Cir. 1969), *cert. denied,* 369 U.S. 1049 (1970)); Edwards v. National Audubon Soc'y, Inc., 556 F.2d 113, 121 (2d Cir.), *cert. denied,* 434 U.S. 1002 (1977); Nader v. de Toledano, 408 A.2d 31, 40 (D.C. App. 1979), *cert. denied,* 444 U.S. 1078 (1980).

[259] 418 U.S. 323 (1974).

[260] Gertz v. Robert Welch, Inc., 680 F.2d 527, 539 (7th Cir. 1982), *cert. denied,* 103 S. Ct. 1233 (1983) (emphasis supplied).

Publishing Co. v. Butts,[261] in which he found that a finding of actual malice by the *Saturday Evening Post* was warranted in part by evidence that the *Post* was anxious to change its image by instituting a policy of "sophisticated muckraking" designed to "provoke people" and "make them mad."[262]

Similarly, in *Burnett v. National Enquirer, Inc.,*[263] in an unusually candid statement the trial court intimated (in language cited with approval on appeal) that the *Enquirer*'s editorial predispositions may have entered into the calculation of the actual malice standard. The court stated that the *Enquirer* "has absolutely no remorse for its misdeeds," and then stated that "it is the policy of the *National Enquirer* to publish two or three unflattering articles about celebrities every week."[264] This amounts, the court said, to "a form of legalized pandering designed to appeal to the readers' morbid sense of curiosity," a "style of journalism that has been enormously profitable."[265] These statements seem to indicate that the court believed that the *Enquirer* may have a predisposition to believe the worst and indeed to sensationalize the underlying facts in stories about celebrities, and that that predisposition was probative of the existence of actual malice.

More recently, the panel Court of Appeals decision in *Tavoulareas v. Washington Post Co.*[266] held that the *Washington Post*'s predisposition toward "hard-hitting investigative journalism" could be considered as evidence relevant to actual malice. The court stated that "[t]he *Post* is a newspaper which seeks, among other things, hard-hitting investigative stories."[267] Bob Woodward, the *Post*'s Assistant Managing Editor, testified at trial that he was looking for something called "a holy shit" story. The Court of Appeals opinion made a great deal of this perceived predisposition:

> What Woodward meant in exhorting his reporters to come up with the "holy shit" stories is not exactly clear, but a reasonable inference is that Woodward, as editor, wanted from his reporters the same kind of stories on which he built his own reputation: high-impact investigative stories of wrong doing . . . .

---

261 388 U.S. 130, 169 (1967) (Warren, C.J., concurring).

262 *Id.*

263 7 Med. L. Rep. (BNA) 1321 (Cal. Super. Ct., Los Angeles County, 1981), *modified,* 144 Cal. App. 3d 991, 193 Cal. Rptr. 206 (1983), *appeal dismissed,* 104 S. Ct. 1260 (1984).

264 7 Med. L. Rep. (BNA) at 1324.

265 *Id.*

266 759 F.2d 90 (D.C. Cir. 1985), *vacated,* 817 F.2d 762 (D.C. Cir.) (en banc), *cert. denied,* 108 S. Ct. 200 (1987).

267 *Id.* at 120.

> . . . From Woodward's testimony it was proper for the jurors to infer that the *Post* put some pressure on its reporters to come up with "holy shit" stories—a category into which the Tavoulareas story . . . presumably fit. Regardless of whether one chooses to characterize this policy as conducive to "hard-hitting investigative journalism," or (to borrow Chief Justice Warren's description of the policy of *The Saturday Evening Post* in *Butts*) "sophisticated muckraking," it certainly is relevant to the inquiry of whether a newspaper's employees acted in reckless disregard of whether a statement is false or not.[268]

This passage in *Tavoulareas,* coupled with the Court of Appeals somewhat restrictive interpretation of the doctrine of independent appellate review,[269] would have been a substantial inroad on the protections the press enjoys under the actual malice standard if followed.[270] The panel decision in *Tavoulareas* was vacated, however, by the entire court, en banc.[270.1] The en banc opinion turned the analysis of the panel directly on its head. The *Post*'s aggressive, adversarial style, the court noted, was in the highest tradition of serious investigative journalism.[270.2] If the adversarial system is regarded as an engine of truth by the legal system, the court argued, it would be astonishing for the law not to recognize that the system works just as effectively as an engine of truth for journalists.[270.3]

In an extremely important insight, the court differentiated between two types of pressure to produce high impact stories within a media organization. Pressure to produce such stories with little or no regard for their accuracy, the court held, *would* be legitimately probative of actual malice.[270.4] That type of pressure, however, did not exist at the *Post.*[270.5] Pressure to produce high impact stories accurately—pressure both to get the tough story *and* to get it right—is *not* probative of actual malice, however.[270.6] Only that second type of pressure existed at the *Post.*[270.7]

---

[268] *Id.* at 121.

[269] *See* Chapter 13, *infra.*

[270] For a similar prediction *see* J. Goodale, "Survey of Recent Media Verdicts, Their Disposition on Appeal, and Media Defense Costs," in Media Insurance and Risk Management 1985, at 71 (J. Lankenau, ed.) (P.L.I. publication, 1985).

[270.1] Tavoulareas v. Washington Post Co., 817 F.2d 762 (D.C. Cir.) (en banc), *cert. denied,* 108 S. Ct. 200 (1987).

[270.2] *Id.* at 795-96.

[270.3] *Id.* at 795.

[270.4] *Id.* at 796-97.

[270.5] *Id.*

[270.6] *Id.* at 797.

[270.7] *Id.*

[6] Doubt Within the Media Organization

If, prior to a publication of a story, reporters or editors connected with the media outlet in question state that they doubt the story's veracity or reliability, this may be used as evidence of actual malice.[271] In William Westmoreland's case against CBS news,[272] for example, Westmoreland presented testimony by a former CBS employee to the effect that he had voiced doubts about the premise of the broadcast, and also to the effect that the paid CBS consultant on the broadcast who originally conceived the basic story line had also expressed doubts about the underlying premises of the broadcast after first viewing it as a whole.[273]

In *Rebozo v. Washington Post Co.*,[274] Charles G. ("Bebe") Rebozo, the long time friend and confidant of former President Richard Nixon, sued the *Washington Post* because of an article that purported to link Rebozo to the cashing of stolen stock. In ruling that a material issue of fact existed as to whether the *Post* had printed the story with actual malice, the Fifth Circuit emphasized that the reporter responsible for the story had written a memorandum to his editor expressing uncertainty about whether a bank in Key Biscayne, Florida, or Rebozo himself, had cashed the stock in question.[275] The reporter stated in the memorandum that if the bank rather than Rebozo had actually cashed the stock, then the article's lead paragraph, which contained the gist of the sting of the piece, would have to be modified. The court took into consideration (1) the uncertainty expressed in the reporter's memo; (2) the fact that the reporter's final resolution of this uncertainty cast Rebozo in the worst possible light; and (3) the fact that the piece ran as a front page story, when the episode might not otherwise have commanded very much attention. For purposes of the motion for summary judgment, these factors were sufficient to raise an issue of material fact as to whether reckless disregard for the truth existed.[276]

Sometimes it is difficult to determine whether doubt expressed within a news organization about a story points to reckless disregard for the

---

[271] *See* Tavoulareas v. Washington Post Co., 759 F.2d 90, 114-17 (D.C. Cir. 1985), *vacated*, 817 F.2d 762 (D.C. Cir.) (en banc), *cert. denied*, 108 S. Ct. 200 (1987); Rebozo v. Washington Post Co., 637 F.2d 375, 382 (5th Cir.), *cert. denied*, 454 U.S. 964 (1981).

[272] Westmoreland v. CBS, 596 F. Supp. 170 (S.D.N.Y. 1984).

[273] *See* Farber, *At CBS Trial, Film Editor Cites His Complaints Concerning Documentary*, New York Times, Jan. 8, 1985, at B4, cols. 1-6.

[274] 637 F.2d 375 (5th Cir.), *cert. denied*, 454 U.S. 964 (1981).

[275] *Id.* at 382.

[276] *Id.*

truth, or just the opposite: that the publisher or broadcaster has carefully analyzed the implications of the story and decided that the story warrants publishing or broadcasting. A good example of the problem is posed by an incident in *Tavoulareas v. Washington Post Co.*[277] Prior to the appearance of the article, a copy editor at the *Washington Post* wrote a memorandum to her superior in which she stated: "I've read the Mobil story several times and while I'm impressed with the amount of work the reporter obviously did, I'm still left with an overwhelming sense of so-what?"[278] After discussing other deficiencies in the angle of the story the copy editor's memorandum stated: "A far more interesting angle, it seems to me, is Mobil's concern about Saudi preference shipping—a concern so profound that it led to the formation of an entire dummy corporation."[279] And then, in a passage heavily relied on by the plaintiff Tavoulareas, the copy editor stated: "It's impossible to believe that Tavoulareas alone could put together such a scheme for the sake of his son's business career, or that he would want to."[280]

The plaintiff underscored that final statement as proof that the *Post* published the article despite the fact that one of its editors had substantial subjective doubts about its accuracy.[281] In ruling on the *Post*'s motion for a judgment n.o.v., however, the district court held that this was a misinterpretation of the memorandum.[282] The court held that the memorandum merely stated the copy editor's subjective and uninformed opinion that she found the story implausible. She had no personal or inside information about the reporter's sources, she had not personally investigated the substance of those sources, and she presented no actual evidence in her memorandum. The memorandum, therefore, did not demonstrate that the article contained any inaccuracy. The district court noted, however, that if the copy editor had in fact personally investigated the article's substance and sources and thereafter expressed a similar statement of doubt as to the article's veracity, the plaintiff's argument might prevail.[283]

---

277 759 F.2d 90 (D.C. Cir. 1985), *vacated,* 817 F.2d 762 (D.C. Cir.) (en banc), *cert. denied,* 108 S. Ct. 200 (1987).

278 *Id.* at 114.

279 *Id.* at 115.

280 *Id.*

281 *See generally* Brill, *Inside the Jury Room at the Washington Post Libel Trial,* The American Lawyer, Nov. 1982.

282 567 F. Supp. 651, 655 (D.D.C. 1983).

283 *Id.*

The analysis was overturned by the panel Court of Appeals decision in the *Tavoulareas* case, however.[284] The Court of Appeals reasoned that the copy editor did play some "substantive" role in the editing process, and that "those *Post* employees who unquestionably had final responsibility for the article's content took her comments seriously."[285] The Court of Appeals held that the memorandum "permitted the jury to find that at least one *Post* editor who exercised some responsibility for the story had a serious doubt about the accuracy of the charge."[286]

This ruling by the panel, however, was subsequently overturned yet again by the entire Court of Appeals, reviewing the decision en banc.[286.1] The memorandum, the court held, is subject to two reasonable interpretations. It may plausibly be understood to state that the copy editor found the story impossible to believe because the story stated or suggested that Tavoulareas's primary motivation in establishing the business arrangement was to benefit his son.[286.2] As a matter of law, however, the court held that the *Post* story could not sustain that interpretation.[286.3] Second, the editor's memorandum could be interpreted more narrowly to express disbelief that Tavoulareas "set up" his son. The court held, however, that the evidence was overwhelming that the charge was substantially true.[286.4] Thus, the memorandum simply could not be connected to any false statement.

[7] A Cautionary Note

The trend that may be emerging in cases such as *Burnett, Tavoulareas,* and *Westmoreland*—taking into account such notions as "editorial balance" or "predisposition" toward sensational, muckraking, or hard-hitting journalism in assessing actual malice—carries with it some serious dangers. At the very core of our first amendment jurisprudence lies the elemental wisdom that government has no business prescribing

(*Text continued on page 3-61*)

[284] *See* 759 F.2d at 114-17.

[285] *Id.* at 116.

[286] *Id.*

[286.1] Tavoulareas v. Washington Post Co., 817 F.2d 762 (D.C. Cir.) (en banc), *cert. denied,* 108 S. Ct. 200 (1987).

[286.2] *Id.* at 794.

[286.3] *Id.* at 781.

[286.4] *Id.* at 794.

what is orthodox, genteel, or polite in politics and culture.[287] A publication or broadcast outlet is not to be penalized because of its unique boldness, style, or flair. Indeed, in an era in which one of the great *economic* tendencies in the media is toward consolidation and centralization, often resulting in "play it safe" editorial styles that make all news sound the same, the first amendment's protection for those media outlets with special courage or uniqueness is more vital then ever. To actually preconceive a story line is one thing—such an act is quite properly probative af actual malice—but merely to have an editorial image or slant is quite another. Such a slant may have little to do with actual malice, but may heavily prejudice a jury. Although as a strict matter of evidentiary relevance it may be legitimate to permit consideration of "editorial slant" to enter the actual malice determination, from the first amendment perspective admission of such evidence may well be seen by a jury as an invitation to penalize a defendant for its *image alone*, and on balance, such evidence would usually be better off excluded.

§ 3.21 Effect of Deadline Pressures on Actual Malice

[1] "Hot News" vs. Time to Investigate

Courts frequently take into account the presence or absence of time pressure in assessing the existence of actual malice, evidencing a much greater tendency to excuse errors made in a "hot news"situation.[288]

---

[287] In the words of the Supreme Court: "If there is any fixed star in our constitutional constellation, it is that no official, high or petty, can prescribe what shall be orthodox in politics, nationalism, religion, or other matters of opinion." West Virginia State Bd. of Educ. v. Barnette, 319 U.S. 624, 642 (1943).

[288] *See, e.g.,* Curtis Publishing Co. v. Butts, 388 U.S. 130, 169-70 (1967) (Warren, C.J., concurring); Associated Press v. Walker, 388 U.S. 130, 159 (1967); Golden Bear Distributing Sys. v. Chase Revel, Inc., 708 F.2d 944 (5th Cir. 1983); Goldwater v. Ginzburg, 414 F.2d 324 (2d Cir. 1969), *cert. denied,* 396 U.S. 1049 (1970); Washington Post Co. v. Keogh, 125 U.S. App. D.C. 32, 39, 365 F.2d 965, 972 (1966), *cert. denied,* 385 U.S. 1011 (1967); Simonson v. UPI, 500 F. Supp. 1261 (E.D. Wis. 1980), *aff'd,* 654 F.2d 478 (7th Cir. 1981); Shutt v. Harte-Hanks Communications, Inc., 7 Med. L. Rep. (BNA) 2559 (E.D. Mich. 1981); Widener v. Pacific Gas & Elec. Corp., 75 Cal. App. 3d 415, 434, 142 Cal. Rptr. 304 (1977), *cert. denied,* 436 U.S. 918 (1978); Briscoe v. Reader's Digest Ass'n, 4 Cal. 3d 529, 535, 93 Cal. Rptr. 866, 483 P.2d 34 (1971); Burns v. McGraw-Hill, 659 P.2d 1351 (Colo. 1983); Times Publishing Co. v. Huffstetler, 409 So. 2d 112, 113 (Fla. Dist. Ct. App.), *pet. denied,* 417 So. 2d 329 (Fla. 1982); Rood v. Finney, 418 So. 2d 1 (La. Ct. App.), *cert. denied,* 420 So. 2d 979 (La. 1982), *cert. denied,* 460 U.S. 1013 (1983); Glover v. Herald Co., 549 S.W.2d 858 (Mo.), *cert. denied,* 434 U.S. 965 (1977).

Robert Sack has cautioned against too much emphasis on the "hot news" factor, emphasizing that "[n]o publication is made without time pressure or with the ability to doublecheck every fact."[289] Courts continue, however, to pay attention to the presence or absence of deadlines, perhaps because it represents one of the more tangible elements of proof often available. Thus, for example, a California decision admonished that: "Where the defamatory statements made by the defendant do not involve an element of 'hot news' and the need for expeditious release is not present, reckless disregard for the truth may be evidenced in part by failure to investigate thoroughly and verify the facts."[290]

[2] Live Broadcasts

A live broadcast involving on-the-air callers represents the best example of "hot news," and the failure to screen out a defamatory remark uttered live is not actual malice.[291] The repetition of such a remark, however, when there has elapsed time to investigate, may constitute actual malice.[292]

§ 3.22 Bearing of a Retraction on Actual Malice

[1] Determination of Actual Malice Made at Time of Publication

It is well established that the presence or absence of actual malice must be assessed as of the time of publication of the defamatory statement.[293]

---

289 R. Sack, Libel, Slander and Related Problems § V.5.2.1. at 216, n.175 (1980).

290 Widener v. Pacific Gas & Elec. Corp., 75 Cal. App. 3d 415, 435, 142 Cal. Rptr. 304 (1977), *cert. denied*, 436 U.S. 918 (1978). *See also* Burns v. McGraw-Hill, 659 P.2d 1351 (Colo. 1983).

291 *See* Adams v. Frontier Broadcasting, Inc., 555 P.2d 556 (Wyo. 1975).

292 *See* Aku v. Lewis, 477 P.2d 162 (Hawaii 1970).

293 *See, e.g.*, New York Times v. Sullivan, 376 U.S. 254, 286 (1964); Fitzgerald v. Penthouse International, Ltd., 525 F. Supp. 585 (D. Md. 1981), *aff'd in part and rev'd in part*, 691 F.2d 666 (4th Cir. 1982), *cert. denied*, 460 U.S. 1204 (1983); Simmons Ford v. Consumers Union of the United States, Inc., 516 F. Supp. 742 (S.D.N.Y. 1981); Samborsky v. Hearst Corp., 2 Med. L. Rep. (BNA) 1638, 1640 (D. Md. 1977); Peisner v. Detroit Free Press, 104 Mich. App. 59, 304 N.W.2d 814 (1981); Dupler v. Mansfield Journal, 64 Ohio St. 2d 116, 413 N.E.2d 1187 (1980), *cert. denied*, 452 U.S. 962 (1981); Taylor v. Miskovsky, 7 Med. L. Rep. (BNA) 2408, 2410 (Okla. 1981).

[2] Failure to Retract

The mere failure of a defendant to retract or correct a story does not constitute actual malice. The leading decision on this point is the *New York Times*[294] case. The Supreme Court held that the failure by the *Times* to retract upon Sullivan's demand, although it later retracted upon the demand of Governor Patterson, was not adequate evidence of malice for constitutional purposes. "Whether or not a failure to retract may ever constitute such evidence,"[295] the Court stated, it could not in the *Sullivan* case, first, because of reasonable doubt on the part of the *Times* as to whether the advertisement could reasonably be taken to refer to Sullivan at all, and second, because the *Times* had not made a final refusal, since it asked for an explanation on how the ad referred to Sullivan.[296] Nor did the retraction upon the demand of the Governor supply the necessary proof; the Court stated, "It may be doubted that a failure to retract which is not itself evidence of malice can retroactively become such by virtue of a retraction subsequently made to another party. But in any event that did not happen here, since the explanation given by the *Times'* Secretary for the distinction drawn between respondent and the Governor was a reasonable one, the good faith of which was not impeached."[297]

Although failure to retract, or the issuance of an evasive or half-hearted retraction, is not itself actual malice,[298] there is authority for the proposition that the failure to retract may be probative of the existence of actual malice.[299] In *Golden Bear Distributing Systems v. Chase Revel, Inc.*,[300] the Fifth Circuit held that under certain circumstances evidence of a refusal by a publisher to retract a statement after it has been demonstrated to him to be both false and defamatory might be relevant in showing recklessness at the time the statement was published.[301] Similarly, in *Burnett v. National Enquirer*,[302] the court found that a finding of actual malice was in part supported by evidence that the

---

294 376 U.S. 254 (1964).

295 *Id.* at 286.

296 *Id.*

297 *Id.*

298 *See id.;* Sambrosky v. Hearst Corp., 2 Med. L. Rep. (BNA) 1638 (D. Md. 1977).

299 *See* Restatement (Second) of Torts §580A, comment d at 219 (1977).

300 708 F.2d 944 (5th Cir. 1983).

301 *Id.*

302 144 Cal. App. 3d 991, 193 Cal. Rptr. 206 (1983), *appeal dismissed,* 104 S. Ct. 1260 (1984).

"retraction proffered was evasive, incomplete, and by any standard legally insufficient."[303]

It is worth noting that the failure to retract may in some cases work to the defendant's advantage, as circumstantial evidence that no actual malice existed, because the defendant continued to believe the story not libelous.[304] In the *New York Times* case, for example, the refusal to retract was actually used by the Supreme Court as evidence of the *Times*'s reasonable belief that it had not defamed Mr. Sullivan.[305]

[3] Retraction as Evidence to Rebut Actual Malice

The issuance of a prompt retraction may be utilized by a defendant to prove the absence of actual malice.[306] While a prompt retraction is evidence of a lack of actual malice, it is not sufficient, standing alone, to establish an absence of actual malice as a matter of law.[307]

§ 3.23 Other Issues Bearing on Actual Malice

[1] Faulty Memory

A faulty memory may involve negligence, but it is not equivalent to knowledge of falsity or reckless disregard for the truth.[308] Reliance on the "faulty memory" defense, however, is not likely to be of much comfort to defense lawyers, who must worry that the trier of fact will find a reporter's protest that he or she "just forgot" the accurate information somewhat lame and self-serving.

---

303 193 Cal. Rptr. at 219.

304 *See* Tavoulareas v. Washington Post Co., 759 F.2d 90, 132 n. 51, *rehearing en banc granted,* 763 F.2d 1472 (D.C. Cir. 1985); Sack, *supra* note 289, § V.5.2.4., at 223-24.

305 New York Times Co. v. Sullivan, 376 U.S. 254 (1964).

306 *See, e.g.,* Logan v. District of Columbia, 447 F. Supp. 1328 (D.D.C. 1978); Hoffman v. Washington Post Co., 433 F. Supp. 600, 605 (D.D.C. 1977), *aff'd without opinion,* 578 F.2d 442 (D.C. Cir. 1978); Cape Publications v. Teri's Health Studio, 385 So. 2d 188 (Fla. App. 1980); Peisner v. Detroit Free Press, 104 Mich. App. 59, 304 N.W.2d 814, 816 (1981); Kuan Sing Enterprises v. T.W. Wang, Inc., 86 A.D.2d 549 (1st Dept.), *aff'd,* 58 N.Y.2d 708 (1982); DiLorenzo v. New York News, 81 A.D.2d 844, 432 N.Y.S.2d 483 (2d Dept. 1980) (substituted opinion).

307 *See* Kerwick v. Orange County Publications, 53 N.Y.2d 625, 43 N.Y.S.2d 778 (1981); DiLorenzo v. New York News, 81 A.D.2d 844, 432 N.Y.S.2d 483 (2d Dept. 1980) (substituted opinion).

308 *See* Brewer v. Memphis Publishing Co., 626 F.2d 1238, 1259 (5th Cir. 1980), *cert. denied,* 452 U.S. 962 (1981).

[2] Misuse of Language or Legal Terminology

Errors of a technical nature in the use of language, particularly errors in the use of legal terminology, normally do not create an issue of actual malice.[309] The failure, for example, to include the word "alleged,"[310] or the misdescription of what was really second degree sexual assualt as "rape"[311] does not demonstrate actual malice.[312]

In *Masson v. The New Yorker Magazine, Inc.*[312.1] the court held that actual malice in a public figure case cannot be inferred from the fabrication of quotations as long as the quotations remain relatively faithful to the substance of what was said. The case arose from a two-part article in *The New Yorker* magazine by author Janet Malcolm, on the termination of psychoanalyst Jeffrey M. Masson from his position as projects director of the Sigmund Freud archives. Malcolm had tape-recorded extensive interviews with Masson, and the article was based primarily on those tapes. Malcolm was not always faithful to the verbatim statements on the tapes, however, at times fabricating quotations.[312.2] According to Malcolm, the fabricated quotations made him appear "unscholarly, irresponsible, vain" and lacking in honesty and integrity.

The court stated that actual malice could be inferred from fabricated quotes in some circumstances, as where "the language attributed to the plaintiff is wholly the product of the author's imagination." But malice "will not be inferred from evidence showing that the quoted language does not contain the exact words used by the plaintiff provided that the fabricated quotations are either 'rational interpretations' of ambiguous remarks made by the public figure," or "do not 'alter the substantive

---

[309] *See* Orr v. Argus-Press Co., 586 F.2d 1108, 1117 (6th Cir. 1978), *cert. denied,* 440 U.S. 960 (1979); Ross v. Gore, 48 So. 2d 412, 415 (Fla. 1950).

[310] *See* Time, Inc. v. Pape, 401 U.S. 279 (1971).

[311] Simonson v. UPI, 654 F.2d 478 (7th Cir. 1981).

[312] *See* Piracci v. Hearst Corp., 263 F. Supp. 511 (D. Md. 1966), *aff'd,* 371 F.2d 1016 (4th Cir. 1967). *Cf.* Robart v. Post-Standard, 74 A.D.2d 963, 425 N.Y.S.2d 891 (1980), *aff'd,* 52 N.Y.2d 843 (1981) (decided under New York gross negligence private figure standard).

[312.1] 881 F.2d 1452, 16 Med. L. Rep. (BNA) 2089 (9th Cir. 1989).

[312.2] The quotations as they appeared in *The New Yorker* articles and the quotations on the actual tapes were frequently different. Janet Malcolm claimed that many of her quotes came from statements made by Masson when the tape recorder was not on. Nevertheless, for the purposes of the summary judgment motion in the case, the court assumed that the inconsistencies existed because Malcolm had fabricated the quotes. In several instances the closeness of the recorded version to the printed version appeared to raise the inference that Malcolm may have taken some editorial license to modify quotes to make them more pithy, biting, or literary.

content' of unambiguous remarks actually made by the public figure."[312.3]

The court's ruling on the actual malice issue in *Masson* was intertwined with its analysis of the issues of defamatory meaning. The court frequently emphasized, for example, that the incremental additional harm to Masson's reputation caused by the fabricated quotes was insignificant when measured against what Masson had in fact said. The fabricated quotes, in other words, were only marginally more damaging than the actual quotes.[312.4]

[3] Republications and Follow-Up Stories

Sometimes a media outlet will undertake republications, reaction stories, sequels, and other follow-ups to an original story. In the interregnum period between the publication or broadcast of the original story and the follow-up or sequel, new information may come to light that may shed doubt on the accuracy of the original story. When in such a republication or follow-up story no new investigation is undertaken, despite the appearance of new reasons for doubt, actual malice may exist with regard to the sequel even if the first story was protected.[313] If the new information is not brought to the publisher's attention before the time of republication or follow-up, however, or if the new information would not trigger a subjective doubt, then no issue of actual malice would be created with regard to either the follow-up or the original story.[314]

312.3 16 Med. L. Rep. (BNA) at 2092.

312.4 *See* the discussion of this problem *infra* §§ 5.08-5.11.

313 *See, e.g.*, Bindrim v. Mitchell, 92 Cal. App. 3d 61, 155 Cal. Rptr. 29, *cert. denied*, 444 U.S. 984 (1979); Good Government Group of Seal Beach, Inc. v. Superior Court, 22 Cal. 3d 672, 150 Cal. Rptr. 258, 586 P.2d 572 (1978), *cert. denied sub nom.* Good Government Group, Inc. v. Hogard, 441 U.S. 961 (1979); Walker v. Colorado Springs Sun, Inc., 188 Colo. 86, 538 P.2d 450, *cert. denied*, 423 U.S. 1025 (1975); Holter v. WLCY-TV, Inc., 366 So. 2d 445 (Fla. Dist. Ct. App. 1978), *cert. denied*, 373 So. 2d 462 (Fla. 1979); Cochran v. Indianapolis Newspapers, Inc., 175 Ind. App. 48, 372 N.E.2d 1211 (1978); Rinaldi v. Viking Penguin, Inc., 101 Misc. 2d 928 (Sup. Ct. 1979), *aff'd in part*, 73 A.D.2d 43 (1st Dept. 1980), *order aff'd*, 52 N.Y.2d 422 (1981); Restatement (Second) of Torts § 560A, comment d at 219 (1977).

314 *See* Bandelin v. Pietsch, 98 Idaho 337, 563 P.2d 395 (1976), *cert. denied*, 434 U.S. 891 (1977); Dupler v. Mansfield News Journal Co., 64 Ohio St. 2d 116, 413 N.E.2d 1187 (Ct. App. 1980), *cert. denied*, 452 U.S. 962 (1981).

[4] Hostile Investigation and Questioning

Just as the existence of common law ill will malice may be admitted as evidence probative of actual malice,[315] evidence of hostile, belligerent, or accusatory reporting or interviewing techniques may be used as circumstantial evidence of actual malice.[316] Even an offhand joke to another journalist may come back to haunt a reporter. In *Tavoulareas v. Washington Post Co.*,[317] for example, the court found relevant to the actual malice issue a statement a *Post* reporter made after an interview with a source. "It is not every day you knock off one of the seven sisters,"[318] the reporter said, referring to Mobil Oil, one of the nation's seven largest oil companies.

[5] Letters to the Editor

Letters to the editor are sometimes vituperative and defamatory, and may raise issues of actual malice with regard to both the publisher of the letter and the person who writes it. With letters to the editor, it is generally extremely difficult for the plaintiff to prevail against the publisher under the actual malice standard; in such cases the defendants normally prevail, often at summary judgment.[319] Where the letter writer acts with actual malice but the publisher is unaware of this, the publisher cannot be liable and is normally not under a duty to investigate the statements in the absence of suspicions that they are not credible.[320] The policy basis for exonerating the publisher of a letter to the editor is specially strong. As a New York court recently put it, quoting

(*Text continued on page 3-67*)

---

[315] *See supra* §3.16.

[316] *See* Jenoff v. Hearst Corp., 453 F. Supp. 514 (D. Md. 1978), *aff'd*, 644 F.2d 1004 (4th Cir. 1981); DiLorenzo v. New York News, 81 A.D.2d 844, 432 N.Y.S.2d 483 (2d Dept. 1980) (substituted opinion).

[317] 759 F.2d 90, *rehearing en banc granted*, 763 F.2d 1472 (D.C. Cir. 1985).

[318] *Id.* at 119.

[319] *See* Moriarty v. Lippe, 162 Conn. 371, 294 A.2d 326 (1972); LaPrade v. H.S. Gere & Sons, Inc., 36 N.E.2d 915 (Mass. App. 1977); Pollnow v. Poughkeepsie Newspapers, Inc., 11 Med. L. Rep. (BNA) 1528, 1532 (N.Y. App. Div., 2d Dept., 1985) (decided under New York's *Chapadeau* standard); Safarets, Inc. v. Gannett Co., 80 Misc. 2d 109, 361 N.Y.S.2d 276, *aff'd*, 49 A.D.2d 666, 373 N.Y.S.2d 858 (3d Dept. 1974); Kruteck v. Schimmel, 27 A.D.2d 837, 278 N.Y.S.2d 25 (2d Dept. 1967); Cera v. Mulligan, 79 Misc. 2d 400, 358 N.Y.S.2d 642, *aff'd*, 47 A.D.2d 797, 365 N.Y.S.2d 99 (4th Dept. 1974); El Paso Times, Inc. v. Trexler, 447 S.W.2d 403 (Tex. 1969).

[320] *See generally supra*, §3.17. For one of the few exceptions holding a publisher potentially liable in such a situation *see* Weaver v. Pryor Jeffersonian, 569 F.2d 967 (Okla. 1977) (reversing grant of summary judgment).

Lord Denning: "when a citizen is troubled by things going wrong, he should be free to write to the newspaper, and the newspaper should be free to publish his letter. It is often the only way to get things put right."[321] As letters to the editor are very much in the American tradition of free speech, courts ought to be extremely cautious before imposing liability on the publishers of such letters.[322]

§ 3.24 The Constitutional Definition of Negligence Under *Gertz*

The combined impact of *Gertz v. Robert Welch, Inc.*[323] and *Dun & Bradstreet, Inc. v. Greenmoss Builders, Inc.*[324] is to require a demonstration of negligence by all private figure plaintiffs in cases involving defamatory speech on matters of public concern.[325]

The Court's opinion in *Gertz* did not actually use the word "negligence." Instead, the Court stated that "so long as they do not impose liability without fault, the States may define for themselves the appropriate standard of liability for a publisher or broadcaster of defamatory falsehood injurious to a private individual."[326] Across the country, however, lower courts interpreted the "fault" requirement as establishing negligence as the minimum standard of culpability that the first amendment would tolerate in a suit by a private figure subject to *Gertz.*[327] Although a handful of states adopted standards for such cases of fault

---

[321] Pollnow v. Poughkeepsie Newspapers, Inc., 11 Med. L. Rep. (BNA) 1528, 1532 (N.Y. App. Div., 2d Dept., 1985) (quoting Slim v. Daily Telegraph, 1 All Eng. Rep. 497, 503 (1968) (per Lord Denning)).

[322] Actions directly against the writer of the letter appear to be easier for plaintiffs under the actual malice standard; the reported cases indicate more mixed results. *Compare* De Loach v. Maurer, 130 Ga. App. 824, 204 S.E.2d 776 (1974) (held actionable) *and* Wright v. Haas, 586 P.2d 1093 (Okla. 1978) (same), *with* Sparks v. Boone, 560 S.W.2d 236 (Ky. App. 1977) (held not actionable) *and* Cera v. Mulligan, 79 Misc. 2d 400, 358 N.Y.S.2d 642, *aff'd,* 47 A.D.2d 797, 365 N.Y.S.2d 99 (4th Dept. 1974) (not actionable). In Pollnow v. Poughkeepsie Newspapers, Inc., 11 Med. L. Rep. (BNA) 1528 (N.Y. App. Div., 2d Dept., 1985), for example, the defendant newspaper was granted summary judgment, but the court refused to dismiss the cause of action against the individual letter writer. *Id.* at 1533.

[323] 418 U.S. 323 (1974).

[324] 105 S. Ct. 2939 (1985).

[325] *See supra* §§ 3.01-3.05.

[326] 418 U.S. at 346.

[327] *See, e.g.,* Troman v. Wood, 62 Ill. 2d 184, 340 N.E.2d 292 (1975); Gobin v. Globe Publishing Co., 216 Kan. 223, 531 P.2d 76 (1975); Franklin, *What Does "Negligence" Mean in Defamation Cases,* 6 Comm/Ent L.J. 259, 260 (1984). *See* the roster of citations in §3.10, *supra.*

more onerous than conventional negligence,[328] none attempted to dip below that standard.

To say that "negligence" is required in cases brought against the media by private figure litigants, however, is not to say that the term is necessarily translatable with complete ease from the realm of physical torts such as car accidents or slips on banana peels to the realm of publishing or broadcasting.[329] The states have essentially been faced with two approaches to the negligence standard: the "professional negligence" standard, which equates negligence on the part of journalists with negligence for professionals such as doctors and lawyers,[330] and an "ordinary reasonable person" standard, which approaches negligence in the more routine sense employed for nonprofessional torts.[331]

§ 3.25 The "Professional Malpractice" Model of Negligence

[1] In General

A number of states have adopted the professional model in analyzing negligence cases when a media outlet is the defendant.[332] Presumably, states that follow the professional model would revert to an ordinary reasonable person standard when the defendant is not a media outlet.[333] The rationale for the professional negligence model is that the purpose of the negligence requirement of *Gertz* is to ensure the existence of adequate breathing space for free expression. Although *Gertz* does not require *as much* breathing space in private figure cases as in public figure cases subject to the actual malice standard, it still fulfills an important role as a first amendment buffer zone for the press, and as

---

328 *See* citations in §§ 3.11-3.12, *supra.*

329 *See* Anderson, *Libel and Press Self-Censorship,* 53 Tex. L. Rev. 422, 480 (1975).

330 *See infra* § 3.20.

331 *See infra* § 3.21.

332 *See* Triangle Publications v. Chumley, 317 S.E.2d 534, 537 (Ga. 1984); Gobin v. Globe Pub. Co., 216 Kan. 223, 531 P.2d 76 (1975); Martin v. Griffin Television, Inc., 549 P.2d 85 (Okla. 1976); Benson v. Griffin Television, Inc., 593 P.2d 511, 513 (Okla. App. 1978); Maressa v. New Jersey Monthly, 89 N.J. 176, 445 A.2d 376, 388, *cert. denied,* 459 U.S. 907 (1982) (citing Curtis Publishing Co. v. Butts, 388 U.S. 130, 155 (1967) (opinion of Harlan, J.)); Seegmiller v. KSL, Inc., 626 P.2d 968 (Utah 1981).

333 *Cf.* Restatement (Second) of Torts § 580B comment g, at 228 (1977) (contrasting role of custom in media and nonmedia cases).

such must take into account the realities of the newsroom.[334] Just as malpractice cases against doctors and lawyers tend to turn on compliance with custom in the profession, the states that adopt the professional negligence standards in defamation cases essentially treat such cases as journalistic malpractice suits. Borrowing from medical and legal malpractice trends, such a standard could import differing treatment for the "local" journalistic outlet than for the "national" outlet, just as medical cases may apply the "locality rule,"[335] or they may adopt the more flexible approach of examining the resources, time pressures, and content of the publication or broadcast outlet and comparing the conduct of the defendant to conduct at comparable outlets.[336] Similarly, just as specialists in medical cases are held to the level of care of others within the speciality, journalists could theoretically be subcategorized and held to prevailing customs in each area—radio, television, newspaper, magazine, or, even more radically, "gossip magazine," "investigative journalism," or "mainstream network" news.[337] The development of these sorts of detailed subdivisions within the professional model, however, does not seem very likely; courts will probably look to industry standards in a more generalized sense.

The professional model necessarily requires the plaintiff to embark on the tricky business of establishing the journalistic standard. The complexity of this enterprise alone may be enough to dissuade some courts from using the professional approach. How are the procedures of the *Washington Post* to be compared with those of *The Nation, People Magazine, Penthouse, The National Enquirer,* or *Atlantic Monthly,* when each publication is likely to develop its own ethics, procedures, and practices? As one commentator has observed:

> Responsible publishers do not have the generally recognized standards

---

[334] *See* Seegmiller v. KSL, Inc., 626 P.2d 968, 976 (Utah 1981).

[335] Although the locality rule in medical cases still has adherents, it is on the decline. For applications of the rule, *see, e.g.*, Fisk v. Soland, 8 Ariz. App. 585, 448 P.2d 429 (1968); Stanley v. Fisher, 417 N.E.2d 932 (Ind. App. 1981). For recent rejections of the locality rule in favor of a national standard of professional medical care, *see, e.g.*, Robbins v. Footer, 553 F.2d 123 (D.C. Cir. 1977); Sullivan v. Henry, 160 Ga. App. 791, 287 S.E.2d 652 (1982).

[336] For discussion of the analogous approach in modern medical cases *see* W. Prosser, W. Keeton, D. Dobbs, R. Keeton, and D. Owen, Prosser and Keeton on Torts § 32, at 188 (5th ed. 1984). For a case taking into account the financial resources of the defendant in a media context, *see* Greenberg v. CBS, Inc., 69 A.D.2d 693, 419 N.Y.S.2d 988 (2d Dept. 1979).

[337] *See* Franklin, *supra* note 327, at 265.

normally associated with traditional, learned professions. They possess no equivalent of generally accepted accounting principles, the Financial Accounting Standards Board statements, the American Institute of Architects' standards, or a Code of Professional Responsibility.

Furthermore, I doubt that universal standards could be adopted by the press. Aside from the constitutional problems inherent in adopting even self-imposed rules of professional conduct for journalists, nothing suggests that the profession could reach consensus on the issue. Every press room has an established mode of operation and a set of journalistic ethics that is unique. Guidelines in one organization are not even an issue for discussion in another.[338]

[2] The *Restatement*'s Adoption of the Professional Model

The *Restatement of (Second) Torts* has adopted the professional model of negligence for defamation cases.[339] The *Restatement's* position in this regard is consistent with its overall approach to negligence in professions or trades. The *Restatement*'s general pronouncement of the standard of care applicable to someone undertaking a profession or trade states: "Unless he represents that he has greater or less skill or knowledge, one who undertakes to render services in the practice of a profession or trade is required to exercise the skill and knowledge normally possessed by members of that profession or trade in good standing in similar communities."[340]

Section 229 of the *Restatement* applies to any person who undertakes to render services to another in the practice of a profession, such as a physician or surgeon, dentist, pharmacist, attorney, accountant, or engineer.[341] It also applies, the *Restatement* maintains, to any person who undertakes to render services for others in the practice of a skilled trade, such as an airline pilot, a precision machinist, an electrician, a carpenter, a blacksmith, or a plumber.[342] In defending its adoption of a professional standard for defamation, the *Restatement* explicitly refers to these other professional applications.

---

338 Daniels, *Public Figures Revisited,* 25 Wm. & Mary L. Rev. 957, 959 (1984). *See also* Anderson, *supra* note 329, at 455 ("Fundamental disagreements exist within the profession concerning what constitutes responsible journalism").

339 Restatement (Second) of Torts §580B comment g (1977).

340 *Id.* at § 299A.

341 *Id.* at § 299A comment b.

342 *Id.*

[3] The Role of Custom and Expert Testimony

The *Restatement* takes the position that a professional disseminator of news, a newspaper, magazine, or broadcasting station for example, or an employee of such a disseminator, such as a reporter, should be held to the skill and experience normally possessed by members of that profession, and that "[c]ustoms and practices within the profession are relevant in applying the negligence standard, which is, to a substantial degree, set by the profession itself."[343] Custom, however, is *not* controlling.[344]

Evidence of custom within the profession of news dissemination would normally come from a person shown to be qualified on that subject.[345] Presumably the expert would be required to establish his or her expertise in the particular form of media involved—radio or television broadcasting, magazine reportage, or newspaper reportage, for example. As a practical matter, however, expert testimony at trial to establish journalistic standards has been extremely rare.[346]

§ 3.26 The "Ordinary Reasonable Person" Model of Negligence

Many jurisdictions have eschewed the *Restatement* approach and simply adopted the traditional tort "ordinary reasonable person" standard of care in defamation cases governed by the fault requirement of *Gertz*.[347] The rationale for the ordinary negligence standard is the argument that the professional negligence model is too solicitous of the media, and not sufficiently protective of private figure plaintiffs.[348] Be-

---

343 *Id.* at § 580B comment g, at 228.

344 *Id.*

345 *See* Seegmiller v. KSL, Inc., 626 P.2d 968 (Utah 1981); McCrory, "Development of the Defense of Constitutional Privilege in Libel Law," 667, at 821, in Communications Law 1984 (J. Goodale, ed.) (Practising Law Institute Publication 1984).

346 McCrory, *supra* note 345, at 821.

347 *See, e.g.*, Little Rock Newspapers v. Dodrill, 281 Ark. 25, 660 S.W.2d 933, 938 (1983); Troman v. Wood, 62 Ill. 2d 184, 340 N.E.2d 292 (1975); McCall v. Courier-Journal & Louisville Times, 623 S.W.2d 882 (Ky. 1981), *cert. denied*, 456 U.S. 975 (1982); Schrottman v. Barnicle, 386 Mass. 627, 437 N.E.2d 205 (1982); Memphis Publishing Co. v. Nichols, 569 S.W.2d 412 (Tenn. 1978).

348 Professor David Anderson offers an interesting critique of the professional model from a somewhat different perspective: that it would "discriminate unjustifiably against media or outlets whose philosophies and methods deviate from those of the mainstream." Anderson, *supra* note 329, at 455.

cause the professional model invites the members of the profession to set their own standards of care, there is the concern that the whole industry will collectively downgrade its officially recognized principles of conduct.[349] Since proof of deviation from professional standards normally requires expert testimony, there is also the concern that the sort of "conspiracy of silence" that makes it difficult for plaintiffs to obtain testimony of malpractice from a medical practitioner's peers might also plague the legitimate efforts of plaintiffs in libel suits. Furthermore, some courts have reasoned that the professional model is only justified when the field involved cannot be understood without resort to technical expert testimony, whereas media negligence cases normally involve issues that a layperson can readily comprehend.[350] The Arkansas Supreme Court, for example, faced with the assertion that a plaintiff's evidence was insufficient because he "failed to provide any expert witness to testify to the standard of care of a publisher," responded: "We think the jury is capable of making that determination without being dependent on expert testimony."[351] Anyone, these cases seem to intimate, can understand the job of a reporter or editor.

§ 3.27 Application of Res Ipsa Loquitur

It is conceivable that in some circumstances the doctrine of res ipsa loquitur may be applicable in a defamation case.[352] Traditionally, the res ipsa loquitur doctrine, which permits the trier of fact to draw an inference of negligence, requires three conditions: (1) the event must be of a kind which ordinarily does not occur in the absence of negligence; (2) it must be caused by an agency or instrumentality in the exclusive control of the defendant; (3) it must not have been due to any voluntary action or contribution on the part of the defendant.[353] Although some types of journalistic errors may meet all these conditions, defamation actions do not on the whole seem appropriate for res ipsa loquitur. Courts should be circumspect in permitting the doctrine of res ipsa loquitur to act as a substitute for actual testimony on the negligence issue, for permitting a jury to indulge its own inference that the media

---

349 *See* Troman v. Wood, 62 Ill. 2d 184, 198, 340 N.E.2d 292, 298-99 (1975).

350 *See* Little Rock Newspapers v. Dodrill, 281 Ark. 25, 660 S.W.2d 933, 938 (1983); Kohn v. West Hawaii Today, Inc., 656 P.2d 79, 83 (Hawaii 1982).

351 Little Rock Newspapers v. Dodrill, 281 Ark. 25, 660 S.W.2d 933, 938 (1983).

352 *See* Restatement (Second) of Torts § 580B comment g, at 228 (1977).

353 *See* Prosser and Keeton, *supra* note 336, § 39, at 244.

defendant acted negligently from the mere fact of publication of the defamation comes perilously close to an invitation to slip into strict liability analysis. The *Restatement* cautions against the use of res ipsa loquitur, expressing the concern that lay inferences of negligence may inadvertently result in a jury nullification of the constitutional standard of negligence and permit a de facto decision by the jury to impose strict liability.[354]

§ 3.28 Determination of Negligence

[1] The Cost/Benefit Approach

In general courts appear to apply traditional tort cost/benefit style analysis[355] in assessing the negligence issue, weighing such matters as the cost of further investigation, the cost of further delay in publishing the story (i.e., whether it is "hot news"), and the importance of the interests being promoted by the speech, against the probability of foreseeable harm to the plaintiff's reputation, including the reliability of the sources for the story, the seriousness of the defamatory charges, and their inherent plausibility.[356]

[2] Contexts in Which Negligence May Arise

The *Restatement (Second) of Torts* lists five contexts in which the question of fault may arise. They are:

(1) Fault in the publication to a third party. (A communication mailed directly to the defamed through the fault of the defendant comes to the attention of a third party, for example.)
(2) Fault regarding the truth or falsity of the communication. (A

---

[354] Restatement (Second) of Torts § 580B comment g, at 228.

[355] This sort of cost/benefit analysis is a major component of modern tort law; it is usually traced to the famous algebraic formula of Judge Learned Hand in United States v. Carroll Towing Co., 159 F.2d 169, 173-74 (2d Cir. 1947), under which a party is deemed negligent if the "burden" (B) is less than the injury (L) multiplied by the probability of its occurrence (P), or, if $B < PL$.

[356] *See, e.g.*, Triangle Publications, Inc. v. Chumley, 317 S.E.2d 534, 537 (Ga. 1984); Troman v. Wood, 62 Ill. 2d 184, 340 N.E.2d 292 (1975); Memphis Publishing Co. v. Nichols, 569 S.W.2d 412 (Tenn. 1978); Torres-Silva v. El Mundo, 106 D.P.R. 15, 3 Med. L. Rep. (BNA) 1508, 1511 (Puerto Rico 1977); Restatement (Second) of Torts § 580B comment h (1977); Franklin, *supra* note 327, at 266.

statement is false, for example, despite a bona fide but unreasonable belief in its truth.)

(3) Fault concerning the defamatory character of the communication. (For example, a statement not defamatory on its face is made so because of extrinsic facts which should have been known to the defendant.)

(4) Fault in the content of the communication. (For example, a statement is rendered defamatory through a typographical error or slip of the tongue or use of words with more than one meaning.)

(5) Fault in the reference to the plaintiff. (For example, a reference to another person or fictitious person is, through the defendant's fault, reasonably understood as referring to the plaintiff.)[357]

The common law always required fault for liability to be imposed in regard to the first of these possible types of fault, publication to a third party.[358] The remaining four species of fault all deal with whether the communication falsely defamed the plaintiff. For each of them the common law position was to impose liability despite the lack of fault, although a special exception existed in the case of the "secondary publisher," who was not liable unless he was at fault in failing to discover a defamatory passage.[359]

In *Gertz*,[360] the Supreme Court was concerned with the second sort of fault listed, the truth or falsity of the communication, and thus negligence is clearly also required in cases subject to *Gertz* on the truth or falsity issue. With regard to the final three instances of fault listed in the *Restatement*, the common law position of strict liability was not explicitly overruled in *Gertz*. The logic of the *Gertz* opinion, however, would seem to apply to those three species of fault as well. The only reference to any of them in the majority opinion in *Gertz* is the statement in the Court's conclusion that fault should be required "at least . . . where . . . the substance of the defamatory statement makes substantial danger

---

357 Restatement (Second) of Torts § 580B comment b (1977). For an excellent review of the fault issues relevant to truth or falsity, applicability to the plaintiff, and the defamatory character of the speech, *see* Franklin & Bussel, *The Plaintiff's Burden in Defamation: Awareness and Falsity,* 25 Wm. & Mary L. Rev. 825 (1984).

358 *See* Restatement (Second) of Torts § 577A (1977).

359 *Id.* at § 580B comment b, and § 581.

360 Gertz v. Robert Welch, Inc., 418 U.S. 323 (1974).

to reputation apparent."[361] This reference apparently refers to fault with regard to the defamatory character of the communication, item (3) on the *Restatement* list, intimating that strict liability would be inappropriate with regard to the question of the defamatory character of the defamation.[362] Similarly, the logic of *Gertz* would seem to require fault with regard to both the content of the communication, item (4), and the reference to the plaintiff, item (5). It does not seem sensible under *Gertz* to impose liability because of a typographical error, for example, or to permit liability to be imposed when the speaker intended to refer to one person and reasonably expected the recipient of the communication to understand that reference, but was, without fault, misunderstood as referring to the plaintiff.[363]

[3] Typical Recurring Negligence Problems

Below is a nonexhaustive list of typical recurring negligence issues, each of which is discussed in greater detail in the sections that follow. Negligence problems typically arise because of:

(1) failure to pursue further investigation;
(2) unreasonable reliance on sources;
(3) unreasonable formulation of conclusions, inferences, or interpretations;
(4) errors in note-taking and quotation of sources;
(5) misuse of legal terminology;
(6) mechanical or typographical errors;
(7) unreasonable screening or checking procedures;
(8) the failure to follow established internal practices and policies.

In dealing with these sorts of errors, courts give them greater or lesser weight depending on the overall assessment of costs and benefits in the case (as discussed in subsection [1] above), and pay particular attention to the presence or absence of time pressures.[364]

---

[361] *Id.* at 348 (quoting Curtis Publishing Co. v. Butts, 388 U.S. 130, 155 (1967)).

[362] Fong v. Merena, 655 P.2d 875, 877 (Hawaii 1982).

[363] *See generally* Restatement (Second) of Torts § 580B, comments d, e and f (1977); Franklin & Bussel, *supra* note 357, at 842-46.

[364] The relevance of the time element is discussed in § 3.35, *infra*.

§ 3.29 Negligence Arising from General Failure to Pursue Further Investigation

Under the actual malice standard it is a settled proposition that actual malice is not established by the mere failure to pursue further investigation of a story before publishing.[365] The opposite is true under the negligence standard: Failure to pursue further investigation when an ordinary reasonable person or (in the case of the professional negligence model) when an ordinary reasonable publisher would have further investigated is negligence.[366] Findings of negligence from breakdowns in investigation most frequently involve either unreasonable reliance on sources[367] or the drawing of damaging inferences and conclusions without further checking.[368]

§ 3.30 Unreasonable Reliance on Sources as Negligence

[1] In General

The single most common predicate for a finding of negligence in media cases involves a determination that the defendant unreasonably relied on the original source for the story.[369] Although other areas of the law have developed reasonably detailed guidelines for when an informant's tip can reasonably be trusted,[370] very little analogous guidance exists concerning when journalists may safely rely on a source. Very few media outlets follow the famous "two source" rule that evolved at the *Washington Post* during Watergate coverage.[371] In the rare situation in

---

365 *See* St. Amant v. Thompson, 390 U.S. 727, 733 (1968). *See generally supra* § 3.17.

366 *See, e.g.*, Mathis v. Philadelphia Newspapers, Inc., 455 F. Supp. 406 (E.D. Pa. 1978); Kohn v. West Hawaii Today, 656 P.2d 79 (Hawaii 1982); E.W. Scripps Co. v. Cholmondelay, 569 S.W.2d 700 (Ky. Ct. App. 1978); Gazette v. Harris, 325 S.E.2d 713 (Va. Sup. Ct. 1984).

367 *See infra* § 3.24.

368 *See infra* § 3.25.

369 *See, e.g.*, Mathis v. Philadelphia Newspapers, Inc., 455 F. Supp. 406 (E.D. Pa. 1978); Jenoff v. Hearst Corp., 453 F. Supp. 541 (D. Md. 1978), *aff'd*, 644 F.2d 1004 (4th Cir. 1978); Peagler v. Phoenix Newspapers, Inc., 114 Ariz. 308, 560 P.2d 1216 (1977); Thomas H. Maloney & Sons v. E.W. Scripps Co., 43 Ohio App. 2d 105, 334 N.E.2d 494 (1975); Franklin, *supra* note 327, at 267.

370 The issue is reasonably well developed in the field of criminal procedure, for example.

371 *See* Daniels, *supra* note 338, at 959 ("The famous two-source rule from Watergate days is a procedure that was followed by one group of reporters, on one story, at one newspaper") (citing C. Bernstein & B. Woodward, All the President's Men 79 (1974)

which two sources are required, it is usually because the sources remain anonymous or confidential.[372] Verification by two sources does not automatically insulate the media from liability; even reliance on two sources can sometimes be negligent.[373]

[2] Official Sources

Reliance on an official source will not always insulate a media outlet from liability under the negligence standard. In *Mathis v. Philadelphia Newspapers, Inc.*,[374] the plaintiff's picture was wrongly included by the defendant newspaper in a list of local bank robbery suspects, because it had been included in photographs of suspects provided by the FBI. The court held that reliance on the FBI report would not, as a matter of law, insulate the defendant from a finding of negligence.[374.1] On the other hand, *Wilson v. Capital City Press*,[375] held that reliance on an address list provided by the Louisiana State Police was not negligent as a matter of law.

§ 3.31 Negligence in the Formulation of Conclusions, Inferences, and Interpretations

[1] In General

Again, in contrast to the actual malice standard, which normally permits the drawing of even the harshest inferences from available evidence against a plaintiff if not done in the face of subjective doubt about a story,[376] under the negligence standard the drawing of unreasonable conclusions, inferences, and interpretations is sufficient to impose liabil-

---

("Gradually, an unwritten rule was evolving: unless two sources confirmed a charge involving activity likely to be considered criminal, the charge was not used in the paper.")).

372 *See* Franklin, *supra* note 327, at 268, n.55 (citing G. Tuchman, Making News 85 (1978)).

373 *See* E.W. Scripps Co. v. Cholmondelay, 569 S.W.2d 700 (Ky. Ct. App. 1978).

374 455 F. Supp. 406 (E.D. Pa. 1978).

374.1 *See also* Boettiger v. Loverro, 555 A.2d 1234 (Pa. 1989) (newspaper could be held liable for invasion of privacy for publishing parts of a wiretap transcript obtained from a criminal case file made available by a court clerk. The printing was in violation of state wiretap laws which makes such transcripts confidential and the fact that the government discloses them does not convert them to public information).

375 315 So. 2d 393 (La. App. 1975).

376 *See supra* § 3.15[3].

ity. In *KARK-TV v. Simon*,[377] for example, a television station broadcast an erroneous news report concerning an alleged robbery; included in the report was film footage of the plaintiffs being placed in a police squad car. The report was based only upon uncorroborated information received over a police scanner, and upon an eyewitness account by a reporter who did not know the circumstances surrounding the events she had observed. The Arkansas Supreme Court held that the TV station could not, as a matter of law, be said to have acted with due care.

Similarly, in *Memphis Publishing Co. v. Nichols*,[378] the defendant printed an article stating that Mrs. Nichols, the plaintiff, had been shot by a Mrs. Newton, after Mrs. Newton appeared at the Nichols home and found Mr. Newton with Mrs. Nichols. The story clearly created the implication of an adulterous relationship between Mrs. Nichols and Mr. Newton. This was in fact erroneous, for Mrs. Nichols and Mr. Newton were not alone at the Nichols home—also there at the time were Mr. Nichols and two neighbors, all of whom were talking together in the living room. The newspaper based the story on the arrest record of the shooting incident, which made no mention of those at the house other than Mrs. Nichols and the Newtons. The trial court directed a verdict for the defendant on the grounds, among others, that basing the story on the arrest record precluded a finding of fault. This judgment was reversed on appeal, the court reasoning that a trier of fact could find negligence in the reporter's drawing of conclusions merely on the arrest report, and in the reporter's failure to further investigate the story or to wait for a more complete police report, which was actually filed a few days later.

By contrast, in *Benson v. Griffin Television, Inc.*,[379] the defendant broadcast a story implying that the police suspected that the plaintiff was involved in a bank robbery, a story that was incorrect. The reporter had concluded that the plaintiff was a suspect because the police, having converged on a house that might have been the plaintiff's, had questioned the occupants of the house about the plaintiff's whereabouts. The reporter also gathered information that some police officials had said that the plaintiff had been seen in a car thought to have been used in the robbery. The truth was that the plaintiff was never actually con-

---

377 280 Ark. 228, 656 S.W.2d 702 (1983). *See also* Seegmiller v. KSL, Inc., 626 P.2d 968 (Utah 1981) (broadcast gave misleading portrait of plaintiff's horse business because of certain erroneous conclusions on the part of the reporter).

378 569 S.W.2d 412 (Tenn. 1978).

379 593 P.2d 511 (Okla. Ct. App. 1978).

sidered a suspect. The defendant's summary judgment verdict was upheld on appeal, the appellate court observing that although the report was erroneous, it "reasonably reflects what a reporter could have concluded based on the undisputed facts. The reporter noted what he observed, was reasonably faithful to those observations, and displayed no indifference or negligence regarding their accuracy."[380]

[2] Contradictory Information

Sometimes a reporter or editor becomes aware of contradictory evidence concerning the story. Arguably, the existence of contradictory information should trigger a duty on the part of the ordinary reasonable reporter to investigate the story further. There is some authority, however, for the position that as long as a reporter who cannot reasonably determine the truth presents a balanced report of the dispute, it cannot be said that the reporter acted without due care.[381] This analysis blends into the controversial doctrine of neutral reportage, an issue discussed later in this volume.[382]

§ 3.32 Negligence in Note Taking and Quoting of Sources

Perhaps no protestation concerning media reportage is more common than the claim that "I was misquoted." However much the press may regard this cliché as the after-the-fact rationalization of an embarrassed source, misquotations and other note-taking errors may constitute sufficient grounds for liability under the negligence standard.

In *Schrottman v. Barnicle,*[383] for example, the purported negligence consisted of quoting the allegedly defamatory and false statement that "life on Blue Hill Avenue . . . is 'o.k. if you're a nigger.' "[384] The plaintiff denied that he ever made the statement. The court held that the trier of facts should "consider the testimony concerning [the reporter's] note-taking and research methods, as well as the clarity and reliability of the notes themselves. This evidence should be viewed in light of circumstances including the relative risk of harm and the presence or ab-

---

380 *Id.* at 514.

381 *See* Peagler v. Phoenix Newspapers, Inc., 131 Ariz. 308, 312, 640 P.2d 1110, 1114 (1982); Robertson, *Defamation and the First Amendment: In Praise of* Gertz v. Robert Welch, Inc., 54 Tex. L. Rev. 199, 264 (1976).

382 *See infra* § 4.15.

383 386 Mass. 627, 437 N.E.2d 205 (1982).

384 *Id.* at 628, 437 N.E.2d at 207.

sence of time constraints against verification."[385] The *Schrottman* example raises the question of whether there is a need in some circumstances to verify a quotation taken directly from a source, even if that quotation does not itself implicate others or create a contradiction within the available evidence.[386] The problem for the journalist is that normally the only way to verify a direct quotation from the source is to rely on a tape recording of the interview, another witness who heard the statement, or to go back to the source itself to ask for a verification. Going back to the source, however, creates both journalistic problems and a problem of proof later at trial, if the story results in litigation. Perhaps, as a journalistic matter, the source should not in some circumstances be given the opportunity to correct the original statement, which might have been embarrassing but accurate. The second time around, a contradictory or sanitized version of the "truth" may come from the source. The better view, and the view more in keeping with the realities, is that if the reporter is confident in and reasonably believes in the accuracy of the original quotation, it is reasonable journalistic practice not to seek a second verification from the source. As a practical matter, of course, when there is no corroboration and such an issue reaches litigation, it will often come down to a credibility choice for the trier of fact.

In *Masson v. The New Yorker Magazine Inc.*,[386.1] malice was not inferred from published quotations that did not contain plaintiff's exact words, since the fabricated quotations were either rational interpretations of ambiguous remarks made by the plaintiff or did not alter the substantive content of any unambiguous remarks actually made by the plaintiff.[386.2]

It is worth noting that the misquotation or transcription error giving rise to the allegations of negligence need not involve the plaintiff's own statements, but may arise from alleged errors in recording the information of other sources.[387]

---

[385] *Id.* at 641, 437 N.E.2d at 214.

[386] Franklin, *supra* note 327, at 269.

[386.1] 881 F.2d 1452, 16 Med. L. Rep. (BNA) 2089 (9th Cir. 1989).

[386.2] *Id.*

[387] *See, e.g.*, Jones v. Sun Publishing Co., 292 S.E.2d 23 (S.C. 1982). *Cf.* Phillips v. Evening Star Newspaper Co., 2 Med. L. Rep. (BNA) 2201 (D.C. Sup. Ct. 1977), *aff'd*, 424 A.2d 78 (D.C. 1980) (error in reporting information from police records).

§ 3.33 Negligence Through Misuse of Language or Legal Terminology

Negligence may exist because of a misuse of language, for example the erroneous use of a corporate name in a manner that carries defamatory meaning,[388] or the misuse of a legal term. The most famous example is *Time, Inc., v. Firestone.*[389] *Time* reported the grounds for the Firestones' divorce as "extreme cruelty and adultery," and quoted the trial judge's remark that the testimony would "make Dr. Freud's hair curl." The trial judge in the Firestone divorce action had in fact stated that there was testimony that both Firestones had engaged in frequent extramarital sex, and that some of the testimony "would have made Dr. Freud's hair curl." The only inaccuracy in the brief two-sentence *Time* article was that the grounds of the divorce were "extreme cruelty and adultery." The trial court actually made no formal finding of adultery, even though adultery had been alleged in Russell Firestone's pleadings. Rather, the trial court made no finding at all as to the grounds for the decree. The Florida Supreme Court concluded that the basis of the judgment was actually "lack of domestication of the parties," a ground not pleaded and not theretofore recognized by Florida law.[390]

What, then, could possibly have been negligent about *Time's* assumption, an assumption that most qualified Florida lawyers probably would have made, that the only pleaded grounds recognized by Florida law at the time of the judgment—extreme cruelty and adultery—were in fact the grounds for the judge's decision? The answer offered by the Florida Supreme Court, which the United States Supreme Court was prepared to accept, was that *Time* had engaged in "flagrant" "journalistic negligence," because it had not realized that adultery could not possibly have been the basis of the decree, since Florida law prohibited an award of alimony to a wife found guilty of adultery, and Mary Alice Firestone had been awarded alimony.[391] This is an extreme, hyperlegalistic view of negligence, and a precedent for misuse of legal terminology that appears to call for great caution by the press in reporting such events.[392]

---

[388] *See* Lake Havasu Estates, Inc. v. Reader's Digest Ass'n, 441 F. Supp. 489 (S.D.N.Y. 1977). *See also* Forrest v. Lynch, 347 So. 2d 1255 (La. Ct. App. 1977).

[389] For a more detailed review of the case, *see supra* § 2.08[1].

[390] *See* Firestone v. Firestone, 263 So. 2d 223, 225 (Fla. 1972).

[391] Firestone v. Time, Inc., 305 So. 2d 172, 178 (Fla. 1974), *vacated and remanded,* 424 U.S. 448 (1976).

[392] For a critique of this aspect of *Firestone, see Smolla, supra* note 29, at 60-61.

§ 3.34 Negligence Arising from Mechanical Errors or Lapses in Internal Procedures

[1] Mechanical Errors

Negligence may be established through lapses in screening and checking procedures,[393] errors in proofreading,[394] or the inadvertent inclusion of defamatory material.[395] These sorts of relatively mechanical errors normally do not entail any journalistic judgment and are the most clearly analogous to the standard fault problems in a routine tort case.[396] Typographical errors are so commonplace, however, particularly in mass daily publications such as newspapers, that courts have shown a willingness to excuse them on the theory that the instance of some typographical errors is simply a constant and virtually unavoidable occurrence in some forms of publication.[397] Even an expert golfer will hit a bad shot from time to time, without being negligent.[398]

[2] Failure to Follow Established Policies and Practices

The failure of a defendant to follow its own established editorial procedures may be sufficient proof to create a finding of negligence. In *Kohn v. West Hawaii Today, Inc.*,[399] for example, a plaintiff demonstrated through testimony of the newspaper's own personnel that in not checking certain police records the paper failed to follow its own normal editorial procedures. The court held this sufficient to allow the trier of fact to conclude that the newspaper was negligent. Despite the plaintiff's failure to produce testimony from any outside expert witnesses as to customs and practices within the newspaper industry, the court held, deviation from the proper standard of care was established through evidence of the defendant's own customs and practices.

The use of proof that the internal rules and procedures of a defen-

---

393 *See* Triangle Publications, Inc. v. Chumley, 317 S.E.2d 534 (Ga. 1984).

394 *See* Franklin, *supra* note 327, at 271 and n.71.

395 *See* Pettengill v. Booth Newspapers, Inc., 88 Mich. App. 587, 278 N.W.2d 682 (1979).

396 *See* Franklin, *supra* note 327, at 271.

397 *See, e.g.*, Nussbaum v. Lacopo, 27 N.Y.2d 311, 319, 317 N.Y.S.2d 347, 353, 265 N.E.2d 762, 767 (1970); Chapadeau v. Utica Observer-Dispatch, Inc., 38 N.Y.2d 196, 200, 341 N.E.2d 569, 572, 379 N.Y.S.2d 61, 65 (1975).

398 Nussbaum v. Lacopo, 27 N.Y.2d 311, 319, 317 N.Y.S.2d 347, 353, 265 N.E.2d 762, 767 (1970).

399 656 P.2d 79, 83 (Hawaii 1982).

dant have been violated to build a negligence case is an increasingly popular tool in tort law generally,[400] and may evolve as a significant plaintiff's weapon in defamation litigation.[400.1]

(*Text continued on page 3-83*)

---

400 *See generally* Thropp v. Bache Halsey Stuart Shields, Inc., 650 F.2d 817 (6th Cir. 1981); Babcock v. Chesapeake & Ohio Railway Co., 83 Ill. App. 3d 919, 38 Ill. Dec. 841, 404 N.E.2d 265 (1979). *See also* Winters, *The Evidentiary Value of Defendant's Safety Rules in a Negligence Action*, 38 Neb. L. Rev. 906 (1959).

400.1 *But see* Florida Star v. B.J.F., 109 S. Ct. 2603 (1989) (the fact that the newspaper breached its own internal policy of not publishing the names of rape victims was mentioned by the Supreme Court, but was not employed by the Court in holding that there was no cause of action as a matter of law).

§ 3.35 Time Pressures and Deadlines

As in the case of the actual malice standard,[401] the existence or nonexistence of deadline pressures has an important bearing on the negligence determination. The *Restatement* strongly emphasizes the time element,[402] calling for inquiry into whether the communication was "a matter of topical news requiring prompt publication to be useful, or was it one in which time and opportunity were freely available to investigate."[403]

§ 3.36 Vicarious Liability (Respondeat Superior)

[1] In General

Vicarious liability principles apply to defamation actions just as they do in tort law generally: The "master" is normally liable for the tortious conduct of the "servant," but not for the tortious conduct of an "independent contractor."[404] There is a division of authority, however, on when an employer is liable for punitive damages arising from a "malicious tort" of an employee.[405] Each of these issues is discussed below.

[2] Employee's Fault Is Imputed to Employer

In *Cantrell v. Forest City Publishing Co.*,[406] the Supreme Court reaffirmed the general principle of vicarious liability in media cases, stating that while there was "no evidence that Forest City Publishing Co. had knowledge of the inaccuracies contained in [the reporter's] article," there was "sufficient evidence for the jury to find that [the reporter's] feature was within the scope of his employment at the *Plain Dealer* and that Forest City Publishing Co. was therefore liable under traditional

---

401 *See supra* § 3.16.

402 *See* Restatement (Second) of Torts § 580B comment h, at 228 (1977).

403 *See, e.g.*, Golden Bear Distributing Sys. v. Chase Revel, Inc., 708 F.2d 944 (5th Cir. 1983); Phillips v. Evening Star Newspaper Co., 424 A.2d 78, 83 (D.C. 1980); Triangle Publications, Inc. v. Chumley, 317 S.E.2d 534, 537 (Ga. 1984); Liquori v. Republican Co., 8 Mass. App. Ct. 671, 678 n.7 (1979); Benson v. Griffin Television, Inc., 593 P.2d 511, 514 (Okla. Ct. App. 1978); Memphis Publishing Co. v. Nichols, 569 S.W.2d 412 (Tenn. 1978).

404 *See generally* Prosser and Keeton, *supra* note 336, §§ 69-71, at 499-516.

405 *See id.*, § 70, at 505-06.

406 419 U.S. 245 (1974).

doctrines of *respondeat superior.*"[407] Both actual malice and negligence on the part of employees may be imputed to the employer, including reporters, staff writers, editors, and any other "in house" personnel.[408]

[3] Must the Employee Have Editorial or Policy-Making Responsibility?

There is some ambiguity as to whether fault by any employee within an employer's organization will be imposed, or whether the employee must have policy-making or editorial responsibility. The issue of threshold liability is in turn sometimes confused with the separate question of who within the corporate hierarchy must "ratify" a malicious act in order to trigger punitive damages.

With regard to cases tried under the negligence standard, courts appear to assume without discussion that the negligence of any employee, from editor to reporter to typesetter, is sufficient.[409] With regard to actual malice, there are decisions holding that the conduct of radio announcers, reporters, and copy editors may be imputed to the employer.[410]

In the *Tavoulareas* litigation, the court, in discussing the relevance of a copy editor's conduct, stated that "[t]he *Post* cannot avoid liability merely by pointing to responsibilities assigned in the newspaper's organizational chart. That an employee's or agent's job duties are so limited is relevant but not dispositive."[411] The proposed jury instructions in *Westmoreland v. CBS*[412] provide an interesting illustration of this issue:

---

407 *Id.*

408 *See, e.g.*, Tavoulareas v. Washington Post Co., 759 F.2d 90, 116-17, *rehearing en banc granted*, 763 F.2d 1472 (D.C. Cir. 1985); Embrey v. Holly, 293 Md. 128, 442 A.2d 966 (1982); Karaduman v. Newsday, 51 N.Y.2d 531, 547, 416 N.E.2d 557, 435 N.Y.S.2d 556 (1980); DiLorenzo v. New York Times, Inc., 81 A.D.2d 844, 432 N.Y.S.2d 483 (2d Dept. 1980).

409 The negligence cases discussed in §§ 3.23-3.29, *supra*, involve the imputed negligence of employees at all levels of the defendants' organizations.

410 *See* Cantrell v. Forest City Publishers Co., 419 U.S. 245 (1974) (reporter); Tavoulareas v. Washington Post Co., 759 F.2d 90 (D.C. Cir. 1985), *rehearing en banc granted*, 763 F.2d 1472 (D.C. Cir. 1985); Embrey v. Holly, 293 Md. 128, 442 A.2d 966 (1982) (radio broadcaster).

411 Tavoulareas v. Washington Post Co., 759 F.2d at 116. This sort of inquiry may involve internal expressions of doubt about a story, which was the case in *Tavoulareas*. *See supra* § 3.15[5].

412 596 F. Supp. 170 (S.D.N.Y. 1984).

> For each defendant . . . you must answer whether that defendant had the prohibited state of mind.
> How do you answer that question for the defendant CBS, which is a corporation and does not have a state of mind? To determine this as to CBS, you look at the beliefs of the persons CBS charged with responsibility for the content of the broadcast.[413]

The instructions then listed as the CBS personnel with responsibility for the content of the broadcast, the producer, the chief correspondent, the paid consultant, the associate producer, the executive producer, the senior producer, and the vice-president and director of public affairs.[414]

[4] Fault of Independent Contractors Normally Not Imputed to Employer

The general rule is that a publisher is not vicariously liable for the fault of an independent contractor, such as a nonstaff author, free-lance writer, independent columnist, or wireservice.[415]

An important caveat to this rule, however, is that the publisher is always liable for its *own* state of mind, and if, for example, information is received to put the publisher on notice of possible falsehood, an independent issue of actual malice or negligence on the part of the publisher itself may arise.[416]

[5] Punitive Damages

The majority rule is that the doctrine of vicarious liability applies to "malicious torts" and renders the employer in a libel case responsible

---

413 Westmoreland v. CBS, Proposed Jury Instructions, *reprinted in* Libel on Trial: The Westmoreland and Sharon Cases, BNA Special Report, Appendix 2, at 17 (1985).

414 *Id.*

415 *See, e.g.*, Hotchner v. Castillo-Puche, 551 F.2d 910 (2d Cir.), *cert. denied*, 434 U.S. 834 (1977); Bindrim v. Mitchell, 92 Cal. App. 3d 61, 155 Cal. Rptr. 29, *cert. denied*, 444 U.S. 984 (1979); Nader v. de Toledano, 408 A.2d 31 (D.C. App. 1979), *cert. denied*, 444 U.S. 1078 (1980); Mehau v. Gannett Pacific Corp., 658 P.2d 312 (Hawaii 1983); Rinaldi v. Holt, Rinehart & Winston, 42 N.Y.2d 369, 336 N.E.2d 1299, *cert. denied*, 434 U.S. 969 (1977).

416 *See* Bindrim v. Mitchell, 92 Cal. App. 3d 61, 155 Cal. Rptr. 29, *cert. denied*, 444 U.S. 984 (1979) (no vicarious liability for first publication of author's book, but when publisher received notice of defamatory falsehood prior to second publication, fault could be found). This is essentially a restatement of the general proposition that suspicious circumstances concerning an independent source's information may trigger a duty to investigate further and create a fault issue. *See, e.g.*, Pep v. Newsweek, Inc., 553 F. Supp. 1000 (S.D.N.Y. 1983); Alioto v. Cowles Communications, Inc., 430 F. Supp. 1363 (N.D. Cal. 1977), *aff'd*, 623 F.2d 616 (9th Cir. 1980), *cert. denied*, 449 U.S. 1102 (1981).

for punitive as well as compensatory damages.[417] A substantial minority of jurisdictions, however, including California, New York, the District of Columbia, Idaho, New Mexico, North Dakota, Ohio, Texas, Vermont, Virginia, and Wisconsin do not permit punitive tort damages to be vicariously imposed unless the employer ratified, participated in, or authorized the employee's conduct.[418] This is the *Restatement* position.[419] The corporate authorization, ratification, or participation may be actual or implied,[420] but generally the activity or acquiescence of executives, high officers, or principal managers within the organizational heirarchy is required.[421]

---

417 *See, e.g.*, Embrey v. Holly, 293 Md. 128, 142 A.2d 966 (1982).

418 Sack, *"Common Law Libel and the Press—A Primer"* in 2 Communications Law 1984, at 607, 653 (J. Goodale, ed.) (Practising Law Institute Publication 1984) (citing Smith-Johnson Motor Corp. v. Hoffman Motors Corp., 411 F. Supp. 670 (E.D. Va. 1975); Remeikis v. Boss & Phelps, Inc., 419 A.2d 986 (D.C. App. 1980); Hartman v. Shell Oil Co., 68 Cal. App. 3d 240, 137 Cal. Rptr. 244 (4th Dist. 1977)).

419 Restatement (Second) of Torts § 909 (1979). *See also* Williams v. New York, 508 F.2d 356 (2d Cir. 1974). On the standards applicable to punitive damages in defamation generally, *see* Chapter 9, *infra.*

420 *See* Bailey v. Gulf Insurance Co., 389 F.2d 889 (10th Cir. 1968).

421 *See* Reiser v. District of Columbia, 563 F.2d 462 (D.C. Cir. 1977); Gill v. Montgomery Ward & Co., 284 A.D. 36, 129 N.Y.S.2d 288 (3d Dept. 1954); Restatement (Second) of Torts § 909 (1979); Sack, *supra* note 428, at 654.

CHAPTER 4

Defamatory Meaning

§ 4.01 The Definition of Defamatory

A substantial number of defamation suits turn on the issue of whether the words involved are capable of sustaining a defamatory meaning. Over the years the various verbal formulas for defining what is defamatory have proliferated; today there are almost as many verbal formulas as there are jurisdictions.[1]

The *Restatement (Second) of Torts* indicates that "a communication is defamatory if it tends so to harm the reputation of another as to lower him in the esteem of the community or to deter third persons from association or dealing with him."[2] William Prosser emphasized a popular, common sense definition, stating that that which is defamatory "tends to injure 'reputation' in the popular sense, to diminish the esteem, respect, good-will, or confidence in which the plaintiff is held, or to excite adverse, derogatory or unpleasant feelings or opinions against him."[3]

One popular approach is to define "defamatory" by stringing together a long litany of colorful pejoratives. Barron Parke's definition is "a publication, without justification or lawful excuse, which is calculated to injure the reputation of another, by exposing him to hatred, contempt or ridicule."[4] Following this example, one frequently encounters definitions of "defamatory" phrased in terms of a communication which "exposes any person to hatred, contempt, ridicule, or obliquy or which causes him to be shunned or avoided or which has a tendency to injure him in his occupation."[5] New York, not to be outdone, defines defamatory as "words which tend to expose one to public hatred, shame, obloquy, contumely, odium, contempt, ridicule, aversion, ostracism, degradation or disgrace, or to induce [an] evil opinion of one in the minds of right-thinking persons, and to deprive one of their confi-

---

[1] *See generally,* W. Prosser, W. Keeton, D. Dobbs, R. Keeton & D. Owen, *Prosser and Keeton on Torts* § 111, at 773 (5th ed. 1984).

[2] Restatement (Second) of Torts § 559 (1977).

[3] Prosser and Keeton, *supra* note 1, § 111, at 773.

[4] Parmiter v. Coupland, 6 M. & W. 105, 109, 151 Eng. Rep. 340, 342 (1840), *quoted in* L. Eldredge, The Law of Defamation § 7, at 31 (1978).

[5] Gallagher v. Johnson, 611 P.2d 613 (Mont. 1980).

dence and friendly intercourse [in] society."[6] Despite the number of colorful variations, however, no complete comprehensive definition is possible, or even desirable,[7] for the essence of the term, whether stated in a long list of adjectives or a short and sweet capsule, is the tendency to injure reputation.[8] As is often the case in the law of torts, the general verbal formulas are of little practical use. Just as general definitions of negligence decide very few cases, general definitions of what is defamatory provide little intelligible guidance to the practical lawyer. The problem of what is "defamatory" is more realistically viewed as a collection of specialized rules developed in recurring situations.

§ 4.02 The Recipient Approach

[1] In General

All of the verbal formulas used to define defamation are recipient-oriented,[9] looking at the effect of the communication on those who receive it.[10] The law has always realized, however, that not all recipients will react to the communication in the same way. The same statement about a person may generate feelings of contempt and ridicule on the part of some and feelings of esteem and honor on the part of others. On emotionally charged issues the value structure of the recipient will be critical in determining whether, in the mind of that recipient, the communication is defamatory.[11]

---

6 Kimmerle v. New York Evening Journal, Inc., 262 N.Y. 99, 102, 186 N.E. 217 (1933).

7 *See* Newell v. Field Enterprises, Inc., 91 Ill. App. 3d 735, 415 N.E.2d 434 (1980)("each case must be decided on its own facts"); Galvin v. Gallagher, 81 Ill. App. 3d 927, 401 N.E.2d 1243 (1980)(same); Catalano v. Pechous, 69 Ill. App. 3d 797, 805, 387 N.E.2d 714, 721 (1978)(same).

8 *See, e.g.*, Schultz v. Reader's Digest Ass'n, Inc., 468 F. Supp. 551 (E.D. Mich. 1979); Burns v. McGraw-Hill Broadcasting Co., 659 P.2d 1351 (Colo. 1983); Byars v. Kolodziej, 48 Ill. App. 3d 1015, 1017, 363 N.E.2d 628, 630 (1977); Denny v. Mertz, 84 Wis. 2d 654, 267 N.W.2d 304 (1978), *subsequent appeal*, 106 Wis. 2d 636, 318 N.W.2d 141, *cert denied*, 459 U.S. 883 (1982).

9 *See* Franklin & Bussel, *The Plaintiff's Burden in Defamation: Awareness and Falsity*, 25 Wm. & Mary L. Rev. 825, 828 (1984).

10 *See* Restatement (Second) of Torts § 559 comment e (1977). *See also* Grant v. Reader's Digest Ass'n, 151 F.2d 733 (2d Cir. 1945)(Hand, J.), *cert. denied*, 326 U.S. 797 (1946).

11 For example, for a doctor to be called an abortionist might raise deeply conflicting responses. Those who basically endorse the Supreme Court's decisions on the issue of abortion would certainly not consider a doctor who assists a woman in exercising this constitutional right as any less deserving of their esteem. On the other hand, to a substan-

[2] The English Approach

In response to the problem created by the differing effects that a communication may have on various recipients, the English tradition evolved an approach that concentrated on the effect of the communication in the eyes of society at large, if there was a clear social consensus as to the societal value system, or, in the alternative, on the effect in the eyes of the "reasonable man."[12] Thus, in *Miller v. David,*[13] it was held that a statement that an artisan favored a nine-hour workday was not defamatory, even though the statement caused the artisan to be blacklisted by local contractors and to suffer other damage, because many other people also approved of the longer workday. Similarly, in *Mawe v. Pigott,*[14] an Irish priest was accused of informing on members of a group of Catholic insurgents, an accusation that would obviously cause deep resentment among many Catholics. The court held, however, that the accusation was not defamatory, because the ordinary reasonable person would not think less of someone for disclosing another's criminal activities. Thus, the consensus as it evolved in England was that "it is not enough to prove that the words spoken rendered the plaintiff obnoxious to a limited class."[15]

[3] The American Approach

The English approach seemed to require that the words be defamatory in the eyes of "right-thinking" people.[16] In the United States, however, this notion was rejected.[17] The "right-thinking" phraseology was laden with problems. The first amendment normally requires that all governmental regulation of speech be content-neutral; the government is not empowered to prescribe what is orthodox or acceptable in mat-

---

tial number of Americans, abortion is a reprehensible act, and any doctor who performs one is likely to trigger deep feelings of contempt and aversion in those persons.

[12] *See* Prosser and Keeton, *supra* note 1, § 111, at 777 (citing Tolley v. J.S. Fry & Sons, 1 K.B. 467, A.C. 333 (1931)).

[13] 9 L.R. - C.P. 118 (1874), *discussed in* Franklin & Bussel, *supra* note 9, at 829 n.14.

[14] 4 Ir. R - C.L. 54 (1869).

[15] Leetham v. Rank, 57 Sol. J. 111 (1912).

[16] *See* Grant v. Reader's Digest, Inc., 151 F.2d 733 (2d Cir. 1945), *cert. denied,* 326 U.S. 797 (1946).

[17] *See* Prosser and Keeton, *supra* note 1, § 111, at 777; Franklin & Bussel, *supra* note 9, at 829 n.14.

ters of politics, religion, or morality.[18] When a court presumes to pick and choose among various false forms of communication—deciding that some false statements are actionable as libelous because "right-thinking" people would find them reprehensible, while other false communications equally damaging to the reputation of the plaintiff among certain segments of society should not be deemed libelous because those segments of society are "wrong-thinking"—the court enters onto extremely dangerous first amendment ground.

Sensitivity to these notions, and a common sense frustration with the "right-thinking" terminology, soon led the formula in this country away from the English approach. The new American version took hold as a result of Justice Holmes's opinion in a 1909 Supreme Court decision, *Peck v. Tribune Co.*[19] An advertisement in the *Tribune* carried the implication that the plaintiff (who abstained from the use of alcohol), a nurse, "enjoyed" the use of malt whiskey. The Court of Appeals, following the English rule, held that although some people would consider the use of whiskey "wrong," and although "there may be people among whom to be a nurse is considered something less desirable than not to be a nurse," the "world has not yet arrived at a consensus of opinion on these matters, that to say these things of a person is, independently of all other considerations, to libel him."[20] The Supreme Court, through Justice Holmes, reversed, concluding that no general consensus need exist as to whether drinking whiskey or being a nurse is discreditable. Justice Holmes wrote:

> [I]t appears to us that such inquiries are beside the point. It may be that the action for libel is of little use, but while it is maintained it should be governed by the general principles of tort. If the advertisement obviously would hurt the plaintiff in the estimation of an important and respectable part of the community, liability is not a question of a majority vote.
>
> We know of no decision in which this matter is discussed upon principle. But obviously an unprivileged falsehood need not entail universal hatred to constitute a cause of action. No falsehood is thought about or even known by all the world, no conduct is hated by all. That it will be known by a large number and will lead *an appreciable fraction of that*

---

[18] *See* West Virginia State Bd. of Educ. v. Barnette, 319 U.S. 624, 642 (1943)("no official, high or petty, can prescribe what shall be orthodox in politics, nationalism, religion, or other matters of opinion").

[19] 214 U.S. 185 (1909).

[20] 154 F. 330, 333 (7th Cir. 1907), *rev'd*, 214 U.S. 185 (1909).

number to regard the plaintiff with contempt is enough to do her practical harm.[21]

The Holmes approach in the *Peck* case became the prevailing American view. In *Grant v. Reader's Digest Association, Inc.*,[22] Judge Learned Hand added his imprimatur to the Holmes approach. In that case, the plaintiff had been accused of being a legislative representative for the Massachusetts Communist Party. Judge Hand noted that although it might be true that right-thinking people would not harbor negative feelings for someone merely because he was an agent for the Communist Party or a sympathizer with its aims and means, the rule, in New York at least, was that the statement could still be actionable. Judge Hand noted that although some defamation decisions seemed to make it a condition that to be actionable the words must be such as would affect "right-thinking" people, and that such appeared to be the recognized rule in England, no such limitation existed in New York. Similarly, in *Katapodis v. Brooklyn Spectator, Inc.*,[23] the court held that the imputation of extreme poverty might be actionable, although certainly "right-thinking" people ought not shun or despise or otherwise condemn a person because he is poor. Following the tradition of these cases, the mainstream American approach today, as expressed in the *Restatement*, is to determine whether the communication would be derogatory in the view of a "substantial and respectable minority."[24]

[4] Limitations on the American Position

Even the liberal American position as to the nature of the group in whose estimation one is defamed has its limits. Under the dominant American approach, for example, "it is not enough that the communication would be derogatory in the view of a single individual or a very small group of persons, if the group is not large enough to constitute a substantial minority."[25]

Aside from the size of the group, the group's position must be at least

---

21 214 U.S. at 189-90 (emphasis supplied).

22 151 F.2d 733 (2d Cir. 1945), *cert. denied*, 326 U.S. 797 (1946).

23 287 N.Y. 17, 38 N.E.2d 112 (1941).

24 Restatement (Second) or Torts § 559 comment e, at 157 (1977).

25 *Id. See also* McBride v. Merrell Dow and Pharmaceuticals, Inc., 717 F.2d 1460 (D.C. Cir. 1983); Brown & Williamson Tobacco Corp. v. Jacobson, 713 F.2d 262 (7th Cir. 1983); Burns v. McGraw-Hill Broadcasting Co., 659 P.2d 1351 (Colo. 1983).

minimally "respectable."[26] Some communication, although obviously defamatory in the eyes of a substantial segment of the community, may be nonactionable because the sentiments of that segment are so antisocial or so against officially recognized public policy that it would not be proper for the court to recognize them.[27] Prior to the Supreme Court's 1954 decision in *Brown v. Board of Education,*[28] for example, a number of defamation decisions, some from the 1950s, held that it was defamatory for a white person to be improperly described as black.[29] A holding like this would be unconscionable today. Even if a plaintiff could show that in a particular community attitudes were such that to be labeled black would indeed lower the plaintiff in the esteem of a substantial number of persons, the views of those persons are antithetical to federal constitutional policies, and hence it would be improper for a state to lend them credence through its tort system.

Similarly, to erroneously call a Democrat a Republican,[30] or to label someone a "liberal,"[31] or a "conservative,"[32] is not defamatory.

---

26 *See* Ingalls v. Hastings & Sons Publishing Co., 304 Mass. 31, 22 N.E.2d 657 (1939)("considerable and respectable class in the community").

27 Restatement (Second) of Torts § 559 comment e, at 158-59 (1977).

28 347 U.S. 483 (1954).

29 *See* Jones v. R.L. Polk & Co., 190 Ala. 243, 67 So. 577 (1915); Upton v. Times-Democrat Publishing Co., 104 La. 141, 28 So. 970 (1900); Natchez Times Publishing Co. v. Dunigan, 221 Miss. 320, 72 So. 2d 681 (1954); Bowen v. Independent Publishing Co., 230 S.C. 509, 96 S.E.2d 564 (1957); Spencer v. Looney, 116 Va. 767, 82 S.E. 745 (1914).

30 *See* W. Prosser, J. Wade & V. Schwartz, Cases and Materials on Torts 985 n.4 (7th ed. 1982).

31 Steinman v. Di Roberts, 23 A.D.2d 693, 257 N.Y.S.2d 695 (1965). *See also* Frinzi v. Hanson, 30 Wis. 2d 271, 140 N.W.2d 250 (1966).

32 Haas v. Evening Democrat Co., 252 Iowa 517, 107 N.W.2d 444 (1961). Nor, apparently, is it defamatory to imply that a law professor teaches an "easy" course. In Kaplan v. Newsweek Magazine, Inc., 10 Med. L. Rep. (BNA) 2142 (N.D. Cal. 1984), Professor John Kaplan, of the Stanford Law School, brought an action for libel and intentional infliction of emotional distress against the publication *Newsweek On Campus*, a special version of *Newsweek* published for college students, for an article entitled "A Giggle of Guts," which appeared both in the regular edition of *Newsweek* and the special *Newsweek On Campus* supplement. Students around the country had responded to interviews requesting their suggestions for "gut" or "mick" courses. One of the nominated courses was Professor Kaplan's criminal law class, taught to undergraduates at Stanford. The court, while sympathizing with his anger and dismay, dismissed Professor Kaplan's claim, stating that the material in the article did not impugn his ability, intellectual standards, or performance as a professor, viewed from the perspective of an average reader, and was not libelous. *Id.* at 2143. The court also dismissed Professor Kaplan's claim for infliction of emotional distress, noting that in a later edition *Newsweek* published Professor Kaplan's letter airing his feelings of outrage at the article, and that the magazine also corrected a factual error it had made regarding the professor's take-home examination. *Id.*

[5] Effect of the Passage of Time

Time is an important component of the social context in which the allegedly defamatory statement must be construed. Time may turn an accusation that would once have been defamatory into an accusation that is not actionable,[33] or turn an accusation once deemed innocent into one now deemed defamatory. To label someone a communist or a communist sympathizer may in one epoch be regarded as not defamatory,[34] but with the fluctuation of attitudes later be almost universally regarded as actionable.[35]

§ 4.03 Name-Calling, Insults, Epithets, and Verbal Abuse

The common law has always differentiated sharply between genuinely defamatory communications as opposed to obscenities, vulgarities, insults, epithets, name-calling, and other verbal abuse. No matter

---

[33] *See* the race example, discussed at text accompanying note 29, *supra.*

[34] Allegations of membership or sympathy with the Communist Party once produced very mixed results. *Compare* Garriga v. Richfield, 174 Misc. 315, 20 N.Y.S.2d 544 (1940) (not defamatory) *and* McAndrew v. Scranton Publishing Co., 364 Pa. 504, 72 A.2d 780 (1950)(same), *with* Grant v. Reader's Digest, Inc., 151 F.2d 733 (1945), *cert. denied,* 326 U.S. 797 (1946)(defamatory) *and* Ward v. League for Justice, 93 N.E.2d 723 (Ohio App.), *appeal dismissed,* 154 Ohio St. 367, 95 N.E.2d 769 (1950).

[35] *See* Herrmann v. Newark Morning Ledger Co., 48 N.J. Super, 420, 138 A.2d 61 (1958)(defamatory), *second appeal,* 49 N.J. Super. 551, 140 A.2d 529 (1958); Toomey v. Farley, 2 N.Y.2d 71, 156 N.Y.S.2d 840, 138 N.E.2d 221 (1956). It is worth remembering that in Gertz v. Robert Welch, Inc., 418 U.S. 323 (1974), there was apparently no dispute that statements calling the plaintiff a "Leninist" and "Communist-fronter" were defamatory.

Some forms of defamatory association have substantial staying power over time—such as implications relating to Nazism. In *Shockley v. Cox Enterprises, Inc.*, 10 Med. L. Rep. (BNA) 1222 (N.D. Ga. 1983), an action was brought by Dr. William Shockley, who shared the Nobel Prize for Physics in 1956 for his part in inventing the transistor, but who in more recent years has become well known for his theories on genetics and human intelligence. *Id.* at 1222. It is Dr. Shockley's belief that human intelligence is largely genetically determined, and that as a general proposition the I.Q.'s of blacks are lower because blacks are genetically inferior to whites. *Id.* An *Atlanta Constitution* article generally critical of Dr. Shockley's theories included the statement that Shockley's proposed program "was tried out in Germany in World War II." The court held that that statement was actionable for libel because the sentence appeared to equate Dr. Shockley's voluntary sterilization program with Nazi experiments conducted on living human beings and the Nazi effort to eliminate all Jews through mass murder. *Id.* at 1223. (At trial, Shockley ultimately prevailed, but the jury award was only one dollar.)

how mean or vulgar, such language is not defamatory.[36] It is not defamatory, for example, to call someone a "bastard,"[37] or a "son of a bitch,"[38] or an "idiot."[39] No matter how obnoxious, insulting, or tasteless such name-calling, it is regarded as a part of life for which the law of defamation affords no remedy. "Mere general abuse and scurrility, however ill-natured and vexatious, is no more actionable when written than spoken, if it does not convey a degrading charge or imputation."[40] The law's traditional position is that vulgar or obscene speech reflects more on the character of the user of the language than on its object.[41]

When the vituperative language goes beyond mere swearing and insult and into the realm of actual factual misstatement about the plaintiff, however, the communication may become defamatory. Thus to call someone a "bitch" may not, standing alone, be defamatory, but to add to it the express statement or implication that the person is sexually promiscuous changes what was at first a mere vulgar insult into a defamatory misstatement of fact. In *Brooks v. Stone*,[42] for example, a publication entitled the *Cadaver*, published by students at a medical college in Georgia, received a "letter to the editor" from a nurse complaining about the allegedly offensive content of the publication. Her letter ended with the statement: "Editors—I appeal to you. Make the *Cadaver* a paper everyone can read. There *is* a difference in humor and trash. If you do—maybe the *Cadaver* will be in the hands of students more—and at the bottom of bird cages less." The editors included the following statement in their reply: "We have backgrounds different from the rest of you. Our mothers were German Shepherds, our fathers were Camels, so naturally we love to hump bitches in heat. Say, Ms.

36 *See, e.g.*, Church of Scientology v. Cazares, 638 F.2d 1272 (5th Cir. 1981); Held v. Pokorny, 583 F. Supp. 1038 (S.D.N.Y. 1984); Lamelza v. Bally's Park Place, Inc., 580 F. Supp. 445 (E.D. Pa. 1984); Crozman v. Callahan, 136 F. Supp. 466 (W.D. Okla. 1955); Moriarty v. Lippe, 162 Conn. 371, 294 A.2d 326 (1972); Rice v. Simmons, 2 Del. 417 (1838); Stanely v. Taylor, 4 Ill. App. 3d 98, 278 N.E.2d 824 (1972); Durr v. Smith, 90 So. 2d 147 (La. Ct. App. 1956); Bartow v. Smith, 149 Ohio St. 301, 305, 78 N.E.2d 735, 737 (1948); Blouin v. Anton, 139 Vt. 618, 431 A.2d 489 (1981).

37 *See* Curtis Publishing Co. v. Birdsong, 360 F.2d 344 (5th Cir. 1966).

38 *See* Moriarty v. Lippe, 162 Conn. 371, 294 A.2d 326 (1972); Notarmuzzi v. Shevack, 108 N.Y.S.2d 172 (1951)(not defamatory to state: "You are a bleached blond bastard, goddamn son of a bitch, and a bum and a tramp; get the hell out of here.").

39 *See* Cowan v. Time, Inc., 41 Misc. 2d 198, 245 N.Y.S.2d 723 (1963).

40 Curtis Publishing Co. v. Birdsong, 360 F.2d 344, 348 (5th Cir. 1966).

41 *Id.*

42 170 Ga. App. 457, 317 S.E.2d 277 (1984).

Brooks, when do you come in season?"[43] A divided Georgia Court of Appeals held that the words were actionable. The majority opinion stated that until the use of the words "When do you come in season" the material was not actionable. The court held, however, that the last sentence, together with the word "bitches," rendered the letter reasonably susceptible of a defamatory meaning.[44]

§ 4.04 Rhetorical Hyperbole

[1] Relation to the Fact/Opinion Distinction

Closely related to the problem of separating mere insults from actual defamatory speech is the problem of separating defamatory communication from rhetorical hyperbole. The problem of rhetorical hyperbole is resolved by the law of defamation under two analytical approaches. The first is to classify the particular word as understood in some sense other than its most literal one, and then to state that the word, as actually understood, did not carry a defamatory meaning. The second approach, which is often intertwined with the first, is to classify the hyperbolic statement not as a statement of fact at all but rather as a statement of opinion, and thus to render it immune from attack for defamation under both the common law and constitutional doctrines that prohibit opinion from forming the basis of a defamation suit. Reli-

---

43 317 S.E.2d at 278.

44 Conflicting affidavits had been provided on the summary judgment motion. The defendant's affidavit stated that the magazine was risqué and off-color but had become accepted as a forum for humor, and as understood in this context was a sort of safety valve for student frustrations within the medical community. Counteraffidavits, however, stated that the understanding of the editorial reply among some readers was that the nurse's character and chastity had been impugned by the suggestion that she was a "bitch in heat," with the connotation that she was sexually promiscuous and someone with whom the editors would like to have sex. The dissenting judges argued that however crude and insulting the letter may have been, it did not make any factual statement at all with regard to the nurse, *id.* at 281-82 (Banke, J., dissenting), nor did it even purport that the editors knew her. While the reply demonstrated sarcastic contempt for her morals and good taste, any defamatory implications in the reply were directed to the editors themselves rather than to the nurse. A second dissenting Judge added the point that the nurse, in writing to the *Cadaver* and calling its contents "sick," "junk," "trash," and something "to be dug out of the garbage chute," purposefully instigated the exchange of words. She "deliberately poked at a hornet's nest, she should not now be allowed to seek salve for her stings from this court." *Id.* (Sognier, J., dissenting).

ance on the fact/opinion distinction[45] is probably the more common solution, but in many situations it may be a shorter and simpler matter to hold that the particular word, although defamatory when used in its literal sense, was not understood in its literal sense, and in the sense that it actually was understood was not defamatory.

[2] *Greenbelt v. Bresler*

The classic case illustrating this problem is the Supreme Court decision from 1970, *Greenbelt Cooperative Publishing Association v. Bresler.*[46] In the *Greenbelt* case, a real estate developer sought a zoning variance from the city council. At the same time the city council was seeking to acquire an unrelated tract of land owned by the same developer. The developer took advantage of this leverage and drove an extremely hard bargain with the city. A newspaper reporter stated that some persons at a public meeting involving the city's dealings with the developer had characterized the developer's behavior as "blackmail." The plaintiff claimed that the newspaper's use of the term "blackmail" was defamatory, arguing that the newspaper knew that the developer had committed no such crime, and that the use of the phrase in the article constituted an intentional and knowing use of a falsehood. The Supreme Court rejected this claim, however, and held that as a matter of constitutional law the use of the word "blackmail" in the particular circumstances was not defamatory:

> It is simply impossible to believe that a reader who reached the word "blackmail" in either article would not have understood exactly what was meant: it was Bresler's [the real estate developer's] public and wholly legal negotiating proposals that were being criticized. No reader could have thought that either the speakers at the meeting or the newspaper articles reporting their words were charging Bresler with the commission of a criminal offense. On the contrary, even the most careless reader must have perceived that the word was no more than rhetorical hyperbole, a vigorous epithet used by those who considered Bresler's negotiating position extremely unreasonable.[47]

The Court stated that it would have been a very different case had the article been distorted or truncated in such a way as to extract the word

---

45 *See* Chapter 6, *infra,* which is devoted solely to discussion of the distinction.
46 398 U.S. 6 (1970).
47 *Id.* at 14.

"blackmail" from the context in which it had been used at the public meeting.[48]

Almost any word, no matter how emotionally charged or pejorative, can in a given context be merely a hyperbolic figure of speech, not a literal misstatement of fact injurious to reputation. A President accused of being a "murderer" because of his steadfast prosecution of an unpopular war is not being accused literally of a common law crime, rather, he is being accused of misconduct in a political sense, a sense that ranges into the realm of opinion. Similarly, a doctor who performs lawful abortions may be faced with the specter of protesters marching in front of his or her clinic with signs declaring that the doctor is a "murderer." The word "murderer" in this context, again, is obviously not intended to be taken in its literal sense, but rather as an expression of the protesters' view that abortion is tantamount to murder.[49]

When these sorts of problems arise, they are often analyzed under any or all of the related rubrics of "name-calling," "hyperbole," and "opinion."[50]

---

[48] *Id.* at 13.

[49] *But see* Commonwealth v. Canter, 269 Mass. 359, 168 N.E. 790 (1929)(Canter, prosecuted for criminal libel, was carrying a sign calling the Governor of Massachusetts a murderer for not sparing the lives of Sacco and Vanzetti).

[50] *See, e.g.,* Smith v. McMullen 589 F. Supp. 642 (S.D. Tex. 1984). In the *Smith* case, Tal Smith, the former general manager of the Houston Astros baseball team, brought an action for libel against John J. McMullen, the owner. McMullen had made a statement about Tal Smith in response to suggestions that Smith had been the architect of the Astros' success. McMullen stated "How can you keep writing that?" He then added "You'd better start writing the truth. Tal Smith is a despicable human being. It's unfair and wrong for people to keep giving him credit." McMullen moved to dismiss the claim on the grounds that the statements were mere rhetorical hyperbole. The court said that the statement that Smith was a "despicable human being," standing alone, was no more than a vigorous epithet, which would not be actionable as libelous. However, the court stated, evaluating the statement in context, the defendant had engaged in far more than mere name-calling: The totality of his statements, when viewed as a whole, was reasonably capable of defamatory meaning. The defendant also moved to dismiss on the grounds that the statement amounted to mere opinion, and thus was not actionable as a matter of law. The court ruled that although pure opinion which includes derogatory remarks and metaphorical language clearly does fall within the protection of the first amendment, "hybrid statements," by contrast, fall somewhere between "pure opinion" and "misstatements of fact," and are entitled to an absolute privilege as opinion only when accompanied by a full and accurate narration of the material background facts. The court held that the plaintiff's statements were hybrid in nature, rather than pure opinion, and that his failure to set forth any facts whatsoever in support of his assertion rendered the statements actionable. *Id.*

The fact/opinion distinction is discussed at length in Chapter 6, *infra.*

[3] *Hustler v. Falwell*

In 1988, the Supreme Court decided an important case impacting on the defamatory meaning problem. In *Hustler Magazine v. Falwell*[50.1] the Court reviewed a jury verdict of $200,000 in favor of the Reverend Jerry Falwell against *Hustler Magazine*, for intentional infliction of emotional distress. The case arose from a parody of a Campari liqueur advertisement run by *Hustler* in which the Reverend Falwell was depicted as having had sex with his mother in an outhouse, and as being a hypocritical drunk.[50.2] The Supreme Court reversed the verdict awarded to Falwell, in a ruling with enormously important implications for the attempted use of the tort of intentional infliction of emotional distress as a substitute for defamation.[50.3] The entire litigation, however, is also instructive with regard to the problem of defamatory meaning.

Clearly, to depict a prominent religious leader as an incestuous drunk is the quintessential of a "defamatory" accusation. But just as the word "blackmail" had not been understood in *Greenbelt v. Bresler*[50.4] as a literal accusation that the real estate developer was a blackmailer, the parody of the Reverend Falwell in the *Hustler* case was not understood by anyone who saw the mock advertisement as a genuine factual assertion that Falwell had actually engaged in such activity. In the trial of the case the jury was asked, in the first interrogatory submitted to it, to determine if the *Hustler* ad could "reasonably be understood as describing actual facts about plaintiff or actual events in which plaintiff participated."[50.5] The jury returned a verdict that the ad could not so be understood, thus eliminating the libel count from the trial, since there could be no actionable defamation if no reasonable reader understood the statements as factual. The Reverend Falwell was thus forced to stake his claim on the alternative theory of intentional infliction of emotional distress.

In his opinion for the Supreme Court, Chief Justice Rehnquist held:

> We conclude that public figures and public officials may not recover for the tort of intentional infliction of emotional distress by reason of publications such as the one here at issue without showing in addition that the

---

50.1 108 S. Ct. 876 (1988).

50.2 The facts of this landmark case are discussed in detail *infra* § 11.01.

50.3 *See* Smolla, *Emotional Distress and the First Amendment: An Analysis of* Hustler v. Falwell, 20 Ariz. St. L. J. 423 (1988).

50.4 Greenbelt Cooperative Publishing Ass'n v. Bresler, 398 U.S. 6 (1970).

50.5 *See* R. Smolla, Jerry Falwell v. Larry Flynt: The First Amendment on Trial 156 (1988).

> publication contains *a false statement of fact* which was made with "actual malice," *i.e.*, with knowledge that the statement was false or with reckless disregard as to whether it was true.[50.6]

This statement is pregnant with implications for many torts other than defamation, including intentional infliction of emotional distress and the branch of invasion of privacy known as "publication of private facts."[50.7] The statement is also significant for defamation, however, in its clear insistence on a *false statement of fact*—an insistence that serves as strong reinforcement for the constitutional doctrine emanating from *Greenbelt v. Bresler* prohibiting liability for mere rhetorical hyperbole.

§ 4.05 Defamation Through Implication

[1] The Significance of Context

The reputational injury caused by a communication may result not from what is said but from what is implied.[51] One of the more famous examples came in *Cooper v. Greeley*,[52] in which Horace Greeley wrote in the *New York Tribune* that he was not worried about a suit filed against him by James Fenimore Cooper because "Mr. Cooper will have to bring his action to trial somewhere. He will not bring it in New York, for we are known here, nor in Ostego, for he is known there."[53] The law's treatment of the defamatory communication conveyed through implication is a subset of the more general problem of determining the meaning of an allegedly defamatory communication by examining the

50.6 Hustler Magazine v. Falwell, 108 S. Ct. 876, 882 (1988).

50.7 *See infra* § 10.04.

51 *See* Restatement (Second) of Torts § 563 comment b (1977); Prosser and Keeton, *supra* note 1, § 111, at 782. *See also* McBride v. Merrell Dow and Pharmaceuticals, Inc., 717 F.2d 1460 (D.C. Cir. 1983); MacLeod v. Tribune Publishing Co., 52 Cal. 2d 536, 547, 343 P.2d 36, 41 (1959); Mullins v. Theirot, 19 Cal. App. 3d 302, 304, 97 Cal. Rptr. 27, 28 (1971).

52 1 Denio 347 (N.Y. 1845).

53 *Id.* There are many modern examples of defamation through implication. In Meadows v. Taft Broadcasting Co., 98 A.D.2d 959, 470 N.Y.S.2d 205 (1983), for example, it was held that a television station's news report that "there may be a connection" between a fatal fire and an investigation into alleged fraud by a funeral home and its director could be construed by the average person as implying that the funeral director committed homicide by arson. The broadcast was thus reasonably susceptible of a defamatory meaning. Similarly, in McBride v. Merrell Dow and Pharmaceuticals, Inc., 717 F.2d 1460 (D.C. Cir. 1983), the court held that a statement that a physician was paid $5,000 per day to testify as an expert witness in a trial, in contrast to much lower sums paid to other expert witnesses, could lead a reader to conclude that the physician's testimony was for sale; the statement thus could not as a matter of law be ruled nondefamatory.

words in their context.[54] Because of the subtleties in any language the task of construing words in context is often complex. Words that appear at first blush to convey a defamatory meaning may be explained away as innocuous when their context is made clear. Conversely, words innocent on their face may, when explained in context, convey a defamatory meaning.[55] The classic example is the statement that John Smith was

(*Text continued on page 4-15*)

---

[54] The defamatory meaning of words must always be determined not from naked words but in light of their context. *See, e.g.,* Greenbelt Cooperative Ass'n v. Bresler, 398 U.S. 6 (1970); Sharon v. Time, Inc., 575 F. Supp. 1162 (S.D.N.Y. 1983); H.O. Merren & Co. v. A.H. Belo Corp., 228 F. Supp. 515, 518 (N.D. Tex. 1964), *aff'd,* 346 F.2d 568 (5th Cir. 1965); Thomson v. Cash, 119 N.H. 371, 402 A.2d 651, 653 (1979); James v. Gannett Co., Inc., 40 N.Y.2d 415, 386 N.Y.S.2d 871, 353 N.E.2d 834 (1976); Westby v. Madison Newspapers, Inc., 81 Wis. 2d 1, 259 N.W.2d 691, 693 (1977); Franklin & Bussel, *supra* note 9, at 830.

[55] *See, e.g.,* Sharon v. Time, Inc., 575 F. Supp. 1162 (S.D.N.Y. 1984). In *Sharon,* General

seen walking into a hotel room with Mary. On its face, the statement does not communicate anything intending to injure reputation. If, however, there is added to the statement the fact that John Smith is married to someone other than Mary, the inference that the ordinary reasonable recipient may draw—that John is involved in an adulterous relationship with Mary—becomes defamatory.[56]

[2] Extrinsic Facts—"Inducement" and "Innuendo"

In determining the meaning of a communication, account must be taken of all the circumstances under which the communication is made. Those circumstances often involve pleading and proof of extrinsic facts. The common law developed technical terms to describe the introduction of extrinsic information rendering the communication defamatory. Under common law pleading, in framing the complaint for defamation when the meaning of the communication or its applicability to the plaintiff depended on extrinsic facts, the plaintiff alleged their existence in a preliminary statement known as the "inducement."[57]

The actual communication was set forth verbatim, and then in the

---

Ariel Sharon, former Minister of Defense of Israel, charged that *Time* magazine had libeled him as part of a report on the Israeli government commission report on the events surrounding the massacres of Palestinian refugees at the Sabra and Shatilla refugee camps in West Beiruit, Lebanon. (For a further review of the facts, *see* § 3.18[2], *supra.*) Judge Abram Sofaer ruled that, read in context, the *Time* article could reasonably be interpreted as libelous, because the challenged statement might reasonably be read to suggest that Sharon had encouraged the Phalangists to engage in bloodshed. The article's claim that the findings it reported were contained in a "secret appendix" to the commission report enhanced the reasonableness of the defamatory interpretation. A reader of the article would not readily conclude that the commission had hidden from public view evidence favorable to Sharon, the judge reasoned. A reader would more reasonably reach the conclusion that in the secret appendix the commission had withheld additional material adverse to Sharon, possibly under the rationale that Sharon had already been openly condemned and that full exposure would unnecessarily endanger Israel's political interests and moral standing.

[56] *See* Kerr v. Kerr, 134 A.D. 141, 142, 118 N.Y.S. 801 (2d Dept. 1909)(the average reader will assume that they " 'saith not a *pater noster*' there"). *See also* Brewer v. Memphis Publishing Co., 626 F.2d 1238 (5th Cir. 1980), *cert. denied,* 452 U.S. 962 (1981). (newspaper article incorrectly stating that a former entertainer who had been Elvis Presley's "number one girl" had a "reunion" with Presley in Las Vegas and that the entertainer had been divorced from her husband was, under Mississippi law, capable of sustaining a defamatory meaning). *Cf.* Gariepy v. Pearson, 207 F.2d 15 (D.C. Cir.), *cert. denied,* 346 U.S. 909 (1953); Thackery v. Patterson, 157 F.2d 614 (D.C. Cir. 1946).

[57] *See* McLaughlin v. Fisher, 136 Ill. 111, 24 N.E. 60 (1890); Ten Broeck v. Journal Printing Co., 166 Minn. 173, 207 N.W. 497 (1926).

"innuendo" there was an explanation of the meaning of the word.[58] Thus, to use William Prosser's example, a statement that the plaintiff had burned his own barn was not defamatory on its face, since he was perfectly free to do so, but when it was pleaded as inducement that he had insured his barn, and as innuendo that the words were understood to mean that he was defrauding the insurance company, the charge that was at first innocent became defamatory, for it imputed to the plaintiff the crime of arson.[59] When extrinsic evidence was necessary in order to link the defamatory statement to the plaintiff, this linkage was pleaded through "colloquium."[60]

These technical common law terms of art, which posed a number of traps for lawyers,[61] may still have relevance, and at times a double meaning—in some circumstances referring to pleading rules, and in others to the actual introduction of extrinsic facts. Thus, the term innuendo has two possible meanings in the law of libel. The technical meaning of the term is associated with the common law pleading requirement that the actual explanation of the defamatory meaning of the communication as explained by extrinsic circumstances be averred in the prefatory statement containing those extrinsic facts—the inducement.[62] The second, less technical meaning of innuendo is closer to that in everyday speech: simply that the insinuation or implication of the statement arises from the literal language when understood in context.[63]

[3] Examples

Although the United States Supreme Court had never even hinted that defamation accomplished through implication should be treated any differently from any other form of defamation,[64] in recent years some state supreme court decisions have declined to permit liability for statements that are made defamatory through implication. In *Schaefer*

58 *See* Pfeifly v. Henry, 269 Pa. 533, 112 A. 768 (1921); Kee v. Armstron, Byrd & Co., 75 Okla. 84, 182 P. 494 (1919).

59 Prosser and Keeton, *supra* note 1, § 111, at 782.

60 *See* Davis v. R.K.O. Radio Pictures, 191 F.2d 901 (8th Cir. 1951).

61 *See generally* Wyse, *The Complaint in Libel and Slander: A Dilemma for Plaintiff*, 33 Chi. Kent. L. Rev. 313 (1955).

62 Pierce v. Capital Cities Communications, Inc., 576 F.2d 495, 499 n.7 (3d Cir.), *cert. denied*, 439 U.S. 861 (1978).

63 *Id.*

64 *See* Franklin, *supra* note 9, at 848.

v. Lynch,[65] a newspaper reporter wrote a story about the director of the Louisiana State Retirement System which implied that the director had used his public office to influence commercial lenders to further the director's personal investment. The Louisiana Supreme Court stated that because statements about public officials are privileged in the absence of actual malice under *New York Times v. Sullivan,*[66] the result "surely [is] that all truthful statements are also constitutionally protected. Even though a false implication may be drawn by the public, there is no redress for its servant. Where public officers and public affairs are concerned, there can be no libel by innuendo."[67]

Similarly, a Massachusetts Appeals Court refused to impose liability in *Mihalik v. Duprey,*[68] involving a local school board member. The school board was engaged in labor negotiations with the local teachers' association. An article published in the association's newspaper during the course of the negotiations asserted, among other things, that the board member had had furniture made at the district's trade school. The article failed to note that any resident who supplied or paid for the necessary materials could have furniture made at the school. The newspaper article thus implied that by having furniture made the board member had abused his office. The jury concluded that, taken in context, the statement was defamatory, but the Massachusetts Court of Appeals held that the defendant, under the *New York Times* rules, could not be held liable for a statement that was literally true, even if that statement had a defamatory insinuation.

One cannot use the theory of "defamatory by implication" to manufacture defamation from words not reasonably capable of sustaining a defamatory meaning. For example, statements by a mayor describing the Church of Scientology as "Helter Skelter," "gung ho," a "rip-off,

---

[65] 406 So. 2d 185 (La. 1981).

[66] 376 U.S. 254 (1964).

[67] 406 So. 2d at 188.

[68] 11 Mass. App. 602, 417 N.E.2d 1283 (1981). Marc Franklin and Daniel Bussel have properly criticized the *Schaefer* and *Mihalik* decisions. Both decisions mistakenly assume that those who defame by implication must be protected. What these decisions fail to appreciate is the distinction between a defendant who unintentionally defames another through implications that the reader brings to the speech, contrary to the speaker's intent, and a defendant who intentionally or recklessly communicates a defamatory statement "in between the lines," hoping to hide behind the fact that the literal statement is not defamatory. Franklin & Bussel, *supra* note 9, at 850. No special constitutional privilege exists to defame by implication. *See* Burns v. McGraw-Hill Broadcasting Co., 659 P.2d 1351 (Colo. 1983); Buratt v. Capital City Press Co., 399 So. 2d 687 (La. Ct. App. 1981), *cert. denied,* 416 So. 2d 116 (La. 1982).

money motivated operation," and a "paramilitary religious organization" were not defamatory.[69] The Church of Scientology claimed that the mayor's use of the phrase "Helter Skelter" was meant to refer to a book dealing with mass murderer Charles Manson. The listener was then to infer that since Manson was considered by some to be a "clear" —a term used in Scientology to describe a person who learns to control his mind—some would understand the mayor as connecting the Church of Scientology to Charles Manson. As Manson is a mass murderer, the mayor's comment was therefore suggestive that Scientology promoted mass murder, the Scientologists reasoned. The court held that it was not prepared to build "inference upon inference" in order to find the statement defamatory, and that the mayor's "Helter Skelter" remark was not defamatory as a matter of law. The court similarly disposed of the other statements.

Similarly, a newspaper's description of a gun dealer as a seller of "heavy artillery," "assault rifles," and "barricade penetrating canister launchers" was held not libelous.[70] The gun seller argued that the innuendo in the article was that the seller engaged in illegal gun traffic with terrorists. The court held that this innuendo was not supported by the words in the article. The court further held that the author's opinion in the article (that a certain semi-automatic weapon sold by the plaintiff could be modified into a machine gun which would be an "assassination weapon") was protected opinion. The article disclosed the underlying facts concerning the particular automatic weapon, and the possibility of converting it into a fully automatic weapon.[71] And in *Grund v. Bethlehem Globe*,[72] the court held that a letter to the editor of a newspaper which stated in regard to the arrest of three minors for widespread criminal activity that "many people must wonder" how parents remain ignorant of their children's criminal activities, and which asked whether the parents were "sharing the loot," but which did not imply the existence of undisclosed facts, was not capable of defamatory meaning.

---

69 Church of Scientology v. Cazares, 638 F.2d 1272 (5th Cir. 1981).

70 B & B Group v. Los Angeles Herald Examiner, 10 Med. L. Rep. (BNA) 1892 (Cal. Ct. App. 2d Dist. 1984)(unpublished opinion).

71 *Id.* at 1894-95.

72 9 Med. L. Rep. (BNA) 1320 (Pa. Ct. Comm. Pleas 1982).

§ 4.06 Rules of Construction

[1] The Reasonable Construction Rule

Every jurisdiction in the United States save Illinois applies the "reasonable construction rule" to the interpretation of allegedly defamatory language, which is really nothing more than an application of the general principle that words are to be construed in context to determine their effect on recipients.[73] "The meaning of a communication is that which the recipient correctly, or mistakenly but reasonably, understands it was intended to express."[74] Words are to be given their natural, plain, ordinary, and obvious meanings whenever possible,[75] not a strained interpretation,[76] but they must always be viewed in total context[77] to determine their impact on the "common"[78] or "average"[79] or "reasonable"[80] recipient. No "artificial and unreasonable construction placed upon innocent words by the evil-minded can add a defamatory meaning not fairly to be found in the light of the circumstances."[81]

[2] The Innocent Construction Rule

Illinois stands alone in its adherence to the so-called innocent construction rule.[82] As explained in *Chapski v. Copley Press, Inc.,*[83] the rule is: "A written or oral statement is to be considered in context, with the words and implications therefrom given their natural and obvious meaning; if, as so construed, the statement may reasonably be innocently interpreted as referring to someone other than the plaintiff it cannot be actionable *per se.*"[84]

---

73 *See* cases cited in note 54, *supra.*

74 Restatement (Second) of Torts § 563 (1977).

75 McGraw v. Thomason, 265 Ala. 635, 639, 93 So. 2d 741 (1957); Church of Scientology v. Minnesota State Med. Ass'n Foundation, 264 N.W.2d 152 (Minn. 1978).

76 *See* Thomson v. Cash, 119 N.H. 371, 402 A.2d 651 (1979).

77 *See* Sharon v. Time, Inc., 575 F. Supp. 1162 (S.D.N.Y. 1983); Ledger-Enquirer Co. v. Grimes, 214 Ga. 422, 105 S.E.2d 229 (1958); Marcuda v. Lewiston Journal Co., 109 Me. 53, 82 A. 438 (1912); Houston v. Interstate Circuit, 132 S.W. 903 (Tex. Civ. App. 1939).

78 Thomson v. Cash, 119 N.H. 371, 402 A.2d 651, 653 (N.H. 1979).

79 *See* Kaplan v. Newsweek Magazine, Inc., 10 Med. L. Rep. (BNA) 2142, 4143 (N.D. Cal. 1984); MacRae v. Afro-American Publishing Co., 172 F. Supp. 184, 186 (E.D. Pa. 1959), *aff'd,* 274 F.2d 287 (3d Cir. 1960).

80 *See* Wheeler v. Dell Publishing Co., 300 F.2d 372, 376 (7th Cir. 1962).

81 Prosser and Keeton, *supra* note 1, § 111, at 781.

82 *See* Smolla & Malone, *The Future of Defamation in Illinois After* Colson v. Steig *and* Chapski v. Copley Press, Inc., 32 De Paul L. Rev. 219, 274-297 (1983).

83 92 Ill. 2d 344, 442 N.E.2d 195 (1982).

84 *Id.* at 352, 442 N.E.2d at 199.

The rule, which is often internally contradictory, confusing, and on the whole significantly biased in favor of defendants,[85] has produced some bizarre results,[86] and has come in for substantial criticism.[87] For the time being, however, the rule that if a statement may reasonably be given an "innocent" construction it must be given that construction appears well entrenched as the law of Illinois.[88]

---

[85] *See* Smolla & Malone, *supra* note 81.

[86] *See, e.g.*, Rasky v. CBS, Inc., 103 Ill. App. 3d 577, 431 N.E.2d 1055 (1st Dist. 1981)(suit dismissed because reference to plaintiff as "slumlord" was capable of innocent construction and did not impugn plaintiff's professional fitness as lawyer and real estate operator); Newell v. Field Enters., 91 Ill. App. 3d 735, 415 N.E.2d 434 (1st Dist. 1980)(newspaper article stating that the plaintiff chose to save a parrot rather than a woman from a fire lowered community respect for plaintiff and hence was not subject to an innocent interpretation); Garber Pierre Food Prods. v. Crooks, 78 Ill. App. 3d 356, 397 N.E.2d 211 (1st Dist. 1970)(attorney's letter accusing nursing home food supplier of "blackmail" and "extortion" not libelous per se because language could be construed as merely a criticism of supplier's policy decision regarding prices and delivery of goods to nursing home); Makis v. Area Publication Corp., 77 Ill. App. 3d 452, 395 N.E.2d 1185 (1st Dist. 1979)(newspaper article stating that the closing of a sky sailing school could have been attributed to accident, argument, or crime could be innocently construed, because crime was only one of three given possibilities and therefore did not amount to libel per se regarding plaintiff's business reputation); Bruck v. Cincotta, 56 Ill. App. 3d 260, 371 N.E.2d 874 (1st Dist. 1977)(article suggesting that plaintiffs made building alterations without permit did not imply that plaintiffs committed a crime, because failure to obtain permit was not an indictable offense); Moricoli v. Schwartz, 46 Ill. App. 3d 481, 361 N.E.2d 74 (1st Dist. 1977)(plaintiff nightclub singer had cause of action against defendants for calling him "fag," but plaintiff was required to prove actual damages); Watson v. Southwest Messenger Press, Inc., 12 Ill. App. 3d 968, 299 N.E.2d 409 (1st Dist. 1973)(statement in article which referred to village mayor's "ticket fixing" could be innocently construed); Delis v. Sepsis, 9 Ill. App. 3d 217, 292 N.E.2d 138 (1st Dist. 1972)(letter describing plaintiff as a "liar," "dishonorable," and "deluded" was construed as mere name-calling and therefore could not damage plaintiff's reputation); Lorlland v. Field Enters., 65 Ill. App. 2d 65, 213 N.E.2d 1 (1st Dist. 1965)(statement in newspaper article that plaintiff's former wife had initiated bigamy suit falsely implied plaintiff had committed a crime and thus was not susceptible of innocent construction), *cited in* Chapski v. Copley Press, Inc., 92 Ill. App 2d at 348, 442 N.E.2d at 197 (1982).

[87] *See, e.g.*, Polelle, *The Guilt of the "Innocent Construction Rule" in Illinois Defamation Law*, 1 N.I.U.L. Rev. 181 (1981); Smolla & Malone, *supra* note 81; Note, *The Illinois Defamation of Innocent Construction: A Minority of One*, 30 U. Chi. L. Rev. 524 (1963).

[88] *See* Sweeney v. Sengstacke Enters., 180 Ill. App. 3d 1044, 536 N.E.2d 823 (1989); Lowe v. Rockford Newspaper, Inc., 179 Ill. App. 3d 592, 534 N.E.2d 549 (1989); Matchett v. Chicago Bar Association, 467 N.E.2d 271 (Ill. App. 1984); Crinkley v. Dow Jones & Co., 119 Ill. App. 3d 147, 456 N.E.2d 138 (1983); Chapski v. Copley Press, Inc., 92 Ill. 2d 344, 442 N.E.2d 195 (1982); Catalano v. Pechous, 83 Ill. 2d 146, 419 N.E.2d 350 (1980); John v. Tribune Co., 24 Ill. 2d 43, 181 N.E.2d 105, *cert. denied*, 371 U.S. 877 (1962).

[3] The Single Instance Rule

In what appears to be a relatively obscure rule, perhaps followed only in New York, an allegation that the plaintiff was guilty of a "single instance" of negligent conduct is not regarded as actionable in the absence of proof of special damages,[89] on the theory that everybody makes mistakes: "infallibility is not a human trait and even the most skillful may make a mistake on a single occasion."[90] The literal statements of this rule should probably be taken with a grain of salt, and not read beyond the applications of the policy behind them. Certainly *some* single instances of impropriety remain actionable without proof of special damage—an allegation of a "single instance" of murder or treason, for example. What is probably intended by the rule is no more than the commonsense view that single acts of simple negligence do not usually, without more, diminish one's reputation.

§ 4.07 Special Contexts for Defamatory Meaning

[1] Headlines, Captions, "Teases," and Publicity Efforts

[a] In General

The headline of a story, the caption above a photograph, the opening "tease" of a broadcast story (the equivalent of a printed headline), or the pre-story publicity ("hype") and advertising that may appear prior to the story's actual publication—all these may turn what would otherwise have been a nonactionable article or broadcast into a defamatory communication. In a number of recent highly publicized libel actions, a substantial amount of attention revolved around the story headline, the pre-story publicity, or the opening "tease" of the broadcast. In *Tavoula-*

---

[89] Duci v. Daily Gazette, 102 A.D.2d 924, 477 N.Y.S.2d 760 (3d Dept. 1984)(a plaintiff accused of a single instance of impropriety may not recover unless he pleads and proves "special damages"); Lyons v. New American Library, 432 N.Y.S.2d 536, 78 A.D.2d 723 (3d Dept. 1980)("[g]enerally, there can be no liability where a professional is charged with ignorance or mistake on a single occasion only and not accused of general ignorance or lack of skill").

[90] Twiggar v. Ossining Printing & Publishing Co., 161 A.D. 718, 146 N.Y.S. 529 (2d Dept. 1914), *appeal dismissed,* 220 N.Y. 716, 116 N.E. 1080 (1917). Robert Sack states that the rule may also have adherents in Florida, and perhaps in Illinois. R. Sack, Libel, Slander and Related Problems, § II. 4.11, at 70-71 (1980) (citing Craig v. Moore, 4 Med. L. Rep. (BNA) 1402, 1405 (Fla. Cir. Ct. 1978)).

reas v. Washington Post Co.,[91] the *Post* ran its story about William Tavoulareas under the headline "Mobil Chief Sets Up His Son in Business." The actual text of the article was a somewhat more reasonably balanced account of the complicated oil shipping arrangements involved.[92] The plaintiffs (and apparently, the jury)[93] concentrated, however, on the basic charge set forth in the headline—that Tavoulareas had "set up" his son in business, and the innuendo that that "set up" was either unethical or illegal.

Similarly, in *Sharon v. Time, Inc.*,[94] *Time* magazine's accusations against former Israeli Defense Minister Ariel Sharon were allegedly aggravated by *Time's* inflammatory advertising leading up to the publication of the *Time* issue containing the alleged defamation.[95] And in General William Westmoreland's lawsuit against CBS,[96] one of the more explicit negative statements came in the so-called tease of the broadcast —the brief opening segment of the documentary. It was in the tease segment that Mike Wallace stated explicitly that CBS would present evidence of what it had come to believe was a "conspiracy" at the highest levels of American military intelligence to suppress information about the strength of enemy troops in Vietnam.

Problems posed by headlines, captions, teases, and publicity will probably appear with increasing frequency, because so much of the output of modern journalism is now packaged to give quick, capsule summaries of the news, often in an attention-grabbing manner. Competitive forces within the media and the fast pace of American life thus make the defamatory headline a likely staple in libel litigation.

[b] Jurisdictions that Construe the Headline Independently

The problem of headlines and other similar "packaging" elements of a story has resulted in some conflicting rulings among courts. In some

91 Tavoulareas v. Washington Post Co., 759 F.2d 90, *rehearing en banc granted*, 763 F.2d 1472 (D.C. Cir 1985).

92 *See supra* § 3.19[4].

93 *See* Brill, *Inside the Jury Room at the Washington Post Libel Trial*, American Lawyer (Nov. 1982).

94 599 F. Supp. 538 (S.D.N.Y. 1984).

95 *See generally* Kaplan, *The Judge's Post Mortem on the Sharon Libel Trial*, National Law Journal, March 18, 1985, at 1; Lubasch, *Sharon, Completing His Testimony, Says Time Article Created Hatred*, New York Times, Nov. 28, 1984, at B6, cols. 1-6; Lubasch, *Sharon's Lawyer Gives Final Statement at Trial*, New York Times, Jan. 12, 1985, at 24, cols. 1-2; Brill, *Say It Ain't So, Henry*, American Lawyer (Feb. 1985).

96 Westmoreland v. CBS, Inc., 596 F. Supp. 1170 (S.D.N.Y. 1984).

jurisdictions, a headline that is defamatory may in itself support an action for libel, even though the body of the article diffuses the defamatory nature of the headline, or sufficiently explains the headline to eliminate the defamation altogether.[97] The logic of those holdings would appear to be that some readers, particularly in a society where news is often packaged in quick, easily digestable bits, gather their basic information from headlines and brief lead paragraphs,[98] and therefore a defamatory statement made in a headline can stand on its own footing even if the defamation is undercut by the text of the article.[99]

[c] Jurisdictions that Construe the Headline in Conjunction with the Text

The majority approach is not to construe the headline alone, but to construe it in conjunction with the article as a whole, to determine whether it is capable of sustaining a defamatory meaning.[100] The majori-

---

[97] *See, e.g.*, Schermerhorn v. Rosenberg, 73 A.D.2d 276, 287, 426 N.Y.S.2d 274, 283 (2d Dept. 1980)("[I]f [the headline] is not a fair index of the article, then the headline must be examined independently to determine whether it is actionable under the general principles of libel."); Las Vegas Sun, Inc. v. Franklin, 74 Nev. 282, 329 P.2d 867 (1958). *Cf.* Forrest v. Lynch, 347 So. 2d 1255 (La. App. 1977), *cert. denied sub nom.* Times-Picayune Publishing Co. v. Forrest, 455 U.S. 971 (1978)(the court in Forrest apparently refused to consider the headline in conjunction with the story, but its analysis on this point is ambigious).

[98] *See* Las Vegas Sun, Inc. v. Franklin, 74 Nev. 282, 329 P.2d 867 (1956)(court held that headline may be construed apart from its accompanying article because public frequently reads only the headline).

[99] *See* Schermerhorn v. Rosenberg, 73 A.D.2d 276, 287, 426 N.Y.S.2d 274, 283 (2d Dept. 1980)("That the defamatory meaning of the headline may be dispelled by a reading of the entire article is of no avail to the publisher.").

[100] *See, e.g.*, Fairbanks Publishing Co. v. Pitka, 376 P.2d 190 (Alaska 1962); Reardon v. News-Journal Co., 53 Del. 29, 164 A.2d 263 (1960); Floyd v. Atlanta Newspaper, Inc., 102 Ga. App. 840, 117 S.E.2d 906 (1960); Ledger-Enquirer Co. v. Brown, 214 Ga. 422, 105 S.E.2d 229, *conformed to* 98 Ga. 462, 106 S.E.2d 61 (1958); Fernandes v. Tenbruggencate, 65 Haw. 226, 649 P.2d 1144 (1982); Cook v. Atlanta Newspaper, Inc., 98 Ga. App. 818, 107 S.E.2d 260 (1959); Naked City, Inc. v. Chicago Sun-Times, 77 Ill. App. 3d 188, 395 N.E.2d 1042 (1979); Reed v. Albanese, 78 Ill. App. 2d 53, 223 N.E.2d 419 (1966); Cochran v. Indianapolis Newspaper, Inc., 178 Ind. App. 53, 372 N.E.2d 1211 (Ct. App. 1978); Hein v. Lacy, 228 Kan. 249, 616 P.2d 277 (1980); Steenson v. Wallace, 144 Kan. 730, 62 P.2d 907 (1936); Cross v. Guy Gannett Publishing Co., 151 Me. 491, 121 A.2d 355 (1956); Hylsky v. Globe Democrat Publishing Co., 348 Mo. 83, 152 S.W.2d 119 (1941); Grossman v. Globe-Democrat Publishing Co., 347 Mo. 869, 149 S.W.2d 362 (1941); Painter v. E.W. Scripps Co., 104 Ohio App. 237, 148 N.E.2d 503, 506 (1957); Dunlap v. Philadelphia Newspapers, Inc., 301 Pa. Super. 475, 448 A.2d 6 (1982); Bray v. Providence Journal Co., 101 R.I. 111, 220 A.2d 531, 535 (1966); Ross v. Columbia Newspapers, 266 S.C. 75, 221 S.E.2d 770 (1976); Jones v. Garner, 250 S.C. 479, 158 S.E.2d 909 (1968).

ty approach is more consistent with the general common law principle that the alleged defamatory speech is to be construed in context.[101] This approach "necessitates that the whole publication be considered. . . . The place and position of the item are to be considered . . . as are the headlines of the articles."[102] In so examining the issue, "both the headline and the body of the article [are] to be considered as one document."[103]

[d] Distinguishing Between Normal and Sensationalized Headlines

In *Sprouse v. Clay Communications, Inc.*,[104] the West Virginia Supreme Court devised a very intelligent synthesis of the two positions:

> Generally, where the headline is of normal size and does not lead to a conclusion totally unsupported by the body of the story, both story and headlines are to be considered together for their total impression. However, where oversized headlines are published which reasonably lead the average reader to an entirely different conclusion than the facts recited in the body of the story, and where the plaintiff can demonstrate that it was the intent of the publisher to use such misleading headlines to create a false impression on the normal reader, the headlines may be considered separately with regard to whether a known falsehood was published.[105]

This is an eminently sensible compromise; it has been cited with apparent approval in several other decisions.[106]

The tensions in this area are caused by the fact that no headline can contain all the details of a complicated story. The defendant must be allowed some leeway in reducing a complicated story into an intelligible headline. On the other hand, a media defendant should not be able to exploit the headline, caption, broadcast tease, or publicity to falsely and misleadingly sensationalize a story so as to create an overall impact more damaging to the plaintiff than the actual facts of the story will

[101] *See* Fernandes v. Tenbruggencate, 65 Haw. 226, 649 P.2d 1144 (1982)("[t]he law does not dwell on isolated passages, but judges the publication as a whole")(quoting Kahanamoku v. Advertiser, 25 Haw. 701, 714 (1920)).

[102] Cochran v. Indianapolis Newspaper, Inc., 178 Ind. App. 53, 372 N.E.2d 1211 (Ct. App. 1978).

[103] Bray v. Providence Journal Co., 101 R.I. 111, 220 A.2d 531, 535 (1966).

[104] 211 S.E.2d 674 (W. Va. 1974), *cert. denied*, 423 U.S. 882 (1975).

[105] *Id.* at 686.

[106] *See* Dostert v. Washington Post Co., 531 F. Supp. 165 (N.D. W. Va. 1982); Fernandes v. Tenbruggencate, 65 Haw. 226, 649 P.2d 1144 (1982); Hodges v. Oklahoma Journal Publishing Co., 617 P.2d 191 (Okla. 1980).

bear. In *Burnett v. National Enquirer,*[107] for example, the gossip column piece that led to Carol Burnett's suit against the *National Enquirer* carried the headline "Carol Burnett and Henry K. in Row." The *Enquirer* was found to have stretched the statement in that headline well beyond what the actual facts of Carol Burnett's evening at the restaurant would bear; Burnett had exchanged pleasantries with Henry Kissinger and had in no sense been involved in a "row."

[e] A Note on Photograph Captions

Closely related to the problem of headlines is the problem of captions for photographs that accompany a story. Like headlines, photograph captions are eye-catching and tend to simplify the information contained in the text of a story. Such captions may become the focal point of libel actions because, like headlines, the captions sometimes reduce the facts of a story to a single statement that may carry a defamatory meaning which the entire story parsed line by line might itself refute. A caption that misidentifies the person in the photograph may carry a defamatory meaning if the activity portrayed in the photograph is defamatory.[108]

---

[107] 144 Cal. App. 3d 991, 193 Cal. Rptr. 206 (1983), *appeal dismissed,* 104 S. Ct. 1260 (1984).

[108] In *Lerman v. Flynt Distributing Co., Inc.*, 745 F.2d 123 (2d Cir. 1984), *cert. denied,* 105 S. Ct. 2114 (1985), for example, writer Jackie Collins Lerman sued the Flynt Distributing Company. The magazine *Adelina* contained two still photographs from a movie, "The World Is Full of Married Men." In one of the photos an anonymous actress was seen nude from the waist up, and the other photo depicted her completely nude, participating in an orgy. The caption to the two photographs identified the writer Jackie Collins as the actress appearing in the film. Although Jackie Collins had written the screenplay for the film and her husband had directed the movie, in fact Jackie Collins was not the woman identified in the photograph, nor had she ever appeared nude in that movie or anywhere else in public. Lerman sued for libel, violation of her right of publicity, and false light invasion of privacy. A New York jury awarded the plaintiff $40 million, but the Court of Appeals reversed for lack of actual malice.

In *Dunlap v. Philadelphia Newspapers, Inc.*, 301 Pa. Super. 475, 448 A.2d 6 (1982), a newspaper article contained the headline "Wide Police Corruption Revealed" and was accompanied by a photograph of a police car stopped outside of a "known gambling location." The article described the plaintiff police officer as "more likely than not" to have been the officer in the photographed car. The court held that the article was capable of a defamatory meaning, since a reasonable person could construe the article, photograph, and caption to indicate that the plaintiff had been bribed. *See also* Martin v. Municipal Publications, 510 F. Supp. 255, 256 (E.D. Pa. 1981)(unnamed photograph with derogatory caption in humorous section of magazine held capable of defamatory meaning).

[2] "Visual Defamation"

[a] Photographs

If a picture is worth a thousand words, it may also lie, and be defamatory.[109] Even photographs that in a technical sense reflect the "truth" of what the camera lens sees may carry an optical illusion sufficiently damaging to be considered defamatory. In a famous case, *Burton v. Crowell Publishing Co.*,[110] an ad for Camel cigarettes displayed a well-known steeple chaser who was quoted as declaring that Camel cigarettes "restored" him after a "crowded business day." Two photographs of the plaintiff were inserted below the statement. The caption to one stated, "Get a lift with a Camel," and the other photograph showed the steeple chaser coming from a race to be weighed in, carrying his saddle in front of him. The line of the seat was about a foot below the plaintiff's waist, and over the seat, at about the middle of the plaintiff's body, a loose white girth fell in such a manner that it appeared at first to be attached to the plaintiff's body, giving the false impression that the plaintiff had grotesquely monstrous and obscene genitals. The trial court dismissed the complaint as nondefamatory, but that decision was reversed on appeal, in a famous opinion by Judge Learned Hand. Judge Hand wrote:

> everybody would at once see that it was the camera and the camera alone that had made the unfortunate mistake. If the advertisement is libel, it is such in spite of the fact that it asserts nothing whatever about the plaintiff, even by the remotest implication. It does not profess to depict him as he is. It does not exaggerate any part of his person so as to suggest that he is deformed. It is patently an optical illusion and carries its correction on its face as much as though it were a verbal utterance which expressly declared that it was false. It would be hard for words so guarded to carry any sting. But the same is not true of characters and this is an example. For notwithstanding all we have just said, it exposed the plaintiff to overwhelming ridicule.[111]

Judge Hand's statement that the photograph in the *Burton* case

---

[109] *See* Regan v. Sullivan, 557 F.2d 300, 308-09 (2d Cir. 1977); Kennedy v. Ministries, Inc., 10 Med. L. Rep. (BNA) 2459 (E.D. Pa. 1984)(use of plaintiff's photograph on book cover and in advertisements which could create impression that plaintiff had been branded with the "Mark of the Beast" and is associated with the "Antichrist" is capable of defamatory meaning); Deay v. Curtis Publishing Co., 78 F. Supp. 305, 306 (D.D.C. 1948).

[110] 82 F.2d 154 (2d Cir. 1936).

[111] *Id.* at 155.

carried a defamatory meaning probably remains good law.[112] It is essentially an extension of the sort of problem posed by headlines. The immediate visceral reaction to the photograph does in fact subject the plaintiff to ridicule, and the fact that a later examination reveals that one's initial reaction was caused by optical trickery of sorts does not completely undo the original defamatory act.

Photographs are not always true representations of reality. Photographs are capable of carrying a defamatory meaning when they have been altered to tell a lie. When the head of one person is cropped from a picture and placed on another's torso, for example, the photograph is "false" in a very literal sense—and if it is also injurious to reputation it may be defamatory and actionable. In *Guccione v. Hustler Magazine, Inc.*,[113] a photograph of Bob Guccione, the publisher of *Penthouse* magazine, appeared with Guccione's head superimposed on the body of another model, who was depicted as involved in an act of anal intercourse. Guccione sued *Hustler* for the defamatory implication in the photograph that Guccione had engaged in deviant sexual activity, and the court held the photograph to be libel per se.[114]

[b] Broadcasts

Film and television broadcast depictions can present the same prob-

---

[112] Because the optical illusion was apparently an inadvertent effect, the continuing vitality of *Burton* in light of the fault rules in Gertz v. Robert Welch, Inc., 418 U.S. 323 (1974), is problematic. If the *Gertz* fault rules apply to matters other than falsity—an issue previously discussed (*see supra* § 3.28[2]—then *Burton* arguably could not withstand *Gertz*. The whole area, however, has been thrown a wrench by the decision in Dun & Bradstreet, Inc. v. Greenmoss Builders, Inc., 105 S. Ct. 2939 (1979)(*see supra* §§ 3.02-3.05). Presumably, the plaintiff in *Burton* would still be a public figure, and actual malice rules would still apply, though arguably the optical illusion did not involve an issue of "public concern." *See supra* §§ 3.03-3.05. This discussion aside, there seems little question that *Burton* remains very much alive as authority on a more limited point: that, notwithstanding fault questions, such an optical trick in a photograph is capable of being defamatory.

[113] 7 Med. L. Rep. (BNA) 2077 (Ohio Ct. App. 1981).

[114] *Id.* at 2087. The jury awarded the plaintiff $3,150,000 in compensatory damages and $37,000,000 in punitive damages. The court ordered a new trial because the awards were so grossly excessive as to indicate passion and prejudice. *Id.* at 2088-92. The court in McCabe v. Village Voice, 550 F. Supp. 525 (E.D. Pa. 1982), on the other hand, held that the publication of the plaintiff's photo in the *Village Voice*, as part of the paper's "centerfold" series of nonobscene photographs of nude or partially nude women in bathtubs, was not capable of defamatory meaning. Plaintiff was identified as a model and she was not depicted in a sexually suggestive or lewd manner.

lems as photographs. In *Duncan v. WJLA-TV, Inc.*,[115] a television station, as part of its general reporting concerning medical treatment for the disease genital herpes, showed plaintiff as one of several people on the street. The court said that the footage on the six o'clock report was not reasonably capable of defamatory meaning, because the reporter's position on the street made it clear that the pedestrians shown were merely background for the film. The court held, however, that the shortened report at eleven o'clock, in which the plaintiff's photograph was broadcast while an off-screen narrator stated that "for the 20 million Americans who have herpes, it's not a cure," could support the inference that the plaintiff had herpes, and thus was capable of a defamatory meaning.

In *Clark v. American Broadcasting Companies, Inc.*,[116] a television broadcast concerning the effects of street prostitution on a middle class neighborhood included footage of a well-dressed woman walking down a public street. According to the court, the broadcast was reasonably capable of a defamatory meaning, in view of its ambiguity as to whether the woman was a resident of the neighborhood or a prostitute.

[3] Cartoons

One of the recent vogues in libel litigation has been the suit based on an unflattering depiction in a cartoon. Former Governor Edward King sued *Boston Globe* cartoonist Paul Szep in a $3.6 million libel suit; former Philadelphia Mayor Frank Rizzo sued cartoonist Rob Lawler, formerly of the *Philadelphia Daily News;* cartoonist Milt Priggee of the *Dayton Journal Herald* was sued by former Ohio Supreme Court Justice James Celebrezze; former Los Angeles Mayor Sam Yorty sued cartoonist Paul Conrad of the *Los Angeles Times*—and these are not the only

---

115 10 Med. L. Rep. (BNA) 1395 (D.D.C. 1984).

116 684 F.2d 1208, 1213-14 (6th Cir. 1982), *cert. denied,* 103 S. Ct. 1433 (1983). On the other hand, in Harrison v. Washington Post Co., 391 A.2d 781, 783-84 (D.C. 1978), the court held that a television report showing two men being escorted by police into a bank which had just been robbed, reporting that both men were being released, was not reasonably capable of being construed as defamatory. In Hallmark Builders v. Gaylord Broadcasting, 733 F.2d 1461 (11th Cir. 1984), in a story reporting problems of new homeowners, a close-up television camera shot revealed a hair-line masonry crack in a house constructed by the plaintiff; the crack was photographed so as to make it appear larger than it really was, plaintiff alleged. Saying that the close-up accurately reflected the size of the crack from the distance shown, the court held that the broadcast was not defamatory.

suits in what seems to be a burgeoning field for libel litigation.[117]

Few of these suits have completed the litigation process. Of those that have, most have ended unfavorably for the plaintiff. In Mayor Yorty's suit, for example, the California Court of Appeals held the cartoons not actionable, on the grounds that they were rhetorical hyperbole.[118] Similarly, in *Miller v. Charleston Gazette,*[119] an attorney who was under consideration for appointment as a U.S. Attorney was depicted as a circus animal trainer using a whip and chain to control an elephant dressed in a corset and holding a parasol. The court held that the newspaper cartoon constituted artistic rhetorical hyperbole and was not reasonably susceptible of a defamatory meaning.

Since cartoons, unlike photographs, are almost always "false" in the limited sense that they intentionally distort and elaborate on reality, they do carry with them the inherent threat of libel litigation. The protection that cartoons receive, however, is extremely high, almost to the point of absolute immunity, not so much because they are incapable of being defamatory as that no reasonable reader will normally understand them as anything but hyperbole and opinion.[120]

---

117 *See generally* Duke, *If a Cartoonist's Pen Draws Blood, Victim Can Return the Favor,* Wall St. Journal, August 2, 1985, at 1, col. 4, and 14, col. 6.

118 Yorty v. Chandler, 13 Cal. App. 3d 467, 91 Cal. Rptr. 709 (1970).

119 9 Med. L. Rep. (BNA) 2540 (W. Va. Cir. Ct. 1983).

120 *See infra* § 6.20. One of the few cases holding a cartoon depiction to be defamatory and actionable is Buller v. Pulitizer Publishing Co., 11 Med. L. Rep. (BNA) 1289 (Mo. Ct. App. 1984). In *Buller* a cartoon accompanying an article depicted the plaintiff, a psychic, as a bizarrely dressed figure in bed surrounded by a chaotic array of charts and diagrams. The terms "hokey," "bizarre costumes," and "crystal ball" were employed. The plaintiff alleged that the cartoon depicted her as having no skill or capacity as a psychic, as conducting her business as if it were an assembly line, with the sole purpose of acquiring money and with little or no concern for her clients. In a somewhat startling opinion, the court held that "defendant's drawing cunningly depicted . . . Buller's [the plaintiff's] business and her lack of skill and integrity. There is in our minds no question that the article and drawing are actionable as libel per se." *Id.* at 1292-93. The court further rejected the position that the cartoon constituted constitutionally protected opinion, stating that "the facts set out visually in the drawing go beyond the protection afforded opinion." *Id.* at 1293.

In another extremely interesting case, Mullenmeister v. Snap-On Tools Corp., 587 F. Supp. 868 (S.D.N.Y. 1984), a cartoon published in a company's in-house newsletter contained a caricature of the plaintiff, a former employee, wearing a helmet inscribed with a swastika. The court dismissed the claim on the grounds that the cartoon was not libelous per se, and therefore not actionable under New York law without pleading and proof of special damages. (New York law on what "libel per se" means is, it should be noted, far from clear. *See infra* § 7.07[4] and *infra* note 60.) The court noted that the "harsh experiences of the Second World War transformed the swastika into the universally recognized symbol of Hitler and his Nazis," and that "[w]hile the depth and diversity of polit-

The Supreme Court's decision in *Hustler Magazine v. Falwell*[120.1] has significant implications for cartoons. The case arose out of a "cartoon" of sorts—a parody depicting the Reverend Jerry Falwell hawking Campari Liqueur.[120.2] One of the most effective *amicus curiae* briefs submitted in the Supreme Court was written by Ms. Roslyn A. Mazer and Mr. George Kaufmann on behalf of the American Editorial Cartoonists, The Authors League of America, and the political satirist Mark Russell.[120.3] The brief contained a compendium of political cartoons from throughout American history, and was very effective in demonstrating how such satiric visual lampoons are a time-honored and important component of the American political landscape.

In *Hustler,* the question of defamatory meaning intersected with the tort of intentional infliction of emotional distress.[120.4] Reverend Falwell had argued that the rules emanating from *New York Times* did not apply to the emotional distress tort, and that the state's interest in protecting its citizens from emotional distress far outweighed any interest the speaker may have in propagating vulgar and shocking speech. It should adequately protect first amendment interests, he argued, to require that the plaintiff prove intent to inflict the distress and to prove that the speech is offensive and outrageous. This formulation, had it been accepted by the Court, would have threatened the very foundations of political cartooning—for many satirists might very well be guilty of intending to inflict distress on their victims, and many juries might be willing to label their lampoons "offensive and outrageous."

In his opinion for the Supreme Court, Chief Justice Rehnquist pointed out, however, that in the world of debate over public affairs, many things are done with motives that are less than admirable, and they do not for that reason alone forfeit first amendment protection. That an utterance is spoken out of hatred does not mean it is false. Chief Justice Rehnquist thus wrote that "while such a bad motive may be deemed controlling for purposes of tort liability in other areas of the law, we

---

ical passions make the identification of defamatory inference in political libels a dangerous task, courts have often found libel per se in false political designations." Nonetheless, the court held, in the context in which it appeared, the drawing was reasonably susceptible of only one interpretation: a "merely epithetic identification of national heritage." This, the court said, was not actionable in New York without special damage.

120.1 108 S. Ct. 876 (1988).

120.2 *See infra* § 11.01.

120.3 *See* Smolla, *supra* note 50.5, at 179.

120.4 *See supra* § 4.04[2].

think the First Amendment prohibits such a result in the area of public debate about public figures."[120.5]

This conclusion, the Chief Justice argued, was necessary to avoid censoring the work of political cartoonists and satirists. The art of caricature, he argued, is based on deliberate distortion or exaggeration for satirical effect. The cartoonist's method is often not reasoned or even-handed, but slashing and one-sided, full of black scorn and ridicule. Chief Justice Rehnquist then engaged in a moving tribute to the great American tradition of spirited satire and parody of public figures. He described the cartoons of Thomas Nast, who published in *Harper's Weekly* in the post-Civil War era. Nast engaged in a graphic vendetta against William M. "Boss" Tweed and his corrupt "Tweed Ring" in New York City. Nast was effective because he constantly went beyond the bounds of good manners and taste. Rehnquist recalled caricatures of George Washington, James G. Blaine, and Abraham Lincoln, and cartoonists' renditions of "Teddy Roosevelt's glasses and teeth, and Franklin D. Roosevelt's jutting jaw and cigarette holder."[120.6] From the viewpoint of history, he argued, "it is clear that our political discourse would have been considerably poorer without them."[120.7]

But could not these famous caricatures in political cartoons be distinguished from the coarse *Hustler* parody? Chief Justice Rehnquist conceded that the *Hustler* parody was at best a distant cousin of the conventional political cartoon, "and a rather poor relation at that."[120.8] In what may have been the single most important analytic step in his opinion, however, Chief Justice Rehnquist argued that there was simply no way to draw a principled distinction between the *Hustler* parody and other satiric efforts. "If it were possible," stated Rehnquist, "by laying down a principled standard to separate the one from the other, public discourse would probably suffer little or no harm."[120.9] But the Supreme Court was doubtful, the Chief Justice explained, that any reasonably concrete standard could ever be articulated. One thing was certainly clear: the amorphous pejorative "outrageous" was too subjective to withstand first amendment requirements. To permit a jury to impose liability for mere "outrageousness" would invite jurors to base liability on the basis of their tastes and prejudices.[120.10]

120.5 Hustler Magazine v. Falwell, 108 S. Ct. 876, 881 (1988).

120.6 *Id.*

120.7 *Id.*

120.8 *Id.*

120.9 *Id.*

120.10 *Id.* at 882.

The *Hustler* decision does not, of course, absolutely immunize cartoons from defamation liability. But it certainly does go a long way in that direction. The strong endorsement of the great American tradition of satirical cartooning in the Supreme Court's opinion should make it extremely difficult for future plaintiffs to demonstrate that a cartoon, no matter how mean-spirited, qualifies as a defamatory statement of fact. After *Hustler,* courts should be inclined to presume that such lampooning is simply not to be construed as a "straight" factual assertion concerning the plaintiff, but rather as exaggeration, ridicule, satire, and opinion.

[4] Song Lyrics

Even a song lyric may draw allegations of defamatory meaning. In *Valentine v. CBS, Inc.,*[121] the plaintiff, Patricia Valentine, sued singer Bob Dylan and others involved in the writing and marketing of a Dylan song written in 1975 entitled "Hurricane." The song tells of the murder trial of prizefighter Rubin "Hurricane" Carter and mentions Valentine as a witness; it portrays a perceived conspiracy among witnesses and police to unjustly convict Carter. In the song, Valentine is said to have cried out, "My God, they killed them all," and later the song speaks of other witnesses with the phrase "boldly lied." Valentine's theory was that, construed together, the stanzas imply that she acquiesced in the story of certain other witnesses and participated in the lie. The court held that the song is not reasonably capable of sustaining a defamatory meaning because, in the lyrics of the song, Valentine's involvement was limited to her testimony as an eyewitness, and the song cannot reasonably be understood as alleging Valentine's participation in a conspiracy.

[5] Misquotations

A misquotation may have defamatory meaning. In *Schrottman v. Barnicle,*[122] a reporter for the *Boston Globe* set out to write an article on "regular working people in the neighborhoods who are not usually covered by newspapers." The reporter interviewed the plaintiff, the owner of a gas station, and subsequently, in an article published by the *Globe,* reference was made to the plaintiff by name. In response to the question, "How's business?" the plaintiff was quoted as saying "Business

---

121 698 F.2d 430 (11th Cir. 1983).

122 386 Mass. 627, 437 N.E.2d 205 (1982).

is okay. It's just changed color." The article continued, "According to Eddie, life on Blue Hill Avenue in 1972 is 'o.k. if you're a nigger.' "[123] The plaintiff claimed he was misquoted, and the court found that the use of the word "nigger" was capable of a defamatory meaning. The court held that the use of the racial slur suggested that the plaintiff was a bigot, and that bigots might reasonably be held up to scorn, hatred,

(*Text continued on page 4-31*)

---

[123] *Id.* at 628, 437 N.E.2d at 207.

ridicule, or contempt by respectable members of the community, both black and white. The court noted that the fact that some blacks may themselves use the same term in a nonpejorative context did not drain the word of its historically hateful content.

The misquotation problem is a particularly important one when the story involves the assembling and editing of a substantial amount of quoted material. A major component of William Westmoreland's suit against CBS, for example, was Westmoreland's allegation that CBS, in editing the interview with Westmoreland, eliminated those clarifying and qualifying statements by Westmoreland that tended to support his version of events prior to the 1968 Tet offensive in Vietnam, and accentuated those parts of his testimony which, taken out of their context, appeared to support the thesis of the CBS broadcast.[124]

[6] Future Conduct

Allegations about a plaintiff's future conduct cannot be defamatory because they can amount to no more than the speaker's opinion about what may happen in the future. (Allegations concerning future conduct may thus be held nonactionable either because they are inherently incapable of being defamatory or because they are always deemed opinion as a matter of law.) In *Shiver v. Apalachee Publishing Co.*,[125] for example, prior to an election a newspaper ran a fictional letter to the editor which alleged that the plaintiff (a political candidate) would engage in illegal or unethical conduct if he were to be elected. The alleged defamation took place in the form of a rhetorical question asking if the plaintiff, if elected, would engage in unethical activity. The court held that since the alleged fabrication was only speculation by the author regarding events that would take place in the future, and was not even an affirmative assertion that those events would ever take place, the statement was not actionable. The court said that the rhetorical question was merely an opinion regarding a future event and as such could not be either true or false. Therefore, a libel action could not be sustained.[126]

---

[124] *See* Westmoreland v. CBS, Inc., 596 F. Supp. 1170 (S.D.N.Y. 1984).

[125] 425 So. 2d 1173 (Fla. 1st Dist. Ct. App. 1983), *aff'g* Med. L. Rep. (BNA) 2160 (Fla. Cir. Ct. 1981).

[126] 7 Med. L. Rep. (BNA) at 2162, *aff'd*, 425 So. 2d 1173 (Fla. 1st Dist. Ct. App. 1983).

[7] Use of Social Science Evidence or Linguistic Experts

In *Rudin v. Dow Jones & Co.*,[127] *Barron's* had printed a headline referring to the plaintiff, an attorney, as a "mouthpiece" for Frank Sinatra. The plaintiff established that among attorneys the term "mouthpiece" had a distinctly defamatory meaning.[128] One of the plaintiff's witnesses was Justice Bruce Kauffman, a former Justice of the Pennsylvania Supreme Court, who testified that the word "mouthpiece," when used to describe an attorney, "clearly communicates one who is more concerned with fulfilling the directions and instructions of a client, usually a criminal client, and even more specifically an underworld client, and has little or no concern with the code of professional responsibility, the rules of court and the applicable law."[129] In an aggressive and creative trial tactic, the plaintiff called as an expert witness a professor of psychology, who conducted two studies to determine the contrast, if any, between a reader's impression of an attorney referred to as another's "spokesman," on the one hand, and an attorney referred to as another's "mouthpiece," on the other. In the first study, the psychologist analyzed responses from 89 persons interviewed in New York City's financial district. Approximately half of those interviewed were given a questionnaire asking for their impression of an attorney referred to as "John Doe's spokeman" in a headline over a letter to the editor. The remaining interviewers were given an identical questionnaire, except that "John Doe's mouthpiece" was substituted for "John Doe's spokesman." The results of the study established that to a statistically significant degree the respondents rated "John Doe's mouthpiece" as more negative than "John Doe's spokesman." In a second study the same procedure was used, but instead of the reference to John Doe, the questionnaires actually used Frank Sinatra's name, asking the respondents for their reactions to the phrases "Sinatra's spokesman" and "Sinatra's mouthpiece." The psychologist testified that the substitution of the name Sinatra for John Doe did not significantly affect the outcome of the study, and that once again the word "mouthpiece" created a statistically significant—more negative—impression on readers than did the word "spokesman."

Barron's presented its own expert, who also conducted a social science study. That study indicated that although "mouthpiece" was a

---

[127] 557 F. Supp. 535 (S.D.N.Y. 1983).

[128] *Id.* at 537-40.

[129] *Id.*

"somewhat negative term," it became significantly less negative when used in connection with Frank Sinatra's name. The bottom-line conclusion of the defendant's expert was that the difference between the ratings of the word "spokesman" and the word "mouthpiece" was less salient when used in conjunction with Sinatra's name.

The court concluded that this battle of psycholinguistics research, as well as the expert testimony of a number of prestigious lawyers including Justice Kauffman, was still not enough to establish the plaintiff's burden that the word "mouthpiece" would be understood as defamatory to the ordinary and average reader. The defendant had claimed that among most readers of *Barron's* the word "mouthpiece" would be seen as little more than a slang term for a lawyer, just as "sawbones" might be used for a member of the medical profession.[130] The court concluded that the word "mouthpiece" did not invariably convey a defamatory meaning, that its meaning can depend upon the context in which it appears. The court said that two factors led it to conclude that the evidence was insufficient to establish the claim of defamatory meaning. First, the witnesses clearly attributed a defamatory meaning to the word only when it was used of a lawyer. The plaintiff, however, was not identified as a lawyer in the publication, and readers were not likely to recall that the plaintiff was identified as a lawyer in an article that appeared two months earlier. Second, although the attorney's testimony, standing alone, was not wholly irrelevant to the question of how *Barron's* readers viewed the caption, that testimony could not be viewed as persuasively establishing that *Barron's* readers were unlikely to have understood the word in the innocent sense of "spokesman." With regard to the social science studies conducted by the two experts in the case, the court stated that they were intriguing examples of psycholinguistics research, but they at best provided ambiguous evidence as to how *Barron's* readers were likely to have perceived the disputed word. Although both studies tended to lend support to the conclusion that "mouthpiece" is generally perceived as a somewhat negative term, and certainly as a more negative term than "spokesman," that was not enough to establish that the phrase was defamatory. To prevail in a defamation action it is necessary to demonstrate not only that the term applied to the plaintiff was more negative than a possible alternative, but also that the word was understood by the ordinary

130 *Id.* at 541-45.

reasonable reader as being defamatory.[131]

§ 4.08 Role of Judge and Jury

The judge determines in the first instance whether a statement is capable of sustaining a defamatory meaning.[132] If it is so capable, then the jury (or, in nonjury cases, the judge as trier of fact) must determine if the statement was in fact understood as defamatory by the recipients of the communication.[133] When the Illinois innocent construction rule is applied,[134] the court must first determine whether the statement may reasonably be given an innocent construction, and if it may be, it is nonactionable as a matter of law.[135] If the court concludes that no innocent construction is reasonable, however, "whether the publication was in fact understood to be defamatory or to refer to the plaintiff is a question for the jury."[136] This is one of the internal contradictions in the Illinois approach, for after the court apparently decides in the first instance that only one construction is reasonable—the noninnocent construction—the case still goes to a jury to determine how it was in fact construed.[137]

---

131 *Id.* For an interesting example of the use of a linguistics expert to attempt to demonstrate the absence of defamatory meaning, *see* Fong v. Merena, 655 P.2d 875, 877 (Hawaii 1982).

132 Restatement (Second) of Torts § 614 (1977). *See also, e.g.*, Pierce v. Capital Cities Communications, Inc., 576 F.2d 495 (2d Cir.), *cert denied*, 439 U.S. 861 (1978); Slawik v. News-Journal Co., 428 A.2d 15 (Del. 1981); Thompson v. Cash, 119 N.H. 371, 402 A.2d 651 (1979); James v. Gannett Co., 40 N.Y.2d 415, 419, 386 N.Y.S.2d 871, 353 N.E.2d 834 (1976); Westby v. Madison Newspapers, Inc., 81 Wis. 2d 1, 259 N.W.2d 691 (1971).

133 Restatement (Second) of Torts § 614 (1977). *See also, e.g.*, Hallmark Builders, Inc. v. Gaylord Broadcasting Co., 733 F.2d 1461 (11th Cir. 1984); Clark v. American Broadcasting Companies, 684 F.2d 1208 (6th Cir. 1982), *cert. denied*, 103 S. Ct. 1433 (1983); Yorty v. Chandler, 13 Cal. App. 3d 467, 475, 91 Cal. Rptr. 709, 714 (1970); Rodriguez v. Nishiki, 65 Haw. 430, 653 P.2d 1145 (1982); Cochran v. Indianapolis Newspapers, Inc., 178 Ind. App. 53, 372 N.E.2d 1211 (1978); Ryan v. Shreveport Times Publishing Co., 344 So. 2d 114 (La. App. 1977); Haas v. Painter, 62 Or. App. 719, 662 P.2d 768, *petition denied*, 295 Or. 297, 668 P.2d 381 (1983).

134 *See supra* § 4.06[2].

135 Chapski v. Copley Press, Inc., 92 Ill. 2d 344, 352, 442 N.E.2d 195, 199 (1982).

136 *Id.*

137 *See generally* Smolla & Malone, *supra* note 82, at 277 ("The primary flaw in the innocent construction rule is the illogical method for determining which statements are to be nonactionable as a matter of law and which are to be sent to the jury").

§ 4.09 Identity: The "Of and Concerning the Plaintiff" Requirement

[1] The Requirement in General

To be actionable the defamatory statement must be understood as being "of and concerning" the plaintiff.[138] It is axiomatic that there is no such thing as defamation in the air; the defamatory words must refer to someone, and because defamation is a recipient-centered tort,[139] the reference must be understood.[140]

[2] The Reference Need Not Be by Name—Colloquium

The plaintiff need not be cited by name for the defamation to be "of and concerning" him.[141] If there is no explicitly literal reference, the plaintiff must sustain the burden of pleading and proof, by way of "colloquium," that the defamatory statement refers to him.[142] If the burden is not met there is no defamation and the case is dismissed.[143]

[3] Strict Liability

If the defendant *intends* to refer to a particular person, the communication will be deemed "of and concerning" that person, if it is so understood by the recipient of the communication, no matter how bizarre or extraordinary it is that the communication was in fact so understood.[144] This is simply an application of the very expansive construction of proximate cause that the law of torts has always granted in intentional conduct situations; the defendant cannot complain that his intended result was accomplished through a circuitous route. "[I]t is

---

[138] *See* Restatement (Second) of Torts § 564 (1977).

[139] *See* Franklin & Bussel, *supra* note 9, at 828.

[140] *See generally* L. Eldredge, The Law of Defamation § 10, at 50 (1978) ("[t]here can be no defamation of the plaintiff unless the recipient of the communication believes it refers to . . . the plaintiff").

[141] *See, e.g.*, Peagler v. Phoenix Newspapers, Inc., 114 Ariz. 309, 560 P.2d 1216 (1977); Bindrim v. Mitchell, 92 Cal. App. 3d 61, 155 Cal. Rptr. 29, *cert. denied*, 444 U.S. 984 (1979); Scripps Co. v. Cholmondelay, 569 S.W.2d 700 (Ky. App. 1978).

[142] *See* Prosser and Keeton, *supra* note 1, § 111, at 783.

[143] *See, e.g.*, Weidman v. Ketcham, 278 N.Y. 129, 15 N.E.2d 426 (1938); Gnapinsky v. Goldyn, 23 N.J. 243, 128 A.2d 697 (1957); Arnold v. Sharpe, 296 N.C. 533, 251 S.E.2d 452 (1979); Brodsky v. Journal Publishing Co., 73 S.D. 343, 42 N.W.2d 855 (1950); Sims v. Kiro, 20 Wash. App. 229, 580 P.2d 642 (1978), *cert. denied*, 441 U.S. 945 (1979).

[144] Restatement (Second) of Torts § 564 comment a (1977); Eldredge, *supra* note 140, § 10, at 50; Prosser and Keeton, *supra* note 1, § 111, at 783.

unimportant that the recipient was extraordinarily perceptive, and that Sherlock Holmes himself would not have identified the plaintiff as being the person described."[145]

[4] The Accidental Reference

If the defendant did *not* intend to refer to the plaintiff, but the communication is in fact so understood by a recipient, there is some ambiguity as to the correct modern position. The original common law view was that the issue was governed by strict liability principles; the question was "not so much who was aimed at as who was hit."[146] A newspaper article about an alleged forger named Harry Kennedy could thus result in a recovery for libel from a *different* Harry Kennedy because some readers thought the article was about him;[147] a novel featuring a fictitious character named Cornigan who was a city magistrate could give rise to liability in a suit by a real Magistrate Corrigan, although the defendant did not know the real Corrigan even existed.[148] The harsh realities of the common law were encapsulated by

---

145 Eldredge, *supra* note 140, § 10, at 50. When the plaintiff's photograph is used in a publication, but not the plaintiff's name, courts will almost always find the communication to be "of and concerning" the plaintiff, apparently treating the matter as an "intentional use" case. In *Triangle Publications v. Chumley*, 317 S.E.2d 534 (Ga. 1984), for example, a *TV Guide* advertisement for a program on teenage pregnancies included in bold letters the statement "Guess what Lori found out today." The middle portion of the advertisement contained a photograph of a diary lying open on a desktop; written across the page was the following entry:"Dear Diary, I found out today that I am pregnant. What will I do now?" Directly below the diary page was a photograph of a teenage girl embracing a young man. The bottom quarter of the ad told the reader the details of the upcoming series on teenage pregnancies. The plaintiff, alleging that she was the girl pictured in the advertisement and that neither she nor anyone else had authorized the use of her photograph, sued for libel and invasion of privacy. She claimed that she had never been pregnant and had never engaged in sexual relations with the young man in the photograph, or with anyone else. The defendants claimed that the advertisement was not of and concerning the plaintiff, basing their contention on the fact that the plaintiff's name had not been used—rather, a substitute name had been printed in the ad—and also that the photograph was not offensive but merely depicted two wholesome, smiling young people. The court held that this argument was without merit, and that the ad was reasonably susceptible of a defamatory meaning. The bold print in the advertisement and the strategic placement of the plaintiff's picture could lead a jury reasonably to perceive the photograph as depicting the plaintiff as the pregnant teenager.

146 Corrigan v. Bobbs-Merrill Co., 228 N.Y. 58, 126 N.E. 260, 262 (1920). *See also* Sims v. Kiro, Inc., 20 Wash. App. 229, 234, 580 P.2d 642, 645 (1978), *cert. denied*, 441 U.S. 945 (1979) ("not who is meant, but who is hit").

147 Washington Post Co. v. Kennedy, 3 F.2d 207 (D.C. Cir. 1925).

148 Corrigan v. Bobbs-Merrill Co., 228 N.Y. 58, 64, 126 N.E. 260, 262 (1920). *See also*

the first *Restatement:* "If a statement sufficiently describes two or more persons and is reasonably capable of being understood as applicable to any one of them, although it is clearly intended to refer only to a single person, the defamer may be liable to *any or all such persons.*"[149]

The tough-minded position of the common law has generally been regarded as displaced by the Supreme Court's decision in *Gertz v. Robert Welch, Inc.*[150] Although there are some dissenters, the consensus appears to be that in cases governed by *Gertz,* fault is required not merely on the truth or falsity issue, but for all aspects of the cause of action, including reference to the plaintiff.[151] Authority for the view that the fault requirements of the first amendment extend to the of and concerning requirement can actually be traced back to *New York Times Co. v. Sullivan,*[152] in which the Court placed constitutional restrictions on the of and concerning requirement when public officials are involved.[153]

The *Restatement (Second) of Torts* thus takes the position that "[a] defamatory communication is made concerning the person to whom its recipient correctly, or mistakenly but reasonably, understands that it was intended to refer."[154] An unintended reference, therefore, will result in liability only if the recipient's understanding is "reasonable." Normally, if the recipient's understanding concerning identity is reasonable, but the defendant did not intend for the identity connection to be made, the defendant must have somehow acted unreasonably, or the mistake would never have occurred. In this sense, the *Restatement* now requires fault in connection with the of and concerning requirement. It is possible, however, for the recipient's understanding that the communication refers to the plaintiff to be reasonable because of facts that the ordinary reasonable defendant was not aware of and could not be expected to anticipate. To handle this problem the *Restatement* adds the caveat that it "is therefore necessary for the plaintiff to prove that a reasonable understanding on the part of the recipient that the com-

---

Memphis Commercial Appeal, Inc. v. Johnson, 96 F.2d 672 (6th Cir. 1938).

149 Restatement of Torts § 579 comment b (1938).

150 418 U.S. 323 (1974).

151 *See* Restatement (Second) of Torts § 580 B comments b-f (1977) (The *Restatement* position on this issue is discussed in § 3.28[2], *supra*); Eldredge, *supra* note 140, § 5, at 25; Sack, *supra* note 90, § II.8.1, at 113, and § II.8.6, at 123-24; Franklin & Bussel, *supra* note 9, at 834-38.

152 376 U.S. 254, 292 (1964).

153 *See supra* § 2.01.

154 Restatement (Second) of Torts § 564 (1977).

munication referred to the plaintiff was one that the defamer was negligent in failing to anticipate."[155]

[5] The Impact of *Dun & Bradstreet*

These attempts to bring all aspects of the of and concerning inquiry into synchronization with what was once thought by many to be the universal negligence requirement of *Gertz* have now been placed in some doubt by the holding in *Dun & Bradstreet, Inc. v. Greenmoss Builders, Inc.*[156] If *Dun & Bradstreet* authorizes a return to strict liability principles,[157] then the common law view that it is "not so much who was aimed at as who was hit"[158] may still apply to cases outside of matters of "public concern."[159]

[6] Not Everyone Must Identify the Plaintiff

It is not necessary that every recipient of the communication identify the plaintiff, as long as there are at least some who reasonably do.[160] However, if the number of people who make the identification is very small, or if only one person makes it, that fact is important in assessing the reasonableness of the belief.[161] Sometimes certain readers may reach a reasonable inference that an "of and concerning" connection exists merely from the syntax of the language used and juxtaposition of the plaintiff's name with the name of another.[162]

---

155 *Id.*, § 564 comment f, at 167.

156 105 S. Ct. 2939 (1985).

157 *See id.* at 2953 (White, J., concurring) ("it must be that the *Gertz* requirement of some kind of fault on the part of the defendant is also inapplicable in cases such as this"). *See supra* §§ 3.03-3.05.

158 Corrigan v. Bobbs-Merrill Co., 228 N.Y. 58, 64, 126 N.E. 260, 262 (1920).

159 *See* Dun & Bradstreet, Inc. v. Greenmoss Builders, Inc., 105 S. Ct. 2939, 2946 (1985) (*Gertz* rules on punitive and presumed damages apply only to speech on matters of public concern). *See supra* §§ 3.03-3.05.

160 Geisler v. Petrocelli, 616 F.2d 636 (2d Cir. 1980); Fetler v. Houghton Mifflin Co., 364 F.2d 650, 651 (2d Cir. 1966); Bindrim v. Mitchell, 92 Cal. App. 3d 61, 75-76, 155 Cal. Rptr. 29, 37-38, *cert. denied*, 444 U.S. 984 (1979); Julian v. American Business Consultants, Inc., 2 N.Y.2d 1, 17, 155 N.Y.S.2d 1, 16 (1956); Prosser and Keeton, *supra* note 1, § 111, at 783 (citing Fitzpatrick v. Age-Herald Publishing Co., 184 Ala. 510, 63 So. 980 (1913); Colvard v. Black, 110 Ga. 642, 36 S.E. 80 (1900)).

161 Restatement (Second) of Torts § 564 comment b, at 165 (1977).

162 *See* Golden Bear Distributing Sys. v. Chase Revel, Inc., 708 F.2d 944 (5th Cir. 1983), in which the Fifth Circuit, applying Texas law, reached the unusual but fully justified conclusion that true statements about one company in juxtaposition to other true statements about a second company could be libelous with regard to the second company. The

[7] Fictional Works

[a] The Problems in General

The fact that a work is labeled fiction does not talismanically immunize it from exposure to defamation liability. A story, novel, play, or film intended to depict only fictitious characters, if it is reasonably understood by the audience as portraying the plaintiff, may because of similarities in plot, character, name, physical resemblance, and other factors libel a real person.[163] For a number of reasons, the normal vocabulary of the law of libel often translates somewhat uneasily into the realm of fiction, posing unique issues and problems.[164]

---

case involved an article by *Entrepreneur* magazine, which includes a regular monthly column entitled "Fraud," in which the magazine exposes alleged instances of consumer and investor fraud. The article in question described investigations by the California Attorney General into the Golden Bear Corporation of California. Appearing throughout the article were statements about the operation of a separate corporation, Golden Bear of Texas, a corporation that shared advertising and sales techniques with Golden Bear of California, but had no apparent other financial connections to the California concern. The court held that the evidence at trial suggested that statements in the magazine article concerning the fraudulent activities of Golden Bear of California, when juxtaposed with statements about Golden Bear of Texas, could create the impression in the eyes of the ordinary reader that Golden Bear of Texas had also engaged in similar illegal activities, even though the extremely careful or literal reader might have realized that the article did not specifically state that Golden Bear of Texas had been investigated by law enforcement authorities, or was in any way implicated in the fraud perpetrated by the California corporation. The law of Texas, the court held, looks to the effect the article has on the mind of the ordinary reader.

163 *See generally* Felcher & Rubin, *Privacy, Publicity and the Portrayal of Real People by the Media,* 88 Yale L.J. 1577 (1979); Franklin & Trager, *Literature and Libel,* 4 Comm/Ent L. Rev. 205 (1982); Silver, *Libel, the "Higher Truths" of Art, and the First Amendment,* 126 U. Pa. L. Rev. 1065 (1978); Wilson, *The Law of Libel and the Art of Fiction,* 44 Law & Contemp. Probs. 27 (1981); Comment, *Defamation in Fiction, The Case for Absolute First Amendment Protection,* 29 Am. U.L. Rev. 571 (1980); Comment, *"Hey That's Me!"—The Conundrum of Identification in Libel and Fiction,* 18 Cal. W. L. Rev. 442 (1982); Note, *Fiction Based on Fact: Writer's Liability for Libel on Invasion of Privacy,* 14 U.C. Davis L. Rev. 1029 (1981).

Although there certainly are contemporary examples of successful defamation actions in suits based on fictional works, *see, e.g.,* Fetler v. Houghton Mifflin Co., 364 F.2d 650 (2d Cir. 1966); Bindrim v. Mitchell, 92 Cal. App. 3d 61, 155 Cal. Rptr. 29, *cert. denied,* 444 U.S. 984 (1979), examples that tend to raise great alarm within the industry, such suits seem to fail more often than they succeed. *See, e.g.,* Wheeler v. Dell Publishing Co., 300 F.2d 372 (7th Cir. 1962); Hicks v. Casablanca Records and Filmworks, 464 F. Supp. 426 (S.D.N.Y. 1978); Springer v. Viking Press, 90 A.D.2d 315, 60 N.Y.2d 916, 470 N.Y.S.2d 579, 458 N.E.2d 1256 (1st Dept. 1982), *aff'd,* 60 N.Y.2d 916 (1983); Wojtowicz v. Delacorte Press, 43 N.Y.2d 858, 403 N.Y.S.2d 218, 374 N.E.2d 129 (1978); Franklin & Trager, *supra* note 163.

164 *See* Smolla, *Let the Author Beware: The Rejuvenation of the American Law of*

For the fiction writer, the problem posed by the of and concerning requirement is that all fiction is to a greater or lesser degree drawn from reality. Henry James was once accused of using the character Miss Birdseye in his novel *The Bostonians* as a vehicle for drawing a vicious caricature of Nathaniel Hawthorne's sister-in-law, Miss Peabody. James remarked that the character Miss Birdseye was drawn "entirely from my moral consciousness, like every other person I have ever known." From Orson Welles's movie "Citizen Kane"—a thinly disguised portrayal of William Randolph Hearst—to Robert Penn Warren's *All the King's Men*—a powerful fictional exploration of a character very much like Huey Long—to the hundreds of roman-à-clefs and docudramas that fill the nation's voracious appetite for entertainment, writers constantly draw directly or obliquely from real life for their characters and events. When they do, they often take liberties with the facts.[165] As Nathaniel Hawthorne wrote in *The Scarlet Letter:* "I have allowed myself as to such points nearly or altogether as much license as if the facts had been entirely of my own invention. What I contest for is the authenticity of the outline."

When a real person is portrayed in a fictional work, it is relatively common for the plaintiff to join various invasion of privacy claims with a libel action, and cross-reference to those areas should be made when handling problems in this area.[166]

[b] Factors Used to Establish Identity in Fiction

In determining whether a character in a fictional work is "of and concerning" the plaintiff, courts consider a broad range of factors, including:

(1) whether the plaintiff's name, or a very similar name, is used;[167]

Libel, 132 U. Pa. L. Rev. 1, 42-47 (1983).

165 *See generally* Silver, *supra* note 163. In the case of a "gonzo journalist" such as Hunter Thompson, powerful and controversial insights are often achieved through the constant and outrageous manipulation of reality.

166 *See* Note, *Fiction Based on Fact: Writer's Liability for Libel or Invasion of Privacy, supra* note 163. *See* Chapters 11 and 12, *infra.*

167 *See* Geisler v. Petrocelli, 616 F.2d 636 (2d Cir. 1980); Corrigan v. Bobbs-Merill Co., 228 N.Y. 58, 126 N.E. 260 (1920); Smith v. Huntington Press, 410 F. Supp. 1270 (S.D. Ohio 1975); Kerby v. Hal Roach Studios, 53 Cal. App. 2d 207, 127 P.2d 577 (2d Dist. 1942); Springer v. Viking Press, 90 A.D.2 315, 60 N.Y.2d 916, 470 N.Y.S.2d 579, 458 N.E.2d 1256 (1st Dept. 1982), *aff'd,* 60 N.Y.2d 916 (1983). *See also* Spahn v. Julian Messner, Inc., 21

(2) whether there are physical appearance similarities between the plaintiff and the character;[168]

(3) whether the ages of the plaintiff and the character are close;[169]

(4) whether there are similarities in geographic location and setting;[170]

(5) whether there are similarities in occupation or career progress;[171]

(6) whether there are similarities in relationships and personality characteristics;[172]

N.Y.2d 124, 286 N.Y.S.2d 832, 223 N.E.2d 840 (1967), *appeal dismissed*, 393 U.S. 1046 (1969) (privacy case); Corr v. Sun Printing & Publishing Co., 177 N.Y. 131, 69 N.E. 288 (1904); E. Hulton Co. v. Jones, 26 T.L.R. 128 (1909).

[168] *See, e.g.*, Wheeler v. Dell Publishing Co., 300 F.2d 372, 276 (7th Cir. 1962); Bindrim v. Mitchell, 92 Cal. App. 3d 61, 155 Cal. Rptr. 29, 37, *cert. denied*, 444 U.S. 984 (1979); Springer v. Viking Press, 90 A.D.2d 315, 60 N.Y.2d 916, 470 N.Y.S.2d 579, 458 N.E.2d 1256 (1st Dept. 1982), *aff'd*, 60 N.Y.2d 916 (1983).

[169] *See, e.g.*, Middlebrooks v. Curtis Publishing Co., 413 F.2d 141, 143 (4th Cir. 1969); Wheeler v. Dell Publishing Co., 300 F.2d 372, 376 (7th Cir. 1962).

[170] *See, e.g.*, Middlebrooks v. Curtis Publishing Co., 413 F.2d 141, 143 (4th Cir. 1969); Wheeler v. Dell Publishing Co., 300 F.2d 372, 375 (7th Cir. 1962); Bindrim v. Mitchell, 92 Cal. App. 3d 61, 155 Cal. Rptr. 29, 37, *cert. denied*, 444 U.S. 984 (1979); Lyons v. New American Library, 78 A.D.2d 723, 432 N.Y.S.2d 536, 536-37 (3d Dept. 1980); Toscani v. Hersey, 271 A.D. 445, 65 N.Y.S.2d 814 (1946).

[171] *See, e.g.*, Middlebrooks v. Curtis Publishing Co., 413 F.2d 141 (4th Cir. 1969); Levey v. Warner Brothers Pictures, 57 F. Supp. 40 (S.D.N.Y. 1944); Bindrim v. Mitchell, 92 Cal. App. 3d 61, 155 Cal. Rptr. 29, 37, *cert. denied*, 444 U.S. 984 (1979); Corrigan v. Bobbs-Merrill Co., 228 N.Y. 58, 126 N.E. 260 (1920). In the Bindrim v. Mitchell case, *supra*, Dr. Paul Bindrim, who led "nude marathon" group therapy sessions, brought a defamation action against Gwen Davis Mitchell over a novel entitled *Touching*. Mitchell attended a Bindrim therapy session and signed a contract stating she would not write about the experience; nonetheless, two months later she received a $150,000 advance from Doubleday to write *Touching*, a book depicting nude encounter sessions run by a fictitious Dr. Simon Herford. Bindrim claimed that the fictitious character was really he, and that the portrayal, which painted him as abusive and insensitive to patients, was libelous. Although the real Bindrim was clean shaven with short hair, the physical description of Herford was that of "a fat Santa Claus type with long white hair, white sideburns, a cherubic rosy face, and rosy forearms." The main evidence that linked the fictitious character with the real plaintiff consisted of several tape recordings of actual sessions for comparison with depictions of the sessions in the novel, and testimony by three witnesses that the nude encounter sessions depicted in the book closely resembled the actual nude encounter sessions conducted by Bindrim. The court found that the evidence was sufficient to support the identification requirements, and applied the *New York Times* actual malice standard to find liability.

[172] *See, e.g.*, Bindrim v. Mitchell, 92 Cal. App. 3d 62, 155 Cal. Rptr. 29, *cert. denied*, 444 U.S. 984 (1979); Springer v. Viking Press, 90 A.D.2d 315, 60 N.Y.2d 916, 470 N.Y.S.2d 579, 458 N.E.2d 1256 (1st Dept. 1982), *aff'd*, 60 N.Y.2d 916 (1983).

(7) whether the work as a whole is clearly presented as fiction;[173]

(8) whether a disclaimer labeling the work as fiction and similarities as "coincidental" is employed;[174]

(9) whether there are similarities between the plot of the fictional work and the real events in the plaintiff's life;[175]

(10) whether the use of the plaintiff's name or the fictional character allegedly representing the plaintiff play prominent roles in the fictional work or have only "fleeting and incidental" significance;[176]

---

173 *See, e.g.*, Geisler v. Petrocelli, 616 F.2d 636 (2d Cir. 1980); Middlebrooks v. Curtis Publishing Co., 413 F.2d 141 (4th Cir. 1969); Hicks v. Casablanca Records & Filmworks, 464 F. Supp. 426 (S.D.N.Y. 1978) (film based on clearly fictionalized incident in Agatha Christie's life not actionable); Bindrim v. Mitchell, 92 Cal. App. 3d 61, 155 Cal. Rptr. 29, *cert. denied*, 444 U.S. 984 (1979). *See also* Leopold v. Levin, 45 Ill. 2d 434, 259 N.E.2d 250 (1970) (heavily fictionalized film based on lives of Leopold and Loeb nonactionable on first amendment grounds).

174 A typical disclaimer such as "All characters in this book are fictitious, and any resemblence to real persons, living or dead, is purely coincidental" is helpful to a finding that the work is not of and concerning the plaintiff, but it is by no means a bar to identification. *See, e.g.*, Allen v. Gordon, 86 A.D.2d 514 (1st Dept. 1982), *aff'd*, 56 N.Y.2d 780 (1982); Lyons v. New American Library, 78 A.D.2d 723, 432 N.Y.S.2d 536 (3d Dept. 1980). *See also* Fetler v. Houghton Mifflin Co., 364 F.2d 650 (2d Cir. 1966) (fictional setting alone not enough to insulate defendant from liability); Corrigan v. Bobbs-Merrill Co., 228 N.Y. 58, 65, 126 N.E. 260, 262 (1920) ("Reputations may not be traduced with impunity, whether under the literary forms of a work of fiction, or in jest.").

175 *See, e.g.*, Fetler v. Houghton Mifflin Co., 364 F.2d 650, 651 (2d Cir. 1966) (both plaintiff and fictional character were oldest sons of minister and part of families of thirteen children giving concerts in Europe on a bus tour in the 1930s); Bindrim v. Mitchell, 92 Cal. App. 3d 61, 70-71, 155 Cal. Rptr. 29, 34, *cert. denied*, 444 U.S. 984 (1979) (similarities between therapy sessions of plaintiff and those conducted by fictional character); Lyons v. New American Library, Inc., 78 A.D.2d 723, 432 N.Y.S.2d 536, 538 (3d Dept. 1980) (lack of similarity between character in novel based on "Son of Sam" killings and plaintiff—fictional character hindered investigation, while plaintiff played no role in real investigation).

176 When the fictional character's role is relatively inconspicuous, courts are unlikely to find the of and concerning requirement satisfied. *See, e.g.*, Wheeler v. Dell Publishing Co., 300 F.2d 376 (7th Cir. 1962) (character occupied "an inconspicuous part in the novel" and "[n]o average reader of the book would remember the very minor subplot" in which the character was involved); Wojtowicz v. Delacorte Press, 58 A.D.2d 45, 395 N.Y.2d 205 (1977), *aff'd mem.*, 43 N.Y.2d 858, 374 N.E.2d 129, 403 N.Y.S.2d 218 (1978).

On the other hand, if the plaintiff was "a prominent character throughout the novel," and thus memorable to the average reader, courts are more likely to find that the identity element is satisfied. *See* Fetler v. Houghton Mifflin Co., 364 F.2d 650, 652 (2d Cir. 1966).

The fleeting and incidental use of the plaintiff's name is normally, standing alone, not enough to sustain a modern action for defamation or invasion of privacy. *See, e.g.*, Hooker v. Columbia Pictures, 551 F. Supp. 1060 (N.D. Ill. 1982); Ladany v. William Morrow & Co., 465 F. Supp. 870 (S.D.N.Y. 1978); Cohn v. NBC, 67 A.D.2d 140 (1st Dept. 1979), *aff'd*, 50 N.Y.2d 885, 430 N.Y.S.2d 265, *cert. denied*, 449 U.S. 1022 (1980); Peterfreund v. United Artists, 6 Med. L. Rep. (BNA) 1754 (N.Y. Sup. Ct. 1980); Koczka v. Avon, 7 Med. L. Rep.

(11) whether the events that take place in the fictional work are so fantastical or bizarre that no reasonable reader would treat them as realistic depictions.[177]

(BNA) 1919 (N.Y. Sup. Ct. 1981). *But see* Polakoff v. Harcourt Brace Jovanovich, 3 Med. L. Rep. (BNA) 2516 (N.Y. Sup. Ct. 1979).

One court has stated that "the fictional character must be so closely akin to the real person . . . that a reader of the book, knowing the real person, would have no difficulty linking the two. *Superficial similarities are insufficient,* as is a common first name." Springer v. Viking Press, 90 A.D.2d 315, 470 N.Y.S.2d 579, 458 N.E.2d 1256 (1st Dept. 1982), *aff'd,* 60 N.Y.2d 916 (1983) (emphasis added).

[177] *See* Pring v. Penthouse International Ltd., 695 F.2d 438 (10th Cir. 1982). The *Pring* facts are worth reviewing, for they demonstrate how depictions may be so outrageous as to be beyond reasonable defamatory construction. The *Pring* case arose from a *Penthouse* article, described as "humor," entitled "Miss Wyoming Saves the World." Set at a Miss America Pageant, the story depicts the exploits of a fictional beauty queen named "Charlene," who has entered the contest as Miss Wyoming. In the story, Charlene, a baton twirler, is about to perform her act when her thoughts wander back to an incident from college. She remembers performing fellatio on a Wyoming football player, an act that mystically caused him to levitate. Once on stage, Charlene begins to simulate fellatio on her baton, a performance that stops the orchestra. Charlene does not make it to the finals of the competition, but she thinks she has a "real talent" nonetheless. While at the edge of the stage watching the finalists answer questions, Charlene's thoughts again wander, this time to how she might answer one of the "poise and intelligence" questions. She fantasizes about how she could "save the world" with her "real talent," with the "entire Soviet Central Committee," "Marshal Tito," and "Fidel Castro." Charlene would be the ambassador of love and peace. She then begins to perform fellatio on her coach at the edge of the stage. As the audience is applauding the new Miss America, this act of fellatio causes the coach to levitate. The story ends with the television cameras leaving the image of the new Miss America to focus on Charlene and the sight of her coach floating on the air.

The plaintiff was Ms. Kimerli Jayne Pring, the real Miss Wyoming of 1978; she was victorious at trial, winning a staggering $1.5 million in compensatory damages and $25 million in punitive damages. The Tenth Circuit reversed, in a 2-1 decision. The court held that "the charged portions of the story described something physically impossible in an impossible setting" and a reader would have "understood that the charged portions were pure fantasy and nothing else." *Id.* The *Pring* case is enormously important precedent for the more unorthodox forms of "gonzo journalism" or fictional works in which authors purposefully interweave real persons and events with fantastical or dreamlike plots—situations that deserve full first amendment protection. (Note that in such instances, the protection may come from the lack of a serious "of and concerning" nexus, or a lack of defamatory meaning, or through the fact/opinion distinction—the essential point is that the reasonable reader understands the portrayals are not to be taken literally.) *See generally* Silver, *supra* note 163, at 1070-76; Smolla, *supra* note 164, at 86-89.

[c] A Cross-Reference to Fault Requirements, and a Proposed Framework for Handling the Special Problems Posed by Fiction

When an author wishes to draw from a real person as the basis for a fictional character, there are two relatively "safe" courses of action from a legal perspective: First, the author may make little or no attempt to disguise the character, but refrain from any defamatory and false embellishments on the character's conduct or personality; second, the author may engage in creative embellishments that reflect negatively on the character's reputation, but make substantial efforts to disguise the character, by changing name, age, geographic setting, personality, occupation, or other factors sufficiently to avoid identification. When an author takes a middle ground, however, neither adhering perfectly to the real person's attributes and behavior nor engaging in elaborate disguise, there is a threat of defamation liability.[178]

The modern law of defamation is particularly unresponsive to this sort of fiction. In evaluating fiction when claims of defamation are raised, courts too often seem ready to conclude that the only significant legal question is the of and concerning requirement. Once identity is established, it often seems as if the barriers that would normally impede recovery for a nonfiction work—standards of intent, or the nonactionability of opinion—have quickly come tumbling down.[179]

The objective in devising a coherent approach to handling libel claims in fiction should be to create a standard that would give fiction the same rough quantum of constitutional and common law protection enjoyed by nonfiction. Because the same verbal formulations under *New York Times, Gertz,* and *Dun & Bradstreet* apply to both fiction and nonfiction, there is a surface equality in the treatment they receive. The equivalency is spurious, however, because it often tends to produce liability in a mechanistic and superficial sense when applied to fiction. One might argue that fiction deserves this fate because it is, after all, a "lie," and there is no first amendment value to false statements of fact.[180] But that argument is wholly unpersuasive, and it is doubtful that courts, if they reflected on the point, would maintain that fiction grounded in reality is undeserving of treatment substantially the same

[178] No case illustrates this problem better than *Bindrim v. Mitchell,* 92 Cal. App. 3d 61, 155 Cal. Rptr. 29, *cert. denied,* 444 U.S. 984 (1979). *See supra* note 171.

[179] *See* Smolla, *supra* note 164, at 86-87.

[180] *See* Gertz v. Robert Welch, Inc., 418 U.S. 323, 340 (1974).

as that applied to nonfiction depicting the same reality. To make the glib statement that fiction authors "lie for a living" totally misconstrues the conventions under which readers read and writers write. Fiction is a critical component of a robust and open culture. It may help a reader escape or transcend reality, or it may incisively explore reality. Authors portray life in an infinite variety of ways for an infinite variety of reasons, among them the search for truths deeper than those revealed by surface facts.[181] Fictional portrayals are drawn with infinite gradations of grace and skill. Courts need just enough literary insight to realize that they are not literary critics, and would be poor judges if they tried to be.[182] Regardless of the perceived quality of the work at issue, courts should ensure that it receives approximately the same level of insulation from liability that would apply to information about the same subject if it were written as something other than fiction.

The problem, however, is to come up with a legal standard that accomplishes this result without warping the basic law of defamation as applied in other cases. One recurring suggestion is to give fiction an absolute privilege against liability.[183] It is possible to rationalize such an absolute privilege by arguing that all fiction is properly classified as "pure idea," which can never be either true or false.[184] But that rationalization goes too far, farther than courts will ever venture. An absolute privilege would not provide equivalent protection for fiction and nonfiction; it would instead remedy the present imbalance with a counterimbalance. Some device is required to allow defamed plaintiffs recompense when a work of fiction is nothing but a shield for an intentional attack on reputation.

There are two important considerations in handling this problem. The first is a conscientious application of the factors listed in the previous section to determine whether the of and concerning requirement has been satisfied, with a recognition that the burden of establishing

---

[181] *See* Silver, *supra* note 163, at 1066-70.

[182] *See* Smolla, *supra* note 164, at 87. *Cf.* Bleistein v. Donaldson Lithographing Co., 188 U.S. 239, 251 (1903) (Holmes, J.) ("It would be a dangerous undertaking for persons trained only to the law to constitute themselves final judges of the worth of pictorial illustrations, outside of the narrowest and most obvious limits.") (Holmes was warning against judges' deciding, on the basis of their personal preferences, what works of art were worthy of copyright.).

[183] *See* Comment, *Defamation in Fiction, The Case for Absolute Protection*, *supra* note 163.

[184] *See* Smolla, *supra* note 164, at 87. *See also* Franklin & Trager, *supra* note 163, at 221-23; Wilson, *supra* note 163, at 44-46.

identity is on the plaintiff, and that in fiction cases *the burden is not a light one.*[185] The second method for handling the problem of libel in fiction is to use the same "knowing or reckless disregard" or negligence standards employed by *New York Times* or *Gertz,* but to change the focus of the inquiry from the author's culpable fault regarding truth or falsity to whether the ordinary reasonable reader would conclude that the author intended the reader to understand the events described in the work as depictions of real life events.[186] There is usually no real harm in an author's drawing characters and events from real life, even if those characters are readily identifiable as actual people, as long as the author does not attempt to identify his or her fantasy as reality. As long as the ordinary reasonable reader is not led to believe that what is packaged as fiction is meant to be taken as fact, conventional first amendment and common law doctrine should make the work nonactionable. As a matter of first amendment jurisprudence, speech that is neither intended nor understood as fact should fall within the protections of *Gertz,* assuming such speech qualifies as related to matters of "public concern" under *Dun & Bradstreet.*[187] There is no better example of "idea" than fantasy, whether it be the dreams in our minds or the dreams we commit to paper. Similarly, even if the fictional character is clearly understood as depicting an actual person, as a matter of common law doctrine, linkage in identity is not enough. The communication must also be defamatory, and it cannot be defamatory as a matter of law if the ordinary reasonable reader would not treat the *actions* of the character as real, even if the reality of the character is conceded.[188]

---

185 *See* Geisler v. Petrocelli, 616 F.2d 636 (2d Cir. 1980) (burden is on plaintiff and it is "not a light one") (quoting Fetler v. Houghton Mifflin Co., 364 F.2d 650, 653 (2d Cir. 1966)). *See also* Hicks v. Casablanca Records and Filmworks, 464 F. Supp. 426, 430-31 (S.D.N.Y. 1978).

186 *See* Smolla, *supra* note 164, at 87-88; Wilson, *supra* note 163, at 43-49.

187 In dealing with fictional works, it should be hoped that courts, sensitive to values of artistic freedom, will interpret the phrase "public concern" with particular openmindedness and flexibility. *See generally supra* §§ 3.02-3.05.

188 *See* Pring v. Penthouse International, Ltd., 695 F.2d 438 (10th Cir. 1982). *See supra* note 177.

§ 4.10 Group Defamation

[1] In General

As a general proposition no action lies for the publication of a general defamatory statement about a large group or class of persons, on the principle that such a general condemnation could not reasonably be construed as of and concerning each individual member of the group, and the disparagement is too diffuse to create a realistic likelihood of reputational injury to any individual member.[189] This general proposition, however, must be qualified by the statement that individuals frequently *are* successful in maintaining actions for defamation arising from statements about a group, either because the size of the group is small or the plaintiff is singled out in some way, or some collection of other factors creates reputational injury that is sufficiently well focused to satisfy the of and concerning requirement. The subsections that follow discuss the factors and fact patterns governing this area.

[2] Racial, Ethnic, or Religious Disparagement

Civil liability is not permitted for defamation aimed at racial, ethnic, or religious groups. Although slurs directed against Blacks, Hispanics, Jews, Catholics, or any other group are repugnant and hateful, they are regarded as beyond the pale of the civil law of defamation.[190] Thus, a defamatory statement aimed at 600 million Muslims was not actionable;[191] "if the court were to permit an action to lie for defamation of such a multitudinous group we would render meaningless the right guaranteed by the First Amendment to explore issues of public import."[192] Similarly, a statement by Joseph Grace, chairman of President Reagan's task force on the Private Sector on Cost Control, that "900,000 [Puerto

---

[189] Prosser and Keeton, *supra* note 1, § 111, at 784. *See generally* Arcand v. Evening Call Publishing Co., 567 F.2d 1163 (7th Cir. 1977); McCullough v. Cities Service Co., 676 P.2d 833 (Okla. 1984); Lewis, *The Individual Member's Right to Recover for Defamation Levelled at the Group*, 17 U. Miami L. Rev. 519 (1963); Reisman, *Democracy and Defamation: Control of Group Libel*, 42 Colum. L. Rev. 727 (1942); Wittenberg, *Individual Recovery for Defamation of a Group*, 15 Ohio St. L.J. 273 (1954); Note, *Liability for Defamation of a Group*, 34 Colum. L. Rev. 1322 (1934).

[190] *See* Puerto Rican Legal Defense Fund, Inc. v. Grace, 9 Med. L. Rep. (BNA) 1514, 1516 (N.Y. Sup. Ct. 1983).

[191] Khalid Abdullah Tario Al Mansour Faissal Fahd Al Talal v. Fanning, 506 F. Supp. 186 (N.D. Cal. 1980).

[192] *Id.* at 187.

Ricans] live in New York and they're all on food stamps" was held nonactionable:[193]

> When an attack is made upon an ethnic or racial group the type of harm likely to be suffered by a member of the group is indirect. It is not the type of focused, individual harm contemplated by the defamation laws. No person is singled out and damaged in his individual capacity. At worst, the defamatory remark increases the general level of prejudice encountered by all members of the defamed group. This is, to be sure, an undesirable result, but one that is harmful to society, rather than to a particular individual.[194]

[3] Criminal Liability for Racial, Ethnic, or Religious Group Defamation

As an alternative to civil liability as a means of dealing with racial, ethnic, or religious disparagement, some states have, over the years, enacted criminal libel laws aimed at creating criminal sanctions for group libel.[195] In *Beauharnais v. Illinois*[196] the Supreme Court upheld the constitutionality of the Illinois criminal group libel statute. *Beauharnais* was a pre-*New York Times* decision, however, and the continued viability of that holding is today in substantial doubt.[197]

[4] Factors Used to Establish or Deny Civil Liability for Group Defamation

[a] Size of the Group

Although there is growing judicial sensitivity to the notion that the size of the group should not be the sole determinative factor in assessing liability to individuals for group defamation,[198] it is certainly an enor-

---

193 Puerto Rican Legal Defense Fund, Inc. v. Grace, 9 Med. L. Rep. (BNA) 1514 (N.Y. Sup. Ct. 1983).

194 *Id.* at 1516.

195 *See generally* Beth, *Group Libel and Free Speech*, 39 Minn. L. Rev. 167 (1954); Reisman, *supra* note 189; Scott, *Criminal Sanctions for Group Libel: Feasibility and Constitutionality*, 1 Duke B.J. 218 (1951); Tanenhaus, *Group Libel*, 35 Corn. L.Q. 261 (1950).

196 343 U.S. 250 (1952).

197 *See* Garrison v. Louisiana, 379 U.S. 64 (1964) (striking down Louisiana criminal libel law for failing to satisfy *New York Times* requirement); Tollet v. United States, 485 F.2d 1087, 1094-99 (8th Cir. 1983) (striking down as unconstitutional federal act prohibiting mailing of "libelous, scurrilous, defamatory, or threatening" material). *See also* Kelly, *Criminal Libel and Free Speech*, 6 Kan. L. Rev. 295 (1958).

198 *See* Brady v. Ottaway Newspaper, Inc., 84 A.D.2d 226, 445 N.Y.S.2d 786 (1981); McCullough v. Cities Service Co., 676 P.2d 833 (Okla. 1984); Fawcett Publications, Inc. v. Morris, 377 P.2d 42 (1962), *cert. denied*, 376 U.S. 513 (1964).

mously important factor and at times a conclusive one.[199] Some groups are so large that assertions of individual liability are almost frivolous; the number of persons affected by references to 600 million Muslims,[200] 900,000 Puerto Ricans,[201] 19,686 doctors of osteopathy,[202] 12,500 members of the Freeway Association,[203] 204 businessmen in Butte, Montana,[204] or 5,000 Kentucky Fried Chicken outlets[205] is simply too large to make claims of individualized reputational harm plausible. As groups get smaller, however, courts often begin to play a relatively fine-tuned "numbers game."

In *Neiman-Marcus v. Lait,*[206] for example, the defendants were authors of a book entitled *U.S.A. Confidential.* They wrote about a department store in Dallas, saying that "some" of the store's models were "call girls—the top babes in town," and that "the salesgirls are pretty good too—pretty and often much cheaper." Additionally, they stated that "Neiman's put in a men's store . . . You wonder how all the faggots got to the wild and woolly . . . Now most of the sales staff are fairies too." The plaintiffs included 30 of Neiman's 382 salesgirls, 15 of the store's 25 salesmen, and all 9 of the store's models. The defendants did not challenge the "of and concerning" element for the 9 models, but did move to dismiss the actions of the salesgirls and the salesmen. The court found that the salesgirls class was too large, and dismissed as to them.

---

[199] The *Restatement,* for example, places primary emphasis on size, stating that liability may exist only if "the group or class is so small that the matter can reasonably be understood to refer to the member" or "the circumstances of publication reasonably give rise to the conclusion that there is a particular reference to the member." Restatement (Second) of Torts § 564A (1977). To the extent that there is any "rule of thumb" concerning judicial analysis based primarily on numbers, groups of less than 25 appear to fare better than groups above that number. *See id.,* comment b. ("it is not possible to set definite limits as to the size of the other group or class, but the cases in which recovery has been allowed usually have involved numbers of 25 or fewer"). *See also* Barger v. Playboy Enterprises, Inc., 564 F. Supp. 1151 (N.D. Cal. 1983), *aff'd,* 732 F.2d 163 (9th Cir. 1984); Golden North Airways, Inc. v. Tanann Publishing Co., 218 F.2d 612 (9th Cir. 1954).

[200] Khalid Abdullah Tariq Al Mansour Faissal Fahd Al Talal v. Fanning, 506 F. Supp. 186 (N.D. Cal. 1980).

[201] Puerto Rican Legal Defense Fund, Inc. v. Grace, 9 Med. L. Rep. (BNA) 1514 (N.Y. Sup. Ct. 1983).

[202] McCollough v. Cities Service Co., 676 P.2d 833 (Okla. 1984).

[203] Macaulay v. Bryan, 75 Nev. 339, 339 P.2d 377 (1959).

[204] Granger v. Time, Inc., 568 P.2d 535 (Mont. 1977).

[205] Kentucky Fried Chicken of Bowling Green, Inc. v. Sanders, 563 S.W.2d 8 (Ky. 1978).

[206] 13 F.R.D. 311 (S.D.N.Y. 1952).

The salesmen did have a cause of action, the court found, specifically holding that it made no difference that the book referred to "most" rather than "all" of the 25 salesmen as "faggots." Given the court's holding regarding the salesmen, it is clear that the court would also have upheld the claim of the 9 models had their action been challenged.

[b] Reference to All or Only Part of a Group

When a defamatory statement refers to less than everyone in a group, courts tend to be less likely to find the "of and concerning" requirement satisfied, but if the statement is sufficiently well focused on a particular subset of the group, or if a significant percentage of a relatively small group is referred to, the requirement may still be satisfied. Thus, a defamatory statement concerning one unidentified member of a police force with a staff of 21 was held nonactionable, with the court drawing an analogy to a suit by an entire baseball team based on a report that one unidentified player has been in a brawl.[207] On the other hand, suits were permitted when the defamatory statement was that either *A* or *B* had altered a note,[208] or when a defamatory charge concerned "some" of the 11 engineers employed by one company,[209] or when "a number" of 13 township commissioners were claimed to be involved in corruption,[210] or when "most" of a sales staff of 25 were said to be "fairies,"[211] or when the defamatory charge was levelled at "all except one" of 12 radio critics in New York City.[212]

[c] The Intensity of Suspicion Test

Several well-reasoned decisions have begun to discard this narrow focus on the size of the group, substituting a more flexible "intensity of suspicion" test in group defamation cases. The earliest case employing this more subtle analysis was *Fawcett Publications, Inc. v. Morris,*[213] in which the court stated that "[w]hile there is substantial precedent from other jurisdictions to the effect that a member of a 'large group' may

---

207 Arcand v. Evening Call Publishing Co., 567 F.2d 1163 (1st Cir. 1977).

208 Farrell v. Johnson, 50 Ky. 48 (1850).

209 Hardy v. Williamson, 86 Ga. 551, 12 S.E. 874 (1841). *See also* American Broadcasting—Paramount Theatres, Inc. v. Simpson, 106 Ga. App. 230, 126 S.E.2d 873 (1962) (charge concerned one of two persons).

210 Farrell v. Triangle Publications, 339 Pa. 102, 159 A.2d 734 (1960).

211 Neiman-Marcus Co. v. Lait, 13 F.R.D. 311 (S.D.N.Y. 1952).

212 Gross v. Kantor, 270 N.Y. 93, 200 N.E. 592 (1936).

213 377 P.2d 42 (Okla. 1962), *cert. denied,* 376 U.S. 513 (1964).

not recover in an action for a libelous publication unless he is referred to personally, we have found no substantial reason why size alone should be conclusive."[214] The plaintiff in the *Morris* case was a fullback on the alternate squad of a football team made up of 60 to 70 players. An article alleged that members of the team were using amphetamines. In upholding the plaintiff's claim, the court refused to follow a mechanical group size rule, "where, as here, the complaining member of the group is as well known and identified in connection with the group as was the plaintiff in this case."[215]

Similarly, in *Brady v. Ottaway Newspapers, Inc.*,[216] the court concluded that 53 members of a 71 member police department in Newburgh, New York, could maintain a defamation action for a statement suggesting that although they were not indicted for misdeeds along with 18 colleagues, the other 53 must have known what was going on. The court eschewed a numbers-oriented analysis and instead considered the defined nature of the group, the prominence of the group, and the role of the plaintiffs within the group. And most recently, in another extremely thoughtful opinion, the Oklahoma Supreme Court, elaborating on the *Morris* and *Brady* decisions, set forth an elaborate analysis in *McCullough v. Cities Service Co.*[217] The court made a number of useful observations:

(1) Size alone "is too narrow a focus" to determine the issue of individual reference arising from a group libel.[218]

(2) An "impersonal reproach" of an "indeterminate class" is generally not actionable. The underlying premise is that "the larger the collectivity named in the libel, the less likely it is that a reader would understand it to refer to a particular individual." Thus, the "incidental and occasional injury to the individual resulting from the defamation of large groups is balanced against the public's right to know."[219]

(3) A reference to a small group is different because "reference to the individual plaintiff reasonably follows from the statement."[220]

---

[214] *Id.* at 51.
[215] *Id.*
[216] 84 A.D.2d 226, 445 N.Y.S.2d 786 (1981).
[217] 676 P.2d 833 (Okla. 1984).
[218] *Id.* at 837.
[219] *Id.* at 836-37.
[220] *Id.* at 837.

(4) The "intensity of suspicion test" recognizes the fact that "even a general derogatory reference to a group may affect the reputation of every member." In order to make the determination, "a factual inquiry [must] be made to determine the degree that the group accusation focuses on each individual member of the group. The numerical size of the group is a consideration, but it is not the only factor. . . . One element to be considered is the prominence of the individual within the group."[221]

---

221 *Id.* In Barger v. Playboy Enterprises, 564 F. Supp. 1151 (N.D. Cal. 1983), *aff'd*, 732 F.2d 163 (9th Cir. 1984), it was held that a magazine article which, in relating the experiences of an undercover police officer who had infiltrated the Hells Angels motorcycle gang, described alleged sexual activities of unnamed "Hells Angels brides" was not sufficiently of and concerning the individual lives of specific Hells Angels members to give them a cause of action for libel. In Lins v. Evening News, 9 Med. L. Rep. (BNA) 2380 (Mich. Ct. App. 1983), an action filed by the president and the secretary-treasurer of a union, the court held that a newspaper column which referred to "thieves who run the teamster's union" and "thugs who run Local 299," "stupid men" who make "stupid moves" and "crooked officials," "animals," and "union hoods" was defamatory, although only the statements referring to these individuals were actionable. Statements pertaining in general to the teamsters' union leadership were not sufficiently of and concerning the plaintiffs.

In Loeb v. Globe Newspaper Co., 489 F. Supp. 481 (D. Mass. 1980), the *Boston Globe* ran three articles attacking the *Manchester Union Leader*, the influential New Hampshire newspaper owned by William Loeb. The *Boston Globe* pieces included statements that the *Union Leader* is "probably the worst newspaper in America" and that the publisher of the *Union Leader* "runs a newspaper by paranoids for paranoids." The *Boston Globe* articles further stated that Loeb "edits his paper like a 19th century yellow journal," that his views are "venomous," and that his newspaper is a "daily drip of venom." A *Globe* cartoon depicted Loeb with a cuckoo springing from his forehead. The *Globe* also ran an editorial that stated that Loeb had "never backed a presidential winner."

The *Boston Globe*'s attack on the *Manchester Union Leader* and its publisher precipitated a number of libel suits. One suit was brought by William Loeb himself, a second by three of the *Union Leader*'s editors, and a third by twenty-four other employees, among them office boys, reporters, and assistant editors. With regard to the twenty-four employees the court held that the *Globe* articles did not give rise to any special application or particular reference to those twenty-four persons, and that their membership in a general group associated with the *Union Leader* was not sufficient to support defamation liability on their behalf. With regard to the three editors the court noted that their case was arguably different, because the group was much smaller and they occupied positions of editorial responsibility. Nevertheless, the court held that neither their pleadings nor affidavits suggested that the *Globe* text provided a reasonable basis to focus on those three editors, and that as to those three there was no special application or particular reference that could reasonably be inferred from the general commentary published by the *Globe*. With regard to William Loeb's action, the court held that certain statements were "of and concerning" him individually, but they were nonetheless nonactionable on other grounds (rhetorical hyperbole and lack of actual malice).

§ 4.11 Who May Sue

[1] No Defamation of the Dead

[a] In General

There is no liability for defamation of the dead, either to the estate of the deceased or to the deceased's descendants or relatives.[222] "Although the memory of the dead may be desecrated and the desecration may constitute a crime, there can be no defamation of the dead."[223] A defamatory statement concerning a deceased person may, however, *independently* also defame someone living, who may then of course maintain an action in his or her own right.[224]

[b] Survival of Action

Whether an action for defamation of a living person survives his death depends on the survival statute in a particular state.[225] The original common law position was that such an action was strictly personal and did not survive,[226] but a number of states have altered that position to permit survival.[227]

[2] No Vicarious Defamation

In what is really merely a specific application of the general "of and concerning" requirement, there can be no vicarious defamation, or defamation through guilt by association. A mere statement that one is

---

222 *See, e.g.*, Gruschus v. Curtis Publishing Co., 342 F.2d 775 (10th Cir. 1965); Mahaffey v. Official Detective Stories, Inc., 210 F. Supp. 251 (W.D. La. 1962), *aff'd*, 389 F.2d 525 (5th Cir. 1968); Insul v. New York World Telegram Corp., 172 F. Supp. 615 (N.D. Ill. 1959), *aff'd*, 273 F.2d 166 (7th Cir.), *cert. denied*, 362 U.S. 942 (1960); Kelly v. Johnson Publishing Co., 160 Cal. App. 2d 718, 325 P.2d 659 (1958); Hughes v. New England Newspaper Publishing Co., 312 Mass. 178, 43 N.E.2d 657 (1942); Bello v. Random House, Inc., 422 S.W.2d 339 (Mo. 1968); Gillikin v. Bell, 254 N.C. 244, 118 S.E.2d 609 (1961).

223 Restatement (Second) of Torts § 560 comment a (1977).

224 *See* Eagles v. Liberty Weekly, Inc., 137 Misc. 575, 244 N.Y.S. 430 (1930); Restatement (Second) of Torts § 560 comment a, and § 564 comment e (1977).

225 Restatement (Second) of Torts § 560 comment a (1977).

226 *See, e.g.*, Gruschus v. Curtis Publishing Co., 342 F.2d 775 (10th Cir. 1965); Prosser & Keeton, *supra* note 1, § 126, at 943. State survival statutes often retain the common law position against survival of defamation. *See, e.g.*, Ky. Rev. Stat. § 411.140; N.C. Gen. Stat. § 28-175.

227 *See, e.g.*, Moyer v. Philips, 462 Pa. 395, 341 A.2d 441 (1975). There has been a great deal more recent litigation on the question of the survivability of "right of publicity" claims, an issue discussed in Chapter 11, *infra*.

related to an infamous person, for example, is not defamatory. In *Torres-Silva v. El Mundo, Inc.*,[228] the Puerto Rico Supreme Court held that a well-known local band leader, who had sued because of a false report that he was the father of a man arrested on drug charges, could not bring his action for libel because erroneous information that the band leader was related to the criminal could not be libelous. In our society, the court held, people are judged by their own actions and not those of their relatives. Similarly, in *Hamilton v. UPI*,[229] UPI ran a story reporting that a Phyllis D. Hamilton had been charged with public indecent exposure. The story also reported that "her husband, Jack Hamilton, owned nightclubs in Washington and Morning Sun." Jack Hamilton was in fact married to Janice Hamilton, not Phyllis Hamilton, the woman arrested for indecent exposure. In Jack Hamilton's suit against UPI, the court ruled that because the article stated only that Jack Hamilton was married to a person who had been arrested, it could not be read to accuse Mr. Hamilton of any criminal act or moral wrong, and the mere association with a person allegedly arrested was not libelous. The court also held, however, that Janice D. Hamilton, the wife of Jack Hamilton, could pursue her suit against UPI, since the article, although it did not mention Janice D. Hamilton by name, did refer to the arrested person as the wife of Jack Hamilton.[230] As with the problems of group defamation and defamation of the dead, however, there is a distinction between an action based on the defamation of another, and one grounded in defamation that is independently of and concerning the plaintiff.[231]

---

[228] 3 Med. L. Rep. (BNA) 1508 (P.R. 1977). *See also* Cohn v. NBC, 50 N.Y.2d 885, 430 N.Y.S.2d 265 (1980) (in a television film depicting the career of the late Senator Joseph McCarthy, references to one of McCarthy's aides were not defamatory of the aide, nor was the cumulative effect of all the passages involving the aides); DiPortanova v. New York News, Inc., 6 Med. L. Rep. (BNA) 1376 (N.Y. Sup. 1980) (in a newspaper article about the Shah of Iran, a photograph depicting a house actually owned by the plaintiff but identified by the paper as having been built by the Shah was not capable of a defamatory meaning).

[229] 9 Med. L. Rep. (BNA) 2453 (S.D. Iowa 1983).

[230] *Id.* at 2454-55.

[231] *See, e.g.*, Redco Corp. v. CBS, 10 Med. L. Rep. (BNA) 1536 (M.D. Pa. 1984) (court held that a television program that discussed the safety of multi-piece tire rims, not naming the particular manufacturer Redco Corporation, but clearly referring to multi-piece manufacturers in general, could reasonably be understood by the average viewer to concern Redco and its products and thus was of and concerning Redco); Patzer v. Liberty Communications, 650 P.2d 141 (Or. Ct. App. 1982) (a plaintiff who was the president and sole stockholder of a corporation and whose surname was part of the corporation's name could have a cause of action for defamation if he could show that the

[3] Corporations

Although a corporation has no reputation in any "personal" sense,[232] it does have reputational interests of a more circumscribed nature that are protected by the law of defamation.[233] "[S]ince it has no character to be affected by a libel it can only be protected against false and malicious statements affecting its credit or property;"[234] or against statements impugning corporate honesty,[235] efficiency,[236] or matters of business performance.[237]

A nonprofit corporation may also maintain an action for defamation, "if, although not for profit, it depends upon financial support from the public, and the matter tends to interfere with its activities by prejudicing it in public estimation."[238]

---

allegedly defamatory remarks directed against the corporation also concerned him personally).

232 *See* El Meson Espanol v. NYM Corp., 521 F.2d 737 (2d Cir. 1975); Prosser and Keeton, *supra* note 1, § 111, at 779. *See also* Gilbert v. Crystal Foundation Lodge, 80 Ga. 284, 4 S.E. 905 (1887) ("The venereal disease was not a partnership malady. That was individual property.").

233 *See* Restatement (Second) of Torts § 561 (1977). *See generally* Note, *Corporate Defamation and Product Disparagement: Narrowing the Analogy to Personal Defamation*, 75 Colum. L. Rev. 963 (1975).

234 El Meson Espanol v. NYM Corp., 521 F.2d 737 (2d Cir. 1975). *See also* Dun & Bradstreet, Inc. v. Greenmoss Builders, Inc., 105 S. Ct. 2939 (1985); Brayton v. Crowell-Collier Publishing Co., 205 F.2d 644 (2d Cir. 1953); Aetna Life Insurance Co. v. Mutual Benefit Health & Accident Ass'n, 82 F.2d 115 (8th Cir. 1936); Maytag Co. v. Meadows Manufacturing Co., 45 F.2d 299 (7th Cir.), *cert. denied*, 283 U.S. 843 (1930).

235 *See* Pullman Standard Car Manufacturing Co. v. Local Union No. 2928, 152 F.2d 493 (7th Cir. 1945).

236 *See* Prosser and Keeton, *supra* note 1, § 111, at 779.

237 *See* DiGiorgio Fruit Corp. v. American Federation of Labor, 215 Cal. App. 2d 560, 30 Cal. Rptr. 350 (1963); R.H. Bouligny, Inc. v. United Steelworkers of America, 270 N.C. 160, 154 S.E.2d 344 (1967). In Golden Place, Inc. v. National Broadcasting Co., 386 F. Supp. 107 (D.D.C. 1974), *aff'd without opinion*, 530 F.2d 1094 (D.C. Cir. 1976), a television show reported that the chef and several other employees of a restaurant had moved to another location, implying a decline in food quality. The court held that this was not sufficient to defame the corporation, because it did not speak to the financial soundness or business ethics of the restaurant, but might state a cause of action for "injurious falsehood" if special damages could be established. On the injurious falsehood tort, *see* Chapter 12, *infra.*

238 Restatement (Second) of Torts § 561 (1977). *See also* Boston Nutrition Soc'y v. Stare, 342 Mass. 439, 173 N.E.2d 812 (1961); New York Soc'y for the Suppresssion of Vice v. MacFadden Publications, 129 Misc. 408, 221 N.Y.S. 563, *aff'd without opinion*, 222 A.D. 739, 226 N.Y.S. 870 (1927).

[4] Governmental Entities

There is strong case authority, supported by several powerful policy rationales, for the proposition that a municipal corporation may not sue for defamation.[239] The English authority traces back to *Mayor, Alderman, and Citizens of Manchester v. Williams,*[240] which refused to permit the city to maintain an action grounded in charges of corruption. The leading American decision is *City of Chicago v. Tribune Co.,*[241] an eloquent opinion from the Illinois Supreme court that has been praised several times by other state courts[242] and quoted by the United States Supreme Court.[243] In the *City of Chicago* case the court emphasized that "[i]t is one of the fundamental principles . . . of American government, that the people have the right to discuss their government without fear of being called to account in the courts for their expressions of opinion."[244] An action by the city, the court stated, " is out of tune with the American spirit, and has no place in American jurisprudence."[245]

In *New York Times Co. v. Sullivan,*[246] the Supreme Court stated that "for good reasons, no court of last resort in this country has ever held, or even suggested, that prosecutions for libel on government have any place in the American system of jurisprudence."[247] The first amendment forbids, the Court stated, the turning of "an otherwise impersonal attack on governmental operations" into a "libel of an official responsi-

---

239 *See, e.g.,* City of Philadelphia v. Washington Post Co., 482 F. Supp. 897 (E.D. Pa. 1979); City of Albany v. Meyer, 99 Cal. App. 651, 279 P. 213 (1929); Capital District Regional Off-Track Betting Corp. v. Northeastern Harness Horseman's Ass'n, 92 Misc.2d 232, 234, 399 N.Y.S.2d 597, 598 (1977); Grafton v. American Broadcasting Companies, Inc., 7 Med. L. Rep. (BNA) 1134 (Ohio Ct. App. 1980); Johnson City v. Cowles Communications, Inc., 477 S.W.2d 750 (Tenn. (1972); Mayor, Alderman, and Citizens of Manchester v. Williams, 1 Q.B. 94, 63 L.T. 805 (1891). *See also* Progress Development Corp. v. Mitchell, 219 F. Supp. 156 (N.D. Ill. 1963) (park district).

240 1 Q.B. 94, 63 L.T. 805 (1891).

241 307 Ill. 595, 601, 139 N.E. 86, 88 (1927).

242 *See, e.g.,* Capital District Regional Off-Track Betting Corp. v. Northeast Harness Horseman's Ass'n, 92 Misc.2d 232, 234, 399 N.Y.S.2d 597, 598 (1977); Grafton v. American Broadcasting Companies, Inc., 7 Med. L. Rep. (BNA) 1134, 1136-37 (Ohio Ct. App. 1980); Johnson City v. Cowles Communications, Inc., 477 S.W.2d 750 (1972).

243 New York Times v. Sullivan, 376 U.S. 254, 291 (1964).

244 307 Ill. at 601-02, 139 N.E. at 88.

245 *Id.* at 610, 139 N.E. at 91.

246 376 U.S. 254 (1964).

247 *Id.* at 291 (quoting City of Chicago v. Tribune Co., 307 Ill. 595, 601, 139 N.E. 86, 88 (1923)).

ble for those operations."[248] This language would seem to foreclose *any* defamation action by a governmental entity as such—indeed, the tradition of American antipathy for seditious libel is the central theme of the *New York Times* case, and perhaps the central meaning of the first amendment itself.[249]

There are, in fact, at least four reasons for forbidding the maintenance of defamation actions by municipalities and other governmental entities: first, the core first amendment concerns attendant to any attempt by the government to use defamation litigation as a retaliation for speech that is critical of the governmental body;[250] second, the normal skepticism with which the common law of defamation has always looked at any suit by a corporate entity (essentially limiting such suits to attacks on the business capabilities of the corporation);[251] third, the proposition under the internal common law or statutory law of some states that a municipal corporation is not a "person" and is thus unable to maintain a tort action aimed at "personal" redress;[252] and fourth, the symmetrical fairness in barring governmental entities from suing, in light of the absolute privilege from defamation actions that such entities frequently enjoy.[253]

It might be argued that when a municipal corporation is defamed, not with regard to the exercise of its "sovereign" powers, but in its "proprietary" capacity—the capacity in which it owns and operates public utilities, for example—it should be permitted the same rights to sue for redress of damage to its "business reputation" as any other corporation.[254] Such a distinction cuts too fine a line to be practical, however, and ignores the essential fact that governmental corporations

---

248 376 U.S. at 292.

249 See Kalven, *The* New York Times *Case: A Note on "The Central Meaning of the First Amendment,"* 1964 Sup. Ct. Rev. 191 (1964). *See generally supra* §§ 2.01 and 2.07.

250 *See* New York Times v. Sullivan, 376 U.S. 254 (1964); City of Chicago v. Tribune Co., 307 Ill. 595, 139 N.E. 86 (1923).

251 *See* Mayor, Alderman, and Citizens of Manchester v. Williams, 1 Q.B. 94, 63 L.T. 805 (1891). *See generally supra* § 4.12[3].

252 *See* Grafton v. American Broadcasting Companies, 7 Med. L. Rep. (BNA) 1134, 1337-38 (Ohio Ct. App. 1980); Johnson City v. Cowles Communications, Inc., 347 S.W.2d 750 (1972).

253 Many governmental entities (and many governmental officials) enjoy absolute immunity from defamation liability. *See generally* Chapter 9, *infra.*

254 This argument perhaps explains the faint suggestion in the Prosser text that a municipal corporation's ability to sue should turn on the individual facts. *See* Prosser and Keeton, *supra* note 1, § 111, at 780. This is one of the few statements (such as it is) in that text that appears clearly unsound.

are *not* like other corporations for first amendment purposes, precisely because they are the government. As the Illinois Supreme Court put it in rejecting this proposed distinction: "While for certain limited purposes it is often said that a municipality owns and operates its public utilities as a private corporation, and not in the exercise of its powers of local sovereignty, yet, because of its proprietary rights, it does not lose its governmental character."[255]

In sum, the only position consistent with the common law traditions and constitutional principles is that all governmental and quasi-governmental[256] entities are flatly barred from maintaining an action for defamation.

§ 4.12 Publication

[1] General Principles

Publication is a term of art in the law of defamation, defined as communication of defamatory matter "intentionally or by a negligent act to one other than the person defamed."[257] Publication is an essential element of the cause of action; it may be effectuated by any form of communication to a third person—to someone other than the originator and the person defamed.[258] Thus, it is not enough that the words are heard only by the plaintiff, since the essence of the tort is diminution of reputation in the eyes of others.[259] The term "publication" is technical, and does not in any sense refer to printing or mass dissemination; rather, it applies to both slander and libel cases, and refers to any form of defamatory communication to a third party, whether written or oral or through gestures, symbols, or another means.[260] The third person

255 City of Chicago v. Tribune Co., 307 Ill. 595, 609-10, 139 N.E. 86, 91 (1923). *See also* Grafton v. American Broadcasting Companies, 7 Med. L. Rep. (BNA) 1134, 1136-38 (Ohio Ct. App. 1980).

256 *See* Progress Development Corp. v. Mitchell, 219 F. Supp. 156 (N.D. Ill. 1963) (suit by park district rejected); Capital District Regional Off-Track Betting Corp. v. Northeastern Harness Horsemen's Ass'n, 92 Misc. 2d 232, 399 N.Y.S.2d 598 (1977) (rejecting suit by public benefit corporation).

257 Restatement (Second) of Torts § 577 (1977).

258 *See* Prosser and Keeton, *supra* note 1, § 113, at 797.

259 *See* McGuire v. Adkins, 284 Ala. 602, 226 So. 2d 659 (1969); Sheffill v. Van Deusen, 13 Mass. (Gray) 304 (1859); Barnes v. Clayton House Motel, 435 S.W.2d 616 (Tex. Civ. App. 1968).

260 *See* Restatement (Second) of Torts § 577 comment a (1977); Prosser and Keeton, *supra* note 1, § 113, at 797.

must understand the defamatory communication. In *Economopoulos v. A.G. Pollard Co.*,[261] for example, a clerk at the defendant store stated in English to the plaintiff, a Greek who did not understand English, that he (plaintiff) had stolen a handkerchief. A Greek clerk repeated the same statement to the plaintiff in Greek. No one else present in the store heard the first statement in English, and no one in the store other than the Greek clerk and the plaintiff understood the second statement, spoken in Greek. The court properly held that there was no publication.[262]

There is some authority for the position that a statement to a third person who is an indispensible element in the transmission process, e.g., dictation to a stenographer, is essentially an extension of one's own writing or voice, and thus is not a publication.[263] This view, however, has been criticized as confusing the issue of publication with the existence of a common law privilege,[264] and the majority position is solidly in favor of treating such acts as dictation to a stenographer as publication (although it may still be privileged).[265]

This entire area has undergone dramatic changes with regard to the unique publication rules that have arisen in the context of defamation in the workplace. An extended discussion of recent publication developments may be found in Chapter 15.[265.1]

[2] Publication Must Be Intentional or Negligent

Publication must be intentional, or the result of a negligent act.[266] In *Smith v. Jones*,[267] for example, the defendant was unaware that the plaintiff's children were listening in to a conversation on extension phones; the court found that no publication existed because the communication to third parties was neither intentional nor negligent. Similarly, if the defamatory statement is sent by the defendant to the plain-

---

261 218 Mass. 294, 105 N.E. 896 (1914).

262 *See also* Douchan v. Godeau, 167 Cal. 692, 140 P. 952 (1914).

263 *See* Insurance Research Serv. v. Associate Finance Corp., 134 F. Supp. 54 (M.D. Tenn. 1955); Watson v. Wanamaker, 216 S.C. 295, 57 S.E.2d 477 (1950); Sutterfield v. McLellan Stores Co., 215 N.C. 582, 2 S.E.2d 709 (1939).

264 *See* Prosser and Keeton, *supra* note 1, § 113, at 799.

265 *See, e.g.*, Avrey Corp. v. Peterson, 178 F. Supp. 132 (E.D. Pa. 1959); Berry v. City of New York Insurance Co., 210 Ala. 369, 98 So. 290 (1923); Ostrowe v. Lee, 256 N.Y. 36, 175 N.E. 505 (1931); Hambrill v. Schooley, 93 Md. 48, 48 A. 730 (1901); Rickbeil v. Grafton Deaconess Hospital, 74 N.D. 525, 23 N.W.2d 247 (1946).

265.1 *See infra* § 15.03.

266 Restatement (Second) of Torts § 577 (1977).

267 335 So. 2d 896 (Miss. 1976).

tiff in a sealed letter with no reasonable expectation that it will be seen by others, there is no publication when the letter is unexpectedly opened by a third person.[268] Liability will exist, however, where the plaintiff's repetition to a third person, or the interception by a third person, is a "natural and probable consequence of the originator's actions,"[269] as where the contents are not sealed (a postcard, for example) or the defendant is blind and will have someone else read the letter, or the defendant knows that the plaintiff's spouse, secretary, or assistants are in the habit of opening and reading the plaintiff's mail.[270]

[3] Defamation by Will

Decisions are divided over whether defamation in a will is actionable.[271] There is an inherent unfairness in charging the executor, who is under legal compulsion to probate the will, with liability, and the general common law position is that the dead can neither defame nor be defamed, leading some courts to say that no defamation by will is possible.[272] Other courts, however, permit defamation by will by holding the estate liable, on the view that the operation of traditional common law rules would unfairly deprive the victim of all remedies.[273]

[4] Repetition by the Plaintiff

The general rule is that the defendant is not liable for publication effectuated by the plaintiff, since such publication is the responsibility of the plaintiff rather than the defendant.[274] As discussed earlier, however,[275] when repetition by the plaintiff is a natural and probable occurrence, such as when the plaintiff is disabled and requires assistance to

---

268 *See* Youngling v. Dane, 122 Iowa 539, 98 N.W. 371 (1904); Barnes v. Clayton House Motel, 435 S.W.2d 616 (Tex. Civ. App. 1968).

269 *See* McKinney v. County of Santa Clara, 110 Cal. App. 3d 787, 168 Cal. Rptr. 89 (1980).

270 *See* Roberts v. English Mfg. Co., 155 Ala. 414, 46 So. 752 (1908); Rummey v. Worthley, 186 Mass. 144, 71 N.E. 316 (1904); Thomson v. Cash, 119 N.H. 371, 402 A.2d 651, 653-54 (1979); Hedgpeth v. Coleman, 183 N.C. 309, 11 S.E. 517 (1922).

271 *See generally* Freifield, *Libel by Will*, 19 A.B.A.J. 575 (1933).

272 *See* Citizens & Southern Nat'l Bank v. Hendricks, 176 Ga. 692, 168 S.E. 313 (1933); Carver v. Morrow, 213 S.C. 199, 48 S.E.2d 814 (1948).

273 *See* Brown v. DuFrey, 1 N.Y.2d 190, 151 N.Y.S.2d 649, 134 N.E. 469 (1956); Harris v. Nashville Trust Co., 128 Tenn. 573, 162 S.W. 584 (1913).

274 *See* Rilely v. Askin & Marine Co., 134 S.C. 198, 132 S.E. 584 (1926); Lyle v. Waddle, 144 Tex. 90, 188 S.W.2d 770 (1945).

275 *See* § 4.12[2], and nn. 269-70, *supra*.

receive communications, or requires consultation regarding them, liability may exist.[276]

[5] Publication Through Act of Omission

In unusual cases an act of omission may be a publication, such as a failure to remove a defamatory statement posted on one's property.[277] In *Hellar v. Bianco*,[278] for example, an anonymous person put the plaintiff's name and telephone number on the bathroom wall of the defendant's tavern with a commentary on her sexual proclivities and availability. The plaintiff's husband learned of the offensive message and demanded its removal; the court held that the failure to remove the graffiti within a reasonable time after the demand constituted publication by the defendant.[279] In *Scott v. Hull*,[280] on the other hand, it was held that the defendant's failure to remove defamatory graffiti from the side of his building was mere "nonfeasance" and not a sufficient predicate for defamation liability, despite the fact that numerous persons passed by the message each day and the plaintiff had demanded its removal.

§ 4.13 Republication

[1] Liability for Republication

[a] In General

On the quaint homespun logic that "[t]alebearers are as bad as talemakers,"[281] each repetition of a defamatory statement by a new person

[276] *See* Lane v. Schiling, 130 Or. 119, 279 P. 267 (1929).

[277] Restatement (Second) § 577(2)(1977)("one who intentionally and unreasonably fails to remove defamatory matter that he knows to be exhibited on land or chattels in his possession or under his control is subject to liability for its continued publication").

[278] 111 Cal. App. 2d 424, 244 P.2d 757 (1952).

[279] *Id. See also* Tidmore v. Mills, 33 Ala. App. 243, 32 So. 2d 769, *cert. denied*, 249 Ala. 648, 32 So. 2d 782 (1947); Fogg v. Boston & Lynn R., 148 Mass. 513, 20 N.E. 109 (1899).

[280] 22 Ohio App. 2d 141, 259 N.E.2d 160, 162 (1970).

[281] Cavalier v. Original Club Forest, 59 So. 2d 489 (La. App. 1952); Harris v. Minvielle, 48 La. App. 908, 915, 19 So. 925, 928 (1896). This rule apparently was not uniformly followed in very early cases. *Compare* Johnson v. St. Louis Dispatch Co., 65 Mo. 539, 541 (1877)(no liability for repetition if repeater believes story), *with* Terwilliger v. Wands, 17 N.Y. 54, 72 Am. Dec. 420 (1858) ("Where words are spoken to one person and he repeats them to another, in consequence of which the party of whom they are spoken sustains damages, the repetition is, as a general rule, a wrongful act, rendering the person repeating them liable in like manner as if he alone had uttered them."). The evolution of the view that one is normally liable for repeating a defamatory statement is probably attributable to the basic instinct in human nature that finds gossipmongers repulsive.

constitutes a new publication, rendering the repeater liable for that new publication.[282] Each republication is a new tort subjecting the repeater to liability independent of the original publisher: The law deems the repeater to "adopt as his own" the defamatory statement.[283]

[b] Expressions of Disbelief

Liability for republishing defamation is not excused by the fact that the repeater states that he disbelieves the story, though such a caveat may be considered in determining damages.[284] Merely stating that the statement is not that of the repeater, [285] or using the word "alleged,"[286] or naming the source,[287] or identifying the information as mere "rumor,"[288] or expressly stating that the story is not believed by the repeater[289] does *not* relieve the repeater of independent liability for the new publication. (These rules, however, are modified in those jurisdictions recognizing the emerging neutral reportage privilege.)[290]

---

282 Restatement (Second) of Torts § 578 (1977). *See also* Schiavone Construction Co. v. Time, Inc., 735 F.2d 94 (3d Cir. 1984); Dixson v. Newsweek, Inc., 562 F.2d 626, 631 (10th Cir. 1977); Cepeda v. Cowles Magazines and Broadcasting, Inc., 328 F.2d 869, 871 (9th Cir.), *cert. denied*, 379 U.S. 844 (1964); Lubone v. Pittsburgh Courier Publishing Co., 101 F. Supp. 234 (D.D.C. 1951), *aff'd*, 200 F.2d 355 (1952); Nance v. Flaugh, 221 Ark. 352, 253 S.W.2d 207 (1952); Vegod Corp. v. American Broadcasting Companies, 25 Cal. 3d 763, 160 Cal. Rptr. 97, 603 P.2d 14 (1979); Terwilliger v. Wands, 17 N.Y. 54, 72 Am. Dec. 420 (1858); Falwell v. Providence Journal Co., 19 R.I. 551 (1896).

283 *See* Robertson, *Defamation and The First Amendment: In Praise of* Gertz v. Robert Welch, Inc., 54 Tex. L. Rev. 199, 262-63 (1976).

284 Restatement (Second) of Torts § 578 comment e, at 214 (1977).

285 *See, e.g.*, Weaver v. Pryor Jeffersonian, 569 P.2d 967 (Okla. 1977)(newspaper could be liable for letter to editor when views clearly those of letter writer).

286 *See, e.g.*, Maloof v. Post Publishing Co., 306 Mass. 279, 28 N.E.2d 458 (1940); Lancour v. Herald & Globe Ass'n, 111 Vt. 371, 17 A.2d 253 (1941).

287 *See* Pittsburgh Courier Pub. Co. v. Lubone, 200 F.2d 355 (D.C. Cir. 1952); Lorilland v. Field Enterprises, Inc., 65 Ill. App. 2d 65, 213 N.E.2d 1 (1965); Vanover v. Wells, 264 Ky. 461, 94 S.W.2d 999 (1936).

288 *See* Cobbs v. Chicago Defender, 308 Ill. App. 55, 31 N.E.2d 323 (1941).

289 Restatement (Second) of Torts § 578 comment e, at 213-14 (1977). *See also* Cobbs v. Chicago Defender, 308 Ill. App. 55, 31 N.E.2d 323 (1941); Branstetter v. Dorrough, 81 Ind. 527, 530 (1882); Morse v. Times-Republican Printing Co., 124 Iowa 707, 100 N.W. 867 (1904); Nicholson v. Merritt, 109 Ky. 369, 371, 59 S.W. 25 (1900); Bishop v. Journal Newspaper Co., 168 Mass. 327, 47 N.E. 119 (1897).

290 *See infra* § 4.15.

[c] Fault Still Required

The rule that the repeater of a defamatory statement "is subject to liability as if he had originally published it"[291] refers only to the issue of *publication;* constitutional fault requirements under *New York Times, Gertz,* and *Dun & Bradstreet* (actual malice, negligence, or strict liability, as the case may be)[292] still apply, and must be established against the repeater. Often, however, these actual malice or negligence requirements do not help the repeater, because in fact the repeater does not believe the statement. A newspaper that repeats someone's newsworthy but false and defamatory statement in the face of the newspaper's own disbelief is thus both liable as a publisher in its own right *and* guilty of actual malice, since it does not believe the story it has technically "adopted as its own." This is the very problem that has generated the new neutral reportage privilege.[293]

[d] Wire Service Defense

Liability for republishing by newspapers and radio stations may be excused when there was a reliance on statements received from a news gathering agency.[293.1] The wire service defense is available if four elements are established: (1) The defendant received a wire release from a reputable news gathering agency; (2) the defendant did not actually know the story was false; (3) nothing on the face of the story itself reasonably would have alerted the defendant that the story may be incorrect; and (4) the defendant reprinted the wire release without substantial change.[293.2]

[2] Liability of Originator

The early position was that the defendant was not liable for the repe-

---

[291] Restatement (Second) of Torts § 578 (1977).

[292] *See supra* §§ 3.01-3.05.

[293] *See infra* § 4.15.

[293.1] *See generally* Nelson v. Associated Press, 667 F. Supp. 1468 (S.D. Fla. 1987) (discussion of the wire service defense provided).

[293.2] Brown v. Courier Herald Publishing Co., 700 F. Supp. 534 (S.D. Ga. 1988) (newspapers' and radio station's failure to compare an allegedly defamatory wire service release with an earlier and non-defamatory release did not create liability); Nelson v. Associated Press, 667 F. Supp. 1468 (S.D. Fla. 1987); Appleby v. New Hampshire Gazette, 395 Mass. 22, 478 N.E.2d 721 (1985) (there is no duty to verify wire service stories).

tition of a statement by others, but only for his own publication.[294] This gave way to an intermediate position which rendered the originator liable for republication if it occurred with the originator's consent or authorization.[295] The more modern rule, however, has simply brought liability for republication by another into consonance with the general proximate cause rules in the law of torts: Liability for republication by another exists if it is "reasonably forseeable"[296] or "a natural and probable consequence of the originator's actions."[297]

[3] Distinction Between Primary and Secondary Publishers

The mere "transmittal" of defamatory material, such as delivery by the post office or transmission by a phone or telegraph company, is normally not a publication.[298] The *Restatement* states that "one who only delivers or transmits defamatory matter published by a third person is subject to liability if, but only if, he knows or has reason to know of its defamatory character."[299] Mere "transmitters" are known as "secondary publishers," and they include those, such as news dealers, video rental outlets, bookstores, libraries, and other distributors and vendors, who merely "distribute" the material in a mechanical sense.[300] "Primary" publishers, on the other hand, are subject to the normal republication liability rules. Primary publishers include most media outlets, such

---

294 *See* Maytag v. Cummins, 260 F. 74 (1919); Age-Herald Publishing Co. v. Waterman, 188 Ala. 272, 66 So. 16 (1914); Hastings v. Stetson, 126 Mass. 329, 30 Am. Rep. 683 (1879); Vicars v. Wilcocks, 8 East 1, 103 Eng. Rep. 244 (1806).

295 *See* Oberman v. Dun & Bradstreet, Inc., 586 F.2d 1173, 1175 (7th Cir. 1978)(applying Illinois law), *relying on* Clifford v. Cochrane, 10 Ill. App. 570 (1882)("no liability attaches to the author of the libel for such reproduction, unless it is made by his authority or consent, either express or implied").

296 *See* Brown v. First National Bank of Mason City, 193 N.W.2d 547 (Iowa 1972).

297 *See, e.g.*, Davis v. National Broadcasting Co., 320 F. Supp. 1070, 1072 (E.D. La. 1972); McKinney v. County of Santa Clara, 110 Cal. App. 3d 787, 168 Cal. Rptr. 89 (1980); Elms v. Crane, 118 Me. 261, 107 A. 852 (1919); Fitzgerald v. Young, 89 Neb. 693, 132 N.W. 127 (1911); Sawyer v. Gilmer's, Inc., 189 N.C. 7, 126 S.E. 183 (1925); Cobb v. Garlington, 193 S.W. 463, 468 (Tex. Civ. App. 1917); Weaver v. Beneficial Finance Co., 199 Va. 196, 98 S.E.2d 687 (1957). Standing alone, mere "acquiescence" in another's republication is not enough to render the originator liable. *See, e.g.*, Davis v. Costa-Gavras, 580 F. Supp. 1082 (S.D.N.Y. 1984); Karaduman v. Newsday, Inc., 51 N.Y.2d 531, 435 N.Y.S.2d 556, 416 N.E.2d 557 (1980).

298 *See* Anderson v. New York Tel. Co., 35 N.Y.2d 746, 361 N.Y.S.2d 913, 320 N.E.2d 647 (1974).

299 Restatement (Second) of Torts § 581(1) (1977).

300 *Id.*, comments b-f. *See also* Lewis v. Time, Inc., 83 F.R.D. 455, 463 (E.D. Cal. 1979); Hartmann v. American News Co., 171 F.2d 581 (7th Cir. 1948), *cert. denied*, 337 U.S. 907 (1949).

as the newspaper or book publisher that prints the statement,[301] or the radio or television station that broadcasts it.[302] The importance of the special common law "scienter" requirement for secondary publishers such as distributors, vendors, or libraries has been obviated to some degree by modern constitutional fault standards, which would normally require some notice of the defamatory character of the statement to impose liability in any event,[303] and have also been blunted by the recognition in some jurisdictions of the "neutral reportage" privilege.[304]

[4] Single Publication Rule

As discussed later in connection with conflict of laws issues,[305] the original common law position was to treat each individual copy of a defamatory statement as a separate publication giving rise to a distinct cause of action,[306] so that a newspaper that sold a million copies of a defamatory statement distributed across fifty states could theoretically be liable in a million different lawsuits litigated in fifty states.

The common law position has proved untenable for modern life: The gigantic circulation of many newspapers and magazines and the development of nationwide radio and television networks have made oppressive the treatment of each separate copy of a defamatory statement as a separate tort.[307]

As a result, the "single publication rule" evolved. It provides that a single communication heard at the same time by two or more persons is a single publication, that any one edition of a book or newspaper, or any one radio or television broadcast, is a single publication, and that as to any single publication there may be only one cause of action, in which recovery for damage in all jurisdictions is recoverable, and which acts as a bar to any other cause of action by the plaintiff in all jurisdic-

---

301 *See* Eldredge, *supra* note 4, § 44, at 231-32.

302 Restatement (Second) of Torts § 581(2) (1977)("One who broadcasts defamatory matter by means of radio or television is subject to the same liability as an original publisher").

303 *See supra* §§ 3.01-3.05.

304 *See infra* § 4.15.

305 *See* Chapter 13, *infra.*

306 *See* The Duke of Brunswick v. Harmer, 14 Q.B. 185, 117 Eng. Rep. 75 (1849), *discussed in* Ogden v. Association of the United States Army, 177 F. Supp. 498 (1959). *See also* Anselmi v. Denver Post, Inc., 552 F.2d 316 (10th Cir.), *cert. denied sub nom.* Times-Mirror Co. v. Anselmi, 432 U.S. 911 (1977); Hartmann v. Time, Inc., 166 F.2d 127 (3d Cir.), *cert. denied,* 334 U.S. 838 (1948).

307 *See* Graham v. Today's Spirit, 503 Pa. 52, 468 A.2d 454 (1983); Eldredge, *supra* note 4, § 38, at 209; Prosser, *Interstate Publication*, 51 Mich. L. Rev. 959 (1953).

tions.[308] As the Supreme Court recently recognized, by statute or judicial decision "[t]he great majority of the States now follow the 'single publication rule.' "[309]

Each new edition of a book is treated as a separate new publication, giving rise to a new cause of action.[310] The subsequent publication of a paperback edition of a book, for example, gives rise to a new cause of action separate from the original action that accrued from the hardcover publication.[311] Subsequent editions of a same day's newspaper,[312] or reprintings of one edition of a book,[313] or the rebroadcast of the same story[314] are also considered new publications triggering a new cause of action, and commencing a new statute of limitations period.

§ 4.14 The Neutral Reportage Privilege

[1] The Inadequacy of Common Law Republication Rules

The traditional common law rules regarding liability for republication often hamstring the press in its coverage of newsworthy events and controversies. Because of the common law fiction that in republishing a defamatory statement the republisher "adopts" it as his own, the press may become liable for merely repeating a defamatory charge made by some other person, even when the original speaker's *very making of the charge itself* is newsworthy.

Imagine that two days before an election a local political candidate charges an opponent with having taken a bribe. Imagine that the local

---

308 Restatement (Second) of Torts § 577A.

309 Keeton v. Hustler Magazine, Inc., 104 S. Ct. 1473, n.8 (1984)(citing Restatement (Second) of Torts § 577A (1977)(Reporter's Note)). *See also* Morrissey v. William Morrow & Co., 739 F.2d 962 (4th Cir. 1984); Fleury v. Harper & Row Publishers, Inc., 698 F.2d 1022 (9th Cir. 1983); Stephenson v. Triangle Publications, Inc., 104 F. Supp. 215 (S.D. Tex. 1952); Rinaldi v. Viking Penguin, Inc., 52 N.Y.2d 422, 438 N.Y.S.2d 496, 420 N.E.2d 377 (1981); Gregoire v. G.P. Putman's Sons, 298 N.Y. 119, 81 N.E.2d 45 (1948); McGuire v. Brightman, 79 Cal. App. 3d 776, 145 Cal. Rptr. 256 (1978); Graham v. Today's Spirit, 503 Pa. 52, 468 A.2d 454 (1983); Holloway v. Butler, 662 S.W.2d 688 (Tex. Civ. App. 1983); Leflar, *The Single Publication Rules,* 25 Rocky Mt. L. Rev. 263 (1953).

310 *See, e.g.,* Wheeler v. Dell Publishing Co., 300 F.2d 372 (7th Cir. 1962); Gregoire v. G.P. Putman's Sons, 298 N.Y. 119, 81 N.E.2d 45 (1948).

311 *See, e.g.,* Kanarek v. Bugliosi, 108 Cal. App. 3d 327, 166 Cal. Rptr. 526 (1980); Rinaldi v. Viking Penguin, Inc., 52 N.Y.2d 422, 438 N.Y.S.2d 496, 420 N.E.2d 377 (1981). *See also* Church of Scientology v. Dell Publishing Co., 362 F. Supp. 767 (N.D. Cal. 1973).

312 Restatement (Second) of Torts § 577A comment d, at 210 (1977). *See also* Cox Enterprises, Inc. v. Gilreath, 142 Ga. App. 297, 235 S.E.2d 633 (1977).

313 Johnson v. Harcourt, Brace, Jovanovich, Inc., 43 Cal. App. 3d 880, 894-96 (1974).

314 Restatement (Second) of Torts § 577A comment d, at 210 (1977).

newspaper editor is absolutely certain that the charge is a lie—the paper has thoroughly investigated the whole alleged incident and found that it was fabricated. Under the common law republication rules the paper will be deemed to have "adopted" the defamatory falsehood if it publishes the candidate's charge, even if the paper also prints its counterevidence and the other candidate's denials. Furthermore, because the newspaper does not believe in the truth of the charge, it is technically publishing with actual malice—knowledge of falsity.

The editor would of course maintain that the charge is newsworthy, for the very making of such a false charge signifies the dishonesty of the candidate who made it. Some might maintain, on the other hand, that the newspaper should not print the lie, particularly so close to election day, because some voters will be swayed by the falsehood, either because they will believe the candidate who made the accusation more than they will believe the counterevidence presented, or because, out of misunderstanding or confusion, they will "register" the bribery charge but fail to read or appreciate the counterevidence and denials. For better or for worse, most editors in the United States would probably run the story, presenting both the defamatory statements and the counterevidence and denials. The common law position would subject the newspapers managed by these editors to liability for defamation. There is a growing recognition by courts, however, that the common law rules are inadequate in these circumstances, for they act to inhibit the flow of information about the very existence of the charges and accusations various persons and groups are hurling at each other in the midst of public controversies. To alleviate this chill on the dissemination of valuable information about what parties are saying about each other in the midst of public disputes, a new doctrine of "neutral reportage" is emerging as a substitute for common law republication rules.

[2] Origins of the Privilege: *Edwards v. National Audubon Society*

The modern neutral reportage privilege had its genesis in a 1977 decision by the United States Court of Appeals for the Second Circuit, *Edwards v. National Audubon Society.*[315] The court framed the new doctrine in the following statement:

[315] 556 F.2d 113 (2d Cir.), *cert. denied sub nom.* Edwards v. New York Times, 434 U.S. 1002 (1977).

> Succinctly stated, when a responsible, prominent organization like the National Audubon Society makes serious charges against a public figure, the First Amendment protects the accurate and disinterested reporting of those charges, regardless of the reporter's private view regarding their validity. . . . *What is newsworthy about such accusations is that they were made.* We do not believe that the press may be required under the First Amendment to suppress newsworthy statements merely because it has serious doubts regarding their truth. Nor must the press take up cudgels against dubious charges in order to publish them without fear of liability for defamation. . . . The public interest in being fully informed about controversies that often rage around sensitive issues *demands that the press be afforded the freedom to report such charges without assuming responsibility for them.*[316]

[3] Elements of the Privilege

To receive the benefit of the neutral reportage privilege, four principal requirements must be satisfied:

(1) "Charges of a serious nature must be made in a context in which the very leveling of the charges is newsworthy in and of itself."[317] This generally means that the charges must either relate to a preexisting public controversy or generate a public controversy in their own right.[318]

(2) The charges must be made by a public official or public figure, or by a prominent organization.[319] (Some formulations, including *Edwards,* would add the caveat that the person or prominent organization be "responsible." Since, however, the purpose of the privilege is to protect charges that are newsworthy in themselves, although they may be false, it would seem that even statements from an "irresponsible" source—Senator

---

[316] *Id.* at 120 (emphasis added).

[317] *See* Barry v. Time, Inc., 584 F. Supp. 1110, 1126-27 (N.D. Cal. 1984)(charges must be "serious"); Krauss v. Champaign News Gazette, 59 Ill. App. 3d 745, 375 N.E.2d 1362 (1978)("If the journalist believes, reasonably and in good faith, that his story accurately conveys information asserted about a personality or program, and such assertion is made under circumstances wherein the mere assertion is, in fact, newsworthy, then he need inquire no further.").

[318] *See* McManus v. Doubleday & Co., 513 F. Supp. 1383, 1391 (S.D.N.Y. 1981)(holding that controversy must be preexisting; no neutral reportage privilege exists for "journalist-induced charges").

[319] *See* Cianci v. New Times Publishing Co., 639 F.2d 54, 67-69 (2d Cir. 1980); McManus v. Doubleday & Co., 513 F. Supp. 1383, 1391 (S.D.N.Y. 1981; DiSalle v. P.G. Publishing Co., 375 Pa. Super. 510, 533 A.2d 1345, 1354 (1989), *cert. denied,* 109 S. Ct. 3216 (1989).

Joseph McCarthy, for example—may often merit publication, because they are still newsworthy.)[320]

(3) The charges must be about a public figure or public official (including, of course, corporations or organizations that qualify for that status).[321]

(4) The reportage of the charges must be "neutral," that is, accurately and disinterestedly republished.[322] (This does not mean, however, that denials or responses to the charge, or accurate reportage of counterevidence, may not be included.)

[4] Judicial Acceptance of the Concept

Although a number of decisions since *Edwards v. National Audubon Society*[323] have rejected the neutral reportage privilege outright,[324] on the theory that the constitutional rules of *New York Times* and *Gertz* already give the press adequate protection,[325] and several other decisions have expressed various degrees of skepticism about the rationale

---

320 *See* Barry v. Time, Inc., 584 F. Supp. 1110, 1126-27 (N.D. Cal. 1984)("[T]he neutral reportage privilege does not depend solely upon the 'trustworthiness' of the individual or organization making the allegedly defamatory statements. . . . A much more sensible approach is to extend the neutral reportage privilege to all republications of serious charges made by one participant in an existing public controversy against another participant in that controversy, regardless of the 'trustworthiness' of the original defamer.").

321 *See* Dixson v. Newsweek, Inc., 562 F.2d 626, 630-31 (10th Cir. 1977).

322 *See* Cianci v. New Times Publishing Co., 639 F.2d 54, 67-69 (2d Cir. 1980)(a "balanced report" required); Dixson v. Newsweek, 562 F.2d 626, 630-31 (10th Cir. 1977) ("publisher may not escape liability for defamation when it takes words out of context and uses them to convey a false representation of fact"); Barry v. Time, Inc., 584 F. Supp. 1110, 1126-27 (N.D. Cal. 1984)("It is the neutrality of the report which is critical."); Krauss v. Champaign News Gazette, 59 Ill. App. 3d 745, 375 N.E.2d 1362 (1978)("Unless it is shown that the journalist deliberately distorts these statements to launch a personal attack of his own upon the public figure or program, that which he reports under such circumstances is privileged."); Orr v. Lynch, 60 A.D.2d 949, 950, 401 N.Y.S.2d 897 (3d Dept.), *aff'd*, 45 N.Y.2d 903, 411 N.Y.S.2d 10, 383 N.E.2d 562 (1978).

323 556 F.2d 113 (2d Cir.), *cert. denied sub nom.* Edwards v. New York Times, 434 U.S. 1002 (1977).

324 *See* Dickey v. CBS, Inc., 583 F.2d 1221, 1225-26 (3d Cir. 1978)(dicta); Tunney v. American Broadcasting Companies, 109 Ill. App. 3d 796, 441 N.E.2d 86 (1st Dist. 1982); Newell v. Field Enterprise, 91 Ill. App. 3d 735, 415 N.E.2d 434 (1st Dist. 1980); McCall v. Courier-Journal, 623 S.W.2d 882 (Ky. 1981), *cert. denied*, 456 U.S. 975 (1982); Postill v. Booth Newspapers, Inc., 118 Mich. App. 608, 325 N.W.2d 511 (1982); Hellman v. McCarthy, 10 Med. L. Rep. (BNA) 1789, 1794 (N.Y. Sup. 1984).

325 *See* Postill v. Booth Newspapers, Inc., 118 Mich. App. 608, 325 N.Y.2d 511, 518 (1982)("We decline to embrace *Edwards*, as the press is adequately protected by the burden of proof required in *Sullivan.*").

of the doctrine,[326] on the whole the doctrine appears to be gaining slow but steady acceptance.[327] The emergence of the neutral reportage privilege is one of the most significant developments in the law of defamation today.[328] The common law republication rules are anachronisms. In light of the careful circumscription given the neutral reportage doctrine by the courts—such as the requirements that the original speaker and plaintiff be public figures or officials, that a public controversy exist, that the charges be newsworthy, and that the report be balanced and neutral—the new doctrine does not seem gratuitously generous to the media, and it contributes significantly to the free flow of information concerning public controversies.[329]

---

326 *See* Medico v. Time, Inc., 643 F.2d 134, 145 (3d Cir.), *cert. denied,* 454 U.S. 836 (1981); Hogan v. Herald Co., 84 A.D.2d 470 (4th Dept. 1982), *aff'd without opinion,* 58 N.Y.2d 630 (1982); Jones v. Palmer Communications, Inc., 16 Med. L. Rep. (BNA) 2137 (Iowa 1989) (court discusses neutral reportage defense at length, but declines to pass judgment on whether to adopt it in Iowa. The court's discussion, however, seemed to collapse its analysis of neutral reportage into the less protective Iowa rule governing the fair report privilege.).

327 *See, e.g.,* Barry v. Time, Inc., 584 F. Supp. 1110, 1126-28 (N.D. Cal. 1984); Whitaker v. Denver Post, Inc., 401 F. Supp. 60 (D. Wyo. 1975), *rev'd on other grounds sub nom.* Anselmi v. Denver Post, Inc., 552 F.2d 316 (10th Cir.), *cert. denied,* 432 U.S. 911 (1977); Bair v. Palm Beach Newspapers, 8 Med. L. Rep. (BNA) 2028 (Fla. 5th Cir. 1982), *aff'd,* 444 So. 2d 1131 (Fla. 4th Dist. Ct. App. 1984); El Amin v. Miami Herald, 9 Med. L. Rep. (BNA) 1079 (Fla. 11th Cir. 1983); Victor v. News and Sun Sentinel, 10 Med. L. Rep. (BNA) 2073 (Fla. 5th Cir. 1984); J.V. Peters & Co. v. Knight Ridder Co., 10 Med. L. Rep. (BNA) 1576 (Ohio App. 1984); Burns v. Times Argus, 430 A.2d 773 (Vt. 1981). In addition, a number of decisions have apparently accepted the doctrine in principle, but with restrictions, or finding the doctrine inapplicable on the facts of the case. *See, e.g.,* Cianci v. New Times Publishing Co., 639 F.2d 54, 67-69 (2d Cir. 1980); Dixson v. Newsweek, 562 F.2d 626, 630-31 (10th Cir. 1977); McManus v. Doubleday & Co., 513 F. Supp. 1383, 1391 (S.D.N.Y. 1981).

328 As is often the case when an emerging and controversial new doctrine is involved, the neutral reportage doctrine has fomented a substantial amount of internal division and confusion within some jurisdictions. *Compare,* for example, Dickey v. CBS, Inc., 583 F.2d 1221, 1225-26 (3d Cir. 1978)(rejecting *Edwards* in dicta), *with* Medico v. Time, Inc., 643 F.2d 134, 145 (3d Cir.), *cert. denied,* 454 U.S. 836 (1981)(suggesting that policies underlying *Edwards* may justify adoption of the doctrine); *and compare* Newell v. Field Enterprises, 91 Ill. App. 3d 735, 415 N.E.2d 434 (1980); Tunney v. American Broadcasting Companies, 109 Ill. App. 3d 769, 441 N.E.2d 86 (1982)(rejecting doctrine), *with* Kraus v. Champaign News Gazette, 59 Ill. App. 3d 745, 375 N.E.2d 1362 (1978) (accepting doctrine); Catalano v. Pechous, 83 Ill. 2d 146 (1980) *and* Fogus v. Capital Cities Media, 111 Ill. App. 3d 1060, 1063 (5th Dist. 1982) (reserving resolution of the issue); *and compare* Orr v. Lynch, 60 A.D.2d 949, 950, 401 N.Y.S.2d 897 (3d Dept.), *aff'd,* 45 N.Y.2d 903, 411 N.Y.S.2d 10, 383 N.E.2d 562 (1978)(endorsing doctrine), *with* Hogan v. Herald Co., 84 A.D.2d 470 (4th Dept. 1982), *aff'd,* 45 N.Y.2d 903 (1978); *and* Hellman v. McCarthy, 10 Med. L. Rep. (BNA) 1789, 1794 (N.Y. Sup. 1984)(rejecting doctrine).

329 *See generally* Sowle, *Defamation and the First Amendment: The Case for a Constitutional Privilege of Fair Report,* 54 N.Y.U. L. Rev. 469 (1979).

CHAPTER 5

Truth as a Constitutional Defense

§ 5.01 Overview

[1] The Early Common Law Rules

If in a libel or slander action the defamatory statement can be shown to be the truth, the defendant, consistent with the Biblical admonition "Ye shall know the truth and the truth shall make you free" shall indeed be freed. The rule in England has always been that truth is an absolute defense in a civil suit for libel or slander.[1] Although in English criminal law, prosecution for criminal libel did not recognize truth as a defense, and in fact followed what to American sensibilities was the almost perverse maxim "the greater the truth the greater the libel,"[2] for libels resulting in mere civil causes of action it was early on established that truth was an absolute defense.

The English criminal law position that truth was not only not a defense but an aggravating circumstance was consistent with the purpose of criminal libel, which was not to compensate victims but rather to protect the Crown against seditious speech and preserve peace and order.[3] Defamatory truth was more likely to hurt the Crown and more likely to provoke a duel or some other breach of peace.[4]

Blackstone explained the very different common law position on the tort side, which recognized truth as a total defense, in terms that to some degree presaged modern first amendment thinking: "it was meritorious for the defamer to give warning about a bankrupt tradesman, a quack physician, a crooked lawyer and a heretic divine," and thus "if the fact be true, it is *damnum absque injuria,* and where there is no injury, the law gives no remedy."[5] Pollack put the English rule more in terms of the plaintiff getting what he deserves by the libel or slander if it turns out to be true. The truth defense exists, Pollack claimed, "because of the demerit attaching to the plaintiff if the imputation is true, whereby he is deemed to have no ground for complaint

---

[1] *See* Gatley on Libel and Slander § 351, at 152 (8th ed. 1981); Holdsworth, *Defamation in the Sixteenth and Seventeenth Centuries,* 41 L.Q.R. 13, 28 (1925).

[2] *See* Tollett v. United States, 485 F.2d 1087, 1098 n.27 (8th Cir. 1973); L. Eldredge, The Law of Defamation § 64, at 324-25 (1978) (citing Blackstone, Commentaries 151).

[3] *See* Garrison v Louisiana, 379 U.S. 64, 67-73 (1964); Tollett v. United States, 485 F.2d 1087, 1094-99 (8th Cir. 1973).

[4] *See* Eldredge, *supra* note 2, § 64, at 325 (citing Blackstone, Commentaries 151).

[5] 3 Blackstone, Commentaries 118-19 (Kerr's 4th ed. 1876).

for the fact being communicated to his neighbors."[6] For Pollack the common law truth defense was simply a matter of barring the plaintiff "of redress which he does not deserve."[7]

[2] The American Position

In the United States, the common law position was originally followed by the overwhelming majority of jurisdictions.[8] The first *Restatement of Torts* summarized the majority position by declaring that "[t]he truth of a defamatory statement of fact is a complete defense to an action for defamation."[9] About a dozen states, however, either intentionally or because of confusion with the English criminal law rule, modified the traditional common law position to make truth a more limited defense in a tort action for defamation.[10] A 1909 New Hampshire judicial decision abrogated the common law rule by restricting the defense of truth to cases in which the defendant published the defamation in good faith and for justifiable purpose.[11] A number of other states, through judicial decision, state constitutional amendment, or statute, similarly departed from the common law position. In some, truth was a defense unless the defamation was published with "malicious motives;" in others there was a requirement of both good motive and "justifiable ends;" and in still others the defamatory communication had to have some nexus to matters of "public information" or "subjects of public concern."[12]

§ 5.02 The Emergence of Truth as a Constitutional Defense in Public Official and Public Figure Cases

When the law of defamation became constitutionalized in 1964, by way of *New York Times Co. v. Sullivan,*[13] the doctrine of truth as an absolute defense began its ascent to constitutional status. Although the

---

6 Pollack, Torts 266 (13th ed. 1929).

7 *Id.*

8 *See generally* Franklin, *The Origins and Constitutionality of Limitations on Truth as a Defense in Tort Law,* 16 Stan. L. Rev. 789 (1964).

9 Restatement of Torts § 582 (1938).

10 Franklin and Bussel, *The Plaintiff's Burden in Defamation: Awareness and Falsity,* 25 Wm. & Mary L. Rev. 825, 851 (1984).

11 Hutchins v Page, 75 N.H. 215, 72 A. 689 (1909).

12 *See* Ray, *Truth: A Defense to Libel,* 16 Minn. L. Rev. 43, 52-53 (1931).

13 376 U.S. 254 (1964).

Times decision did not in so many words declare that the first amendment required that truth be an absolute defense in a civil action for defamation against a public official, the requirement of knowledge of falsity or reckless disregard for the truth[14] seemed implicitly to carry with it the principle that truth would be an absolute defense. In the same year of the *Times* decision, *Garrison v. Louisiana*[15] presented the Court with a criminal libel action brought under a Louisiana statute that permitted truth to be interposed as a defense only when the communication was uttered "with good motives and for justifiable ends."[16] The Court struck down the statute, and stated that its holding would apply to civil actions as well as criminal prosecutions. Observing that *New York Times* permitted a civil remedy for a public official "only if he establishes that the utterance was false and that it was made with knowledge of falsity or in reckless disregard of whether it was false or true,"[17] the Court declared: "Truth may not be the subject of either civil or criminal sanction where discussion of public affairs is concerned."[18]

§ 5.03 Truth as a Constitutional Defense in Private Figure Cases

[1] The *Gertz* and *Dun & Bradstreet* Cases

Although the language in *Garrison v. Louisiana* was cast in terms of "public affairs" rather than "public figures," it nonetheless remained unclear whether truth was an absolute defense as a matter of constitutional law in all libel actions, or merely in all actions involving "public affairs," or in all actions involving public officials and public figures. In *Gertz v. Robert Welch, Inc.*,[19] the Court imposed a fault requirement in private figures cases.[20] *Gertz* was modified in *Dun & Bradstreet, Inc. v. Greenmoss Builders, Inc.*,[21] however, and the full implications of *Dun & Bradstreet* remain unknown.[22] It seems safe to say that at least in the types of cases subject to a fault requirement, proof of the statement's

---

14 *Id.* at 279-80.

15 379 U.S. 64 (1964).

16 *Id.* at 70.

17 *Id.* at 74.

18 *Id.*

19 418 U.S. 323 (1974).

20 *Id.* at 347.

21 105 S. Ct. 2939 (1985).

22 *See infra* § 5.05.

falsity is necessary to sustain a defamation action, as a matter of constitutional law.[23] As to whether truth is an absolute first amendment defense in cases not subject to fault requirements, where common law strict liability rules might apply there is still some doubt.

[2] The *Cox Broadcasting* Case

In *Cox Broadcasting Corp. v. Cohn,*[24] Chief Justice Burger's majority opinion refused to address the question "whether truthful publications may ever be subjected to civil or criminal liability consistent with the First and Fourteenth Amendments."[25] The Chief Justice claimed that the Court had "carefully left open the question whether the First and Fourteenth Amendments require that the truth be recognized as a defense in a defamation action brought by a private person as distinguished from a public official or public figure."[26] Justice Powell, in a concurring opinion, took issue with the majority opinion's intimation that the questions had been "carefully left open," arguing that "[t]he requirement that the state standard of liability be related to the defendant's failure to avoid publication of 'defamatory falsehood' limits the grounds on which a normal action for defamation can be brought. It is fair to say that if the statements are true, the standard contemplated by *Gertz* cannot be satisfied."[27]

[3] The *Firestone* Case

Two years after *Cox Broadcasting,* the Court in *Time, Inc. v. Firestone*[28] again strongly hinted that truth was a complete constitutional defense even in a private figure case. The Court cited Justice Powell's concurrence in *Gertz* for the proposition that "[b]ecause demonstration that an article was true would seem to preclude finding the publisher at fault," the Court had "examined the predicate for" the defendant *Time's* contention that the article about Mary Alice Firestone was substantially true.[29]

The broad intimation in *Firestone* that truth is an absolute defense

---

23 *See* Franklin and Bussel, *supra* note 10, at 853 n.101.
24 420 U.S. 469 (1975).
25 *Id.* at 491.
26 *Id.* at 490.
27 *Id.* at 499 (Powell, J., concurring).
28 424 U.S. 448 (1976).
29 *Id.* at 458.

in all cases involving fault requirements is consistent with the position of the *Restatement (Second) of Torts,* which declares that: "[o]ne who publishes a defamatory statement of fact is not subject to liability for defamation if the statement is true."[30] This position is supported by a number of lower court holdings.[31]

[4] *Philadelphia Newspapers, Inc. v. Hepps*

Whatever doubt may have existed concerning the status of truth as a constitutionally mandated defense in private figure cases was virtually eliminated by the Supreme Court's 1986 decision in *Philadelphia Newspapers, Inc. v. Hepps.*[31.1] *Hepps* held that the plaintiff bears the burden of establishing falsity in private figure cases, at least when the speech involves issues of public concern and a media defendant.[31.2] This ruling on burden of proof necessarily also means that in such cases truth is a constitutional defense.

§ 5.04 The Truth Issue in Cases Governed by *Dun & Bradstreet*

Because the general applicability of the *New York Times* and *Gertz* fault rules in private figure cases governed by *Dun & Bradstreet* (cases not issues of public concern) remains somewhat clouded,[32] the application of the constitutional absolute truth defense in private figure cases not involving matters of public concern is also thrown into doubt. If the constitutional truth defense is viewed as a mere corollary to fault requirements, then it is plausible that truth would not be a constitutionally mandated defense in cases that fall outside of fault rules after *Dun & Bradstreet.* The better view, however, is that the first amendment's

---

[30] Restatement (Second) of Torts § 581A (1977).

[31] *See, e.g.,* Redco Corp. v. CBS, Inc., 10 Med. L. Rep. (BNA) 1536, 1542 (M.D. Pa. 1984); Corabi v. Curtis Publishing Co., 441 Pa. 432, 450, 273 A.2d 899, 908 (1971); Dunlap v. Philadelphia Newspapers, Inc., 301 Pa. Super. Ct. 475, 486, 448 A.2d 6, 11 (1982); Commonwealth Motor Parts, Ltd. v. Bank of Nova Scotia, 44 A.D.2d 375, 355 N.Y.S.2d 138 (1st Dept. 1974), *aff'd,* 37 N.Y.2d 824, 377 N.Y.S.2d 482, 339 N.E.2d 888 (1975); Gantry Construction Co. v. American Pipe & Construction Co., 49 Cal. App. 3d 186, 122 Cal. Rptr. 834 (2d Dist. 1975); Jolly v. Fossum, 59 Wash. 2d 20, 365 P.2d 780 (1961); Farnsworth v. Tribune Co., 43 Ill. 2d 286, 253 N.E.2d 408 (1969); Koren v. Capital Gazette Newspapers, Inc., 22 Md. App. 576, 581, 325 A.2d 140, 143 (1974).

[31.1] 106 S. Ct. 1558 (1986).

[31.2] *See infra* § 5.07.

[32] *See supra* §§ 3.02–3.06.

protection of truth, like its protection of opinion, stands on its own footing, and is analytically distinct from fault rules. The first amendment's protection of truth and opinion should be regarded as completely outside of the balancing process employed by *Gertz* and *Dun & Bradstreet* when false factual speech is at issue. Just as under the first amendment there is "no such thing" as a false idea, there should be "no such thing" as liability for defamation for speaking the truth.

§ 5.05 Burden of Proving the Truth

Is truth an affirmative defense that must be pleaded and proved by the defendant, or is falsity an element of the plaintiff's prima facie case that must be pleaded and proved by the plaintiff? The common law position was that truth was an affirmative defense and the burden of proof rested with the defendant.[33] Once the plaintiff at common law established that the communication was defamatory, it was presumed false, and it was up to the defendant to rebut the presumption.[34] Some courts have held that this burden was shifted back to the plaintiff in cases in which a common law privilege applied.[35] Other authority held that the burden of proving truth remained on the defendant even if a qualified common law privilege existed.[36]

Today the weight of authority supports the proposition that the constitutional requirements emanating from *New York Times* have shifted the burden of proving falsity to the plaintiff, eliminating the presumption of falsity and making proof of falsity part of the plaintiff's case in chief. *New York Times,* in holding that the plaintiff must prove with "convincing clarity" that the defamatory statement was published "with knowledge that it was false or with reckless disregard of whether it was false,"[37] has, "as a practical matter, made it necessary for the plaintiff to allege and prove the falsity of the communication, and from a realistic standpoint, has placed the burden of proving falsity on the

---

[33] *See* Restatement of Torts § 613(2)(a) (1938).

[34] *See, e.g.,* Memphis Publishing Co. v. Nichols, 569 S.W.2d 412, 420 (Tenn. 1978); Eldredge, *supra* note 2, § 63, at 323 (1978).

[35] *See* Ross v. Gallant, Farrow & Co., P.C., 27 Ariz. App. 89, 551 P.2d 79 (1976); Munsell v. Ideal Food Stores, 208 Kan. 909, 494 P.2d 1063 (1972); Wetherby v. Retail Credit Co., 235 Md. 237, 201 A.2d 344 (1964); Stukuls v. State, 42 N.Y.2d 272, 397 N.Y.S.2d 740, 366 N.E.2d 829 (1977); Smith v. Smith, 194 S.C. 247, 9 S.E.2d 584 (1940). *Cf.* Ripps v. Herrington, 241 Ala. 209, 1 So. 2d 899 (1941).

[36] Corabi v. Curtis Publishing Co., 441 Pa. 432, 273 A.2d 899 (1971).

[37] New York Times v. Sullivan, 376 U.S. 254, 280 (1964).

plaintiff."[38] In *Garrison v. Louisiana,*[39] the Court stated that it "held in *New York Times* that a public official might be allowed the civil remedy only if he establishes that the utterance was false."[40] In *Curtis Publishing Co. v. Butts,*[41] Justice Harlan stated that under the *New York Times* doctrine public officials could recover for defamation "only when they could prove that the publication involved was deliberately falsified, or published recklessly despite the publisher's awareness of probable falsity."[42] Although the "truth" issue is now properly classified as part of the plaintiff's principal case, lawyers continue to refer colloquially to the "truth defense," and the term is employed throughout this chapter, though it would be more technically correct to drop the word "defense."

§ 5.06 The Burden of Proof in Public Official and Public Figure Cases

In public official and public figure cases, those courts that have explicitly considered the issue have interpreted *New York Times* and its progeny as placing the burden of proving falsity on the plaintiff.[43] A number of courts have held that in public official and public figure cases this burden must be discharged with "convincing clarity."[44]

---

[38] Restatement (Second) of Torts § 613 comment j (1977).

[39] 379 U.S. 64 (1964).

[40] *Id.* at 74.

[41] 388 U.S. 130 (1967).

[42] *Id.* at 153.

[43] *See, e.g.,* Steaks Unlimited, Inc. v. Deaner, 623 F.2d 264, 774-75 n.49 (3d Cir. 1980)(dicta); Meiners v. Moriarity, 563 F.2d 343 (7th Cir. 1977); Goldwater v. Ginzberg, 414 F.2d 324 (2d Cir. 1969), *cert denied,* 396 U.S. 1049 (1970); Redco Corp. v. CBS, Inc., 10 Med. L. Rep. (BNA) 1536 (M.D. Pa. 1984); Field Research Corp. v. Patrick, 30 Cal. App. 3d 603, 106 Cal. Rptr. 473, *cert denied,* 414 U.S. 922 (1973); Farnsworth v. Tribune Co., 43 Ill. 2d 286, 253 N.E.2d 408 (1969); Michaud v. Inhabitants of Town of Livermore Falls, 381 A.2d 1110 (Me. 1978); Kapiloff v. Dunn, 27 Md. App. 514, 343 A.2d 251 (Ct. Spec. App. 1975); Reaves v. Foster, 200 So. 2d 453 (Miss. 1967); Fairley v. Peekskill Star Corp., 83 A.D.2d 294, 445 N.Y.S.2d 156 (2d Dept. 1981); Rinaldi v. Holt, Rinehart & Winston, Inc., 42 N.Y.2d 369, 397 N.Y.S.2d 943, 366 N.E.2d 1299 (1977), *cert denied,* 434 U.S. 969 (1977); Duffy v. Kipers, 26 A.D.2d 127, 271 N.Y.S.2d 338 (4th Dept. 1966); Dunlap v. Philadelphia Newspapers, Inc., 301 Pa. Super. 475, 448 A.2d 6 (1982).

[44] *See* Pape v. Time, Inc., 294 F. Supp 1087 (N.D. Ill.), *rev'd on other grounds,* 419 F.2d 980 (7th Cir. 1969), *rev'd,* 401 U.S. 279 (1971); Whitmore v. Kansas City Star Co., 499 S.W.2d 45 (Mo. App. 1973).

§ 5.07 The Burden of Proof in Private Figure Cases

With regard to private figure plaintiffs, there was authority for the position that the burden of proof on the truth issue remains with the defendant, as in the original common law position.[45] In a decision rendered as this treatise was going to press, however, the Supreme Court held that in private figure cases involving matters of public concern, the burden of proving falsity has been shifted to the plaintiff as part of the prima facie case.

In *Philadelphia Newspapers, Inc. v. Hepps,*[46] the *Philadelphia Inquirer* ran a series of stories purporting to link the plaintiffs, operators of a chain of "thrifty" stores, to organized crime. The articles further claimed that those crime links had been exploited by the plaintiffs to influence Pennsylvania's legislative and governmental processes. The question in the case, as it reached the Supreme Court, was whether Pennsylvania's adherence to the common law rule[47] that defendants have the burden of proving the truth of the defamatory charges which they have leveled against the plaintiff was inconsistent with the first amendment.[47.1] In a significant victory for the press, one that may well have taken many Court watchers by surprise, the Court held that the Constitution requires that the burden of proof on truth or falsity be placed on the plaintiff.[47.2]

Lest there be too much dancing in the streets by the press, however, it is important to emphasize the limited contours of the *Hepps* ruling. The Court's opinion began much as *Dun & Bradstreet* began, with

---

[45] *See* Rogozinski v. Airstream by Angell, 152 N.J. Super. 133, 377 A.2d 807 (1977), *modified on other grounds,* 164 N.J. Super 465, 397 A.2d 334 (1979); Memphis Publishing Co. v. Nichols, 569 S.W.2d 412 (Tenn. 1978).

[46] 106 S. Ct. 1558 (1986). The discussion of *Hepps* contained in this section is drawn substantially from Smolla, Dun & Bradstreet, Hepps, *and* Liberty Lobby: *A New Analytic Primer on the Future Course of Defamation,* Geo. L.J., Summer 1987.

[47] Pennsylvania followed "the common law's presumption that an individual's reputation is a good one." 106 S. Ct. at 1560.

[47.1] *Hepps* had been anticipated by a number of lower court decisions that had also placed a burden on plaintiffs. *See, e.g.,* Wilson v. Scripps-Howard Broadcasting Co., 642 F.2d 371 (6th Cir.), *cert. granted,* 454 U.S. 962, *cert. dismissed,* 454 U.S. 1130 (1981); Williams v. WCAU-TV, 555 F. Supp. 198 (E.D. Pa. 1983); Health Unlimited, Inc. v. Loyola University, 434 So. 2d 133 (La. Ct. App.), *appeal denied,* 435 So. 2d 445 (La. 1983); Jacron Sales Co. v. Sindorf, 276 Md. 580, 350 A.2d 688 (1976); Madison v. Yunker, 180 Mont. 54, 589 P.2d 126 (1978); Fairley v. Peekskill Star Corp., 83 A.D.2d 294, 445 N.Y.S.2d 156 (2d Dept. 1981); Horvath v. Ashtabula Telegraph, 8 Med. L. Rep. (BNA) 1657 (Ohio Ct. App. 1982).

[47.2] *Id.* at 1564-65.

carefully chosen words narrowing the precise question being addressed. The plaintiffs were private figures, but in this case the speech, the Court emphasized, involved an issue of public concern.[47.3] In a footnote later in the opinion, the Court further emphasized the precision of its holding, stating that it had no occasion to consider the *quantity* of proof of falsity that a private figure plaintiff must present to recover damages.[47.4] In a final caveat, the Court emphasized that the *Philadelphia Inquirer* was a media defendant, and that the Court's opinion expressed no view as to whether the same rule would apply in the nonmedia context.[47.5] This fastidious concern for delimiting the scope of its ruling stands in marked contrast to the style and method of the Court's opinion twelve years before in *Gertz*, in which the Court went well beyond the facts of the case before it to announce a whole matrix of new constitutional rules.[47.6]

The holding in *Hepps* leaves unresolved a number of important burden of proof questions. In emphasizing the media status of the defendant, the Court left open the burden of proof rule when nonmedia defendants are involved. Presumably, public *officials* would bear the burden of proof as plaintiffs in media and nonmedia cases alike.[47.7] *New York Times Co. v. Sullivan*,[47.8] it should be remembered, was both a media and a nonmedia case—Commissioner Sullivan sued not only the *Times* but also four individual black ministers who had signed the advertisement. The burden of proof in the remaining types of nonmedia cases (involving public figure and private figure plaintiffs), however, remains somewhat problematic. *Hepps* also fails to establish the burden of proof when the subject matter of the speech does not involve an issue of public concern. If the preoccupation with the "issue of public concern" factor exhibited in both *Hepps* and *Dun & Bradstreet* evolves into the dominant analytic principle of the modern law of defamation, then conceivably the burden of proof even in public official and public figure cases could be placed on defendants when the speech involves private issues. Again, because it is unclear whether the "issue of public concern" test is to be the gatekeeper for *any* first

47.3 *Id.* at 1559.

47.4 *Id.* at 1565 n.4.

47.5 *Id.* (citing Hutchinson v. Proxmire, 443 U.S. 111, 133 n.16 (1979)).

47.6 *See* Gertz v. Robert Welch, Inc., 418 U.S. 323 (1974). For a description of the *Gertz* rules, *see supra* §§ 2.04-2.08.

47.7 *See* Restatement (Second) of Torts § 613 comment j (1977). *See also supra* § 5.06.

47.8 376 U.S. 254, 280 (1964).

amendment protection, this area remains unresolved.[47.9]

Hepps is, however, an important victory for the press, a victory that was by no means foreordained. Many Americans consider defamatory charges made by the media at least symbolically equivalent to criminal charges instituted by the state, and from that equation conclude that the victim (the "accused") should be deemed innocent until proven guilty. Something is grossly amiss, this line of reasoning goes, when the plaintiff is given the license to drag someone through the mud and then force the hapless victim to clear himself if he can.[47.10]

That the Court resisted the substantial emotional pull of this argument was, from the media's perspective, grounds for a sigh of relief. Justice O'Connor's opinion, with utmost clarity, went for the jugular on this conflict. There will always be cases in which the crucible of litigation fails to convincingly melt away the lies and leave a dispositive core of truth about the events giving rise to the lawsuit. Litigation must end with a victory for someone; somehow ties must be broken. Any arbitrary assignment of victory to one side or the other when the evidence is in equipoise will result in cases "wrongly decided," in the sense that we are statistically certain that the outcome will at times be at variance with what the outcome would be if the triers-of-fact were omniscient. Justice O'Connor resolved the unavoidable dilemma in favor of free expression values:

> This dilemma stems from the fact that the allocation of the burden of proof will determine liability for some speech that is true and some that is false, but *all* of such speech is *unknowably* true or false. Because the burden of proof is the deciding factor only when the evidence is ambiguous, we cannot know how much of the speech affected by the allocation of the burden of proof is true and how much is false. In a case presenting a configuration of speech and plaintiff like the one here, and where the scales are in such an uncertain balance, we believe that the Constitution requires us to tip them in favor of protecting free speech. To ensure that true speech is not deterred, we hold that the common law presumption that defamatory speech is false cannot stand when a plaintiff seeks damages against a media defendant for speech of public concern.[47.11]

Under *Hepps,* therefore, ties go to the press. There should be no

---

[47.9] *See also supra* § 3.02.

[47.10] *See also* Martin v. Griffin Television, Inc., 549 P.2d 85, 87-94 (Okla. 1976); Memphis Publishing Co. v. Nichols, 569 S.W.2d 412 (Tenn. 1978); Frank B. Hall & Co. v. Buck, 678 S.W.2d 612, 623-25 (Tex. App. 1984), *cert. denied,* 472 U.S. 1009 (1985); Denny v. Mertz, 106 Wis. 2d 636, 654-58, 318 N.W.2d 141, 150-51, *cert. denied,* 459 U.S. 883 (1982).

[47.11] 106 S. Ct. 1558, 1564 (1986).

illusion that this resolution does not extract a substantial social cost—it surely does. *Hepps* is only meaningful in cases in which the media has misbehaved. By hypothesis, the power of *Hepps* lies in its protection of stories concerning matters of public interest that were negligently, recklessly, or intentionally prepared, since the fault requirements of *Gertz* and *New York Times* must be satisfied at the threshold in cases involving public plaintiffs or private plaintiffs and public speech.[47.12] In theory, *Hepps* invites the unscrupulous publisher who does not believe in the truth of the story but is confident that at any trial the truth would ultimately prove to be unknowable to go ahead and publish. Even assuming that some publishers are sufficiently amoral and brazen to make this calculation, however, there are many other disincentives to publishing the story. If litigation does ensue, it will be costly whether won or lost, and the uncertainties of trials are such that the niceties of the burden of proof allocation may give way to the vengeance of the outraged jury. Realistically, however, *Hepps* does surely provide safe harbor for at least some sloppy, unprofessional journalism. The powerful message of the majority opinion is that this social subsidy must be paid to give breathing space to good journalism, journalism that is aggressive, insistent, conscientious, but sometimes wrong. And so for defenders of the press, *Hepps*, for all its limitations and wrinkles, was a crucial victory.

To summarize, the holding in *Hepps* decides that the burden of proof on the issue of truth or falsity is on the plaintiff in the following types of cases:

47.12 This point lies at the heart of Justice Stevens's dissent in *Hepps. Id.* at 1566. (Stevens, J., dissenting). Justice Stevens's argument that the only publishers who benefit from *Hepps* are those who act negligently or recklessly is, as stated in the text, technically correct, but it may overly dramatize the practical impact of *Hepps*. The probability is that a plaintiff able to meet the burden of proving negligence or recklessness usually will also be able to meet the burden of proving falsity. Falsity, in fact, is an issue that is typically either intertwined with fault or resolved as an issue antecedent to fault. Evidence of fault is not marshaled and presented in a vacuum. It is extremely difficult to imagine a plaintiff establishing actual malice or negligence in a case, while still unable to prove that he or she was lied about. *See* Restatement (Second) of Torts § 613 comment j (1964). Nevertheless, there may at times be cases where reckless or negligent journalistic behavior is well demonstrated, despite the fact that the ultimate judgment on truth or falsity remains hopelessly clouded. A reporter, for example, might be egregiously sloppy in verification procedures (and thus negligent), or might even subjectively doubt the story but publish anyway (and thus be reckless). Yet, in both cases the reporter may be the beneficiary of the burden of proof rule when later litigation efforts by both sides reveal the underlying truth or falsity of the story to be impossible to determine. In such a case Justice Stevens's observation would be accurate.

(1) Media defendant cases involving public officials or public figures and issues of public concern.
(2) Media defendant cases involving private figures and issues of public concern.

Hepps technically leaves the burden of proof issue open in the following cases:

(3) Media defendant cases involving public officials or public figures and issues of private concern.
(4) Media defendant cases involving private figures and issues of private concern.
(5) Nonmedia defendant cases involving public figures and public officials and issues of public concern.
(6) Nonmedia defendant cases involving private figures and issues of public concern.
(7) Nonmedia defendant cases involving public officials and public figures and issues of private concern.
(8) Nonmedia defendant cases involving private figures and cases of private concern.

The wisest choice in those cases left open by *Hepps* (cases 3-8) is to place the burden of proof on the plaintiff, creating one uniform rule for all defamation cases. The two easiest cases to decide are cases 5 and 6, both of which involve issues of public concern. The only distinguishing element between those cases and *Hepps* is the nonmedia status of the defendant. Whatever the wisdom of engaging in a media/nonmedia distinction on fault issues,[47.13] it seems perverse to engage in such a distinction in the context of litigating truth or falsity. If anything, we should be harder on media defendants on the truth issue than on nonmedia defendants, first, because media defendants have greater capacity to cause harm by lying, and second, because media defendants are more likely to make financial profits from lies. If the general policy judgment of *Hepps* as to the importance of not penalizing speech on matters of public concern protects media defendants, then it is hard to see how the *same speech* would be less worthy of protection because of the "amateur status" of the defendant. To the extent that the popular "innocent until proven guilty" cliché is the source of the old common law rule putting the burden on the defendant, the force of that cliché

[47.13] *See supra* § 3.02[2].

is substantially diminished in nonmedia cases, where the analogy between defamation and the state's power to convict completely breaks down.

Cases 3, 4, 7 and 8 present a tougher problem, for all involve speech on issues not of public concern. Even in private speech cases, however, plaintiffs should bear the burden of proof. The only significant rationale for adherence to the old common law rule placing the burden of proof on the defendant was the theory that a person's reputation is "presumed to be good," and therefore the injurious statement presumed false until the defendant demonstrates otherwise.[47.14] The presumption, however, was purely a legal fiction: one's first human reaction upon hearing derogatory information about another is not necessarily "that can't be true . . . it must be wrong," nor is it necessarily "I believe it, I thought as much." What we in fact do when we receive defamatory information about others is filter that information through our own internal judgments of credibility and plausibility, as colored by our individual predilections. The common law presumption, in short, is not a common sense presumption, for there is no universal common sense to be had on the subject. Rather, the common law presumption reflects two normative judgments: first, that those who bear bad tales should have the facts to back them up, and second, that a person accused of wrongdoing should be deemed innocent until proven guilty.

These are not frivolous concerns. There may well be a sort of internal psychological burden of proof at work in the common law rule, a burden that partakes of the judgment that those who make accusations really should be able to put up or shut up, and if they can't, then a defamation suit is what they have coming. And to the extent that the speaker of the defamation is the original "aggressor" in the dispute and the accused victim the person against whom that aggression was targeted, there is a certain appeal to the notion that the victim should not be forced to defend at his or her peril, but should have the option of remaining dignified and mute, "innocent unless proven guilty."

Hepps answers most of these arguments. *Our model* for defamation *is not borrowed from* the criminal *law,* with the awesome power of the official accuser pitted against an individual defendant, *but is, rather, the model of a* vigorous and open *marketplace,* where different versions of the truth vie for acceptance. To encourage the free trade of information in that market we place the burden on plaintiffs, so that in all "unknow-

[47.14] *See* Philadelphia Newspapers, Inc. v. Hepps, 106 S. Ct. 1558, 1560 (1986).

able truth" situations the law exacts no sanctions, leaving judgments on truth to the marketplace of public opinion.[47.15] We value the pursuit of truth so highly, in fact, that we prefer to force victims to fight back rather than stand silent.

The force of these judgments in *Hepps* is only slightly diminished when the speech is not about issues of public concern. Private truth is as valuable as public truth; for most of us the private facts of our family lives, workplaces, schools, churches and neighborhoods are as vital as the more public facts of politics, art, and science.[47.16]

More significantly, the "innocent until proven guilty" aphorism should actually operate to put the burden on the plaintiff, not the defendant, if we intend to operate defamation rules to be at all consistent with the rest of the law of torts. For the traditional tort rule in every area but defamation is that because the plaintiff is invoking the heavy machinery of state power against a fellow citizen, the plaintiff bears the burden—it is the defendant who is deemed innocent of tortious activity until proven guilty. The only reason defamation has survived in some jurisdictions as an exception to this rule is the psychological transposition of roles that defamation suits invite: the plaintiff is thought of as the person "really on trial," for it is the plaintiff's reputation at stake. But once again, the law of torts routinely puts the burden of proof on

---

[47.15] *Id.* at 1564-65.

[47.16] *See* Smolla, *Let the Author Beware: The Rejuvenation of the American Law of Libel,* 132 U. Pa. L. Rev. 1, 68-71 (1983). An excellent example of how libel litigation can chill valuable private speech, creating a substantial practical social detriment, is the growing number of libel suits filed by employees who were fired. The trend is toward increasing use of libel theories as part of termination litigation. The *Wall Street Journal* recently published an estimate that one third of all defamation suits arise from cases filed by discharged employees against their former employers. Stricharchuk, *Fired Employees Turn the Reason for Dismissal into a Legal Weapon,* Wall St. Journal, Oct. 2, 1986, § 2, at 1, col. 4. This litigation has become extraordinarily expensive to defend, to the point that many major corporations are refusing to release information concerning the reasons for termination or the employee's job performance. Some companies are not even explaining the reasons for discharge to the employee who is being fired. The social costs here are obvious. First, the flow of information about employees is diminished, resulting in less informed hiring decisions and increased turnover. *Id.* Second, libel rules may actually work to decrease other forms of legal protection for employees: procedural due process (for public employers) and more generalized fairness and good faith considerations (for private employers). To the extent that treating employees with fairness and dignity is a function of explaining personnel decisions to them, libel litigation may in the long run work at cross-purposes with these values. Though this sort of "chilling effect" has nothing to do with the media, it is a considerable drag on the economy, and a vivid example of why libel litigation in all contexts, public and private, should at *least* be made to adhere to the normal rules of other civil litigation. *See* Chapter 15, *infra.*

plaintiffs when interests every bit as precious as reputation are being litigated—the common law exception for defamation simply cannot stand up to logical scrutiny.

§ 5.08 The Substantial Truth Test

"Truth" will protect the defendant from liability even if the precise literal truth of the defamatory statement cannot be established. Slight inaccuracies are tolerated; the test is whether the statement is "substantially true."[48] There are four useful guidelines in applying the "substantial truth" test:

[1] Specific Defamatory Charges

The more the defamatory charge is particularized and specific, the more evidence used to establish "substantial truth" must be particularized and specific.[49]

[48] *See,eg.*, Wehling v. CBS, 721 F.2d 506 (5th Cir. 1983); Alioto v. Cowles Communications, Inc., 623 F.2d 616 (9th Cir. 1980), *cert. denied*, 449 U.S. 1102 (1981); Anderson v. Stanco Sports Library, Inc., 542 F.2d 638 (4th Cir. 1976); Robinson v. U.S. News & World Report, Inc., 16 Med. L. Rep. 1695 (BNA) (U.S. Dist. Ct., N.D. Ill. 1989); Alabama Ride Co. v. Vance, 235 Ala. 263, 178 So. 438 (1938); Kirkpatrick v. Journal Publishing Co., 210 Ala. 10, 97 So. 58 (1923); Fairbanks Publishing Co. v. Francisco, 390 P.2d 784 (Alaska 1964); Fendler v. Phoenix Newspapers, Inc., 130 Ariz. 475, 636 P.2d 1257 (Ct. App. 1981); Pritchard v. Times Southwest Broadcasting, Inc., 277 Ark. 458, 642 S.W.2d 877 (1982); Gantry Construction Co. v. American Pipe & Construction Co., 49 Cal. App. 3d 186, 122 Cal. Rptr. 834 (1975); Strada v. Connecticut Newspapers, 193 Conn. 313, 10 Med. L. Rep. (BNA) 2165 (1984); Goodrich v. Waterbury Republican-American, Inc., 188 Conn. 107, 448 A.2d 1317 (1982); Gomba v. McLaughlin, 180 Colo. 232, 504 P.2d 337 (1972); Hill v. Lakeland Ledger Publishing Corp., 231 So. 2d 254 (Fla. Dist. Ct. App. 1970); Hammond v. Times Publishing Co., 162 So. 2d 681 (Fla. Dist. Ct. App. 1964); McCormick v. Miami Herald Publishing Co., 139 So. 2d 197 (Fla. Dist. Ct. App. 1962); Jones v. Neighbor Newspapers, Inc., 142 Ga. App. 365, 236 S.E.2d 23 (1977); Griffin v. Kentucky Post, 10 Med. L. Rep. (BNA) 1159 (Ky. Cir. 1983); Bell v. Courier-Journal & Louisville Times Co., 402 S.W.2d 84 (Ky. 1966); Hopkins v. Keith, 348 So. 2d 999 (La. Ct. App. 1977), *cert. denied*, 350 So. 2d 893 (La. 1977); Herrmann v. Newark Morning Ledger Co., 48 N.J. Super. 420, 138 A.2d 61 (1958); Franklin v. Blank, 86 N.M. 585, 525 P.2d 945 (Ct. App. 1974); Akins v. Altus Newspapers, Inc., 609 P.2d 1263 (Okla. 1977), *cert. denied*, 449 U.S. 1010 (1980); Kilian v. Doubleday & Co., Inc., 367 Pa. 117, 79 A.2d 657 (1951); Ross v. Columbia Newspapers, Inc., 266 S.C. 75, 221 S.E.2d 770 (1976); Stones River Motors, Inc. v. Mid-South Publishing Co., 651 S.W.2d 713 (Tenn. App. 1983).

[49] Kilian v. Doubleday & Co., 367 Pa. 117, 79 A.2d 657 (1951); Restatement (Second) of Torts § 581A comment c (1976); W. Prosser, W. Keeton, D. Dobbs, R. Keeton & D. Owen, Prosser & Keeton on Torts § 116, at 841 (5th ed. 1984).

[2] Generalized Defamatory Charges

As the character of the defamatory charge becomes more generalized and unspecified, the evidence used to establish substantial truth may encompass a broader range of conduct and events.[50]

[3] Minor Inaccuracies

Whether the defamatory charge is specific (requiring specific proof) or more general (permitting more generalized proof), minor inaccuracies of terminology or detail do not prevent the story from being substantially true as long as the "gist" or "sting" of the defamation is true.[51]

Closely related to the rule governing minor inaccuracies is the "incremental harm" branch of the libel-proof doctrine.[51.1] A "libel-proof" plaintiff is a plaintiff with a reputation so bad that it cannot be further damaged.[51.2] The "incremental harm" doctrine measures the incremental reputational harm inflicted by the challenged statements beyond the harm imposed by the nonactionable remainder of the publication. If this additional "incremental" damage is deemed nominal or nonexistent, the statements are not actionable.[51.3] While the incremental harm doctrine has been cited as a branch of the libel-proof doctrine, in fact it is closely related to the issue of substantial truth, and is indeed simply another variation of the principle that liability of defamation cannot exist when the "gist" or "sting" of the defamatory statement in not actionable.[51.4]

---

[50] Restatement (Second) of Torts § 581A comment c (1976). *Cf.* Smith v. Byrd, 225 Miss. 331, 83 So. 2d 172 (1955).

[51] Wehling v. CBS, Inc., 721 F.2d 506 (5th Cir. 1983); Maheu v. Hughes Tool Co., 569 F.2d 459 (9th Cir. 1977); Gantry Construction Co. v. American Pipe & Construction Co., 49 Cal. App. 3d 186, 122 Cal. Rptr. 834 (1975); Swaffield v. Universal Esco Corp., 271 Cal. App. 2d 147, 76 Cal. Rptr. 680 (1969); Kurata v. Los Angeles News Publishing Co., 4 Cal. App. 2d 224, 40 P.2d 520 (1935); Kohn v. West Hawaii Today, Inc., 65 Haw. 584, 656 P.2d 79 (1982); Sivulich v. Howard Publications, 10 Med. L. Rep. 2013, 2015 (Ill. App. Ct. 1984); Herrmann v. Newark Morning Ledger Co., 48 N.J. Super. 420, 138 A.2d 61 (1958); Edwards v. Bell, 1 Bing. 403, 130 Eng. Rep. 162 (1824); Prosser & Keeton, *supra* note 49, § 116, at 842.

[51.1] *See* Herbert v. Lando, 781 F.2d 298, 310-11 (2d Cir.), *cert. denied*, 476 U.S. 1182 (1986).

[51.2] *See infra* § 9.10[4][d].

[51.3] Masson v. The New Yorker Magazine, Inc., 881 F.2d 1452, 16 Med. L. Rep. (BNA) 2089, 2093-94 (9th Cir. 1989).

[51.4] *See infra* §§ 5.09-5.11.

[4] Repetition of Another's Defamatory Communication

Repetition of a defamatory charge made by someone else normally cannot be defended on the grounds that the repetition was "true" in the narrow literal sense that the other person in fact made the defamatory statement.[52] The substantial truth of the defamatory accusations thus repeated must normally be established.[53] This rule is qualified, however, by inroads made by the emerging neutral reportage privilege.[54]

§ 5.09 The Substantial Truth Test: Specific Defamatory Charges

[1] Overview

When the defamatory allegation is narrow and specific, the evidence of truth must more strictly conform to the allegation.[55] An allegation that the plaintiff embezzled $50 from the First State Bank cannot be proved substantially true with evidence that the plaintiff embezzled $100 from the Second National Bank.[56] A statement that John committed adultery with Mary is not justified as substantially true by proof that John committed adultery with Sue.[57] In *Himango v. Prime Time Broadcasting*,[58] for example, a radio station alleged that the plaintiff had been caught "in a somewhat compromising position" with the wife of a person who was later charged with assaulting the plaintiff. It was held proper not to permit the introduction of evidence concerning plaintiff's

---

52 *See* Dement v. Houston Printing Co., 14 Tex. Civ. App. 391, 37 S.W. 985 (1896); Restatement (Second) of Torts § 581A comment e (1976); Eldredge, *supra* note 2, § 67, at 331.

53 Fountain v. West, 23 Iowa 9 (1867); Watkin v. Hall, 3 Q.B. 396, 37 L.J.Q.B. 125 (1868); Restatement (Second) of Torts § 581A comment f (1976); Eldredge, *supra* note 2, § 68, at 332, Prosser & Keeton, *supra* note 49, § 116, at 841.

54 *See supra* § 4.15.

55 Kilian v. Doubleday & Co. 367 Pa. 117, 79 A.2d 657 (1951); Restatement (Second) of Torts § 581A comment c (1976); Prosser & Keeton, *supra* note 49, § 116, at 841.

56 *See* Sun Printing & Publishing Ass'n v. Schenck, 98 F. 925 (2d Cir. 1900); Eastland v. Caldwell, 5 Ky. (Bibb.) 21 (1810); Self v. Gardner, 15 Mo. 480 (1852); Kariavainean v. MacFadden Publications, 305 Mass. 573, 26 N.E.2d 538 (1940); Downs v. Hawley, 112 Mass. 237 (1873); Haddock v. Naughton, 74 Hun. 390 (N.Y. 1893); Kilian v. Doubleday & Co., 367 Pa. 117, 79 A.2d 657 (1951); Eldredge, *supra* note 2, § 8, at 332-33; Prosser & Keeton, *supra* note 49, § 116, at 841.

57 Pallet v. Sargent, 36 N.H. 496 (1858).

58 10 Med. L. Rep. (BNA) 1724 (Wash. Ct. App. 1984).

other alleged extramarital sexual activity.[59] Specific charges of particularized crimes cannot be refuted with general evidence of other, similar activity, or by an attack on the general bad character or misconduct of the plaintiff.[60]

The relative strictness of the common law position on substantial truth when specific defamatory charges are made can be justified on the grounds that more detailed charges of misconduct often tend to create greater reputational injury, simply because the existence of detail tends to lend credibility to the accusation. The art of successful lying, as Huck Finn was so adept at demonstrating, is frequently the art of embellishment.

Nevertheless, a distinction should be made between (1) inaccuracies that amount to charges of *an act of misconduct different from the one plaintiff actually engaged in,* and (2) cosmetic inaccuracies *that correctly identify the act but err in describing minor details* concerning the act. Reporting that the plaintiff robbed a bank, but putting the amount of money stolen at $50,000, when in fact it was $25,000, would still be "substantial truth."[61] To use a contemporary example, if in *Westmoreland v. CBS, Inc.,*[62] CBS had demonstrated that a conspiracy existed to underestimate the strength of enemy forces in Vietnam, but the broadcast reported that more troops were cut during the conspiracy than the actual evidence at trial established, the test of "substantial truth" would be satisfied.

[2] Relationship to Fault Requirements

Although the common law requirement of strict adherence to the truth when very specific charges are made remains intact, it should be

[59] *Id.* at 1727 (citing McCormick, Evidence § 189, at 445 (2d ed. 1972)(Evidence of specific acts or of a character trait is generally not admissible to show that a party acted in conformity therewith on a particular occasion.)). *See also* Fed. R. Evid. 404.

[60] *See, e.g.,* Himango v. Prime Time Broadcasting, 10 Med. L. Rptr. (BNA) 1724, 1727 (Wash. Ct. App. 1984); Crane v. New York World Telegram Corp., 308 N.Y. 470, 126 N.E. 2d 753 (1955); Dowie v. Priddle, 216 Ill. 553, 75 N.E. 243 (1905); Prosser & Keeton, *supra* note 49, § 116, at 841; Fed. R. Evid. 404.

[61] Fort Worth Press Co. v. Davis, 96 S.W.2d 416 (Tex. Civ. App. 1936); Prosser & Keeton, *supra* note 49, § 116, at 842.

[62] Westmoreland v. CBS, Inc., 596 F. Supp 1170 (S.D.N.Y. 1984). *See also related proceedings in* Westmoreland v. CBS, Inc., 11 Med. L. Rep. (BNA) 1013 (2d Cir. 1984); Westmoreland v. CBS, Inc., 97 F.R.D. 703 (S.D.N.Y. 1983); Westmoreland v. CBS, Inc., 9 Med. L. Rep. (BNA) 2316 (S.D.N.Y. 1983); Westmoreland v. CBS, Inc., 9 Med. L. Rep. (BNA) 1521 (S.D.N.Y. 1983); Westmoreland v. CBS, Inc., 8 Med. L. Rep. (BNA) 2493 (D.S.C. 1982).

remembered that the force of the rule is still considerably blunted by constitutional fault requirements.[63] Thus, although the defense of truth may not exist when the defendant mistakenly accuses the plaintiff of robbing a certain bank on a certain day, the circumstances that led the defendant to level the accusation may be sufficient to preclude a finding of negligence or recklessness. The "nearer the miss," so to speak, the less likely the miss is attributable to "fault."[64]

§ 5.10 The Substantial Truth Test: Generalized Defamatory Charges

Evidence of "substantial truth" must be "as broad, and as narrow, as the defamatory imputation itself."[65] As the defamatory charge against the plaintiff increases in generality, the range of evidence that will establish substantial truth similarly broadens. A charge that the plaintiff is an embezzler can be shown to be substantially true by evidence of one act of embezzlement.[66] On the other hand, if the gist of the charge is repeated misconduct, the evidence must show repetition.[67] One does not show that a woman is a prostitute with proof of one act of unchastity.[68]

§ 5.11 Minor Inaccuracies in Detail

[1] Errors in Terminology

Errors in labeling or in terminology, usually legal terminology, do not prevent the charge from being substantially true.[69] In *Griffin v.*

---

63 *See supra* §§ 3.01-3.05.

64 *See generally* discussions of proof of fault in Chapter 3, *supra.*

65 Prosser & Keeton, *supra* note 49, § 116, at 841.

66 Restatement (Second) of Torts § 581A comment c (1976).

67 *Id.*

68 *Id.*

69 *See, e.g.*, Sivulich v. Howard Publications, 10 Med. L. Rep. (BNA) 2013 (Ill. App. Ct. 1984); Griffin v. Kentucky Post, 10 Med. L. Rep. (BNA) 1159 (Ky. Cir. Ct. 1983); Orr v. Argus-Press Co., 586 F.2d 1108 (6th Cir. 1978), *cert. denied*, 440 U.S. 960 (1979); Herrmann v. Newark Morning Ledger Co., 48 N.J. Super. 420, 138 A.2d 61 (1958); Grab v. Poughkeepsie Newspapers, Inc., 91 Misc. 2d 1003, 399 N.Y.S. 2d 97 (Dutchess Co. 1977); Piracci v. Hearst Corp., 263 F. Supp 511 (D. Md. 1966), *aff'd*, 371 F.2d 1016 (4th Cir. 1967); Pritchard v. Times Southwest Broadcasting, Inc., 277 Ark. 458, 642 S.W.2d 877 (1982); Saleeby v. Free Press, Inc., 197 Va. 761, 91 S.E.2d 405 (1956); Coronado Credit Union v. KOAT Television, Inc., 99 N.M. 233, 656 P.2d 896 (Ct. App. 1982); Williams

Kentucky Post,[70] for example, the plaintiff was a dancer at a lounge. A police officer observed her, in the words of the court, "dancing topless at the lounge and upon investigating found her to be naked of an occupational license; whereupon he cited her in violation of [the occupational license] ordinance."[71] A newspaper article reported that the plaintiff had "pled guilty to nude dancing," when in fact the plaintiff had pled guilty to performing such dancing without the requisite occupational license. The court held the newspaper report was substantially true, since at the time of her citation for violation of the ordinance she "was dancing 'bare breasted' (nude) without the license to cover her occupation."[72] Similarly, to describe a violation of the securities laws as "fraud" is substantially true.[73] So, too, is it substantially true to report of a person involved in an altercation that "charges of aggravated battery have been filed" even though the person was actually sued in a civil action, when, despite the fact that aggravated battery is a criminal felony charge, the reader would gather from the entire article that the nature of the legal action was civil, not criminal.[74]

[2] Minor "Literary" Embellishments

In a popularization of an event, or in the reducing of a complex set of facts into an intelligible story, the writer or broadcaster will often exercise literary or editorial judgment, making cosmetic additions to or subtractions from the raw events.[75] In *Meeropol v. Nizer,*[76] for exam-

v. Pasma, 656 P.2d 212 (Mont. 1982), *cert. denied,* 103 S. Ct. 2122 (1983); Handelsman v. San Francisco Chronicle, 11 Cal. App. 3d 381, 90 Cal. Rptr. 188 (Ct. App. 1970).

[70] 10 Med. L. Rep. (BNA) 1159 (Ky. Cir. Ct. 1983).

[71] *Id.* at 1160.

[72] *Id.* at 1160.

[73] Orr v. Argus-Press Co., 586 F.2d 1108 (6th Cir. 1978), *cert. denied,* 440 U.S. 960 (1979).

[74] Sivulich v. Howard Publications, 10 Med. L. Rep. (BNA) 2013 (Ill. App. Ct. 1984).

[75] Ryan v. Brooks, 634 F.2d 726, 733 (4th Cir. 1980); Hotchner v. Castillo-Puche, 551 F.2d 910, 914 (2d Cir.), *cert. denied sub nom.* 434 U.S. 834 (1977); Time, Inc. v. Johnston, 448 F.2d 378, 384 (4th Cir. 1971); Loeb v. Globe Newspaper Co., 489 F. Supp. 481, 486 (D. Mass. 1980); Meeropol v. Nizer, 381 F. Supp. 29, 35 (S.D.N.Y. 1974), *aff'd in part, rev'd on other grounds,* 560 F.2d 1061 (2d Cir. 1977), *cert. denied,* 434 U.S. 1013 (1978); Gomba v. McLaughlin, 180 Colo. 232, 504 P.2d 337 (1973); Strada v. Connecticut Newspapers, 193 Conn. 313, 10 Med. L. Rep. (BNA) 2165 (1984); Rinaldi v. Holt, Rinehart & Winston, Inc., 42 N.Y.2d 369, 397 N.Y.S.2d 943, 366 N.E.2d 1299 *cert. denied,* 434 U.S. 969 (1977).

[76] 381 F. Supp. 29 (S.D. N.Y. 1974), *aff'd in part, rev'd on other grounds,* 560 F.2d 1061 (2d Cir. 1977), *cert. denied,* 434 U.S. 1013 (1978).

ple, the court noted that "any 'deviations from or embellishments upon' the information obtained from the primary sources relied upon were miniscule and can be attributed to the leeway afforded an author who attempts to recount and popularize [a] historic event."[77] The omission of inconsequential or minor details is "largely a matter of editorial judgment in which the courts, and juries, have no proper function."[78] The "author's job is not simply to copy statements verbatim."[79] Rather, it is in the very nature of the writing and reporting process "to interpret and rework them into the whole."[80] As observed in *Loeb v. Globe Newspaper Co.*,[81] "[a] fussy insistence upon literal accuracy 'would condemn the press to an arid, desiccated recital of bare facts.' "[82] "Where 'the main charge, or gist, of the libel' is true, minor errors that do not change a reader's perception of the statement do not make the statement actionable."[83] The test is "whether the libel, as published, would have a different effect upon the reader than the pleaded truth would have produced."[84]

Defendants may also usefully invoke the "incremental harm" doctrine in such cases.[84.1] The "incremental harm" doctrine measures the incremental reputational harm inflicted by the challenged statements beyond the harm imposed by the nonactionable remainder of the publi-

---

77 381 F. Supp. at 35.

78 Rinaldi v. Holt, Rinehart & Winston, Inc., 42 N.Y.2d 369, 383, 397 N.Y.S.2d 943, 952, 366 N.E.2d 1299, *cert. denied*, 434 U.S. 969 (1977).

79 Strada v. Connecticut Newspapers, 193 Conn. 313, 10 Med. L. Rep. (BNA) 2165, 2168 (1984).

80 Ryan v. Brooks, 634 F.2d 726, 733 (4th Cir. 1980).

81 489 F. Supp 481 (D. Mass. 1980).

82 *Id.* at 486 (quoting Time, Inc. v. Johnston, 448 F.2d 378, 384 (4th Cir. 1971)).

83 Strada v. Connecticut Newspapers, 193 Conn. 313, 10 Med. L. Rep. (BNA) 2165, 2168-2169 (1984). *See also* Wehling v. Columbia Broadcasting Sys., 721 F.2d 506 (5th Cir. 1983); Gomba v. McLaughlin, 180 Colo. 232, 504 P.2d 337 (1973); Goodrich v. Waterbury Republican-American, Inc., 188 Conn. 107, 113, 448 A.2d 1317 (1982); Kohn v. West Hawaii Today, Inc., 65 Haw. 584, 656 P.2d 79 (1982); Lawrence v. Bauer Publishing & Printing, Ltd., 89 N.J. 451, 446 A.2d 469, *cert. denied*, 459 U.S. 999 (1982).

84 Goodrich v. Waterbury Republican-American, Inc., 188 Conn. 107, 113, 448 A.2d 1317, 1322 (1982). *See also* Gomba v. McLaughlin, 180 Colo. 232, 504 P.2d 337 (1973); Strada v. Connecticut Newspapers, 193 Conn. 313, 10 Med. L. Rep. (BNA) 2165, 2169 (1984); Hill v. Lakeland Ledger Pub. Corp., 231 So. 2d 254 (Fla. Dist. Ct. App. 1970); Hammond v. Times Pub. Co., 162 So. 2d 681 (Fla. Dist. Ct. App. 1964); McCormick v. Miami Herald Pub. Co., 139 So. 2d 197 (Fla. Dist. Ct. App. 1962); Fleckenstein v. Friedman, 266 N.Y. 19, 193 N.E. 537 (1934); Hayward v. Watsonville Register-Pajaronian & Sun, 265 Cal. App. 2d 255, 262, 71 Cal. Rptr. 295, 300 (1968).

84.1 *See supra* § 5.08[3].

cation.[84.2] In the case of fabricated quotes and other similar embellishments, there will be no liability if the embellishments are deemed trivial or nominal in comparison to the actual reality.[84.3]

In *Masson v. The New Yorker Magazine, Inc.*[84.4] the court denied liability in a public figure case involving the outright fabrication of quotations, on the grounds that the manufactured quotations were relatively faithful to the substance of what was actually said. The case arose from a two-part article in *The New Yorker* magazine by author Janet Malcolm, on the termination of psychoanalyst Jeffrey M. Masson from his position as projects director of the Sigmund Freud archives. Malcolm had tape-recorded extensive interviews with Masson, and the article was based primarily on those tapes. Malcolm was not always faithful to the verbatim statements on the tapes, however, at times fabricating quotations.[84.5] According to Malcolm, the fabricated quotations made him appear "unscholarly, irresponsible, vain" and lacking in honesty and integrity.

The court stated that actual malice could be inferred from fabricated quotes in some circumstances, as where "the language attributed to the plaintiff is wholly product of the author's imagination." But malice "will not be inferred from evidence showing that the quoted language does not contain the exact words used by the plaintiff provided that the fabricated quotations are either 'rational interpretations' of ambiguous remarks made by the public figure," or "do not 'alter the substantive content' of unambiguous remarks actually made by the public figure."[84.6]

The court's ruling on the actual malice issue in *Masson* was intertwined with its analysis of the issues of defamatory meaning. The court frequently emphasized, for example, that the incremental additional

---

[84.2] *See* Herbert v. Lando, 781 F.2d 298, 310-11 (2d Cir.), *cert. denied*, 476 U.S. 1182 (1986).

[84.3] Masson v. The New Yorker Magazine, Inc., 881 F.2d 1452, 16 Med. L. Rep. (BNA) 2089, 2093-94 (9th Cir. 1989).

[84.4] *Id.*

[84.5] The quotations as they appeared in the *New Yorker* articles and the quotations on the actual tapes were frequently different. Janet Malcolm claimed that many of her quotes came from statements made by Masson when the tape recorder was not on. Nevertheless, for the purposes of the summary judgment motion in the case, the court assumed that the inconsistencies existed because Malcolm had fabricated the quotes. In several instances the closeness of the recorded version to the printed version appeared to raise the inference that Malcolm may have taken some editorial license to modify quotes to make them more pithy, biting, or literary.

[84.6] 16 Med. L. Rep. (BNA) at 2092.

harm to Masson's reputation caused by the fabricated quotes was insignificant when measured against what Masson had in fact said. The fabricated quotes, in other words, were only marginally more damaging than the actual quotes.[84.7]

There were many alleged misquotations in the *Masson* case, and the court painstakingly analyzed each of them. The most striking quotation involved the author's fabrication of the phrase "Intellectual Gigolo." In the actual interview Masson had described himself this way:

> [Eisler and Anna Freud] felt, in a sense, I was a private asset but a public liability. They like me when I was alone in their living room, and I could talk and chat and tell them the truth about things and they would tell me. But that I was, in a sense, much too junior within the hierarchy of analysis, for these important training analysis to be caught dead with me.

What Janet Malcolm wrote, however, was this:

> Eisler and Anna Freud told me the same thing. They like me well enough "in my own room." They loved to hear from me what creeps and dolts analysts are. I was like an intellectual gigolo—you get your pleasure from him, but you don't take him out in public.

Although Masson had never used the phrase "intellectual gigolo" to describe himself, and although the phrase certainly does create a somewhat different effect than the actual self-description Masson used, the court was convinced that the differences were too inconsequential to support liability. The court reached this conclusion over the protests of a vigorous dissent, which argued that quotation marks are special, and the material within them should have a special integrity, in which embellishments are not permitted.

The *Masson* case is a close call, in which the entire record must be weighed to make an intelligent judgment. On the whole, the majority's opinion is probably correct. Many of the things that Masson did in fact say on the tapes were heavily damaging. He bragged, for example, of having had sex with over 1,000 women. His striking ego and eccentricities surely had an influence on the result, convincing the court that Malcolm's license with the quotations was for the most part a trivial extrapolation of the substance and tone of his interview.

[3] Is the Statement Actually Defamatory?

An important connection exists between the substantial truth defense and the threshold question of whether the inaccurate information

84.7 *See* the discussion of this problem in *supra* §§ 5.08-5.11.

is defamatory.[85] The two defenses often dovetail, because the same basic policies that undergird the rule that minor inaccuracies going to the gist or sting of the defamation do not subtract from the "substantial truth" defense also underlie the distinction between defamatory and nondefamatory speech. Plaintiffs sometimes sue when the underlying sting of what was said about them is true but surrounding details are false. Inaccuracies concerning those details, however, may have absolutely no tendency to injure reputation, and therefore are not defamatory. The test for "substantial truth" that looks to whether the reader would think differently of the plaintiff if the literal truth had been

(*Text continued on page 5-23*)

---

[85] *See supra* §§ 4.01-4.05.

communicated[86] is essentially parallel to the test for measuring whether the speech was defamatory in the first place.[87] Perhaps the classic example was the allegation in *New York Times v. Sullivan*[88] that black students protesting in Montgomery, Alabama, had been singing not "My Country, 'Tis of Thee" but the "Star Spangled Banner" when police arrived.[89] Anytime the factual error leads the reasonable recipient of the information to react, "So what?" the error of detail is probably not defamatory. When all errors of detail are of this nature, the defendant actually has two defenses—that the "gist or sting" is substantially true, and that whatever falsehoods do exist are not defamatory. In *Gomba v. McLaughlin,*[90] for example, the court articulated the test for substantial truth in terms of "whether the statement produces a different effect upon the reader than that which would be produced by the literal truth of the matter."[91] The defendant in *Gomba* had accused the plaintiff of having assaulted an elderly man at a dog show in Cheyenne. The court held the charge was substantially true when it was proved that the assault was actually upon a man from Cheyenne at a dog show in Brighton. An equally valid rationale, however, would have been that nothing in the "falsehood"—the confusion of Brighton and Cheyenne—was defamatory.

§ 5.12 Substantial Truth and Accurate Repetition of Another's Defamation

The common law views "tale beareres" as being just as responsible for repeating defamatory falsehood as the original "tale maker."[92] Thus

[86] *See, e.g.,* Goodrich v. Waterbury Republican-American, Inc., 188 Conn. 107, 448 A.2d 1317 (1982). *See also* Gomba v. McLaughlin, 180 Colo. 232, 504 P.2d 337 (1973); Strada v. Connecticut Newspapers, 193 Conn. 313, 10 Med. L. Rep. (BNA) 2165, 2169 (1984); Hill v. Lakeland Ledger Pub. Corp., 231 So. 2d 254 (Fla. Dist. Ct. App. 1970); Hammond v. Times Pub. Co., 162 So. 2d 681 (Fla. Dist. Ct. App. 1964); McCormick v. Miami Herald Pub. Co., 139 So. 2d 197 (Fla. Dist. Ct. App. 1962); Fleckenstein v. Friedman, 266 N.Y. 19, 193 N.E. 537 (1934); Hayward v. Watsonville Register-Pajaronian & Sun, 265 Cal. App. 2d 255, 262, 71 Cal. Rptr. 295 (1968).

[87] *See supra* §§ 4.01-4.05.

[88] 376 U.S. 254 (1964).

[89] *Id.* at 258-59, and Appendix at 292.

[90] 180 Colo. 232, 504 P.2d 337 (1973).

[91] *Id.* at 234, 504 P.2d at 339.

[92] Harris v. Minvielle, 48 La. App. 908, 915, 19 So. 925, 928 (1896). *See also* Cobbs v. Chicago Defender, 308 Ill. App. 55, 31 N.E.2d 323 (1941); Lancour v. Herald & Globe Ass'n, 111 Vt. 371, 17 A.2d 253 (1941); Restatement (Second) of Torts §§ 578, 581A comment e (1977).

the publication of rumors is not justified by the fact that the rumors existed.[93] A newspaper's publication of a story that the plaintiff "was jailed last night on the charge of horse stealing," for example, was actionable when the plaintiff was in fact arrested, charged, and jailed overnight for horse theft, but then released.[94]

This common law position has been considerably tempered by constitutional fault requirements,[95] and by the growing recognition of the neutral reportage privilege.[96] Today an accurate report by the media of criminal charges against the plaintiff thus frequently receives complete first amendment protection even if the underlying charges ultimately prove false, and the media's neutral and unembellished reportage of defamatory charges leveled by parties to a public controversy may in some jurisdictions be completely protected.[97] The neutral reportage concept may thus be conceptualized as either an exception to common law republication rules, or as a modern adjunct to the truth defense.[98]

§ 5.13 Increasing Use of Truth as a Defense

[1] Traditional Caution

At one time it was regarded as axiomatic that defendants should generally avoid relying on the truth defense, because truth was often difficult to prove and failure to meet the burden of proof could be disastrous. The Prosser hornbook,[99] for example, admonished that "[t]he defense of truth frequently is a hazardous venture for the defendant, since if he fails to sustain it the jury may be permitted to find that he has reiterated the defamation, and to consider the fact in aggrava-

93 *See, e.g.*, Cobbs v. Chicago Defender, 308 Ill. App. 55, 31 N.E.2d 323 (1941); Lancour v. Herald & Globe Ass'n, 111 Vt. 371, 17 A.2d 253 (1941); L. Eldredge, *supra* note 2, § 44, at 233.

94 Dement v. Houston Printing Co., 14 Tex. Civ. App. 391, 37 S.W. 985 (Tex. Civ. App. 1896).

95 *See supra* §§ 3.01-3.05.

96 *See* Edwards v. National Audubon Society, Inc., 556 F.2d 113, 120 (2d Cir. 1977), *cert. denied sub nom.* Edwards v. New York Times Co., 434 U.S. 1002 (1977). Barry v. Time, Inc., 584 F. Supp. 1110, 1126-28 (N.D. Cal. 1984). *But see* McCall v. Courier Journal, 623 S.W.2d 882 (Ky. 1981), *cert. denied,* 456 U.S. 975 (1982); Postill v. Booth Newspapers, Inc., 118 Mich. App. 608, 325 N.W.2d 511, 518 (1982). *See generally supra* § 4.15.

97 *See infra* § 4.15.

98 *See infra* § 4.15.

99 Prosser & Keeton, *supra* note 49.

tion of the damages."[100] Since the defamatory statement was normally presumed false at common law, all the legal and psychological momentum on the truth issue was with the plaintiff, and it was often thought more prudent to defend the case obliquely, relying on other privileges and defenses, than to hazard having the truth defense backfire. Professor Laurence Eldredge thus cautioned that "truth . . . should never be pleaded unless defense counsel has the evidence to prove it,"[101] and further asserted that truth "is the most dangerous plea there is and can boomerang upon the defendant with deadly effect in an award of punitive damages."[102]

[2] New Boldness in Asserting the Defense

In recent years these strategy tables have turned. Although it is not yet time for defense counsel to toss such cautions to the winds, they are to some degree anachronisms. The old litigation saw that truth is too dangerous a defense to hazard has been displaced by a new aggressiveness on the part of defendants in emphasizing the truth issue.

[3] Impact of Modern Fault Rules

The growing tendency of defendants to boldly litigate the truth issue is a general strategy adjustment made in light of the changes brought on by cases such as *Gertz* and *Hepps.*[103] Since, the plaintiff now carries the burden of proof on the truth issue,[104] the defense has the legal and psychological edge on the issue, so that heavily contesting the truth issue is no longer the gamble it might once have been. Cases in which the truth cannot be determined are now defense victories. This assumes, of course, that the jury follows the law, or that the trial court or appellate court reviews the evidence properly.[105]

More important, however, is the view among many defense lawyers that by heavily emphasizing the truth issue, the defense increases its

---

100 *Id.*, § 116 at 842 (1984) (citing Hall v. Edwards, 138 Me. 231, 23 A.2d 889 (1942); Coffin v. Brown, 94 Md. 190, 50 A. 567 (Md. 1901); Krulic v. Petcoff, 122 Minn. 517, 142 N.W. 897 (1913); Will v. Press Publishing Co., 309 Pa. 539, 164 A. 621 (1932)).

101 *See* Eldredge, *supra* note 2, § 98, at 588.

102 *Id.*

103 *See* Philadelphia Newspapers, Inc. v. Hepps, 106 S. Ct. 1558 (1986).

104 *See supra* §§ 5.06 and 5.07.

105 This assumption, unfortunately, is not always valid, and must be weighed in the strategy balance. *See* Smolla, *Let the Author Beware: The Rejuvenation of the American Law of Libel*, 132 U. Pa. L. Rev. 1 (1983).

chances of winning on the "reckless disregard" standard in public official and public figure cases, and the negligence issue in private figure cases. If the defendant does not give an inch in conceding that the substance of the reported story was true, that same subjective certitude may at trial have a spillover effect on judgments concerning the state of mind of the defendant at the time of the publication or broadcast. The theory is that the jury will reason that if the defendant believes absolutely in its story at trial, then it surely must have believed the story when it first released it.

[4] Modern Examples

In three of the most celebrated libel suits of the last several years, General William Westmoreland's suit against CBS,[106] General Ariel Sharon's suit against *Time*,[107] and Mobil Oil President William Tavoulareas' suit against *The Washington Post*,[108] the media defendants stood by their stories to the bitter end.

Irving Younger, who headed the defense team in the *Post* case, analogized the aggressive adherence to the truth claim to a criminal trial.[109] Juries, Younger claimed, are looking for compromises. In a criminal trial, the defense must aim for absolute innocence, knowing that the "compromise" position that "the defendant may have done it but the prosecutor did not prove it beyond a reasonable doubt" will still result in acquittal.[110] In a libel case, Younger reasons, the "reckless disregard" standard similarly should serve as a fallback "compromise" position.[111]

In Ariel Sharon's suit against *Time*, it is possible that this sort of psychology was at work. *Time* very aggressively stood by the substance of its story concerning Sharon. The jury decided against *Time* on the truth issue, announcing that *Time* had been negligent, but they held that *Time* had not been reckless. Similarly, CBS's no-holds-barred litigation of the truth issue in the Westmoreland case was surely part of what ultimately wore General Westmoreland down to the point of settle-

---

106 Westmoreland v. CBS, Inc., 596 F. Supp. 1170 (S.D.N.Y. 1984).

107 Sharon v. Time, Inc., 599 F. Supp. 538 (S.D.N.Y. 1984).

108 Tavoulareas v. Washington Post Co., 759 F.2d 90 (D.C. Cir. 1985), *rehearing en banc granted*, 763 F.2d 1472 (D.C. Cir. 1985).

109 Brill, *Inside the Jury Room at the Washington Post Trial*, American Lawyer, November 1982.

110 *Id.*

111 *Id.*

ment. Some of CBS's journalistic practices in putting together the documentary at issue in the Westmoreland case were, by its own admission, less than ideal. Had CBS *not* placed truth in issue the jury might well have been tempted to jump to the decision that CBS had acted with the requisite level of actual malice. CBS, however, countered with a long line of witnesses to attempt to prove the charges in its broadcast were true. This could not help but influence the jurors' thinking on the recklessness issue, for even if they were to decide that Westmoreland had not been guilty of conspiracy, they could at least see how CBS could nonrecklessly arrive at that belief. No one will ever know what a jury would have decided in the Westmoreland case, or how the post-verdict appeals process would have ended, but it seems clear in hindsight that CBS's decision to hold fast on the truth issue certainly increased the percentages in its favor.

[5] "Psychological Cost" to the Plaintiff

Emphasis on the truth issue is also a way to "increase the cost" in emotional terms for the plaintiff. Most plaintiffs probably believe that they have been lied about when they sue for defamation, but *some* plaintiffs undoubtedly sue even though they know (or should know) the allegations are true. Some plaintiffs may actually convince themselves that the truth is other than actual reality. Others may feel it desperately essential to fight for lost honor. (Oscar Wilde sued the Marquis of Queensberry because of the latter's allegations that Wilde was homosexual, despite the truth of the allegations; Wilde even lied to his own attorneys.) It is one thing to take such risks when the plaintiff anticipates that the defendant will concede falsity, and quite another when the defamatory charges will be vigorously defended. From a defense perspective, taking a hard line in standing by a story may deter some plaintiffs from blindly purusing lost (but expensive) causes.

[6] Risks

None of this is to say that hard line adherence to the truth position is not without risks for the media defendant. If the jury decides the story is false, the momentum of that decision may not always result in a "compromise"—the defendant's defeat on the truth issue may well subtly influence jurors to find against the defendant on the recklessness issue as well. Adherence to the position that the story is true in the face of evidence to the contrary may also be perceived by some juries as arrogance, thereby producing a backlash effect in the jury room.

The computation of pluses and minuses of litigation strategy, particularly in jury cases, is obviously a matter for individual judgment on the facts of each case. But it is fair to say that the changes in burden of proof brought on by *New York Times* and its progeny have increased the benefits and decreased the risks involved in vigorously asserting the truth defense.

CHAPTER 6

Opinion and Fair Comment

§ 6.01 Introduction

At both the common law and constitutional law levels, courts and commentators have long struggled over the distinction between "fact" and "opinion." Although the law of defamation has to some degree always sought to protect opinion more than misstatements of fact, more than one commentator has observed that the distinction is "more announced than defined."[1] The fact/opinion distinction has "proved to be a most unsatisfactory and unreliable one, difficult to draw in practice."[2] The distinction has been criticized as merely furnishing "vague familiar terms into which one can pour whatever meaning is desired."[3] The Alaska Supreme Court has remarked that "the distinction between a fact statement and an opinion or comment is so tenuous in most instances, that any attempt to distinguish between the two will lead to needless confusion."[4] As Judge Robert Bork has written in discussing the fact/opinion issue, the "temptation to adhere to sharply defined categories is understandable," and inevitably judges will generalize, enunciating "such things as four-factor frameworks, three-pronged tests, and two-tiered analysis in an effort, laudable by and large, to bring order to a universe of unruly happenings and to give guidance for the future," but it is certain that "life will bring up cases whose facts simply cannot be handled by purely verbal formulas, or at least not handled with any sophistication and feeling for the underlying values at stake."[5] Quoting Professor Wigmore, Judge Bork warned against analyzing the fact/opinion distinction with mechanical rigidity.[6] In the sections that follow one is tempted to get wrapped up in the arcania of the various tests different courts now use to separate opinion from fact. Indeed, today there are as many tests for identifying opinion as there are home

---

1 *See* Franklin & Bussel, *The Plaintiff's Burden in Defamation*, 25 Wm. & Mary L. Rev. 825, 870-71 (1984) (quoting Note, *Fair Comment*, 62 Harv. L. Rev. 1207, 1212 (1949).

2 W. Prosser, Handbook of the Law of Torts § 118, at 820 (4th ed. 1971).

3 Titus, *Statement of Fact Versus Statement of Opinion — A Spurious Dispute in Fair Comment*, 15 Vand. L. Rev. 1203, 1205-06 (1962).

4 Pearson v. Fairbanks Publishing Co., 413 P.2d 711, 714 (Alaska 1966). *See also* 1 F. Harper & F. James, Torts § 5.28, at 458 (1956).

5 Ollman v. Evans, 750 F.2d 970, 994 (D.C. Cir. 1984) (en banc) (Bork, J., concurring), *cert. denied*, 105 S. Ct. 2662 (1985).

6 7 J. Wigmore, Evidence § 1919, at 14-16 (J. Chadbourn rev. ed. 1978).

> In the first place no such distinction is scientifically possible. . . . As soon as we come to analyze and define these terms for the purpose of that accuracy which is necessary in legal rulings, we find that the distinction vanishes. . . . If then our notion of the supposed firm distinction between "opinion" and "fact" is that the one is certain and sure, the other is not, surely a just view of their psychological relations serves to demonstrate that in strict truth nothing is certain. Or if we prefer the suggestion of Sir G.C. Lewis that the test is whether "doubt can reasonably exist," then certainly it must be perceived that the multiple doubts which ought to exist would exclude vast masses of indubitably admissible testimony. Or if we prefer the idea that "opinion" is inference and fact is "original perception," then it may be understood that no such distinction can scientifically be made, since the processes of knowledge and the sources of illusion are the same for both.

remedies for hiccups. But it is best to keep Wigmore's observations in mind, and realize that in any given case an intelligent argument concerning the fact/opinion distinction cannot be marshalled without resort to discussion of the true purposes served by the fact/opinion distinction in defamation law: an accommodation between protection of valuable interests in reputation and the provision of sufficient breathing space for critical and sometimes caustic free expression.[7]

§ 6.02 The Original Common Law Position—Fair Comment

[1] The Evolution of Fair Comment

The majority common law position prior to *New York Times Co. v. Sullivan*[8] did not immunize all expressions of "opinion." Rather, an expression of opinion could be defamatory if it was sufficiently derogatory to cause injury to the plaintiff's reputation.[9] Though many opinions are inherently incapable of being proved or disproved,[10] the common law deemed actionable an expression of opinion that would tend to be injurious to reputation.[11] This position was adhered to even though the truth or falsity of the opinion at issue might not be objectively determinable at all, and even though the common law simultaneously maintained the position that truth was a complete defense in a civil action for defamation.[12]

In the tentative piecemeal fashion characteristic of the common law, courts gradually began to acknowledge the contradictions of the early position, and to recognize that "valuable discourse might be furthered by intuitive, evaluative statements that could not be proved either true or false by the rigorous deductive reasoning of the judicial process."[13]

---

7 *See, e.g.*, Pearson v. Fairbanks Publishing Co., 413 P.2d 711, 714 (Alaska 1966); Snively v. Record Publishing Co., 185 Cal. 565, 198 P. 1 (1921); Coleman v. MacLennan, 78 Kan. 711, 98 P. 281 (1908).

8 376 U.S. 254 (1964).

9 Restatement (Second) of Torts § 566 comment a (1977).

10 *See* Grech v. Odhams Press Ltd., 2 Q.B. 275, 281-82 (1958); Christie, *Defamatory Opinions and the Restatement (Second) of Torts*, 75 Mich. L. Rev. 1621, 1625-28 (1977); Franklin & Bussel, *supra* note 1, at 871, and 878-79 n.207.

11 Restatement (Second) of Torts §566 comment a (1976); Franklin & Bussel, *supra* note 1, at 871.

12 *See* Christie, *supra* note 10, at 1621-28.

13 Franklin & Bussel, *supra* note 1, at 871.

Concern for the need to give some shelter to these evaluative statements was vented through limited protection for opinion, primarily through the gradual recognition of a "fair comment" privilege.[14]

The original coverage of the fair comment privilege was quite modest. Opinions were protected only if based upon "true facts" that "fully and fairly justified" the opinion.[15] Over time, however, the privilege embraced opinions about matters of public concern based on true facts, whether the opinion was "reasonable" or not.[16] This common law "safety valve" for fair comment emerged for much the same reasons that ultimately came to inform modern first amendment jurisprudence.[17] As early as the 1808 English case *Tabart v. Tipper*,[18] for example, it was explained that "[l]iberty of criticism must be allowed, or we should have neither purity of taste nor of morals. Fair discussion is essentially necessary to the truth of history, and the advancement of science."[19] The majority position was that the fair comment privilege protected only expressions of opinion and not false facts expressly stated or implied from the expression of the opinion.[20] The fair comment privilege was

---

14 *See* Note, *Fair Comment, supra* note 1, at 1212-13.

15 *See generally* Restatement (Second) of Torts § 566 comment a (1977).

16 *Id.*

17 *See, e.g.*, Sweeny v. Patterson, 128 F.2d 457 (D.C. Cir.), *cert. denied*, 317 U.S. 678 (1942); Phoenix Newspapers v. Choisser, 82 Ariz. 271, 276-77, 312 P.2d 150, 154 (1957); Snively v. Record Publishing Co., 185 Cal. 565, 571-76, 198 P. 1 (1921); Parmelee v. Hearst Pub. Co., 341 Ill. App. 339, 347-48, 93 N.E.2d 512, 515 (1950); Salinger v. Cowles, 195 Iowa 873, 889, 191 N.W. 167, 174 (1922); Cherry v. Des Moines Leader, 114 Iowa 298, 86 N.W. 323 (1901); Stice v. Beacon Newspaper Corp., 185 Kan. 61, 65-67, 340 P.2d 396, 400-01 (1959); Coleman v. MacLennan, 78 Kan. 711, 98 P. 281 (1908); Lawrence v. Fox, 357 Mich. 134, 146, 97 N.W.2d 719, 725 (1959); Friedell v. Blakely Printing Co., 163 Minn. 226, 230, 203 N.W. 974, 975 (1925); Chagnon v. Union Leader Corp., 103 N.H. 426, 438, 174 A.2d 825, 833 (1961), *cert. denied*, 369 U.S. 830 (1962); Ponder v. Cobb, 257 N.C. 281, 299, 126 S.E.2d 67, 80 (1962); McLean v. Merriman, 42 S.D. 394, 175 N.W. 878 (1920); Bailey v. Charleston Mail Ass'n, 126 W. Va. 292, 307, 27 S.E.2d 837, 844 (1943). *See also* Chase, *Criticism of Public Officers and Candidates for Public Office*, 23 Am. L. Rev. 46, 367-71 (1884); Hallen, *Fair Comment* 8 Tex. L. Rev. 41, 61 (1929); Noel, *Defamation of Public Officers and Candidates*, 49 Col. L. Rev. 875, 891-95, 903 (1949); Smith, *Charges Against Candidates*, 18 Mich. L. Rev. 1, 115 (1919).

18 170 Eng. Rep. 981 (1808).

19 *Id.* at 982

20 *See* Kirkland v. Constitution Pub. Co., 38 Ga. App. 632, 144 S.E. 821 (1928); Smith v. Pure Oil Co., 278 Ky. 430, 128 S.W.2d 931 (1939); Bander v. Metropolitan Life Ins. Co., 313 Mass. 337, 47 N.E.2d 595 (1943); Starks v. Comer, 190 Ala. 245, 67 So. 440 (1914); Eikhoff v. Gilbert, 124 Mich. 353, 360, 83 N.W. 110, 113 (1900); Van Arsdale v. Time, Inc., 35 N.Y.S.2d 951 (Sup. Ct. 1942), *aff'd mem.*, 265 App. Div. 919, 39 N.Y.S.2d 413 (1st Dept. 1942); Restatement of Torts § 606 (1938); Noel, *supra* note 17, at 877.

lost if the statement was published with "malice," in the common law sense of spite or ill will,[21] or if the opinion was not "sincerely" held.[22]

[2] Persons and Institutions Subject to the Privilege

The "fair comment" privilege ultimately came to encompass comment concerning "persons, institutions or groups who voluntarily injected themselves into the public scene or affected the community's welfare, such as public officials, political candidates, community leaders from the private sector or private enterprises which affected public welfare, persons taking a public position on a matter of public concern, and those who offered their creations for public approval, such as artists, performers, and athletes."[23] In short, the fair comment privilege came to embrace a range of plaintiffs at least as broad as,[24] and arguably, broader than, the modern constitutional protections defined in *Gertz v. Robert Welch, Inc.*[25] Institutions and individuals subject to the fair comment privilege thus included politicians,[26] entertainers,[27] owners of art galleries,[28] art experts,[29] athletes,[30] high school principals,[31] authors,[32] the doctors of professional athletes,[33] restaurants,[34] and others

---

[21] Restatement of Torts § 606 (1) (c) (1934). *See also* Beauharnais v. Pittsburg Courier Publishing Co., 243 F.2d 705, 708 (7th Cir. 1957); Potts v. Dies, 132 F.2d 734 (D.C. Cir. 1942), *cert. denied,* 319 U.S. 762 (1943); Herman v. Labor Co-op Educational & Pub. Soc'y, 139 F. Supp. 35, 38 (D.D.C. 1956); Fisher v. Washington Post Co., 212 A.2d 335, 337 (D.C. Ct. App. 1965); Wehringer v. Newman, 60 A.D.2d 385, 400 N.Y.S.2d 553 (1st Dept. 1978).

[22] *See* Hallen, *supra* note 17, at 41; Noel, *supra* note 17, at 878.

[23] Mashburn v. Collin, 355 So. 2d 879, 882 (La. 1977).

[24] *See* Carman, Hutchinson v. Proxmire *and the Neglected Fair Comment Defense: An Alternative to "Actual Malice,"* 30 De Paul L. Rev. 1, 32 (1980).

[25] 418 U.S. 323 (1974). *See supra* § 2.02.

[26] *See* Post Publishing Co. v Hallam, 59 F. 530, 539-42 (6th Cir. 1893); Coleman v. MacLennan, 78 Kan. 711, 723, 98 P. 281, 285 (1908); Hall v. Binghamton Press Co., 263 A.D. 403, 412, 33 N.Y.S.2d 840, 849 (1942), *aff'd,* 296 N.Y. 715, 70 N.E.2d 538 (1946).

[27] Julian v. American Business Consultants, Inc., 2 N.Y.2d 1, 155 N.Y.S. 2d 1, 137 N.E.2d 1 (1956); Cherry v. Des Moines Leader, 114 Iowa 298, 86 N.W. 323 (1901).

[28] Fisher v. Washington Post Co., 212 A.2d 335, 337 (D.C. Ct. App. 1965).

[29] Porcella v. Time, Inc., 300 F.2d 162 (7th Cir. 1962).

[30] Cepeda v. Cowles Magazine & Broadcasting, Inc., 328 F.2d 869 (9th Cir.), *cert. denied,* 379 U.S. 844 (1964).

[31] Kapiloff v. Dunn, 27 Md. App. 514, 343 A.2d 251 (1975), *cert. denied,* 426 U.S. 907 (1976).

[32] Guitar v. Westinghouse Electric Corp., 396 F. Supp. 1042, 1048 (S.D.N.Y. 1975), *aff'd without opinion,* 538 F.2d 309 (2d Cir. 1976); Buckley v. Vidal, 327 F. Supp. 1051 (S.D.N.Y. 1971); Berg v. Printer's Ink Publishing Co., 54 F. Supp. 795, 791 (S.D.N.Y. 1943), *aff'd on opinion below,* 141 F.2d 1022 (2d Cir. 1944); Pearson v. Fairbanks Publishing Co., 413 P.2d 711 (Alaska 1966); Triggs v. Sun Printing and Publishing Ass'n, 179 N.Y. 144, 71 N.E. 739 (1904).

who mount the rostrum[35] and invite public judgment for any purpose.[36]

[3] The Comment Must Be "Fair"

"One who enters the public arena must expect latitude in the give-and-take of public debate, extending to sharp and coarse comment, and to excessive and perhaps unwarranted characterization."[37] The traditional majority position was that the fair comment privilege existed only if based on facts "truly stated,"[38] and even then, the comment had to be "fair."[39] Defendants thus resorted to (and still do resort to) the so-called rolled-up plea: that all statements of fact contained in the publication are true, and all other statements contained therein are "fair" comment on those facts.[40] Courts thus inquired into whether a "reasonable man may honestly entertain such an opinion."[41] Other courts emphasized full factual disclosure, holding that the comment must be "fair

---

33 Shenkman v. O'Malley, 2 A.D.2d 567, 157 N.Y.S.2d 290 (1956).

34 Twenty-five East 40th St. Restaurant Corp. v. Forbes, Inc., 37 A.D.2d 546, 322 N.Y.S.2d 408 (1st Dept. 1971), *aff'd,* 30 N.Y.2d 595, 331 N.Y.S.2d 29, 282 N.E.2d 118 (1972). *Cf.* Mashburn v. Collin, 355 So. 2d 879 (La. 1977) (reaching same result regarding restaurant criticism under first amendment principles, as Louisiana had not theretofore acknowledged the fair comment doctrine).

35 Brewer v. Hearst Publishing Co., 185 F.2d 846, 850 (7th Cir. 1950); Kellems v. California CIO Council, 68 F. Supp. 277, 278 (N.D. Cal. 1946); Edmonds v. Delta Democrat Publishing Co., 230 Miss. 583, 93 So. 2d 171 (1957).

36 Afro-American Publishing Co. v. Jaffe, 366 F.2d 649, 656-57 (D.C. Cir. 1966) (en banc); Porcella v. Time, Inc., 300 F.2d 162 (7th Cir. 1962); Potts v. Dies, 132 F.2d 734 (D.C. Cir. 1942), *cert. denied,* 319 U.S. 762 (1943); Guitar v. Westinghouse Electric Corp., 396 F. Supp. 1042 (S.D.N.Y. 1975), *aff'd,* 538 F.2d 309 (2d Cir. 1976); Julian v. American Business Consultants, Inc., 2 N.Y.2d 1, 155 N.Y.S.2d 1, 137 N.E.2d 1 (1956); Cohalan v. New York Tribune, Inc., 172 Misc. 20, 15 N.Y.S.2d 58 (Sup. Ct. 1939); Carman, *supra* note 24, at 32.

37 Afro-American Publishing Co. v. Jaffe, 366 F.2d 649, 657 (D.C. Cir. 1966).

38 *See, e.g.,* Washington Times Co. v. Bonner, 86 F.2d 836 (D.C. App. Ct. 1936); Guitar v. Westinghouse Electric Corp., 396 F. Supp. 1042, 1051 (S.D.N.Y. 1975), *aff'd,* 538 F.2d 309 (2d Cir. 1976); Parsons v. Age-Herald Publishing Co., 181 Ala. 439, 450, 61 So. 345, 350 (1913); Briarcliff Lodge Hotel v. Citizen-Sentinel Publishers, Inc., 260 N.Y. 106, 183 N.E. 193 (1932); Foley v. Press Publishing Co., 226 App. Div. 535, 235 N.Y.S. 340 (1st Dept. 1929).

39 *See* Guitar v. Westinghouse Electric Corp., 396 F. Supp. 1042, 1050-51 (S.D.N.Y. 1975), *aff'd,* 538 F.2d 309 (2d Cir. 1976); Julian v. American Business Consultants, Inc., 2 N.Y.2d 1, 7-9, 155 N.Y.S.2d 1, 5, 137 N.E.2d 1, 5 (1956); Noel, *supra* note 17, at 880.

40 *See* Noel, *supra* note 17, at 880; Note, *Libel Actions Brought by Public Officials,* 51 Yale L.J. 693, 697 (1942).

41 Grower v. State, 23 A.D.2d 506, 255 N.Y.S.2d 135 (3d Dept. 1965), *aff'd,* 19 N.Y.2d 625, 278 N.Y.S.2d 408, 224 N.E.2d 899 (1967). *See also* Restatement of Torts §607 comment i (1934); Noel, *supra* note 17, at 882.

in the sense that the reader can understand the factual basis for the opinions containing the criticism."[42] The "fairness" or "reasonableness" of the comment was usually left to the relatively unguided judgment of the jury.[43] Since this practice permitted juries to pass judgment on the "worth" of the speaker's opinion, it carried the potential for being quite inimical to free expression.[44]

A minority position did exist, however, that protected the comment even if based upon false factual statements, and in some holdings, even if the facts are not stated at all.[45] This more expansive definition of the fair comment privilege tended to be reserved for commentary on political candidates and public officials.[46]

[4] Continued Vitality of the Privilege

[a] Has the First Amendment Swallowed Fair Comment?

The Supreme Court has constitutionalized much of the common law's "fair comment" and "opinion" defenses,[47] and there is substantial support for the position that the common law doctrines are obsolete, having been taken over by broader and stronger first amendment defenses.[48] Virtually all significant discussion of the fact/opinion dichoto-

---

42 Edmonds v. Delta Democrat Publishing Co., 230 Miss. 583, 93 So. 2d 171, 173 (1957). *See also* Restatement of Torts § 607 comment i (1934); Noel, *supra* note 17, at 882.

43 *See* Julian v. American Business Consultants, Inc., 2 N.Y.2d 1, 8-9, 155 N.Y.S.2d 1, 6-7, 137 N.E.2d 1, 8-9 (1956); Van Arsdale v. Times, Inc., 35 N.Y.S.2d 951 (Sup. Ct.), *aff'd*, 265 App. Div. 919, 39 N.Y.S.2d 413 (1st Dept. 1942); Triggs v. Sun Printing & Publishing Ass'n, 179 N.Y. 144, 154, 71 N.E. 739, 742 (1904). *But see* Hay v. Reid, 85 Mich. 296, 307, 48 N.W. 507, 510 (1891).

44 *See* Hill, *Defamation and Privacy Under the First Amendment*, 76 Colum. 1. Rev. 1205, 1233 (1974) ('Such an approach threatens the free expression of opinion.").

45 *See* Coleman v. MacLennan, 78 Kan. 711, 98 P. 281 (1908); Hallen, *supra* note 17, at 61; Noel, *supra* note 17, at 891; Smith, *supra* note 17, at 115.

46 *See* Noel, *supra* note 17, at 401-03 (citing Sweeney v. Caller-Times Publishing Co., 41 F. Supp. 163 (S.D. Tex. 1941); Hills v. Press Co., 122 Misc. 212, 215, 202 N.Y.S. 678, 682 (Sup. Ct. 1924), *aff'd*, 214 App. Div. 752, 209 N.Y. S. 848 (3d Dept. 1925); Tanzer v. Crowley Publishing Corp., 240 App. Div. 203, 268 N.Y. Supp. 620, 622 (4th Dept. 1934); Cotulla v. Kerr, 74 Tex. 89, 94, 11 S.W. 1058, 1059 (1889).

47 *See infra* § 6.03.

48 *See, e.g.*, Hoffman v. Washington Post Co., 433 F. Supp. 600, 603 (D.D.C. 1977), *aff'd without opinion*, 578 F.2d 442 (D.C. Cir. 1978); Kotlikoff v. The Community News, 444 A.2d 1086, 89 N.J. 62 (1982); Mashburn v. Collin, 355 So. 2d 879, 891 (La. 1977) ("Because an expression of opinion without knowing or reckless falsity about a matter of public concern by the press is fully protected under the First Amendment aegis, we did not consider to what extent our state constitution, jurisprudence and statutes also protect expressions of such opinions."); Restatement (Second) of Torts §§ 566, 606-10 (1977); Franklin & Bussel, *supra* note 1, at 875.

my in recent years has been conducted under the rubric of the first amendment, rather than the common law.[49] Some courts have suggested that the need for a common law fair comment privilege has totally been obviated by first amendment doctrine.[50] The *Second Restatement of Torts* has unceremoniously dropped fair comment from the common law roster, on the logic that under the first amendment a statement of opinion which does not imply a defamatory statement of fact is no longer actionable, and no privilege is needed.[51]

[b] The Doctrine Remains Useful in Some Situations

Reports of the demise of the fair comment privilege may, like the premature reports of the death of Mark Twain, be greatly exaggerated.[52] The doctrine retains its utility for two reasons. First, although the Supreme Court has brought "opinion" and "fair comment" beneath the umbrella of the first amendment,[53] courts have been struggling on a case-by-case basis to give definition to those terms. A variety of constitutional tests have proliferated to define "opinion" and segregate it from "fact."[54] Some judges may prefer not to venture into uncharted first amendment territory, and simply rest their judgment in a particular case on more modest common law doctrine. It remains a canon of constitutional litigation that constitutional law issues normally should not be reached if they can be avoided by deciding a case on statutory or "independent and adequate" state grounds.[55] If a decision to protect

---

[49] *See also infra* §§6.03-6.05.

[50] *See* Ollman v. Evans, 750 F.2d 970, 975 n.8 (D.C. Cir. 1984) (en banc), *cert. denied,* 105 S. Ct. 2662 (1985) ("Although [the] claim arises under the District of Columbia common law of libel, . . . the issue whether the allegedly libelous statements are protected opinion is to be decided as a matter of federal constitutional law.") (citing Lewis v. Time, Inc., 710 F.2d 549, 552-53 (9th Cir. 1983)). *See also* Yerkie v. Post-Newsweek Stations, Michigan, Inc., 470 F. Supp. 91, 94 (D. Md. 1979); Hoffman v. Washington Post Co., 433 F. Supp. 600, 603 (D.C. Cir. 1977), *aff'd without opinion,* 578 F.2d 442 (D.C. Cir. 1978); Bucher v. Roberts, 595 P.2d 239 (Colo. 1979); Naked City, Inc. v. Chicago Sun-Times, 77 Ill. App. 3d 188, 395 N.E.2d 1042 (1979); Mashburn v. Collin, 355 So. 2d 879, 891 (La. 1977).

[51] Restatement (Second) of Torts § 566 comment c (1977).

[52] *See* R. Sack, Libel, Slander, and Related Problems 180-83 (1980); Carman, *supra* note 24; Franklin & Bussel, *supra* note 1, at 875 n.192.

[53] *See infra* § 6.03.

[54] *See infra* §§ 6.04-6.12.

[55] *See generally* Ashwander v. TVA, 297 U.S. 288, 346-48 (1936) (Brandeis, J., concurring) (the Court will not "anticipate a question of constitutional law in advance of the necessity of deciding it," nor "pass upon a constitutional question, although properly

a particular statement can be decided under a state's fair comment privilege, therefore, some courts may prefer that method.

Second, some courts may feel bolder in experimenting with more expansive protection for opinion on a common law basis than as a matter of constitutional law.[56] The various tests that have emerged to define "opinion" vary significantly in the level of protection that they give to speech.[57] Some jurisdictions may wish to provide more protection for speech than the rock bottom requirements of the first amendment demand.[58] One of the principal methods for accomplishing that purpose is to give opinions broader common law "breathing space" than is strictly necessary under the first amendment through more expansive interpretations of the common law fair comment doctrine.[59]

§ 6.03 The Supreme Court and the Fact/Opinion Dichotomy

[1] Early Statements

The Supreme Court's earliest expositions on the fact/opinion issue came in relatively oblique references in *New York Times Co. v. Sulli-*

---

presented by the record, if there is also present some other ground upon which the case may be disposed of"). *But see* Gunther, *The Subtle Vices of the 'Passive Virtues'—A Comment on Principle and Expediency in Judicial Review,"* 64 Colum. L. Rev. 1 (1964). It should be noted that the Supreme Court largely ignored the *Ashwander* limitations in *Gertz,* in which it went out of its way to establish a matrix of rules that were not strictly necessary to the disposition of the case, including *dicta* on the fact/opinion distinction. *See* Justice Rehnquist's remarks in a dissent from a denial of certiorari in Miskovsky v. Oklahoma Publishing Co., 654 P.2d 587 (Okla.), *cert. denied,* 459 U.S. 923 (1982) (Rehnquist, J., dissenting).

56 *See* Smolla, *The Rejuvenation of the American Law of Libel,* 132 U. Pa. L. Rev. 1, 77-78 and n.372 (1983).

57 *Compare* Ollman v. Evans, 750 F.2d 970 (D.C. Cir. 1984) (en banc), *cert. denied,* 105 S. Ct. 2662 (1985) (applying four factor test), *with* Shiver v. Apalachee Publishing Co., 425 So. 2d 1173 (Fla. Dist. Ct. App. 1983) (distinction "a judgment call") *and* Hotchner v. Castillo-Puche, 551 F.2d 910, 913 (2d Cir.), *cert. denied sub nom.* Hotchner v. Doubleday & Co., 434 U.S. 834 (1977) (emphasizing "verifiability") *and* Information Control Corp. v. Genesis One Computer Corp., 611 F.2d 781 (9th Cir. 1980); Cole v. Westinghouse Broadcasting Co., 386 Mass. 303, 435 N.E.2d 1021, 1025, *cert. denied,* 459 U.S. 1037 (1982); Burns v. McGraw-Hill Broadcasting Co., 659 P.2d 1351, 1360 (Colo. 1983) (applying three factor test).

58 *See* Smolla, *supra* note 56, at 68-78.

59 *See* Franklin & Bussel, *supra* note 1, at 875 n.192 (citing Desert Sun Publishing Co. v. Superior Court for Riverside County, 97 Cal. App. 3d 49, 158 Cal. Rptr. 519 (1979); Marchiondo v. New Mexico State Tribune Co., 98 N.M. 282, 648 P.2d 321 (Ct. App. 1981)).

van[60] and *Garrison v. Louisiana.*[61] In *New York Times,* the Court essentially placed the fair comment privilege on a constitutional footing, stating that "[s]ince the Fourteenth Amendment requires recognition of the conditional privilege for honest misstatements of fact, it follows that a defense of fair comment must be afforded for honest expression of opinion based upon privileged, as well as true, statements of fact."[62] In *Garrison,* a prosecution for criminal libel, the Court again alluded to the fair comment privilege, though finding it unnecessary to decide in the context of the case whether the statement involved "was factual or merely comment, or whether a State may provide any remedy, civil or criminal, if defamatory comment alone, however vituperative, is directed at public officials."[63]

[2] *Greenbelt v. Bresler*

Greenbelt Cooperative Publishing Association v. Bresler[64] was a case that did not expressly refer to the fact/opinion issue. Nonetheless it has repeatedly been treated by later cases (including later Supreme Court decisions) and by commentators as a fact/opinion case.[65] The plaintiff Bresler, a real estate developer and builder, engaged in negotiations with the City Council of Greenbelt, Maryland, for zoning variances so that he could build high density housing on land he owned. Simultaneously, the city was trying to acquire another tract of land from Bresler to construct a high school. The concurrent negotiations gave each side bargaining leverage. (Bresler, for example, could adjust the price for the tract depending on the city's attitude toward the variances.) A newspaper accurately reported the public debate at city council meetings where Bresler's negotiating demands were denounced as "blackmail." Bresler sued for libel, alleging that the articles imputed a crime to him. The Supreme Court held that the "accusation" was a constitutionally protected statement, since in context the word "blackmail" was no more than hyperbole, a vigorous epithet used by those who consid-

---

[60] 376 U.S. 254 (1964).

[61] 379 U.S. 64 (1964).

[62] 376 U.S. at 292 n.30.

[63] 379 U.S. at 76 n.10.

[64] 398 U.S. 6 (1970).

[65] *See* Old Dominion Branch No. 496, National Association of Letter Carriers v. Austin, 418 U.S. 264, 283-86 (1974); Ollman v. Evans, 750 F.2d 970, 1017 (D.C. Cir. 1984) (en banc) (Robinson, J., dissenting in part), *cert. denied,* 105 S. Ct. 2662 (1985).

ered Bresler's negotiating position extremely unreasonable."[66] The context in which the words appeared was such that no reader could have thought that Bresler was being charged with a crime. The *Bresler* decision is understandable either as a constitutionalization of limits on the extent to which rhetorical hyperbole may be construed as defamatory or, alternatively, as a holding expressing constitutional limitations surrounding the fact/opinion dichotomy. It is frequently relied upon for both purposes.[67]

[3] The *Gertz* Pronouncement

The Supreme Court's most important statements on the fact/opinion distinction came in *Gertz v. Robert Welch, Inc.*,[68] where the Court in *dicta* seemed to provide absolute first amendment immunity from defamation actions for all opinions. The Court began its analysis of the case by stating:

> We begin with the common ground. Under the First Amendment there is no such thing as a false idea. However pernicious an opinion may seem, we depend for its correction not on the conscience of judges and juries but on the competition of other ideas. But there is no constitutional value in false statements of fact. Neither the intentional lie nor the careless error materially advances society's interest in "uninhibited, robust, and wide-open" debate on public issues . . . They belong to that category of utterances which "are no essential part of any exposition of ideas, and are of such slight value as a step to truth that any benefit that may be derived from them is clearly outweighed by the social interest in order and morality."[69]

By this statement, *Gertz* apparently elevated to constitutional status the distinction between fact and opinion, which at common law had

---

66 398 U.S. at 14.

67 *See also supra* §4.04[2].

68 418 U.S. 323 (1974).

69 *Id.* at 339-40 (quoting New York Times v. Sullivan, 376 U.S. 254, 270 (1964), and citing Chaplinsky v. State of New Hampshire, 315 U.S. 568, 572 (1942)). It is theoretically arguable that this statement from *Gertz* no longer applies in private figure plaintiff cases not involving issues of public concern, following Dun & Bradstreet, Inc. v. Greenmoss Builders, Inc., 105 S. Ct. 2939 (1985), for the reasons articulated in § 5.04, *supra*. The better view is that the *Gertz* pronouncements on the issues of opinion and truth announce first amendment principles that apply to all defamation cases, without regard to the status of the plaintiff or the speech as "public" or "private." This statement from *Gertz* stands on its own footing, independent of fault rules.

formed the basis of the fair comment privilege.[70] *Gertz's* command thus imposed upon both state and federal courts the duty, as a matter of constitutional obligation, to distinguish facts from opinions in order to provide opinions with the requisite absolute first amendment protection.[71] As a number of lower courts have noted, however, the Supreme Court provided little guidance in *Gertz* itself as to the manner in which the distinction between fact and opinion is to be discerned.

In truth, *Gertz* did not focus on the fact/opinion distinction at all. Rather, assuming without lengthy discussion that the statements in that case could be construed as statements of fact, the Court ruled that the plaintiff, who was held to be a private rather than a public figure, need prove only that the statements at issue were negligently made.[72] In the 1984 case of *Bose Corporation v. Consumers Union of the United States, Inc.*,[73] the Supreme Court referred to the *Gertz* dicta with approval. But two members of the Court—Justices White and Rehnquist—have noted that "the problem of defamatory opinion was not remotely an issue in *Gertz* and there is no evidence that the Court was speaking with an awareness of the rich and complex history of the struggle of the common law to deal with this problem."[74]

---

70 Ollman v. Evans, 750 F.2d 970, 975 (D.C. Cir. 1984) (en banc), *cert. denied,* 105 S. Ct. 2662 (1985).

71 Although the quoted statement from *Gertz* was unabashed dicta, it has been accepted by subsequent decisions as controlling law. *See, e.g.*, Bose Corp. v. Consumers Union of the United States, Inc., 104 S. Ct. 1949, 1961 (1984) (quoting the *Gertz* dicta with approval); Ollman v. Evans, 750 F.2d 970, 974-75 n.6 (D.C. Cir. 1984) (en banc), *cert. denied,* 105 S. Ct. 2662 (1985); McBride v. Merrell Dow and Pharmaceuticals Inc., 717 F.2d 1460, 1464 & n.7 (D.C. Cir. 1983); Lewis v. Time, Inc., 710 F.2d 549, 552-53 (9th Cir. 1983); Hammerhead Enterprises, Inc., v. Brezenoff, 707 F.2d 33, 40 (2d Cir.), *cert. denied,* 104 S. Ct. 237 (1983); Rinsley v. Brandt, 700 F.2d 1304, 1307 (10th Cir. 1983); Bose Corp v. Consumers Union, Inc., 692 F.2d 189, 192-94 (1st Cir. 1982), *aff'd on other grounds,* 104 S. Ct. 1949 (1984); Orr v. Argus-Press Co., 586 F.2d 1108, 1114 (6th Cir. 1978), *cert. denied,* 440 U.S. 960 (1979); Church of Scientology v. Cazares, 638 F.2d 1272, 1286 (5th Cir. 1981); Avins v. White, 627 F.2d 637, 642 (3d Cir.), *cert. denied,* 449 U.S. 982 (1980).

72 *See* Ollman v. Evans, 750 F.2d 970, 975 (D.C. Cir. 1984) (en banc), *cert. denied,* 105 S. Ct. 2662 (1985).

73 Bose Corp. v. Consumers Union, Inc., 104 S. Ct. 1949, 1961 (1984).

74 The view of Justices White and Rehnquist was expressed in an unusual opinion by Justice Rehnquist, who was dissenting from the Court's denial of certiorari. *See* Miskovsky v. Oklahoma Publishing Co., 654 P.2d 587 (Okla.), *cert. denied,* 459 U.S. 923 (1982) (Rehnquist, J., dissenting).

[4] The *Letter Carriers* Holding

Old Dominion Branch No. 496, National Association of Letter Carriers v. Austin[75] was argued and handed down on the same day as *Gertz.* In the case, a union newsletter had published under the heading "List of Scabs" the names of the plaintiffs and other employees who had not joined the union. Just above the list was printed a particularly derogatory definition of the term "scab" attributed to Jack London.[76]

Letter Carriers was, technically, based not on the first amendment but on the protection that the federal labor laws extend to communications made in the course of a labor dispute.[77] Nevertheless, the Court's interpretation of the labor laws relied heavily on first amendment defamation cases, including *Gertz.*[78] It has generally been understood that *Letter Carriers* serves as a further explication of *Gertz.*[79]

The Court in *Letter Carriers* quoted the reasoning of *Bresler* about the meaning imparted by context, and then stated:

> It is similarly impossible to believe that any reader of the *Carrier's Corner* would have understood the newsletter to be charging the appellees with committing the criminal offense of treason. As in *Bresler*, Jack London's "definition of a scab" is merely rhetorical hyperbole, a lusty and

---

75 418 U.S. 264 (1974).

76 *Id.* at 268.

After God had finished the rattlesnake, the toad, and the vampire, He had some awful substance left with which He made a *scab.*

A scab is a two-legged animal with a corkscrew soul, a water brain, a combination backbone of jelly and glue. Where others have hearts, he carries a tumor of rotten principles.

When a scab comes down the street, men turn their backs and Angels weep in Heaven, and the Devil shuts the gates of hell to keep him out.

No man (or woman) has a right to scab so long as there is a pool of water to drown his carcass in, or a rope long enough to hang his body with. Judas was a gentleman compared with a scab. For betraying his Master, he had character enough to hang himself. A scab has not.

Esau sold his birthright for a mess of pottage. Judas sold his Savior for thirty pieces of silver. Benedict Arnold sold his country for a promise of a commission in the British Army. The scab sells his birthright, country, his wife, his children and his fellowmen for an unfulfilled promise from his employer.

Esau was a traitor to himself; Judas was a traitor to his God; Benedict Arnold was a traitor to his country; a SCAB is a traitor to his God, his country, his family and his class.

77 *Id.* at 283 n.15.

78 *See id.* at 282-86.

79 *See* Ollman v. Evans, 750 F.2d 970, 999 n.4 (D.C. Cir. 1984) (en banc) (Bork, J., concurring), *cert. denied,* 105 S. Ct. 2662 (1985).

imaginative expression of the contempt felt by union members towards those who refuse to join.[80]

[5] A Synthesis of *Bresler, Gertz,* and *Letter Carriers*

Although it may be true in a sense that the Supreme Court managed to constitutionalize the fact/opinion distinction without much exploration of "the rich and complex history of the struggle of the common law to deal with this problem,"[81] it is also true that a comparison of *Bresler, Gertz,* and *Letter Carriers* reveals that the Supreme Court, judging by what it *does* instead of what it says, has not been mechanistic, but rather has been sensitive to the richness and complexity of the problem. The fact that the epithets "Leninist" and "Communist-fronter" were deemed actionable, while the epithets "blackmail," "scab," and "traitor" were not, demonstrates that when it comes to first amendment analysis, the Supreme Court does not employ a simplistic fact/opinion distinction.[82] The Court has been sensitive to the context in which the words are spoken, looking to surrounding circumstances to determine how the language involved is to be construed. The Court, at this point, has basically set the outer "ground rules" —opinion is absolutely protected, but misstatements of fact are not—and left it to case-by-case development (in essence, a continuation of the "rich and complex" common law process) to work out more sensitive and refined definitions.

[6] The *Hustler v. Falwell* Decision

The Supreme Court's latest foray into the fact/opinion distinction came in its decision in *Hustler Magazine v. Falwell.*[82.1] Whatever doubts may have existed about the constitutional status of the opinion defense were erased by the opinion of Chief Justice Rehnquist in that case.

Chief Justice Rehnquist began his analysis with an essay on the purposes of the first amendment. "At the heart of the First Amendment," he wrote, "is the recognition of the fundamental importance of the free

---

[80] 418 U.S. at 285-86.

[81] Miskovsky v. Oklahoma Publishing Co., 654 P.2d 587 (Okla.), *cert. denied,* 459 U.S. 923 (1982) (Rehnquist, J., dissenting). Justice Rehnquist's observation was based on a quote from the work of Professor Hill. *See* Hill, *supra* note 44, at 1239.

[82] Ollman v. Evans, 750 F.2d 970, 1000 (D.C. Cir. 1984) (en banc) (Bork, J., concurring), *cert. denied,* 471 U.S. 1127, 105 S. Ct. 2662 (1985).

[82.1] 108 S. Ct. 876 (1988).

flow of ideas and opinions on matters of public interest and concern."[82.2] He then recognized the two principal functions of free speech, the self-fulfillment of the individual speaker, and the broader social search for enlightenment. Quoting from the Court's 1984 decision, *Bose v. Consumers Union*,[82.3] he noted that " 'the freedom to speak one's mind is not only an aspect of individual liberty—and thus a good unto itself—but also is essential to the common quest for truth and the vitality of society as a whole.' "[82.4] The Court has been particularly vigilant, he observed, to ensure that ideas remain free from governmentally imposed sanctions, because the "First Amendment recognizes no such thing as a 'false' idea."[82.5] Chief Justice Rehnquist capped off his introductory remarks by invoking one of the most sacred passages in the first amendment tradition, the haunting appeal for tolerance by Justice Oliver Wendell Holmes in his dissent in *Abrams v. United States:*

> "When men have realized that time has upset many fighting faiths, they may come to believe even more than they believe the very foundations of their own conduct that the ultimate good desired is better reached by a free trade in ideas—that the best test of truth is the power of the thought to get itself accepted in the competition of the market."[82.6]

If the marketplace of ideas was to be robust and wide-open, what did that bode for public figures? The next section of Chief Justice Rehnquist's analysis went to great lengths to establish that in America the prevailing ethos is not to encourage people to enter the public arena by guaranteeing them shelter from caustic and virulent attack; it is rather to require as a cost of entering the public arena a certain toughening of the hide. Good but sensitive people may be discouraged in America from stepping forward into public life, but that is part of the price of an open society and a spirited democracy. In this nation, a public figure must be able to take as well as give.

Public figures, observed Chief Justice Rehnquist, have a substantial capacity to shape events. Quoting Felix Frankfurter, he noted that one " 'of the prerogatives of American citizenship is the right to criticize

82.2 *Id.* at 879.

82.3 Bose Corp. v. Consumers Union of United States, Inc., 466 U.S. 485 (1984).

82.4 108 S. Ct. at 879, quoting Bose v. Consumers Union, 466 U.S. at 503-04.

82.5 108 S. Ct. at 879, citing Gertz v. Robert Welch, Inc., 418 U.S. 323, 339 (1974).

82.6 Abrams v. United States, 250 U.S. 616, 630 (1919) (Holmes, J., dissenting).

public men and measures.' "[82.7] And in this country, such criticism will not always be reasoned and moderate. Quoting from *Monitor Patriot Co. v. Roy,*[82.8] Chief Justice Rehnquist made a point that seemed aimed personally at Jerry Falwell: " 'The candidate who vaunts his spotless record and sterling integrity cannot convincingly cry 'Foul!' when an opponent or an industrious reporter attempts to demonstrate the contrary.' "[82.9] This quote was a diplomatic way of stating to the Reverend Falwell that moralists must expect attacks on their morality.

This does not mean, cautioned Chief Justice Rehnquist, "that *any* speech about a public figure is immune from sanction in the form of damages."[82.10] Speech that is libelous in the conventional sense—speech that contains genuine misstatements of fact and that injures reputation—may be penalized in some circumstances. But even here, Chief Justice Rehnquist admonished, the Constitution requires that the rules of libel be fashioned to provide sufficient breathing space for free speech. In what was, to most observers, a remarkable paragraph, Chief Justice Rehnquist proceeded to wholeheartedly endorse *New York Times Co. v. Sullivan* and its progeny. For public figures and public officials, it was critical that they prove that the offending statement was *both* false and made with actual malice.[82.11] If the Chief Justice had any doubts about the wisdom of the *New York Times*[82.12] ruling, they were not apparent here; in both letter and spirit, he was reaffirming *New York Times* with relish. The decision in *Hustler* was, by any measure, a landmark reaffirmation of the first amendment's absolute protection for opinion.

[82.7] 108 S. Ct. at 879-80, quoting Baumgartner v. United States, 322 U.S. 665, 673-74 (1944).

[82.8] 401 U.S. 265 (1971).

[82.9] 108 S. Ct. at 880, quoting Monitor Patriot v. Roy, 401 U.S. at 274.

[82.10] 108 S. Ct. at 880 (emphasis in original).

[82.11] *Id.*

[82.12] Chief Justice Rehnquist's record on libel and invasion of privacy cases involving the press prior to the *Hustler* decision had been largely antagonistic to press interests and the basic values articulated in the *New York Times Co. v. Sullivan* line of precedent. *See* R. Smolla, Jerry Falwell v. Larry Flynt: The First Amendment on Trial, 252-54 (1988). In that respect, Chief Justice Rehnquist's ringing endorsement of *New York Times* in his *Hustler* opinion may mark a significant sea change on the Court, in which the *Times* decision will now be accepted as absolutely settled law.

§ 6.04 "Pure Opinion" vs. "Mixed Opinion": The *Restatement (Second)* Approach

The *Restatement (Second) of Torts* uses as the sole test for determining the actionability of a statement cast in the form of an opinion the question of whether the opinion implies the existence of undisclosed defamatory facts.[83] In Section 566 of the *Restatement* the rule is expressed: "A defamatory communication may consist of a statement in the form of an opinion, but a statement of this nature is actionable only if it implies the allegation of undisclosed defamatory facts as the basis for the opinion."[84] The *Restatement* recognizes two types of opinion: "pure" and "mixed."

[1] Pure Opinion

With "pure" opinion, as that term is used in the *Restatement,* either the maker of the comment states the facts on which the opinion is based, or the recipient of the communication is already aware of the facts upon which the opinion is based.[85] A pure opinion does not lose its protected status merely because it is ostensibly cast in factual form, if it is clear from the context that the maker does not intend to assert *another* objective fact, but only his personal view on the objective facts *already* stated.[86]

Contrary to what the terminology of the *Restatement* might suggest, the "pure" opinion always includes facts as part of the total "communication package;" the facts are either stated by the speaker or already known to the recipient. The point, however, is that the opinion and the factual predicate are to be treated separately. The underlying facts, if stated by the speaker, may be true or false, and their actionability is

---

[83] Restatement (Second) of Torts § 566 (1977). *See also* Lewis v. Time, Inc., 710 F.2d 549, 555-56 (9th Cir. 1983) (applying *Restatement* § 566).

[84] Restatement (Second) of Torts § 566 (1977).

[85] *Id.*, comment b. *See* Lewis v. Time, Inc., 710 F.2d 549, 555 (9th Cir. 1983); Orr v. Argus-Press Co., 586 F.2d 1108, 1114-15 (1978), *cert. denied,* 440 U.S. 960 (1979); Okun v. Superior Court of Los Angeles County, 29 Cal. 3d 442, 175 Cal. Rptr. 157, 162, 629 P.2d 1369, 1374, *cert. denied,* 454 U.S. 1099 (1981); Burns v. Denver Post, Inc., 43 Colo. App. 325, 606 P.2d 1310, 1311 (Colo. App. 1979); National Ass'n of Government Employees, Inc. v. Central Broadcasting Corp., 379 Mass. 220, 396 N.E.2d 996, 1001-02 (1979), *cert. denied,* 446 U.S. 935 (1980); Anton v. St. Louis Suburban Newspapers, Inc., 598 S.W.2d 493, 498-99 (Mo. App. 1980); Pease v. Telegraph Publishing Co., 121 N.H. 62, 426 A.2d 463, 465 (1981); Rinaldi v. Holt, Rinehart & Winston, Inc., 42 N.Y.2d 369, 380, 397 N.Y.S.2d 943, 950, 366 N.E.2d 1299, 1306, *cert. denied,* 434 U.S. 969 (1977).

[86] Restatement (Second) of Torts § 566 comment b (1977).

judged by looking at them simply as statements of fact, in the usual manner.[87] The "comment" that the speaker draws from those facts, however, is "pure opinion," and is never actionable.[88] If the factual predicate for the opinion is true, the opinion, no matter how unfair,

(*Text continued on page 6-17*)

---

[87] *Id.*

[88] *See, e.g.,* Avins v. White, 627 F.2d 637, 642-43 (3d Cir.), *cert. denied,* 449 U.S. 982 (1980); Pritsker v. Brudnoy, 389 Mass. 776, 452 N.E.2d 227, 229 (1983); Bruno v. New York News, Inc., 89 A.D.2d 260, 264 (3d Dept. 1982); Holy Spirit Ass'n for Unification of World Christianity v. Sequoia Elsevier Publishing Co., 75 A.D.2d 523, 426 N.Y.S.2d 759, 760 (1st Dept. 1980); Braig v. Field Communications, 456 A.2d 1366, 1372 (Pa. Super. 1983).

unreasonable, or outrageous, is itself immune from actionability.[89] Thus in *Pritsker v. Brudnoy*,[90] the court, applying the *Restatement's*[91] "pure" opinion formulation, stated that such opinion by itself is not actionable "no matter how unjustified and unreasonable the opinion may be or how derogatory it is."[92]

[2] Mixed Opinion

"Mixed" opinions, somewhat contrary to the name, do not disclose the facts upon which they are based, but rather imply the existence of undisclosed defamatory facts that justify the opinion expressed.[93] The mixed type of opinion may be actionable if the trier of fact finds that undisclosed defamatory facts would be inferred by the recipient. For the mixed type of opinion to exist, the speaker cannot disclose the factual predicate for his statement, nor can the recipient already be aware of the factual predicate upon which the speaker relies.[94] Rather, the touchstone of the mixed opinion is that, in addition to expressly stating an opinion, the speaker is simultaneously implying the existence of defamatory facts.[95]

[3] Examples

The first two of five illustrative examples used by the *Restatement* to explain the distinction between "pure" and "mixed" opinions repeat the facts of the Supreme Court's decisions in the *Bresler*[96] and *Letter*

---

[89] *See* Restatement (Second) of Torts § 566 comment c (1977).

[90] 389 Mass. 776, 452 N.E.2d 227 (1983).

[91] Restatement (Second) of Torts § 566, comment c (1977).

[92] Pritsker v. Brudnoy, 389 Mass. 776, 452 N.E.2d 227, 228 (1983). *See also* Holy Spirit Ass'n for Unification of World Christianity v. Sequoia Elsevier Publishing Co., 75 A.D.2d 523, 426 N.Y.S.2d 759, 760 (1st Dept. 1980) ("Such opinions, even if bizarre, and even if they have no sound basis in the facts which the writer characterizes by these opinions, are still constitutionally protected.").

[93] Restatement (Second) of Torts § 566 comment b (1977).

[94] *Id.*

[95] *See, e.g.*, Lewis v. Time, Inc., 710 F.2d 549, 555 (9th Cir. 1983); Hotchner v. Castillo-Puche, 551 F.2d 910, 913 (2d Cir.), *cert. denied*, 434 U.S. 834 (1977); Pritsker v. Brudnoy, 389 Mass. 776, 452 N.E.2d 227, 229-30 (1983); Rinaldi v. Holt, Rinehart & Winston, Inc., 42 N.Y.2d 369, 380-82, 397 N.Y.S.2d 943, 949-51, 366 N.E.2d 1299, 1205-06, *cert. denied*, 434 U.S. 969 (1977); Nevada Independent Broadcasting Corp. v. Allen, 664 P.2d 337, 342 (Nev. 1983).

[96] Greenbelt Cooperative Publishing Ass'n v. Bresler, 398 U.S. 6 (1970).

Carriers[97] decisions. In *Bresler,* the newspaper stated the facts underlying the conclusion that the plaintiff was a "blackmailer;"[98] in *Letter Carriers,* the facts underlying the depiction of the characteristics of a "scab" were already known as part of the general background of the labor dispute involved.[99] The next three examples used by the *Restatement* more sharply illustrate the disclosure principle. If *A* writes to *B* of his neighbor *C,* "I think he must be an alcoholic," the statement might be construed as implying the existence of undisclosed defamatory facts about *C,* and would therefore be of the mixed type, and potentially actionable.[100] On the other hand, it would not be actionable if the letter stated that "He moved in six months ago. He works downtown and I have seen him during that time only twice—in his backyard around 5:30 seated in a deck chair with a portable radio listening to a news broadcast with a drink in his hand. I think he must be an alcoholic."[101] In this case, the writer, having disclosed the underlying facts, is treated as engaging in "pure opinion" in reaching the conclusion that *B* is an alcoholic. The final example, one of pure opinion, is that *A* says to *B* about *C,* a city official: "He and his wife took a trip on city business a month ago and he added her expenses in as part of his own." *B* responds: "If he did that, he is really a thief."[102] Since *A* already knows the factual predicate for *B's* judgment, it is pure opinion.

§ 6.05 Elaborations on the *Restatement*

A three part classification scheme for opinions is put forward in the latest edition of the Prosser and Keeton hornbook on Torts.[103] This classification scheme can be used in conjunction with the *Restatment* approach to give it greater depth. Under the Prosser and Keeton tripartite scheme, opinions can be of three types: "deductive opinions only," "evaluative opinions only," and opinions (either deductive or evaluative) that are "informational."

---

97 Old Dominion Branch No. 496, National Association of Letter Carriers v. Austin, 418 U.S. 264 (1974).

98 *See supra* § 6.03[2].

99 *See supra* § 6.03[4].

100 Restatement (Second) of Torts §566, illustration 3 (1977).

101 *Id.,* illustration 4.

102 *Id.,* illustration 5.

103 W. Prosser, W. Keeton, D. Dobbs, R. Keeton, and D. Owen, *The Law of Torts* § 113A, at 813-14 (5th ed. 1984).

[1] Deductive Opinions

An opinion is deductive if it implies or deduces misconduct or a disparaging fact about the plaintiff on the basis of true information supplied to the public or already generally known to the public.[104] An example is a statement by Holmes to Watson, "Given facts A, B, and C, it must have been John who committed the murder." The "deduction" is the publisher's judgment that a particular fact exists, given the existence of other known or disclosed true facts. The early common law position would often permit the "deductive only" opinion to be actionable if the deduction proved to be erroneous, but under the *Restatement (Second)* approach, all "deductive only" opinions would be nonactionable, since the underlying facts from which such opinions are drawn are, by definition, disclosed.[105]

[2] Evaluative Opinions

The "evaluative only" opinion is an opinion involving a value judgment on the basis of true information disclosed to or known by the public.[106] Some evaluative opinions simply convey the publisher's tastes, such as "it was the worst movie I've ever seen" or "this wine is not worth its price." Other evaluative statements go beyond taste, to matters of political, moral, or social value judgments. An example would be the statement, "Given what John Dean told Richard Nixon, Nixon was corrupt and dishonest." Unlike the deductive opinion, the evaluative opinion conveys the publisher's judgment as to the value of another's behavior or work product, rather than the publisher's judgment as to the existence of facts. Such characteristics as "goodness" or "badness" are, in short, concepts rather than facts.[107]

The common law position was generally more protective of evaluative opinions than deductive opinions. The evaluative opinion was treated as actionable, however, if the evaluator did not in reality enter-

---

[104] *Id.*

[105] *Id.*, § 113A, at 814. Restatement (Second) of Torts § 566 (1977).

[106] Prosser & Keeton, *supra* note 103, § 113A, at 814. *See* Ollman v. Evans, 750 F.2d 970, 1021 (D.C. Cir. 1984) (en banc) (Robinson, J., dissenting in part), *cert. denied*, 105 S. Ct. 2662 (1985) ("Matters of personal taste, aesthetics, literary criticism, religious beliefs, moral convictions, political views and social theories would fall within this category.") (citing Avins v. White, 627 F.2d 637, 640 (3d Cir.), *cert. denied*, 449 U.S. 982 (1980). *See also* Keeton, *Defamation and Freedom of the Press*, 54 Tex. L. Rev. 1221, 1250-51 (1976).

[107] Prosser & Keeton, *supra* note 103, § 113A, at 814.

tain the opinion, or if a reasonable and fair-minded person could not have entertained the derogatory opinion on the basis of the disclosed true information upon which it was based.[108]

Under the *Restatement (Second)* virtually all "evaluative only" opinions would be nonactionable, since they are by definition based on disclosed facts.[109] Certainly neither the *Restatement* nor the first amendment would permit an evaluative statement based on true disclosed facts to be actionable merely because it is not "reasonable" or "fair-minded."[110] The statement that "Jane Doe did not deserve the Oscar for her movie role because it was a shallow, two-bit, hack performance" is not actionable even in the face of ironclad proof that every other living being who has ever seen the movie loved the performance.

[3] Dishonestly Maintained Evaluative Opinions

[a] In General

It is not completely clear that the dishonestly maintained evaluative opinion should be nonactionable under either the *Restatement* or the first amendment. Suppose a movie critic sets out to pan a film, telling her readers not to see it, when in fact the critic loved the movie. Like Antonio Salieri, who (as portrayed in the movie *Amadeus*) set out to sabotage the career of Mozart by demeaning Mozart's compositions, though in fact Salieri thought they were works of genius, a modern critic might, out of jealousy, envy, or spite, choose to pan a film. Should such a "dishonest evaluative opinion" be actionable? The Prosser and Keeton hornbook appears to reach the conclusion that it should not be, on the theory that the inquiries necessary to prove the dishonesty would be impractical and too injurious to free speech.[111] This conclusion, however, may confuse problems of proof with problems of actionability.[112]

---

108 *See* Restatement (Second) of Torts § 566 comment a. *See supra* § 6.02.

109 Prosser & Keeton, *supra* note 103, § 113A, at 814 (5th ed. 1984).

110 *See, e.g.*, Avins v. White, 627 F.2d 637, 642-43 (3d Cir. 1980), *cert. denied*, 449 U.S. 982 (1980); Pritsker v. Brudnoy, 389 Mass. 776, 452 N.E.2d 227, 229 (1983); Bruno v. New York News, Inc., 89 A.D.2d 260, 264 (3d Dept. 1982); Holy Spirit Ass'n for Unification of World Christianity v. Sequoia Elsevier Publishing Co., Inc., 75 A.D.2d 523, 426 N.Y.S.2d 759, 760 (1st Dept. 1980); Braig v. Field Communications, 456 A.2d 1366, 1372 (Pa. Super. 1983).

111 Prosser & Keeton, *supra* note 103, § 113A, at 814.

112 This is the common law position. To be protected as opinion the criticism must represent the critic's actual opinion. *See* Fisher v. Washington Post Co., 212 A.2d 335, 337

[b] The Proof Problem

If the critic says, "I really believed in the opinion I pronounced," perhaps that should end the inquiry. To permit a trier of fact to inquire into the bona fides of that alleged belief is to invite a jury to make credibility choices that may be influenced by the "fair-mindedness" of the belief. To give all evaluative opinions sufficient breathing space, a prophylactic rule making them all immune from actionability might arguably be warranted.[113]

[c] A Compromise Position

It might be feasible, however, to fashion a compromise position: In the absence of direct documentary or eyewitness testimony that the speaker did not believe in his own professed evaluative opinion, it should be nonactionable. In the rare case of hard evidence that the opinion was misrepresented—a memorandum by the critic, or a telltale statement to the contrary in the presence of witnesses—the suit should be permissible. This would preserve the common law position that the opinion must be sincerely held,[114] while still giving the publisher sufficient breathing space.

[4] Informational Opinions

An "informational opinion" may be either deductive or evaluative.[115] The touchstone of the informational opinion is that the publisher can reasonably be regarded as using the superficial form of an opinion to convey information other than those facts explicitly disclosed or already known to the recipient of the statement.[116] The Prosser and Keeton definition of the informational opinion tracks the *Restatement*

(D.C. Ct. App. 1965) (citing Brewer v. Hearst Pub. Co., 185 F.2d 846 (7th Cir. 1950)); Halen, *supra* note 17, at 41; Noel, *supra* note 17, at 878. *See also* Prosser & Keeton, *supra* note 103, § 113A, at 114 ("it can be said that the state of a person's mind is a fact and if a publisher misrepresents his state of mind, he misrepresents a fact even though it is only an opinion").

[113] *Id. See also* Rinaldi v. Holt, Rinehart & Winston, Inc., 42 N.Y.2d 369, 381, 397 N.Y.S.2d 943, 366 N.E.2d 1299, *cert. denied,* 434 U.S. 969 (1977); Franklin & Bussel, *supra* note 1, at 868-69 n.165; Keeton, *supra* note 106, at 1257.

[114] *See* Sierra Breeze v. Superior Court of El Dorado County, 86 Cal. App. 3d 102, 149 Cal. Rptr. 914 (3d Dist. 1978); Coleman v. Newark Morning Ledger Co., 29 N.J. 357, 149 A.2d 193 (1959); Fisher v. Washington Post Co., 212 A.2d 335 (D.C. App. Ct. 1965).

[115] Prosser & Keeton, *supra* note 103, § 113A, at 814.

[116] *Id.*

(Second) approach to actionable opinion by characterizing it as an opinion that creates an inference that undisclosed facts exist that justify the opinion expressed; if those undisclosed facts "do not justify the conclusion drawn, the statement made is to be regarded as a misstatement of the undisclosed facts."[117]

§ 6.06 Judicial Variations on the *Restatement*

A number of courts have expressed the fact/opinion dichotomy in language which resembles the *Restatement (Second)* approach, but which employs somewhat different terminology and methodology, analyzing the problem in terms of "pure" vs. "hybrid" opinions. The "hybrid" opinion is not exactly the same as the *Restatement's* "mixed" opinion, rather, it refers to the more general character and context of the statement as "laden with factual content."[118] Judge Robinson of the District of Columbia Court of Appeals recently offered an expansive explication of this approach.[119]

[1] Elaborations on "Pure Opinion"

"Pure opinions," Judge Robinson argued, are commonly understood as incapable of being adjudged true or false, and include matters of personal taste, aesthetics, literary criticism, religious beliefs, moral convictions, political views, and social theories.[120] Also at the end of Judge Robinson's pure opinion spectrum would be " 'loosely definable, variously interpretable' " derogatory remarks of the sort frequently flung about in colloquial argument.[121] Finally, he would include as pure opinion metaphorical language used figuratively or imaginatively without any intention to rely on its literal meaning, such as the statement in

---

117 *Id.*

118 Cianci v. New Times Publishing Co., 639 F.2d 54, 63 (2d Cir. 1980).

119 750 F.2d 970, 1016 (D.C. Cir. 1984) (en banc) (Robinson, J., dissenting in part), *cert. denied*, 105 S. Ct. 2662 (1985).

120 *Id. See also* Avins v. White, 627 F.2d 637, 640 (3d Cir.), *cert. denied*, 449 U.S. 982 (1980); Loeb v. Globe Newspaper Co., 489 F. Supp. 481, 486 & n.6 (D. Mass. 1980).

121 Ollman v. Evans, 750 F.2d 970, 1021 (D.C. Cir. 1984) (en banc) (Robinson, J., dissenting in part), *cert. denied*, 105 S. Ct. 2662 (1985). *See also* Hotchner v. Castillo-Puche, 551 F.2d 910, 912 (2d Cir.), *cert. denied sub nom.* Hotchner v. Doubleday & Co., 434 U.S. 834 (1977); Buckley v. Littell, 539 F.2d 882, 893-95 (2d Cir. 1976), *cert. denied*, 429 U.S. 1062 (1977).

Loeb v. Globe Newspaper Co.[122] that the plaintiff "runs a paper by paranoids for paranoids."[123]

[2] "Hybrid" or "Factually Laden" Opinions

In Judge Robinson's view, however, "pure opinion" constitutes only a small portion of the "opinions" that become the subject of defamation litigation.[124] More common are opinions "laden with factual content,"[125] opinions that he, and a number of other courts and commentators, have begun to describe as "hybrid" opinions.[126] "Hybrid opinions" vary in their proportional mixture of opinion and fact. The statement that "John Doe is an incompetent worker" suggests a low degree of factual content and a relatively high degree of subjective judgment. The statement that "John Doe is a murderer" has a much richer mix of fact than subjective opinion. From a coldly logical analysis, however, neither statement is obviously pure fact or opinion, for both represent an amalgamation and interpretation of underlying data.[127]

All pure opinions are nonactionable, but hybrid opinions can be either actionable or nonactionable. The question of whether a hybrid opinion should be actionable turns on the extent to which it is "laden" with false defamatory factual content.

[3] Examples

Judge Robinson poses his own series of hypotheticals to demonstrate how the determination in "hybrid" cases should be made. Imagine that an author makes the following statement:

> One evening, Smith went to White's house. She had with her a small gun which she customarily carried in her purse for protection. She and White began a discussion which escalated into a heated argument. White became enraged, grabbed a butcher knife and lunged across the room toward Smith with the weapon raised. Smith drew out her gun, aimed it

---

122 489 F. Supp. 481 (D. Mass. 1980).

123 *Id.* at 486.

124 Ollman v. Evans, 750 F.2d 970, 1022 (D.C. Cir. 1984) (en banc) (Robinson, J., dissenting in part), *cert. denied,* 105 S. Ct. 2662 (1985).

125 Cianci v. New Times Publishing Co., 639 F.2d 54, 63 (2d Cir. 1980).

126 Ollman v. Evans, 750 F.2d 970, 1021-25 (D.C. Cir. 1984) (en banc) (Robinson, J., dissenting in part), *cert. denied,* 105 S. Ct. 2662 (1985).

127 *Id.* at 1023-25, and nn.67, 70, 71.

at White's heart, and pulled the trigger. White died from the wound. Smith is a murderer.[128]

A court faced with this sort of statement can apply an analysis basically parallel to that urged by the *Restatement (Second)*. Judge Robinson, for example, would argue that for most readers, the hybrid statement "Smith is a murderer" would be an irrational and thus nondamaging conclusion, for "presumably their view of Smith would not be adversely affected by what commonly would be regarded as an unwarranted application of the charge by the author. The readers possess the relevant background data. Having supplied an accurate account of those facts, "the author cannot be said to have misled or deceived the reader about the matter discussed, even if the author's ultimate conclusion—the hybrid statement—may in some sense be erroneous." Although the author's derogatory judgment may carry some power to damage reputation simply by virtue of his stature in the reader's estimation, it is safe to assume that whatever damage is inflicted will turn primarily on the reader's personal appraisal of how reasonable that judgment is in light of the facts set forth.

If, however, the bold statement is made that "Smith is a murderer," with no further factual elaboration, most reasonable readers will assume that such a drastic charge would not be made without factual support. Readers would not reasonably expect that the author holds a bizarre definition of "murder" which would discount the justifiability of homicide in self-defense. This statement, containing a higher "fact content," would be actionable.[129]

Finally, assume that an author tells the story of Smith's encounter with White, giving all the factual details save one: that White lunged at Smith with a knife. Now the hybrid statement would be the most factually laden, and in Judge Robinson's scheme the most actionable, since the statement "Smith is a murderer" (or even, "In my opinion, Smith is a murderer") would apparently be accompanied by a complete set of facts—the omission of just one critical fact is actually more deceptive than the omission of all the facts.[130] "Partial truths are not necessarily even mitigating in this branch of the law, for the defamer may be the

---

[128] *Id.* at 1023 n.67.

[129] *See* DeSavitsch v. Patterson, 81 U.S. App. D.C. 358, 360, 159 F.2d 15, 17 (1946).

[130] *Cf.* Restatement (Second) of Torts § 529 comment a (1977) ("A statement containing a half truth may be as misleading as a statement wholly false. Thus, a statement that contains only favorable matters and omits all reference to unfavorable matters is as much a false representation as if all the facts stated were untrue.").

more successful when he baits the hook with truth."[131]

[4] Loss of the Absolute Privilege for Hybrid Opinions

Under the "hybrid opinion" analysis, a hybrid statement is absolutely privileged as opinion only if accompanied by "a reasonably full and accurate narration of the facts" pertinent to the formulation of the opinion, unless those facts are already known to the recipient of the communication.[132]

§ 6.07 The Verifiability Factor

[1] In General

One approach to the fact/opinion problem is to avoid the dichotomy altogether, and instead concentrate solely on whether the statement is verifiable.[133] Courts sometimes simply define opinions as statements that cannot be proved or disproved;[134] other courts list a variety of factors but appear to employ verifiability as the controlling element.[135]

An emphasis on verifiability arguably dissolves a confusion that has long existed in the *Restatement of Torts* approach to the fact/opinion distinction.[136] As Professor George Christie has explained,[137] the *Restatement (First)* defined the cause of action for defamation in terms of communications both "false and defamatory." Yet the *Restatement* permitted liability for the expressions of certain opinions despite the fact that their truth or falsity was undeterminable.[138] Marc Franklin and Daniel Bussel argue that the current tendency of courts to engage in

---

131 Afro-American Publishing Co. v. Jaffe, 125 U.S. App. D.C. 70, 76, 366 F.2d 649, 655 (1966) (en banc).

132 *See* Ollman v. Evans, 750 F.2d 970, 1024 (D.C. Cir. 1984) (en banc) (Robinson, J., dissenting in part), *cert. denied,* 105 S. Ct. 2662 (1985).

133 *See* Franklin & Bussel, *supra* note 1, at 871-87.

134 *See* Hotchner v. Castillo-Puche, 551 F.2d 910, 913 (2d Cir.), *cert. denied sub nom.* Hotchner v. Doubleday & Co., 434 U.S. 834 (1977); Goodrich v. Waterbury Republican-American, Inc., 448 A.2d 1317, 1319 (Conn. 1982); Buckley v. Littell, 539 F.2d 882 (2d Cir. 1976), *cert. denied,* 429 U.S. 1062 (1977); Cole v. Westinghouse Broadcasting Co., 386 Mass. 303, 435 N.E.2d 1021, *cert. denied,* 459 U.S. 1037 (1982); McHale v. Lake Charles American Press, 390 So. 2d 556 (La. Ct. App. 1980), *cert. denied,* 452 U.S. 941 (1981).

135 *See* Marchiondo v. Brown, 98 N.M. 394, 649 P.2d 462 (1982); Franklin & Bussel, *supra* note 1, at 879.

136 Franklin & Bussel, *supra* note 1, at 879.

137 *See* Christie, *supra* note 10, at 1621-28.

138 *Id.* at 1625-28.

confusing analysis over the definition of "opinion" should be supplanted by a simpler focus on "disprovability."[139] Reliance on "disprovability" will not eliminate hard judgment calls, but it arguably will focus attention on the degree to which the statement is susceptible of disproof.[140]

[2] Relationship to the Burden of Proof on Falsity Issue

There is an important linkage between the verifiability factor and the burden of proof on truth or falsity. Statements will cover a broad range of relative provability or disprovability.[141] If the verifiability of a statement is somewhere in the middle of the continuum, should it be actionable or nonactionable? The answer to the question is obviously connected to the issue of who has the burden of proof on the issue of truth or falsity. Since plaintiffs in cases involving issues of public concern clearly have the burden of proof[142]—an issue resolved in *Philadelphia Newspapers, Inc. v. Hepps*[143]—then defendants ought to prevail when the verifiability of the statement is doubtful, since a plaintiff unable to demonstrate that the truth or falsity of a statement is provable by definition cannot meet the burden of establishing falsity.[144] In those jurisdictions that require falsity to be established by clear and convincing evidence[145] the range of protection for nondisprovable statements is, correspondingly, even greater.

§ 6.08 The Totality of Circumstances Approach

[1] In General

Concerned that the *Restatement (Second)* approach may be overly mechanistic, a number of courts have begun to emphasize a more flexible "totality of circumstances" approach to the fact/opinion prob-

139 Franklin & Bussel, *supra* note 1, at 879-80.

140 *See* Schauer, *Language, Truth, and the First Amendment: An Essay in Memory of Harry Canter*, 64 Va. L. Rev. 263, 276-81 (1978) ("Verifiability is not a property that either does or does not obtain. Rather, it is a property that may be present in varying degrees.").

141 *Id.*

142 *See supra* § 5.05-5.06.

143 106 S. Ct. 1558 (1986).

144 *See generally* Franklin & Bussel, *supra* note 1, at 885-87.

145 *See supra* § 5.05.

lem.[146] In *Cole v. Westinghouse Broadcasting Company,*[147] for example, the court stated that the statement at issue should be examined "in its totality in the context in which it was uttered or published."[148] Under the totality of circumstances methodology, "the court must consider all the words used, not merely a particular phrase or sentence."[149] The court is to consider cautionary terms that accompany the statement[150] and all other circumstances that surround the statement, including the medium used and the audience.[151] Where the defamatory statements are part of a heated public debate, or a labor dispute, or some other setting in which the audience naturally anticipates attempts "to persuade . . . by use of epithets, fiery rhetoric, or hyperbole,"[152] language which generally might be considered as statements of fact might well assume the character of statements of opinion.[153] Other factors listed by courts as part of the totality of the circumstances include the verifiability of the statement[154] and the extent to which the plaintiff has voluntarily injected himself into the public controversy out of which the opinion arose.[155]

[2] The *Information Control* Three Part Version

In an influential decision, *Information Control Corp. v. Genesis One*

---

146 *See, e.g.,* Ollman v. Evans, 750 F.2d 970, 977-80 (D.C. Cir. 1984)(en banc), *cert. denied,* 105 S. Ct. 2662 (1985); Information Control Corp. v. Genesis One Computer Corp., 611 F.2d 781, 784 (9th Cir. 1980); Cole v. Westinghouse Broadcasting Co., 386 Mass. 303, 435 N.E.2d 1021, 1025, *cert. denied,* 459 U.S. 1037 (1982).

147 386 Mass. 303, 435 N.E.2d 1021, 1025, *cert. denied,* 459 U.S. 1037 (1982).

148 *Id.*

149 *Id.*

150 *See* Ollman v. Evans, 750 F.2d 970, 982-83 (D.C. Cir. 1984)(en banc), *cert. denied,* 105 S. Ct. 2662 (1985); Information Control Corp. v. Genesis One Computer Corp., 611 F.2d 781, 784 (9th Cir. 1980); Cole v. Westinghouse Broadcasting Co., 386 Mass. 303, 435 N.E.2d 1021, 1025, *cert. denied,* 459 U.S. 1037 (1982).

151 Information Control Corp. v. Genesis One Computer Corp., 611 F.2d 781, 784 (9th Cir. 1980); Cole v. Westinghouse Broadcasting Co., 386 Mass. 303, 453 N.E.2d 1021, 1025, *cert. denied,* 459 U.S. 1037 (1982).

152 Gregory v. McDonnell Douglas Corp., 17 Cal. 3d 596, 131 Cal. Rptr. 641, 644, 552 P.2d 425, 428 (1976).

153 Information Control Corp. v. Genesis One Computer Corp., 611 F.2d 781, 784 (9th Cir. 1980).

154 Ollman v. Evans, 750 F.2d 970, 981 (D.C. Cir. 1984)(en banc), *cert. denied,* 105 S. Ct. 2662 (1985).

155 *Id.* at 1002-05 (Bork, J., concurring).

Computer Corp.,[156] the Ninth Circuit Court of Appeals announced a three part test designed as a more specific elaboration on the totality of circumstances test. At least three states appear to have adopted the *Information Control* approach.[157] The *Information Control* court held that, in determining whether a statement was opinion or fact, three factors should be analyzed. First, the "words are not defamatory unless they are understood in a defamatory sense. . . . Thus, the words alone are not determinative; the facts surrounding the publication must also be considered."[158] Second, "even apparent statements of fact may assume the character of statements of opinion and thus be privileged when made in public debate, heated labor disputes, or other circumstances in which an 'audience may anticipate efforts by the parties to persuade others to their positions by use of epithets, fiery rhetoric or hyperbole.' "[159] Third, the court noted the importance of the language itself: "Where the language of the statements is 'cautiously phrased in terms of apparency' or is of a kind typically generated in a spirited legal dispute in which judgment, loyalties and subjective motives of the parties are reciprocally attacked and defended in the media and other public forums, the statement is less likely to be understood as a statement of opinion rather than as a statement of fact."[160]

[3] *Ollman v. Evans:* A Case Study

[a] Significance of the Decision

The most exhaustive exploration of the fact/opinion problem in recent years was undertaken in a series of opinions written by various judges in the District of Columbia Court of Appeals' *en banc* decision in *Ollman v. Evans.*[161] In light of the considerable depth and breadth of the various opinions in *Ollman*, the case promises to be one of the most influential ones in the defamation area in the years ahead. The

---

156 611 F.2d 781 (9th Cir. 1980).

157 *See* Burns v. McGraw-Hill Broadcasting Co., 659 P.2d 1351, 1360 (Colo. 1983); From v. Tallahassee Democrat, Inc., 400 So. 2d 52, 57 (Fla. Dist. Ct. App. 1981), *petition denied*, 412 So. 2d 465 (Fla. 1982); Cole v. Westinghouse Broadcasting Co., 386 Mass. 303, 435 N.E.2d 1021, 1025, *cert. denied*, 459 U.S. 1037 (1982).

158 Information Control Corp. v. Genesis One Computer Corp., 611 F.2d 781, 783-784 (9th Cir. 1980).

159 *Id.* at 784 (quoting Gregory v. McDonnell Douglas Corp., 17 Cal. 3d 596, 131 Cal. Rptr. 641, 644, 552 P.2d 425, 428 (1976)).

160 611 F.2d at 784.

161 750 F.2d 970 (D.C. Cir. 1984)(en banc), *cert. denied*, 105 S. Ct. 2662 (1985).

majority opinion in *Ollman*, written by Judge Starr, announced a four factor test for analyzing the fact/opinion issue.

[b] Factual Background

The plaintiff in *Ollman* was Bertell Ollman, a political science professor at New York University, who had been nominated by a departmental search committee to head the Department of Government and Politics at the University of Maryland. Professor Ollman was an expert on and a proponent of Marxism. His nomination generated substantial controversy, and was the subject of a column by the conservative, nationally syndicated columnists Rowland Evans and Robert Novak.[162]

---

[162] *Id.* at 992-93 (Appendix). The column began by stating:

> What is in danger of becoming frivolous public debate over the appointment of a Marxist to head the University of Maryland's department of politics and government has so far ignored this unspoken concern within the academic community: the avowed desire of many political activists to use higher education for indoctrination.

The column went on to state that:

> [t]he proposal to name Bertell Ollman, professor at New York University, as department head has generated wrong-headed debate. Politicians who jumped in to oppose Ollman simply for his Marxist philosophy have received a justifiable going-over from defenders of academic freedom in the press and the university. Academic Prince Valiants seem arrayed against McCarthyite know-nothings.

The authors then posed what they deemed the pivotal issue:

> But neither side approaches the central question: not Ollman's beliefs, but his intentions. His candid writings avow his desire to use the classroom as an instrument for preparing what he calls "the revolution." Whether this is a form of indoctrination that could transform the real function of a university and transcend limits of academic freedom is a concern to academicians who are neither McCarthyite nor know-nothing.

Evans and Novak stated that "[w]hile Ollman is described in news accounts as a 'respected Marxist scholar,' he is widely viewed in his profession as a political activist. Amid the increasingly popular Marxist movement in university life, he is distinct from philosophical Marxists. Rather, he is an outspoken proponent of 'political Marxism.' "

The authors then related Ollman's two unsuccessful efforts to win election to membership on the council of the American Political Science Association. In these elections, the column stated, Professor Ollman ran as a candidate of the Caucus for a New Political Science and each time finished last out of 16 candidates. The column went on to observe, "Whether or not that represents a professional judgment by his colleagues, as some critics contend, the verdict clearly rejected his campaign pledge: 'If elected . . . I shall use every means at my disposal to promote the study of Marxism and Marxist approaches to politics throughout the profession.' "

Evans and Novak then discussed an article by Ollman, entitled "On Teaching Marxism and Building the Movement," in the Winter 1978 issue of *New Political Science*. In the article, Ollman claimed that most students conclude his political science course with a "Marxist outlook.' " Evans and Novak observed:

[c] The Test Set Forth in *Ollman*

The court held, by a 6-5 vote, in a decision that included seven separate opinions,[163] that all of the allegedly defamatory statements made by Evans and Novak were absolutely privileged as opinion. Judge Starr's opinion for the court,[164] and the concurring opinions of Judges Bork[165] and MacKinnon,[166] all emphasized flexible "totality of circumstances" approaches.[167] Judge Starr's opinion argued that to evaluate the totality of the circumstances, four factors should be assessed.[168]

[i] The Common Usage or Meaning of the Language

The first factor of the *Ollman* test is to analyze the common usage or meaning of the allegedly defamatory words themselves.[169] The object is to determine whether the allegedly defamatory statement has a precise meaning and thus is likely to give rise to clear factual implications. "A classic example of a statement with a well-defined meaning is

---

Ollman concedes that will be seen "as an admission that the purpose of my course is to convert students to socialism."

> That bothers him not at all because "a correct understanding of Marxism (as indeed of any body of scientific truths) leads automatically to its acceptance." . . . The "classroom" is a place where the students' "bourgeois ideology is being dismantled." "Our prior task" before the revolution, he writes, "is to make more revolutionaries."

Moving to a brief discussion of Ollman's principal work, *Alienation: Marx's Conception of Man in Capitalist Society*, the authors described the work as "a ponderous tome in adoration of the master (Marxism 'is like a magnificently rich tapestry'). Published in 1971, it does not abandon hope for the revolution forecast by Karl Marx in 1848." The columnists then made the statement most vigorously contested in the litigation:

> Such pamphleteering is hooted at by one political scientist in a major eastern university, whose scholarship and reputation as a liberal are well known. "Ollman has no status within the profession, but is a pure and simple activist," he said. Would he say that publicly? "No chance of it. Our academic culture does not permit the raising of such questions."

163 Opinions were written by Judges Starr, Bork, MacKinnon, Robinson, Wald, Edwards, and Scalia.

164 750 F.2d at 971.

165 *Id.* at 993 (Bork, J.).

166 *Id.* at 1010 (MacKinnon, J.).

167 *See id.* at 996, 1012-13.

168 *Id.* at 997.

169 *Id.* at 980. The court emphasized that in employing this factor it was not invoking the unusual Illinois "innocent construction rule." *Id.*, n.18. *See* Chapski v. Copley Press, Inc., 92 Ill. 2d 344, 442 N.E.2d 195 (1982); John v. Tribune Co., 24 Ill. 2d 437, 181 N.E.2d 105, 108, *cert. denied*, 371 U.S. 877 (1962); Malone and Smolla, *The Future of Defamation in Illinois After* Colson v. Steig *and* Chapski v. Copley Press, Inc., 32 De Paul L. Rev. 219, 274-97 (1983). *See also supra* § 4.06[2].

an accusation of a crime. To be sure, such accusations are not records of sense perceptions. Quite to the contrary, they depend for their meaning upon social normative systems. But those norms are so commonly understood that the statements are seen by the reasonable reader or hearer as implying highly damaging facts."[170] On the other hand, the court observed, statements that are "loosely definable" or "variously interpretable" cannot in most contexts support an action for defamation.[171] Statements that a political writer is a "fascist,"[172] or that a judge is "incompetent," are examples of words too vague and imprecise to support a defamation claim.[173] Similarly, the accusation that a reporter had engaged in "sloppy and irresponsible reporting,"[174] or that a law school was deficient because of an "intangible . . . ennui that pervades the institution," with faculty and students missing "intellectual spark," is too amorphous a statement to be actionable.[175]

[ii] Verifiability

The second factor used in *Ollman* (and in a number of other "tests" advanced by other courts)[176] is the degree to which the statement is objectively capable of proof or disproof. "The reason for this inquiry is simple: a reader cannot rationally view an unverifiable statement as conveying actual facts."[177]

[iii] Context and Cautionary Language

The *Ollman* court's third factor is the context in which the statement

---

[170] Ollman v. Evans, 750 F.2d 970, 980 (D.C. Cir. 1984)(en banc), *cert. denied,* 105 S. Ct. 2662 (1985).

[171] *Id.*

[172] Buckley v. Littell, 539 F.2d 882, 895 (2d Cir. 1976), *cert. denied,* 429 U.S. 1062 (1977).

[173] Rinaldi v. Holt, Rinehart & Winston, Inc., 42 N.Y.2d 369, 397 N.Y.S.2d 943, 947, 366 N.E.2d 1299, 1303, *cert. denied,* 434 U.S. 969 (1977).

[174] Cole v. Westinghouse Broadcasting Co., 386 Mass. 303, 435 N.E.2d 1021, 1025, *cert. denied,* 459 U.S. 1037 (1982).

[175] Avins v. White, 627 F.2d 637, 642 (3d Cir.), *cert. denied,* 449 U.S. 982 (1980).

[176] *See* Hotchner v. Castillo-Puche, 551 F.2d 910, 913 (2d Cir.), *cert. denied sub nom.* Hotchner v. Doubleday & Co., 434 U.S. 834 (1977); Goodrich v. Waterbury Republican-American, Inc., 188 Conn. 107, 448 A.2d 1317, 1319 (Conn. 1982); Buckley v. Littell, 539 F.2d 882 (2d Cir. 1976), *cert. denied,* 429 U.S. 1062 (1977); Cole v. Westinghouse Broadcasting Co., 386 Mass. 303, 435 N.E.2d 1021, *cert. denied,* 459 U.S. 1037 (1982); McHale v. Lake Charles American Press, 390 So. 2d 556 (La. Ct. App. 1980), *cert. denied,* 452 U.S. 941 (1981).

[177] Ollman v. Evans, 750 F.2d 970, 981 (D.C. Cir. 1984)(en banc), *cert. denied,* 105 S. Ct. 2662 (1985). *See generally supra* § 5.07.

was made.[178] Unfortunately, the word "context" is itself rather vague, and, when used without elaboration, conveys nothing more definite than the equally vague "totality of circumstances" phraseology. The *Ollman* court apparently intended "context" to mean the actual language surrounding the allegedly defamatory statement.[179] When other language used reveals that the allegedly offending words are being used metaphorically, or humorously, they should be treated as nonfactual.[180] Similarly, cautionary language such as the prefaces "In my opinion" or "Is it not true that?" may alert the recipient of the communication not to take the words literally.[181]

In discussing the cautionary language issue, the court noted that authority existed against giving weight to cautionary or interrogatory language. In *Cianci v. New Times Publishing Co.*,[182] for example, Judge Henry Friendly argued that it "would be destructive of the law of libel if a writer could escape liability for accusations of crime simply by using, explicitly or implicitly, the words 'I think.' "[183] But the *Ollman* court maintained that although on its particular facts—involving the accusation of criminal activity—the mere inclusion of cautionary language would not magically turn what was otherwise a factual statement into mere opinion, that did not mean that in other more ambiguous cases cautionary language should not play a role as one of the factors to be weighed in the totality of circumstances balance.[184]

[iv] The Broader Social Context of the Speech

In addition to looking to the immediate context of the allegedly defamatory statement, the *Ollman* court required as the fourth prong of its analysis an inquiry into the broader social context into which the statement fits.[185] Some types of writing or speech, the court argued, by custom or conversation, signal to readers or listeners that what is being

---

178 *Id.* at 782-83.

179 *See id.* at 783.

180 *See* Myers v. Boston Magazine Co., Inc., 380 Mass. 336, 403 N.E.2d 376, 377 (1980).

181 *See* Rinsley v. Brandt, 700 F.2d 1304, 1309 (10th Cir. 1983); Burns v. McGraw-Hill Broadcasting Co., 659 P.2d 1351, 1360 (Colo. 1983); Pease v. Telegraph Publishing Co., 121 N.H. 62, 426 A.2d 463, 465 (1981).

182 639 F.2d 54 (2d Cir. 1980).

183 *Id.* at 64.

184 Ollman v. Evans, 750 F.2d 970, 983 (D.C. Cir. 1984)(en banc), *cert. denied,* 105 S. Ct. 2662 (1985)(citing Burns v. McGraw-Hill Broadcasting Co., 659 P.2d 1351, 1360 n.4 (Colo. 1983)).

185 Ollman v. Evans, 750 F.2d 970, 983 (D.C. Cir. 1984)(en banc), *cert. denied,* 105 S. Ct. 2662 (1985).

read or heard is likely to be opinion, not fact.[186] "It is one thing to be assailed as a corrupt public official by a soapbox orator and quite another to be labelled corrupt in a research monograph detailing the causes and cures of corruption in public service."[187]

Among the "broader social context" factors to be considered is the medium in which the speech occurs. When, for example, the statement occurs on the Op-Ed page of a newspaper, it is more likely to be understood as opinion, for it is "well understood that editorial writers and commentators frequently 'resort to the type of caustic bombast traditionally used in editorial writing to stimulate public reaction.' "[188] Courts should thus take into account the different social conventions or customs that surround different types of communication.

[d] The *Ollman* Test Applied

The court in *Ollman* had no great difficulty in determining that most of the statements complained of in the Evans and Novak column were opinion under its four part test. The one highly problematic statement, however, was the quotation in the column of an anonymous political science professor that "Ollman has no status within the profession but is a pure and simple activist."[189] This statement sharply divided the court, and was primarily responsible for the close 6-5 split among the judges. Typical of the dissenters' positions was Judge Edwards' state-

---

[186] *See* Restatement (Second) of Torts § 566 comment e (1977)("There are some statements that are in form statements of opinion, or even of fact, which cannot reasonably be understood to be meant literally and seriously and are obviously mere vituperation and abuse."). As the court in *Ollman* notes, it was taking this comment in the *Restatement* one step further, by applying it to whole genres of writing or speaking. 750 F.2d at 983 n.25.

[187] Ollman v. Evans, 750 F.2d 970, 983 (D.C. Cir. 1984)(en banc), *cert. denied,* 105 S. Ct. 2662 (1985).

[188] *Id.* at 984. *See also* National Rifle Ass'n v. Dayton Newspapers, Inc., 555 F. Supp. 1299 (S.D. Ohio 1983)(statement in an editorial that the National Rifle Association "happily encourages . . . murders and robberies" was protected as opinion); Loeb v. Globe Newspaper Co., 489 F. Supp. 481 (D. Mass. 1980)(disparaging remarks about the publisher of the *Manchester Union Leader* appearing on the *Boston Globe's* editorial page were protected opinion); National Association of Gov't Employees, Inc. v. Central Broadcasting Corp. 379 Mass. 220, 396 N.E.2d 996, 1001 (1979), *cert. denied,* 446 U.S. 935 (1980)(the charge of communism levied against a union on a radio call-in talk show called "Sound-Off" would have been understood by listeners as "pejorative rhetoric" and was protected opinion).

[189] Ollman v. Evans, 750 F.2d 970, 989 (D.C. Cir. 1981)(en banc), *cert. denied,* 105 S. Ct. 2662 (1985) (The majority opinion of Judge Starr referred to this as "the most troublesome statement" in the column).

ment that "[a]fter agonizing over this case, I have finally concluded that it is untenable even to suggest that the ['no status' statement] is an absolutely privileged 'opinion.' "[190] Noting his own background as an academic, Judge Edwards remarked that "I am somewhat taken aback by the notion that one's reputation within the profession (which is *easily* verifiable) may be so freely and glibly libeled. I can find no meaningful case authority to convince me that the First Amendment is designed to condone such loose muckraking."[191]

Nonetheless, the majority in *Ollman* found the "no status" statement to be more the stuff of opinion than fact. Judge Starr, admonishing against "a Talmudic parsing of a single sentence or two" emphasized both the specific and broader social contexts of the statement.[192] Appearing in the column after other relevant facts and opinions had alerted the reader that Ollman was a controversial figure, the quote, attributed to an anonymous political science professor, would caution the reader not to treat the statement as factual. In the broader social context, the statement appeared on the Op-Ed page; it was made by two columnists with an identity as generally conservative and provocative; and "the thrust of the column, taken as a whole," was "to raise questions about Mr. Ollman's scholarship and intentions, not to state conclusions."[193]

[4] The Political Arena and Public Controversy Factors

[a] Judge Robert Bork's "Political Arena" Innovation

In a concurring opinion in *Ollman v. Evans*,[194] Judge Robert Bork (in an opinion joined by Judges Wikley, Ginsburg, and MacKinnon) emphasized the "public arena" and "public controversy" notions as part of the totality of circumstances to be considered in dealing with the fact/opinion problem. The totality of circumstances test, Judge Bork confessed, "is a balancing test and risks admitting into the law an element of judicial subjectivity."[195] Nonetheless, as admirable as "sharply defined principles" may be, they often fail to reflect the realities of life.[196]

---

190 *Id.* at 1035-36. (Edwards, J., concurring in part and dissenting in part).
191 *Id.* at 1036.
192 *Id.* at 991.
193 *Id.* at 990.
194 *Id.* at 993 (Bork, J., concurring).
195 *Id.* at 997.
196 *Id.* at 994.

Judge Bork analyzed the "totality of circumstances" in *Ollman* first in more or less traditional terms, and then added his own innovation: "[W]e ought to accept the proposition that those who place themselves in a political arena must accept a degree of derogation that others need not."[197] The corollary to this proposition is that when a person is derogated in connection with his activity in the public arena, courts should be more inclined to construe negative statements made about the person as opinion. Judge Bork was thus importing the public figure and public official analysis of *Gertz* as an aid to construing a statement as fact or opinion under the totality of circumstances. Under this theory, "opinion" would have a broader meaning for public figure plaintiffs than for private figure plaintiffs. Judge Bork thus contrasted the "activist" political scientist with the more reclusive ivory tower scholar.[198]

[b] Usefulness of the Political Arena Approach

[i] The Assumption of Risk Rationale

Judge Bork's insight makes sense on two levels. First, as a normative matter, the rationale of *Gertz* that those who enter the political kitchen must accept the heat is as logically applicable to the construction and interpretation elements of the plaintiff's case as it is to the fault elements. Rough and ready commentary about one's political positions on issues is a price that ought to be paid for entering the arena; to borrow a phrase from Cardozo, "the timorous may stay at home."[199]

[ii] The Recipient's Understanding Rationale

Second, purely as a guide to reasonable construction of the meaning of words, Judge Bork's analysis is eminently sensible. The ordinary reasonable recipient of a communication naturally discounts to some degree statements made in the heat of vitriolic battle, because the recipient understands and anticipates the human tendency to exaggerate positions during the passions and prejudices of the moment. The plaintiff's entry into a public controversy is to some degree a warning

---

197 *Id.* at 1002.

198 *Id.* at 1002-03.

199 Murphy v. Steeplechase Amusement Co., 250 N.Y. 479, 166 N.E. 173, 174 (1929). In other apt language from one of Cardozo's tersest opinions: "The antics of the clown are not the paces of the cloistered cleric. The rough and boisterous joke, the horseplay of the crowd, evokes its own guffaws, but they are not the pleasures of tranquility. The plaintiff was not seeking a retreat for meditation." *Id.*

bell to recipients of information about the controversy that what the plaintiff says and what is said about him may have to be taken with a grain of salt. As Judge Bork put it, the plaintiff Ollman should not be permitted "to have it both ways: acting as a political man but suing as if he were a private scholar."[200]

Although Judge Bork's opinion did not represent the holding of the court in *Ollman,* it did draw the concurrence of three other judges, and like all of the thoughtful opinions on both sides in that case, it is likely to be drawn upon by other courts across the country for its persuasive value.

§ 6.09 Defamatory Opinions

[1] In General

The statement that "Jane Smith is a blackmailer" might in some contexts be nonactionable, because it could not reasonably be understood by a recipient of the communication as defamatory.[201] The context may make it clear that the statement as used in the particular circumstances was totally innocuous. The same statement might also be nonactionable even if it was clear from the context that it was defamatory or injurious to reputation, if it could also be shown that in context it was an expression of pure opinion. One of the red herrings in understanding the fact/opinion problem is the misconception that "pure opinions" cannot be defamatory. For although some statements may be both nondefamatory and "opinion," there is no necessary correlation between the two.

[2] "Defamatory" Opinions—"Defamatory" Not a Synonym for "Actionable"

Opinions, even of the purest evaluative variety, can be defamatory—that is, they can have a tendency to be injurious to reputation, subjecting the victim to ridicule or contempt. If Walter Cronkite were to state in a *People* magazine interview, "I do not like Dan Rather," it might well injure Rather's reputation, because readers might be influenced by Walter Cronkite's view. The statement would not be actionable, how-

---

200 Ollman v. Evans, 750 F.2d 970, 1010 n.10 (D.C. Cir. 1984)(en banc), *cert. denied,* 105 S. Ct. 2662 (1985).

201 *See* Greenbelt Cooperative Publishing Ass'n v. Bresler, 398 U.S. 6 (1970).

ever, and some courts might say—incorrectly—that the reason is that such a statement is not defamatory. But that obviously cannot be the reason, since, by any realistic appraisal, to be negatively spoken of by Walter Cronkite would surely tend to cause reputational injury in the eyes of some recipients of the statement.

Opinions, therefore, can be defamatory; they can inflict great reputational damage. Although it would be nice to believe that the "ordinary reasonable person" would never think less of another because a third party has expressed negative "opinion" as opposed to "negative factual information" about the other, reasonable people are in fact constantly judging the reputations of persons on the basis of the "opinions" of others. Even the purest opinion—that *X* is a "bad" person—can work gigantic reputational injury to *X* if the speaker is influential. We have, in fact, come to include the phrase "opinion-maker" as part of our cultural vocabulary. The legal shelter given to the hypothetical statement by Walter Cronkite that "I do not like Dan Rather" thus exists *in spite* of the statement's defamatory character, not because it lacks that character. The real truth, in fact, is that negative opinions are *supposed* to be defamatory—their very function is to injure reputation. When the critic says she does not like the movie, her purpose is to do harm. The first amendment does not embrace the trite wallflower politeness of the cliché that "if you can't say anything good about a person you should say nothing at all." Rather, the first amendment is built on the notion that individuals are free to form their own judgments, and then to speak their mind about them. As much as the first amendment encourages the open venting of value judgments, tastes, and ideas, however, it generally does not encourage the communication of false statements of fact. The important point to bear in mind is that the often difficult question of whether a particular communication should be treated as nonactionable opinion or as actionable misstatement of fact will not always yield the same answer as the question whether the communication is "defamatory," for both "opinion" and "facts" have the capacity to defame. The legal decision that a particular statement is "opinion" makes the statement absolutely nonactionable, even though it might well remain defamatory, that is, injurious to reputation.

§ 6.10 Role of the Judge and Jury

[1] General Rule

Courts frequently state the proposition that the judgment as to whether a statement is fact or opinion is a question of law for the court to determine.[202] There appears to be a divergence of viewpoints, however, as to what this general proposition means.

[2] Majority Position

Many courts simply state that the fact/opinion issue is a question of law.[203] One can interpret this majority position as meaning that the jury plays no role at all, or as meaning that the question of whether the language used is fact or opinion is a question of law for the court *in the first instance.*

If the court rules that the statement is not one of opinion but of fact, one can argue that the jury must still determine that the recipient of the communication *understood* it as a statement of defamatory fact. This elaboration on the majority rule is actually the most protective of the publisher, for it preserves the proposition that the fact/opinion distinction is an issue of law, thereby avoiding the problem of run-away jury nullification. At the same time, if the publisher loses the question in front of the judge, this elaboration prevents the plaintiff from being home free: The publisher gets a second bite at the apple if he can show that no recipients of the publication *actually* understood it as defamatory fact. Under this version of the majority position, the jury cannot hurt the defendant on the fact/opinion issue, but may help him. The judge's duty is to determine how the communication would be understood by

---

202 *See, e.g.*, Ollman v. Evans, 750 F.2d 970, 978 (D.C. Cir. 1984)(en banc), *cert. denied*, 105 S. Ct. 2662 (1985); Lewis v. Time, Inc., 710 F.2d 549, 553 (9th Cir. 1983); Rinsley v. Brandt, 700 F.2d 1304, 1309 (10th Cir. 1983); Orr v. Argus Press Co., 586 F.2d 1108, 1114 (6th Cir. 1978), *cert. denied*, 440 U.S. 960 (1979); Utah State Farm Bureau v. National Farm U.S. Corp., 198 F.2d 20, 33 (10th Cir. 1952); Dowd v. Calabrese, 589 F. Supp. 1206 (D.D.C. 1984); Held v. Pokorny, 583 F. Supp. 1038, 1039 (S.D.N.Y. 1984); Walker v. Southeastern Newspapers, 9 Med. L. Rep. 1516, 1518 (Ga. 1982); Naked City, Inc. v. Chicago Sun Times, 77 Ill. App. 3d 188, 395 N.E.2d 1042 (1979); Pritsker v. Brudnoy, 389 Mass. 776, 452 N.E.2d 227, 229 (1983); Silsdorf v. Levine, 59 N.Y.2d 8, 449 N.E.2d 716, *cert. denied*, 104 S. Ct. 109 (1983); Golden v. Elmira Star Gazette, 9 Med. L. Rep. 1183, 1184 (N.Y. Sup. 1983); Rinaldi v. Holt, Rinehart & Winston, Inc., 42 N.Y.2d 369, 381, 397 N.Y.S.2d 943, 366 N.E.2d 1299, *cert. denied*, 434 U.S. 969 (1977).

203 *See, e.g.*, Ollman v. Evans, 750 F.2d 970, 978 (D.C. Cir. 1984)(en banc), *cert. denied*, 105 S. Ct. 2662 (1985); Lewis v. Time, Inc., 710 F.2d 549, 553 (9th Cir. 1983).

the average recipient.[204] The plaintiff always has the burden of showing as part of his cause of action, however, that recipients who understood the communication as defamatory in fact really existed.[205] Thus, even if a court were to rule that a particular statement would be understood by the average recipient as factual, the defendant can still prevail if the jury finds that the only people who actually heard or read the information treated it as opinion.

[3] Minority Position

A number of courts have stated that if the average reader could reasonably understand the statement as either fact or opinion, the question should be submitted to the jury.[206] If the court concludes "that the average reader could not reasonably understand the statement as anything other than opinion, no genuine issue of material fact exists and summary judgment for the defendant may be entered."[207] Thus, under this view, when the statements at issue "are unambiguously fact or opinion," it is for the court to make the determination as a matter of law.[208] "However, where the alleged defamatory remarks could be determined either as fact or opinion, and the court cannot say as a matter of law that the statements were not understood as fact, there is a triable issue of fact for the jury."[209]

---

[204] *See, e.g.*, Ollman v. Evans, 750 F.2d 970, 978 (D.C. Cir. 1984)(en banc), *cert. denied*, 105 S. Ct. 2662 (1985); Caron v. Bangor Publishing Co., 470 A.2d 782 (Me.), *cert. denied*, 104 S. Ct. 3512 (1984); Good Government Group of Seal Beach, Inc. v. Superior Court of Los Angeles County, 22 Cal. 3d 672, 150 Cal. Rptr. 258, 586 P.2d 572 (1978), *cert. denied sub nom.* Good Government Group of Seal Beach, Inc. v. Hogard, 441 U.S. 961 (1979).

[205] *See supra* § 4.08.

[206] *See, e.g.*, Bindrim v. Mitchell, 92 Cal. App. 3d 61, 77-78, 155 Cal. Rptr. 29, 39, *cert. denied*, 444 U.S. 984 (1979); Good Government Group of Seal Beach, Inc. v. Superior Court of Los Angeles County, 22 Cal. 3d 672, 150 Cal. Rptr. 258, 586 P.2d 572 (1978), *cert. denied sub nom.* Good Government Group of Seal Beach, Inc. v. Hogard, 441 U.S. 961 (1979); Myers v. Boston Magazine Co., Inc., 380 Mass. 336, 403 N.E.2d 376 (1980); Caron v. Bangor Publishing Co., 470 A.2d 782 (Me.), *cert. denied*, 104 S. Ct. 3512 (1984); Pease v. Telegraph Publishing Co., 121 N.H. 62, 426 A.2d 463 (1981); Thomas v. Cash, 119 N.H. 371, 401 A.2d 651, 653 (1979).

[207] Caron v. Bangor Publishing Co., 470 A.2d 782 (Me.), *cert. denied*, 104 S. Ct. 3512 (1984). *See also* Myers v. Boston Magazine Co., Inc., 380 Mass. 336, 403 N.E.2d 376 (1980).

[208] Bindrim v. Mitchell, 92 Cal. App. 3d 61, 77-78, 155 Cal. Rptr. 29, 39, *cert. denied*, 444 U.S. 984 (1979).

[209] *Id. See also* Good Government Group of Seal Beach, Inc. v. Superior Court of Los Angeles County, 22 Cal. 3d 672, 150 Cal. Rptr. 258, 586 P.2d 572 (1978), *cert. denied sub nom.* Good Government Group of Seal Beach, Inc. v. Hogard, 441 U.S. 961 (1979); Myers

[4] Comparison of Majority and Minority Views

The minority position on the fact/opinion question is actually closer to the reasonable construction rule that applies to the question of whether the language at issue is defamatory.[210] If the language is susceptible of two meanings, one defamatory and one nondefamatory, the view in every state except Illinois is that the question of defamatory meaning is for the jury.[211] The majority position—to the extent that it envisions that where an average reader could reasonably interpret the language as either fact or opinion, the judge must still "make the call" as to how it would be understood—appears to give the judge a stronger role on the fact/opinion question than he or she has on most other elements of the cause of action. This greater intrusiveness by the court may be the result of the language in *Gertz,* to the effect that the fact/opinion distinction states a principle of "constitutional law" and therefore requires greater judicial superintendence.[212] For example, the weight of authority is that the issue of whether the plaintiff is a public figure or a private figure is a question of law.[213] Even this principle is subject to some ambiguity, however, for the Supreme Court in *Rosenblatt v. Baer*[214] qualified its statement that the public figure/private figure question is one of law for the court by adding the phrase "in the first instance."[215] Similarly, with regard to some issues relating to constitutional standards, such as the existence of *New York Times* actual malice, the question is treated as one of "constitutional fact," in which juries do make the determination, but the determination is then independently scrutinized by the trial and appellate courts.[216] Although the position that permits language "that could go either way" to be present-

v. Boston Magazine Co., 380 Mass. 336, 403 N.E.2d 376 (1980); Caron v. Bangor Publishing Co., 470 A.2d 782 (Me.), *cert. denied,* 104 S. Ct. 3512 (1984).

210 *See* Myers v. Boston Magazine Co., 380 Mass. 336, 403 N.E.2d 376 (1980)("This approach is analogous to the allocation between judge and jury on the issue of whether a statement is defamatory."). *See also* Pease v. Telegraph Publishing Co., 121 N.H. 62, 426 A.2d 463 (1981)(citing W. Prosser, Handbook on the Law of Torts § 111, at 747-48 (4th ed. 1971)).

211 *See supra* §§ 4.06[2], 4.08.

212 *See* Ollman v. Evans, 750 F.2d 970, 978 (D.C. Cir. 1984)(en banc), *cert. denied,* 105 S. Ct. 2662 (1985).

213 *See* Rosenblatt v. Baer, 383 U.S. 75, 88 (1966); Waldbaum v. Fairchild Publications, Inc., 627 F.2d 1287 (D.C. Cir.), *cert. denied,* 449 U.S. 898 (1980); Stone v. Essex County Newspapers, Inc., 367 Mass. 849, 330 N.E.2d 161 (1975). *See supra* § 3.30.

214 383 U.S. 75 (1966).

215 *Id.* at 88.

216 *See* Bose Corp. v. Consumers Union of United States, Inc., 104 S. Ct. 1949 (1984).

ed to the jury remains the minority position, as of yet there is no clear statement from the Supreme Court that the more restrictive majority approach is constitutionally mandated.

§ 6.11 Private Figures vs. Public Officials and Public Figures; the Protection for Opinion

The distinction between public figures and officials and private figures that was created by *Gertz*[217] "does not directly bear on the distinction between fact and opinion."[218] The logic of the constitutional principle protecting opinions announced in *Gertz* "would appear to apply to all expressions of opinion," whether they concern public or private matters.[219] Expressions of opinion are therefore protected whether the subject of the comment is a public or private figure.[220]

§ 6.12 The Fact/Opinion Distinction in Specific Situations

As in all other areas of defamation, it is perilous to rely to any great extent on lists of certain words or categories of language as the litmus test for separating fact from opinion.[221] Some patterns and tendencies do emerge from the cases, however, in recurring fact situations. With the caveat that every case involves judgment and must turn on its own facts,[222] some of these recurring patterns are discussed in the sections that follow.

[1] Lawyers and Judges

It has been held to be protected opinion to call a judge "incompe-

---

217 *See supra* § 2.02.

218 Ollman v. Evans, 750 F.2d 970, 975 (D.C. Cir. 1984) (en banc), *cert. denied,* 105 S. Ct. 2662 (1985).

219 Restatement (Second) of Torts § 566 comment c (1977).

220 *See, e.g.,* Ollman v. Evans, 750 F.2d 970, 975 (D.C. Cir. 1984)(en banc), *cert. denied,* 105 S. Ct. 2662 (1985); Lewis v. Time, Inc., 710 F.2d 549, 555 (9th Cir. 1983); Burns v. Denver Post, Inc., 606 P.2d 1310 (Colo. App. 1979); Anton v. St. Louis Suburban Newspapers, Inc., 598 S.W.2d 493, 499 n.9 (Mo. App. 1980). *But see* the "political arena" concept advanced by Judge Bork in his concurring opinion in *Ollman v. Evans,* discussed in § 6.08[4], *supra.*

221 *See supra* § 4.07.

222 *See* Shiver v. Apalachee Publishing Co., 425 So. 2d 1173 (Fla. Dist. Ct. App. 1983).

tent" and urge that he be removed from office.[223] To imply that an attorney is one of the bar's "shadier practitioners," after setting forth the facts in two malpractice judgments involving the attorney, was held protected as opinion.[224] Similarly, it was protected opinion to state that an attorney gave "incompetent" legal advice.[225] It was held to be opinion to refer to an attorney's "sleazy sleight of hand."[226] Statements that a candidate for appointment to the post of United States Attorney was a "second-rater" who lacked the "experience or temperament for the job" were held to be opinion.[227] In *Belli v. Berryhill*,[228] attorney Melvin Belli had filed a class action charging more than 200 California financial institutions with having improperly invested homeowner property tax payments. In a press conference, Belli described the suit as "the largest such suit ever filed."[229] A representative of one of the defendants stated that the suit was "without merit," that Belli was "in a time warp," and that "Belli is not known for his research, and probably doesn't even know the difference between state and federally chartered S & L associations."[230] Using an analysis similar to that of Judge Bork in *Ollman v. Evans*,[231] the court held the statements to be opinion, quoting the words of Harry Truman: "If you can't stand the heat, get out of the kitchen."[232] In another case involving Melvin Belli, however, a story falsely accusing Belli of taking advantage of an invitation to speak at a Florida Bar Association meeting to run up purchases charged to his hotel account was held factual and capable of defamatory meaning, and not mere "caustic comment."[233]

---

223 Rinaldi v. Holt, Rinehart & Winston, Inc., 42 N.Y.2d 369, 381, 397 N.Y.S.2d 943, 366 N.E.2d 1299, *cert. denied*, 434 U.S. 969 (1977).

224 Lewis v. Time, Inc., 710 F.2d 549, 550-51 (9th Cir. 1983)("If the legal system has been reluctant to discipline its shadier practitioners, it has been swift to crack down on anyone threatening to cut fees or reduce business.").

225 Plough v. Schneider, 8 Med. L. Rep. (BNA) 1620 (Ohio Ct. App. 1982).

226 Anton v. St. Louis Suburban Newspapers, 598 S.W.2d 493 (Mo. Ct. App. 1980).

227 Miller v. Charleston Gazette, 9 Med. L. Rep. (BNA) 2540 (W. Va. Cir. Ct. Ohio County 1983).

228 11 Med. L. Rep. (BNA) 1221 (Cal. Ct. App. 1st Dist. 1984). (an editorial note states that the court has indicated that the opinion is "not to be published in official reports").

229 *Id.* at 1222.

230 *Id.*

231 Ollman v. Evans, 750 F.2d 970, 993 (D.C. Cir. 1984)(en banc)(Bork, J., concurring), *cert. denied*, 105 S. Ct. 2662 (1985). *See supra* §6.08[3].

232 Belli v. Berryhill, 11 Med. L. Rep. (BNA) 122, 1224 (Cal. Ct. App. 1st Dist. 1984)(citing Botos v. Los Angeles County Bar Ass'n, 151. Cal App. 3d 1083, 1090 (1984)).

233 Belli v. Orlando Daily Newspapers, Inc., 389 F.2d 579 (1967), *cert. denied*, 393 U.S. 825 (1968).

[2] Labor Disputes

Few confrontations in American society are more prone to violent disagreement than disputes between management and labor. American history since the industrial revolution has been punctuated by bitter struggles between labor and capital, and in light of this history courts tend to give broad compass to remarks flung about in the context of labor disputes.[234] Perhaps no case more strongly illustrates the point than the Supreme Court's decision in *Letter Carriers*,[235] in which the Court found the hard-bitten sarcasm of the great Jack London to be legally protected opinion. London's definition of a "scab," used by the defendants to describe the plaintiffs, included the statements that the "scab sells his birthright, country, his wife, his children, and his fellowmen for an unfulfilled promise from his employer," and "is a traitor to his God, his country, his family and his class."[236]

Gregory v. McDonnell Douglas Corp.,[237] held allegations that union leaders were willing to sacrifice the interests of their union members to further their own personal political ambitions and aspirations constituted protected opinion.

[3] Political Campaigns

Generally, courts tend to be more liberal in construing as opinion statements made by participants in, and by those who comment on, political campaigns. In *Miskovsky v. Oklahoma Publishing Co.*,[238] the Supreme Court of Oklahoma held that attacks by a newspaper on the behavior of a senatorial candidate, who repeated allegations of another candidate's homosexuality, were protected opinion.[239] One of the articles quoted another party's description of the plaintiff as a "hatchet man,"[240] another called the plaintiff's attack "despicable and stupid."[241] The paper accused the plaintiff of having "sunk to a new low

---

[234] *See* Gregory v. McDonnell Douglas Corp., 17 Cal. 3d 596, 131 Cal. Rptr. 641, 643, 552 P.2d 425 (1976); National Ass'n of Gov't Employees, Inc. v. Central Broadcasting Corp., 379 Mass. 220, 396 N.E.2d 996 (1979), *cert. denied,* 446 U.S. 935 (1980).

[235] Old Dominion Branch No. 496, National Association of Letter Carriers v. Austin, 418 U.S. 264 (1974). *See supra* § 6.03[4].

[236] 418 U.S. at 268.

[237] 17 Cal. 3d 596, 552 P.2d 425, 131 Cal. Rptr. 641 (1976).

[238] 654 P.2d 587 (Okla.), *cert. denied,* 459 U.S. 923 (1982).

[239] 654 P.2d at 594.

[240] *Id.* at 593.

[241] *Id.* at 594.

in Oklahoma political rhetoric—and for him that takes some doing."[242] The United States Supreme Court, over the dissent of Justices Rehnquist and White, denied certiorari.[243]

In contrast to the high level of protection in *Miskovsky*, the court in *Silsdorf v. Levine*[244] held that the plaintiff, a candidate for village mayor, was not precluded by the opinion doctrine from maintaining an action against the defendants, who had sent an open letter to the village containing allegedly defamatory charges. The court was not impressed with the "defendants' concern over undue limitations upon expression in the course of political campaigns."[245] The court admonished that "[e]ven privilege has its limitations and even a public figure in the midst of a political campaign is entitled to some degree of protection."[246]

The cryptic decision in *Silsdorf* is somewhat difficult to evaluate, for it may be that the court was essentially holding that the plaintiff's allegations stated a cause of action because they alleged that the letter contained false and defamatory factual statements, in addition to opinions. At other points in the court's decision, however, there are implications that the opinions themselves may in certain circumstances be actionable. The court held that the charges, "although constituting opinions and therefore entitled to a measure of constitutional protection, may nevertheless form the basis of a defamation claim, inasmuch as plaintiff has alleged that the facts set forth by defendants in support of their opinions are false."[247] The court held that "the immunity afforded to expression of opinion obtains only when the facts supporting the opinion are set forth,"[248] *and* if those underlying facts are true.[249] Since the plaintiff had alleged that the underlying facts were false, the court reasoned, the plaintiff should be entitled to establish actual malice.[250] The holding in *Silsdorf* had overtones suspiciously reminiscent of the restrictive common law approach prior to *Gertz*,[251] and is arguably out of step with post-*Gertz* first amendment developments.

---

242 *Id.*
243 459 U.S. 923 (1982).
244 59 N.Y.2d 8, 462 N.Y.S.2d 822, 449 N.E.2d 716 (1983).
245 462 N.Y.S.2d at 827.
246 *Id.*
247 *Id.* at 823.
248 *Id.* at 825.
249 *Id.* at 825-26.
250 *Id.* at 826-27.
251 *See supra* § 6.02.

[4] Op-Ed Articles, Letters to the Editor, and Political Cartoons

On the whole, the decisions run strongly in favor of finding statements on the Op-Ed pages,[252] or in letters to the editor,[253] or in political cartoons[254] protected opinions. The Op-Ed page is one of the great American forums for the free exchange of vitriolic debate, and readers can be expected to discount the statements made in that context as more likely to be the stuff of opinion than fact.[255] Although statements made in an editorial forum can be and at times are construed as action-

[252] *See, e.g.*, Ollman v. Evans, 750 F.2d 970, 990 (D.C. Cir. 1984)(en banc), *cert. denied*, 105 S. Ct. 2662 (1985); Loeb v. Globe Newspaper Co., 489 F. Supp. 481 (D. Mass. 1980); Block v. Desert Sun, 6 Med. L. Rep. (BNA) 1367 (Cal. App. 1980); Russell v. McMillen, 10 Med. L. Rep. (BNA) 1888 (Colo. Ct. App. 1984); Slawik v. News Journal Co., 428 A.2d 15 (Del. Sup. Ct. 1981); Whitfield v. Southeastern Newspapers, 10 Med. L. Rep. (BNA) 1777 (Ga. Sup. Ct. 1984); Walker v. Southeastern Newspapers, 9 Med. L. Rep. 1516 (Ga. 1982); Caron v. Bangor Publishing Co., 470 A.2d 782 (Me.), *cert. denied*, 104 S. Ct. 3512 (1984); Anton v. St. Louis Suburban Newspapers, Inc., 598 S.W.2d 493 (Mo. App. 1980); LaRocca v. New York News, Inc., 156 N.J. Super. 59, 383 A.2d 451 (App. Div. 1978); Marchiondo v. Brown, 98 N.M. 394, 649 P.2d 462 (1982); Ritter v. Matthes, 9 Med. L. Rep. (BNA) 1744 (N.Y. Sup. Ct. 1983); Ferguson v. Dayton Newspapers, 7 Med. L. Rep. (BNA) 2502 (Ohio Ct. App. 1981); Dupler v. Mansfield Journal Co., 64 Ohio St.2d 116, 413 N.E.2d 1187 (Sup. Ct. 1980), *cert. denied*, 452 U.S. 962 (1981); Miskovsky v. Oklahoma, 654 P.2d 587 (Okla.), *cert. denied*, 459 U.S. 923 (1982); Haas v. Painter, 62 Or. App. 719, 662 P.2d 768 (1983); Miller v. Charleston Gazette, 9 Med. L. Rep. (BNA) 2540 (W. Va. Cir. Ct. Ohio County 1983). *But see* Brooks v. Stone, 6 Med. L. Rep. (BNA) 1823 (Ga. County Ct. 1983); McHale v. Lake Charles American Press, 390 So. 2d 556 (La. Ct. App. 1980)(holding that statement in editorial that "no bond buyer would buy a nickel's worth of securities" on city attorney's opinion was statement of fact, not opinion); Costello v. Capital Cities Media, Inc., 445 N.E.2d 13, 9 Med. L. Rep. (BNA) 1434 (Ill. App. 1982)(editorial statement that county board chairman deliberately lied was fact, not opinion).

[253] *See, e.g.*, Hay v. Independent Newspapers, 10 Med. L. Rep. (BNA) 1928 (Fla. Ct. App. 1984); Sepmeier v. Tallahassee Democrat, 10 Med. L. Rep. (BNA) 1285 (Fla. Cir. Ct. 1984); Shiver v. Apalachee Publishing Co., 425 So. 2d 1173 (Fla. Dist. Ct. App. 1983); Medeiros v. Northwest Publishing, 8 Med. L. Rep. (BNA) 2500 (Mass. Sup. Ct. 1982); Nash v. Keen Publishing, 10 Med. L. Rep. (BNA) 2281 (N.H. Sup. Ct. 1984); Pease v. Telegraph Publishing Co., 121 N.H. 62, 426 A.2d 463 (1981); Kotlikoff v. The Community News, 89 N.J. 62, 444 A.2d 1086 (1982). *Cf.* Ratner v. Young, 465 F. Supp. 386 (D.V.I. 1979)(newspaper published letter written to federal district judge during controversial murder trial arising from famous Fountain Valley murder case in St. Croix).

[254] *See, e.g.*, Yorty v. Chandler, 13 Cal. App. 3d 467, 91 Cal. Rptr. 709 (1970); Russell v. McMillen, 10 Med. L. Rep. (BNA) 1888 (Colo. Ct. App. 1984); Walker v. Southeastern Newspapers, 9 Med. L. Rep. (BNA) 1516 (Ga. 1982); Miller v. Charleston Gazette, 9 Med. L. Rep. (BNA) 2540 (W. Va. Cir. Ct. Ohio County 1983); Ferguson v. Dayton Newspapers, 7 Med. L. Rep. (BNA) 2502 (Ohio Ct. App. 1981). For additional citations to and discussion of cases involving cartoons, *see supra* §4.07[3].

[255] *See* Ollman v. Evans, 750 F.2d 970, 984 (D.C. Cir. 1984)(en banc), *cert. denied*, 105 S. Ct. 2662 (1985); Loeb v. Globe Newspaper Co., 489 F. Supp. 481 (D. Mass. 1980).

able fact rather than opinion,[256] it is clear that the editorial context is regarded by the courts as a powerful element in construing as opinion what might otherwise be deemed fact. In *Kotlikoff v. Community News*,[257] for example, a letter to the editor charged the mayor and the tax assessor with covering up the names of deliquent taxpayers, suggesting they might be "engaged in a huge coverup;" the charges, considered in their "editorial forum" context, were held to be opinion,[258] though from a strictly semantic perspective they might normally have been treated as fact. Similarly, in the context of a radio talk show called "Sound Off," the normally libelous charge that a labor union is communist was held to be nonactionable opinion because, in the context of the program format, it would likely have been understood as "pejorative rhetoric."[259]

In the field of television, a statement by commentator Andy Rooney on the effectiveness of a product sent to him was not actionable because Rooney's comments and the context in which they were made were understood as "humorous, satirical, full of ridicule, and often to be taken with a grain of salt."[259.1]

[5] Ideologically Amorphous Statements

To call someone a communist is often held to be a defamatory statement of fact.[260] More amorphous "political epithets," however, are usually characterized as opinion. In *Buckley v. Littell*,[261] a writer of a book on the political right labeled conservative columnist and author William

256 *See* McHale v. Lake Charles American Press, 390 So. 2d 556 (La. Ct. App. 1980), *cert. denied*, 452 U.S. 941 (1981); Silsdorf v. Levine, 59 N.Y.2d 8, 462 N.Y.S.2d 822, 449 N.E.2d 716, *cert. denied*, 104 S. Ct. 109 (1983).

257 89 N.J. 62, 444 A.2d 1086 (1982).

258 *Id.*

259 National Ass'n of Gov't Employees v. Central Broadcasting Corp., 379 Mass. 220, 396 N.E.2d 996 (1979), *cert. denied*, 446 U.S. 935 (1980).

259.1 Unelko Corp. v. Rooney, 16 Med. L. Rptr. 1737 (BNA) (U.S. Dist. Ct., Dist. of Ariz. April 25,1989).

260 *See, e.g.*, Grant v. Reader's Digest Ass'n, 151 F.2d 733 (2d Cir. 1945), *cert. denied*, 326 U.S. 797 (1946); Herrmann v. Newark Morning Ledger Co., 49 N.J. Super. 551, 140 A.2d 529 (1958). *Cf.* Gertz v. Robert Welch, Inc., 418 U.S. 323 (1974). *But see* National Ass'n of Gov't Employees v. Central Broadcasting Corp., 379 Mass. 220, 396 N.E.2d 996 (1979), *cert. denied*, 446 U.S. 935 (1980); Garriga v. Richfield, 174 Misc. 315, 20 N.Y.S.2d 544 (1940); McAndrew v. Scranton Republican Publishing Co., 364 Pa. 504, 72 A.2d 780 (1950). For a related discussion on the issue of whether such an allegation carries defamatory meaning, *see supra* § 4.02.

261 539 F.2d 882 (2d Cir. 1976), *cert. denied*, 429 U.S. 1062 (1977).

F. Buckley, Jr. a "fellow traveler" of "fascists."[262] Noting that the writer and William F. Buckley embraced widely differing world views and different definitions of "fascism," the Second Circuit held that the pivotal term lacked a sufficiently well defined meaning in the context of the

(*Text continued on page 6-47*)

[262] *Id.* at 893-95.

case to be characterized as factual.[263] Such expressions, the court stated, "cannot be regarded as having been proved to be statements of facts, among other reasons, because of the tremendous imprecision of the meaning and usage of these terms in the realm of political debate, an imprecision which is similarly echoed in the book."[264]

Echoing the *Buckley* ruling, in the exhaustively analytical and scholarly opinions authored in *Ollman v. Evans*,[265] it was held that statements about a political science professor that he was widely viewed as "a political activist," that he was "an outspoken proponent of 'political Marxism,' " and that he had "no status within the profession, but [was] a pure and simple activist," were held to be protected opinion.[266] Similarly, courts have held to be opinion, charges of racial prejudice,[267] "Nazi-style anti-Semitism,"[268] and "spiritual fascism."[269]

[6] Religious Opinion

Allegedly defamatory statements that implicate issues intertwined with religious beliefs receive protection from the religion clauses of the first amendment in addition to the normal protections of the speech and press clauses.[270] The double-edged danger posed by the entry of a court into a religious fray is that the court may interfere with the free exercise clause by favoring one party, and with the establishment clause by favoring the other. The normal breathing space given to opinions under the first amendment is thus even broader when religious matters

---

263 *Id.*

264 *Id.* at 893.

265 750 F.2d 970 (D.C. Cir. 1984)(en banc), *cert. denied*, 105 S. Ct. 2662 (1985).

266 *See supra* § 5.11.

267 Cibenko v. Worth Publishers, Inc., 510 F. Supp. 761 (D.N.J. 1981).

268 Holy Spirit Ass'n for Unification of World Christianity v. Sequoia Elsevier Publishing Co., 75 A.D.2d 523, 426 N.Y.S.2d 759 (1980).

269 New Testament Missionary Fellowship v. E.P. Dutton & Co., 9 Med. L. Rep. (BNA) 1174 (N.Y. Sup. Ct. 1982). *See also* Labor Party v. Anti-Defamation League, 6 Med. L. Rep. (BNA) 2209 (N.Y. Sup. Ct. 1980)(charges that group was "anti-Semitic" held to be opinion).

270 The first amendment bars attempts to litigate the truth or falsity of religious beliefs. *See* United States v. Ballard, 322 U.S. 78 (1944); Founding Church of Scientology v. United States, 409 F.2d 1146, 1160 (D.C. Cir.), *cert. denied*, 396 U.S. 963 (1969). Courts thus must refrain from making ecclesiastical determinations. *See* Serbian Eastern Orthodox Diocese for U.S.A. and Canada v. Milivojevich, 426 U.S. 696 (1975); Presbyterian Church in the United States v. Hull Memorial Presbyterian Church, 393 U.S. 440 (1969).

are implicated.[271] In *Holy Spirit Ass'n v. Harper & Row Publishers, Inc.*,[272] for example, the court stated that where "the issue involves the validity of a religious denomination's beliefs, the First Amendment would bar such a claim, as it would embroil the state in an inquiry into the truth or falsity of beliefs or teachings."[273] In *New Testament Missionary Fellowship v. E.P. Dutton & Co.*,[274] it was held protected opinion to label a group of coreligionists "spiritual fascists." It was held in *Holy Spirit Ass'n of the Unification for World Christianity v. Sequoia Elsevier Publishing Co.*[275] that the accusation that a religious group was characterized by "elements of Nazi-style anti-Semitism" was protected opinion. And it was opinion to describe Scientologists as a "gung-ho" organization engaging in "helter-skelter" tactics to infiltrate the community.[276] In short, whenever the question of whether a particular statement of fact or opinion involves disputes concerning religious practices or doctrine, courts have quite properly leaned toward construing the offending language as opinion.

[7] Literary and Artistic Criticism

In *Hellman v. McCarthy*,[277] writer Mary McCarthy, during the course of an interview on the "Dick Cavett Show," described writer Lillian Hellman as "dishonest," and added: "Every word she writes is a lie, including 'and' and 'the.' "[278] The court held, in denying defendant Mary McCarthy's motion for summary judgment, that it could not be said as a matter of law that the statements were opinion.[279]

It was held to be fact, not opinion, to say of a sports writer that he "is not a graceful wordsman" and is "quite possibly the worst writer" on a sport magazine's staff, and that he continued as head football writer "not least because" he was the managing editor's "longtime

---

271 *See* Church of Scientology v. Siegelman, 475 F. Supp. 950 (S.D.N.Y. 1979).

272 101 Misc. 2d 30, 420 N.Y.S.2d 56 (N.Y. Sup. 1979).

273 420 N.Y.S.2d at 60. The court further stated, however, that "the alleged libelous statements involved in the case at bar do not involve the validity of beliefs and practices." *Id.*

274 9 Med. L. Rep. (BNA) 1174 (N.Y. Sup. Ct. 1982).

275 75 A.D.2d 523, 426 N.Y.S.2d 759 (1980).

276 Church of Scientology of California v. Cazares, 638 F.2d 1272 (5th Cir. 1981).

277 10 Med. L. Rep. (BNA) 1789 (N.Y. Sup. Ct. 1984).

278 *Id.* at 1790.

279 *Id.* at 1793-94.

drinking companion."[280] The court held that the "reasonable reader must be able to discern that what is being presented is a statement of the author's opinion based on stated facts and not a statement of fact in itself."[281] The court continued, "A statement of fact, even a conclusory one, is not an opinion and merely juxtaposing a factual statement and a conclusory allegation does not transform either the statement or the allegation into constitutionally protected opinion."[282] A statement by the president of a publishing company that he did not want the company's subsidiary to publish a book because it was "trash" was held not protected as fair comment.[283]

In *Cole v. Westinghouse Broadcasting Co.*,[284] however, it was held that a statement that a reporter had engaged in "sloppy and irresponsible reporting" was opinion.[285] A newspaper theater critic's columns concerning a change in ownership of the county's only legitimate dinner theater were privileged as fair comment.[286] Statements that "not even libel" bothers a publisher who has a "stranglehold" on the life of a state were held protected as opinion,[287] as were statements that a publisher runs a newspaper "by paranoids for paranoids."[288] It was held to be opinion to describe a newspaper reporter as "journalistic scum of the earth."[289]

A book review characterizing a book on gambling as the "number one fraud ever perpetrated upon the gambling reader" was held to be protected as opinion.[290] And in *Myers v. Boston Magazine Co.*,[291] a statement that a television sports reporter was "the only newscaster in town who is enrolled in a course for remedial speaking" was held to be opinion.[292] As a general principle, authors, journalists, and artists invite criticism of their work product, and although there are cases holding

280 Maule v. NYM Corp., 10 Med. L. Rep. (BNA) 1962 (N.Y. Sup. Ct. 1984).

281 *Id.* at 1964.

282 *Id.* at 1964-65.

283 Coniff v. Dodd, Mead, 10 Med. L. Rep. (BNA) 2272 (S.D.N.Y. 1984).

284 386 Mass. 303, 435 N.E.2d 1021, *cert. denied*, 459 U.S. 1037 (1982).

285 *Id.* at 1025.

286 Victor v. News and Sun Sentinel Co., 10 Med. L. Rep. (BNA) 2188 (Fla. Cir. Ct. 1984).

287 Loeb v. New Times Communications Corp., 497 F. Supp. 85 (S.D.N.Y. 1980).

288 Loeb v. Globe Newspaper Co., 489 F. Supp. 481 (D. Mass. 1980).

289 Pease v. Telegraph Publishing Co., 121 N.H. 62, 426 A.2d 463 (1981).

290 Stuart v. Gambling Times, 534 F. Supp. 170 (D.N.J. 1982).

291 380 Mass. 336, 403 N.E.2d 376 (1980).

292 *Id.* at 336, 403 N.E.2d at 377.

that such criticism in certain circumstances is actionable as fact,[293] the mainstream position is clearly to construe such criticism as opinion or fair comment.[294]

[8] Restaurant and Food Critiques

Although restaurant reviews seem to generate a substantial amount of libel litigation, the plaintiffs are almost never successful. Perhaps nothing is more quintessentially subjective as one's tastes in food and drink, and courts are loath to describe such reviews as anything other than opinion.[295] In a recent Second Circuit opinion, Judge Thomas Meskill noted that the plaintiff could not cite "a single case that has found a restaurant review libelous."[296] The decision involved a review of a Chinese restaurant in which the reviewers claimed that it was "impossible" to get basic condiments served, that the sweet and sour pork contained "more dough than meat," that the green peppers were "still frozen," that the fried rice was "soaking" in oil, and that the pancakes were "the thickness of a finger."[297] Judge Meskill wrote, "[T]he natural function of the review is to convey the critic's opinion of the restaurant reviewed."[298] Similarly, in *Golden v. Elmira Star Ga-*

---

293 *See* Maule v. NYM Corp., 10 Med. L. Rep. (BNA) 1962 (N.Y. Sup. Ct. 1984); Hellman v. McCarthy, 10 Med. L. Rep. (BNA) 1789 (N.Y. Sup. Ct. 1984).

294 *See, e.g.*, Guitar v. Westinghouse Electric Corp., 396 F. Supp. 1042, 1048 (S.D.N.Y. 1975), *aff'd*, 538 F.2d 309 (2d Cir. 1976); Buckley v. Vidal, 327 F. Supp. 1051 (S.D.N.Y. 1971); Berg v. Printer's Ink Publishing Co., 54 F. Supp. 795, 791 (S.D.N.Y. 1943), *aff'd on opinion below*, 141 F.2d 1022 (2d Cir. 1944); Pearson v. Fairbanks Publishing Co., 413 P.2d 711 (Alaska 1966); Triggs v. Sun Printing and Publishing Ass'n, 179 N.Y. 144, 71 N.E. 739 (1904).

295 *See, e.g.*, Mr. Chow of New York v. Ste. Jour Azur S.A., 11 Med. L. Rep. (BNA) 1713 (2d Cir. 1985); Ihle v. Florida Publishing Co., 5 Med. L. Rep. (BNA) 2005 (Fla. Cir. Ct. 1979); Mashburn v. Collin, 355 So. 2d 879 (La. 1977); Pritsker v. Brudnoy, 389 Mass. 776, 452 N.E.2d 227 (1983); Golden v. Elmira Star Gazette, 9 Med. L. Rep. (BNA) 1183 (N.Y. Sup. Ct. 1983); Kuan Sing Enterprises v. T.W. Wang, 86 A.D.2d 549, 446 N.Y.S.2d 76 (1st Dept.), *aff'd*, 58 N.Y.2d 708, 444 N.E.2d 1008, 458 N.Y.S.2d 544 (1982); Havalunch, Inc. v. Mazza, 294 S.E.2d 70 (W. Va. 1981); Twenty-five East 40th St. Restaurant Corp. v. Forbes, Inc., 37 A.D.2d 546, 322 N.Y.S.2d 408 (1st Dept. 1971), *aff'd*, 30 N.Y.2d 595, 331 N.Y.S.2d 29, 282 N.E.2d 118 (1972); Steak Bit of Westbury, Inc. v. Newsday, Inc., 70 Misc. 2d 437, 334 N.Y.S.2d 325 (N.Y. Sup. 1972); Greer v. Columbus Monthly, 4 Ohio App. 3d 235, 238, 448 N.E.2d 157, 161 (1982).

296 Mr. Chow of New York v. Ste. Jour Azur S.A., 11 Med. L. Rep. (BNA) 1713, 1719 (2d Cir. 1985).

297 *Id.* at 1714, 1720-21.

298 *Id.* at 1719. *See also* Greer v. Columbus Monthly Publishing Corp., 4 Ohio App. 3d 235, 238, 448 N.E.2d 157, 161 (1982)("By its very nature, an article commenting upon the quality of a restaurant or its food, like a review of a play or a movie, constitutes the opinion of the reviewer.").

zette,[299] a restaurant review was held to be protected opinion, including statements that the vegetables were "under-cooked" and "stringy," the salads were "undistinguished," the lettuce "yellowed," the duck "awash in grease," and the tomato sauce high in "acid content."[300] And in *Mashburn v. Collin,*[301] it was held to be protected opinion to review a restaurant with such critical blasts as "[T]'aint Cajun, t'aint French, t'aint Country American, t'aint good," describing the food as made with "hideous sauces" including an "ugly sauce that tastes too sweet and thick and makes you want to scrape off the glop," and saying the menu included "yellow death on duck," "trout à la green plague," and "badly overcooked fish."[302]

[9] Allegations of Criminal Activity

Accusations of criminal activity tend to put the defendant on dangerous ground under the fact/opinion distinction. At least when phrased in relatively specific terms, such allegations will usually not be construed as protected opinion.[303] Nonetheless, mere charges that the plaintiff's conduct was wrongful, and references to the "repentance of criminals," were held to be opinion.[304] The characterization of a book as a "fraud" on readers[305] and speculation about possible criminal conduct in the future[306] were held protected opinion. Similarly, statements about an attorney's "sleazy sleight of hand" in connection with a change in a governmental board's membership was held protected opinion.[307]

[299] 9 Med. L. Rep. (BNA) 1183 (N.Y. Sup. Ct. 1983).

[300] *Id.* at 1184.

[301] 355 So. 2d 879 (La. 1977).

[302] *Id.* at 888-89.

[303] *See, e.g.*, Cianci v. New Times Publishing Co., 639 F.2d 54 (2d Cir. 1980); Catalano v. Pechous, 83 Ill. 2d 146, 419 N.E.2d 350 (1980), *cert. denied*, 451 U.S. 911 (1981); Silsdorf v. Levine, 59 N.Y.2d 8, 449 N.E.2d 716, *cert. denied*, 104 S. Ct. 109 (1983); Gewurz v. Bernstein, 107 Misc. 2d 857, 436 N.Y.S.2d 142 (N.Y. Sup. Ct. 1981)(accusations that attorney's conduct was analogous to champerty, which is a crime); Rinaldi v. Holt, Rinehart & Winston, Inc., 42 N.Y.2d 369, 397 N.Y.S.2d 943, 366 N.E.2d 1299, *cert. denied*, 434 U.S. 969 (1977); Cushman v. Day, 43 Or. App. 123, 602 P.2d 327 (1979).

[304] Leader v. WSM, Inc., 10 Med. L. Rep. (BNA) 1343 (Tenn. Cir. 1984).

[305] Stuart v. Gambling Times, 534 F. Supp. 170 (D.N.J. 1982).

[306] Shiver v. Apalachee Pub. Co., 425 So. 2d 1173 (Fla. Dist. Ct. App. 1983).

[307] Anton v. St. Louis Suburban Newspapers, 598 S.W.2d 493 (Mo. App. 1980).

[10] Abusive Language, Name-Calling, Ridicule, and Jest

Name calling, epithets, and abusive language, no matter how vulgar or offensive, are not actionable.[308] To be called a "stupid son of a bitch,"[309] a "bleached blond bastard,"[310] a "fucker,"[311] or "nothing but a Lee Harvey Oswald and a Jack Ruby"[312] gives rise to no cause of action. Sometimes these decisions are reached on the ground that such accusations are opinion, but more commonly they are simply disposed of on the ground that mere epithets are not considered to carry a defamatory meaning.[313]

Similarly, it is well established that the context of the language as part of a parody, satire, ridicule, or jest will be a factor against finding the language actionable.[314] Again, these holdings can be cast under the rubric of the "opinion" rationale, or on the grounds that the language lacks defamatory meaning.

---

308 *See, e.g.*, Beauharnais v. Pittsburg Courier Pub. Co., 243 F.2d 705 (7th Cir. 1957); Klahr v. Winterble, 4 Ariz. App. 158, 418 P.2d 404 (1966); Good Government Group of Seal Beach, Inc. v. Superior Court of Los Angeles County, 22 Cal. 3d 672, 150 Cal. Rptr. 258, 586 P.2d 572 (1978), *cert. denied sub nom.* Good Government Group of Seal Beach, Inc. v. Hogard, 441 U.S. 961 (1979); Gregory v. McDonnell Douglas Corp., 17 Cal. 3d 596, 131 Cal. Rptr. 641, 552 P.2d 425 (1976); Moriarty v. Lippe, 162 Conn. 371, 294 A.2d 326 (1972); Delis v. Sepsis, 9 Ill. App. 3d 217, 202 N.E.2d 138 (1972); Stanley v. Taylor, 4 Ill. App. 3d 98, 278 N.E.2d 824, *cert. denied*, 409 U.S. 983 (1972); Notarmuzzi v. Shevack, 108 N.Y.S.2d 172 (1951).

309 Moriarty v. Lippe, 162 Conn. 371, 294 A.2d 326 (1972).

310 Notarmuzzi v. Shevack, 108 N.Y.S.2d 172 (1951).

311 Spence v. Washington Post Co., 8 Med. L. Rep. (BNA) 296 (D.C. Sup. Ct. 1982).

312 Stanley v. Taylor, 4 Ill. App. 3d 98, 278 N.E.2d 824, *cert. denied*, 409 U.S. 983 (1972).

313 *See supra* § 4.03.

314 *See, e.g.*, Blake v. Hearst Publishers, Inc., 75 Cal. App. 2d 100 (1946); Cherry v. Des Moines Leader, 114 Iowa 298, 86 N.W. 323 (1901); Myers v. Boston Magazine Co., 380 Mass. 336, 403 N.E.2d 376 (1980); Lamberti v. Sun Printing & Pub. Ass'n, 111 App. Div. 437, 97 N.Y.S. 694 (1906).

CHAPTER 7

Special Harm—
Libel and Slander Per Se Rules

§ 7.01 An Overview of Special Harm

The distinction between libel and slander[1] retains contemporary significance in only one respect: as an element in the classification system utilized to determine when a plaintiff must allege and prove the existence of "special damages" or "special harm."[2] Special harm need not be established in defamation cases classified as "libel per se" or "slander per se." Special harm must be established in defamation cases classified as "libel per quod" or "slander per quod."

This ostensibly simple classification system, however, has gone through so many bizarre twists and turns over the last two centuries that the entire area is now a baffling maze of terms with double meanings, variations upon variations, and multiple lines of precedent. To minimize the confusion, it is important to define terms precisely; for, more than any other area in the law of defamation, the variety of state rules governing special damages is as much the product of imprecision in the use of terminology as it is any coherent logical plan.

§ 7.02 Special Harm, Actual Harm, and Presumed Harm

[1] Special Harm

The term "special harm" (or its synonym, "special damage") is a narrow term of art in the law of defamation that refers to "the loss of something having economic or pecuniary value."[3] Special harm requires an " 'actual temporal loss,' " a loss that is " 'pecuniary' or 'capable of being estimated in money.' "[4] Special harm is a smaller *subset* of a much broader term of art, "actual harm."

---

1 *See Chapter 1*, §1.04, *supra*.

2 Throughout this text the term "special harm" is employed, following the usage of the Restatement (Second) of Torts: *See id.*, § 569 (1977).

3 Restatement (Second) of Torts § 575 comment b (1977).

4 L. Eldredge, The Law of Defamation § 16, at 92 (1978) (quoting Gatley, Libel and Slander § 203 (7th ed. 1974).

[2] Actual Harm

Actual harm is an extremely broad term used in the law of defamation to define any form of harm, pecuniary or nonpecuniary, that is established through some form of evidence. In *Gertz v. Robert Welch, Inc.*,[5] the Supreme Court held that in cases subject to the *Gertz* holding, plaintiffs who do not establish actual malice are restricted "to compensation for actual injury."[6] The Court made it clear, however, that "actual injury" is "not limited to out-of-pocket loss" but includes "impairment of reputation and standing in the community, personal humiliation, and mental anguish and suffering."[7] The *Gertz* actual injury requirement "must be supported by competent evidence concerning the injury, although there need be no evidence which assigns an actual dollar value to the injury."[8] This stands in contrast with the narrower concept of special harm, for which a "dollar value" always exists.[9]

[3] Presumed Harm

The term "presumed harm" (or "presumed damage") refers to a procedural device that permits a jury to return a damages award without any proof whatsoever of injury or damage.[10] Actual damages, on the other hand, must be supported by evidence of injury, but the injury need not be pecuniary loss. Thus, mere evidence (including the plaintiff's testimony alone) of personal humiliation or anguish may suffice as actual harm.[11]

[4] The Significance of the Distinctions

Special harm, therefore, is a subset of the larger set of actual harm. The practical importance of the distinction between actual and special harm lies in the fact that some proof of actual harm is almost always

---

[5] 418 U.S. 323 (1974).

[6] *Id.* at 349.

[7] *Id.*

[8] *Id.*

[9] Eldredge, *supra* note 4, § 16, at 92.

[10] *See generally* Anderson, *Reputation, Compensation, and Proof*, 25 Wm. & Mary L. Rev. 747 (1984); McCormick, *The Measure of Damages for Defamation*, 12 N.C. L. Rev. 120, 127 (1934) ("The plaintiff is relieved from the necessity of producing any proof whatsoever that he had been injured.").

[11] *See* Time, Inc. v. Firestone, 424 U.S. 448 (1976).

possible to muster—if nothing else, the plaintiff himself can testify. But special harm, i.e., some actual pecuniary loss arising from the defamation, will not always exist. It is possible, therefore, to "control the gates" to defamation by using the requirement of "special harm" as the gatekeeper. Because many plaintiffs will not be able to point to any palpable pecuniary loss, they are likely to find the requirement of special harm an impediment impossible to overcome. Unfortunately, the rules that evolved for determining when special harm would be required were more the product of arbitrary developments than any coherent set of logical principles. Before turning to the common law classification system, however, it is worth summarizing the extent to which constitutional damages rules affect this area.

§ 7.03 Constitutional Minimums Set by *Gertz* and *Dun & Bradstreet*

[1] The Constitution Does Not Require Special Harm

To avoid confusion in this area it is best to emphasize what the Constitution does *not* require rather than what it does. No Supreme Court opinion has ever required special harm in any defamation case. When special harm is mandated in a case it is purely a requirement of state law. As far as the first amendment is concerned, a state is free to abolish special harm requirements entirely if it wishes, wiping the concept from the face of its law of defamation.

[2] The Constitutional Issues When State Law Does Not Require Special Harm

The traditional common law position put the plaintiff in a sort of all or nothing game with regard to proof of injury: Either special harm was required, in which case the plaintiff was faced with the harsh task of demonstrating pecuniary loss, or damages were presumed, in which case the plaintiff had no burden whatsoever regarding evidence of injury.

In combination, *Gertz* [12] and *Dun & Bradstreet* [13] now set a series of different "floors" for damages in cases in which states do not require

[12] Gertz v. Robert Welch, Inc., 418 U.S. 323 (1974).

[13] Dun & Bradstreet, Inc. v. Greenmoss Builders, Inc., 105 S. Ct. 2939 (1985).

special harm.[14] In a nutshell, the rules are:

(1) Presumed harm is constitutionally permitted in private figure cases not involving speech implicating matters of public concern.[15]

(2) Presumed harm is constitutionally permitted in *any* case in which actual malice is established.[16] (And actual malice must always, of course, be established in public official and public figure cases.)[17]

(3) In private figure cases involving speech implicating issues of "public concern," presumed harm is prohibited, and actual harm (but *not* special harm) is the constitutional minimum.[18]

§ 7.04 The Original Common Law Position

The original common law position was that all libels were actionable without proof of special harm.[19] This rule, which has persisted in many American jurisdictions throughout this century,[20] and which still claims many adherents, including the First[21] and Second[22] *Restatements*, recognized no subdivision at all among libels; all libels were actionable without special harm, and thus all were properly denominated "libel per se." Libels received this preferred treatment on the view that as a class they were more likely to be harmful than were slanders, and thus should never be encumbered by special harm requirements to be actionable.[23]

---

14 These issues are discussed in greater detail in Chapter 9, on damages.

15 Dun & Bradstreet, Inc. v. Greenmoss Builders, Inc., 105 S. Ct. 2939 (1985).

16 Gertz v. Robert Welch, Inc., 418 U.S. 323, 349-50 (1974).

17 *See supra* § 3.05.

18 Gertz v. Robert Welch, Inc., 418 U.S. 323, 349-50 (1974). *See supra* §§ 3.01-3.05.

19 *See* Thorley v. Lord Kerry, 128 Eng. Rep. 367 (1812); Prosser, *Libel Per Quod*, 46 Va. L. Rev. 839, 842 (1960).

20 Approximately ten states continued to treat all libels as actionable without proof of special damages at the time of the adoption of the Restatement (Second) of Torts (1977). *See* Restatement (Second) of Torts at 84-85 (Tent. Draft No. 11). In many of the jurisdictions counted, however, precedent was ambigious, due to confusion in the use of terminology. *Id.* at 85. The jurisdictions so classified were Delaware, Iowa, Minnesota, Mississippi, New Jersey, Texas, Washington, Wisconsin, and Tennessee.

21 Restatement of Torts § 569 (1938).

22 Restatement (Second) of Torts § 569 (1977).

23 *See* M. Franklin & R. Rabin, Tort Law and Alternatives 875 (3d ed. 1983). For modern cases endorsing the position that all libels are actionable without special harm, *see, e.g.*, Newson v. Henry, 443 So. 2d 817 (Miss. 1984); Herrman v. Newark Morning Ledger Co., 48 N.J. Super. 420, 138 A.2d 61 (1958); Hinkle v. Alexander, 244 Or. 267, 417 P.2d 586

Slanders, unlike libels, were subdivided into two categories, those actionable without proof of special harm (per se) and those requiring special harm (per quod). Whether a slander was categorized as per se or per quod was determined soley by the *content of the charges*: slanders were actionable per se *only* if they fell within one of four defined categories: (1) imputations of criminal conduct; (2) allegations injurious to another in his or her trade, business, or profession; (3) imputations of loathsome disease; and (4) imputations of unchastity in a woman.[24]

§ 7.05 The Four Common Law Slander Per Se Categories

[1] A Note on Mechanical Use of the Categories

The four slander per se categories are arbitrary and archaic, reflecting sensibilities that are no longer completely relevant to contemporary values. Nonetheless, because of the crazy quilt of confusion that already surrounds the whole slander and libel per se terminology, courts have tended to follow the four categories mechanically. The retention of the rule concerning unchastity in a woman is particularly outmoded, for example. An allegation that a woman is sexually promiscuous is slanderous per se, but a similar allegation about a man is not. This division is based on sexual stereotypes that probably could not withstand a modern equal protection clause attack.[25] The four categories certainly do not encompass the full range of extremely serious forms of defamation, and they encompass some allegations that many Americans would regard as not serious at all. Nonetheless, until this libel/slander dichotomy is dissolved and the byzantine per se and per quod rules overhauled, courts can be expected to follow the old categories with rigid fidelity.

(1966); Memphis Publishing Co. v. Nichols, 569 S.W.2d 412 (Tenn. 1978); Lent v. Huntoon, 143 Vt. 539, 470 A.2d 1162 (1983); Pitts v. Spokane Chronicle Co., 63 Wash. 2d 763, 388 P.2d 978 (1964); Martin v. Outboard Marine Corp., 15 Wis. 2d 452, 113 N.W.2d 135 (1962).

[24] *See generally* Spelson v. CBS, 11 Med. L. Rep. (BNA) 1900 (7th Cir. 1985); Brown & Williamson Tobacco Corp v. Jacobson, 713 F.2d 262 (7th Cir. 1983); Lamelza v. Bally's Park Place, Inc., 580 F. Supp. 445 (E.D. Pa. 1984); Lowe v. Rockford Newspaper, Inc., 179 Ill. App. 3d 592, 534 N.E.2d 549 (1989); American Pet Motels v. Chicago Veterinary Medical Ass'n, 106 Ill. App. 3d 626, 435 N.E.2d 1297 (1982); Kirk v. Village of Hillcrest, 31 Ill. App. 3d 1063, 1065, 335 N.E.2d 535 (1935); Gnapinsky v. Goldyn, 23 N.J. 243, 128 A.2d 697, 701 (1957); Lent v. Hunton, 143 Vt. 539, 470 A.2d 1162 (1983).

[25] *See* W. Prosser, J. Wade, & V. Schwartz, Cases and Materials on Torts 1015 (7th ed. 1982), (citing Sauerhoff v. Hearst Corp., 588 F. Supp. 117 (D. Md. 1977); Restatement (Second) of Torts § 574 (1977)).

[2] Imputations of Criminal Conduct

[a] In General

The imputation to another of conduct that constitutes a criminal offense is slanderous per se and is traditionally actionable without proof of special damages if the imputed criminal conduct would be punishable by imprisonment or is generally regarded by public opinion as involving moral turpitude.[26] In examining the nature of the offense, its criminality is judged by the law of the place of publication rather than the law of the place of commission.[27] This rule exists because the damage to reputation lies in the statement's effect upon the minds of those who hear the accusation.[28] The focus is on the alleged criminality of the conduct, not the risk of punishment. The accusation is not less actionable when the victim of the accusation is for one reason or another immune from conviction or imprisonment. The fact that the accused has been pardoned, or that the statute of limitations has run, or that he or she has been acquitted and thus cannot be placed again in jeopardy has no bearing on the actionability of the slander.[29] The imputation need not be made in the technical language of the criminal law, and need not even refer to a specific crime.[30] Thus, the statement that "John is a felon" or that "John has served time in the penitentiary" is actionable as slander pe se.[31]

[b] Moral Turpitude

The formula most often used by modern courts to describe slander per se is that the crime must involve moral turpitude.[32] For the most

---

[26] Restatement (Second) of Torts § 571. *See, e.g.*, Sweeney v. Sengstacke Enters., 180 Ill. App. 3d 1044, 536 N.E.2d 823, 825 (1989); Agnew v. Hiatt, 466 N.E.2d 781 (Ind. Ct. App. 1984); Mitchell v. Peoria Journal Star, Inc., 76 Ill. App. 2d 154, 160, 221 N.E.2d 516 (1966); Walker v. Tucker, 220 Ky. 363, 295 S.W. 138 (1927); Stevens v. Wilber, 136 Or. 599, 300 P.2d 329 (1931).

[27] Restatement (Second) of Torts § 571 comments b & e (1977). *See also* Klumph v. Dunn, 66 Pa. 141 (1870).

[28] Restatement (Second) of Torts § 571 comment b (1977).

[29] *Id.*

[30] *See* W. Prosser, W. Keeton, D. Dobbs, R. Keeton, & D. Owen, Prosser and Keeton on Torts § 112, at 790 (1984).

[31] *Id.*

[32] *See, e.g.*, American Pet Motels v. Veterinary Medical Ass'n, 106 Ill. App. 3d 626, 435 N.E. 1297 (1982); Mitchell v. Peoria Journal-Star, Inc., 76 Ill. App. 2d 154, 160, 221 N.E.2d 516 (1966); Walker v. Tucker, 220 Ky. 383, 295 S.W. 138 (1927).

part this additional category is duplicative of the imprisonment category, since most crimes involving moral turpitude—treason, espionage, murder, rape, burglary, larceny, arson, kidnapping, bribery, perjury, for example—also are punishable by imprisonment. A few crimes, however, may involve moral turpitude even though in the particular jurisdiction in which the accusation is published the criminal would not be subject to either state or federal imprisonment for the crime. Indecent exposure and the uttering of a bad check, for example, might be regarded as crimes of moral turpitude by the general public even though they might not be punishable by imprisonment. The test is whether public opinion in the place of publication would treat the crime as one involving moral turpitude as that term has traditionally been defined by the common law: an offense involving so extreme a deviation from recognized standards of honesty, good morals, justice, or ethics that it can be characterized as "shocking to the moral sense of the community"[33]

[3] Allegations Tending to Injure Another in His or Her Trade, Business, Profession, or Office

[a] In General

The imputation of conduct tending to injure another in his or her trade, business, profession, or office is slanderous per se and is actionable without proof of special damages.[34] This is the broadest and most important of the traditional four slander per se categories. An attorney should be careful in applying this category, for its very breadth frequently places it in potential conflict with the rule that statements of opinion, as opposed to mistatements of fact, are not actionable.[35] Similarly, the common law rule includes allegations imputing incompetence to an official in public office, allegations that may in some circumstances be absolutely privileged under emerging first amendment principles.[36]

---

33 Restatement (Second) of Torts § 571 comment g (1977).

34 *See* Brown & Williamson Tobacco Corp. v. Jacobson, 713 F.2d 262 (7th Cir. 1983); Thompson v. Bridges, 209 Ky. 710, 273 S.E. 529 (1925); Louisville Taxicab & Transfer Co. v. Ingle, 229 Ky. 578, 17 S.W.2d 709 (1929); Calwell v. Crowell-Collier Publishing Co., 161 F.2d 333 (5th Cir. 1947); Foley v. Hoffman, 188 Md. 273, 52 A.2d 476 (1947); Nolan v. Standard Publishing Co., 67 Mont. 212, 216 P. 571 (1923); Dietrich v. Hauser, 45 Misc. 2d 805, 257 N.Y.S.2d 716 (1965); Walter v. Duncan, 15 N.Y.S.2d 916 (Sup. Ct. 1956).

35 *See supra* §§ 6.17 and 6.24.

36 *See supra* § 2.01.

[b] The Nexus Requirements

Two important principles define this slander per se category. First, the accusation need not involve an element of dishonesty, moral failing, or other culpable evil to be actionable; it is enough for the accusation to impugn the skill or competence of another, as long as the accusation would adversely affect that person's fitness for his or her trade, business, profession, or office.[37] Second, there must be a nexus between the defamatory statement and the competence, performance, or fitness for the business, trade, profession, or office. The disparagement must be more than general defamation of the victim's character, it must go to a characteristic peculiarly relevant to the victim's occupation.[38] To say that a fiction writer is a habitual drunk, for example, is not slander per se (though it could be libel per se if written), because alcoholism is not generally thought to be a character trait that impugns one's ability to carry on the profession of fiction writing.[39] To make the same statement about a surgeon, however, would be slander per se.[40] Similarly, to say that a surgeon frequently consorts with prostitutes is not slander per se; but to make the same statement of a Roman Catholic Bishop is.[41]

[4] Imputations of Loathsome Disease

The common law rule is that an imputation of loathsome disease is slanderous per se and actionable without proof of special damages.[42] There are very few American cases applying this category. The diseases considered loathsome have tended to be limited to venereal diseases such as syphilis or gonorrhea, and leprosy.[43] The inclusion of venereal disease arguably makes some sense, since it would normally carry an

---

[37] *See generally* Restatement (Second) of Torts § 573 comment c, at 193 (1977); Prosser and Keeton, *supra* note 25, § 112, at 791.

[38] *See* Liebel v. Montgomery Ward & Co., 103 Mont. 370, 62 P.2d 667 (1936); Hudson v. Pioneer Service Co., 218 Or. 561, 346 P.2d 123 (1959); Restatement (Second) of Torts § 573 comment e (1977); Prosser & Keeton, *supra* note 25, § 112, at 791-92.

[39] Prosser & Keeton, *supra* note 25, § 112, at 792 ("The effect of a charge that the plaintiff is insolvent, illiterate, a coward or had been seen drunk, may depend upon whether he is a merchant, a professor, a soldier, or a clergyman."].

[40] *See* Amick v. Montross, 206 Iowa 51, 220 N.W. 51 (1928) ("Dr. Amick was drunk the night the Goodman baby was born and that was the reason another doctor was called").

[41] *See* Cobbs v. Chicago Defender, 308 Ill. App. 55, 31 N.E.2d 323 (1941).

[42] Eldredge, *supra* note 4, § 20, at 109 (describing the rule as "ancient law"); Prosser & Keeton, *supra* note 25, § 112, at 790.

[43] Restatement (Second) § 572 comment b (1977); Eldredge, *supra* note 4, § 20, at 109.

indirect imputation of sexual misconduct. The inclusion of leprosy, however, merely reflects a sort of dark ages social prejudice that is no longer reflective of our cultural sensibilities. Some broader statements of the rule would treat as slanderous per se any disease that society might consider particularly contagious or repugnant, such as would normally cause a person to be excluded from society.[44] The modern American paranoia over AIDS, for example, would presumably qualify that disease as "loathsome." Courts have generally not been willing, however, to extend the list, particularly when the imputed disease is a mental one. The law of defamation would probably do well to abandon this category entirely; it is an anachronism, a remnant of a period in English history when the sick were shunned.

[5] Imputations of Unchastity

The traditional common law position is that the imputation of unchastity in a woman is slander per se and is actionable without proof of special damages.[45] It does not matter under the traditional rule whether the conduct is criminal.[46] The woman, under the orthodox view, may be married or unmarried;[47] and "unchaste" conduct includes fornication and adultery.[48] Two strong objections can be made to the modern adherence to this rule. The first is that many forms of sexual activity once regarded as particularly egregious are today thought of in many quarters as not justifying special legal condemnation.

The more substantial objection to this category of slander per se is that it is quite blatantly sexist and discriminatory, and is based on outmoded assumptions about sexual behavior. Sex-based classifications very similar to the "unchastity of a woman" rule have been struck down by the United States Supreme Court as violative of the equal protection clause.[49] The traditional rule clearly appears unconstitutional. An alle-

---

[44] *See* Brown & Williamson Tobacco Corp. v. Jacobson, 713 F.2d 262 (7th Cir. 1983)("a communicable disease which would exclude one from society").

[45] *See* Hollman v. Brady, 233 F.2d 877 (9th Cir. 1956); Biggerstaff v. Zimmerman, 108 Colo. 194, 114 P.2d 1098 (1941); Gnapinsky v. Goldyn, 23 N.J. 243, 128 A.2d 697 (1957); Crellin v. Thomas, 122 Utah 122, 247 P.2d 264 (1952).

[46] Restatement [Second) of Torts § 547 comment b (1977).

[47] *Id.*

[48] Illinois, for example, has dropped the chastity category. *See* Brown & William Tobacco Corp. v. Jacobson, 713 F.2d 262 (7th Cir. 1983).

[49] *See, e.g.*, Mississippi University for Women v. Hogan, 458 U.S. 718 (1982); Craig v. Boren, 429 U.S. 190 (1976); Frontiero v. Richardson, 411 U.S. 677 (1973).

gation of unchastity is either sufficient to be slanderous per se for both men and women, or for neither.[50] The *Restatement (Second)* takes a laudable lead in this area, modifying the traditional rule to a sex-neutral standard that renders any imputation of "sexual misconduct" by a man or woman slanderous per se.[51] States should either apply the sex-neutral rule or discard this category entirely.

§ 7.06 The Introduction of Libel Per Quod

[1] Overview

Professor Dan Dobbs has put it nicely: "it apparently occurred to someone that if there were cases of slander per se, there must be cases of libel per se, and if cases of libel per se, then cases in which libel was something else."[52] Gradually, an increasing number of states began to subdivide the once unified class of libels into those libels actionable without special damage (per se) and those requiring special damage (per quod).

But rather than accomplish this objective through the relatively simple device of importing the four slander per se categories into the libel area, the common law, with an almost perverse ingenuity, hit upon an entirely different classification device for libels, a device that hinged on an entirely different meaning for the phrase "per se."

[2] The Use of "Per Se"

A second, entirely different use of the term "per se" refers to defamation whose defamatory meaning is apparent on the face of the communication, or in other words, defamation whose defamatory character can be established without the introduction of extrinsic evidence. Thus, when used in this sense, the statement that "Mary, John's wife, had

---

[50] *See* Prosser, Wade, & Schwartz, *supra* note 25, at 1014-15 ("Recent holdings on the constitutional requirements of equality of treatment between the sexes, while not specifically applicable to this problem, may affect the holding that an imputation of unchastity for a woman is slanderous per se while a similar imputation for a man is not. If the Constitution is held to require that they [must] be treated similarly, there is no indication as to which of the two applicants will be changed." (citing Restatement (Second) of Torts § 574 (1977); Sauerhoff v. Hearst Corp. 388 F. Supp. 117 (D. Md. 1974)).

[51] Restatement (Second) of Torts § 574 (1977). *Cf.* Nowark v. Maquire, 22 A.D.2d 901, 255 N.Y.S.2d 318 (1964) (homosexual conduct); Buck v. Savage, 323 S.W.2d 363 (Tex. Civ. App. 1959)(same).

[52] D. Dobbs, Dobbs on Remedies § 7.2, at 512 (1973).

sexual intercourse with Frank" would be actionable "per se," whereas the statement "Mary had sexual intercourse with Frank" would not be actionable "per se," because proof of the extrinsic fact that Mary is married to John and not Frank would be necessary to establish the defamatory meaning.

[3] The Emergence of Libel Per Quod

A number of jurisdictions have over the years confused the original meaning of the term "per se," which was really significant only for slander and referred only to the four categories, with the secondary meaning of "per se," in the sense of the statement being understood as defamatory without resort to extrinsic fact.[53] Those jurisdictions no longer exempt all libels from the special damages requirement. Instead, for those libels that require proof of extrinsic facts to establish their defamatory meaning, the plaintiff must establish special harm.[54] Libels that require extrinsic facts (and thus special harm) are labeled libel per quod. In these states, the classification system for libel is totally different from the one for slander. The libel classification is based on the "apparent on its face" versus "extrinsic fact" division, while the slander classification is based on the four categories. In sum, these jurisdictions have the following rules:

---

53 This development provoked one of the great (and at times, caustic) academic debates in the history of the law of defamation, between William Prosser and Laurence Eldredge. *See* Prosser, *Libel Per Quod*, 46 Va. L. Rev. 839 (1960); Eldredge, *The Spurious Rule of Libel Per Quod*, 79 Harv. L. Rev. 733 (1966); Prosser, *More Libel Per Quod*, 79 Harv. L. Rev. 1629 (1966); Eldredge, *Variation on Libel Per Quod*, 25 Vand. L. Rev. 79 (1972). The debate may well have overlooked the most significant issue of all: the essential illogic of the whole common law approach to special harm. *See* Anderson, *supra* note 10, at 750-51; Murnaghan, *From Figment to Fiction to Philosophy—The Requirement of Proof of Damages in Libel Actions*, 22 Cath. U. L. Rev. 1, 27 (1972).

54 *See, e.g.*, Brayton v. Crowell-Collier Publishing Co., 205 F.2d 644 (2d Cir. 1953); Peagler v. Phoenix Newspapers, Inc., 114 Ariz. 309, 560 P.2d 1223 (1977); Ilitzky v. Goodman, 57 Ariz. 216, 112 P.2d 860 (1941); Karrigan v. Valentine, 184 Kan. 783, 339 P.2d 52 (1959); Campbell v. Post Publishing Co., 94 Mont. 12, 20 P.2d 1063 (1933); Ellsworth v. Martindale-Hubbell Law Directory, 66 N.D. 578, 268 N.W. 400 (1936); Waite v. Stockgrowers Credit Corp., 63 N.D. 763, 249 N.W. 910 (1933); J.V. Peters & Co. v. Knight Ridder Co., 10 Med. L. Rep. (BNA) 1576 (Ohio Ct. App. 1984); Shifflet v. Thompson Newspapers, Inc., 69 Ohio St. 2d 179, 431 N.E.2d 1014 (1982).

[a] Libel Per Se

Libels whose defamatory meanings are apparent on their face do not require special damages. These are libels "per se." A libel can be "per se" even if it falls outside of the four categories, because the four categories are not used for libel.

[b] Libel Per Quod

Libels that require proof of extrinsic facts also require proof of special harm. These are libels "per quod." A libel that falls within one of the four special categories is still only libel per quod, because the special categories are not used for libel.

[c] Slander Per Se

Slanders that fall into the four categories are "per se," and special damages are not required. The extrinsic fact issue is not used for slander.

[d] Slander Per Quod

Slanders that do not fit into the four categories are "per quod," and special damages are required. The extrinsic fact issue is irrelevant.

§ 7.07 Hybrids of the Per Se/Per Quod Distinction

[1] Classification System for Both Libel and Slander

Some jurisdictions pay no attention to the extrinsic fact requirement, but also do not make all libels actionable. Instead, they use the four traditional categories for libel per se for both libel and slander. Virginia is the clearest example of this approach.[55] Illinois also is arguably in this camp—the Illinois courts quite clearly state that "Illinois has abolished the distinction between slander and libel and in the process has assimilated libel per se to the quite different concept of slander per se,

---

[55] Virginia, for example, recognizes no distinction between libel and slander; in Virginia all special harm issues are resolved by use of the four traditional slander categories—libel per se and slander per se must fit into one of the four categories, and all other libels and slanders are per quod and require special harm. *See* Fleming v. Moore, 221 Va. 884, 889, 275 S.E.2d 632, 635 (1981); Carwile v. Richmond Newspapers, 196 Va. 1, 7, 82 S.E.2d 588, 591 (1954).

rather than vice versa."[56] The Illinois picture is complicated, however, by its unique adherence to the "innocent construction rule,"[57] which results in suggestions in some cases that to be "per se" the defamation must *both* fit into one of the slander categories *and* be clear without resort to extrinsic facts.[58]

[2] Combining the Approaches

Some jurisdictions have combined the original common law and newer positions, by retaining the extrinsic fact system for libel while transferring the use of the four categories for slander to libel also. Special damages are normally required for libel when the defamatory meaning is not apparent on its face, but if the libel requiring extrinsic facts happens to fit into one of the four traditional categories for slander, no special damages are required.[59]

[3] Requirement of Fault Regarding Extrinsic Facts

Another variation renders the defendant liable for communications that require reference to extrinsic facts to disclose their defamatory meaning only if the defendant knew or should have known of these extrinsic facts.[60]

[4] Multiple Lines of Precedent

Finally, some jurisdictions waver between different approaches, at times appearing to require special damages when proof of extrinsic facts is necessary, and at times appearing to adhere to the common law rule that rendered all libels actionable without special damages.[61] Fur-

---

56 Brown & Williamson Tobacco Corp. v. Jacobson, 713 F.2d 262 (7th Cir. 1983); American Pet Motels, Inc. v. Chicago Veterinary Medical Ass'n, 106 Ill. App. 3d 626, 629 and n.1, 435 N.E.2d 1297, 1300 and n.1 (1982); Gragavoy v. Wilson, 87 Ill. App. 2d 193, 202, 230 N.E.2d 581, 585 (1967); Mitchell v. Peoria Journal-Star, Inc., 76 Ill. App. 2d 154, 158-60, 221 N.E.2d 516, 519-20 (1966).

57 *See* Smolla and Malone, *The Future of Defamation in Illinois After* Colsen v. Stieg *and* Chapski v. Copley Press, Inc., 32 De Paul L. Rev. 219, 274-96 (1983). *See also supra* § 4.06[2].

58 *See* Makis v. Area Publications Corp., 77 Ill. App. 3d 452, 395 N.E.2d 1185 (1979).

59 *See* R. Sack, *Libel, Slander, and Related Problems* § 11.7.3., at 98 (1980).

60 *See* Marchiondo v. New Mexico State Tribune Co., 98 N.M. 282, 648 P.2d 321 (Ct. App. 1981), *cert. quashed*, 98 N.M. 336, 648 P.2d 794 (1982).

61 The law in New York is in exceptional disarray. *See* Mullenmeister v. Snap-On Tools, Inc., 587 F. Supp. 868 (S.D.N.Y. 1984); Rinaldi v. Holt, Rhinehart & Winston, Inc., 42

ther, some jurisdictions appear to apply the per se/per quod dichotomy, not to the question of whether extrinsic facts are necessary to establish defamatory meaning, but to whether the statement is capable of both a defamatory and a nondefamatory construction—if it is, special harm must be established.[62]

§ 7.08 A Proposal for a Simplified, Fair Reform

The common law special harm rules were illogical enough when they were originally created. When the many historical variations and complicated first amendment rules that now must be superimposed upon them are added in, the result is a quagmire of archiac, arbitrary, internally inconsistent rules. The chaos that now exists under this regime does neither plaintiffs nor defendants any long term good. Some of the most serious and damaging defamatory statements are treated as requiring proof of special damages, artificially penalizing deserving plaintiffs. Some defamatory statements that are relatively innocuous to the modern ear, however, receive the hallowed status of being actionable per se. Courts constantly misuse the terminology, confusing concepts and precedent, precisely because they bear no connection to everyday thought, common sense, or any coherent legal policies. The only certainty in the confusion is that cases too often turn on the very sort of hypertechnical distinctions that have given the law of defamation a bad

N.Y.2d 369, 397 N.Y.S.2d 943, 366 N.E.2d 1299, *cert. denied*, 434 U.S. 969 (1977); Hinsdale v. Orange County Publications, Inc., 17 N.Y.2d 284, 270 N.Y.S.2d 592, 217 N.E.2d 650 (1966); Sydney v. MacFadden Publishing Co., 242 N.Y. 208, 151 N.E. 209 (1926); O'Connell v. Press Publishing Co., 214 N.Y. 352, 108 N.E. 556 (1915). After an exhaustive and excellent analysis of the confusing precedent, Robert Sack has concluded that the "best guess" is that New York follows the libel per se/per quod dichotomy, requiring special harm for libels in which the defamatory meaning must be established with extrinsic facts. Sack, *supra* note 59, § 11.7.6.4 at 104-109. Robert Sack's esteem in the field is such that the New York Court of Appeals might very well treat his analysis as dispositive when it ultimately seeks to clarify the issue.

[62] *See, e.g.*, Dietrich v. Pulitizer Publishing Co., 422 S.W.2d 330 (Mo. 1968); Langworthy v. Pulitizer Publishing Co., 368 S.W.2d 385 (Mo. 1963); Renwick v. News & Observer Publishing Co., 310 N.C. 312, 312 S.E.2d 405 (1984); Arnold v. Sharpe, 296 N.C. 533, 251 S.E.2d 452 (1979); McLean v. Nichter, 42 N.C. App. 184, 256 S.E.2d 261 (1979); Gallagher v. Johnson, 611 P.2d 613 (1980); Sellars v. Oklahoma Publishing Co., 687 P.2d 116 (Okla. 1984); Akins v. Altus Newspapers, Inc., 609 P.2d 1263 (Okla.), *cert. denied*, 101 S. Ct. 564 (1980); Winters v. Morgan, 576 P.2d 1152 (Okla. 1978).

name, inviting exploitation by both sides.[63] The following reforms, which might be implemented either by statute or judicial decision, would make this area of the law of defamation extremely straightforward, without tilting the balance toward either plaintiffs or defendants. A simplified reformed system would include the following elements:

[1] Abolish Libel/Slander Distinction

The distinction between libel and slander should be abolished. One action, for "defamation," should exist.

[2] Eliminate All Special Harm Rules

Special harm (pecuniary loss) should never be required in any case. Special harm has always been a crude and clumsy screening device for separating deserving from undeserving plaintiffs. It is as if the special harm rules have popped up like wild cards. Fault requirements, the existence of defamatory meaning, the fact/opinion distinction, and the various common law privileges are, in the aggregate, well equipped to perform all screening functions.

[3] Require Actual Harm in All Cases

Actual damages (proof of actual "injury," which need not be pecuniary) should be required in all cases. If there was ever any hope that this would become an across-the-board requirement as a matter of constitutional law, that hope was dashed by the Supreme Court's decision in *Dun & Bradstreet*[64] permitting presumed damages in private figure cases not involving matters of public concern. The reform might still be imposed as a matter of state law, however.

[4] Permit Jury to Weigh All Factors

In assessing damages, juries should be instructed to take into account the full range of factors that were traditionally embraced by the arbitrary common law rules. Thus in judging the extent of damage caused,

---

[63] *See* Smolla, *Let the Author Beware: The Rejuvenation of the American Law of Libel*, 132 U. Pa. L. Rev. 1, 63 (1983)("The law of defamation should be streamlined, simplified, stripped of internal contradictions, and generally made more coherent.").

[64] Dun & Bradstreet, Inc. v. Greenmoss Builders, Inc., 105 S. Ct. 2939 (1985). *See supra* § 3.02.

the jury may consider the seriousness of the defamatory communication, or the fact that its meaning was not obvious on its face, or any other relevant factors.

This system is eminently simple, for it does away completely with the strange and dimly understood vocabulary of libel and slander per se and per quod. At the same time it preserves the essential screening purposes that were so crudely and arbitrarily captured by the common law system, by allowing juries to consider all the relevant factors as part of the damages calculus.

CHAPTER 8

Common Law Privileges

§ 8.01 Introduction

[1] The Function of Common Law Privileges

Long before the decision in *New York Times Co. v. Sullivan*[1] sparked the modern era of constitutional privileges in defamation actions, the common law had evolved its own set of safety valves immunizing defendants from liability for what would otherwise have been actionable defamation. Common law privileges grew out of a recognition that in certain circumstances the social interest in the free flow of information is so important that allowance for mistakes must be made, even at the expense of leaving the victims of defamatory speech remediless.[2]

[2] The Division Between Absolute and Conditional Privileges

In weighing the trade-offs between protection of reputation and the encouragement of free expression the common law has always been sensitive to the relative importance of the speech involved. In a few narrowly defined situations the public interest in the information at issue is deemed so vital that the privilege is absolute. In a true absolute privilege situation, liability is totally foreclosed without regard to the fault or mental state of the defendant.[3] With the exception of the abso-

---

[1] 376 U.S. 254 (1964). *See supra* §2.01.

[2] *See* W. Prosser, W. Keeton, D. Dobbs, R. Keeton, & D. Owen, Prosser and Keeton on Torts § 114, at 815 (5th ed. 1984).

[3] *See, e.g.*, Boston Mutual Life Ins. Co. v. Varone, 303 F.2d 155 (1st Cir. 1962); Read v. News-Journal Co., 474 A.2d 662 (Del. 1984); Shafer v. Lamar Publishing Co., 621 S.W.2d 709 (Mo. App. 1981); Restatement (Second) of Torts § 611 comment b (1977).

lute privilege for consent,[4] which is grounded in its own special policy rationale, the common law absolute privileges tend to be limited to speech concerning certain defined governmental proceedings. The absolute privileges exist because of the paramount public interest in obtaining information about official actions,[5] and because of the need to encourage participants in governmental proceedings to speak freely without fear of vexatious reprisals in the form of defamation suits.[6]

"Conditional" or "qualified" privileges, on the other hand, involve speech deserving of some enhanced protection, but not the complete immunity that accompanies absolute privileges. Common law conditional privileges do not attach to certain speakers or forums but are triggered by particular "occasions" or "contexts" in which the speech is published, governed by the interrelationships between the speaker, the listener, the victim, and the content of the speech.[7] The protection of a conditional privilege is forfeited if the privilege is "abused," which may, depending on the jurisdiction, mean that the defamation was published with "common law (ill-will) malice," or "actual malice" (knowing or reckless disregard of the truth), or published beyond the scope of those who were legitimately entitled to receive it, or published with simple negligence.[8]

[3] The "Fair Report" Privilege

A special common law privilege, analogous to the emerging privilege of neutral reportage previously discussed,[9] permits the press (and in some formulations, any person[10]) to republish "fair and accurate reports" of certain defined judicial, legislative, or executive proceedings.[11] Like its neutral reportage counterpart, the fair report privilege

---

4 *See infra* § 8.10.

5 *See generally* Medico v. Time, Inc., 643 F.2d 134 (3d Cir.), *cert. denied*, 454 U.S. 836 (1981).

6 *See* L. Eldredge, The Law of Defamation § 72, at 340 (1978) (quoting Munster v. Lamb, 11 Q.R.D. 588, 607 (C.A. 1883)).

7 *See* Smolla, *Let the Author Beware: The Rejuvenation of the American Law of Libel*, 132 U. Pa. L. Rev. 1, 64-65 (1983); Restatement (Second) of Torts §§ 593-598A (1977).

8 *See infra* § 8.09.

9 *See supra* § 4.15.

10 *See* Restatement (Second) of Torts § 611 comment c (1977); Okla. Stat. tit. 12, § 1443 (1971).

11 *See, e.g.*, Cal. Civ. Code § 47 (West 1954); Ga. Code Ann. § 105-704 (1978); N.Y. Civil Rights Law § 74 (McKinney 1976); Ohio Rev. Code Ann. § 2317.04 (Page 1953); Wis. Stat. § 895.05 (1975); Medico v. Time, Inc., 643 F.2d 1134 (3d Cir.), *cert. denied*, 454 U.S. 836 (1981); Restatement (Second) of Torts § 611 (1977).

is an exception to the normal common law rule rendering a speaker liable for republication of another's defamatory statement.[12]

Some jurisdictions treat the fair reports privilege essentially as a form of qualified privilege, employing the rule, for example, that the privilege is lost if the defamatory statement is made with "malice."[13] Other states treat it as a form of absolute privilege, insulating the defendant from liability without regard to fault or state of mind.[14]

§ 8.02 The Absolute Privilege of Consent

The maxim *volenti non fit injuria*—to one who is willing, no wrong is done—expresses one of the fundamental principles of the common law of torts.[15] Consistent with this general principle, the plaintiff's consent to the publication of defamatory matter about him is a complete defense to his action for defamation.[16] The consent may be actual or constructive.[17] The "extent of the privilege is determined by the terms of the consent.[18] One of the more typical modern consent situations involves the plaintiff's instigation of or participation in investigations, hearings, or other proceedings in which findings, results, or commentary will be published; defamation arising from such publication will usually be absolutely privileged because of the plaintiff's consent[19] (or,

---

12 *See supra* §§ 4.14-4.15

13 *See, e.g.*, Pearce v, Courier-Journal & Louisville Times Co., 683 S.W.2d 633 (Ky. Ct. App. 1985); Molnar v. Star-Ledger Co., 193 N.J. Super. 12, 471 A.2d 1209 (1984). States differ as to whether the malice needed to defeat the fair report privilege must be "actual malice" or common law "ill-will malice." *See infra* § 8.10.

14 *See, e.g.*, Read v. News-Journal Co., 474 A.2d 662 (Del. 1984); Restatement (Second) of Torts § 611 (1977). *See infra* § 8.10.

15 *See generally* Prosser & Keeton, *supra* note 2, § 18, at 112; Restatement (Second) of Torts § 892 (1977).

16 *See, e.g.*, Walters v. Linhof, 559 F. Supp. 1231 (D. Colo. 1983); Costa v. Smith, 601 P.2d 661 (Colo. App. 1979); Ling v. Whittemore, 140 Colo. 247, 343 P.2d 1048, 1049 (1959); Taylor v. McDaniels, 139 Okla. 262, 281 P. 967 (1929); Lee v. Paulsen, 273 Or. 103, 539 P.2d 1079 (1975); Restatement (Second) of Torts § 583 (1977).

17 *See* Walters v. Linhof, 559 F. Supp. 1231 (D. Colo. 1983).

18 Restatement (Second) of Torts § 583 comment d, at 240 (1977).

19 *See, e.g.*, Walters v. Linhof, 559 F. Supp. 1231 (D. Colo. 1983) (constructive consent found when plaintiffs were proponents in a rezoning proceeding); Merritt v. Detroit Memorial Hosp., 81 Mich. App. 279, 265 N.W.2d 124 (1978) (consent found in employee's statement as to why he was disharged by former employer when former employer communicated reasons to prospective new employer); Borden, Inc. v. Wallace, 570 S.W.2d 445 (Tex. Civ. App. 1978) (consent found in submission to polygraph test when conclusions reported by polygraph operator); Restatement (Second) of Torts § 583 comment d, illustrations 2 and 3 (consent derived from submission to investigation).

to use what is probably a more apt description, because of the plaintiff's assumption of risk).

§ 8.03 The Absolute Privilege for Participants in Judicial Proceedings

[1] Who Is Protected

The absolute privilege for statements made in the course of judicial proceedings is one of the oldest absolute common law privileges.[20] Care should be taken not to confuse this privilege, which attaches to various *participants* in the proceedings, with the distinct "fair report" privilege, which refers to the republication of information about the proceedings, and which is not always an absolute privilege.[21]

[a] Judges

There is perhaps no more powerful privilege known to the law of defamation than the absolute immunity that shields judges from liability for statements made by them within the ambit of judicial proceedings.[22] The social interest in a free and independent judiciary requires that judges be able to function in an environment unfettered by fear of liability for defamation, for otherwise "no man but a beggar or a fool would be a judge."[23] The scope of the privilege is enormously broad, encompassing statements in trials,[24] pretrial proceedings,[25] communications to other officials within the scope of a judge's duties,[26] memoranda or opinions,[27] and in any other context colorably within the sphere of

20 *See* Yates v. Lansing, 5 Johns 282, 291 (N.Y. 1810). ("It is to be found in the earliest judicial records, and it has been steadily maintained by an undisturbed current of decisions.") *See also* Imbler v. Pachtman, 424 U.S. 409, 423 n.20 (1976).

21 The separate fair report privilege is discussed in § 8.10, *infra.*

22 *See, e.g.*, Bradley v. Fisher, 80 U.S. 335 (1871); Ginger v. Bowles, 369 Mich. 680, 120 N.W.2d 842, *cert. denied,* 375 U.S. 856 (1963); Scott v. Stansfield, L.R., 3 Ex. 220, 223 (1868); Restatement (Second) of Torts § 585 (1977); Eldredge, *supra* note 6, § 72, at 340.

23 Prosser & Keeton, *supra* note 2, § 114, at 816 and n.8 (quoting Miller v. Hope, 2 (Shaw) Sc. App. Cases 125 (1824)).

24 Restatement (Second) of Torts § 585 (1977).

25 La Placa v. Lowery, 134 Vt. 56, 349 A.2d 235 (1975).

26 Brech v. Seacat, 84 S.D. 264, 170 N.W.2d 348 (1969) (letter to state pardons board).

27 *See, e.g.*, Lowenschuss v. West Publishing Co., 542 F.2d 180 (3d Cir. 1976); Garfield v. Palmieri, 297 F.2d 526 (1962); Lucas v. Central Missouri Trust Co., 349 Mo. 537, 162 S.W.2d 569, 591 (1942); Nadeau v. Texas Co., 104 Mont. 558, 69 P.2d 586 (1937); Reller v. Ankeny, 160 Neb. 47, 68 N.W.2d 686 (1955); Francis v. Branson, 168 Okla. 24, 31 P.2d

the judge's official duties or jurisdiction.[28] The privilege is absolute; it exists even if the judge knows the statement is false and acts out of ill will.[29]

[b] Attorneys

Subject to the rules governing relevance,[30] attorneys are covered by an absolute privilege for statements made during the course of their participation as counsel in judicial proceedings.[31] Furthermore, statements made *prior* to the commencement of judicial proceedings are absolutely privileged if made "in connection with possible litigation"[32] that is "contemplated in good faith and under serious consideration."[33] Similarly, statements made during pretrial discovery,[34] pretrial conferences,[35] and the filing of briefs, documents or letters to the

---

870 (1933); Dodge v. Henriod, 21 Utah 2d 277, 444 P.2d 753 (1968); Restatement (Second) of Torts § 585, comment d (1977). An aberration that seems clearly out of line with the mainstream of authority is Murray v. Brancatto, 290 N.Y. 52, 48 N.E.2d 257 (1943), in which it was held that only a qualified privilege attached to "unofficial" publication in the *New York Law Journal* and the *New York Supplement Reports.* This 4-3 decision, aptly described by Laurence Eldredge as "silly," has been substantially criticized and undermined. *See* Garfield v. Palmieri, 297 F.2d 526, 527 (2d Cir. 1962) (transmission of opinion to West Publishing Company absolutely privileged).

[28] *See* Restatement (Second) of Torts § 585 comment c (1977) (privilege extends to any matter in which judge possesses "some slight colorable jurisdiction over the subject matter before him").

[29] *See* Prosser & Keeton, *supra* note 2, § 114, at 816 (citing Scott v. Stansfield, L.R. 3 Ex. 220, 223 (1868); Irwin v. Ashurst, 158 Or. 61, 74 P.2d 1127 (1938)).

[30] *See supra* § 8.03[2][b].

[31] *See, e.g.,* Johnston v. Cartright, 355 F.2d 32 (8th Cir. 1966) (Blackmun, J.); Ginsburg v. Black, 192 F.2d 823 (7th Cir.), *cert. denied,* 343 U.S. 934 (1951); Carpenter v. Ashley, 148 Cal. 422, 83 P. 444 (1906); Campbell v. Lo Pucki, 345 So. 2d 860 (Fla. Ct. App. 1977); Cuddy v. Kueker, 7 Mass. App. 896, 387 N.E.2d 213, 214 (1979); Kipp v. Kueker, 7 Mass. App. 206, 386 N.E.2d 1282, 1286 (1979); Bull v. McCuskey, 96 Nev. 706, 615 P.2d 957, 961 (1980); Irwin v. Ashurst, 158 Or. 61, 74 P.2d 1127 (1938); Russell v. Clark, 620 S.W.2d 865, 868-70 (Tex. Civ. App. 1981); McNeal v. Allen, 95 Wash. 2d 265, 621 P.2d 1285, 1286 (1980); Restatement (Second) of Torts § 586 (1977).

[32] Johnston v. Cartright, 355 F.2d 32, 38 (8th Cir. 1966); Russell v. Clark, 620 S.W.2d 865, 868-70 (Tex. Civ. App. 1981).

[33] Restatement (Second) of Torts § 586 comment e (1977). *See also* Lerette v. Dean Witter Organization, Inc., 60 Cal. App. 3d 573, 131 Cal. Rptr. 592 (1976).

[34] *See* Thorton v. Rhoden, 245 Cal. App. 2d 80, 53 Cal. Rptr. 706 (1966); Sussman v. Damian, 355 So. 2d 809 (Fla. Ct. App. 1977); Beezley v. Hansen, 4 Utah 2d 64, 286 P.2d 1057 (1955).

[35] Spoehr v. Mittelstadt, 34 Wis. 2d 653, 150 N.W.2d 502 (1967).

court[36] in connection with litigation are absolutely privileged.

[c] Parties and Statements in Documents

Again, subject to the requirement of relevancy,[37] a party to a judicial proceeding is absolutely privileged to publish defamatory statements during the course of the proceeding in which he participates.[38] The rule covers communications "preliminary to a proposed judicial proceeding, or in the institution of or during the course and as part of, a judicial proceeding."[39] The rule applies to both civil and criminal proceedings[40] and encompasses communications made by a client to his attorney[41] as well as information given to prosecuting attorneys or other proper officers preliminary to a proposed criminal prosecution.[42]

Statements made in bona fide pleadings, or in other documents pertinent to the proceeding, such as answers to interrogatories, are also absolutely privileged.[43]

---

36 Mohler v. Houston, 356 A.2d 646 (D.C. App. 1976); Richeson v. Kessler, 73 Idaho 548, 255 P.2d 7097 (1953); Simon v. Stim, 11 Misc. 2d 653, 176 N.Y.S.2d 475 (1958), *aff'd*, 10 A.D.2d 647, 199 N.Y.S.2d 405 (1960).

37 *See infra* § 8.03[2]

38 *See, e.g.*, Drummond v. Stahl, 127 Ariz. 122, 618 P.2d 616, 619 (1980), *cert. denied*, 450 U.S. 967 (1981); Magnan v. Anaconda Industries, Inc., 37 Conn. Sup. 38, 429 A.2d 492, 495 (1980); Sailboat Key, Inc. v. Gardner, 378 So. 2d 47, 49 (Fla. Ct. App 1979); Sullivan v. Birmingham, 11 Mass. App. 359, 416 N.E.2d 528, 530-31 (1981); McGranahan v. Dahar, 119 N.H. 758, 408 A.2d 121, 126 (1979); Lann v. Third National Bank in Nashville, 198 Tenn. 70, 277 S.W.2d 439 (1955); McNeal v. Allen, 95 Wash. 2d 265, 621 P.2d 1285, 1286-87 (1980); Restatement (Second) of Torts § 587 (1977).

39 Restatement (Second) of Torts § 587 (1977).

40 *See* McGranahan v. Dahar, 119 N.H. 758, 408 A.2d 121, 125-26, 128 (1979); Ducosin v. Mott, 292 Or. 764, 642 P.2d 1168, 1169 (1982); Trotman v. Dunn, 4 Camp. 211, 66 Eng. Rep. 297 (1915); Restatement (Second) of Torts § 587 comment b (1977).

41 *See* McGrahahan v. Dahar 119 N.H. 758, 408 A.2d 121, 126 (1979); Restatement (Second) of Torts § 587 comment b (1977).

42 *See* McGrahahan v. Dahar, 119 N.H. 758, 408 A.2d 121, 125-26 (1979); Ducosin v. Mott, 292 Or. 764, 642 P.2d 1168, 1169 (1982); Cushman v. Edgar, 44 Or. App. 297, 605 P.2d 1210, 1212 (1980); Restatement (Second) of Torts § 587 comment b (1977). Reports to law enforcement officers are often classified, however, as not falling within this absolute privilege, but within the somewhat parallel qualified privilege to report matters to public officials under a duty to act thereon. *See infra* § 8.08[4].

43 Taliaferro v. Sims, 187 F.2d 6 (5th Cir. 1951) (pleadings); Fletcher v, Maupin, 138 F.2d 742 (4th Cir.), *cert. denied*, 322 U.S. 750 (1943)(pleadings); Sacks v. Stecker, 60 F.2d 73 (2d Cir. 1932) (affidavit); Drummon v. Stahl, 127 Ariz. 122, 618 P.2d 616, 619 (1980), *cert. denied*, 450 U.S. 967 (1981) (pleadings); Allstate Insurance Co. v. Shupack, 335 So. 2d 620 (Fla. Ct. App. 1976)(answers to interrogatories); DiBlasio v. Kolodner, 233 Md. 512, 197 A.2d 245 (1964)(pleadings); Sullivan v. Birmingham, 11 Mass. App. 359, 416 N.E.2d 528, 530-31 (1981)(pleadings); Greenberg v. Aetna Insurance Co., 427 Pa. 511, 235 A.2d

[d] Witnesses

If the statement has some relation to the proceeding, a witness enjoys an absolute privilege to publish defamatory matter in communications preliminary to or as part of a judicial proceeding in which he is testifying.[44]

[e] Judicial Personnel

Clerks, officers of the court, and related judicial personnel are absolutely privileged to publish defamatory matter related to judicial proceedings.[45]

[f] Jurors

Members of grand and petit juries are absolutely privileged to publish defamatory matter in the performance of their functions as jurors, if the statement bears some relation to the proceedings in which the juror is acting.[46]

[2] The Defamatory Statement Must Be Relevant to the Judicial Proceeding

[a] In General

To fall within the absolute privilege for participants in judicial pro-

---

576, *cert. denied*, 392 U.S. 907 (1967)(pleadings); Janklow v. Keller, 241 N.W.2d 364 (S.D. 1976)(petition for removal); McNeal v. Allen, 95 Wash. 2d 265, 621 P.2d 1285, 1286-87 (1980)(pleadings); McClure v. Stretch, 20 Wash. 2d 460, 147 P.2d 935 (1944)(pleadings).

[44] *See, e.g.*, Sweet v. Middlesex Mutual Insurance Co., 397 F. Supp. 1101, 1103 (D.N.H.), *aff'd without opinion*, 527 F.2d 642 (1st Cir. 1975); Todd v. Cox, 20 Ariz. App. 347, 512 P.2d 1234 (1973); Johnson v. Dover, 201 Ark. 175, 143 S.W.2d 1112 (1940); Tiedemann v. Superior Court, 83 Cal. App. 3d 918, 925, 148 Cal. Rptr. 242, 247 (1978); Thorton v. Roden, 245 Cal. App. 2d 80, 53 Cal. Rptr. 706 (1966); Aborn v. Lipson, 357 Mass. 71, 256 N.E.2d 442 (1970); Greenberg v. Ackerman, 41 N.J. Super. 146, 124 A.2d 313 (1956); Massey v. Jones, 182 Va. 200, 28 S.E.2d 623 (1944); Restatement (Second) of Torts § 588 (1977).

[45] Restatement (Second) of Torts § 585 comment b (1977). *See also* Vasquez v. Courtney, 276 Or. 1053, 557 P.2d 672 (1976).

[46] *See, e.g.*, Irwin v. Murphy, 129 Cal. App. 713, 19 P.2d 292 (1933); Ryon v. Shaw, 77 So. 2d 455 (Fla. 1955); Greenfield v. Courier-Journal & Louisville Times Co., 283 S.W.2d 839 (Ky. 1955); Hayslip v. Wellford, 195 Tenn. 621, 263 S.W.2d 136, *cert. denied*, 346 U.S. 911 (1953); Restatement (Second) of Torts § 589 (1977).

ceedings the defamatory statement must be "relevant" or "pertinent" to the proceeding.[47]

[b] Relevancy Requirement Is Broad

The so-called English Rule, which has been adopted by the *Restatement (Second) of Torts,*[48] imposes virtually no relevancy requirement whatsoever, applying the absolute privilege to any statement made during the course of the judicial proceeding.[49] The "American Rule" is in theory narrower, requiring a somewhat closer nexus between the defamatory statement and the subject matter of the litigation, but as a practical matter the American Rule is so broadly applied that it may be stated that in effect American courts have all but adopted the English Rule.[50]

The requirement of relevancy is very liberally construed; statements will be deemed relevant as long as they have "some relation" or a "reasonable relation" or "may possibly" be pertinent to the subject of the inquiry.[51] Technical relevancy within the rules of evidence is not required.[52]

---

47 *See, e.g.,* Adams v. Alabama Lime & Stone Corp., 225 Ala. 174, 142 So. 424 (1932); Laing v. Mitten, 185 Mass. 233, 70 N.E. 128 (1904); Mathis v. Kennedy, 243 Minn. 219, 67 N.W.2d 413, 418 (1954); Magelo v. Roundup Coal Mining Co., 109 Mont. 293, 96 P.2d 932 (1939); Vieira v. Meredith, 84 R.I. 299, 123 A.2d 743 (1956).

48 *See* Restatement (Second) § 585 comment e, and Reporter's Note (1977).

49 *See, e.g.,* Munster v. Lamb, 11 Q.B.D. 588 (1883); Seaman v. Netherclift, 2 C.P.D. 53 (1876); Scott v. Stansfield, L.R. 3 Ex. 220 (1868); Gatley, Libel and Slander, § 383, at 161-62 (7th ed. 1974).

50 *See* Prosser & Keeton, *supra* note 2, § 114, at 818 (discussing American approach "which seems in effect to adopt the English rule"). *See also* Butler v. Lilly, 533 S.W.2d 130 (Tex. Civ. App. 1976)(following English approach).

51 *See, e.g.,* Lowenschuss v. West Publishing Co., 542 F.2d 180 (3d Cir. 1976); Ginsburg v. Black, 192 F.2d 823 (7th Cir.), *cert. denied,* 343 U.S. 934 (1951); Bleecker v. Drury, 149 F.2d 770 (2d Cir. 1945); Young v. Young, 57 U.S. App. D.C. 157, 18 F.2d 807 (1927); Johnson v. Dover, 201 Ark. 175, 143 S.W.2d 1112 (1940); Mohler v. Houston, 356 A.2d 646 (D.C. 1976); Mathis v. Kennedy, 243 Minn. 219, 67 N.W.2d 413 (1954); McGranahan v. Dahar, 119 N.H. 758, 408 A.2d 121, 127 (1979); McKinney v. Cooper, 163 Or. 512, 98 P.2d 711 (1940); Greenberg v. Aetna Insurance Co., 427 Pa. 511, 235 A.2d 576 (1967); Johnston v. Schlarb, 7 Wash. 2d 528, 110 P.2d 190 (1941).

52 *See, e.g.,* Taliaferro v. Sims, 187 F.2d 6 (5th Cir. 1951); Brown v. Shimabukuro, 73 U.S. App. D.C. 194, 118 F.2d 17 (1940); Johnston v. Schlarb, 7 Wash.2d 528, 110 P.2d 190 (1941); Prosser & Keeton, *supra* note 2, § 114, at 818.

[3] What Qualifies as a "Judicial Proceeding"

[a] Any Governmental Body or Proceeding Engaging in Judicial or Quasi-Judicial Function

There is no precise definition of what qualifies as a "judicial proceeding" for the purposes of the absolute privilege; but it clearly extends to tribunals other than courts. The term is employed in a flexible fashion to embrace any governmental proceeding involving the exercise of a judicial or quasi-judicial function,[53] including a wide variety of administrative boards,[54] commissions,[55] or other tribunals[56] which may engage in judicial or quasi-judicial action though not part of the court system. When an agency at times exercises quasi-judicial functions and at times exercises nonquasi-judicial authority, the absolute privilege for judicial proceedings will apply only when the agency performs in its quasi-judicial capacity.[57] (Even in such cases, however, some other absolute privilege may be deemed applicable.[58])

[b] Privilege Extends to All Aspects of the Proceeding

The privilege extends to all aspects of a proceeding, including pre-

---

[53] *See* Restatement (Second) of Torts § 585 comment b (1977).

[54] *See, e.g.*, White v. Holderby, 192 F.2d 722 (5th Cir. 1951)(board of education); Bleecker v. Drury, 149 F.2d 770 (2d Cir. 1945)(industrial board); Parker v. Kirkland, 298 Ill. App. 340, 18 N.E.2d 709 (1939)(board of tax appeals); Schulze v. Board of Education, School District No. 258, 221 Kan. 351, 559 P.2d 367 (1977)(school board disciplinary proceeding); Richards v. Ellis, 233 A.2d 37 (Me. 1967)(licensing board).

[55] *See, e.g.*, Lininger v. Knight, 123 Colo. 213, 226 P.2d 809 (1951)(liquor commission); Robertson v. Industrial Insurance Co., 75 So. 2d 198 (Fla. 1954)(insurance commission); Fisher v. Payne, 93 Fla. 1085, 113 So. 378 (1927)(lunacy commission); James v. Brandon, 61 Ga. App. 719, 7 S.E. 305 (1940)(attorney grievance committee); Kimball v. Ryan, 283 Ill. App. 456 (1936)(election commission); Corcoran v. Jerrel, 185 Iowa 532, 170 N.W. 776 (1919)(lunacy commission); McAlister & Co. v. Jenkins, 214 Ky. 802, 284 S.W. 88 (1926)(real estate commission); Marino v. Wallace, 65 A.D.2d 946, 410 N.Y.S.2d 488 (1978) (public service commission).

[56] *See* Fenning v. S.G. Holding Corp., 47 N.J. Super 110, 135 A.2d 346 (1957)(rent control authority); Rainier's Dairies v. Raritan Valley Farms, Inc., 19 N.J. 552, 117 A.2d 889 (1955)(office of milk industry); Hanzimanolis v. City of New York, 88 Misc. 2d 681, 388 N.Y.S.2d 826 (1976)(police department investigation).

[57] *See* Richardson v. Dunbar, 95 Ill. App. 3d 254, 419 N.E.2d 1205, 1208 (1981)(involving members of police committee).

[58] *See infra* §§ 8.04[3], 8.05.

proceeding steps taken in contemplation of initiation, through the final termination.[59]

[c] Does Not Extend to Press Conferences or Other Extra-Judicial Activity

Statements made at press conferences or in other circumstances not related to the proceeding are not covered by the absolute privilege,[60] nor are statements made after termination of the proceeding.[61] Care should be taken, however, to distinguish statements which are made away from the tribunal setting before or during a proceeding, but which nonetheless fall within the privilege (e.g., complaints to prosecutors, communications between attorneys or between attorneys and clients, or statements during discovery or in litigation documents),[62] from truly extra-judicial statements (statements to the press, for example).

[4] Questions of Law

The determination of whether the statement is relevant to a judicial proceeding, or whether the proceeding is properly classified as judicial, is for the court to decide as an issue of law.[63]

---

59 *See, e.g.*, Brown v. Shimabukuro, 73 U.S. App. D.C. 194, 118 F.2d 17 (1941)(motion for rehearing); Libco Corp. v. Adams, 100 Ill, App. 3d 314, 426 N.E.2d 1130, 1131-32 (1982)(correspondence between attorneys); Stone v. Hutchinson Daily News, 125 Kan. 715, 266 P. 78 (1928) (application for search warrant); Schmitt v. Mann, 291 Ky. 80, 163 S.W.2d 281 (1942)(motion for new trial); Cushman v. Edgar, 44 Or. App. 297, 605 P.2d 1210, 1212 (1980)(letter to governor requesting investigation); McKinney v. Cooper, 163 Or. 512, 98 P.2d 711 (1940)(final accounting); Hammett v. Hunter, 189 Okla. 455, 117 P.2d 511 (1941)(modification of decree); Brech v. Seacat, 84 S.D. 264, 170 N.W.2d 348 (1969) (letter to pardoning board); Spoehr v. Mittlestadt, 34 Wis. 2d 653, 150 N.W.2d 502 (1967)(pretrial conference).

60 *See, e.g.*, Kennedy v. Cannon, 29 Md. 92, 182 A.2d 54 (1962); Barto v. Felix, 250 Pa. Super. 262, 378 A.2d 927 (1977); Twelker v. Shannon & Wilson, Inc., 88 Wash. 2d 473, 564 P.2d 1131 (1977); Eldredge, *supra* note 6, § 73, at 355-56; Prosser & Keeton, *supra* note 2, § 114, at 820; R. Sack, Libel, Slander and Related Problems § VI.2.1.8, at 277 (1980).

61 Burlingame v. Burlingame, 8 Cow. 141 (N.Y. 1828); Paris v. Levy, 9 C.B. (N.S.) 342, 142 Eng. Rep. 135 (1860); Prosser & Keeton, *supra* note 2, § 114, at 819. *See also* Bigner v. Hodges, 82 Miss. 215, 33 So. 980 (1903)(does not extend to statement to person not concerned with case).

62 *See supra* §§ 8.03[b] and [c].

63 *See* Ginsburg v. Black, 192 F.2d 823 (7th Cir. 1951); Macie v. Clark Equipment Co., 8 Ill. App. 3d 613, 290 N.E.2d 912 (1972); Matthis v. Kennedy, 243 Minn. 219, 67 N.W.2d 413 (1954); Vieira v. Meredith, 84 R.I. 299, 123 A.2d 743 (1956); Eldredge, *supra* note 6, § 73, at 356.

§ 8.04 Absolute Immunity for Participants in Legislative Proceedings

[1] The Federal Rule

[a] In General

Members of the United States Congress enjoy an absolute privilege to publish defamatory matter in communications arising from their legislative activities. The immunity is derived from the federal Constitution's speech or debate clause, which provides that "for any Speech or Debate in either House, they shall not be questioned in any other Place."[64] The clause has "direct kinship in the English Bill of Rights of 1689."[65] As the Supreme Court has explained, "[s]ince the Glorious Revolution in Britain, and throughout United States history, the privilege has been recognized as an important protection of the independence and integrity of the legislature."[66]

A literal construction of the clause would confine its application only to members of the House and Senate for statements made "*in* either House." The Supreme Court, however, has given the clause "a practical rather than strictly literal reading."[67] The Court has developed a distinction between "legislative" acts, which are covered by the clause, and "political" acts, which are not.[68] In *Gravel v. United States*,[69] the Court declared:

> Legislative acts are not all-encompassing. The heart of the Clause is speech or debate in either House. Insofar as the Clause is construed to reach other matters, *they must be an integral part of the deliberative and communicative processes* by which Members participate in committee and House proceedings with respect to the consideration and passage or rejection of proposed legislation or with respect to other matters which the Constitution places within the jurisdiction of either House.[70]

[b] Aides and Assistants

Gravel held that in light of the complexities of the modern legislative process, which render it "literally impossible . . . for Members of Con-

---

[64] U.S. Const. art. I, § 6, cl. 1.

[65] J. Nowak, R. Rotunda, & J. Young, Constitutional Law 257 (2d ed. 1983).

[66] United States v. Johnson, 383 U.S. 169, 178 (1966).

[67] *See* Hutchinson v. Proxmire, 443 U.S. 111, 130-33 (1979).

[68] *See generally* Nowak, Rotunda, & Young, *supra* note 65, at 260-63.

[69] 408 U.S. 606 (1972).

[70] *Id.* at 625.

gress to perform their legislative tasks without the help of aides and assistants,"[71] that a member of Congress and his assistant are to be treated as one.[72] Any act which would be protected if performed by the member of Congress personally is equally protected if performed by a legislative aide or assistant on his or her behalf.[73]

[c] Committee Reports and Staff

In *Doe v. McMillan*,[74] the Court held that the speech or debate clause immunizes members of Congress and committee staff from civil liability arising from the dissemination of material in a committee report.[75] The Court refused, however, to extend the clause's protection to employees of the Government Printing Office, which acts at the direction of Congress to distribute material to the public.[76]

[d] The Holding in *Hutchinson v. Proxmire*

The Supreme Court's most extensive elaboration on the immunity from defamation liability under the speech or debate clause came in *Hutchinson v. Proxmire*.[77] Senator William Proxmire and his legislative assistant were sued by Hutchinson, a research behavioral scientist, for defamation arising from one of Proxmire's "Golden Fleece of the Month Awards" — "awards" given by the Senator to publicize incidents of what he perceived as wasteful federal spending. Proxmire gave his award to Hutchinson, the National Science Foundation, NASA, and the Office of Naval Research, for what he saw as wasteful expenditures for Hutchinson's research on the behavior of primates. Senator Proxmire sarcastically belittled Hutchinson's work in a speech written by his aide, which the Senator read on the Senate floor. The text of the speech was also incorporated in a press release distributed to 275 media outlets, and a summary of the speech was contained in a newsletter sent to approximately 10,000 persons, primarily the Senator's constituents in Wisconsin.

The Court held that the Senator would be "wholly immune" for his

[71] *Id.* at 616-17. The aide is in effect the member's "alter ego." *Id.*

[72] *Id.* at 616.

[73] *Id.* at 616-18.

[74] 412 U.S. 306 (1973).

[75] *Id.* at 308-13.

[76] *Id.* at 314.

[77] 443 U.S. 111 (1979).

statements about Hutchinson, but only for those statements made on the Senate floor or in a committee hearing.[78] "[N]either the newsletters nor the press release was 'essential to the deliberations of the Senate' and neither was part of the deliberative process."[79] Thus newsletters and press releases do not fall within the immunity created by the clause; nor do "follow-up telephone calls to executive agencies and . . . radio and television interviews."[80]

[2] State Legislators

At least 41 states have versions of speech or debate clauses in their state constitutions.[81] The classic state case is *Coffin v. Coffin*,[82] which declared that the absolute immunity conferred by such clauses is granted "not with the intention of protecting the members against prosecutions for their own benefit, but to support the rights of the people, by enabling their representatives to execute the functions of their office without fear of prosecutions, civil or criminal."[83] The immunity provided by such state provisions has rarely been tested, but the consensus appears to be that such clauses provide at least as much protection as their federal counterpart.[84]

[3] Subordinate Legislative Bodies

There is a division of authority as to whether the absolute privilege applies to subordinate legislative bodies, such as city councils. The decisions appear to be about evenly divided between those holding that an absolute privilege applies to members of such bodies,[85] and those hold-

---

78 *Id.* at 130.

79 *Id.* at 133.

80 *Id.* at 121 n.10.

81 *See* the listing compiled in Tenney v. Brandhove, 341 U.S. 367, 375 n.5 (1951).

82 4 Mass. 1, 3 Am. Dec. 189 (1808).

83 4 Mass. at 27.

84 *See* Abercrombie v. McClung, 55 Hawaii 595, 525 P.2d 594 (1974)(extending protection to statements made to newspaper reporter in interview concerning Senator's speech before legislature). *See generally* Field, *The Constitutional Privileges of Legislators*, 9 Minn. L. Rev. 442 (1925). *See also* Cole v. Richards, 108 N.J.L. 356, 158 A. 466 (1932).

85 McNayr v. Kelly, 184 So. 2d 428 (Fla.), *conformed to* 185 So. 2d 194 (1966); Larson v. Donner, 32 Ill. App. 2d 471, 178 N.E.2d 399 (1961); Bolton v. Walker, 197 Mich. 699, 164 N.W.420 (1917); Board of Education v. Buffalo Council of Supervisors, 52 A.D.2d 220, 383 N.Y.S.2d 732 (1976); Tanner v. Gault, 20 Ohio App. 243, 153 N.E.24 (1925). *See also* Harnish v. Smith, 138 Cal. App. 2d 307, 291 P.2d 532 (1956) (applying California statute, West Cal. Civ. Code § 47); Jacobs v. Underwood, 484 S.W.2d 855 (Ky. 1972)(applying

ing that only a qualified privilege applies.[86]

[4] Witnesses in Legislative Proceedings

As in the case of judicial proceedings, an absolute privilege protects witnesses in legislative proceedings from liability for defamatory statements made during testimony or in communications preliminary to the proceeding, if they have some relation to the proceeding.[87]

§ 8.05 Absolute Immunity for Executive and Administrative Officials

[1] The Federal Rule

[a] All Officials Covered

All federal executive and administrative officers enjoy absolute immunity from liability for statements made in the performance of their official duties.[88] The federal rule, which began as an immunity for cabinet rank officers,[89] now extends to all federal executive and administrative personnel.[90]

Kentucky statute, Ky. Rev. Stat. 84.050(5), as amended Ky. Rev. Stat. 83A.060(15)); Carter v. Jackson, 10 Utah 2d 284, 351 P.2d 957 (1960)(applying Utah statute, Utah Code Ann. 1953, 45-2-3).

[86] *See, e.g.*, McClendon v. Coverdale, 57 Del. 568, 203 A.2d 815 (1964); Gardner v, Hollifield, 97 Idaho 607, 549 P.2d 266 (1976); Cowman v. LaVine, 234 N.W.2d 114 (Iowa 1975); Mills v. Denny, 245 Iowa 584, 63 N.W.2d 222 (1954); Cohen v. Bowdoin, 288 A.2d 106 (Me. 1972); Jones v. Monico, 276 Minn. 371, 150 N.W.2d 213 (1967); Richards v. Gruen, 62 Wis. 2d 99, 214 N.W.2d 309 (1974).

[87] Restatement (Second) of Torts § 590A (1977). *See also* Kelly v. Daro, 47 Cal. App. 2d 418, 118 P.2d 37 (1941); McClendon v. Coverdale, 57 Del. 568, 203 A.2d 815 (1964); Mills v. Denny, 245 Iowa 584, 63 N.W.2d 222 (1954); Jennings v. Cronin, 256 Pa. Super. 398, 389 A.2d 1183 (1978); Logan's Super Markets, Inc. v. McCalla, 208 Tenn. 68, 343 S.W.2d 892 (1961).

[88] *See, e.g.*, Barr v. Matteo, 360 U.S. 564 (1959); Howard v. Lyons, 360 U.S. 593 (1959); Expeditions Unlimited Aquatic Enterprises, Inc. v. Smithsonian Institution, 566 F.2d 289 (D.C. Cir. 1977), *cert. denied*, 438 U.S. 915 (1978); Johnson v. Aldredge, 488 F.2d 820 (3d Cir.), *cert. denied*, 419 U.S. 882 (1973); Sauber v. Gliedman, 283 F.2d 941 (7th Cir.), *cert. denied*, 366 U.S. 906 (1960); Preble v. Johnson, 275 F.2d 275 (10th Cir. 1960); Gorst v. Ferguson, 431 F. Supp. 125 (W.D. Okla. 1977); Nester v. O'Donohue, 429 F. Supp. 25 (D. Hawaii 1977).

[89] *See* Spalding v. Vilas, 161 U.S. 483 (1896) (Postmaster General); Standard Nut Margarine Co. v. Mellon, 63 U.S. App. D.C. 339, 72 F.2d 557, *cert. denied*, 293 U.S. 605 (1934)(Secretary and Assistant Secretary of Treasury).

[90] *See* cases cited in note 88, *supra*.

[b] Scope of Immunity

The federal absolute immunity encompasses any publication within the "outer perimeter" of their "line of duty."[91] Although this formulation is extremely expansive, it is not unbounded. As in all tort immunity problems for federal officials,[92] acts that form no part of any official's duty,[93] or acts that are clearly unconstitutional, are not protected.[94]

[2] State Officials

[a] States that Follow the Federal Model

Some jurisdictions have adopted the federal rule of *Barr v. Matteo*[95] granting all state executive and administrative officers absolute immunity for statements made in the performance of their duties.[96]

[b] States that Limit Absolute Immunity to Superior State Officials

A majority of states do not follow the federal model, instead restricting the absolute privilege to superior ranking state officers.[97] To determine whether the official qualifies for absolute immunity, courts in such jurisdictions appear to proceed on a case-by-case basis, examining such

---

[91] Barr v. Matteo, 360 U.S. 564, 575 (1959).

[92] *See generally* Prosser & Keetan, *supra* note 2, § 114, at 822; Handler and Klein, *The Defense of Privilege in Defamation Suits Against Government Executive Officials*, 75 Harv. L. Rev. 44 (1960); Becht, *The Absolute Privilege of the Executive in Defamation*, 15 Vand. L. Rev. 1127 (1962).

[93] Colpoys v. Gates, 73 U.S. App. D.C. 193, 118 F.2d 16 (1940).

[94] *See* Butz v. Economou, 438 U.S. 478 (1978).

[95] 360 U.S. 564 (1959).

[96] *See, e.g.*, Wyatt v. Ruck Construction, Inc., 117 Ariz. 186, 571 P.2d 683 (Ariz. App. 1977)(contract administrator); Grande v. State, 115 Ariz. 394, 565 P.2d 900 (Ariz. App. 1977)(tax commission officials); White Mountain Apache Indian Tribe v. Shelley, 107 Ariz. 4, 480 P.2d 654 (1971); Long v. Metz, 2 Ariz. App. 215, 407 P.2d 404 (1965) (highway engineer); Cripe v. Board of Regents, 358 So. 2d 244 (Fla. Ct. App.), *cert. denied*, 365 So. 2d 710 (Fla. 1978) (university official); Cobb's Auto Sales, Inc. v. Coleman, 353 So. 2d 922 (Fla. Ct. App. 1978)(sheriff); McNayr v. Kelly, 184 So. 2d 428 (Fla. 1966)(county manager); Blair v. Walker, 64 Ill. 2d 1, 349 N.E.2d 385 (1976)(governor); Larson v. Donner, 32 Ill. App. 2d 471, 178 N.E.2d 399 (1961) (mayor); Shearer v. Lambert, 274 Or. 449, 547 P.2d 98 (1976)(university official).

[97] *See* Restatement (Second) of Torts § 591(b), and Reporter's Notes (1977).

factors as the official's rank, duties, and breadth of policy-making responsibility.[98]

[c] States that Recognize No Executive or Administrative Absolute Immunity

A few states appear to recognize no absolute immunity whatsoever for state executive or administrative officers, limiting such protection to the judicial and legislative branches.[99]

§ 8.06 Miscellaneous Absolute Privileges

[1] Spouses

A husband or wife "is absolutely privileged to publish to the other spouse defamatory matter concerning a third person."[100]

[2] Publication Required by Law

The *Restatement (Second)* has adopted the position that one who is required by law to publish defamatory matter is absolutely privileged to publish it.[101]

---

98 *Compare* Saroyan v. Burkett, 57 Cal. 2d 706, 21 Cal. Rptr. 557, 371 P.2d 293 (1962)(absolute immunity for superintendent of banks); Ryan v. Wilson, 231 Iowa 33, 300 N.W. 707 (1941)(absolute immunity for governor); Hackworth v. Larson 83 S.D. 674, 165 N.W.2d 705 (1969)(absolute immunity for secretary of state); Gold Seal Chinchillas, Inc. v. State, 69 Wash. 2d 828, 420 P.2d 698 (1966)(absolute immunity for attorney general), *with* Barry v. McCollom, 81 Conn. 293, 70 A. 1035 (1908)(no absolute immunity for school superintendent); Carr v. Watkins, 227 Md. 578, 177 A.2d 841 (1962)(no absolute immunity for police).

99 *See* Browning v. Birmingham News, 348 So. 2d 455 (Ala. 1977); Goolsby v. Wilson, 146 Ga. App. 288, 246 S.E.2d 371 (1978)(no absolute privilege for mayor; applying Georgia statute which grants only qualified privilege to public officials, Ga. Code Ann. § 105-709(1)(1968)).

100 Restatement (Second) of Torts § 592 (1977). *See also* Dyer v. MacDougall, 93 F. Supp. 484 (E.D.N.Y. 1950); Lawler v. Merritt, 182 Misc. 648, 48 N.Y.S.2d 843, *aff'd*, 269 A.D. 662, 53 N.Y.S.2d 465 (1944).

101 Restatement (Second) of Torts § 592A (1977). *See also* Becker v. Philco Corp., 372 F.2d 771 (4th Cir.), *cert. denied*, 389 U.S. 979 (1967); Lamb v. Sutton, 274 F.2d 705 (6th Cir.), *cert. denied*, 363 U.S. 830 (1960).

[3] Sovereign Immunity

Whether a governmental entity itself may be sued for defamation depends on the internal sovereign immunity law of the jurisdiction.[102]

§ 8.07 Conditional Privileges: An Overview

[1] The Traditional Common Law Function

Prior to *New York Times* the law of defamation was a strict liability tort,[103] but the common law nonetheless recognized a series of absolute and conditional privileges out of a developing ackowledgment that in certain recurring factual situations, free and open communication should transcend concern for reputation.[104]

[2] Conditional and Absolute Privileges Compared

The conditional privileges operate differently from the absolute privileges in two ways. First, the absolute privileges are not subject to defeasance for "abuse" or "fault" or "malice" — once they are found applicable, they are, as their name implies, truly absolute.[105] Conditional privileges, however, may be defeated through "abuse," which has a number of specific meanings, such as "excessive publication,"[106] publication despite a lack of belief in the necessity for publication in light of the purpose of the privilege,[107] certain forms of negligence,[108] common law "ill-will malice,"[109] or "actual malice."[110] Depending on the jurisdic-

---

[102] *Compare* Federal Tort Claims Act, 28 U.S.C. § 2680(h)(United States has not waived its sovereign immunity for libel), *with* New York Court of Claims Act § 8 (1963)(New York has not retained sovereign immunity for libel).

[103] *See supra* § 1.03[1].

[104] *See generally* Eaton, *The American Law of Defamation Through* Gertz v. Robert Welch, Inc. *and Beyond: An Analytical Primer,* 61 Va. L. Rev. 1349, 1359-64 (1975).

[105] *See supra* §§ 8.01-8.06.

[106] *See* Restatement (Second) of Torts § 604 (1977).

[107] *See id.*, §§ 603, 605.

[108] *See, e.g.*, Zuschek v. Whitmoyer Laboratories, Inc., 430 F. Supp. 1163, 1166 (E.D. Pa. 1977), *aff'd mem.*, 571 F.2d 573 (3d Cir. 1978)(privilege lost if defendant "does not believe in the truth of the statements" or "has no reasonable ground for so believing").

[109] *See, e.g.*, Hardee v. North Carolina Allstate Servs., Inc., 537 F.2d 1255, 1259-60 (4th Cir. 1976); Arsenault v. Allegheny Airlines, Inc., 485 F. Supp. 1373, 1379-80 (D. Mass.), *aff'd mem.*, 636 F.2d 1199 (1st Cir. 1980), *cert. denied*, 454 U.S. 821 (1981).

[110] *See* Restatement (Second) of Torts § 600 (1977).

tion, "abuse" or defeasance of a conditional privilege might be triggered through some or all of these factors.

Conditional privileges differ from absolute privileges in a second way: Where absolute privileges are generally geared to the identity of the speaker (judge, legislator, high public official, for example) or to the forum in which the speech takes place (a judicial proceeding or legislative chamber, for example), conditional privileges are governed by far more flexible standards, which involve relationships between the speaker, the audience, and the subject of the speech—such as speech serving a "common interest" of the speaker and recipient.[111]

Conditional privileges are thus in one sense less valuable to defendants, because they are subject to defeasance, but in another sense *more* valuable to defendants, because they are sufficiently malleable and flexible to cover a much wider field of application.

[3] Relationship to Modern Constitutional Fault Rules

[a] The Partial Duplication of Functions Problem

With the emergence of post-*New York Times* constitutional fault rules, some of the functions traditionally served by conditional privileges have been subsumed by first amendment fault requirements. In a public figure case requiring actual malice as a prerequisite to recovery, for example, assertion of a common law conditional privilege is an essentially worthless addition to the defense case, for if actual malice is demonstrated most jurisdictions would treat the conditional privilege as lost, and if actual malice is not demonstrated the defendant will prevail under the first amendment rules anyway.

Similarly, most jurisdictions treat the conditional privilege as lost if the defendant is guilty of negligence. In private figure cases subject to the *Gertz* fault requirement, however, negligence is required automatically as part of the plaintiff's prima facie case, rendering the conditional privilege a meaningless defense that adds nothing to the burden already imposed on the plaintiff.[112]

---

111 *See infra* § 8.08[3].

112 *See* Prosser & Keeton, *supra* note 2, § 115, at 85; Smolla, *supra* note 7, at 79.

[b] The Renewed Significance of Conditional Privileges After *Dun & Bradstreet*

In light of the Supreme Court's holding in *Dun & Bradstreet, Inc. v. Greenmoss Builder's, Inc.*,[113] which may authorize a return to common law strict liability standards in private figure cases not involving matters of public concern,[114] the traditional common law privileges, which were originally designed to operate as safety valves for the strict liability defamation system, may undergo a rejuvenation. Defense counsel who rely primarily on first amendment defenses will be challenged to give renewed attention to the matrix of common law conditional privileges in cases governed by strict liability as the "base" liability principle. When these common law privileges are dusted off and refitted for new use, one of the "surprises" in store may be the recognition that many of them are extremely broad, at least in their verbal formulas, inviting creative growth as litigation defenses.

[c] Solutions to the Duplication Problem in *Gertz* Fault Cases

In cases in which *Gertz* is applicable and fault is required as part of the plaintiff's prima facie case, there are a number of possible responses to the duplication of functions problem.

[i] Requiring Fault Greater than Negligence to Defeat the Privilege

One response in cases subject to the *Gertz* fault rule is to "upgrade" the level of fault necessary to defeat a common law conditional privilege, by imposing a requirement of some form of conduct beyond mere negligence to defeat it.[115] Recognizing the potential for *Gertz* to swallow up the conditional privileges, for example, the *Restatement (Second)* requires "actual malice" in the constitutional sense of knowledge of falsity or reckless disregard for the truth in order to establish abuse of the privilege.[116] Alternatively, a state might require that in addition to negligence, a plaintiff must establish common law ill-will malice to

---

113 105 S. Ct. 2939 (1985).

114 *See supra* §§ 3.02-3.05.

115 *See* Smolla, *supra* note 7, at 79.

116 *See* Hoesl v. United States, 451 F. Supp. 1170, 1179 (N.D. Cal. 1978)(actual malice, not mere negligence, required to defease common law conditional privilege); Marchesi v. Franchino, 283 Md. 131, 381 A.2d 1129, 1131-33 (1978)(same); Restatement (Second) of Torts § 600 (1977)(same)(the *Restatement (Second)* continues to recognize other grounds for abuse, however, such as excessive publication—*see id.*, § 604).

overcome a conditional privilege. A third possibility would be to ground defeasance of the privilege on either actual malice or common law ill-will malice, so long as something beyond mere negligence is established.

[ii] The Alternative of Discarding Conditional Privileges in *Gertz* Fault Cases

As an alternative approach to upgrading common law conditional privileges to make them meaningful in *Gertz* fault cases some jurisdictions may prefer to essentially downgrade them out of existence, on the theory that "[m]ost private interests would be adequately protected without the necessity for a recognition of a qualified privilege" in such cases.[117]

These options are summarized subsequently as part of the overview of "abuse of privilege."[118]

§ 8.08 The "Interest-Related" Conditional Privileges

Several related common law conditional privileges are based on the defendant's acting to further his self-interest, the interest of others, or a "common" interest.

[1] Statements Made to Protect the Publisher's Interest

There is a conditional common law privilege to make statements for the protection of the speaker's own legitimate interests.[119] Examples include statements made to defend one's reputation in response to attack by another,[120] statements made in connection with the retrieval

---

117 Prosser & Keeton, *supra* note 2, § 115, at 2.

118 *See infra* § 8.09.

119 *See, e.g.*, British American & Eastern Co. v. Wirth, Ltd., 592 F.2d 75 (2d Cir. 1979); Nichols v. J.J. Newberry Co., 150 F.2d 15 (9th Cir. 1945); Ripps v. Herrington, 241 Ala. 209, 1 So. 2d 899 (1941); Emde v. San Joaquin County Central Labor Council, 23 Cal. 2d 146, 143 P.2d 20 (1943); Newark Trust Co. v. Bruwer, 51 Del. 188, 141 A.2d 615 (1958); Davidson v. Walter, 93 Ga. App. 290, 91 S.E.2d 520 (1956); Southwestern Bell Telephone Co. v. Dixon, 575 S.W.2d 596 (Tex. Civ. App. 1978); Restatement (Second) of Torts § 594 (1977).

120 *See, e.g.*, Shenkman v. O'Malley, 2 A.D.2d 567, 157 N.Y.S.2d 290 (1956); Craig v. Wright, 182 Okla. 68, 76 P.2d 529 (1936); Haycox v. Dunn, 200 Va. 212, 104 S.E.2d 800 (1958).

of property that has been stolen,[121] or statements made in the course of collecting a bona fide debt.[122] The privilege is roughly analogous to the common law privilege of self-defense in response to physical attack, or the privilege of self-help to defend property.[123] As is the case with those privileges, the conditional privilege to defend legitimate self-interest is usually regarded as forfeited if the speaker publishes more than is reasonably required to defend his or her interest, or if the speaker publishes beyond the circle of persons to whom the self-defensive action is relevant.[124] (In this sense the analogy to self-defense of one's person and property is particularly apt: Excessive publication is conceptually parallel to the use of excessive force in self-defense.) In applying this privilege, courts are to weigh the interest of the publisher to determine whether it is "sufficiently important" as well as the extent to which publication of the defamatory matter was of service to the furtherance of that interest.[125]

[2] Statements Made in Furtherance of the Interests of Others

[a] In General

If in recognizing a self-interest privilege the common law appears to reward selfishness, it also rewards altruism, because it recognizes a conditional privilege to make statements for the protection of the legitimate interests of another.[126] The conditional privilege applies particularly when the party whose interests are being protected occupies such a close relationship to the speaker that the speaker has a moral or legal obligation to act to protect those interests.[127] This privilege finds its analogue in the more general common law privilege to use force to protect the safety of another, and, like its counterpart, the privilege to defame in furtherance of another's interest is lost if the publication extends beyond what is necessary to effectuate the defense. A wide

---

121 *See, e.g.*, Faber v. Byrle, 171 Kan. 38, 229 P.2d 718 (1951).

122 *See* Prosser & Keeton, *supra* note 2, § 115, at 826.

123 *See* Restatement (Second) of Torts §§ 63, 68, 77-86 (1975).

124 *See infra* § 8.09[1].

125 *See* Restatement (Second) of Torts § 594 (1977).

126 *See, e.g.*, Zuschek v. Whitmoyer Labs, Inc., 430 F. Supp. 1163 (E.D. Pa. 1977), *aff'd*, 571 F.2d 573 (3d Cir. 1978); Dillard Department Stores, Inc. v. Felton, 276 Ark. 304, 634 S.W.2d 135, 136 (1982); Institute of Athletic Motivation v. University of Illinois, 114 Cal. App. 3d 1, 170 Cal. Rptr. 411, 417 (1980); Gengler v. Phelps, 92 N.M. 465, 589 P.2d 1056, 1058-59 (1978); Restatement (Second) of Torts § 595 (1977).

127 *See* Restatement (Second) of Torts § 595(1)(b) and (2)b, and comment b (1977).

variety of statements are covered by the privilege, e.g., a warning that a prospective fiancé is an ex-convict,[128] a doctor's statement to protect a patient,[129] or an attorney's statement on behalf of a client.[130]

[b] Requested vs. Volunteered Information

The privilege may exist whether the information is requested by the person whose interest is being advanced,[131] or is simply volunteered.[132] Consistent with the common law's general suspicion of officious intermeddlers,[133] however, courts are generally more favorably inclined to grant the privilege when the information is furnished in response to a request.[134] The presence or absence of a request is not conclusive; it is merely one of the factors to be considered in determining whether the privilege applies.[135]

[c] Credit Reports

[i] The Rules Prior to *Dun & Bradstreet*

Defamation actions arising from credit reports bring the conditional privilege to further the interest of another into play; because such suits are so common, a number of special approaches have evolved in the credit reporting context.[136]

The majority of states recognize a qualified privilege of some sort for

---

128 *See* Prosser & Keeton, *supra* note 2, § 115, at 826.

129 Cash Drug Store v. Cannon, 47 S.W.2d 861 (Tex. Civ. App. 1932).

130 Kruse v. Rabe, 80 N.J.L. 378, 79 A. 316 (1910).

131 Restatement (Second) of Torts § 595(2)(a)(1977).

132 *See* Morton v. Knipe, 28 A.D. 94, 112 N.Y.S. 451 (1908).

133 *See* Prosser & Keeton, *supra* note 2, § 115, at 827 ("A point is reached at which the line must be drawn against officious intermeddling, where a reasonable person would conclude that the matter is none of his affair.").

134 *Compare* Willis v. Dimopolis Nursing Home, 336 So. 2d 1117 (Ala. 1976)(privilege upheld in response to request); Zenfield v. Hayes Freight Lines, Inc., 41 Ill. 2d 345, 243 N.E.2d 217 (1968)(same); Stevenson v. Baltimore Baseball Club, 250 Md. 482, 243 A.2d 533 (1968), *with* Henderson v. Teamsters Local 313, 90 Wash. 2d 666, 585 P.2d 147 (1978)(volunteered information not privileged).

135 Restatement (Second) of Torts § 595 comment j (1977).

136 *See generally* Maurer, *Common Law Defamation and the Fair Credit Reporting Act*, 72 Geo. L. Rev. 95, 99-105 (1983). *See also, e.g.*, Luster v. Retail Credit Co., 575 F.2d 609 (8th Cir. 1978); Anderson v. Dun & Bradstreet, Inc., 543 F.2d 732 (10th Cir. 1976); Hood v. Dun & Bradstreet, Inc., 486 F.2d 25 (5th Cir. 1973), *cert. denied*, 415 U.S. 985 (1974); Bartels v. Retail Credit Co., 185 Neb. 304, 175 N.W.2d 292 (1970).

credit reports.[137] A number of decisions require a showing of at least recklessness to defeat the privilege, essentially treating the matter as a public figure case subject to the actual malice test.[138] Most courts, however, have not applied the actual malice standard to credit reports.[139] Many courts have focused on whether the report was in good faith or bad faith,[140] or whether common law malice existed.[141] Finally, a few states recognize no privilege whatsoever for credit reports.[142]

The rationale favoring a strong conditional privilege for credit reports is that the person seeking the credit information normally has a strong interest in obtaining it, and the free flow of such commercial information is vital to society.

The counterargument, used to establish a weaker version of the privilege (such as one defeated by mere negligence) or even to justify total elimination of the privilege, is that credit information is simply not the sort of speech worthy of any special protection.[143] In *Grove v. Dun & Bradstreet, Inc.*,[144] for example, the Third Circuit in an influential decision refused to apply an actual malice test to such reports, noting the selective, finite audience to whom they are issued, the fact that subscribers agree to keep the information confidential, and the fact that the person reported on often has little or no chance to respond or gain

---

137 *See* Dun & Bradstreet, Inc. v. Greenmoss Builders, Inc., 105 S. Ct. 2939, 2963 (1985)(Brennan, J., dissenting); Maurer, *supra* note 147, at 99-105; Restatement (Second) of Torts § 595 comment h (1977).

138 *See, e.g.*, Luster v. Retail Credit Co., 575 F.2d 609 (8th Cir. 1978); Datacon, Inc. v. Dun & Bradstreet, Inc., 465 F. Supp. 706, 708 (N.D. Tex. 1979), *aff'd*, 601 F.2d 584 (5th Cir. 1979); Dun & Bradstreet, Inc. v. O'Neil, 46 S.W.2d 896, 900-01 (Tex. 1970).

139 *See, e.g.*, Hood v. Dun & Bradstreet, Inc., 486 F.2d 25, 28-29 (5th Cir. 1973), *cert. denied*, 414 U.S. 985 (1974); Oberman v. Dun & Bradstreet, Inc., 460 F.2d 1381, 1384 (7th Cir. 1972); Kansas Electric Supply Co. v. Dun & Bradstreet, Inc., 448 F.2d 647, 649 (10th Cir. 1971), *cert. denied*, 405 U.S. 1026 (1972); Grove v. Dun & Bradstreet, Inc., 438 F.2d 433 (3d Cir.), *cert. denied*, 404 U.S. 898 (1971); Roemer v. Retail Credit Co., 44 Cal. App. 3d 926, 933-34, 119 Cal. Rptr. 82, 86 (1975); Tom Olesker's Exciting World of Fashion, Inc. v. Dun & Bradstreet, Inc., 61 Ill. 2d 129, 137-38, 334 N.E.2d 160, 164 (1975).

140 *See* Anderson v. Dun & Bradstreet, Inc., 543 F.2d 732 (10th Cir. 1976); Krumholz v. TRW, Inc., 152 N.J. Super. 80, 88-89, 360 A.2d 413, 417 (1976).

141 *See* Dun & Bradstreet, Inc., v. Greenmoss Builders, Inc., 105 S. Ct. 2939 (1985)(no privilege in Vermont); Retail Credit Co. v. Russell, 234 Ga. 765, 771-75, 218 S.E.2d 54, 58-51 (1975)(no privilege in Georgia); Johnson v. Bradstreet Co., 77 Ga. 172 (1886)(same); Pacific Packing Co. v. Bradstreet Co., 25 Idaho 696, 139 P. 1007 (1914).

142 *See* Restatement (Second) of Torts § 595 comment h (1977).

143 *See* Watkins & Schwartz, Gertz *and the Common Law of Defamation: Of Fault, Nonmedia Defendants, and Conditional Privileges*, 15 Tex. Tech. L. Rev. 823, 856-57 (1984).

144 438 F.2d 433 (3d Cir.), *cert. denied*, 404 U.S.898 (1971).

access to the credit agency or its sources.[145] In *Hood v. Dun & Bradstreet, Inc.*,[146] the Fifth Circuit noted that while most jurisdictions do recognize a qualified privilege for credit reports, in those states that do not recognize the privilege there is a thriving credit reporting business and commercial credit transactions are not inhibited. The court cited an empirical study comparing credit transactions in Boise, Idaho, where no privilege exists, with those in Spokane, Washington, where a privilege is recognized.[147] Justice Powell's opinion in *Dun & Bradstreet* cited the Fifth Circuit analysis with approval.[148]

[ii] The Potential Influence of the *Dun & Bradstreet* Decision

Although the Supreme Court's opinion in *Dun & Bradstreet*[149] dealt with first amendment doctrine, and as a strict matter has no precedential value on the issue of common law conditional privilege, the Court's decision will undoubtedly have some collateral impact on how lower courts in the future analyze the conditional privilege problem for credit reports. As previously discussed,[150] the Court gave extremely short shrift to the argument that credit information has social value of sufficient moment to justify special first amendment protection.[151] Quoting from Professor Shiffrin, the Court noted that: "with respect to 'the case of a commercial supplier of credit information that defames a person applying for credit'—the case before us today—'If the first amendment requirements outlined in *Gertz* apply, there is something clearly wrong with the first amendment or with *Gertz*.' "[152] Given the Supreme Court's general denigration of the social importance of credit reporting information in *Dun & Bradstreet*, it seems reasonable to surmise that a spillover influence will be that credit reports will receive less favorable common law conditional privilege protection as well.

---

145 *Id.* at 436-38. *See also* Watkins & Schwartz, *supra* note 143, at 856-57.

146 486 F.2d 25 (5th Cir. 1973), *cert. denied*, 415 U.S. 985 (1974).

147 *Id.* at 32.

148 Dun & Bradstreet, Inc. v. Greenmoss Builders, Inc., 105 S. Ct. 2939, 2947 n.9 (1985).

149 *Id.*

150 *See supra* §§ 3.02-3.04.

151 105 S. Ct. at 2946-47.

152 *Id.* at 2946 n. 6 (quoting Shiffrin, *The First Amendment and Economic Regulation: Away From a General Theory of the First Amendment*, 78 Nw. L. Rev. 1212, 1268 (1983)).

[d] Reports on Employees

A second common invocation of the privilege to publish defamatory matters in furtherance of the interest of others involves defamation arising from reports evaluating employees. A conditional privilege does extend to such evaluations, whether they be from a present or past employer to a prospective employer[153] or "within the chain of command" by one employee charged with evaluating a fellow employee and reporting to a superior.[154]

Very few defamatory statements carry more potential for devastating harm to the victim than false and defamatory evaluations of an employee's work performance. Careers may turn on such evaluations and courts are thus faced with a powerful conflict between protecting the substantial social interest in candid and honest appraisals of an employee's competence and the equally substantial interest in safeguarding the employee from undeserved injury. The conditional privilege to publish such evaluations is thus well established, but by the same token courts are alert to potential abuses of the privilege, such as circulation of unfavorable evaluations to those with no need to see them, particularly when the charges involved are serious.[155]

The privilege has been extended to others who make employee evaluations, such as physicians[156] or private investigation agencies.[157]

---

153 *See, e.g.*, Zuschek v. Whitmoyer Laboratories, 430 F. Supp. 1163, 1166 (E.D. Pa. 1977), *aff'd without opinion*, 571 F.2d 573 (3d Cir. 1978); Weenig v. Wood, 169 Ind. App. 413, 349 N.E.2d 235, 248 (1976); Sindorf v. Jacron Sales Co., 27 Md. App. 53, 341 A.2d 856, 865-66 (Md. Sp. App. 1975), *aff'd*, 276 Md. 580, 350 A.2d 688 (1976); Gengler v. Phelps, 92 N.M. 465, 589 P.2d 1056, 1058-59 (N.M. App. 1978); Cribbs v. Montgomery Ward & Co., 202 Or. 8, 272 P.2d 978, 981 (1954); Swanson v. Speidel Corp., 110 R.I. 335, 293 A.2d 307, 310 (1972); Duncantell v. Universal Life Insurance Co., 446 S.W.2d 934, 937 (Tex. Civ. App. 1969).

154 *See, e.g.*, Dillard Department Stores, Inc. v. Felton, 276 Ark. 304, 634 S.W.2d 135, 136 (1982); Dobbyn v. Nelson, 2 Kan. App. 2d 358, 579 P.2d 721, *aff'd*, 225 Kan. 56, 587 P.2d 315 (1978); Berger v. Gilbert, 65 A.D.2d 882, 410 N.Y.S.2d 427 (1978). *See also* Gaines v. Cuna Mutual Ins. Soc'y, 681 F.2d 982, 987 (5th Cir. 1982).

155 *See* Dillard Department Stores, Inc v. Felton, 276 Ark. 304, 634 S.W.2d 135, 136 (1982); Weenig v. Wood, 169 Ind. App. 413, 349 N.E.2d 235, 248-49 (1976).

156 Hoesl v. United States, 451 F. Supp. 1170 (N.D. Cal. 1978).

157 Cambell v. Willmark Service System, 123 F.2d 204 (3d Cir. 1941); Roscoe v. Schoolitz, 105 Ariz. 310, 464 P.2d 333 (1970); Freeman v. Mills, 97 Cal. App. 2d 161, 217 P.2d 687 (1950); Dierson v. Robert Griffin Investigations, Inc., 92 Nev. 605, 555 P.2d 843 (1976).

[e] The Petitions Clause

When recommendations for employment involve the fitness of a prospective appointee to public office, common law conditional privileges take on a federal constitutional dimension. In *McDonald v. Smith*,[158] the plaintiff, who was being considered for an appointment as a United States Attorney in North Carolina, was allegedly libeled in two letters sent by the defendant to President Ronald Reagan, with copies to Presidential Advisor Edwin Meese, Senator Jesse Helmes, and others, disparaging the defendant's fitness for office.[159] Construing the rarely invoked petitions clause of the first amendment, which guarantees "the right of the people . . . to petition the Government for a redress of grievances," the Supreme Court rejected the defendant's claim of absolute immunity, holding that the first amendment merely imposes an obligation on a state to provide qualified immunity for such communications.[160] Under North Carolina's common law, an actual malice standard equivalent to *New York Times* protection was required to defeat the privilege;[161] the Supreme Court held that North Carolina's common law satisfied the demands of the first amendment.[162]

[3] Statements Made to Protect a Common Interest

[a] In General

A conditional privilege exists when the speaker and the recipient have legitimate common interests and the communication is made in furtherance of those interests.[163] The common interest privilege is frequently invoked when the defamatory communication involves persons with common interests in organizations or enterprises in which information is exchanged relevant to the group's conduct or activities.

158 105 S. Ct. 2787 (1985).

159 *Id.* at 2789.

160 *Id.* at 2790-91. *See also* White v. Nichols, 3 How. 266, 11 L. Ed. 591 (1845).

161 Dellinger v. Belk, 34 N.C. App. 488, 490, 238 S.E.2d 788, 789 (1977).

162 105 S. Ct. at 2791.

163 *See, e.g.*, Rush-Hampton Industries, Inc. v. Home Ventilating Inst., 419 F. Supp. 19 (M.D. Fla. 1976); Lull v. Wick Constuctions Co., 614 P.2d 321, 324 (Alaska 1980); Judge v. Rockford Memorial Hospital, 17 Ill. App. 2d 365, 376-77, 150 N.E.2d 202, 208 (2d Dist. 1958); Stevenson v. Baltimore Baseball Club, Inc., 250 Md. 482, 243 A.2d 533, 536 (1968); McBride v. Sears, Roebuck & Co., 306 Minn. 93, 235 N.W.2d 371, 374 (1975); Iacco v. Bohannon, 70 Mich. App. 463, 245 N.W.2d 791 (1976); Buckley v. Litman, 57 N.Y.2d 516, 457 N.Y.S.2d 221, 223, 443 N.E.2d 469 (1982).

Communications with religious groups,[164] professional groups,[165] fraternal organizations,[166] labor unions,[167] educational organizations,[168] between officials or directors of a corporation and stockholders,[169] or within an association of property owners[170] are examples. The privilege is rooted in situations in which there is a legal obligation to speak,[171] but in its modern form encompasses a broad range of circumstances involving shared interests and the need for a free interchange of information. There is even some support for the somewhat expansive proposition that the press may avail itself of the common interest privilege when reporting newsworthy events,[172] but for the most part the privilege has been circumscribed within more defined and limited relationships, such as within organizations.[173]

[b] Family Relationships

The *Restatement (Second)* classifies defamatory statements concerning the well-being of an immediate family member between one member of the family and the third person as subject to a special conditional privilege encompassing family relationships.[174] Although there is no question as to the validity or existence of this privilege, it probably does not require any independent classification as a special privilege; it is, rather, merely an application of either the interest-of-another privilege or the common-interest privilege, or both.

---

164 Pinn v. Lawson, 63 U.S. App. D.C. 370, 72 F.2d 742 (1934); Creswell v. Pruitt, 239 S.W.2d 165 (Tex. Civ. App. 1951); Rankin v. Phillippe, 206 Pa. Super. 27, 211 A.2d 56 (1965).

165 Judge v. Rockford Memorial Hospital, 17 Ill. App. 2d 365, 150 N.E.2d 202 (1958); Campbell v. St. Mary's Hospital, 312 Minn. 379, 252 N.W.2d 581 (1977); Buckley v. Litman, 57 N.Y.2d 516, 457 N.Y.S.2d 221, 223, 443 N.E.2d 469 (1982); Mick v. American Dental Ass'n, 49 N.J. Super. 262, 139 A.2d 570 (1958); Zito v. American Fed'n of Musicians, 60 A.D.2d 967, 401 N.Y.S.2d 929 (4th Dept. 1978).

166 Bayliss v. Grand Lodge of State of Louisiana, 131 La. 579, 59 So. 996 (1912); Reiniger v. Prickett, 192 Okla. 486, 137 P.2d 595 (1943).

167 Ward v. Painters' Local Union No. 300, 41 Wash. 2d 859, 252 P.2d 253 (1953).

168 Jamison v. Roberson, 21 Ill. App. 2d 364, 158 N.E.2d 82 (1959); Dobbyn v. Nelson, 2 Kan. App. 358, 579 P.2d 721 (1978).

169 Garey v. Jackson, 197 Mo. App. 217, 193 S.W. 920 (1917).

170 Bufalino v. Maxon Brothers, 368 Mich. 140, 117 N.W.2d 150 (1962).

171 *See* Eaton, *supra* note 104, at 1361.

172 *See* Maidman v. Jewish Publications, Inc., 54 Cal. 2d 643, 7 Cal. Rptr. 617, 355 P.2d 265 (1980); Seegmiller v. KSL, Inc., 626 P.2d 968 (Utah 1981).

173 *See supra* notes 175-81.

174 Restatement (Second) of Torts § 597 (1977). *See also* MacConnell v. Mitten, 131 Ariz. 22, 638 P.2d 689, 691 (1981); Faber v. Byrle, 171 Kan. 38, 229 P.2d 719, 723 (1951).

[4] Statements to Those Who Act in the Public Interest

A conditional privilege exists to communicate information to public officials relevant to the discharge of their official duties in the public interest.[175] The privilege embraces a wide spectrum of communications, including reports to law enforcement or other authorities concerning the prevention or detection of crime,[176] and complaints about the performance of public officials or institutions.[177] To a large degree, however, the functions of the public interest privilege are performed by other, more specific absolute or conditional common law privileges —such as the privilege for witnesses in legislative or judicial proceedings[178]—or they have been swallowed up by constitutional doctrines—such as the actual malice standard, which applies to any critique of a government official.[179]

[5] A Cross-Reference to the Common Law Fair Comment Privilege

The common law fair comment privilege was once routinely classified among the common law conditional privileges.[180] Fair comment issues have now been essentially subsumed into the fact/opinion distinction, and the *Restatement (Second)* has eliminated fair comment as a privilege, reclassifying it under the rubric of the rule that statements of opinion are no longer actionable.[181] The fair comment issue is similarly discussed in this volume as part of the general fact/opinion distinction issue.[182]

---

175 *See, e.g.*, Foltz v. Moore McCormack Lines, Inc., 189 F.2d 537 (2d Cir.), *cert. denied*, 342 U.S. 871 (1951); Tschinsky v. Superior Court, 124 Cal. App. 3d 534, 177 Cal. Rptr. 357, 600 (1981); Newark Trust Co. v. Bruwer, 51 Del. 188, 141 A.2d 615 (1958); Segall v. Piazza, 46 Misc. 2d 700, 260 N.Y.S.2d 543 (1965); Getchell v. Auto Bar Systems N.W. Inc., 73 Wash. 2d 831, 440 P.2d 843 (1968).

176 *See, e.g.*, Hutchinson v. New England Telephone & Telegraph Co., 350 Mass. 188, 214 N.E.2d 57 (1966)(bomb threat).

177 *See, e.g.*, Ring v. Schlesinger, 502 F.2d 479 (D.C. Cir. 1974); Swaaley v. United States, 180 Ct. Cl. 1, 376 F.2d 857 (1967); Zarate v. Continas, 553 S.W.2d 652 (Tex. Civ. App. 1977).

178 *See supra* §§ 8.03[1][d], 8.04[4].

179 *See supra* § 2.01.

180 *See* Restatement of Torts §§ 606-610 (1939).

181 Restatement (Second) of Torts, explanatory note to omitted Title B, §§ 606-10, at 297 (1977).

182 *See* Chapter 6, *supra*.

§ 8.09 Abuse of Privilege

[1] Excessive Publication

A conditional privilege is considered abused and therefore lost if the defendant knowingly publishes the defamatory matter to persons other than those to whom publication is privileged—those to whom publication is necessary to protect the interest giving rise to the privilege.[183] Publication to persons whose knowledge of the communication is unnecessary to protect the interest involved is normally abuse of the privilege, but this principle is qualified by a rule of reason that permits such publication to uninterested parties when it is incidental to publication to proper parties and the spillover to other recipients is not reasonably avoidable. Thus, to accuse a subordinate of dishonesty in a loud voice in the presence of a lobby full of customers is to abuse the privilege, but to shout "Stop, thief!" to a guard at the door of the same lobby, in light of a belief that someone is absconding with stolen money, would not abuse the privilege.[184]

[2] Publishing for Reasons Other than Protection of the Interest Giving Rise to the Privilege

To publish defamatory matter for purposes other than protection of the interests giving rise to the conditional privilege is an abuse of the privilege.[185] Similarly, to publish defamatory matter when one does not reasonably believe that the publication will further the interest giving rise to the privilege is an abuse of the privilege.[186] These general propositions, which cause defeasance of the privilege whenever the defamatory communication is published for reasons extraneous to the purposes justifying the privilege, are as a practical matter usually distilled in the cases under the rubric of publication for spite or ill will, discussed below.

---

[183] *See, e.g.*, Avins v. White, 627 F.2d 637, 645 (3d Cir.), *cert. denied*, 449 U.S. 982 (1980); Selby v. Savard, 134 Ariz. 222, 655 P.2d 342, 346 (1982); Institute of Athletic Motivation v. University of Illinois, 114 Cal. App. 3d 1, 170 Cal. Rptr. 411 (1980); Arkansas Associated Tel. Co. v. Blankenship, 211 Ark. 645, 201 S.W.2d 1019 (1947); Presnell v. Pell, 39 N.C. App. 538, 251 S.E.2d 692 (1979); Gray v. Allison Division, General Motors, 52 Ohio App. 2d 348, 370 N.E.2d 747 (1977).

[184] *See* Restatement (Second) of Torts § 604 comment a, illustrations (1) and (2) (1977).

[185] Restatement (Second) of Torts § 603 (1977).

[186] *Id.*, § 605.

[3] Publication with Common Law (Ill-Will) Malice

[a] In General

It is frequently held that a conditional privilege is forfeited if the publication is made with "malice" in the traditional common law sense of actual spite or ill will.[187]

[b] Spite and Legitimate Motives May Coexist

Although cases sometimes appear to indicate that any spite or ill will taints the conditional privilege and will result in its forfeiture,[188] the majority view is that when a spiteful or vengeful motive coexists with a legitimate and otherwise privileged interest in publishing the defamatory communication, the privilege will be lost only if the malicious motive predominates.[189] Thus, when a proper motivation falling within one of the recognized privileges exists, the fact that the defendant happens to hate the plaintiff and therefore derived some incidental spiteful glee from the defamatory publication is not enough to defeat the privilege.[190]

[4] Negligence

Some courts have stated that lack of "probable cause" or "reasonable belief" in the truth of a statement constitutes grounds for defeasance of a conditional privilege, essentially holding that it is forfeited through

---

187 *See, e.g.*, Hardee v. North Carolina Allstate Servs., Inc., 537 F.2d 1255, 1259-60 (4th Cir. 1976); Arsenault v. Allegheny Airlines, Inc., 485 F. Supp. 1373, 1379-80 (D. Mass.), *aff'd mem.*, 636 F.2d 1199 (1st Cir. 1980), *cert. denied*, 454 U.S. 821 (1981); Agarwal v. Johnson, 25 Cal. 3d 932, 944, 160 Cal. Rptr. 141 (1979); Newark Trust Co. v. Bruwer, 51 Del. 188, 141 A.2d 615 (1958); Powers v. Lewiston Evening Journal, 174 Me. 286, 86 A.2d 164 (1952); Powers v. Carvalho, 117 R.I. 519, 368 A.2d 1242 (1977); Prosser & Keeton, *supra* note 2, § 115, at 833-34.

188 *See* Stearns v. McManis, 543 S.W.2d 659 (Tex. Civ. App. 1976).

189 Restatement (Second) of Torts § 603 comment a (1977).

190 *See, e.g.*, Manbeck v. Ostrowski, 128 U.S. App. D.C. 1, 384 F.2d 970 (1967), *cert. denied*, 390 U.S. 966 (1968) (motive of ill will a "highly relevant factor"); New York & Puerto Rico S.S. Co. v. Garcia, 16 F.2d 734 (1st Cir. 1926); Prosser & Keeton, *supra* note 2, § 115, at 834. When spite or ill will is the "chief" or "predominate" factor, the privilege is lost. *See, e.g.*, Brewer v. Second Baptist Church of Los Angeles, 32 Cal. 2d 791, 197 P.2d 713 (1948); Mullen v. Lewiston Evening Journal, 147 Me. 286, 86 A.2d 164 (1952); Schafroth v. Baker, 276 Or. 39, 45-48, 553 P.2d 1046, 1049-50 (1976).

negligence.[191] As previously discussed, this position renders the conditional privilege meaningless in cases governed by the *Gertz* fault requirement, because negligence is necessary in any event.[192] This position remains meaningful, however, in cases that would otherwise be tried under a strict liability standard, for it raises the liability rule to negligence in situations encompassed by a conditional privilege.[193] Even prior to *Gertz*, many decisions rejected the view that mere negligence would defeat a conditional privilege, requiring malice of some kind, or excessive publication, to trigger loss of the privilege.[194]

[5] Actual Malice, Knowlege of Falsity, Recklessness

A growing number of decisions are placing conditional common law privileges on a par with the *New York Times* standard, holding that such privileges are lost only if the defendant acted with knowledge of falsity or recklessness (though the decisions do not always employ the specific terminology "actual malice").[195]

§ 8.10 The "Fair Report" Privilege

[1] Function and Rationale

The common law has long recognized the unique privilege to publish fair and accurate reports of certain defined judicial, legislative, and executive proceedings.[196] Known variously as the privilege of "fair re-

---

[191] *See* Mercedes-Benz of North America, Inc. v. Finberg, 58 A.D.2d 808, 809, 396 N.Y.S.2d 260, 262 (1977) (lack of probable cause); Zuschek v. Whitmoyer Laboratories, Inc., 430 F. Supp. 1163, 1166 (E.D. Pa. 1977), *aff'd mem.*, 571 F.2d 573 (3d Cir. 1978)("has no reasonable ground for so believing"); Restatement of Torts § 601 (1938) (lack of reasonable grounds to believe in truth of statement is abuse of privilege).

[192] *See supra* § 8.07[3].

[193] *See supra* § 8.07[3]. Strict liability as the base liability rule may now be permissible in private figure cases not involving issues of public concern. *See* Dun & Bradstreet, Inc. v. Greenmoss Builders, Inc., 105 S. Ct. 2939 (1985). *See also supra* §§ 3.02-3.05, 8.07[3].

[194] *See* Prosser & Keeton, *supra* note 2, § 115, at 834-35.

[195] *See, e.g.*, Hoesl v. United States, 451 F. Supp. 1170, 1179 (N.D. Cal, 1978); Roemer v. Retail Credit Co., 3 Cal. App. 3d 368, 83 Cal. Rptr. 540 (1970); Marchesi v. Franchino, 283 Md. 131, 387 A.2d 1129, 1131-33 (1978); Petition of Retailers Commercial Agency, Inc., 342 Mass. 515, 174 N.E.2d 376 (1961); Dun & Bradstreet, Inc. v. O'Neil, 456 S.W.2d 896 (Tex. 1970); Restatement (Second) of Torts § 600 (1977).

[196] Prosser & Keeton, *supra* note 2, § 115, at 836. The privilege dates back long before first amendment restrictions were implanted on the law of defamation. *See, e.g.*, Wohlfort v. Wohlfort, 125 Kan. 234, 263 P. 1062 (1928); Smith v. Smith, 192 Mich. 566, 159 N.W. 349 (1916); Glass v. Bennett, 89 Tenn. 478, 14 S.W. 1085 (1891); Ratcliffe v. Walker, 117

port," the "record" privilege, or the "reporter's" privilege, it is a somewhat narrower common law antecedent to the emerging modern "neutral reportage" privilege.[197] Like the neutral reportage privilege, the fair report privilege is technically an exception to the normal common law position that one who republishes a libel "adopts it as his own" and becomes liable as if he were the originator of the defamation.[198] The fair report privilege thus permits the publisher of information from covered proceedings to repeat defamatory statements made at those proceedings without the usual republisher's liability. The fair report privilege continues to thrive; it remains one of the most powerful and frequently invoked common law defenses, particularly for the press. The rationale for the privilege is of considerable vintage, but remains as relevant as ever: The reporter is a surrogate for the public, permitting it to observe through the reporter's eyes how the business of government is being conducted.[199] The fair report privilege is thus a common law doctrine that partakes of values at the very core of first amendment jurisprudence, the political enlightenment function of the first amendment.[200] In the words of Justice Holmes, "it is of the highest moment that those who administer justice should always act under the sense of public responsibility, and that every citizen should be able to satisfy himself with his own eyes as to the mode in which a public duty is performed."[201]

Va. 569, 85 S.E. 575 (1915); Baird v. Carle, 157 Wis. 565, 147 N.W. 834 (1914). *But see* Lowe v. Rockford Newspaper, Inc., 179 Ill. App. 3d 592, 534 N.E.2d 549 (1989) (fair report privilege does not apply when newspaper's article contains allegedly defamatory statements that were not found in the police report the article was based on).

197 *See supra* § 4.15.

198 *See id.*

199 *See* Prosser & Keeton, *supra* note 2, § 115, at 836. *See also* Read v. News-Journal, 474 A.2d 119 (Del. 1984).

200 *See supra* § 1.07[3]. *See also* Medico v. Time, Inc., 643 F.2d 134 (3d Cir.), *cert. denied*, 454 U.S. 836 (1981); Bell v. Associated Press, 584 F. Supp. 128 (D.D.C. 1984); Hauser v. Urchisin, 231 So. 2d 6 (Fla. 1970); Shifflet v. Thomson Newspapers, 69 Ohio St. 2d 179, 431 N.E.2d 1014 (1982).

201 Cowley v. Pulsifer, 137 Mass. 392, 394, 50 Am. Rep. 318 (1884)(quoting Rex v. Wright, 8 Term. R. 293, 101 Eng. Rep. 1396 (1799)).

[2] Proceedings Covered

[a] Judicial Proceedings

[i] In General

Judicial proceedings are clearly covered by the privilege.[202] The defi-

(*Text continued on page 8-35*)

---

[202] *See, e.g.*, Levine v. CMP Publications, 738 F.2d 660 (5th Cir. 1984); Lal v. CBS, Inc., 726 F.2d 97 (3d Cir. 1984); Porter v. Guam Publications, Inc., 643 F.2d 615, 618 (9th Cir.), *cert. denied*, 454 U.S. 940 (1981)("judicial" or "other public" proceedings); Ronwin v. Shapiro, 657 F.2d 1071, 1075 (9th Cir. 1981); Cianci v. New Times Publishing Co., 639

nition of "judicial proceeding" is quite broad, applying not only to in-court proceedings before a judge but to any exercise of judicial power.[203] Appellate as well as trial procedures are clearly covered; a summary of a state supreme court decision in a law review, for example, falls within the privilege.[204]

[ii] Official Action

The older view is that because of the potential for abuse through the strategy of filing a suit with defamatory allegations and then promptly discontinuing the action, or simply permitting it to languish, the fair report privilege for judicial proceedings in not "activated" until some official action in the litigation has transpired.[205] The more modern view, however, is that no official action is necessary; the fair report privilege, for example, thus extends to a summary of the accusations in a complaint, though no official action has taken place.[206]

[b] Arrests and Other Law Enforcement Activity

Reports of arrests are encompassed by the fair report privilege.[207] The mere informal utterances of the police, however, are not covered.[208] Summaries of FBI reports have been held covered by the privilege,[209] as have a summary of a police officer's affidavit in support of an

---

F.2d 54 (2d Cir. 1980); Ricci v. Venture Magazine, Inc., 574 F. Supp. 1563 (D. Mass. 1983); Roberts v. Birmingham Post Co., 10 Med. L. Rep. (BNA) 2208 (Ala. Cir. Ct. 1984); Jamason v. Palm Beach Newspapers, 450 So. 2d 1130 (Fla. Dist. Ct. App. 1984); Pearce v. Courier-Journal & Louisville Times Co., 683 S.W.2d 633 (Ky. Ct. App. 1985); Sibley v. Holyoke Transcript-Telegram Publishing Co., 391 Mass. 468, 461 N.E.2d 823 (1984).

203 *See* Sibley v. Holyoke Transcript-Telegram Publishing Co., 391 Mass. 468, 461 N.E.2d 823 (1984).

204 Ronwin v. Shapiro, 657 F.2d 1071, 1075 (9th Cir. 1981).

205 Prosser & Keeton, *supra* note 2, § 115, at 837.

206 *See, e.g.*, American District Telegraph Co. v. Brink's, Inc., 380 F.2d 131 (7th Cir. 1967); Hanish v. Westinghouse Broadcasting Co., 487 F. Supp. 397 (E.D. Pa. 1980); Johnson v. Johnson Publishing Co., 271 A.2d 696 (D.C. 1970); Newell v. Field Enterprises, Inc., 91 Ill. App. 3d 735, 415 N.E.2d 434 (1980); Langford v. Vanderbilt University, 199 Tenn. 389, 287 S.W.2d 32 (1956).

207 Piracci v. Hearst Corp., 263 F. Supp. 511 (D. Md.), *aff'd mem.*, 371 F.2d 1016 (4th Cir. 1966); Lotrich v. Life Printing & Publishing Co., 117 Ill. App. 2d 15, 253 N.E.2d 899 (1969); Francois v. Capital City Press, 166 So. 2d 84 (La. 1964); Koren v. Capital-Gazette Newspapers, Inc., 22 Md. App. 576, 325 A.2d 140, *cert. denied*, 273 Md. 721 (1974).

208 Medico v. Time, Inc., 643 F.2d 134 (3d Cir.), *cert. denied*, 454 U.S. 836 (1981).

209 Sibley v. Holyoke Transcript-Telegram Publishing Co., 391 Mass. 468, 461 N.E.2d 823 (1984).

application for a search warrant,[210] and a prosecutor's affidavit of probable cause.[211] Reports by private persons to law enforcement agencies, however, are not within the privilege.[212]

[c] Legislative Proceedings

The privilege includes coverage of legislative proceedings,[213] including subordinate legislative bodies such as municipal councils.[214]

[d] Executive, Administrative, and Other Public Proceedings

The privilege has been applied to a wide spectrum of executive, administrative, and other public proceedings. California law, for example, generally protects reports of any "public" meeting;[215] New York extends protection to reports of any "official proceeding."[216]

[3] The Requirement of Accuracy and Fairness

[a] In General

Since the rationale of the fair report privilege is that the reporter acts as a substitute for the citizen's personal observation of public proceedings, the privilege is lost if the report is not an accurate and fair summary of what transpired.[217] Editorializing, or writing a one-sided account, will cause a privilege to be lost.[218]

---

210 Mark v. Seattle Times, 96 Wash. 2d 473, 635 P.2d 1081 (1981), *cert. denied,* 454 U.S. 1124 (1982).

211 Pittsburg Courier Publishing Co. v. Lubore, 200 F.2d 355 (D.C. Cir. 1952).

212 Cresson v. Louisville Courier-Journal, 299 F.2d 487 (6th Cir. 1924).

213 Swede v. Passaic Daily News, 30 N.J. 320, 153 A.2d 36 (1959).

214 *See, e.g.,* Brandon v. Gazette Publishing Co., 234 Ark. 332, 352 S.W.2d 92 (1961)(official report to governor); Begley v. Louisville Times Co., 272 Ky. 805, 115 S.W.2d 345 (1938)(adjutant general); Painter v. E.W. Scripps Co., 104 Ohio App. 237, 148 N.E.2d 503 (1957)(coroner); Restatement (Second) of Torts § 611 comment i (1977).

215 Kilgore v. Younger, 102 Cal. App. 3d 744, 162 Cal. Rptr. 469 (1980), *aff'd,* 30 Cal. 3d 770, 180 Cal. Rptr. 657, 640 P.2d 793 (1982).

216 N.Y. Civil Rights Law § 74 (McKinney 1976).

217 Restatement (Second) of Torts § 611 comment f (1977). *Accord,* Time, Inc. v. Firestone, 424 U.S. 448 (1976); Schiavone Construction Co. v. Time, Inc., 735 F.2d 94 (3d Cir. 1984); Brown & Williamson Tobacco Corp. v. Jacobson, 713 F.2d 262 (7th Cir. 1983); Hartzog v. United Press Associations, 202 F.2d 81 (4th Cir. 1953); Williams v. WCAU-TV, 555 F. Supp. 198 (E.D. Pa. 1983); Newell v. Field Enterprises, Inc., 91 Ill. App. 3d 735, 415 N.E.2d 434 (1980); O'Brien v. Franich, 19 Wash. App. 189, 575 P.2d 258 (1978).

218 Hogan v. New York Times Co., 313 F.2d 354 (2d Cir. 1963); Robinson v. Johnson, 239 F. 671 (8th Cir. 1917); Book v. Plainfield Courier-News, 45 N.J. Super. 302, 132 A.2d 523 (1957).

[b] The Substantial Accuracy Test

Most official proceedings must be condensed and summarized in reports about them to the general public, and perfect accuracy in recounting the proceedings is not required. Rather, borrowing from the test utilized to determine the "truth" issue,[219] courts merely require that the report of the proceeding be "substantially accurate."[220] Similarly, minor errors that do not relate to the sting or gist of the defamatory charge do not cause the privilege to be forfeited.[221] The accuracy requirement, it must be remembered, relates to what transpired at the proceedings, *not* to the objective truth of the underlying defamatory charges.[222]

---

219 *See* Chapter 5, *supra.*

220 *See, e.g.*, Schuster v. United States News & World Report, 459 F. Supp. 973 (D. Minn. 1978), *aff'd*, 602 F.2d 850 (8th Cir. 1979); Hopkins v. Keith, 348 So. 2d 999 (La. App. 1977); Holy Spirit Ass'n v. New York Times Co., 49 N.Y.2d 63, 68, 399 N.E.2d 1185, 1187, 424 N.Y.S.2d 165, 168 (1979); Binder v. Triangle Publications, Inc., 442 Pa. 319, 324, 275 A.2d 53, 56 (1971); Dudley v. Farmers Branch Daily Times, 550 S.W.2d 99 (Tex. Civ. App. 1977).

221 Reeves v. American Broadcasting Companies, 719 F.2d 602 (2d Cir. 1983); Restatement (Second) of Torts § 611 comment f (1977). In the *Firestone* case, however, the Supreme Court appeared willing to countenance an extremely technical error as sufficient to avoid the fair report privilege under Florida law. *See* Time, Inc. v. Firestone, 424 U.S. 448 (1976), dicussed *supra* § 2.07.

222 Mathis v. Philadelphia Newspapers, Inc., 455 F. Supp. 406 (E.D. Pa. 1978). The "truth" in this sense is not that the plaintiff did what the defamatory charges said he did, but that the defamatory charges were in fact made during the course of an official proceeding. *See also* the discussion of neutral reportage, *supra* § 4.15.

CHAPTER 9

Damages and Other Remedies

§ 9.01 Overview

[1] Linkage to Substantive Rules

The rules governing damages and other remedies in the modern law of defamation are, like most of the field today, a composite of common law and constitutional law doctrines. Under *Gertz*[1] and *Dun & Bradstreet*,[2] damages rules are inextricably intertwined with constitutional fault requirements geared to the public or private status of the plaintiff and the public or private status of the speech involved.[3] Similarly, the category of special damages is intimately linked to the confusing array of state common law rules governing libel and slander per se and per quod.[4]

[2] The Interest in Reform

As discussed later in this chapter,[5] juries today are notorious for their free and easy willingness to award often stupendous sums as damages to defamation plaintiffs, while judges and appellate courts continue frequently to trim or eliminate those awards. The fear that some of these gargantuan awards will begin to make it through the litigation gauntlet intact, and the often enormous legal costs attending the defense of a defamation action even if it ends in victory for the defendant, have generated renewed interest among many media lawyers in reforming the structure of defamation remedies.[6]

By the same token, many plaintiffs are deeply frustrated by the current system, which from their perspective as well is costly and often painstakingly slow and cumbersome. Media critics and members of the plaintiff's bar have thus also argued for adjustments in the system, calling for changes to make the remedies available for reputational vindication more plain, speedy, and efficient. Some of the proposals for reform in this area are discussed later in this chapter.[7]

[3] Terminology

The tendency to misuse terms in the damages area, though perhaps not as egregious as in the area of the per se and per quod rules, is none-

---

1 Gertz v. Robert Welch, Inc., 418 U.S. 323 (1974).

2 Dun & Bradstreet, Inc. v. Greenmoss Builders, Inc., 105 S. Ct. 2939 (1985).

3 *See* chart in § 3.05, *supra*, and § 9.09, *infra*.

4 *See* Chapter 7, *supra*.

5 *See infra* § 9.14.

6 *See generally* Lewis, New York Times v. Sullivan *Reconsidered: Time to Return to "The Central Meaning of the First Amendment,"* 83 Colum. L. Rev. 603 (1983); Smolla, *Let the Author Beware: The Rejuvenation of the American Law of Libel*, 132 U. Pa L. Rev. 1 (1983).

7 *See infra* § 9.13.

theless a recurring problem. The various categories of damages should thus be referred to with reasonable attention and precision.

§ 9.02 Nominal Damages

[1] When Appropriate

In any defamation action the plaintiff, if he or she prevails, is at minimum entitled to an award of nominal damages, such as six cents or one dollar.[8] Nominal damages may be awarded in two situations. The (*Text continued on page 9-5*)

---

[8] *See, e.g.,* Buckley v. Littell, 539 F.2d 882 (2d Cir. 1976), *cert. denied,* 429 U.S. 1062 (1977); Elliot v. Roach, 409 N.E.2d 661, 664 (Ind. App. 1980); Kraisinger v. Liggett, 3 Kan. App. 2d 235, 592 P.2d 447, 479 (1979); Restatement (Second) of Torts § 620 (1977).

first involves the preferences of the plaintiff, the second the judgment of the jury.

[a] Plaintiff's Preference

In some cases the plaintiff may for personal reasons not desire a substantial monetary award; rather, the suit may have been brought for the sole purpose of obtaining vindication of the plaintiff's character. Certain plaintiffs may think it unseemly to seek money. Others may wish to have their reputations restored without financially crippling the defendant. When the plaintiff seeks only nominal damages, the defamation suit is in effect a declaratory judgment action.

[b] The Jury's Judgment

[i] Award of Significant Damages Not Appropriate

The more common application of nominal damages occurs when the plaintiff has in fact sought compensatory or punitive damages but the jury for some reason feels that, although the plaintiff has been defamed and the defendant is legally culpable, justice requires only nominal damages. The "signal" from the jury for such an award is usually that the plaintiff's character is so bad that it was not significantly injured by the defamation,[9] or that, although plaintiff's character was good, the defamation was trivial and the plaintiff's suit essentially frivolous.[10]

[ii] As a "Peg" for Punitive Damages

In some cases an award of nominal damages is treated as a sort of peg upon which to hang a more substantial award of punitive damages. In *Goldwater v. Ginzburg*,[11] for example, the jury awarded one dollar in nominal damages and $75,000 in punitive damages.

[2] Constitutional Questions

There is some question whether nominal damages are constitutionally permissible in cases subject to the *Gertz* actual harm requirements—cases involving private figure plaintiffs and matters of public concern—

Nominal damages were recently awarded in physicist and genetics theorist William Shockley's suit against the *Atlanta Constitution*. *See* Shockley v. Cox Enterprises, Inc., 10 Med. L. Rep. (BNA) 1222 (N.D. Ga. 1983).

[9] *See* Restatement (Second) of Torts § 620 comment a (1977).

[10] Elliot v. Roach, 409 N.E.2d 661, 684 (Ind. App. 1979).

[11] 414 F.2d 324 (2d Cir. 1969), *cert. denied*, 396 U.S. 1049 (1970).

on the theory that nominal damages are at times granted without proof of actual harm.[12] The argument is more academic than practical; it is more sensible to treat nominal damages as a form of declaratory judgment in such instances and outside of the *Gertz* actual harm rule.

§ 9.03 Compensatory Damages

[1] Not a Term of Art

In the law of defamation, compensatory damages is not a specific category or term of art as such. The word "compensatory" in a nontechnical descriptive sense merely refers to all damages designed to compensate for injury, rather than those damages that are "punitive," i.e., designed to punish the defendant.[13]

[2] Types

There were four types of compensatory damages at common law prior to *Gertz:* (1) special damages, or damages involving pecuniary injury; (2) general damages involving actual proof of injury to a plaintiff's reputation; (3) general damages involving actual proof of injury to a plaintiff's emotional well-being; and (4) general damages awarded without proof of injury but merely "presumed" to exist. Depending on the jurisdiction and the special new rules created by the combination of *Gertz* and *Dun & Bradstreet,* all four of these forms of compensatory damages continue to have relevance to the modern law of defamation.

§ 9.04 General Damages

[1] Types

The term general damages refers to all forms of compensatory dam-

---

12 *See* Restatement (Second) of Torts § 620 comment c (1977).

13 Although early tort law was a spin-off of the criminal law and included as a primary emphasis policies of deterence and punishment, it is worth observing that the primary mission of modern tort law is to provide just compensation for injured victims. *See* W. Prosser, D. Dobbs, R. Keeton, and D. Owen, Prosser and Keeton on Torts § 2 at 7 (5th ed. 1984); Anderson, *Reputation, Compensation, and Proof,* 25 Wm. & Mary L. Rev. 747 (1984).

ages *other than* pecuniary losses, which fall under the heading of special damages.[14]

General damages include "actual damages," those damages supported by the existence of evidence,[15] and "presumed damages," those presumptively in existence as a matter of law that may be awarded without any evidentiary support.[16] General damages are in turn subdividable into damage to reputation, and damage to the defendant's internal emotional or mental state.

[2] Constitutional Rules

In cases governed by *Dun & Bradstreet*,[17] cases involving private figure plaintiffs and no issue of public concern, and thus subject to no special constitutional damages restrictions, states are free to provide the full range of general damages to plaintiffs, including presumed damages. In cases subject to the *Gertz* damages restrictions,[18] cases involving private figure plaintiffs and matters of public concern, states may only award actual general damages—presumed damages are not permitted. Finally, in cases in which actual malice is established (by definition, all public official and public figure cases in which the plaintiff prevails), no constitutional restrictions on damages exist, and states may again provide plaintiffs the full range of general damages.[19]

§ 9.05 Presumed Damages

[1] Function and Rationale

Presumed damages, a subclass of general damages, continue to play a significant role in modern defamation law. Presumed damages are a form of compensatory damages relatively unique in the world of modern tort law: they may be awarded without any actual evidence of

---

[14] Restatement (Second) of Torts § 621 comment a (1977).

[15] *See infra* § 9.06.

[16] *See infra* § 9.05

[17] Dun & Bradstreet, Inc. v. Greenmoss Builders, Inc., 105 S. Ct. 2939 (1985).

[18] Gertz v. Robert Welch, Inc., 418 U.S. 323 (1974).

[19] *Gertz* by its terms exempted all cases in which *New York Times* actual malice is demonstrated from its restrictions on damages, stating that the "plaintiff who establishes liability under a *less demanding standard* than that stated by *New York Times* may recover only such damages as are sufficient to compensate him for actual injury." *Id.* at 350.

injury.[20] When the doctrine of presumed damages is applied, "[t]he plaintiff is relieved of the necessity of producing any proof whatsoever that he has been injured."[21] Instead, the jury is instructed that it may "presume" that injury took place from the mere fact that defamatory matter was published by the defendant.[22] As the Supreme Court put it in *Dun & Bradstreet*, "[T]he rationale of the common law rules has been the experience and judgment of history that 'proof of actual damage will be impossible in a great many cases where, from the character of the defamatory words and the circumstances of publication, it is all but certain that serious harm has resulted in fact.' "[23] As a result of this bit of common law psychology, "courts for centuries have allowed juries to presume that some damage occurred from many defamatory utterances and publications."[24] The Supreme Court has additionally stated that the common law presumed harm rule "furthers the state interest in providing remedies for defamation by ensuring that those remedies are effective."[25] Indeed, it goes without saying that any remedy involving an award of damages without proof of injury is bound to be *quite* effective.

[2] When Constitutionally Permissible

Presumed damages remain constitutionally permissible today at the top end and the bottom end of the defamation spectrum; like so much else today, only the middle class feels the pinch.

---

20 *See* Belli v. Orlando Daily Newspapers, Inc., 389 F.2d 579 (5th Cir. 1967), *cert. denied*, 393 U.S. 825 (1968); Missouri Pacific R.R. v. Arkansas Sherriff's Boys' Ranch, 280 Ark. 53, 655 S.W.2d 839 (1983); Dalton v. Meister, 52 Wis. 2d 173, 188 N.W.2d 494, *cert. denied*, 405 U.S. 934 (1971); Anderson, *supra* note 12, at 747.

21 McCormick, *The Measure of Damages for Defamation*, 12 N.C. L. Rev. 120, 127 (1934).

22 *Id.*

23 Dun & Bradstreet, Inc. v. Greenmoss Builders, Inc., 105 S. Ct. 2939, 2946 (1985) (quoting W. Prosser, Law of Torts § 112, at 765 (4th ed. 1981)). *See also* Rowe v. Metz, 195 Colo. 424, 425-26, 579 P.2d 83, 84 (1978); Note, *Developments in the Law—Defamation*, 69 Harv. L. Rev. 875, 891-92 (1956).

24 Dun & Bradstreet, Inc. v. Greenmoss Builders, Inc., 105 S. Ct. 2939, 2946 (1985) (citing Restatement of Torts § 568 comment b (1938) (noting that Hale announced that damages were to be presumed for libel as early as 1670)).

25 Dun & Bradstreet, Inc. v. Greenmoss Builders, Inc., 105 S. Ct. 2939, 2946 (1985).

[a] When Actual Malice Is Established

Presumed damages are permitted in any case in which actual malice is established—by definition, any plaintiff's victory involving a public official or public figure.[26]

[b] Cases Governed by *Dun & Bradstreet*

At the opposite end of the spectrum, *Dun & Bradstreet* now authorizes presumed damages when the case is exempt from *Gertz* because it involves a private figure plaintiff and no matter of public concern.[27]

[c] Not Permitted in *Gertz* Negligence Cases

Presumed damages are not permitted, however, in those cases covered by the *Gertz* actual harm requirement: private figure cases involving issues of public concern, when only negligence, and not actual malice, is established.[28] Note that in a case involving a private figure plaintiff and matters of public concern, the plaintiff is always free to attempt to go beyond the basic burden of demonstrating negligence, and also establish actual malice. If the plaintiff does establish actual malice, he or she then becomes constitutionally eligible for presumed damages, and for punitive damages as well. Even in such private figure/public concern cases, therefore, it will often be useful strategically for the plaintiff's attorney to plead and attempt to prove actual malice.

---

[26] Gertz v. Robert Welch, Inc., 418 U.S. 323, 350 (1974). *Gertz* placed restrictions on presumed damages only when actual malice is not established. *See supra* note 19. After *Gertz* the *Restatement (Second)* declined to take a position on whether presumed damages could be recovered when "actual malice" is established, despite *Gertz's* apparent clarity on the point. Restatement (Second) of Torts § 621, caveat at 319 (1977). The question would appear to have been resolved by a statement in the *Dun & Bradstreet* opinion interpreting *Gertz:* "we held that a State could not allow recovery of presumed and punitive damages absent a showing of 'actual malice.' " Dun & Bradstreet, Inc. v. Greenmoss Builders, Inc., 105 S. Ct. 2939, 2944 (1985).

[27] 105 S. Ct. at 2946.

[28] Gertz v. Robert Welch, Inc., 418 U.S. 323, 350 (1985); Little Rock Newspapers, Inc. v. Dodrill, 281 Ark. 25, 660 S.W.2d 933 (1983).

§ 9.06 Actual Damages

[1] Definition

Actual damages consist of those two types of general damages other than pecuniary loss (special damages) and nonproven loss (presumed damages). Actual damages are thus damages established by evidentiary proof, but of a nonpecuniary nature.[29] In contrast to the relatively precise and objective dollar value that will often be assignable to the special damages category, the dollar value attached to actual damages will always of necessity be somewhat subjective.

[2] When Constitutionally Required

Actual damages are required by the Constitution in any case governed by the *Gertz* negligence standard,[30] that is, any private figure plaintiff case involving matters of public concern in which actual malice is not established.[31] Cases in which actual malice is established, and cases that under *Dun & Bradstreet*[32] involve private figure plaintiffs and no matters of public concern, are exempt from constitutional actual harm requirements.[33]

[3] The Two Subdivisions

In *Gertz* the Supreme Court required only that actual harm be supported by proof.[34] Rather than limiting actual harm to reputational injury alone, the Court included within the definition the plaintiff's subjective mental or emotional distress:[35] "Indeed, the more customary types of actual harm inflicted by defamatory falsehood include impairment of reputation and standing in the community, personal humiliation, and mental anguish and suffering."[36] In the aftermath of *Gertz* two approaches developed regarding the mental or emotional distress component of actual harm. Some decisions permitted emotional distress

---

29 *See* Gertz v. Robert Welch, Inc., 418 U.S. 323, 350 (1974).

30 *Id.*

31 *See supra* § 9.05[2] and note 26.

32 Dun & Bradstreet, Inc. v. Greenmoss Builders, Inc., 105 S. Ct. 2939 (1985).

33 *See supra* § 9.05[2].

34 418 U.S. at 350 ("All awards must be supported by competent evidence concerning the injury, although there need be no evidence which assigns an actual dollar value to the injury.").

35 *Id.*

36 *Id.*

damages only "parasitically" to damages based upon proof of reputational injury, while other decisions permitted evidence of emotional distress standing alone to suffice as a basis for an award of actual damages. As explained below, the Supreme Court has made it clear that the choice is a matter of state law; the Constitution permits evidence of emotional distress standing alone to suffice as actual harm.[37]

[4] Decisions Restricting the Award

[a] In General

In the aftermath of *Gertz* a number of state court cases have decided as a matter of state law to reaffirm the classic distinction between the functions of the tort of defamation and the functions of the various invasion of privacy and emotional distress torts by restricting recovery for mental or emotional disturbance in defamation actions to those cases in which the plaintiff first establishes harm to his reputation. In New York, for example, absent proof of harm to reputation, a plaintiff may not recover damages for mental anguish on a claim of defamation unless the plaintiff proves malice.[38] The Kansas and Arkansas Supreme Courts recently endorsed this position, drawing on the historical function of the tort of defamation for support. In *Gobin v. Globe Publishing Co.*,[39] the Kansas Supreme Court held that "damage to one's reputation is the essence and gravamen of an action for defamation" and that "the plaintiff in an action for defamation must first offer proof of harm to reputation; any claim for mental anguish is 'parasitic,' and compensable only after damage to reputation has been established."[40] Similarly, in *Little Rock Newspapers, Inc. v. Dodrill*,[41] the Arkansas Supreme Court declared that "[t]he law of defamation has always attempted to balance

[37] *See* discussion in § 9.05[5], *infra.*

[38] *See* France v. St. Clare's Hospital & Health Center, 82 A.D.2d 1, 441 N.Y.S.2d 79 (1st Dept. 1981)("by naked allegations [of purported emotional trauma and periods of sexual impotence] . . . plaintiff attempts to bootstrap claims for emotional distress. These claims are not compensable, however, since damages are recoverable in a defamation action only when concomitant with a loss of reputation."); Salomone v. MacMillan Publishing Co., 77 A.D.2d 501, 502, 429 N.Y.S.2d 441 (1980)("As to the claim for mental anguish, it has long been held in this state that such damage is compensable only when it is concomitant with loss of reputation.") (citing Terwilliger v. Wands, 17 N.Y. 54, 72 Am. Dec. 420 (1858)).

[39] 232 Kan. 1, 649 P.2d 1239 (1982).

[40] *Id.* at 6-7, 649 P.2d at 1243-44.

[41] 281 Ark. 25, 660 S.W.2d 938 (1983).

the tension between the individual's right to protect his reputation and the right of free speech. To totally change the character of defamation to allow recovery when there has been no loss of the former right would be an unjustified infringement on the First Amendment."[42]

[b] Consistency with the Common Law Tradition

These decisions holding that injury to reputation is a prerequisite to recovery, at least in the absence of a showing of actual malice, are consistent with the mainstream tradition in the American law of defamation. Although recovery for emotional distress has been permitted as a parasitic component of defamation damages, the orthodoxy has been that the law of defamation exists not to provide compensation for emotional disturbance but to remedy a wrongful disruption in the "relational interest" that an individual has in maintaining personal esteem in the eyes of others.[43] The traditional common law position thus was to distinguish between reputational injury and invasion of privacy.[44] In the words of the Massachusetts Supreme Judicial Court, "the fundamental difference between a right to privacy and a right to freedom from defamation is that the former directly concerns one's own peace of mind, while the latter concerns primarily one's reputation."[45]

[5] Emotional Distress as a Free-Standing Component of Actual Damages

[a] The *Firestone* Case

The decisions discussed above requiring evidence of injury to reputation as a prerequisite to recovery of actual damages, although they invoke references to the first amendment,[46] *are purely decisions of state law:* The first amendment does *not* require injury to reputation to establish actual harm—evidence of emotional distress standing alone will suffice.

---

[42] 660 S.W.2d at 936. *See also* Anderson, *supra* note 13, at 758-59.

[43] *See* L. Green, Cases on Injuries to Relations 193-276 (1940); Berney, *Libel and the First Amendment—A New Constitutional Privilege,* 51 Va. L. Rev. 1, 40-41 (1965); Green, *Relational Interests,* 31 Ill. L. Rev. 35, 36 (1936).

[44] Wade, *Defamation and the Right of Privacy,* 15 Vand. L. Rev. 1093, 1094 (1962).

[45] Themo v. New England Newspaper Publishing Co., 306 Mass. 54, 57 27 N.E.2d 753, 755 (1940).

[46] *See* Little Rock Newspapers, Inc. v. Dodrill, 281 Ark. 25, 660 S.W.2d 936 (1983).

In *Time, Inc. v. Firestone*,[47] the plaintiff voluntarily withdrew any claim of injury of reputation prior to trial. The Supreme Court held that the Florida rule, permitting recovery of actual damages without proof of injury to reputation, did not violate the first amendment:

> Florida has obviously decided to permit recovery for other injuries without regard to measuring the effect the falsehood may have had upon a plaintiff's reputation. This does not transform the action into something other than an action for defamation as that term is meant in *Gertz*. In that opinion we made it clear that States could base awards on elements other than injury to reputation, specifically listing "personal humiliation and mental anguish and suffering" as examples of injuries which might be compensated consistently with the Constitution upon a showing of fault.[48]

The plaintiff in *Firestone*, having proffered evidence that *Time's* report of her divorce trial had made her emotionally anxious and concerned, was thus in compliance with the *Gertz* actual injury requirement with regard to the jury's award to her of $100,000 in damages.[49]

[b] The Practical Result: Presumed Harm Through the Back Door

As a practical litigation matter the acceptance of the Florida position that emotional distress alone is enough to establish actual injury and recovery of actual damages in a defamation action may well be to permit the principle of presumed harm to sneak back into the defamation cases governed by *Gertz* through the back door. In *Hearst v. Hughes*,[50] for example, the Maryland Court of Appeals accepted the Florida position, and in so doing actually relied on the very rationales that are conventionally put forward to support the common law position of presumed harm: the difficulty of proving reputational damage and the reasonableness of the inference that the defamatory speech in fact causes some injury.[51]

Because self-serving testimony of personal humiliation and mental anguish will almost always be available to the plaintiff (and in most cases, the testimony will be genuinely sincere) those states that permit

---

47 424 U.S. 448 (1976). *See supra* § 2.07.

48 *Id.* at 460.

49 *Id.* at 461.

50 297 Md. 112, 466 A.2d 486 (1983). *See also* International Bhd. of Elec. Workers, Local 1805 v. Mayo, 281 Md. 475, 379 A.2d 1223 (1977).

51 *Id.* at 129-30; 466 A.2d at 495. These rationales, it should be noted, were recently endorsed by the Supreme Court. Dun & Bradstreet, Inc. v. Greenmoss Builders, Inc., 105 S. Ct. 2939, 2946 (1985). *See supra* § 9.05[2][b].

emotional distress standing alone to support an award of actual damages for defamation are in truth virtually eliminating proof of "actual harm" as a meaningful barrier to a plaintiff's recovery. In so doing such states also substantially blur the distinction between defamation and invasion of privacy.[52]

[6] Proving Actual Harm to Reputation

Professor David Anderson recently authored an extremely perceptive examination of the various components of "actual injury" to reputation.[53] Anderson's analysis is that the common law doctrine of presumed harm actually masked three separate litigation problems in the law of defamation: (1) the problem of proving that any reputational injury has occurred; (2) the difficulties in quantifying the loss; and (3) the problem of proving that the defamation was the cause in fact of the injury.[54]

Classically, the primary function of the damages award in defamation cases is to compensate for injury to so-called "relational interests."[55] Relational interests may be categorized as of four types:

[a] Interference with Existing Relations

The defamatory speech may cause disruption with the plaintiff's existing relationships with third persons such as family friends, employees, customers, or clients.[56]

[b] Interference with Future Relations

Although those who know the plaintiff well may be true-blue and stand by the plaintiff in the midst of the defamation, the charges against him or her may dissuade others from future relationships with the

---

52 The Florida approach endorsed in *Firestone* has drawn its share of harsh criticism. *See, e.g.*, Little Rock Newspapers, Inc. v. Dodrill, 281 Ark. 25, 660 S.W.2d 936 (1983); Anderson, *supra* note 13, at 757-60; Ashdown, Gertz *and* Firestone: *A Study in Constitutional Policy-Making*, 61 Minn. L. Rev. 645, 670-71 (1977); Eaton, *The American Law of Defamation Through* Gertz v. Robert Welch, Inc. *and Beyond: An Analytical Primer*, 61 Va. L. Rev. 1349 (1975).

53 *See* Anderson, *supra* note 13.

54 *Id.* at 764.

55 *See supra* note 43.

56 *See* Anderson, *supra* note 13, at 765.

plaintiff— future business or social relationship that would have prospered may not take place.[57]

[c] Destruction of Favorable Public Image

A defamatory falsehood may injure reputation in ways not directly linked to the actual impairment of relationships, by impairing the plaintiff's favorable public image. Public image as a valuable personal asset is largely a product of our modern cultural environment, in which a positive media image is often a springboard to influence and wealth, as well as a commodity inextricably wrapped up in self-image.[58]

[d] Negative Public Image

Even a plaintiff with no public image to speak of prior to the publication of a defamatory statement may suffer actual reputational injury when exceptionally notorious deeds are attributed to him, creating a lasting negative public image where previously the plaintiff had enjoyed anonymity.[59]

§ 9.07 Special Damages

Special damages (or "special harm") consist of injury of a pecuniary nature.[60] Pecuniary or monetary loss may include any injury of financial value to the plaintiff, but the mere mental distress of the plaintiff, even if it results in physical illness, is not sufficient.[61] Loss of customers or business will qualify as special harm,[62] as will loss of a specific contract,[63] loss of earnings,[64] loss of credit,[65] or loss of employment.[66] Mere loss of

---

57 *Id.* at 765-66.

58 *Id.* at 756-57. *See also* Smolla, *supra* note 6, at 20-21.

59 Anderson uses as an example a person wrongfully accused of assassinating the President. Anderson, *supra* note 13, at 767.

60 *See* Lind v. O'Reilly, 636 P.2d 1319, 1321 (Colo. App. 1981); Restatement (Second) of Torts § 575 comment b (1977).

61 *See* Harrison v. Burger, 212 Ala. 670, 103 So. 842 (1925); Lind v. O'Reilly, 636 P.2d 1319, 1321 (Colo. App. 1981); Scott v. Harrison, 215 N.C. 427, 2 S.E.2d 1 (1939); Terwilliger v. Wands, 17 N.Y. 54, 72 Am. Dec. 420 (1858); Clark v. Morrison, 80 Or. 240, 156 P. 429 (1916).

62 WDM Planning, Inc. v. United Credit Corp., 62 A.D.2d 940, 404 N.Y.S.2d 5 (1978); Ellsworth v. Martindale-Hubbell Law Directory, 68 N.D. 425, 280 N.W. 879 (1938).

63 *See* Storey v. Challands, 8 Car & P. 234, 173 Eng. Rep. 475 (1837).

64 Korry v. International Tel. & Tel. Corp., 444 F. Supp. 193 (S.D.N.Y. 1978).

65 Prettyman v. Shockley, 4 Del. (4 Harr.) 112 (1844).

66 Prosser and Keeton, *supra* note 13, § 112, at 794.

social contacts or friends is not special harm,[67] unless the loss can be linked to actual pecuniary injury.[68]

Special damages may be used to enhance recovery of general damages.[69] As a practical matter, however, the primary significance of special damages in the modern law of defamation is the role pleading and proof of special damage continues to play in the application of the libel and slander per se and per quod rules.[70]

§ 9.08 Punitive Damages

[1] Definition

Punitive (or "exemplary") damages are not aimed at compensation, but at punishment and deterrence.[71] They are "private fines levied by civil juries to punish reprehensible conduct and to deter its future occurrence."[72]

[2] When Constitutionally Permitted

[a] Under *Gertz*

In *Gertz* the Supreme Court held that punitive damages could not be recovered absent a showing of actual malice.[73] As subsequently reinterpreted by *Dun & Bradstreet,*[74] *Gertz* applies only to cases involving matters of public concern. Punitive damages are thus available under the first amendment in any public official or public figure case, since such plaintiffs must always establish actual malice as a prerequisite to

---

67 Lind v. O'Reilly, 636 P.2d 1319, 1321 (Colo. App. 1981); Clark v. Morrison, 80 Or. 240, 156 P. 429 (1976).

68 Pettibone v. Simpson, 66 N.Y. (Barb.) 492 (1873); Restatement (Second) of Torts § 575 comment b (1977).

69 *See* Snowdow v. Pear River Broadcasting Corp., 251 So. 2d 405 (La. App.), *application denied,* 259 La. 887, 253 So. 2d 217 (1971).

70 *See generally* Chapter 7, *supra.*

71 *See, e.g.,* Gertz v. Robert Welch, Inc., 418 U.S. 323, 349-51 (1974); Stevenson v. Hearst Consolidated Publications, Inc., 214 F.2d 902 (2d Cir. 1954), *cert. denied,* 348 U.S. 874 (1954); Burnett v. National Enquirer, Inc., 144 Cal. App. 3d 991, 193 Cal. Rptr. 206 (1983), *appeal dismissed,* 104 S. Ct. 1260 (1984); Dalton v. Meister, 52 Wis. 2d 173, 188 N.W.2d 494 (1971), *cert denied,* 405 U.S. 934 (1972); D. Dobbs, Handbook on the Law of Remedies § 7.2, at 522 (1973).

72 Gertz v. Robert Welch, Inc., 418 U.S. 323, 349 (1974).

73 *Id.*

74 Dun & Bradstreet, Inc. v. Greenmoss Builders, Inc., 105 S. Ct. 2939 (1985). *See supra* §§ 3.02-3.05.

liability, though states are free to impose additional requirements on plaintiffs to make them eligible for the bonus of punitive damages.[75] In private figure cases involving matters of public concern, punitive damages are constitutionally available only if the plaintiff goes beyond the minimum liability requirement of negligence and establishes actual malice.

[b] Under *Dun & Bradstreet*

As previously discussed in the context of presumed damages,[76] *Dun & Bradstreet* completely exempted all private figure cases not involving defamatory speech concerning matters of public concern from first amendment requirements.[77] In such cases, therefore, punitive damages are available as a matter of constitutional law without regard to fault levels; their availability in such cases is purely a matter of state law.

[c] First Amendment Considerations

A number of commentators have called for the outright abolition of punitive damages.[78] Professor William Van Alstyne, with characteristic incisiveness, has offered an outstanding constitutional argument for banning all punitive damages.[79] Drawing on basic first amendment principles that antedate even the *New York Times* case,[80] Van Alstyne demonstrates that the tendency of juries to utilize punitive damages to punish defendants for the general character of their publication rather than for any particular misconduct cannot be reconciled with fundamental first amendment values.

Nevertheless, prior to *Dun & Bradstreet,* the overwhelming weight of authority was that so long as the *Gertz* minimum of actual malice

---

75 *See infra* § 9.08[3].

76 *See supra* § 9.05[2][b].

77 105 S. Ct. at 2946.

78 *See* Rosenbloom v. Metromedia, Inc., 403 U.S. 29, 78 (1971)(Marshall, J., dissenting) (views of Justices Marshall and Stewart that punitive damages should be eliminated); Anderson, *Libel and Press Self-Censorship,* 53 Tex. L. Rev. 422, 477 (1975); Franklin, *Good Names and Bad Law: A Critique of Libel Law and a Proposal,* 18 U.S.F.L. Rev. 1, 39 (1983); Hill, *Defamation and Privacy Under the First Amendment,* 76 Colum. L. Rev. 1205, 1251-53 (1976); Smolla, *supra* note 6, at 92-93.

79 Van Alstyne, *First Amendment Limitations on Recovery from the Press—An Extended Comment on "The Anderson Solution,"* 25 Wm. & Mary L. Rev. 793, 803-07 (1984).

80 *See id.* at 801-07 (quoting Dennis v. United States, 341 U.S. 494, 510 (1951)(quoting Dennis v. United States, 183 F.2d 201, 212 (2d Cir. 1950)(Hand, J.)); Abrams v. United States, 250 U.S. 616, 629 (1919)(Holmes, J., dissenting).

was established, punitive damages did not per se violate the first amendment.[81] *Dun & Bradstreet* obviously now permits punitive damages in any private figure/private speech case,[82] and further reaffirms (in dicta) their availability whenever actual malice is established.[83] For the time being, therefore, any decision by a court to abolish punitive damages in some or all classes of defamation cases will be pursuant to state law and policy[84] and not constitutional requirements.

One of the latest cases to present these problems to the Supreme Court is *CBS v. Brown & Williamson Tobacco Corp.*[84.1] Brown & Williamson filed suit against CBS for a commentary, broadcast on Chicago station WBBM-TV, concerning cigarette advertising. A federal district court jury awarded Brown & Williamson $3 million compensatory damages and $2.5 million in punitive damages, but the court reduced the award of compensatory damages to one dollar. On appeal, the U.S. Court of Appeals for the Seventh Circuit reinstated an award of $1 million compensatory damages and upheld the punitive damages award. "These facts present the strongest possible argument against the constitutionality of presumed and punitive damages in such libel cases," CBS stated in its petition for review. "There was no competent evidence of actual injury to the corporation yet it received an award of more than $3 million—larger than any libel award ever upheld by this court—composed entirely of presumed and punitive damages." This case, CBS stated, "presents the Court with its clearest opportunity to define constitutional limits on the award of presumed and punitive damages for libel where both public issues and public figures are involved." However, on April 4, 1988, the Supreme Court denied *certiorari* in *Brown & Williamson,* declining, at least for the time being, the invitation to address and perhaps resolve the constitutionality of presumed and punitive damages in media libel cases. The Court's action, while perhaps understandable in light of the unique facts of *Brown & Williamson,* is nonetheless significant because the case represents a lost opportunity

---

[81] *See, e.g.,* Buckley v. Littell, 539 F.2d 882, 897 (2d Cir. 1976); Appleyard v. Transamerican Press, Inc., 539 F.2d 1026, 1029-30 (4th Cir. 1976); Carson v. Allied News Co., 529 F.2d 206, 214 (7th Cir. 1976); Davis v. Schucat, 510 F.2d 731, 737-38 (D.C. Cir. 1975); Roemer v. Retail Credit Co., 44 Cal. App. 3d 926, 932, 119 Cal. Rptr. 82, 85 (1975); Foray v. Noveroski, 31 Ill. App. 3d 182, 198, 334 N.E.2d 79, 92 (1975); Newspaper Publishing Corp. v. Burke, 216 Va. 800, 224 S.E.2d 132, 136 (1976); Calero v. Del Chemical Corp., 68 Wis. 2d 737, 228 N.W.2d 737, 747 (1975).

[82] 105 S. Ct. at 2946.

[83] *Id.* at 2944.

[84] Some states have abolished punitive damages in defamation suits. *See infra* § 9.08[4].

[84.1] 108 S. Ct. 1302 (1988).

to address these consequential issues in the seemingly compelling context of huge awards some four times larger than any presumed or punitive damages previously upheld on appeal.

[d] Other Constitutional Challenges

There is a possibility that the Supreme Court will at some point uphold a constitutional challenge to punitive damages outside the specific context of the first amendment and libel.

In *Browning-Ferris Industries of Vermont, Inc. v. Kelco Disposal, Inc.*[84.2] the Supreme Court upheld a jury award of $6 million in punitive damages in a non-media antitrust case involving two competing trash disposal companies. The plaintiff Kelco successfully claimed that Browning Ferris Industries had employed an illegal pricing strategy to attempt to monopolize the garbage collection market in Burlington, Vermont. Kelco was awarded only $51,000 in compensatory damages. Browning-Ferris appealed to the Supreme Court, claiming that the gargantuan award of $6 million in punitive damages was so disproportionate to Kelco's compensatory damages as to constitute an excessive fine violative of the eighth amendment.[84.3]

The Court rebuffed the eighth amendment argument, holding that the amendment's Excessive Fines Clause does not limit punitive damages award in civil cases between private parties.[84.4] The Court did not completely shut the door on constitutional challenges to punitive damages, however. The Court's opinion expressly refused to reach the question of whether uncontrolled jury discretion to award punitive damages could violate the Due Process Clause. The Court stated that there "is some authority in our opinions for the view that the Due Process Clause places outer limits on the size of a civil damages award made pursuant to a statutory scheme,"[84.5] "but we have never addressed the precise question presented here: whether due process acts as a check on undue jury discretion to award punitive damages in the absence of any express statutory limit."[84.6] The Court ruled, however, that because the peti-

---

[84.2] 109 S. Ct. 2909 (1989).

[84.3] The eighth amendment reads: "Excessive bail shall not be required, nor excessive fines imposed, nor cruel and unusual punishments inflicted."

[84.4] 109 S. Ct. at 2920.

[84.5] *Id.* at 2921, *citing* St. Louis, I.M. & S.R. Co. v. Williams, 251 U.S. 63 (1919).

[84.6] 109 S. Ct. at 2921.

tioners had not properly raised and preserved this claim in the courts below, "That inquiry must await another day."[84.7]

This intriguing statement by the Court might be interpreted as sound judicial restraint in not reaching a difficult constitutional question unless absolutely necessary, or as unseemly judicial avoidance of an issue of pressing moment that could and should have been reached, or as a tantalizing hint to litigants and lower courts that it would indeed be willing to create due process limits on unfettered jury discretion to award punitive damages in civil cases in the right factual and procedural circumstances. The positions of the Justices who concurred and dissented are perhaps significant in predicting the future. Justice Brennan, joined by Justice Marshall, stated, "I join the Court's opinion on the understanding that it leaves the door open for a holding that the Due Process Clause constrains the imposition of punitive damages in civil cases brought by private parties."[84.8] Justice O'Connor, joined by Justice Stevens, dissented, and in a long and scholarly opinion argued forcefully that punitive damages in civil cases are subject to the limitations of the eighth amendment.[84.9] Justice O'Connor did not reach the due process question. Her eighth amendment analysis, however, was permeated with sensitivity to the arbitrariness of gigantic punitive damages awards, and to the explosion of such awards in modern civil litigation. As did Justice Brennan, Justice O'Connor went out of her way to point out that nothing in the Court's opinion would foreclose a due process challenge to such awards.[84.10]

If one is keeping score, therefore, it would appear that four Justices, Brennan, Marshall, O'Connor, and Stevens, would be favorably disposed to sustain a due process attack in the right circumstances. Given the Court's careful circumnavigation of the issue in its majority opinion in *Browning-Ferris,* it would appear that such a challenge would have an outstanding chance of reaching the Court for review (only four Justices need vote to accept a case for it to be docketed), and a good fighting chance of prevailing.

If such a constitutional challenge is brought before the Court, of course, it might be in virtually any sort of civil litigation. Would such a challenge be stronger in the context of the first amendment? Would a combination due process and free speech attack on punitive damages

---

84.7 *Id.*

84.8 *Id.* at 2923 (Brennan, J., concurring).

84.9 *Id.* at 2924-34 (O'Connor, J., concurring in part and dissenting in part).

84.10 *Id.* at 2924.

have the strongest chance of all at success? One might like to think that the answer is yes: that is certainly the correct answer as a matter of principle. It is just possible, however, that a due process challenge brought by a media defendant for damages in a libel or invasion of privacy or emotional distress suit might backfire, and actually be weaker than a due process challenge brought in a run-of-the-mill commercial suit, such as an insurance or antitrust case. At times some of the Justices, either out of antipathy for the press, or out of a sense that punitive damages are the only effective remedy in some intangible harm cases, almost act as if speech cases present one of the best examples of the utility of punitive damages.[84.11] Whether the case finally accepted by the Court is a media-related case or not, however, media interests must certainly pursue with vigor the constitutional attack on unchecked punitive jury awards.

[3] When Permitted Under State Law

[a] General Tort Principles

Punitive damages have never been thought of as available as a matter of course in the law of torts; instead they are conceptualized as unusual exercises in punishment reserved for cases of especially egregious or reprehensible tortious misconduct.[85] Punitive damages, it has been said, involve torts which "have the character of outrage frequently associated with crime."[86] It is thus well accepted that ordinary carelessness or negligence, even if it causes severe injury, is not enough to support an award of punitive damages.[87]

(*Text continued on page 9-19*)

84.11 *See supra* § 9.08[2].

85 *See, e.g.*, Smith v. Gray Concrete Pipe Co., Inc., 267 Md. 149, 297 A.2d 721 (1972)("reckless disregard for the rights of others"); Allman v. Bird, 186 Kan. 802, 353 P.2d 216 (1960)("heedless disregard of the consequences"); GRYC v. Dayton-Hudson Corp., 297 N.W.2d 727 (Minn. 1980)("willful or reckless disregard"); Jones v. Fisher, 42 Wis. 2d 209, 166 N.W.2d 175 (1969)(character of "outrage").

86 Prosser & Keeton, *supra* note 13, § 2, at 9.

87 Roginski v. Richardson-Merrell, Inc., 378 F.2d 832 (2d Cir. 1967).

[b] Defamation Rules

[i] In General

Traditionally state courts permit punitive damages in defamation actions only if, in *addition* to whatever threshold standards of fault apply, the defendant is guilty of publishing with common law malice, in the sense of spite, ill will, or vengeance.[88]

[ii] Common Law Malice

It is important to note that in a public official or public figure case, the plaintiff may be required to prove both constitutional actual malice and common law ill-will malice to be eligible for punitive damages. Actual malice is automatically required to establish liability, and common law malice is then imposed to trigger eligibility for punitive damages under state law. If a state does *not* impose an additional common law malice requirement in such cases, it is in the anomalous position of permitting punitive damages automatically in any case in which the threshold liability standard (actual malice) is satisfied. The difficulty with this approach is that it runs counter to the traditional conceptualization of punitive damages as an extraordinary remedy reserved for unusually outrageous cases, a remedy requiring some level of conduct above and beyond that necessary to establish threshold liability. The norm, therefore, is for states to impose common law malice as an additional requirement.[89]

[iii] Evidentiary Standard

There is a division of authority as to whether the "clear and convincing" or the "preponderance of the evidence" standard applies to the showing of malice necessary to trigger punitive damages. In *Burnett v. National Enquirer, Inc.*,[90] the court took the position that while the clear and convincing evidence standard is constitutionally required in connection with the actual malice determination necessary to trigger liability, only the preponderance of the evidence is necessary to estab-

---

[88] *See, e.g.*, Cantrell v. Forest City Publishing Co., 419 U.S. 245, 251-52 (1974); Hunt v. Liberty Lobby, 720 F.2d 631 (11th Cir. 1983); H.E. Crawford v. Dun & Bradstreet, Inc., 241 F.2d 387 (4th Cir. 1957); Lubore v. Pittsburg Courier Publishing Co., 101 F. Supp. 234 (D.D.C. 1951), *aff'd*, 200 F.2d 355 (D.C. Cir. 1952); Hansen v. Stoll, 130 Ariz. 454, 636 P.2d 1236 (Ct. App. 1981); Burnett v. National Enquirer, Inc., 144 Cal. App. 3d 991, 193 Cal. Rptr. 206 (1983), *appeal dismissed*, 104 S. Ct. 1260 (1984).

[89] *See infra* note 90.

[90] 144 Cal. App. 3d 991, Cal. Rptr. 206 (1983), *appeal dismissed*, 104 S. Ct. 1260 (1984).

lish the additional common law malice required in California to support punitive damages.

[c] Other Factors Considered in Assessing Punitive Damages

[i] Financial Condition of Defendant

In light of the fact that the function of punitive damages is punishment and deterrence the defendant's net worth may be admitted in evidence so that a sum appropriate for deterrence may be established.[91]

[ii] Actual Harm

Some decisions hold that punitive damages are not recoverable in the absence of actual damages.[92] Other decisions permit punitive damages to be assessed if nominal damages are awarded,[93] or in the complete absence of actual damages.[94]

[iii] Reasonable Proportionality to Actual Damages

Although courts are extremely loath to engage in any arithmetic formula,[95] one factor that is sometimes employed as an element in reviewing the award of punitive damages is the size of the punitive damages award in comparison to the actual damages award.[96]

---

91 *See, e.g.*, Dobbs, *supra* note 71, § 7.2, at 522-23. *See also* Burnett v. National Enquirer, Inc., 144 Cal. App. 3d 991, 193 Cal. Rptr. 206 (1983), *appeal dismissed*, 104 S. Ct. 1260 (1984); Dalton v. Meister, 52 Wis.2d 173, 188 N.W.2d 494 (1971), *cert denied*, 405 U.S. 934 (1972).

92 *See, e.g.*, Doubleday v. Rogers, 674 S.W.2d 751 (Tex. 1984).

93 *See* Goldwater v. Ginzburg, 414 F.2d 324 (2d Cir. 1969), *cert. denied*, 396 U.S. 1049 (1970)(one dollar nominal damages and $75,000 punitive damages); Reynolds v. Pegler, 223 F.2d 429 (2d Cir.), *cert. denied*, 350 U.S. 846 (1955)(one dollar nominal damages and $100,000 punitive damages).

94 *See* Newson v. Henry, 443 So. 2d 817 (Miss. 1984) (award of $2,500 in punitive damages upheld even though jury awarded zero actual damages); Kent v. City of Buffalo, 36 A.D.2d 85, 319 N.Y.S.2d 305, *rev'd mem. on other grounds*, 29 N.Y.S.2d 653 (1971); Dobbs, *supra* note 71, § 7.2, at 523.

95 *See* Dalton v. Meister, 52 Wis. 2d 173, 188 N.W.2d 494 (1971), *cert. denied*, 405 U.S. 934 (1972)("While there is no arithemetic proportion to which punitive damages should relate to the wealth of the defendant or to the damage done the plaintiff, we think punitive damages in an amount equal to compensatory damages founded on special harm is reasonable.").

96 *See, e.g.*, Thomas v. E.J. Korvette, Inc., 329 F. Supp. 1163 (D. Pa. 1971); Wozniak v. United Elec., Radio and Machine Workers, 57 Wis. 2d 725, 205 N.W.2d 369 (1973).

[4] Jurisdictions that Do Not Permit Punitive Damages

The prospects for the elimination of punitive damages as a matter of federal constitutional law are today quite bleak,[97] but strong policy arguments can nonetheless be marshalled in favor of their elimination as a matter of state law.[98] In *Wheeler v. Green,*[99] for example, the Oregon Supreme Court drew on a provision in the Oregon Constitution[100] to ban punitive damages in defamation suits, holding that the state's interest in protecting reputation was adequately served by limiting damages to compensation, and that in "the sensitive area of free expression, the threat of large damage recoveries can easily inhibit the exercise of freedom of constitutionally protected expression, as well as its abuse."[101]

§ 9.09 Chart of Constitutional Damages Rules

The constitutional minimums that apply to damages in modern defamation actions vary with the level of fault proven, the status of the plaintiff, and the status of the speech. They are summarized graphically in Figure 9.1, below. The term "general damages" is not used on the chart, but instead its subdivisions of actual and presumed damages (which vary with the category) are used. Note that actual damages and special damages, both of which are by definition supported by evidence, are *always* constitutionally permissible. Note, also, the assumption built into the chart that nominal damages are always permitted. Finally, the chart suggests that fault requirements do not now exist under the Constitution for cases governed by *Dun & Bradstreet.*

---

[97] *See supra* § 9.08[2][c].

[98] *See* Stone v. Essex County Newspapers, 367 Mass. 849, 330 N.E.2d 161 (1975); Wheeler v. Green, 286 Or. 99, 593 P.2d 777, 788 (1979); Tasket v. King Broadcasting, 86 Wash. 2d 439, 447, 546 P.2d 81 (1976). *See also* Kewin v. Massachusetts Mutual Life, 409 Mich. 401, 419, 295 N.W.2d 50 (1980); Pettengill v. Booth Newspapers, Inc., 88 Mich. App. 587, 278 N.W.2d 682 (1979)(Michigan, although recognizing exemplary damages by name, limits their award to "compensation" for injury to reputation).

[99] 286 Or. 99, 593 P.2d 777, 788 (1979).

[100] Or. Const. art. I, § 8 ("No law shall be passed restraining the free expression of opinion, or restricting the right to speak, write, or print freely on any subject whatever; but every person shall be responsible for the abuse of this right.").

[101] 286 Or. 99, 593 P.2d 777, 778. *See also* cases cited in note 100, *supra;* text and authorities in § 9.08[2][c], *supra;* Comment, *Punitive Damages and Defamation Litigation: A Clear and Present Danger to Free Speech,* 64 Yale L.J. 610 (1955); Comment, *The Constitutionality of Punitive Damages in Libel Actions,* 45 Ford. L. Rev. 1382 (1977).

Whether this is true or not, the effect on the damages issue is the same: *Dun & Bradstreet* clearly holds that no first amendment restrictions on damages exist in such cases, fault rules notwithstanding.

Figure 9.1

Status of Plaintiff and Status of Speech	*Level of Fault Demonstrated*	*Types of Damages Permitted by First Amendment*
Public Official/ Public Figure; Speech of Public Concern	Plaintiff Proves Actual Malice (Required)	Nominal; Actual; Special; Presumed; Punitive
Private Figure/ Speech of Public Concern	Plaintiff Proves Actual Malice (Optional)	Nominal; Actual; Special; Presumed; Punitive
Private Figure/ Speech of Public Concern	Plaintiff Proves Negligence (Required)	Nominal; Actual; Special
Private Figure/ Speech Not Involving Matters of Public Concern	Plaintiff May Not Be Required to Prove Any Fault After *Dun & Bradstreet*	Nominal; Actual; Special; Presumed; Punitive

§ 9.10 Factors in Mitigation and Aggravation

[1] Nature of the Defamation

In assessing damages the trier of fact will quite naturally take as a starting point the nature of the defamation, awarding more substantial sums for more serious charges.[102]

---

[102] *See* Dobbs, *supra* note 71, § 7.2, at 515. Dobbs compares McKnight v. Scott, 130 So. 2d 681 (La. App. 1961) (award of $1,000 reduced to $500 for calling plaintiff "nothing but a whore"), *with* Faulk v. Aware, Inc., 19 A.D.2d 464, 244 N.Y.S.2d 259 (1963)(award of $400,000 to plaintiff, popular entertainer, wrongfully charged with being communist sympathizer).

[2] Form and Extent of Publication

The form of publication, the extent of publication, and the relative degree of permanency are factors to be considered in increasing or decreasing damages.[103]

[3] Extent to Which Defamation Believed by Recipients

Whether recipients of the defamatory statement believed the statement is a factor to be weighed in assessing damages; testimony that the statement was believed and acted upon or disbelieved by most recipients obviously goes to the heart of the question of the extent of real reputational damage.[104]

[4] Plaintiff's Prior Reputation

[a] Plaintiff's Good Reputation

The plaintiff's prior reputation may be an important factor in assessing damages. A plaintiff who prior to the defamation had a good reputation will quite naturally suffer more from a defamatory publication than a plaintiff whose prior reputational stock was at so low an ebb that he had little or nothing left of his good name to lose. Traditionally, however, most courts apply the principle that the plaintiff's prior good reputation is presumed, and evidence of the plaintiff's prior good reputation is inadmissible as part of the plaintiff's case in chief.[105] General "apple pie and motherhood" evidence by the plaintiff is thus not admissible.[106] This rule, however, may be circumvented. When the defendant controverts that the plaintiff has a good reputation, the plaintiff may in-

---

[103] *See* Eulo v. Deval Aerodynamics, Inc., 47 F.R.D. 35 (D. Pa. 1969), *cert. denied,* 401 U.S. 974 (1971)(jury could consider limited dissemination as factor in assessing damages); Owens v. Scott Publishing Co., 46 Wash. 2d 666, 284 P.2d 296, *cert. denied,* 350 U.S. 968 (1955).

[104] *See* Dobbs, *supra* note 71, § 7.2, at 515 (citing Thomas v. Howard, 168 A.2d 908 (D.C. Mun. App. 1961); Bishop v. New York Times Co., 233 N.Y. 446, 135 N.E. 845 (1922)). *But see* Clay v. Lagiss, 143 Cal. App. 2d 441, 299 P.2d 1025 (1956)(disbelief not a mitigating factor).

[105] *See* L. Eldredge, *The Law of Defamation* § 97, at 564 (1978)(citing Davis v. Hearst, 160 Cal. 143, 185, 116 P. 530, 548 (1911); Chubb v. Gsell, 34 Pa. 114 (1859); Arnold v. National Union of Marine Cooks & Stewards, 44 Wash. 2d 183, 265 P.2d 1051 (1954)).

[106] *See* Dobbs, *supra* note 71, § 7.2, at 516 n.35. *See also* Ogletree v. Marcus, 361 P.2d 689 (Okla. 1961) (inadmissible that plaintiff supported his mother, who was blind and had a broken hip).

troduce such evidence in his case in chief.[107] In the recent Ariel Sharon case against *Time*, for example, the jury was given a virtual history lesson on the life of Ariel Sharon.[108] Other decisions seem to apply the rules of evidence liberally to admit evidence of good reputation in a specific field or activity providing the evidence is probative of whether the defamatory statements adversely affect the plaintiff's future in that field.[109]

[b] Plaintiff's Bad Reputation

The defendant is entitled to introduce evidence of the plaintiff's prior bad reputation in mitigation of damages; a prior bad reputation is an appropriate ground for reducing damages.[110]

[c] Prior Bad Acts

Specific prior acts of misconduct by the defendant concerning actions unrelated to the defamatory charges are traditionally not admissible in mitigation of damages, on the grounds that they too often bear only remotely on the issues in dispute, and may take the trial far afield, yet may well be significantly prejudicial.[111] As with most exclusionary evidentiary rules, however, the prohibition on evidence of unrelated prior bad acts may often be finessed. First, it is worth remembering that evidence of bad acts relating directly to the defamatory charges at issue are always admissible as part of the truth defense. Thus, if the plaintiff was charged with being drunk and disorderly at a restaurant, the defendant may always introduce evidence that the plaintiff was in fact drunk

---

107 *See* Sloneker v. Van Ausdall, 106 Ohio St. 320, 140 N.E. 121 (1922).

108 *See generally* Sharon v. Time, Inc., 599 F. Supp. 538 (S.D.N.Y. 1984)(denying motion for summary judgment) *and* Sharon v. Time, Inc., 575 F. Supp. 1162 (S.D.N.Y. 1983) (Sharon not "libel proof").

109 *See* Toomey v. Farley, 2 N.Y.2d 71, 156 N.Y.S.2d 840, 138 N.E.2d 221 (1956)(plaintiff permitted to show his religious piety on grounds that defamatory charges that plaintiff was sympathetic to communist causes would make him appear hypocritical). *See also* Wegner v. Rodeo Cowboys Ass'n, 417 F.2D 881 (10th Cir. 1969), *cert. denied*, 398 U.S. 903 (1970)(factors peculiar to plaintiff's situation in community may be assessed in calculating damages).

110 *See* Little Rock Newspapers, Inc. v. Dodrill, 281 Ark. 25, 660 S.W.2d 933 (1983); Dunagan v. Upham, 214 Ark. 66, 214 S.W.2d 786 (1948); Sclar v. Resnick, 192 Iowa 669, 185 N.W. 273 (1921); Sickra v. Small, 87 Me. 493, 33 A. 9 (1895); Falwell v. Providence Journal Co., 19 R.I. 551, 37 A. 6 (1896); Towle v. St. Albans Publishing Co., 122 Vt. 134, 165 A.2d 363 (1960); Campbell v. Campbell, 54 Wis. 90, 11 N.W. 456 (1882).

111 *See* Dobbs, *supra* note 71, § 7.2, at 516.

and disorderly. The defendant, however, may not under conventional wisdom introduce evidence of specific instances in which the plaintiff was drunk and disorderly on *other* occasions, either to establish truth or to mitigate damages.[112] Nor may the defendant introduce evidence of specific other bad acts, such as that the plaintiff is a murderer or arsonist.

A defense attorney, however, *will* be permitted to introduce opinion evidence concerning the plaintiff's reputation for prior bad acts,[113] such as opinion evidence that the plaintiff has a reputation for being drunk and disorderly, a murderer, or an arsonist, and in this way usually will be able to accomplish somewhat more obliquely the same purpose as direct evidence of these acts.

[d] The "Libel-Proof" Plaintiff

A plaintiff's reputation may sink so low that he is regarded as "libel proof," a forlorn and ignominious status. The law regards this plaintiff as so notorious that his reputation cannot be made worse than it is.[114] The libel-proof plaintiff is an outcast of the law of defamation whose reputation may be kicked and trod upon with impunity. Thus, a convicted murderer,[115] a habitual criminal,[116] a person with a well-established reputation for taking financial advantage of women,[117] an

---

[112] *See* Register Newspaper Co. v. Stone, 31 Ky. L. Rep. 458, 102 S.W. 800 (1907); Shilling v. Carson, 27 Md. 175 (1867); Small v. Chronicle & Gazette Publishing Co., 96 N.H. 265, 74 A.2d 544 (1950); Bausewine v. Norristown Herald, 351 Pa. 634, 41 A.2d 736 (1945); Dobbs, *supra* note 71, § 7.2, at 516; Eldredge, *supra* note 105, § 97, at 569-70. *But see* Lawlor v. Gallagher President's Report, Inc., 394 F. Supp. 721, 734 n.26 (S.D.N.Y. 1975), *remanded*, 538 F.2d 311 (2d Cir. 1976); Mills v. Kinsport Times-News, 475 F. Supp. 1005 (W.D. Va. 1979)("Of course, in special damage suits it could be argued that the inaccuracy does no more damage than the literal truth and, therefore, would not be actionable. But that is a determination for the jury").

[113] *See, e.g.*, Snively v. Record Publishing Co., 185 Cal. 565, 581, 198 P. 1, 7 (1921)(defendants "had a right to prove that the plaintiff's general reputation for efficiency and competency as chief of police was bad"); Cooper v. Illinois Publishing & Printing Co., 218 Ill. App. 95 (1920)(judge's reputation for his conduct in sex cases admissible); Courier Journal Co. v. Noble, 251 Ky. 527, 65 S.W.2d 703 (1933)(evidence that defendant had reputation for being unlawful dealer in whiskey admissible).

[114] *See generally* Cardillo v. Doubleday & Co., Inc., 518 F.2d 638, 639-40 (2d Cir. 1975); Sharon v. Time, Inc., 575 F. Supp. 1162 (S.D.N.Y. 1983); Wynberg v. National Enquirer, Inc., 564 F. Supp. 924, 927-28 (C.D. Cal. 1982); Urbano v. Sondern, 41 F.R.D. 355 (D. Conn.), *aff'd*, 370 F.2d 13 (2d Cir. 1966), *cert. denied*, 386 U.S. 1034 (1967).

[115] Ray v. Time, Inc., 452 F. Supp. 618, 622 (W.D. Tenn. 1976), *aff'd*, 582 F.2d 1280 (6th Cir. 1977)(Killer of Dr. Martin Luther King, Jr.).

[116] Cardillo v. Doubleday & Co., Inc., 518 F.2d 638 (2d Cir. 1975).

[117] Wynberg v. National Enquirer, Inc., 564 F. Supp. 924, 927-28 (C.D. Cal. 1982).

imprisoned felon,[118] and a confessed murderer with several narcotics convictions[119] have all been found libel proof.

Occasionally the libel-proof defense will be effective outside the criminal context. In *Simmons Ford, Inc. v. Consumers Union of United States, Inc.*,[120] a libel claim by the manufacturer of an electric car was dismissed because the false statements about the car, when compared to a number of other uncontested yet devastating statements concerning the safety of the car, left no more than nominal incremental damage to the plaintiff's reputation possible.[121]

An interesting recent analysis of the libel-proof defense is contained in Judge Sofaer's rejection of the applicability of the defense in *Sharon v. Time, Inc.*[122] *Time's* report concerning Sharon's alleged advance discussion of possible revenge leading to the massacres in Palestinian refugee camps did not damage Sharon, *Time* maintained, in light of the harsh criticism he had already received for his role in the events surrounding the massacres, criticism which Sharon himself had described as having put "the mark of Cain" on him. Judge Sofaer ruled that as severe as the public critique of Sharon's conduct had been, his reputation had not been so completely damaged as to render him libel proof, particularly since that criticism had been aimed primarily at Sharon's alleged "blunders" and "grave mistake," but it did not, as the *Time* article had, impute immoral or possibly illegal misconduct to Sharon.

There is an "incremental harm" branch of the libel-proof doctrine.[122.1] This doctrine measures the incremental reputational harm inflicted by the challenged statements beyond the harm imposed by the nonactionable remainder of the publication. If this additional "incremental" damage is deemed nominal or nonexistent, the statements are not actionable.[122.2] The incremental harm doctrine is closely related to the issue of substantial truth, and is indeed simply another variation of the principle that liability for defamation cannot exist when the "gist" or "sting" of the defamatory statement in not actionable.[122.3]

---

118 Turner v. Harcourt Brace Jovanovich, 5 Med. L. Rep. (BNA) 1437 (W.D. Ky. 1979).

119 Logan v. District of Columbia, 447 F. Supp. 1328 (D.D.C. 1978).

120 516 F. Supp. 742 (S.D.N.Y. 1982).

121 *Id.* at 750-51.

122 575 F. Supp. 1162 (S.D.N.Y. 1983). For the facts in *Sharon, see supra* § 3.18[2].

122.1 *See* Herbert v. Lando, 781 F.2d 298, 310-11 (2d Cir.), *cert. denied*, 476 U.S. 1182 (1986).

122.2 Masson v. The New Yorker Magazine, Inc., 881 F.2d 1452, 16 Med. L. Rep. (BNA) 2089, 2093-94 (9th Cir. 1989).

122.3 *See supra* §§ 5.08-5.11

[5] Prior Publication

The established rule is that damages may *not* be mitigated by proof that the defamatory statement had already been published or in general circulation prior to the publication of the statement giving rise to the suit.[123] "No one can say which of many defamations has destroyed or materially impaired a reputation; or whether, but for the last, the ear-

(*Text continued on page 9-27*)

---

[123] *See* Behrendt v. Times-Mirror Co., 30 Cal. App. 2d 77, 85 P.2d 949 (1938); Wilson v. Fitch, 41 Cal. 363 (1871); Burt v. Advertiser Newspaper Co., 28 N.E. 1, 5 (Mass. 1891); Hayener v. Pulitzer Publishing Co., 172 Mo. App. 436, 158 S.W. 54 (1913); Bragg v. Hammack, 155 Va. 419, 155 S.E. 683 (1930).

lier ones would have made any grave impression upon the opinion of the public."[124] The rule has been criticized, for it seems both illogical and out of consonance with general rules involving multiple tortfeasors and damages, and should perhaps be reexamined.[125]

[6] Prior Recoveries or Settlements

Consistent with the general prohibition in civil litigation on duplicate recoveries for the same injury, prior judgments or settlements from other tortfeasors for the same defamatory publication must be subtracted from any award of compensatory damages.[126]

[7] Defendant's Good Faith or Bad Faith

Although evidence of the defendant's good faith or bad faith is arguably relevant only to the assessment of punitive rather than compensatory damages,[127] some courts permit this sort of evidence to be considered

---

[124] Sun Printing & Publishing Ass'n v. Schneck, 98 F. 925 (1900). The court added that "irritation, if long enough persisted in, will at last accomplish its result; and every repetition of a slander adds to its malign effect." *Id.*

[125] *See* Dobbs, *supra* note 71, § 7.2, at 517-18. It would seem as a matter of logic that the fact that the same libelous statements were previously published and in circulation is analytically indistinguishable from evidence of the plaintiff's prior bad reputation, which traditionally is admissible in mitigation of damages. Perhaps courts have unconsciously distinguished the two on a feeling that, while a prior bad reputation is usually deserved (though the rule does not actually require that the plaintiff's bad reputation be deserved), the prior circulation of the same defamatory charge upon which liability is predicated involves a diminished reputation that is undeserved, so it is unfair to penalize the plaintiff for those prior publications. *See also* Palmer v. New York News Publishing Co., 61 A.D. 210, 52 N.Y.S. 539, 540 (1898)("If 100 persons at 100 different places make 100 separate publications of a libel in 100 different newspapers, that fact that this simultaneous action . . . has ruined the plaintiff's character is no reason why [one] of them, when sued for it, should shelter himself behind the acts of the other 99 [saying] that 99/100 of the plaintiff's character was ruined by the others, and therefore he is liable for only 1/100 part of the damages."); Behrendt v. Times-Mirror Co., 30 Cal. App. 2d 77, 83, 85 P.2d 949, 951 (1938).

[126] *See* Dixson v. Newsweek, Inc., 562 F.2d 626 (10th Cir. 1977); N.Y. Civil Rights Law § 76 (McKinney's 1976).

[127] Professor Dobbs argues that logically the defendant's motivation is relevant only to punitive damages once liability is initially established. Dobbs, *supra* note 71, § 7.2, at 519. *See also* John v. Tribune Co., 28 Ill. App. 2d 300, 171 N.E.2d 432 (1960), *rev'd on other grounds,* 24 Ill. 2d 437, 181 N.E.2d 105, *cert. denied,* 371 U.S. 877 (1962)(good faith relevant to issue of punitive damages).

in mitigation or in aggravation of damages.[128]

[8] Evidence of Provocation by the Plaintiff

Evidence of provocation by the plaintiff may be admitted in mitigation of damages,[129] though courts often restrict evidence of provocation to the issue of punitive damages.[130]

[9] Retraction

The issuance of a retraction is certainly admissible as evidence in mitigation of damages.[131] Because the rules governing retractions have been set to statute in many jurisdictions and are replete with special procedural and substantive details, retractions receive individual coverage later in this chapter.[132]

§ 9.11 Judicial Review of Damages Awards

[1] In General

No realist can deny that there is an inherent subjective arbitrariness to any award of general punitive damages in a defamation suit, for the injury is intangible and unquantifiable. In Professor McCormick's words, "damages in defamation cases are measurable by no standard which different men can use with like results."[133] Nevertheless, "control of the jury's action in respect to amount, exercised by the judges, trial and appellate, . . . is obviously real and constant, in checking extreme results, despite the absence of a tangible standard, under the formula that, while the amount is largely in the jury's discretion, it may be set

128 *See* Massee v. Williams, 207 F. 222 (6th Cir. 1913) (good faith admissible in mitigation); Venn v. Tennessean Newspapers, Inc., 201 F. Supp. 47, 61 (D. Tenn. 1962), *aff'd*, 313 F.2d 639 (6th Cir.), *cert. denied*, 374 U.S. 830 (1963)(bad faith admissible in aggravation); Conroy v. Fall River Herald News Co., 306 Mass. 488, 28 N.E.2d 729 (1940(good faith admissible in mitigation).

129 Schockley v. McCauley, 101 Md. 461, 61 A. 583 (1905); McLeod v. American Publishing Co., 126 S.C. 363, 120 S.E. 70 (1923).

130 *See* Farrell v. Kramer, 159 Me. 387, 193 A.2d 560, 563 (1963)("such factors should be considered only in mitigation of punitive damages").

131 *See generally* Dobbs, *supra* note 71 § 7.2, at 519.

132 *Infra* § 9.11.

133 C. McCormick, Handbook on the Law of Damages § 120, at 443 (1935).

aside if it appears to be the result of passion or prejudice."[134] The extremely deferential "passion or prejudice" standard has its genesis in the colorful language of Chancellor Kent:

> The damages . . . must be so excessive as to strike mankind, at first blush, as being beyond all measure, unreasonable and outrageous, and such as manifestly show the jury to have been actuated by passion, partiality, prejudice, or corruption. In short, the damages must be flagrantly outrageous and extravagant, or the court cannot undertake to draw the line; for they have no standard by which to ascertain the excess.[135]

[2] The Modern Approach

Statistics indicate that modern courts take their review of jury awards quite seriously,[136] policing with particular vigilance the "mega-verdicts" that have recently begun to proliferate. Thus, although the verbal formulas of review remain couched in terms of great deference to juries, such as "passion or prejudice,"[137] "shock the conscience of the court,"[138] "unsupported by competent probative evidence and beyond all reason,"[139] "grossly excessive,"[140] "clear showing of excessiveness or impropriety,"[141] and "palpably excessive or grossly disproportionate,"[142] courts seem *in practice* to employ a rule of common sense that is somewhat more demanding, but impossible to articulate precisely.[143]

[3] First Amendment Considerations

The modern judicial function in controlling jury verdicts should include as a component the first amendment considerations emanating

---

[134] *Id.* at 444 (citing Sandora v. Times Co., 113 Conn. 574, 155 A. 819 (1931); Yates v. Mullins, 233 Ky. 781, 26 S.W.2d 757 (1930)).

[135] Coleman v. Southwick, 9 Johns. 44, 52 (N.Y. 1812).

[136] *See infra* § 9.13.

[137] Moore v. Green, 431 F.2d 584 (9th Cir. 1970); Burnett v. National Enquirer, Inc., 144 Cal. App. 3d 991, 193 Cal. Rptr. 206 (1983), *appeal dismissed,* 104 S. Ct. 1260 (1984); Widener v. Pacific G & E Co., 75 Cal. App. 3d 415, 142 Cal. Rptr. 304, *cert. denied,* 436 U.S. 918 (1978).

[138] Fleck Brothers Co. v. Sullivan, 423 F.2d 155 (7th Cir. 1970).

[139] A.H. Belo Corp. v. Rayzor, 620 S.W.2d 756 (Tex. App. 1981).

[140] Grove v. Dun & Bradstreet, Inc., 438 F.2d 433 (3d Cir.), *cert. denied,* 404 U.S. 898 (1971).

[141] Braun v. Flynt, 726 F.2d 245 (5th Cir. 1984).

[142] Burnett v. National Enquirer, Inc., 144 Cal. App. 3d 991, 193 Cal. Rptr. 206 (1983), *appeal dismissed,* 104 S. Ct. 1260 (1984).

[143] *See infra* § 9.13.

from *New York Times* and its progeny, not only with regard to liability, but with regard to the level of damages. The likelihood is that the *New York Times* line of cases has already had a strong infiltrating impact on review of the size of jury awards even though, in formal language, courts continue to adhere to the deferential terminology of the common law.[144]

When reviewing a jury award of punitive damages, courts should never lose sight of the Supreme Court's admonition that "juries assess punitive damages in wholly unpredictable amounts bearing no necessary relation to the actual harm caused. And they remain free to use their discretion selectively to punish expressions of unpopular views."[145]

Even awards of compensatory damages carry with them the potential for a hidden element of gratuitous punishment, and reviewing courts should not abdicate their vital first amendment function by retreating behind the deferential formulas of the common law.[146]

§ 9.12 Retraction

[1] Overview

[a] At Common Law

A retraction is a withdrawal of the defamatory charge.[147] Merely to state that the victim of the defamation denies the charge is not a retraction; the defamer must himself recant and withdraw the accusation.[148] At common law the issuance of a retraction was not a complete defense, on the view that a renunciation might never quite catch up with the original lie.[149] Thus a retraction was admissible in mitigation of damages, subject to the discretion of the jury.[150]

---

144 *See supra* § 9.10[2] and nn. 140-45.

145 Gertz v. Robert Welch, Inc., 418 U.S. 323, 350 (1974).

146 *See generally* Stone v. Essex County Newspapers, Inc., 367 Mass. 849, 861, 330 N.E.2d 161, 170 (1975).

147 *See* Brogan v. Passaic Daily News, 22 N.J. 139, 123 A.2d 473, 477 (1956).

148 *See* Palmer v. Makin, 120 F. 737, 746 (8th Cir. 1903).

149 *See* Cass v. New Orleans Times, 27 La. Ann. 214, 219 (1875)("Thousands may have read the libelous matter that never saw its refutation.").

150 *See, e.g.*, Webb v. Call Publishing Co., 173 Wis. 45, 180 N.W. 263 (1920).

[b] The Proliferation of Statutes

In the modern law of defamation retraction has been largely overtaken by statutes. Over half the states now have retraction statutes.[151]

[2] Variations in Statutory Approaches

[a] Media vs. Nonmedia

The majority of retraction statutes apply to media defendants only, although a number of states apply statutory retraction rules to media and nonmedia defendants alike.[152]

Some states further differentiate among different types of media outlets. The California statute, for example, applies only to "a libel in a newspaper" or "a slander by radio broadcast." In *Burnett v. National Enquirer, Inc.*,[153] the court held that the *National Enquirer* did not qualify as a newspaper and did not receive the benefits of the statute. The rationale was that media outlets such as the *Enquirer* do not engage in the reportage of "hot news" and do not require the enhanced protection the statute provides.[154] An argument can be made that while a state is not constitutionally *required* to enact a retraction statute at all, if one is enacted the first amendment nonetheless imposes an obligation to treat all elements of the press equally, without regard to the content or format of the outlet, absent compelling state interests for granting some types of media outlets preference over others. Against such a test, the *Burnett* holding would fail, for it seems clear that at times some magazines do face genuine hot news deadline pressures (a newsweekly, for

---

[151] Robert Sack has counted 33. R. Sack, *Libel, Slander and Related Problems*, § VIII.2, at 372 (1980). Sack's overview of the various state approaches to retraction is excellent.

[152] California, for example, follows the majority approach and provides only for certain media defendants in its retractions statute, while Connecticut, Louisiana, Maine, Massachusetts, Nebraska, Texas, and West Virginia apply their statutes to all defendants. *Compare* Cal. Civ. Code § 48a (West 1954), *with* Conn. Gen. Stat. Ann. § 52-237 (West 1960); La. Civ. Code Ann. Art 2315.1 (West 1979); Me. Rev. Stat. Ann. tit. 14 § 153 (1965); Mass. Gen. Laws Ann. ch. 231, § 93 (1956); Mich. Stat. Ann. § 600.2911 (1962); Neb. Rev. Stat. § 25-840.01 (1975); Tex. Rev. Civ. Stat. Ann. art. 5430 (Vernon 1958); W. Va. Code § 57-2-4 (1966).

[153] 144 Cal. App. 3d 991, 193 Cal. Rptr. 206 (1983), *appeal dismissed*, 104 S. Ct. 1260 (1984).

[154] 144 Cal. App. 3d at 1004. *See also* Montandon v. Triangle Publications, Inc., 45 Cal. App. 3d 938, 120 Cal. Rptr. 186 (1975). *But see* Johnson v. Harcourt, Brace, Jovanovich, Inc., 43 Cal. App. 3d 880, 894, 118 Cal. Rptr. 370 (1974); Briscoe v. Reader's Digest Ass'n, 4 Cal. 3d 529, 543, 93 Cal. Rptr 886 (1971).

example, faces such pressures routinely), while some newspapers and broadcasters face little or no deadline pressures for major parts of their output.[155]

[b] Notice Provisions

[i] Timing

The typical retraction statute requires that the defamed person must give the publisher written notice of the alleged defamation and an opportunity to retract. The notice is usually required to be given within a specified time after the defamed person learns of the defamation, such as twenty days.[156]

[ii] Prerequisite to Suit

Florida requires notice and a demand for a retraction before a defamation suit can be filed.[157]

[iii] Prerequisite to Certain Types of Damages

The more common approach of retraction statutes is to condition the award of certain types of damages on compliance with the statute. Some states thus prohibit punitive damages unless the retraction is properly sought,[158] others limit recovery to special damages when the statute is not complied with.[159]

---

155 Equal protection attacks of this sort on retraction statutes have thus far not fared well. *See* Werner v. Southern California Associated Newspapers, Inc., 35 Cal. 2d 121, 216 P.2d 825 (1950), *appeal dismissed,* 340 U.S. 910 (1951); Ross v. Gore, 48 So. 2d 412 (Fla. 1950); Allen v. Pioneer Press, 40 Minn. 117, 41 N.W. 936 (1889). These decisions, however, are all at least 35 years old, and came at a time when first amendment and equal protection jurisprudence was substantially less developed than is the case today. Equality is emerging as a significant modern first amendment principle. *See generally* Karst, *Equality as a Central Principle in the First Amendment,* 43 U. Chi. L. Rev. 20 (1975). It is worth noting that the Court in *Dun & Bradstreet, Inc. v. Greenmoss Builders, Inc.,* 105 S. Ct. 2939 (1985), eschewed an approach based on the status of the speaker as media or nonmedia. *See supra* § 3.02. The time is therefore ripe for a new and serious challenge to many of the restrictions in the coverage of typical retraction statutes.

156 *See* Ariz. Stat. Ann. § 12-653.02; Or. Rev. Stat. § 30.165 (1963).

157 Fla. Stat. Ann. § 770.01 (West 1978). *See* Nazelek v. Sunbeam Television Corp., 413 So.2d 51 (Fla. Dist. Ct. App. 1982)(plaintiff must generally allege compliance with statute to withstand motion to dismiss).

158 Ala. Code § 6-5-186 (1975). *See* Fitzpatrick v. Age-Herald Publishing Co., 184 Ala. 510, 63 So. 980 (1913).

159 *See* Werner v. Southern California Associated Newspapers, Inc., 35 Cal. 2d 121, 216 P.2d 825 (1950), *appeal dismissed,* 340 U.S. 910 (1951).

[c] Effect of Retraction

[i] The Mere Mitigation Approach

Some retraction statutes merely restate the common law position that a retraction may be considered in mitigation or damages.[160]

[ii] Limitation to Special Damages

Some states place retractions on a very powerful footing, restricting to special damages recovery against defendants who make proper retractions.[161]

[iii] Limitation to Actual Damages

The most common effect of a proper retraction by the defendant in compliance with the statute is a limitation on recovery to "actual damages."[162]

[d] Aspects of a Retraction

[i] Content

A half-hearted retraction may be damning by faint praise, doing more damage than repair.[163] Common law doctrine has thus always required that to be effective the retraction must not be limited, partial, equivocal, hesitant, or hypothetical; the law will simply not recognize the retraction with fingers crossed.[164] It must be "frank and full, since a guarded and half-hearted apology will only injure the defendant's position, and a so-called apology is not an apology at all unless it unreservedly withdraws all imputations and expresses regret for having

---

[160] *See* La. Civ. Code Ann. art 2315.1 (West 1979); Me. Rev. Stat. Ann. tit. 14, § 153 (1965); Tex. Rev. Civ. Stat. Ann. art. 5430 (Vernon 1958).

[161] *See* Cal. Civ. Code § 48a(1) (West 1954).

[162] *See, e.g.*, Conn. Gen. Stat. Ann. § 52.237 (West 1960); N.C. Gen. Stat. § 99.2(a) (1979); Okla. Stat. Ann. tit. 12, § 1446a (West 1961).

[163] *See* Burnett v. National Enquirer, Inc., 144 Cal. App. 3d 991, 193 Cal. Rptr. 206 (1983)("evasive" and "incomplete" retraction a factor in *support* of punitive damages); Lehrer v. Elmore, 100 Ky. 56, 37 S.W. 292, 293-94 (1896)(retraction "contributed little, if anything, towards repairing the wrong already inflicted").

[164] *See, e.g.*, Lehrer v. Elmore, 100 Ky. 56, 37 S.W. 292, 293-94 (1896); Monaghan v. Globe Newspaper Co., 190 Mass. 294, 77 N.E. 476 (1906); Orband v. Kalamazoo Telegraph Co., 170 Mich. 387, 136 N.W. 380 (1912); Gray v. Times Newspaper Co., 74 Minn. 452, 77 N.W. 204 (1898); Brogan v. Passaic Daily News, 22 N.J. 139, 123 A.2d 473, 477 (1956); Roth v. Greensboro News Co., 217 N.C. 13, 6 S.E.2d 882 (1940); Goolsby v. Forum Printing Co., 23 N.D. 30, 135 N.W. 661 (1912).

made any."[165] Thus it is not enough merely to report: "We do not know whether our defamatory statement was true, but if it was not, we are sorry we published it."[166] The hedged retraction may thus be considered a second separate libel,[167] or a factor to be considered to enhance, rather than mitigate, damages.[168]

[ii] Form and Placement

Today these common law principles are incorporated into the language or judicial construction of most retraction statutes, and statutes may in addition impose other requirements of form, such as the size of type, the physical placement within the publication, or a heading stating the word "retraction."[169] The general principle underlying these details is, of course, the same: In all respects the retraction should be as conspicuous as the original libel,[170] with sufficient resources dedicated to it to provide some measure of confidence that it will reach as many readers as the original defamatory statement. In the broadcast context, this may mean broadcasting the retraction during the same or equivalent spot in the programming day as the original defamatory broadcast, with the same level of sending power.[171]

[iii] Timing

The common law rule was that a retraction must be issued within a

---

165 Brogan v. Passaic Daily News, 22 N.J. 139, 123 A.2d 473, 477 (1956).

166 W. Prosser, J. Wade, & V. Schwartz, Cases and Materials on Torts 1081 (7th ed. 1982) (citing Monaghan v. Globe Newspaper Co., 190 Mass. 394, 77 N.E. 476 (1906); Goolsby v. Forum Printing Co., 23 N.D. 30, 135 N.W. 161 (1913)).

167 Orband v. Kalamazoo Telegraph Co., 170 Mich. 387, 136 N.W. 380 (1912).

168 *See* Burnett v. National Enquirer, Inc., 144 Cal. App. 3d 991, 193 Cal. Rptr. 206 (1983), *appeal dismissed*, 104 S. Ct. 1260 (1984). This principle that an equivocal retraction may aggravate more than mitigate has old and estimable origins. *See* Hotchkiss v. Oliphant, 2 Hill 510, 516 (N.Y. 1842)("Hesitation, lurking insinuation, an attempted perversion of the plain import of the language used in the libelous article, or a substitution of one calumny for another, only aggravate the original offense and show a consciousness of the wrong done without the manliness or magnanimity to repair it.").

169 *See, e.g.,* Minn. Stat. Ann. § 548.03 (1961); Okla. Stat. Ann. tit. 12, § 1446a (West 1961).

170 *See* Burnett v. National Enquirer, Inc., 144 Cal. App. 3d 991, 193 Cal. Rptr. 206 (1983), *appeal dismissed*, 104 S. Ct. 1260 (1984)(absence of photograph near retraction and headline, as well as less prominent placement within article, factors against adequacy of retraction); Southeastern Newspapers, Inc. v. Walker, 76 Ga. App. 57, 44 S.E.2d 697 (1947)(the retraction not of equivalent prominence).

171 *See, e.g.,* Cal. Civ. Code. § 48a(2) (West 1954); Nev. Rev. Stat. § 41.336 (1975); N.C. Gen. Stat. § 99-2(b) (1979); N.D. Cent. Code § 14.02.08 (1971).

reasonable time following notice and demand;[172] quite obviously the prompter the retraction the better in terms of its effectiveness in mitigating injury. Most statutes today specifically set forth a time limitation. California, for example, requires the retraction to be published in a regular issue or broadcast within three weeks of the demand;[173] Nevada requires it within twenty days.[174] Some states place great time pressure on the defendant to retract. North Dakota, for example, requires the retraction to be "in the next issue of the paper, or in the case of a daily paper, within three days after the mistake was brought to the attention of the publisher."[175] Ohio requires the retraction "in the next regular issue or within forty-eight hours following receipt of such statement or article."[176]

When the defamation is against a candidate for office, North Dakota imposes an additional interesting set of requirements: "[T]he retraction must be made editorially, and in the case of daily paper, at least three days before the election, and in the case of a weekly paper, at least ten days before the election."[177]

§ 9.13 Other Remedies and Reforms

[1] Injunctive Relief

[a] Equity Will Not Enjoin a Libel

One of the unwavering precepts of the American law of remedies has long been the axiom that equity will not enjoin a libel.[178]

---

172 *See* Van Duzer v. Bourizzeau, 23 Mich. App. 720, 179 N.W.2d 214 (1970)(discussing definition of reasonable time for retraction).

173 Cal. Civ. Code § 48a(2) (West 1954). *See also* Neb. Rev. Stat. § 25.840.01 (1975)(three weeks).

174 Nev. Rev. Stat. § 41.336 (1975).

175 N.D. Cent. Code § 14-02-08 (1971).

176 Ohio Rev. Code Ann. § 2739.14 (Page 1954).

177 N.D. Cent. Code § 14-02-08 (1971).

178 *See, e.g.,* Alberti v. Cruise, 383 F.2d 268 (4th Cir. 1967); Parker v. Columbia Broadcasting System, Inc., 320 F.2d 937 (2d Cir.), *cert. denied,* 373 U.S. 911 (1963); Crosby v. Bradstreet, 312 F.2d 483 (2d Cir. 1963); Kukatush Mining Corp v. Securities and Exchange Commission, 114 U.S. App. D.C. 27, 309 F.2d 647 (1962); Robert E. Hicks Corp. v. National Salesman's Training Corp., 19 F.2d 963 (7th Cir. 1927); Reliance Insurance Co. v. Barron's, 428 F. Supp. 200, 205 (S.D.N.Y. 1977); Konigsberg v. Time, Inc., 288 F. Supp. 989 (S.D.N.Y. 1968); American Broadcasting Companies, Inc. v. Smith Cabinet Mfg. Co., 160 Ind. App. 367, 312 N.E.2d 85 (1974); Greenberg v. DeSalvo, 254 La. 1019, 229 So. 2d 83, *cert. denied,* 397 U.S. 1075 (1969); Krebiozen Research Foundation v. Beacon

[b] Rationales for the Principle

There are a number of rationales traditionally cited to support the maxim that equity will not enjoin a libel: (1) equity will afford protection only to property as opposed to personal rights; (2) equity will not enjoin a crime; (3) damages provide an adequate remedy at law for defamation; (4) the defendant would be deprived of a right to a jury trial; and (5) to enjoin defamation is to employ an unconstitutional restraint on freedom of speech.[179]

Of these rationales, none holds up to close scrutiny, except the final one: the first amendment's strong presumption against prior restraints. Equity jurisprudence has abandoned the archaic notion that equity will protect only property and not personal rights; courts of equity today routinely issue injunctions to protect personal rights.[180] The maxim that equity will not enjoin a crime does not apply when private rights otherwise qualifying for injunctive relief are endangered,[181] and most modern libels are not criminal acts in any event.[182] The idea that damages are an adequate remedy at law begs the essential question—a convincing case can in fact be made that defamation is precisely the form of nonquantifiable injury for which damages are ill-suited, and that equitable relief would prevent reputational damage that might never be truly restored by money.[183] The jury trial argument is all but frivolous; if

---

Press, Inc., 334 Mass. 86, 134 N.E.2d 1, *cert. denied,* 352 U.S. 848 (1956); Willing v. Mazzocone, 482 Pa. 377, 393 A.2d 1115 (1978).

179 *See, e.g.,* Mazzocone v. Willing, 246 Pa. Super. 98, 369 A.2d 829 (1976), *rev'd,* 482 Pa. 377, 393 A.2d 1155 (1978); Dobbs, *supra* note 71, § 7.2 at 524; Gold, *Does Equity Still Lack Jurisdiction to Enjoin a Libel or Slander?,* 48 Brooklyn L. Rev. 231 (1982); Leflar, *Legal Remedies for Defamation,* 6 Ark. L. Rev. 423 (1952); Pound, *Equitable Relief Against Defamation and Injuries to Personality,* 29 Harv. L. Rev. 640 (1916).

180 *See, e.g.,* Kenyon v. City of Chicopee, 320 Mass. 528, 70 N.E.2d 241 (1946)(discussing in general the bankruptcy of the personal right/property right distinction).

181 *See* Dobbs, *supra* note 71, §§ 2.11 and 7.2.

182 Most criminal libel laws are today unconstitutional. *See generally* Garrison v. Louisiana, 379 U.S. 64 (1964). The problem is discussed in § 4.10, *supra.*

183 *See* Dobbs, *supra* note 71, § 7.2, at 524. In Mazzocone v. Willing, 246 Pa. Super. 98, 369 A.2d 829 (1976), the defendant persisted in parading in front of a law office with a shopping cart, cowbell, and whistle. He wore a sign proclaiming that the law firm "Stole Money From Me and Sold Me Out to the Insurance Company." The defendant, who was impecunious and unable to pay any damages award, was fixated on this false and defamatory accusation. As a practical matter, therefore, the damages remedy was utterly worthless, a factor that convinced the lower court to discard the weight of authority and issue an injunction to halt the defendant's "bizarre parade." The Pennsylvania Supreme Court reversed, upholding the traditional maxim against enjoining a libel on free expression grounds under the Pennsylvania Constitution. Willing v. Mazzocone, 482 Pa. 377, 393

there is no adequate remedy at law, equitable relief without a jury trial is permitted under federal and state jury trial guarantees,[184] so the jury trial argument can rise no higher than its premise than an adequate remedy at law exists.

If first amendment values were not implicated, therefore, the maxim that equity will not enjoin a libel would probably have succumbed to its harsh critics[185] long ago. First amendment values obviously are implicated, and they are among the most powerful constitutional traditions that exist: the arguments against prior restraint.

[c] Prior Restraints and the First Amendment

The traditional rule of equity jurisprudence was strongly buttressed by the Supreme Court's ruling in *Near v. Minnesota*[186] recognizing that prior restraints are normally invalid under the first amendment.[187] Under *Near,* prior restraints are permitted only in "exceptional cases," such as speech that threatens the nation's military security, obscene speech, or "incitement to acts of violence and the overthrow by force of orderly government."[188] Although the Court has rejected the absolutist "proposition that prior restraints can never be employed,"[189] it is abundantly plain from *Near* and its progeny that the circumstances in which they will be permissible are extremely narrow.[190] The *Near* doctrine is sufficiently powerful and enduring to make the prohibition on injunctions as a remedy for libel unlikely to erode.

A.2d 1155 (1978)(relying on Goldman Theatres v. Dana, 405 Pa. 83, 173 A.2d 59, *cert. denied*, 368 U.S. 897 (1961)(Pennslyvania Constitution prohibits prior restraints)).

[184] Dobbs, *supra* note 71 § 7.2 at 524.

[185] *See* Bertelsman, *Injunctions Against Speech and Writing: A Re-Evaluation*, 59 Kent L.J. 319 (1970); Pound, *supra* note 179; Sedler, *Injunctive Relief and Personal Intergrity*, 9 St. Louis U.L.J. 147 (1964).

[186] 283 U.S. 697 (1931).

[187] *See* Restatement (Second) of Torts § 623 (Special Note on Remedies for Defamation other than Damages, at 329) (1977).

[188] 283 U.S. at 716.

[189] Nebrasks Press Ass'n v. Stuart, 427 U.S. 539, 570 (1970).

[190] *See* Southeastern Promotions, Ltd. v. Conrad, 420 U.S. 546, 559 (1975)(To be valid a prior restraint "first, must fit within one of the narrowly defined exceptions to the prohibition against prior restraints, and second, must have been accomplished with procedural safeguards that reduce the danger of suppressing constitutionally protected speech.").

[d] Recharacterizing the Harm

When the tortious conduct can be characterized as implicating torts other than defamation, injunctive relief tends to be more readily available. Trade libel cases, for example, often permit injunctive relief; courts have enjoined dissatisfied owners from painting lemons or white elephants on automobiles,[191] apparently reflecting the view that commercial speech generally is deserving of less first amendment protection.[192] Similarly, if the tort can be cast in terms of one of the prongs of invasion of privacy, such as false light invasion of privacy[193] or intrusion,[194] injunctive relief may issue.[195] Where the defamation is incident to some other legal invasion for which injunctive relief is available, such as a trespass, or violent picketing, or fraud, both the larger tortious misconduct and the incidental defamation may be enjoined.[196]

[2] Right of Reply and Compulsory Retraction

[a] Right of Reply

From time to time states have experimented with "access remedies" for defamation—statutes that give the victim of a defamatory statement by the media equal time or equal space to present his own side of the story.[197] Wisconsin, for example, permitted "the libeled person's statement of the true facts" to constitute a correction within its right of reply

191 *See* Carter v. Knapp Motor Co., 243 Ala. 600, 11 So. 2d 383 (1943); Menard v. Houle, 298 Mass. 546, 11 N.E.2d 436 (1937).

192 *See generally* Dun & Bradstreet, Inc. v. Greenmoss Builders, Inc., 105 S. Ct. 2939 (1985). *See also supra* § 3.02.

193 *See* Ali v. Playgirl, Inc., 447 F. Supp. 723 (S.D.N.Y. 1978).

194 *See* Galella v. Onassis, 487 F.2d 986 (2d Cir. 1973).

195 *See generally* Note, *Right of Privacy—Availability of Injunctive Relief for Invasions of Privacy,* 39 Mo. L. Rev. 647 (1974).

196 Dobbs, *supra* note 71, § 7.2, at 524. *See also* Horne v. Radiological Health Services, D.C., 83 Misc. 2d 446, 371 N.Y.S.2d 948 (1975), *aff'd mem.*, 51 A.D.2d 544, 379 N.Y.S.2d 374 (2d Dept. 1976).

197 For an excellent overview of "right of access" theory generally, *see* Lange, *The Role of Access Doctrine in the Regulation of the Mass Media: A Critical Review and Assessment,* 52 N. Car. L. Rev. 1 (1973). On the related fairness and equal time doctrines imposed on the broadcast media by the FCC, *see generally* Red Lion Broadcasting Co., Inc. v. Federal Communications Commission, 395 U.S. 367 (1969)(holding fairness doctrine and related rules do no violate first amendment, relying on argument of spectrum scarcity).

statute.[198] More aggressively, a Florida statute declared it a crime for a newspaper to refuse to publish free of charge a reply of equivalent length by any political candidate whom the newspaper had attacked in personal character or the conduct of his or her office.[199] The reply required by Florida was to be in as conspicuous a place and of the same size type as the original attack, and failure to comply was a first degree misdemeanor.[200] In *Miami Herald Publishing Co. v. Tornillo*,[201] the Supreme Court held the Florida right-of-reply statute unconstitutional. Chief Justice Burger, writing for the Court, stated that "[c]ompelling editors or publishers to publish that which ' "reason" tells them should not be published' is what is at issue in this case."[202] The Florida statute, the Court stated, "exacts a penalty on the basis of the content of a newspaper."[203] In a broad endorsement of the ideal of editorial freedom, the Chief Justice continued:

> Even if a newspaper would face no additional costs to comply with a compulsory access law and would not be forced to forgo publication of news or opinion by the inclusion of a reply, the Florida statute fails to clear the barriers of the First Amendment because of its intrusion into the function of editors. A newspaper is more than a passive receptacle or conduit for news, comment, and advertising. The choice of material to go into a newspaper, and the decisions made as to limitations on the size and content of the paper, and treatment of public issues and public officials—whether fair or unfair—constitute the exercise of editorial control and judgment. It has yet to be demonstrated how governmental regulation of this crucial process can be exercised consistent with First Amendment guarantees of a free press as they have evolved to this time.[204]

The opinion in *Miami Herald v. Tornillo* is generally understood as closing the constitutional door on right of reply statutes. The opinion does not, however, address retraction statutes.[205]

---

198 Wis. Stat. § 895.05(2), *discussed and reprinted in* M. Franklin & R. Rabin, Tort Law and Alternatives 941-42 (3d ed. 1983).

199 Fla. Stat. Ann. § 104.38 (1973).

200 *Id.* The statute was upheld by the Florida Supreme Court. Tornillo v. Miami Herald Publishing Co., 287 So. 2d 78 (Fla. 1973).

201 418 U.S. 241 (1974).

202 *Id.* at 256 (internal quotes from Court's quotation of appellee's brief, at 5).

203 *Id.*

204 *Id.* at 258.

205 *See id.* at 258-59 (Brennan, J., concurring). *See also supra* § 9.11.

[b] Compulsory Retraction

The *Tornillo* holding did not *necessarily* foreclose a compulsory retraction as a *post-judgment remedy after a court has determined in a full-fledged defamation suit that liability exists.* At this time there is no statutory authorization for such a remedy in any state. It was long ago reported by the esteemed Dr. Robert A. Leflar that in the Ozark Mountains of North Arkansas there was a cause of action known by the quaint title the "lie bill," which was used as the remedy for its sound-alike "libel," and for slanders.[206] The judgment, if the plaintiff prevailed, would not be for money damages but "would . . . be in the nature of a declaratory judgment, with the defendant required to sign a written statement to the effect that he had lied about the plaintiff."[207]

Prior to World War II, German law provided for compulsory retraction, a remedy that was seldom used, apparently because of the strict interpretation given to criminal statutes and the small maximum fine of 150 marks.[208]

Arguably, compulsory retraction (or compulsory equal space) *after* a full-fledged defamation trial with all appeals exhausted could survive the holding in *Tornillo,* since the defendant would have received the full protections of due process of law and applicable first amendment liability rules prior to being forced to retract or yield equal space. A statute creating such a remedy might even offer it as an alternative to be first elected by the plaintiff and then chosen by the defendant in lieu of damages: either pay the damages or print the retraction. In theory, such a remedy is merely a form of relief *in specie,* a sort of equitable replevin ordering that the defendant, rather than pay damages, return what it actually took, that is, the plaintiff's reputation.

A number of court decisions prior to *Tornillo,*[209] however, evince a general hostility toward compulsory access to the media. This hostility might very well continue to carry the day after *Tornillo.* American law

---

206 Leflar, *supra* note 182, at 423.

207 *Id.*

208 The remedy was known as *Berichtigung. Id.* at 436-37. *See also* Dobbs, *supra* note 73, § 7.2, at 526; Reisman, *Democracy and Defamation: Fair Game and Fair Comment,* 42 Colum. L. Rev. 1085, 1110 (1942).

209 *See* Associates & Aldrich Co., Inc. v. Times Mirror Co., 440 F.2d 133 (9th Cir. 1970); Chicago Joint Board v. Chicago Tribune Co., 435 F.2d 470 (7th Cir. 1970), *cert. denied,* 402 U.S. 973 (1971); Resident Participation of Denver, Inc. v. Love, 322 F. Supp. 1100 (D. Colo. 1971); Cook v. Advertiser Co., 323 F. Supp. 1212 (M.D. Ala. 1971), *aff'd on other grounds,* 458 F.2d 1119 (5th Cir. 1972).

does not even force criminals to admit they committed the crime—a man is free to accept his sentence in silence and pay his debt to society.[210] Although the Supreme Court has ruled that, because of the unique problem of spectrum scarcity, compulsory access to the broadcast media is constitutional,[211] the "function of the press from the days the Constitution was written to the present time has never been conceived as anything but a private enterprise, free and independent of government control and supervision."[212] The draconian remedy of compulsory retraction or right of reply is probably best kept a theory; there is ample room for less drastic reform in other areas of the law of defamation.

[3] Declaratory Judgments

Public vindication through a pronouncement by a court of law that a defendant's reputation has been wrongfully impugned is one of the primary functions of the law of defamation.[213] For many plaintiffs the public declaration is more vital than the money involved. General Westmoreland, for example, planned to give to charity any money he received in his suit against CBS; for him, restoration of his sullied honor was much more significant than dollars.

In most jurisdictions today declaratory relief is authorized by statute in civil cases in lieu of compensatory (damages) or coercive (injunctive) remedies. A declaratory judgment in a defamation action would seem to be a particularly appropriate remedy, for it accomplishes the restoration of the plaintiff's human dignity without the cumbersome effort to establish damages. In recent years the remedy of declaratory relief has often been touted as the desirable alternative to a damages action.[214]

---

210 One wonders what effect compulsory retraction can have when it is not truly heartfelt, except to break the spirit of the one forced to recant.

211 *See* Red Lion Broadcasting Co. v. FCC, 395 U.S. 367 (1969)(upholding FCC fairness doctrine); CBS, Inc. v. FCC, 453 U.S. 367 (1981)(upholding FCC ruling giving federal candidates limited right of access to broadcast media). *But see also* Columbia Broadcasting System, Inc. v. Democratic National Committee, 412 U.S. 94 (1973)(no general public right of access to broadcast media advertising).

212 Chicago Joint Board v. Chicago Tribune Co., 435 F.2d 470, 474 (7th Cir. 1970), *cert. denied,* 402 U.S. 973 (1971), *quoted with approval in* Associates & Aldrich Co. v. Times Mirror Co., 440 F.2d 133, 135 (9th Cir. 1971).

213 *See* Smolla, *supra* note 6, at 19.

214 Professor Stanley Ingber is one of the most thoughtful proponents of such a proposal. He describes such an approach as a "fault free" defamation action. *See* Ingber, *Defamation: A Conflict Between Reason and Decency,* 65 Va. L. Rev. 785, 852-53 (1979).

Among those who have argued for the use of current declaratory judgment procedures as an alternative method of resolving defamation disputes is United States District Judge Pierre N. Leval, of the United States District Court for the Southern District of New York. Judge Leval presided in the *Westmoreland v. CBS* litigation.[214.1] Judge Leval, in an extremely thoughtful article in the *Harvard Law Review* [214.2] argues that: "Recognition of a no-money, no-fault suit would enhance the primary objective of the law of defamation: the restoration of a falsely damaged reputation."[214.3]

Under our present defamation system this alternative may, however, prove to be impractical, for the mechanisms now in place provide no pragmatic incentives to plaintiffs to seek declaratory relief in lieu of the traditional tort action for damages.[215] If new innovations encouraging declaratory relief are to be considered, there will have to be "something in the deal" for both plaintiffs and defendants, something that takes account of litigation costs and incentives as well as first amendment rules. For example, the declaratory judgment as the alternative to damages is appealing to a plaintiff only if that option is much swifter and cheaper than an action for damages. It can be made swifter and cheaper, however, only by eliminating litigation issues such as the existence of actual malice or negligence. This raises a fascinating and largely uncharted first amendment question: Would the fault rules created by the combination of *New York Times, Gertz, Walker* and *Butts,* and *Dun & Bradstreet*[216] apply when the remedy is merely declaratory relief? If the answer is no,[217] then a speedy action for declaratory relief might very well be worthwhile, at least when the question of truth or falsity can be litigated with relative expedition. When the question of truth or falsity is not easily resolved, however, as in recent marathon cases such as *Westmoreland v. CBS, Inc.*[218] and *Sharon v. Time, Inc.,*[219] the expense

214.1 Westmoreland v. CBS, 596 F. Supp. 1170 (S.D.N.Y. 1984).

214.2 Leval, *The No-Money, No-Fault Libel Suit: Keeping Sullivan in its Proper Place,* 101 Harv. L. Rev. 1287 (1988).

214.3 *Id.* at 1302.

215 *See* Restatement (Second) of Torts § 623 (Special Note on Remedies for Defamation other than Damages, at 327-28); Inbger, *supra* note 214, at 852.

216 *See* the summary of these rules in §§ 3.01 and 3.05, *supra.*

217 Justice Brennan has so suggested. *See* Gertz v. Robert Welch, Inc., 418 U.S. 323, 368 n.3 (Brennan, J., concurring).

218 596 F. Supp. 1170 (S.D.N.Y. 1984).

219 599 F. Supp. 538 (S.D.N.Y. 1984).

of litigation may already be so great that plaintiffs simply cannot afford to lose the hope of a damages recovery, a recovery that often pays merely for legal fees.[220]

[4] The Annenberg Libel Reform Proposal

[a] Introduction

The most comprehensive recent proposal for reforming the current American law of defamation was published in October 1988 by the Annenberg Washington Program in Communications Policy Studies of Northwestern University. Entitled *Proposal for the Reform of Libel Law: The Report of the Libel Reform Project of the Annenberg Washington Program,* the report was the result of a project sponsored by the Annenberg Washington Program and directed by the author of this treatise, Rodney A. Smolla.

The Annenberg Report received wide attention in the press and among members of the bar and the journalism community. Because it is likely to be an ongoing focal point for debate on libel reform, the proposed "Libel Reform Act" and accompanying "Section-by-Section Analysis" set forth in the Report are reprinted here in their entirety.

[b] Summary of Annenberg Proposals

The Report of the Annenberg Washington Program Libel Reform Project sets forth a comprehensive model Libel Reform Act, designed to encourage the dissemination of truth in the marketplace by emphasizing remedies other than money damages to facilitate the prompt and efficient resolution of defamation disputes. The driving philosophy behind the proposed Libel Reform Act is the conviction that the first amendment's guarantee of freedom of speech and the law of defamation should not work at cross-purposes, but should function in harmony to serve the compelling public interest in the pursuit of truth.

The idea for the Annenberg Libel Reform Project was conceived by Newton M. Minow, the Director of the Annenberg Washington Program in Communications Policy Studies of Northwestern University. His hypothesis was that the current libel system is not working well for anyone. Plaintiffs, defendants, judges, and academics have all criticized

---

[220] In Tavoulareas v. Washington Post Co., 759 F.2d 90 (D.C. Cir. 1985), *vacated,* 817 F.2d 762 (D.C. Cir.) (en banc), *cert. denied,* 108 S. Ct. 200 (1987), for example, the punitive damages award of $1.8 million was equal to the plaintiff's attorneys fees.

the modern law of libel; in practice it appears neither to adequately protect first amendment values nor to provide plaintiffs with an efficient, meaningful forum for vindicating reputational damage. If a group of thoughtful experts from various libel "constituencies" could be brought together for an extended exploration of the current system, perhaps consensus could emerge on reform.

Eleven persons, from a wide spectrum of backgrounds and viewpoints, and including representatives of the defense and plaintiffs' bars, the judiciary, journalists, academe, and the insurance industry, were assembled for a series of meetings in Washington, D.C., to study and debate the current state of the law of libel, and to propose reforms. The members of the project were Rodney A. Smolla, the Project Director, Sandra S. Baron, Managing General Attorney for the Law Department of the National Broadcasting Company, Bruce E. Fein, a well-known conservative constitutional law expert and former General Counsel of the Federal Communications Commission, Judge Lois G. Forer, former Judge of the Court of Common Pleas in Philadelphia and author of the book, *A Chilling Effect: The Growing Threat of Libel and Invasion of Privacy Actions to the First Amendment,* Samuel E. Klein, of Kohn, Savett, Klein & Graf, P.C., in Philadelphia, Anthony Lewis, columnist for *The New York Times,* Roslyn A. Mazer, of Dickstein, Shapiro, & Morin, in Washington, D.C., Chad Milton, Assistant General Counsel of Media/Professional Insurance, Inc., Anthony Murry, formerly one of the lawyers for William Westmoreland in his suit against CBS, and now an attorney in Washington, D.C., Herbert Schmertz, formerly of Mobil Oil Corporation, and now President of the Schmertz Company, and Richard M. Schmidt, Jr., of Cohn & Marks, Washington, D.C.

It was an experiment—as in the words of Oliver Wendell Holmes "all life is an experiment." The meetings were intense and vigorous, in the true tradition of *New York Times Co. v. Sullivan's* famous celebration of "uninhibited, robust, and wide-open" debate. The experiment proved to be an extraordinary success. Out of the diversity and extended give-and-take of the group, substantial consensus emerged, ending with the Report and its carefully balanced Libel Reform Act.

The Libel Reform Act proceeds from the premise that traditional libel suits for money damages are a poor vehicle for resolving modern defamation disputes. Libel suits tend to drag on interminably, are enormously costly for both sides, and very rarely end in a clearcut resolution of what ought to be the heart of the matter: a determination of the truth or falsity of what was published.

Many of the ideas expressed in the Report have been around for some time. In the last several years a national conversation about libel reform has been carried out in a wide variety of books, articles, conferences, and symposia. Of particular note are Professor Marc Franklin of Stanford and Professor David Anderson of Texas, both of whom have long been the preeminent scholarly voices on the law of libel; Floyd Abrams, a great first amendment lawyer and defender of press liberties; Congressman Charles Schumer of New York; United States District Judge Pierre Leval of New York, who presided in the *Westmoreland v. CBS* litigation; Abraham Sofaer of the Department of State, formerly the United States District Judge who presided in the *Sharon v. Time, Inc.* trial; Steven Brill, Editor of *The American Lawyer;* Professor Gilbert Cranberg and Professor John Soloski of Iowa, and Dean Randall P. Bezanson of Washington & Lee, the authors of the monumental Iowa Libel Research Project; Henry Kaufman, General Counsel of the Libel Defense Resource Center; Professor Paul LeBel of William and Mary; William Tavoulareas, President of Mobil Oil Corporation; Everette Dennis, of the Gannett Center for Media Studies; and Richard Winfield, a leading libel defense lawyer from New York. Several of the participants in the Annenberg Libel Reform Project had also contributed to this rich national debate; Anthony Lewis and Bruce Fein, for example, had written thoughtful articles with proposals for change, and Judge Lois Forer, in her book *A Chilling Effect,* set forth a comprehensive reform statute. These people, along with many other Americans interested in defamation, have proposed a number of thougtful reform measures in recent years, many of which have been incorporated in the Libel Reform Act. The Act, for example, includes the emphasis on declaratory judgment alternatives that have been suggested by people like Judge Pierre Leval and Professor Marc Franklin. The Report has drawn from this rich public discourse, and attempts to combine the best features of many of the thoughtful reform proposals that have surfaced in recent years in a comprehensive, balanced package, a package fair to the interests of both plaintiffs and defendants, a package that places as the highest interest of all the expeditious and efficient dissemination of truth in the marketplace.

[c] Text of Annenberg Libel Reform Act

THE LIBEL REFORM ACT

Preamble

The purpose of this Act is to provide an efficient and speedy remedy for defamation, emphasizing the compelling public interest in the dissemination of truth in the marketplace. The provisions of this Act are intended to encourage the prompt resolution of defamation disputes through remedies other than money damages and should be liberally construed to accomplish that purpose.

Section 1: Scope of Coverage

(a) One Cause of Action. One cause of action, for defamation, shall exist for all claims based on publication of false defamatory statements. The cause of action for false-light invasion of privacy is abolished.

(b) Publication Defined. Publication is the communication of defamatory matter, intentionally or by negligent act, to one other than the person defamed.

(c) No Distinction Between Media and Nonmedia. The provisions of this Act shall apply without regard to the media or nonmedia status of the publisher.

Section 2: False Defamatory Statements of Fact Required

(a) False Statements of Fact Required. All actions for defamation must be based upon publication of false defamatory statements of fact of and concerning the plaintiff. No action may be based upon statements that are expressions of opinion.

(b) Defamatory Defined. A statement is defamatory if, as reasonably construed, it tends to injure the plaintiff's reputation.

(c) Question for Court. Whether the statements giving rise to the action are capable of being reasonably understood as defamatory statements of fact is initially a question of law to be decided by the court. If the court determines that the statements are capable of being reasonably understood as defamatory statements of fact, it shall be for the trier-of-fact to determine whether the statements were actually so understood by recipients of the statements.

(d) Factors to be Considered. In determining whether the statements giving rise to the litigation are defamatory statements of fact or statements of opinion, the court and trier-of-fact shall consider:

(1) The extent to which the statements are objectively verifiable or provable;

(2) The extent to which the statements were made in a context in which they were likely to be reasonably understood as opinion or rhetorical hyperbole and not as statements of fact;

(3) The language used, including its common meaning, and the extent to which qualifying or cautionary language, or a disclaimer, was employed.

Section 3: Retraction or Reply

(a) Request as Prerequisite to Suit. No action for defamation may be brought against any defendant, unless the plaintiff shall allege either:

(1) That the plaintiff made a timely and sufficient request for a retraction and the defendant failed to make a timely and conspicuous retraction; or

(2) That the plaintiff made a timely and sufficient request for an opportunity to reply, and the defendant failed to provide the plaintiff with a timely and conspicuous opportunity to reply or to make a timely and conspicuous retraction; or

(3) That the plaintiff made a timely and sufficient request in the alternative for either a retraction or an opportunity to reply, and the defendant failed to make either a conspicuous retraction or provide the plaintiff with a conspicuous and timely opportunity to reply.

(b) Retraction Defined. A retraction is a good faith publication of the facts, withdrawing and repudiating the prior defamatory statements.

(c) Reply Defined. A reply is the publication of the plaintiff's statement of the facts.

(d) Timely Request. A timely request for retraction or reply is a request made within 30 days of the publication of the defamatory statement.

(e) Requirements for Request. A request for a retraction or reply must be made in writing and signed by the plaintiff or his authorized attorney or agent. It must specify the statements claimed to be false and defamatory and must set forth the plaintiff's version of the facts.

(f) Conspicuous Retraction. A conspicuous retraction is a retraction published in substantially the same place and manner as the defamatory statements being retracted. The placement and timing of the retraction must be reasonably calculated to reach the same audience as the prior defamatory statements being retracted.

(g) Conspicuous Reply. A conspicuous reply is a reply written by the plaintiff and published in substantially the same place and manner as the defamatory statements to which the reply is directed. In the case of a broadcast, the defendant may read the reply or permit the plaintiff or his designate to read it. The defendant may require that the reply not exceed the length of the material in which the defamatory statements of and concerning the plaintiff were published, and that its form reasonably accommodate the nature of the medium in which it is to be published. The reply must be concise and limited to rebuttal of the defamatory statements.

(h) Publication of Retraction or Reply in Customarily Designated Places. When the defendant customarily publishes retractions, corrections or opportunities to reply in a designated place, publication of a retraction or reply in that place shall be deemed conspicuous if notice of the retraction or reply is published in substantially the same place and manner as the statements to which the reply or retraction is directed.

(i) Options of Defendant. Upon receipt of a request for a retraction, the defendant may satisfy the requirements of this Section only by publishing a retraction. Upon receipt of a request for an opportunity to reply, or upon receipt of a request in the alternative for either a retraction or opportunity to reply, the defendant may satisfy the requirements of this Section by electing either to publish a retraction or to provide the plaintiff with an opportunity to reply.

(j) Timely Retraction or Reply. To be timely, the publication of a retraction or reply must be made within 30 days of the request. In the case of a false and defamatory statement about a candidate for public office, however, the retraction or reply shall not be deemed timely unless it is published within a reasonable time under the circumstances prior to the election.

Section 4: Declaratory Judgment

(a) Declaratory Judgment Action Brought by Plaintiff. Subject to the requirements of Section 3, a person who is the subject of any defamation may bring an action in any court of competent jurisdiction for a declaratory judgment that such publication was false and defamatory.

(b) No Damages Permitted. No damages shall be awarded in such an action, and the filing of such an action for declaratory judgment shall forever bar the plaintiff from asserting or recovering for any other claim or cause of action arising out of the publication which is the subject of the action.

(c) Proof of Fault or State of Mind Not Required. Neither the fault nor state of mind of the defendant shall be an element of such an action.

(d) Burden of Proof. In any action for a declaratory judgment, the plaintiff shall bear the burden of proving by clear and convincing evidence that the publication was false and defamatory.

(e) Election of Defendant to Convert Action for Damages to an Action for Declaratory Judgment. A defendant in an action for defamation shall have the right, at the time of filing its answer or within 20 days from the commencement of the action, whichever comes first, to designate the action as an action for a declaratory judgment. Any action designated by the defendant as an action for a declaratory judgment pursuant to this provision shall be treated for all purposes as if it had been filed originally as an action for a declaratory judgment by the plaintiff, and the plaintiff shall be forever barred from asserting or recovering for any other claim or cause of action arising out of the publication which is the subject of such action.

(f) Docket Priority. Actions for declaratory judgments in defamation cases shall be granted priority over other civil actions in setting trial dates, and in all cases must be tried within 120 days of the filing of the complaint, unless the court makes an explicit finding on the record that such an expedited trial date is impracticable under the circumstances. The court may issue such orders as to discovery as are consistent with the expedited trial required by this Section.

Section 5: Neutral Reportage

No cause of action for either a declaratory judgment or damages may be maintained for the reporting of false and defamatory statements involving matters of public interest or concern made by persons or entities other than the defendant if the persons or entities who made the statements are identified and the statements are accurately reported.

Section 6: Truth or Falsity

(a) Burden of Proof. In any action for defamation, whether for declaratory judgment or damages, the plaintiff shall bear the burden of proving by clear and convincing evidence that the defamatory statements of and concerning the plaintiff are false.

(b) Substantial Truth. The plaintiff shall not be deemed to have met the burden of proof required by this Section if the defamatory statements are substantially true.

Section 7: Minimum Fault Requirements

In all defamation actions for damages, at minimum the plaintiff shall bear the burden of proving, through clear and convincing evidence, that the defendant failed to act as a reasonable person under the circumstances.

Section 8: Privileges

(a) Absolute Privileges. Any cause of action for defamation maintained pursuant to this Act, whether for a declaratory judgment or for damages, shall be absolutely barred if the statements were made by:

(1) Judges, attorneys, witnesses, jurors, or other participants in any judicial proceeding;

(2) Legislators, attorneys, aides, witnesses, or other participants in any legislative proceeding; or

(3) Executive and administrative officials, attorneys, witnesses, or other participants in any quasi-judicial or quasi-legislative executive or administrative proceeding.

(b) Conditional Privileges Abolished in Declaratory Judgment Actions. All conditional privileges are abolished in actions for declaratory judgment maintained pursuant to Section 4.

(c) Conditional Privileges in Damages Actions. In actions maintained for damages, the defendant shall be given a conditional privilege for statements made:

(1) In the self-defense of the defendant's own legitimate interests;

(2) In furtherance of the legitimate interests of others;

(3) To protect a common interest between the defendant and the recipient of the communication; or

(4) To persons officially charged with the duty of acting in the public interest.

(d) Abuse of Conditional Privilege. No cause of action based upon statements encompassed by a conditional privilege may be maintained unless the plaintiff proves that the defendant abused the privilege. The privilege shall be deemed abused and forfeited if the defendant deliberately communicated the defamatory matter to persons other than those to whom communication was necessary to serve the interests giving rise to the privilege. If the communication was not made to persons other than those necessary to serve the interest giving rise to the privilege, then the privilege shall be deemed abused and forfeited only if the defendant published the defamatory statements with the knowledge of falsity or reckless disregard for truth or falsity.

Section 9: Damages

(a) Libel and Slander Distinctions Abolished. All distinctions among libel, slander, libel per se, libel per quod, slander per se and slander per quod are abolished.

(b) Recovery Limited to Actual Injury. In any action for damages, recovery shall be limited to reasonable compensation based on proof of actual injury. Presumed damages are abolished. Proof of special damages (specific, pecuniary, out-of-pocket damages) shall not, however, be required. Proof of damage to reputation is a prerequisite to any recovery of damages. If proof of reputational injury is established, the plaintiff may additionally recover damages for personal humiliation, anguish or emotional distress.

(c) All Factors Considered. In awarding compensatory damages for actual injury the trier-of-fact may take into account all factors relevant to the impact of the defamatory statement, including whether it was in written or oral form.

(d) No Punitive Damages. No punitive damages shall be permitted in any action for defamation.

Section 10: Attorneys' Fees

(a) In Litigating the Sufficiency of a Retraction or a Reply. The defendant may move to dismiss any action for defamation on the grounds that the plaintiff failed to comply with the requirements for a request for a retraction or reply set forth in Section 3, or on the grounds that the defendant either published a retraction or provided an opportunity to reply, in compliance with the requirements of Section 3. If the action is so dismissed, the defendant shall be awarded reasonable attorneys' fees. If the action is not so dismissed, attorneys' fees shall be awarded as otherwise provided in this Section.

(b) In Declaratory Judgment Actions. In any action brought as a declaratory judgment or converted to an action for a declaratory judgment, the court shall award the prevailing party reasonable attorneys' fees. The court shall have discretion to deny or reduce the award of attorney's fees to any prevailing party who litigated vexatious or frivolous claims or defenses.

(c) In Damages Actions. In any action for damages, each side shall bear its own attorneys' fees, subject to the applicable general rules of the jurisdiction for civil litigation.

Section 11: Limitations Period One Year

Any action for defamation must be commenced no later than one year after the first date of publication.

Section 12: Single Publication Rule

An action brought pursuant to this Act shall be the exclusive remedy for all injury in all jurisdictions arising from the defamatory statement upon which the action is based.

Section 13: Severability

The provisions of this Act are severable, and any judicial decision declaring any provision of this Act invalid shall not be deemed to invalidate other provisions of the Act.

Section 14: Preemption and Jurisdiction

Alternative A—Federal Statute. The provisions of this Act shall be preemptive of all applicable state laws governing defamation or false-light invasion of privacy. A cause of action pursuant to this Act may be brought in any state or federal court of competent jurisdiction.

Alternative B—State Statute. Except as otherwise provided herein, the provisions of this Act are preemptive of applicable prior law governing defamation or false-light invasion of privacy. A cause of action pursuant to this Act may be brought in any state or federal court of competent jurisdiction.

SECTION-BY-SECTION ANALYSIS

Preamble

The Preamble should be read in conjunction with this Section-by-Section Analysis to illuminate the principal legislative purpose of this statute: to encourage the speedy and efficient resolution of defamation disputes through remedies other than money damages, emphasizing the compelling public interest in the dissemination of truth in the marketplace. The retraction, reply, declaratory judgment and attorneys' fees provisions of this Act are designed to work together in an integrated system of checks and balances. They aim to create incentives for both plaintiffs and defendants to resolve defamation disputes through mechanisms other than prolonged and costly suits for damages. All provisions of this Act should be liberally construed to accomplish that legislative purpose.

Section 1: Scope of Coverage

1. This Section abolishes the common law cause of action for false-light invasion of privacy. It should be construed in conjunction with Section 9(a), which abolishes the distinctions between libel and slander. The Act creates one cause of action, defamation, for all claims based on false defamatory statements.

2. The creation of one cause of action simplifies the law and prevents parties from evading the coverage of this Act by attempting to recast a cause of action for defamation as an action for false-light invasion of privacy.

3. The common law causes of action for defamation and false-light invasion of privacy are largely duplicative. Technically, the common law cause of action for false-light invasion of privacy did not require proof of injury to reputation, but was meant instead to redress injury to the peace of mind of the plaintiff who wishes to be left alone. In practice, however, the overlap between the two torts resulted primarily in needless confusion and duplication. The abolition of the false-light tort should also be construed in light of Section 9(c), which instructs the trier-of-fact to take into account all factors relevant to the impact of the defamatory statement in awarding compensatory damages.

4. This Act covers only actions based on false defamatory statements of fact. It does not encompass or affect actions existing at common law other than libel, slander or false-light invasion of privacy. Actions such as infliction of emotional distress or invasion of privacy actions based on intrusion, publication of private embarrassing facts or appropriation of name or likeness are thus not covered by this Act. Nevertheless, it is the purpose of this Act to preempt all common law causes of action based on false defamatory statements of fact. The Act does not permit causes of action such as infliction of emotional distress or invasion of privacy to be used as surrogates for defamation to avoid the coverage of the Act.

5. "Publication" as defined in this Section adopts the common law position requiring intentional or negligent communication to a third person other than the publisher and the person defamed. Publication is a term of art referring to any form of dissemination of information to a third person. It may include writings, spoken words, symbols, electronic transmissions or any other form of communication.

6. This Act rejects any distinction between media and nonmedia defendants, and encompasses all actions for defamation. The provisions of this Act would thus apply to defamation spoken from one private person to another as well as defamation in a newspaper article or television broadcast. The provisions of this Act are to be flexibly interpreted to accommodate the wide variety of contexts in which defamation may occur. A retraction, for example, may take one form in a newspaper, another in a radio broadcast and yet another in the context of correcting a credit report or employment letter of reference. The statutory purpose in media and nonmedia cases, however, remains the same: encouraging prompt resolution and correction of the record in lieu of prolonged suits for damages. No matter what the context of the defamation, therefore, the Act is to be construed to accomplish that overriding legislative goal.

Section 2: False Defamatory Statements of Fact Required

1. This Section requires that all actions for defamation be based on false defamatory statements of fact. The common law evolved many colorful pejoratives to define "defamatory," employing such terms as "hatred," "contempt," "ridicule" or "obloquy." This Section employs a simplified, common-sense formulation: A defamatory statement is one that tends to injure the plaintiff's reputation.

2. With respect to the language giving rise to the action, the words are to be given a reasonable construction in light of the context of the communication. The court must determine in the first instance whether the words are capable of being reasonably understood as defamatory statements of fact. This is an issue of law for the court. Whether, in the actual circumstances of the case, recipients of the statements in fact understood the statements as defamatory statements of fact remains a fact issue for resolution by the trier-of-fact. One of the most perplexing problems in defamation law is the concept of defamatory implications. Suits often involve accurately reported facts that are alleged to carry a false and defamatory implication. There is a conflict among judicial decisions as to whether defamation actions may be maintained by pub-

lic officials and public figures solely on the basis of implications. It is possible for a valid defamation action to be maintained on the basis of allegedly false and defamatory implications alone, but such an action may be maintained only when the implications alleged to be communicated may reasonably be drawn from the actual statements made. In all instances, of course, the implication must be a false and defamatory factual statement and not an expression of opinion. The "reasonableness" of a defamatory implication drawn from accurate facts depends on such factors as the omission or inclusion of other relevant facts, the use of suggestive language hinting at other implications, and the drawing of conclusions from ambiguous facts. The reasonable construction requirement, in the context of defamatory implications, should be read in conjunction with the retraction provisions of the Act. As set forth below in the analysis of provisions dealing with retractions, in cases in which the action for defamation is grounded in what the words imply, rather than what they actually state, a retraction in compliance with the Act may be perfected by a statement indicating that the alleged defamation was not intended either to state or imply the meaning ascribed to it by the plaintiff.

3. Statements of opinion are never actionable in a cause of action for defamation. This principle is now entrenched in federal constitutional law. This Section draws on the rich constitutional and common law traditions in establishing the factors to be considered in determining whether a statement is one of fact or opinion. The first factor is the extent to which the statements are objectively verifiable or provable. If they cannot be objectively proved they are not statements of fact. The second factor emphasizes the general context of the communication: Statements made in a work of fiction, as part of satire or parody, or in the context of artistic, athletic, literary, academic, culinary, theatrical, religious or political review or commentary should be presumptively construed as opinion. Letters to the editor, editorials and editorial cartoons should be presumptively construed as opinion. Statements made in a straight news story should be presumptively construed as factual, unless qualifying language is employed to indicate otherwise. Mere colorful exaggeration, rhetorical hyperbole, verbal abuse, name-calling, ridicule or jest should be presumptively construed as opinion. In all instances, however, the emphasis must be on the overall context of the communication and on how the statements were reasonably understood in that context. The final factor emphasizes the nature of the language giving rise to the communication, including the extent to which

qualifying, cautionary or disclaiming language was employed. In a work of fiction, the use of a disclaimer shall presumptively establish that the statements giving rise to the action were reasonably understood as imaginary and not factual.

Section 3: Retraction or Reply

1. This Section establishes, as an absolute prerequisite to the maintenance of any suit for defamation, that the plaintiff first demand a retraction or opportunity to reply, and that such demand be refused by the defendant. The rationale for this Section is that the simplest, most efficient remedy for defamation is a prompt and reasonable retraction or reply. This Section should be read in conjunction with the attorneys' fees provisions of Section 10, which include provisions for the awarding of attorneys' fees in cases in which the sufficiency or reasonableness of a retraction or opportunity for reply is litigated.

2. Along with the declaratory judgment provisions of Section 4 and the attorneys' fees provisions of Section 10, this Section establishes a system of checks and balances in which each party has incentives to self-critically assess its own version of the facts and its willingness to litigate disputes over those facts. A defendant who refuses a demand for a retraction or an opportunity to reply may be forced to litigate under penalty of paying the plaintiff's attorneys' fees if the plaintiff's version of the facts prevails. Conversely, a plaintiff who chooses to commence an action after refusal of a demand for a retraction or reply may be penalized by being forced to pay the defendant's attorneys' fees if that action does not prevail in court. The overall effect of these Sections is to encourage the parties to negotiate and settle the dispute prior to litigation.

3. This Section establishes a hierarchy of options for plaintiffs and defendants in choosing between the retraction and reply alternatives. The plaintiff always has an absolute right to demand a retraction in the first instance. (This provision is not to be a trap for the unwary plaintiff. If there is ambiguity as to whether the plaintiff has requested a retraction or a reply, the request is to be construed as one for a retraction.) A plaintiff who specifically demands a retraction, not an opportunity to reply, is entitled to a retraction before litigation is barred. Therefore, a defendant faced with such a plaintiff may not avoid litigation merely by offering an opportunity to reply. The rationale for this provision is that the plaintiff has a right to a full repudiation of the defamation by the defendant, instead of the mere opportunity to reply, before the plaintiff is

stripped of any litigation remedy. Conversely, however, when the plaintiff asks specifically for an opportunity to reply, the defendant may avoid litigation by providing either an opportunity to reply or by publishing a retraction. A retraction, in short, always bars litigation. The rationale for this different treatment is that the plaintiff has no persuasive grounds for insisting on reply time or space when the defendant has voluntarily repudiated the defamation. Similarly, in the case of a plaintiff who demands a retraction or opportunity to reply in the alternative, the defendant has the option of choosing either option.

4. To be sufficient, a retraction must withdraw and repudiate the prior defamatory statements and publish the corrected facts. An equivocal, hypothetical or half-hearted retraction will not suffice. When the allegedly false and defamatory statement giving rise to the plaintiff's demand for a retraction is not a statement actually made by the defendant, but rather an implication allegedly communicated by the actual statements, the defendant may satisfy the retraction requirement by publishing a statement that the defendant did not intend either to state or to imply the meaning ascribed by the plaintiff.

5. To be conspicuous the retraction must be published in substantially the same place or manner as the defamatory statements being retracted. The retraction must be reasonably calculated to reach the same audience as the prior defamatory statements.

6. A reply must also be published in a conspicuous manner—that is, in substantially the same place and manner as the defamatory statements to which the reply is directed. The reply submitted by the plaintiff must be concise and limited to rebuttal of the defamatory statements. Gratuitous statements irrelevant to rebuttal of the facts alleged to be false and defamatory may not be included. No obscene language or material may be included. The precise form and placement of a conspicuous reply may differ, depending on the nature of the medium. So long as the defendant offers the plaintiff an opportunity to reply that is reasonably calculated to reach the same audience as the original defamatory statements, the defendant may require reasonable accommodations in placement or timing of the reply.

7. In some cases the defendant may by custom have designated a particular place or time for the publication of corrections or retractions. A newspaper may customarily print retractions on the first inside page, for example. In a nonmedia context, there may be a particular bulletin board or display area within an office that is customarily set aside for important notices. Publication of a retraction or reply in such a location

will satisfy the requirement that the retraction or reply be conspicuous, so long as notice of that placement is published or "flagged" in substantially the same place and manner as the defamatory statements to which the reply or retraction is directed.

8. The defendant may require that the length of the reply not exceed the length of the material in which the defamatory statements were published. The phrase "length of the material" refers to that portion of the prior communication in which the allegedly defamatory statements of and concerning the plaintiff were made. This length may be as great as that of an entire story or broadcast segment, for example, but only if the entire story or segment contained defamatory material of and concerning the plaintiff. Indeed, the reply will normally be longer than the single sentence or sentences in which the actual defamatory statements were made, if the story or segment included other material that could have been reasonably understood as supporting or explaining the defamatory statements. An entire ten paragraph article, for example, may be completely devoted to defamatory material of and concerning the plaintiff, even though only three sentences contain the actual defamatory language giving rise to the plaintiff's complaint. In such a case, the plaintiff would be entitled to reply space equal to the length of the entire article. On the other hand, a ten paragraph article may contain three sentences actually defamatory of the plaintiff, within three paragraphs elaborating on those sentences. The rest of the article may not concern the plaintiff. In such a case, the length of the reply could be limited by the defendant to three paragraphs.

9. Most retractions or replies must be made within 30 days of the request. In the unique context of elections, however, the retraction or reply must take place within a reasonable time under the circumstances, prior to the election. In determining the reasonableness of the timing of the retraction, the court shall consider the promptness or the delay of the plaintiff in making a demand and the promptness or delay of the defendant in responding, all in light of the strong public interest in accurate information concerning candidates for public office.

Section 4: Declaratory Judgment

1. This Section permits either the plaintiff or the defendant to dictate that the lawsuit be tried as a declaratory judgment action over the truth or falsity of the defamatory statements, with no damages permitted. It must be construed in light of Section 10's provisions for shifting attorneys' fees to the prevailing party in such actions.

2. In a declaratory judgment action the only issue litigated is the truth or falsity of the defamatory statement. All questions of fault or state of mind are eliminated. The plaintiff bears the burden of proving with clear and convincing evidence that the publication was false and defamatory.

3. The court is to expedite trials of declaratory judgment actions. Normally such trials must be set no later than 120 days after the filing of the complaint. The plaintiff in declaratory judgment cases receives no monetary remedy and therefore in fairness is entitled to a speedy trial.

4. A prompt trial on the issue of truth or falsity in which the plaintiff prevails and is awarded attorneys' fees pursuant to Section 10 will normally make the plaintiff whole. In such a case, the plaintiff will have received an expedited judicial declaration that the defamatory facts published were false. Although plaintiffs forfeit any opportunity for money damages in a declaratory judgment action, that loss is offset by the provision for the award of attorneys' fees, by the speed and efficiency of the declaratory judgment remedy and by the elimination of the burden of establishing fault on the part of the defendant.

Section 5: Neutral Reportage

1. This Section adopts the emerging absolute privilege for neutral reportage. The common law employed a fiction that in republishing a defamatory statement the republisher "adopted" the statement as his own. Thus, a defendant could be successfully sued for defamation for merely quoting some other person's defamatory statement, even when the original speaker's very making of the defamatory statement was itself newsworthy.

2. This Section absolutely bars any liability for merely reporting the defamatory statements of others, when the statements involve issues of public interest or concern. The plaintiff's recourse in such event is to pursue the remedies provided in this Act against the person who made the defamatory statements that were reported. Statements made by others include statements accurately reported and identified in documents such as correspondence or the complaint or pleadings filed in litigation. To qualify as neutral reportage, the publication must disclose the identity of the persons or entities that actually made the defamatory statement and those statements must be accurately reported. The phrase "persons or entities" is used to make clear that in addition to statements directly made by natural persons, the privilege encompasses

statements made in identified documents such as committee reports, law enforcement records, exhibits in administrative, legislative or judicial proceedings, and the like. The statement need not be quoted verbatim to satisfy the accuracy requirement; a paraphrase or summary is sufficient. In all cases, however, the report must correctly characterize the gist or sting of the other person's defamatory statement.

3. The neutral reportage privilege does not encompass statements that do not merely report the defamatory statements of others, but instead incorporate such statements into an independent defamatory accusation by the defendant. If the defendant states, for example, that the police chief took a bribe, and that the proof comes from a public statement by the chief's secretary that the chief took a bribe, the neutral reportage privilege would cover the publication of the secretary's statement (assuming it was accurately reported), but not the defendant's separate assertion that the chief took a bribe.

4. The neutral reportage privilege will automatically encompass accurate reports of statements made by identified persons in judicial, legislative or executive branch proceedings, or statements from identified documents in those proceedings; therefore, no separate absolute privileges covering such proceedings are set forth in this Act.

Section 6: Truth or Falsity

1. Constitutional decisions already place the burden of proof on the plaintiff in many defamation cases. This Section establishes that rule as a uniform requirement in all defamation actions. Putting the burden of proof on the plaintiff serves the compelling interest of providing breathing space for the free flow of information. It brings defamation into line with most other tort actions, in which the plaintiff normally has the initial burden of proving all elements of the prima facie case.

2. The substantial truth test codified in this Section has long been an element of the common law. Minor inaccuracies in terminology or detail do not invalidate the substantial truth of a statement if its gist or sting is true. The test is whether those aspects of the communication that are false are the same aspects that tend to injure the reputation.

Section 7: Minimum Fault Requirements

1. This Section establishes negligence as the minimum level of fault that the plaintiff must prove, with clear and convincing evidence, in all defamation actions for damages. Under the First Amendment, ac-

tions for damages brought by public officials or public figures are subject to the higher requirement that the plaintiff prove through clear and convincing evidence that the defendant published the defamatory statements of fact with knowledge of falsity or reckless disregard for truth or falsity. This fault requirement, imposed by the United States Constitution, may not be amended through statute. This Section therefore establishes negligence as a universal minimum statutory fault level but does not attempt to codify through statute the higher levels of fault required by Supreme Court decisions, nor does it affect present or future decisions by state courts in jurisdictions that chose to evolve higher fault standards through judicial decisions. Minimum constitutional fault requirements may be set only by the judiciary, through constitutional adjudication; this Section makes no attempt to interfere with that process. Accordingly, under this Act, fault levels for defamation above the minimum negligence standard are free to move with the evolution of constitutional and common law.

2. This Section should be construed in conjunction with Section 4, which gives either party the right to avoid a damages suit altogether by electing the declaratory judgment alternative.

Section 8: Privileges

1. Absolute privileges are intended to completely immunize defendants from any legal action for statements made in certain narrowly defined circumstances. Absolute privileges thus bar any action under this Act, including both actions for declaratory judgment and actions for damages.

2. This Section does not include a separately defined privilege of fair report for reportage by journalists and other nonparticipants about judicial or other governmental proceedings or activities, because such reports are automatically encompassed by the absolute neutral reportage privilege established in Section 5.

3. This Section establishes an absolute privilege for statements made by participants in judicial and legislative proceedings. The privilege is also extended to executive and administrative proceedings that are quasi-judicial or quasi-legislative in character. Public hearings before administrative agencies such as school boards, power commissions or environmental agencies, for example, are within the scope of the privilege. The rationale for these absolute privileges is that in certain narrowly defined settings the public interest in totally unfettered freedom of speech is so powerful that no action for defamation arising from these

settings should be permitted. Statements made in these settings are subject to the truth-seeking devices of the judicial or legislative processes, and those devices serve to vindicate the public interest in the dissemination of truth in the marketplace, diminishing to at least some degree the need for defamation actions to serve that function. Of overriding significance, however, is the conviction that in judicial or legislative proceedings and quasi-judicial or quasi-legislative executive or administrative proceedings, the public need for complete candor and openness by participants must prevail over any private interest in the vindication of reputation.

4. Conditional privileges function differently from absolute privileges. They provide only qualified protection for defamatory statements and traditionally have been regarded as defeated when the privilege has been abused through the fault of the defendant. Since conditional privileges place the fault of the defendant in issue, they are inappropriate for declaratory judgment actions maintained under Section 4, in which a no-fault standard is employed.

5. In suits for damages, however, conditional privileges remain applicable. The privileges codified in this Section are the four conditional privileges traditionally recognized at common law. They pertain to certain recurring-fact situations in which the interest in free and open communication is particularly high, requiring enhanced legal protection. Although this Section embraces those conditional privileges recognized by current law, it is not intended to freeze or stultify their evolution through judicial interpretation.

6. The privilege of protecting one's own interest is analogous to the privilege of self-defense against physical attack, and covers such communications as statements made in connection with the retrieval of stolen property or the recovery of a debt. The privilege of protecting the interest of others includes such communications as a doctor's statements to protect a patient or an attorney's statement on behalf of a client. Statements made to protect a common interest typically include statements made within an organization or enterprise in which information is exchanged in furtherance of the group's conduct or activities, such as intra-corporate communication or communication within religious, political, professional, fraternal, labor, educational or social organizations.

7. The privilege of communicating information to public officials or others charged with actions in the public interest embraces a wide spectrum of communications, including reports to law enforcement officials

concerning prevention or detection of crime and complaints about the performance of public officials or institutions. This privilege is particularly important in protecting the speech of whistleblowers who report alleged wrongdoing in public or private institutions or organizations.

8. Current law recognizes a wide variety of circumstances in which a conditional privilege would be deemed abused and forfeited, including excessive publication, ill-will or spite, negligence and knowing or reckless falsity. This Act, however, recognizes only two grounds for defeating a conditional privilege: excessive publication and publication with knowledge of falsity or reckless disregard for truth or falsity.

9. When the communication is deliberately spread by the defendant to persons other than those with a legitimate need for the information in light of the interests being served by the privilege ("excessive publication"), the rationale for the privilege dissolves and the privilege should be forfeited.

10. Since this Act establishes negligence as a minimum fault standard in all defamation actions, the notion that a privilege could be forfeited through the mere negligence of the defendant is obsolete, for the privilege would then provide nothing to the defendant not already required by the prima facie case.

11. This Section rejects the view that a conditional privilege may be lost simply because a communication is motivated by "common law malice," in the sense of spite or ill-will. A communication motivated by spite may nonetheless serve the purposes advanced by the privilege and be made in the sincere belief that it is true. A tainted motive does not of itself reduce the social value of the communication and should not cause the privilege to be forfeited.

12. This Section accepts the knowledge of falsity or reckless disregard for truth or falsity standard as the only level of fault that will operate to defeat a conditional privilege when no excessive publication exists. This provides such communications with the breathing space that the privileges are designed to insure, and it advances the additional interest in simplification of defamation rules, by synchronizing the definition of the fault standards applicable to conditional privileges with the prevailing constitutional fault rules.

Section 9: Damages

1. The traditional common law distinction between libel and slander is antiquated and can no longer be justified. Modern forms of technology—such as radio, television and computer communication—have

blurred the distinction between oral and written communication. The confusing and arbitrary rules for slander per se and per quod, pursuant to which some forms of slander require proof of special damages while others are actionable without special damages, work in a haphazard and irrational way, increasing or decreasing the protection for the statements in a manner bearing no logical relation to the actual balance of reputational and speech interests involved. Similarly, the rules of libel per se and libel per quod impose the burden of proving special damages on the plaintiff in a manner different from the slander rules but no less confusing and arbitrary. Finally, the doctrinal quagmire of current law is further complicated by the imposition of constitutional damages rules, rules that generally bear no relation to the common law libel/slander and per se/per quod distinctions.

2. This Section eliminates the entire set of confusing distinctions in current law and replaces it with a simple, unified set of damages rules.

3. There is no longer any distinction between libel or slander, but the trier-of-fact may take the nature of the communication into account in assessing damages. Special damages, in the sense of out-of-pocket pecuniary losses, are never required as a prerequisite to recovery. In any action for damages, recovery is limited to proof of actual injury, which necessarily involves proof of some damage to reputation. Presumed damages, in which no proof of injury is required, are abolished. Once damage to reputation is proved, the plaintiff may enhance the recovery of damages with proof of injury in the form of personal humiliation, anguish or emotional distress. Recovery for such emotional harm is only permitted when reputational injury is first established.

4. This Section absolutely bars the award of punitive damages in all defamation actions. Punitive actions act as an excessive chill on free expression and may be devastating to the defendant. In addition, such awards often bear no relation to reality, sometimes serving to vent distaste for the nature or character of the defendant instead of fulfilling any rational interest in deterrence. Compensatory damages for defamation are already highly subjective and may even contain a hidden punitive component. To permit additional punitive damages, therefore, may punish the defendant twice and provide the plaintiff with a windfall grossly out of proportion to actual injury.

Section 10: Attorneys' Fees

1. This Section serves to insure that the defendant's attorneys' fees incurred in the process of getting a suit dismissed for failure by the

plaintiff to make a proper demand for retraction or reply will be paid by the plaintiff. This Section further insures that when the defendant does retract or provide an opportunity to reply, and the plaintiff files suit anyway, on the grounds that the retraction failed to meet the standards of Section 3 (such as conspicuousness or timeliness), that the defendant's attorneys' fees be paid if the court determines that the retraction or reply was sufficient under Section 3.

2. The plaintiff's interests in this situation are fully protected under the other fee-shifting rules in this Section. In cases in which the court determines that the defendant's retraction or offer of opportunity to reply was not adequate under Section 3, and the plaintiff goes on to prevail in a declaratory judgment action, this Section provides for an award of plaintiff's attorneys' fees, which would include fees incurred in the process of litigating the adequacy of the defendant's retraction or opportunity to reply.

3. The party who prevails in a declaratory judgment action will ordinarily recover reasonable attorneys' fees as a matter of course unless that party has prolonged the litigation through the maintenance of vexatious or frivolous positions. The intent of this Section is to encourage prompt resolution of defamation disputes by establishing a balance of incentives for both parties to self-critically evaluate their versions of the truth and to be forthcoming in providing the evidence upon which their versions are based to the other side. A prevailing party who is guilty of "sandbagging," by not coming forward with evidence that would have ended the litigation promptly if revealed, may in the discretion of the court be penalized for having litigated in a vexatious or frivolous manner.

4. The fee-shifting provisions of this Act do not apply when neither side elects to pursue the declaratory judgment option and the suit is tried for damages.

Section 11: Limitations Period One Year

This provision should be construed in light of the single publication rule in Section 12.

Section 12: Single Publication Rule

This Section adopts the single publication rule, which prevails under current law in most American jurisdictions. The purpose of the Section is to bar a multiplicity of actions filed in separate states for the same publication.

Section 13: Severability

In the event that any court should declare invalid any provision of this Act, all other provisions shall continue to be of full force and effect.

Section 14: Preemption and Jurisdiction

1. The Act is intended to preempt current law with regard to those issues addressed by it and to leave untouched those issues not addressed by it, such as the rules governing disclosure of confidential sources. If enacted as a federal law, the Act will preempt all existing applicable state laws. If enacted as a state law, the Act will preempt current common law rules except where provisions in the Act indicate otherwise.

2. If enacted as federal law, state and federal courts shall have concurrent jurisdiction.

3. If enacted as state law, actions may be brought pursuant to the Act in state courts of competent jurisdiction or federal courts in which diversity and other jurisdictional requirements are met.

[d] Conclusion

The Annenberg Report generated considerable attention in the media bar, and may well serve as a blueprint for legislative changes in the law of libel, should such reform efforts ever achieve realistic possibility.

[5] The Iowa Project

[a] In General

Professors Randall P. Bezanson, Gilbert Cranberg, and John Soloski recently completed a monumental empirical study of the libel litigation process.[220.1] Their outstanding contribution to scholarship concerning the law of libel is currently in a second phase, in which an alternative dispute resolution mechanism is employed. The Iowa Libel Research Project (ILRP), in cooperation with the American Arbitration Association, will select some 30 libel cases nationwide to be resolved through

220.1 R. Bezanson, G. Cranberg, & J. Soloski, Libel Law and the Press: Myth and Realty (1987).

the use of a nonjudicial process. The Iowa Project is an ambitious and highly significant reform effort. Because of its significance, a relatively detailed synopsis of the project's procedures is set forth below.[220.2]

[b] Description of the Project Procedures

[i] How the Program Works

Either party to a media libel dispute may ask the ILRP to ascertain whether the other party or parties are willing to submit the dispute to the Libel Dispute Resolution Program. The dispute should be one that is likely to be seriously litigated and that involves statements of a factual nature.

ILRP staff will explain the procedures available. Except for the basic elements described below, the parties are able to negotiate the details of the process. ILRP staff will assist the parties in fashioning the process. Once ILRP staff have obtained the agreement of the parties to submit the dispute to the program, the parties are requested to complete a submission agreement.

In the submission agreement, the parties agree to submit the dispute to the Libel Dispute Resolution Program under its rules, to abide by the agreed-upon remedy, and to waive legal action. The submission agreement also includes the names and addresses of the parties, their representatives and counsel; a brief statement of the nature of the dispute; and the negotiated specifies of the process (e.g., type of settlement conference, location of the hearing, information exchange, and remedy).

When the submission has been completed, the American Arbitration Association will administer the dispute and will provide a special panel of neutrals for the program. If problems arise, the administrator assigned to each dispute will be available for assistance.

[ii] Summary of Libel Dispute Resolution Procedures

The issues to be adjudicated in the process are the existence of reputational harm and the truth or falsity of the challenged statements. Fault-related questions, such as malice, negligence, and the reasonableness of editorial procedures, will not be relevant, and discovery and evidence relating to such issues will be prohibited. The complainant has

---

220.2 The material describing the Iowa Project is taken from the information pamphlet of the Iowa Research Project, reprinted with permission of Professor Randall Bezanson. Plaintiffs or defendants seeking further information should contact The Iowa Libel Research Project, College of Law, University of Iowa, Iowa City, Iowa 52242.

the burden of defining the specific statements alleged to be false, must show that the challenged statements have caused reputational harm, and, unless the parties agree otherwise, carries the burden of proof on the issue of falsity.

The remedy is subject to negotiation, but is likely to consist of the respondent's agreeing to publish or broadcast in full the neutral's brief written finding on the falsity issue, or to pay to have the finding published or broadcast in other comparable media. The parties, by agreement, may depart from this and determine any other nonmonetary remedy.

The process is strictly scheduled to expedite resolution of the dispute. Discovery, if needed, would take the form of a structured information exchange or would be limited to essential information. The dispute should be resolved within 60 days.

If the parties choose to proceed directly to a hearing, they may do so. In such cases, they need only to have a telephone conference call with a neutral, before the hearing, in order to resolve any remaining questions or conflicts concerning information to be exchanged or the conduct of the hearing.

Many parties, however, may find a prehearing settlement conference to be useful. Parties may choose between a conference that involves mediation and one that involves assessment by a special master. The goals of the conference include reducing the scope of the dispute, encouraging stipulations of uncontested facts, and encouraging settlement discussions.

The settlement conference is private and informal and requires the attendance of the parties as well as counsel. All admissions, proposals, and statements made in the course of the conference are confidential and inadmissible at the hearing or in any other proceeding. Disputes that have not reached an agreement in the settlement conference will proceed to a hearing.

The hearing is public unless both parties agree that it should be closed. The proceedings are informal with relaxed rules of procedure and evidence. One party has full opportunity to present its claims and proofs and to question the other party.

The neutral's brief written finding will state the factual questions at issue; the existence of reputational harm; the truth, falsity, or indeterminacy of the facts as found; and the basics upon which the finding has been made.

The following brief description of the settlement conferences and of the hearing are intended to provide assistance in choosing a procedure.

A Mediator helps the parties analyze their dispute and encourages them to consider how they might be able to reach a mutually satisfactory settlement. Mediation proceedings are confidential and private. The mediator's role is advisory; a mediator cannot make a finding on the dispute.

After each party presents opening statements, the mediator guides the parties' discussion about the relevant information, seeking to devise a formula for settlement. The mediator may offer suggestions and point out things that the parties might have overlooked, helping to clarify the issues.

The mediator may meet separately with each party in a private caucus to get a clearer understanding of the issues in an attempt to bring disputants' offers closer together. The information shared with the mediator in a caucus is confidential and will not be revealed to the other party.

The mediator will work with both sides toward establishing realistic, acceptable claims and offers. Negotiating, with or without the help of a mediator, is a voluntary process. If a party does not like the way negotiations are going, the process can be terminated.

Resolution of the dispute rests with the parties themselves: the settlement must be satisfactory to both sides.

When the parties reach agreement, the terms will be reduced to writing. Any issues not resolved in mediation must be submitted to a hearing for a determination by the neutral.

A special master helps the parties identify areas of agreement and assess their relative positions on areas of disagreement. The proceedings are confidential and private. The special master can indicate the likely outcome in a hearing but cannot make a finding on the dispute.

After each party presents its side of the case, the special master will identify areas of substantial agreement and encourage stipulations. He or she also will note areas of disagreement, probing the support for differing views of the facts. The special master assesses the relative strengths and weaknesses of each side's evidence and arguments on key contested issues.

If the parties are interested, the special master will help them explore settlement options. If the parties are not interested in discussing settlement, or if they try but no settlement is reached, the special master will provide the parties with an evaluation of the likely outcome of the dispute in a hearing and the reasoning behind it.

In the hearing, each side presents its case before a neutral. The neutral issues a written finding on the questions of reputational harm and the truth or falsity of the statements, and the basis upon which the finding has been made.

The parties, by mutual agreement, control the range of issues to be resolved in the hearing, the scope of the remedy, and many of the procedural aspects of the process. Usually, the claiming party presents its case first, followed by the responding party. Hearings are conducted by the neutral in a manner that permits a fair presentation of the case by the parties.

Arbitration hearings are less formal than court trials. Neutrals are not required to follow strict rules of evidence. The neutral decides what evidence offered by the parties is material and relevant to understanding the issues and can reject any evidence or give it the weight he or she thinks is appropriate.

The hearing is ended only after both parties have had a full opportunity to present their case. The neutral will issue a written finding within 10 days.

[iii] The Neutrals

The neutrals selected for this program are drawn from a specially compiled panel of experienced neutrals. The neutrals for the settlement conference are appointed by the AAA. The parties select the neutral to conduct the hearing.

The parties will be provided with information on the neutrals and must advise the AAA of any objections. Any personal, professional, or business contacts must be disclosed by the parties and the neutrals. If there is a disclosure of a disqualifying nature, the AAA will replace the neutral and notify the parties of the replacement.

[iv] Cost

Each party will bear the cost it incurs in preparing for the proceedings. Administrative fees and neutrals' fees will be paid in whole or in part by the ILRP.

[v] Iowa Libel Research Project

The ILRP was established in 1982 at the University of Iowa with a grant from the John and Mary R. Markle Foundation, as a joint research project of the School of Journalism and Mass Communication and the College of Law.

[vi] American Arbitration Association

The AAA, founded in 1926, is a not-for-profit organization offering a broad range of dispute resolution services for a variety of disputes. It administers more than 40,000 disputes each year and has on its panels more than 60,000 impartial experts to hear and decide cases. Services are available through 31 regional offices located in major cities across the country. Hearings may be held at these offices or at any location convenient for the parties.

Although probably best known for its work in labor-management relations, the AAA administers many special programs involving the voluntary submission of disputes to a nonjudicial procedure. These include programs to resolve insurance, computer technology, and business disputes, as well as a medical malpractice program and a court referral project in the U.S. District Court for the Southern District of New York.

§ 9.14 Recent Trends in Damages Awards—A Statistical Summary

The growing visibility of libel and other media-related litigation has generated a substantial amount of new statistical data concerning such suits. The pioneering effort was that of Professor Marc Franklin, consisting of a statistical survey of libel suits decided between January 1976 and mid-June 1979.[221] Sixty-nine percent of the cases studied by Franklin involved nonmedia defendants, and 31 percent involved media defendants.[222] Juries were overwhelmingly more favorable to plaintiffs than were judges, both as to liability and damages. Plaintiffs won judgments *after appeal* in only 5 percent of all media cases, and 12 percent of all nonmedia cases.[223] Appellate courts affirmed 75 percent of the appeals from judgments in favor of defendants, but less than 50 percent of the lower court judgments for plaintiffs.[224] Where plaintiff's verdicts on liability were affirmed, appellate courts frequently found the damages awarded to be excessive.[225]

A second Franklin study was limited to media defendants.[226] On the whole it tended to confirm the conclusions of the first study: Plaintiffs ultimately prevailed in only 5 percent of the cases, after all appeals.[227] Franklin concluded that suits against the media were "not likely to be rewarding," but added the caveat that "even unsuccessful suits may be costly to defend."[228]

---

221 Franklin, *Winners and Losers and Why: A Study of Defamation Litigation,* 1980 Am. B. Found. Research Journal 455.

222 *Id.* at 465.

223 *Id.* at 498.

224 *Id.*

225 *Id.*

226 Franklin, *Suing the Media for Libel: A Litigation Study,* 1981 Am. B. Found. Research J. 795.

227 *Id.* at 800 and n.12.

228 *Id.* at 829; *see also id.* at 800 and n.13.

The task of keeping statistical tab of libel litigation has in recent years been undertaken by the Libel Defense Resource Center (LDRC).[229] One 1982 LDRC study showed that 30 out of 47 damage awards included punitive damages, with 7 of those punitive damages awards for over $1 million.[230]

In a 1984 LDRC study, cases between 1982 and 1984 were examined,[231] and in a 1985 study, an additional 17 cases were analyzed.[232] James Goodale recently summarized these most recent results, and compared them to the 1982 LDRC study.[233] Whereas plaintiffs won 87 percent of the trial verdicts in the 1982 study, they won only 54 percent in the 1984 study, and 59 percent in the 1985 study.[234] Defendants did better in federal court than in state court, winning 75 percent of the cases in the 1984 study in federal court, but only 39 percent in state court.

Plaintiffs at trial did less well when facing the actual malice standard, winning 89 percent in 1982, compared to 47 percent in 1984. Against the negligence standard, plaintiffs won 76 percent of the cases in 1982, and 56 percent in 1984.[235]

Whatever solace defendants may take in the ultimate statistical success rates of libel suits, the *size* of damages awards remains intimidating. In the 1982 LDRC study, the average initial damages award was $2,051,178.20, and the average punitive damages award was $2,520,901.60. In the 1984 study, the figures were $2,033,367.00 and $2,980,093.70.[236] These figures are simply astronomical and out of touch with reality—they are three times as high as the average damages awards in products liability and medical malpractice cases,[237] which involve more palpable injuries.

Million-dollar-plus awards are also on the rise. Prior to 1980, only one damages award was for over $1 million; the 1982 study revealed that

229 *See supra* § 1.02[3], note 27.

230 LDRC Bulliten No. 4, Oct. 15, 1982, at 3, 5, and table 2, 6 and table 2-b.

231 LDRC Bulletin No. 11 (1984).

232 LDRC Bulletin No. 13 (1985).

233 Goodale, "Survey of Recent Media Verdicts, Their Disposition on Appeal and Media Defense Costs," *printed in* Media Insurance and Risk Management 69 (J. Lankenau, ed., PLI 1985).

234 *Id.* at 72-73.

235 *Id.* at 73-74.

236 *Id.* at 78.

237 *Id.*

19 percent of all awards were for over $1 million, and the 1984 study indicated that over one third of all jury awards exceeded that amount.[238]

---

[238] *Id.*

PART II

Invasion of Privacy and Related Torts

CHAPTER 10

Invasion of Privacy

§ 10.01 Overview

[1] History

The area of interrelated torts encompassed by the umbrella term "invasion of privacy" is largely an American contribution to the common law, which is usually said to have its origins in the seminal law review article by Samuel Warren and Louis Brandeis published in 1890.[1] As American society has become more complicated and stressful, concern for the protection of individual dignity and autonomy, or "space," has grown.[2] As solitude and peace become increasingly hard to find, privacy has become ever more precious. American courts, largely undirected by any comprehensive structure, demonstrated growing sensitivity to privacy concerns in the years following the Warren and Brandeis article, but the development of privacy law was still

1 Warren & Brandeis, *The Right to Privacy*, 4 Harv. L. Rev. 193 (1890).

2 *See* Smolla, *Let the Author Beware: The Rejuvenation of the American Law of Libel*, 132 U. Pa. L. Rev. 1, 17-21 (1983).

largely haphazard[3] until 1960, when, with characteristic decisiveness, William Prosser brought a new structure to the law of privacy by subdividing it into four distinct categories.[4] Prosser's four part subdivision has dominated the law of privacy ever since.[5]

[2] Prosser's Four Part Subdivision of the Law of Privacy

Prosser broke invasion of privacy down into four separate torts, each with its own distinct elements. The four categories are:

(1) *False Light Invasion of Privacy.* The essence of this tort, a close cousin of defamation, is the placing of another "in a false light in the public eye."

(2) *Intrusion.* This tort, distinct from but related to trespass, involves an invasion of the plaintiff's "private" space or solitude —eavesdropping on private conversations or peeping through the bedroom window, for example.

(3) *Publication of Private Facts.* This tort involves the publication of true but intimate or private facts about the plaintiff, such as matters concerning the plaintiff's sexual life or health. Since it is premised on publication of facts that are private but nonetheless true, it is the most problematic of the privacy torts in terms of reconciliation with the first amendment.

(4) *The Right of Publicity or Appropriation.* Invasion of the "right of publicity," also known as "appropriation," consists of the exploitation of the plaintiff's name or likeness, usually for commercial gain, as in the unauthorized use of the plaintiff's name in an advertising endorsement for a product.

Of the grouping of these four torts, the first three all involve true invasion of the plaintiff's "privacy," in the sense of disruption of the plaintiff's mental or emotional solitude. The fourth Prosser category, the appropriation of the plaintiff's name or likeness, is in truth a tort less concerned with emotional tranquility and more in the nature of the tort system's own creation of a form of private property interest in the

---

[3] *See generally* W. Prosser, W. Keeton, D. Dobbs, R. Keeton, & D. Owen, *Prosser and Keeton on Torts* § 117, at 849-51 (5th ed. 1984).

[4] Prosser, *Privacy*, 48 Calif. L. Rev. 383 (1960).

[5] Although the judicial response to Prosser's taxonomy of privacy was overwhelming, the classification was not without its academic critics. *See* Bloustein, *Privacy as an Aspect of Human Dignity: An Answer to Dean Prosser*, 39 N.Y.U. L. Rev. 962 (1969).

financial exploitability of one's "persona." Because the right of publicity is somewhat distinct from the other three privacy torts and presents its own special range of issues, coverage of it in this volume is limited to the very brief overview in the text below.

[3] Special Note on the Right of Publicity

[a] In General

The fourth prong of invasion of privacy, known as "the right of publicity," or "appropriation," lends common law or statutory protection to an individual's name or likeness. The *Restatement (Second) of Torts* states simply: "One who appropriates to his own use or benefit the name or likeness of another is subject to liability to another for invasion of privacy."[6]

Courts in the United States and England as far back as the nineteenth century held that it was tortious to use a person's photograph without his or her consent.[7] The influential Warren and Brandeis article on privacy in 1890[8] was followed by a sporadic recognition of a common law tort designed to protect against the unauthorized use of a person's name or likeness, until gradually the cause of action became a generally accepted component of modern tort law.

[b] First Amendment Tensions with the Right

The right of publicity may at times conflict with the first amendment interest in the dissemination of news,[9] and courts have frequently refused to accept right of publicity claims out of solicitude for first amendment considerations. In *Ann-Margret v. High Society Magazine,*[10] for example, the court found that a magazine's reprinting of a photograph of a partially nude Ann-Margret, which had been taken from a fleeting scene in a movie, was protected by the first amendment.

The Supreme Court's contribution to the development of the right of publicity came in the "human cannonball case," *Zacchini v. Scripps-*

---

6 Restatement (Second) of Torts § 652C (1977).

7 *See generally* Gordon, *Right of Property in Name, Likeness, Personality and History,* 55 Nw. L. Rev. 553 (1960).

8 Warren & Brandeis, *supra* note 1.

9 *See generally* Felcher and Rubin, *Privacy, Publicity, and the Portrayal of Real People in the Media,* 88 Yale L.J. 1577 (1979).

10 498 F. Supp. 401 (S.D.N.Y. 1980).

Howard Broadcasting Co.[11] The case involved the entertainment act of Hugo Zacchini, which consisted of his being shot from a cannon 200 yards into a net. Zacchini's act, which he was engaged to perform at the Geauga County Fair, in Burton, Ohio, took place in a fenced area surrounded by grandstands, but patrons of the fair were charged no separate admission to observe the act.

Zacchini noticed a free-lance reporter for a local television station with a small movie camera observing his act. Zacchini asked the reporter not to film the act. The reporter complied at that time, but on the next day, at the behest of the television station's newscast producer, he videotaped the entire act. The film clip, 15 seconds in length, was shown that evening on the eleven o'clock news, with quite favorable commentary.

The Ohio Supreme Court recognized that Zacchini possessed a common law right of publicity, but it ruled for the defendant broadcaster, reasoning that "First Amendment principles require that the right of privacy give way to the right to be informed of matters of public interest and concern."[12] The United States Supreme Court reversed, holding that "the State's interest in permitting a 'right of publicity' is in protecting the proprietary interest of the individual in his act in part to encourage such entertainment. . . . [T]he State's interest is closely analogous to the goals of patent and copyright law, focusing on the right of the individual to reap the reward of his endeavors."[13] In holding that the first amendment did not protect the station's broadcast of Zacchini's performance, the court heavily emphasized Zacchini's proprietary interest:

> The broadcast of a film of petitioner's entire act poses a substantial threat to the economic value of that performance. As the Ohio court recognized, this act is the product of petitioner's own talents and energy, the end result of much time, effort, and expense. Much of its economic value lies in the "right of exclusive control over the publicity given to his performance," if the public can see the act free on television, it will be less willing to pay to see it at the fair.[14]

It is important to emphasize that the Supreme Court in *Zacchini* did not by any means hold that right of publicity claims are completely immune from first amendment restriction. The Court noted that there

---

[11] 433 U.S. 562 (1977).

[12] Zacchini v. Scripps-Howard Broadcasting Co., 47 Ohio St. 2d 224, 234 n.5, 315 N.E.2d 454, 461 n.5 (1976).

[13] 433 U.S. at 573.

[14] *Id.* at 575.

"is no doubt that entertainment, as well as news, enjoys First Amendment protection," and that it "is also true that entertainment itself can be important news."[15] Rather, by analogy to the principle that one may not usually invoke the "fair use" defense in a copyright infringement case when an entire creative work has been appropriated, the first amendment does not insulate the taking of a performer's entire act.

[c] Commercial vs. Noncommercial Uses

Many of the various state formulations of the right of publicity tort are phrased in terms relating to commercial exploitation of the plaintiff's name or likeness.[16] Appropriation for advertising purposes thus falls squarely within the coverage of the tort, and is far and away the most common ground for successful right of publicity suits.[17] Although there are aberrations,[18] courts generally acknowledge that commercial exploitation means something other than the mere gain that comes from selling more issues of the publication in which the plaintiff's name or likeness is used.[19] This is in effect another way of expressing the newsworthiness principle—that the use of the plaintiff's name or likeness in connection with a bona fide story does not infringe the right of publicity.[20]

Newsworthiness principles aside, however, the common law right of publicity action is not strictly limited to commercial appropriations such as product sales, but may include appropriations for political or other purposes involving exploitation of a nonpecuniary nature.[21] Such

---

15 *Id.*

16 498 F. Supp. 401 (S.D.N.Y. 1980).

17 *See, e.g.*, Carson v. Here's Johnny, 698 F.2d 831 (6th Cir. 1983); Grant v. Esquire, Inc., 367 F. Supp. 876 (S.D.N.Y. 1973).

18 Ali v. Playgirl, Inc,. 447 F. Supp. 723 (S.D.N.Y. 1978); Eastwood v. Superior Court, 149 Cal. App. 3d 409, 198 Cal. Rptr. 342 (1983).

19 *See, e.g.*, Benavidez v. Anheuser Busch, Inc., 873 F.2d 102 (5th Cir. 1989); Namath v. Sports Illustrated, 48 A.D.2d 487, 371 N.Y.S.2d 10 (1st Dept. 1975), *aff'd*, 39 N.Y.2d 897, 352 N.E.2d 584, 386 N.Y.S.2d 397 (1976); Booth v. Curtis Publishing Co., 15 A.D.2d 343, 349, 223 N.Y.S.2d 737, 743 (1st Dept), *aff'd*, 11 N.Y.S.2d 907, 182 N.E.2d 812, 208 N.Y.S.2d 468 (1962).

20 Prosser & Keeton, *supra* note 3, § 117, at 853.

21 *See, e.g.*, Hamilton v. Lumberman's Mutual Cas. Co., 82 So. 2d 61 (La. App. 1955) (plaintiff's name used in connection with witnessing of accident); Spellman v. Simon & Schuster, 3 Med. L. Rep. (BNA) 2406 (1978) (plaintiff's photograph used on cover of book for students desiring to go to college); Hinish v. Meier & Frank Co., 166 Or. 482, 113 P.2d 438 (1941) (plaintiff's name used in petition to governor); State ex rel. La Follette v. Hinkle, 131 Wash. 86, 229 P. 317 (1924) (plaintiff's name used as candidate for office by political party).

uses of the tort are often just as properly classifiable as false light claims, for they typically involve misleading inferences of endorsement or association.[22]

Whether the appropriation is for commercial or noncommercial purposes, it is the value of the plaintiff's name or likeness that must be taken, not the mere name itself. The mere use of a name identical to the plaintiff's is, without more, not actionable.[23]

§ 10.02 False Light Invasion of Privacy

[1] Overview

The form of invasion of privacy most akin to defamation is known as placing the plaintiff in a "false light in the public eye." The *Restatement (Second) of Torts* defines this tort as follows:

> One who gives publicity to a matter concerning another that places the other before the public in a false light is subject to liability to the other for invasion of his privacy, if
>
> (a) the false light in which the other was placed would be highly offensive to a reasonable person, and
>
> (b) the actor has knowledge of or acted in reckless disregard as to the falsity of the publicized matter and the false light in which the other would be placed.[24]

This branch of the law of privacy is said to date as far back as 1816, when Lord Byron succeeded in enjoining publication of a poem that had falsely been attributed to his authorship—the "false light" being that he could write so poor a poem.[25]

---

[22] *See, e.g.*, Cher v. Forum International, Ltd., 692 F.2d 634 (9th Cir. 1982), *cert. denied*, 103 S. Ct. 3089 (1983) (advertising in connection with interview created false impression of endorsement); Zim v. Western Publishing Co., 573 F.2d 1318 (5th Cir. 1978) (use of author's name on book editions he had not approved); National Bank of Commerce v. Shaklee Corp., 503 F. Supp. 533 (W.D. Tex. 1980) (held actionable under both appropriation and false light theories to use a corporation's name on cover of author's book and to include author's name in ad on back cover associating author with defendant).

[23] *See* Nebb v. Bell Syndicate, 41 F. Supp. 929 (S.D.N.Y. 1941); Swacker v. Wright, 154 Misc. 822, 277 N.Y.S. 296 (1935).

[24] Restatement (Second) of Torts § 652E (1977).

[25] Lord Byron v. Johnston, 2 Mer. 29, 35 Eng. Rep. 851 (1816).

[2] Relationship to Defamation

[a] The Problem of Distinguishing the Torts

It has been said that the tort of false light invasion of privacy is distinguishable from the tort of defamation in that false light invasion of privacy protects a person's interest "in being let alone," whereas defamation protects one's interest in a good reputation.[26] This distinction is often elusive, however, and not completely satisfactory. As previously discussed, the law of defamation may be primarily concerned with protecting reputation, but it has always served at least secondarily the interest in compensating for injured feelings.[27] More important, however, is the fundamental flaw in any definition of a tort that concentrates more on the species of injury to the victim than on the type of conduct on the part of the plaintiff that makes it actionable. To put the issue squarely, is there any distinction between the *conduct of the actor* giving rise to a claim for defamation and the conduct giving rise to a claim for "false light"? There are in truth at least two factors that make the torts different.

[b] A False Light Claim Need Not Involve Defamatory Speech

The single most important distinguishing characteristic of the false light tort is that the publication need not be defamatory.[28] A false light claim may actually involve statements that say something *good* about the plaintiff, statements that enhance the plaintiff's reputation, yet are nonetheless "false."

---

26 *See* Rinsley v. Brandt, 700 F.2d 1304, 1307 (10th Cir. 1983); Goodrich v. Waterbury Republican-American, Inc., 188 Conn. 107, 120 n.19, 448 A.2d 1317, 1329 n.19 (1982); Froelich v. Adair, 213 Kan. 357, 360, 516 P.2d 993, 996 (1973); Crump v. Beckley Newspapers, Inc., 320 S.E.2d 70 (W. Va. Sup. Ct. App. 1984); Prosser and Keeton, *supra* note 3, § 117 at 864. *See generally* Thema v. New England Newspaper Publishing Co., 306 Mass. 54, 57, 27 N.E.2d 753, 755 (1940) ("the fundamental difference between a right to privacy and right to freedom from defamation is that the former directly concerns one's peace of mind, while the latter concerns primarily one's reputation"); Wade, *Defamation and the Right of Privacy,* 15 Vand. L. Rev. 1093, 1094 (1962).

27 *See supra* § 9.06[3].

28 *See* Wilson v. American Broadcasting Co., 96 F.R.D. 658, 669 (W.D. Ark. 1983); Machleder v. Diaz, 538 F. Supp. 1364, 1375 (S.D.N.Y. 1982); Uhl v. Columbia Broadcasting Systems, Inc., 476 F. Supp. 1134, 1139 (W.D. Pa. 1979); Hinish v. Meier & Frank Co., 166 Or. 482, 113 P.2d 438 (1941); Restatement (Second) of Torts § 652E comment b (1977).

[c] The Statement Must Be Highly Offensive to a Reasonable Person

In place of the requirement that the statement be injurious to reputation, the false light tort requires that the statement be "highly offensive to a reasonable person." It thus is *not* the tendency to lower the person in the esteem of others, but the tendency to be highly offensive, that forms the gravamen of the false light tort.[29]

[d] How Can a Nondefamatory Statement Be Offensive?

The relationship between the false light and defamation tort has caused a good deal of confusion, because for many it is difficult to understand how a statement that is not defamatory might nonetheless be highly offensive to a reasonable person.

The confusion may be eliminated by reflecting on the fact that sometimes even a positive lie is offensive—the lie alone causes injury, even if the lie is laudatory. Imagine, for example, a Vietnam veteran who experienced many episodes of violent combat during the War, saw many comrades die, and witnessed many acts of valor on the part of others. The particular soldier did his duty, served his country well, yet was neither uncommonly brave nor cowardly. Imagine that on the anniversary of the War the local newspaper publishes a story on the veteran, and to embellish the story invents a number of acts of valor by the veteran, making him out as almost a wild-eyed John Wayne hero, when if fact he was just a good soldier. These exaggerated acts of courage might well enhance the veteran's reputation, but he would still have a valid action for false light invasion of privacy. To the reasonable person in the veteran's circumstances, it would very probably be deeply offensive to endure these manufactured stories—the veteran would have seen real valor and real death, and would be profoundly disturbed and embarrassed at being made out as something he is not.

Two false light claims have reached the Supreme Court and both aptly demonstrate this point. In *Cantrell v. Forest City Publishing Co.*,[30] the plaintiff's husband had been killed in a bridge collapse disaster; a newspaper reporter who had visited her home, but not even seen her, painted her as proudly and stoically bearing her grief in the face

---

29 *See* Prosser & Keeton, *supra* note 3, § 117, at 865.
30 418 U.S. 245 (1974).

of abject poverty. By manufacturing the emotions and conditions of her life the story placed her in a false light, and was highly offensive.

Similarly, in *Time, Inc. v. Hill*,[31] the Hill family had been held hostage for nineteen hours by three escaped convicts. The abductors treated the Hills civilly. A novel was written about the event, followed by a Broadway play. *Life* magazine did a pictorial article on the play, which it said was inspired by the Hill family episode. The article and the accompanying pictures (from the play) portrayed the convicts as violent and abusive toward the Hills and the Hills courageously defying them. The lower state courts upheld the false light claims;[32] the Supreme Court, for reasons discussed below, reversed.

[3] First Amendment Fault Standards

[a] The Ambiguities

In the *Hill* case,[33] the Supreme Court held that a false light claim involving "matters of public interest" was precluded "in the absence of proof that the material was published with knowledge of falsity or in reckless disregard of the truth."[34] *Hill*, however, appeared to be decided under the same sort of "public interest" standard characterized by *Rosenbloom v. Metromedia, Inc.*[35] When *Rosenbloom* was overruled by *Gertz*,[36] the question became whether the *Gertz* public figure/private figure dichotomy would apply to false light cases as well, or whether the actual malice standard of *Hill* would govern all false light cases. After *Dun & Bradstreet*[37] the issue is clouded even more, for now it is arguable that no constitutional fault standards apply when the speech does not involve an issue of "public concern."

The Supreme Court might have chosen to resolve at least some of the post-*Gertz* ambiguity in the *Cantrell* case.[38] The Court in *Cantrell* found, however, that on the facts of that case actual malice had been established in any event, and stated that "[c]onsequently, this case

31 385 U.S. 374 (1967).

32 Hill v. Hayes, 18 A.D.2d 485, 240 N.Y.S.2d 286 (1963), *aff'd on opinions below*, 15 N.Y.2d 986, 207 N.E.2d 604, 260 N.Y.S.2d 7 (1965).

33 Time, Inc. v. Hill, 385 U.S. 374 (1967).

34 *Id.* at 388.

35 403 U.S. 29 (1971).

36 Gertz v. Robert Welch, Inc., 418 U.S. 323 (1974). *See supra* §§ 2.03-2.04.

37 Dun & Bradstreet, Inc. v. Greenmoss Builders, Inc., 105 S. Ct. 2939 (1985). *See supra* §§ 3.02-3.05.

38 Cantrell v. Forest City Publishing Co., 419 U.S. 245 (1974).

presents no occasion to consider whether a State may constitutionally apply a more relaxed standard of liability for a publisher or broadcaster of false statements injurious to a private individual under a false-light theory of invasion of privacy, or whether the constitutional standard announced in *Time, Inc. v. Hill* applies to all false light cases."[39]

[b] Division Among Lower Court Decisions

There is a division of authority on the question of whether the *Gertz* ruling permits states to impose liability for false light invasion of privacy in private figure cases on a showing of mere negligence, rather than actual malice. There is now substantial authority on both sides of the issue. A significant number of cases have held that *Hill* should be regarded as modified by *Gertz,* and that actual malice is not required by the first amendment in false light cases with private figure plaintiffs.[40] These rulings have emphasized the pronounced overlap between the defamation and false light privacy torts, and have reasoned that the inconsistency between *Hill* and *Gertz* will eventually be resolved in favor of *Gertz.*[41]

There is also, however, substantial authority, including the *Restatement (Second) of Torts,* for the proposition that all false light claims must meet the actual malice standard.[42] The rationale for retaining the actual malice standard is that the state's interest in false light claims is less substantial than in defamation actions, because false light claims involve *only* injured feelings and need not harm reputation, whereas defamation claims by definition implicate the considerable state interest in protecting reputation.

---

[39] *Id.* at 250.

[40] *See* Braun v. Flynt, 726 F.2d 245 (5th Cir. 1984); Wood v. Hustler Magazine, Inc., 736 F.2d 1084 (5th Cir. 1984); Cantrell v. American Broadcasting Companies, Inc., 529 F. Supp. 746 (N.D. Ill. 1981); Dresbach v. Doubleday, 518 F. Supp. 1285 (D.D.C. 1981); Crump v. Beckley Newspapers, Inc., 320 S.E.2d 70 (W. Va. Sup. Ct. App. 1984).

[41] *See* Crump v. Beckley Newspapers, Inc., 320 S.E.2d 70 (W. Va. Sup. Ct. App. 1984). *See also* Lehmann, *Triangulating the Limits on the Tort of Invasion of Privacy,* 3 Hastings Const. L.Q. 543, 593 (1976); Phillips, *Defamation, Invasion of Privacy, and the Constitutional Standard of Care,* 16 Santa Clara L. Rev. 77, 99 (1975).

[42] *See* Restatement (Second) of Torts § 652E (1977). The *Restatement* waffles a bit, however, for it also includes the caveat that it takes no position as to whether there are any circumstances in which recovery may be obtained on a showing of fault less than actual malice. For decisions imposing the actual malice standard in all false light cases, *see* Dodrill v. Arkansas Democrat Co., 265 Ark. 628, 590 S.W.2d 840 (1979); Goodrich v. Waterbury Republican-American, Inc., 188 Conn. 107, 448 A.2d 1317 (1982); McCall v. Courier-Journal, 623 S.W.2d 882 (Ky. Sup. Ct. 1981).

Because *Dun & Bradstreet*[43] is such a recent case, its impact on the false light area is not yet manifest, but, at least for those courts that found *Hill* to be modified by *Gertz,* the likelihood is that the further modification visited by *Dun & Bradstreet* will also be applied, opening the door to the possibility of a complete absence of constitutional fault requirements when the speech is not about a matter of public concern.[44]

[4] Types of False Light Claims

[a] False Association

A false light claim may involve the attribution to the plaintiff of a false association with some activity, statement, opinion, or work product. This was essentially the basis of Lord Byron's claim involving false attribution of authorship of a poem,[45] and it has been followed in cases of false claims of political affiliation,[46] or inclusion of a person as a plaintiff in a lawsuit without authorization,[47] or false attribution of beliefs, writings, or statements.[48]

[b] Distortion or Exaggeration

When the truth concerning the plaintiff is distorted or embellished through misleading photographs, film footage, or through the omission of significant facts in a printed text, a false light claim may exist.

[i] Photographs

Photographs appear to generate a considerable number of false light claims. It has been held actionable to use a person's photograph without consent in a homosexual magazine,[49] to use the photo of a female minor to illustrate a story on harassment of women minors,[50] or to use the picture of someone other than the artist to illustrate the cover of an

---

43 105 S. Ct. 2939 (1985).

44 *See supra* § 3.02.

45 Lord Byron v. Johnston, 2 Mer. 29, 35 Eng. Rep. 851 (1816).

46 Battaglia v. Adams, 164 So. 2d 195 (Fla. 1964).

47 Steding v. Battistoni, 3 Conn. Cir. 76, 208 A.2d 559 (1964).

48 *See* Goldberg v. Ideal Publishing Corp., 210 N.Y.S.2d 928 (N.Y. Sup. 1969); Wigmore, *The Right Against False Attribution of Belief or Utterance,* 4 Ky. L.J. 83 (1916).

49 Palmisano v. Modernismo Publications, 98 A.D.2d 953, 470 N.Y.S.2d 196 (4th Dept. 1983).

50 Crump v. Beckley Newspapers, Inc., 320 S.E.2d 70 (W. Va. Sup. Ct. App. 1984).

album by a classical guitarist,[51] or to publish a fraudulently obtained photograph of a woman in a sexually explicit magazine.[52]

It was held not actionable, however, to publish a photograph of a group of boys being helped by a policewoman to repair a bicycle on a city street. The photograph featuring the boys was printed in the context of a series of nude photos of the policewoman.[53] Ann-Margret had no cause of action for a partially nude photo of her that was lifted from a movie scene and printed in a magazine;[54] nor was there a cause of action for the use of the plaintiff's photo on the front cover of a magazine as part of a story on upwardly mobile middle class blacks.[55] Other false light cases involving photographs have failed for lack of the requisite level of fault,[56] or because use of the photo was not highly offensive.[57]

[ii] Film and Broadcast Footage

A filmed interview segment on "20/20" implying that the plaintiff has some connection with an arson-for-profit scheme was held to be actionable on a false light theory,[58] as was that part of a television documentary entitled "Sex for Sale" which showed the plaintiff walking on a street in Detroit.[59]

In *Machleder v. Diaz,*[60] a Second Circuit case decided in September 1986, the court very severely restricted exposure to liability under a false light theory for so-called ambush broadcast interviews. A CBS

---

[51] Jumez v. ABC Records, 3 Med. L. Rep. (BNA) 2324 (S.D.N.Y. 1984).

[52] Braun v. Flynt, 726 F.2d 245 (5th Cir. 1984). *See also* Wood v. Hustler Magazine, Inc., 736 F.2d 1084 (5th Cir. 1984) (false light 736 F.2d 1084 (5th Cir. 1984) (false light claim upheld for publication of plaintiff's nude photo submitted by another to magazine as part of its "Beaver Hunt" section (photos submitted by readers) as a prank); Davis v. High Society, 90 A.D.2d 374 (2d Dept. 1983) (held actionable to erroneously identify plaintiff as person depicted in photo of semi-nude boxer).

[53] Jackson v. Playboy Enterprises, 574 F. Supp. 10 (S.D. Ohio 1983).

[54] Ann-Margret v. High Society Magazine, Inc., 498 F. Supp. 401 (S.D.N.Y. 1980).

[55] Arrington v. New York Times, 78 A.D.2d 839, 433 N.Y.S.2d 164 (1st Dept. 1980), *rev'd in part,* 57 N.Y.2d 669, 454 N.Y.S.2d 75 (1982), *cert. denied,* 103 S. Ct. 787 (1983).

[56] *See* Lerman v. Flynt Distributing Co., 745 F.2d 123 (2d Cir. 1984); Cefalu v. Globe Newspaper, 391 N.E.2d 935 (Mass. App. 1979), *cert. denied,* 444 U.S. 1060 (1980).

[57] *See* Fogel v. Forbes, Inc., 500 F. Supp. 1081 (E.D. Pa. 1980). *See also* Cibenko v. Worth Publishers, 510 F. Supp. 761 (D.N.J. 1981) (photo held not actionable in light of caption, which was held to constitute opinion); Byrd v. Hustler, 433 So. 2d 593 (Fla. Dist. Ct. App. 1983) (not actionable as satire).

[58] Cantrell v. American Broadcasting Companies, 529 F. Supp. 746 (N.D. Ill. 1981).

[59] Clark v. American Broadcasting Companies, 684 F.2d 1208 (6th Cir. 1982), *cert. denied,* 460 U.S. 1040 (1983).

[60] 801 F.2d 46 (2d Cir. 1986).

affiliate, in a story on toxic dumping in New Jersey, had run footage part of which showed the plaintiff saying "Get that damn camera out of here."[60.1] CBS edited out the plaintiff's prior, less aggressive statement, "I don't want to be on television, I'm sorry, I'm sorry."[60.2] In all other respects the interview was unedited and accurate. In a very important ruling, the court held that this did not rise to the level of being placed in a false light. In fact the plaintiff appeared exactly as he had been captured by the camera, and the mere editorial decision not to include his less intemperate protest did not render his portrayal false.[60.3] Explaining another quite significant rationale for the holding, the court said that even if this had been a false portrayal, it was nowhere near the level of being "highly offensive," one of the common law requirements. And in an important statement, the court noted that in the first amendment context the common law "highly offensive" standard should be narrowly construed.[60.4]

In a recent Sixth Circuit case, *Angelotta v. ABC*,[60.5] decided in June 1987, an Ohio judge had been interviewed by Geraldo Rivera on rape cases, and had expressed the view that in terms of credibility, juries may not believe "bad girls" as much as "good girls," because, he said, "maybe [they] enticed the m[e]n." Following the interview segment, Barbara Walters commented to Rivera that she was appalled that the judge had said, "We understand that if it's a good girl we understand, but if it's a bad girl, she obviously wanted to be raped." Geraldo Rivera seconded that indignation, referring to it as a "dinosaur attitude."

The Sixth Circuit disposed of the judge's false light claim by expressing the position that Ohio simply does not recognize the tort of false light at all. Even if it did, the court noted, at best Walters and Rivera gave the judge a "cheap shot." But since they ran his actual words, they had a right to express their opinion as to what they believed he was saying.

Angelotta reflects an overall pattern—and of course there are deviations—a pattern of increasing judicial sensitivity to two propositions that have been around for some time. First, false light and defamation often overlap, and when they do overlap, the first amendment restrictions on false light should at least be coextensive with those for defama-

---

60.1 *Id.* at 50-51, 58.

60.2 *Id.*

60.3 *Id.* at 56-58.

60.4 *Id.* at 58.

60.5 14 Med. L. Rep. (BNA) 1185 (6th Cir. 1987).

tion. Second, courts increasingly perceive that the primary *practical* difference between false light and defamation is that false light claims do not need to rise to the level of being defamatory—of being injurious to reputation. (This point was emphasized in *Machleder.*) False light claims may, in short, be based on more amorphous, watered down, less intensely damaging forms of falsity. Courts are perceiving, however, that that very difference marks false light as a tort that protects a much weaker social interest. And in effect, what courts seem to be saying is that once the false light claim no longer overlaps defamation, no longer implicating actual reputational damage, but instead enters this watered down realm of falsity, it may no longer be egregious enough to meet the "highly offensive" standard. This is a very positive trend, if it continues, for it may reflect a judicial resolve not to open the door too wide to what are in fact second class defamation rejects: suits brought for relatively trivial falsehoods that do not qualify as defamation because the plaintiffs have only some vague objection to the tone or slant or balance of a broadcast or story.

Thus, while a false light claim was upheld on behalf of a close-up "pedestrian on the street" shot as background for a story on herpes[61] —a relatively serious and offensive blunder—many false light claims based on broadcasts have failed for lack of the required fault, falsity, or offensiveness.[62]

[iii] Printed Matter

The portrayal of an army officer as "weak" and one who "broke down easily" during prisoner of war training was held to state a claim for false light,[63] as was the false attribution of motives in a book about a murder case,[64] and, in a story concerning a suicide, the emphasis on

---

61 Duncan v. WJLA-TV, 10 Med. L. Rep. (BNA) 1395 (D.D.C. 1984).

62 *See* Bichler v. Union Bank and Trust Co. of Grand Rapids, 745 F.2d 1006 (6th Cir. 1984) (en banc) (no actual malice); Berry v. National Broadcasting Company, 480 F.2d 428 (8th Cir. 1973) (no actual malice); Michigan United Conservation Clubs v. Columbia Broadcasting Company, 485 F. Supp. 893 (W.D. Mich. 1980), *aff'd*, 644 F.2d 110 (6th Cir. 1981) (depiction not sufficiently of and concerning plaintiffs); DeGregoria v. CBS, 123 Misc. 2d 491, 473 N.Y.S.2d 922 (N.Y. Sup. 1984) (film of male and female construction workers holding hands, in segment called "Couples in Love in New York," when both married or engaged to others, held not a false portrayal).

63 Pierson v. News Group Publications, Inc., 549 F. Supp. 635 (S.D. Ga. 1982) (denying motion for summary judgment).

64 Dresbach v. Doubleday, 518 F. Supp. 1285 (D.D.C. 1982).

certain elements of the story and the omission of others.[65] The leading case involving distortion is the *Cantrell* decision,[66] in which the reporter invented out of whole cloth an interview with the widow of a bridge disaster victim, describing her emotional state and the expression on her face.

[5] Minor and Insubstantial Errors

When the distortions are technical,[67] involve insubstantial details, or

(*Text continued on page 10-15*)

65 Varnish v. Best Medium Publishing Co., 405 F.2d 608 (2d Cir. 1968), *cert. denied,* 394 U.S. 987 (1969).

66 Cantrell v. Forest City Publishing Co., 419 U.S. 245 (1974).

67 Rinsley v. Brandt, 700 F.2d 1304 (10th Cir. 1983) (statements critical of a psychiatrist too minor and technical in inaccuracies to support false light claim).

merely involve colorful language and descriptions,[68] no false light claim will exist.[69] In this sense, the false light tort parallels the substantial truth rules that govern defamation.[70]

[6] Fiction and the False Light Tort

[a] In General

Lawsuits generated from works of fiction, or from related forms such as docudramas, frequently involve false light claims, either as appendages to defamation claims or as the primary cause of action. These false light claims involve virtually the same issues as those presented by defamation in fiction.[71]

In *Spahn v. Julian Messner, Inc.*,[72] a case involving both false light and appropriation claims, baseball star Warren Spahn successfully maintained his false light claim arising from a biography filled with fictionalized material, including attribution of thoughts and motives to Spahn, and the statement that he was a war hero. And in *Polakoff v. Harcourt Brace Jovanovich*,[73] a false light claim was sustained (though the jury award was reduced as excessive) when the real name of an attorney who had represented underworld figure Lucky Luciano was used in a wholly fictional episode in a novel. The *Polakoff* case is of special note because the episode was nondefamatory, and the jury's refusal to find for the plaintiff on the defamation claim arising from the same facts was upheld. This illustrates the potential usefulness of the false light claim from the plaintiff's perspective, for it may have a much broader sweep.

[b] Identity Issues

As in defamation cases involving fiction,[74] the problem of identifying

---

[68] Goodrich v. Waterbury Republican-American, Inc., 188 Conn. 107, 448 A.2d 1317 (1977).

[69] *Id.*

[70] *See generally* Chapter 5, *supra*. Courts borrow freely from the far more extensively developed rules governing defamation in fleshing out the technical aspects of the false light tort, including issues such as publication or truth.

[71] *See supra* § 4.09[7].

[72] 18 N.Y.2d 324, 274 N.Y.S.2d 877, 22 N.E.2d 543 (1966), *reaffirmed after remand*, 21 N.Y.2d 124, 286 N.Y.S.2d 832, 233 N.E.2d 840 (1967), *appeal dismissed*, 393 U.S. 1046 (1969).

[73] 3 Med. L. Rep. (BNA) 2516, 67 A.D.2d 871, 413 N.Y.S.2d 537 (1st Dept. 1979).

[74] *See supra* § 4.09[7].

the fictional character as "of and concerning" the plaintiff frequently arises in false light cases, and in fact the same analysis and decisions (many of which involve joinder of defamation and false light theories) are used interchangeably in both areas.[75]

[c] Special First Amendment Considerations

Again, as in the defamation area, false light claims arising from fiction present special problems under the first amendment, both in the application of the fact/opinion distinction and constitutional fault requirements. The defamation and false light cases are interchangeable in these areas.[76] Fictional embellishments so fantastic that no reader would take them as true,[77] or works painted with an aura of genuineness for dramatic effect but not to be seriously understood by readers as true,[78] will generally receive protection from liability for false light invasion of privacy, on either fault or fact/opinion grounds.[79]

[d] Survival

In *Frosch v. Grossett & Dunlap,*[80] a false light claim arising from

---

75 *See, e.g.,* Geisler v. Petrocelli, 616 F.2d 636 (2d Cir. 1980) (jury question on issue of identity presented when similarities in name, characteristics, and acquaintances exist); Fetter v. Houghton-Mifflin, 364 F.2d 650 (2d Cir. 1966) (sufficient similarities to make identity an issue for the jury); Bindrim v. Mitchell, 92 Cal. App. 3d 61, 155 Cal. Rptr. 29, *cert. denied,* 444 U.S. 1040 (1980) (identity upheld); Springer v. Viking Press, 90 A.D.2d 315, 455 N.Y.S.2d 383 (1st Dept. 1982), *aff'd,* 60 N.Y.S.2d 916, 458 N.E.2d 1256, 470 N.Y.S.2d 579 (1983) (no identity as a matter of law; superficial similarities insufficient); Wojtowicz v. Delacorte Press, 43 N.Y.2d 858, 403 N.Y.S.2d 218, 374 N.E.2d 129 (1978) (no identity on behalf of plaintiffs, victims of bank robbery, who were portrayed with different names in fictionalized book and film "Dog Day Afternoon"). For a detailed discussion of the identity issue regarding fiction, *see supra* § 10.02[6].

76 *See supra* § 4.09[7].

77 *See* Pring v. Penthouse International, Ltd., 695 F.2d 738 (10th Cir. 1982), *cert. denied,* 103 S. Ct. 3112 (1983), discussed in § 4.09[7][b], note 177, *supra.*

78 *See* Hicks v. Casablanca Records, 464 F. Supp. 426 (S.D.N.Y. 1978). *But see* Guccione v. Hustler Magazine, Inc., 64 Ohio Misc. 59, 413 N.E.2d 860 (Ohio Ct. App. 1981) (photo of head of Penthouse editor cropped and superimposed upon photo of man engaged in buggery, with caption "Bob Guccione Discovers Vaseline," could support false light claim if meant to be viewed literally and not as expression of opinion).

79 *See* Meeropol v. Nizer, 560 F.2d 1061 (2d Cir. 1977), *cert. denied,* 434 U.S. 1013 (1978) (book involving children of Rosenbergs not actionable); Leopold v. Levin, 45 Ill. 2d 434, 259 N.E.2d 250 (1970) (fictionalized account of famous murders not actionable). *See generally supra* § 4.09[7].

80 4 Med. L. Rep. (BNA) 2307 (N.Y. Sup. 1979), *aff'd,* 75 A.D.2d 768, 427 N.Y.S.2d 828 (1st Dept. 1980).

Norman Mailer's book on Marilyn Monroe was dismissed as not surviving the death of Monroe.

[7] The *Renwick* Case as an Assault on the False Light Tort

In *Renwick v. News and Observer Publishing Co.,*[81] the North Carolina Supreme Court broke new ground by rejecting altogether the existence of the false light tort in that state. The court found the substantial overlap between the false light and defamation torts disturbing, echoing the concerns of William Prosser as to "whether this branch of the tort is not capable of swallowing up and engulfing the whole law of public defamation."[82] The court then went on to pronounce one of the precious few endorsements of the behavior of the press that the media has enjoyed in recent years:

> The conditions which led Warren and Brandeis to argue almost a century ago for a separate tort of invasion of privacy have at least to some extent subsided. Most modern journalists employed in print, television or radio journalism now receive formal training in ethics and journalism entirely unheard of during the era of "yellow journalism."
>
> As a general rule journalists simply are more responsible and professional today than history tells us they were in that era.[83]

The *Renwick* holding may well not attract an immediate following, but its logic is not without substantial weight: The incursion of free expression values recognized by the false light tort is simply not supported by as weighty an interest as the state's interest in protecting reputation—an interest already adequately served by the law of defamation—and so continued recognition of the false light branch of invasion of privacy is not justified.

Assuming that most jurisdictions will continue to acknowledge the false light tort, they may well choose to at least borrow from the reasoning in *Renwick* in keeping the reach of false light channeled within sufficiently narrow banks to avoid engulfing the law of defamation. Short of abolishing false light, the best method of constraining the tort is to take seriously the requirement that the speech be "highly offensive," [84] and to impose the actual malice standard in all cases.[85]

---

[81] 310 N.C. 312, 312 S.E.2d 405 (1984).

[82] 312 S.E.2d at 412 (quoting Prosser, *supra* note 4, at 400-01).

[83] 312 S.E.2d at 413.

[84] *See supra* § 10.02[2][b].

[85] *See supra* § 10.02[3].

§ 10.03 Intrusion

[1] Overview

The "intrusion" branch of invasion of privacy is unlike most of the other torts covered in this volume, in that it is concerned not with the subject matter of what is published by the defendant but with the method whereby the information is obtained. Intrusion is in fact an extremely broad tort concept that is related to the action for trespass, but with the interests protected not limited to physical invasions. An intrusion consists of the intentional invasion of the solitude or seclusion of another in his or her private affairs or concerns, through either physical or nonphysical means.[86] In the context of the media, intrusion is thus of concern as a news-gathering tort rather than a news dissemination tort.

[2] Activities Covered

[a] In General

Surveillance of many varieties may give rise to tort liability for intrusion. Peeping through the windows of a home[87] and eavesdropping by means of wiretap or microphones[88] are common examples. Intrusion will exist when one's mail is surreptitiously opened,[89] or through prying into one's bank account,[90] or through secret photographing, video taping, or tape recording of a subject during an interview.[91]

---

86 Restatement (Second) of Torts § 652B (1977); Prosser & Keeton, *supra* note 3, § 117 at 854-55.

87 Pinkerton National Detective Agency, Inc. v. Stevens, 108 Ga. App. 159, 132 S.E.2d 119 (1963); Souder v. Pendleton Detectives, 88 So. 2d 716 (La. App. 1956).

88 Reitmaster v. Reitmaster, 162 F.2d 691 (2d Cir. 1947); Fowler v. Southern Bell Tel. & Tel. Co., 343 F.2d 150 (5th Cir. 1965); Rhodes v. Graham, 238 Ky. 225, 37 S.W.2d 119 (1931); Nader v. General Motors Corp., 25 N.Y.2d 560, 307 N.Y.S.2d 647, 255 N.E.2d 765 (1970); Elson v. Bowen, 83 Nev. 515, 436 P.2d 12 (1967); Hamberger v. Eastman, 106 N.H. 107, 206 A.2d 239 (1964); Roach v. Harper, 143 W. Va. 869, 105 S.E.2d 564 (1958).

89 Birnbaum v. United States, 588 F.2d 319, 323 (2d Cir. 1978); Vernars v. Young, 539 F.2d 966 (3d Cir. 1976).

90 Zimmerman v. Wilson, 81 F.2d 847 (3d Cir. 1936); Brex v. Smith, 104 N.J. Eq. 386, 146 A. 34 (1929).

91 *See* Dietman v. Time, Inc., 449 F.2d 245 (9th Cir. 1971) (secret photographs and recording of plaintiff as part of story on his alleged unauthorized practice of medicine held to be intrusion).

[b] The Essence of Intrusion

Publication is not an element of the tort of intrusion[92]—the essence of the tort is the invasion itself. The information obtained need not be utilized for the cause of action to exist,[93] and indeed it is not required that any information be obtained at all.[94] In *Pearson v. Dodd,*[95] private documents were stolen from the office of United States Senator Edwin Dodd and the contents were subsequently published in Drew Pearson's national column. The documents had been taken by members of Dodd's staff. Even if Pearson knew the documents were stolen, the court held, there could be no cause of action for intrusion against him because he was not a participant in the theft. Had the thieves been working pursuant to Pearson's direction or under his employ, of course, normal tort *respondeat superior* liability would have attached, and possible criminal liability as well.

In *Galella v. Onassis,*[96] Jacqueline Kennedy Onassis was successful in limiting the activities of Galella, a free-lance photographer who had fashioned himself as a so-called paparazzo (which, translated literally, means a kind of annoying insect). Paparazzi engage in the tactic of making themselves visible and often obnoxious to their photographic subjects to aid in the advertisement and sale of their photographic works. Galella's particular actions included jumping out of bushes as Onassis walked past, bringing his power boat close to her while she was swimming, jumping into one of her children's paths to photograph him riding a bicycle, invading the children's schools, bribing nightclub, restaurant, and hotel doormen, and romancing a family servant to keep apprised of the family's movement. Galella was enjoined from blocking the plaintiff's movement in public places, from "any act foreseeably or reasonably calculated to place the life and safety" of Onassis in jeopardy or that could "reasonably be foreseen to harass, alarm or frighten her," and from coming closer than 25-30 feet of her. The injunction later proved to have teeth; in 1982 Galella was found in contempt for twelve

---

[92] Smith v. Fairman, 98 F.R.D. 445 (E.D. Ill. 1982); Estate of Berthiaume v. Pratt, M.D., 365 A.2d 792 (Me. 1976); Corcoran v. Southwestern Bell Telephone Co., 572 S.W.2d 212 (Mo. App. 1978).

[93] Fowler v. Southern Bell Tel. & Tel. Co., 343 F.2d 150 (5th Cir. 1965).

[94] Hamberger v. Eastman, 106 N.H. 107, 206 A.2d 239 (1964).

[95] 410 F.2d 701 (D.C. Cir.), *cert. denied,* 395 U.S. 947 (1969). *See also* Bilney v. Evening Star, 43 Md. App. 560, 406 A.2d 652 (1979) (no liability for intrusion for publication of confidential academic records of players on University of Maryland basketball team when records obtained from unnamed source).

[96] 487 F.2d 986 (2d Cir. 1973).

violations and was fined $120,000 (suspended on condition that Galella pay Onassis $10,000 in legal fees).[97]

[3] Intrusion and Trespass in News Gathering

[a] Defining Seclusion; Public vs. Private Matters

Surveillance, photographing, or filming persons in public places usually does not qualify as an invasion of the plaintiff's solitude or private affairs[98] unless the means used is somehow unusually harassing or offensive in its own right.[99]

An area not usually regarded as public may become so because of newsworthy events within the area. For example, it was held not to be an intrusion for a photographer to accompany a fire marshall into a home destroyed by fire, with the court relying to some degree on the tradition of such coverage by the news media.[100] On the other hand,

---

[97] Galella v. Onassis, 533 F. Supp. 1076 (S.D.N.Y. 1982).

[98] *See* Wheling v. CBS, Inc., 721 F.2d 506 (5th Cir. 1983) (where broadcast merely depicted what could have been seen from public street, no action for intrusion); Dempsey v. National Enquirer, 687 F. Supp. 692 (D. Me. 1987), *modified on other grounds*, 702 F. Supp. 934 (D. Me. 1989) (intrusion claim was denied because the reporter was taking photographs in a public thoroughfare and in other places open to the public); Machleder v. Diaz, 538 F. Supp. 1364 (S.D.N.Y. 1983) (no liability for intrusion for surprise television interview regarding chemical dumping because interview in semi-public area visible to public eye); Berg v. Minneapolis Star & Tribune Co., 79 F. Supp. 957 (D. Minn. 1948) (no intrusion for photograph in courtroom); Gill v. Hearst Publishing Co., 40 Cal. 2d 224, 253 P.2d 441 (1953) (no intrusion for photograph in farmers' market); Nelson v. Maine Times, 373 A.2d 1223 (Me. 1977) (not an intrusion to take photograph of Indian child in public place); Bisbee v. Conover, 9 Med. L. Rep. (BNA) 1292 (N.J. App. Div. 1982) (no intrusion from publication of details of sale of an historic home, with photograph taken from street); Mark v. KING Broadcasting, 27 Wash. App. 344, 618 P.2d 512, *aff'd*, 96 Wash. 2d 473, 635 P.2d 1081 (Wash. Sup. Ct. 1981) (no intrusion for filming of interior of pharmacy from outside window even though cameraman did trespass on neighbor's property).

[99] *See* Galella v. Onassis, 487 F.2d 986 (2d Cir. 1973) (photographs obtained through "paparazzi" tactics, discussed in text accompanying note 96, *supra*, held to be intrusion); Daily Times-Democrat Co. v. Graham, 276 Ala. 380, 162 So. 2d 474 (1964) (intrusion claim upheld for photograph of plaintiff in "Fun House" with dress blown up over her head); Pinkerton National Detective Agency, Inc. v. Stevens, 108 Ga. App. 159, 132 S.E.2d 119 (1963) (shadowing of plaintiff on street in ostentatious manner that drew public attention held actionable). *But cf.* Neff v. Time, Inc., 406 F. Supp. 858 (D.C. Pa. 1976) (no cause of action under various privacy theories when photograph of professional football player showed his open zipper fly).

[100] Florida Publishing Co. v. Fletcher, 340 So. 2d 914 (Fla. 1976), *cert. denied*, 413 U.S. 930 (1977). *See also* Cape Publications v. Bridges, 431 So. 2d 988 (Fla. App.), *cert. denied*, 104 S. Ct. 239 (1983).

there was no privilege for television reporters to accompany police enforcing a warrant within a private school.[101]

Photographs in jails and prisons have generally been held nonactionable.[102] A film shot from behind a two-way mirror of a police officer's undercover investigation in a massage parlor was held nonactionable in light of the officer's public official status and the public interest in his conduct.[103] To photograph a patient in a hospital bed without his or her consent, however, is an actionable intrusion.[104]

[b] Consent

[i] In General

A frequently litigated issue concerning intrusion claims is consent. The subject of an interview or photograph, for example, might consent to what would otherwise be an actionable intrusion on his or her solitude or seclusion. The subject may later claim that no consent existed, or that the plaintiff exceeded the terms of the consent.[105]

[ii] "Ambush" Interview Techniques

The so-called ambush interview, in which a reporter and film crew come without prior warning to the subject's residence or place of business with "cameras rolling" to question the subject, may present issues concerning intrusion and the scope of consent. No intrusion issue is presented, of course, unless the interview takes place in a setting where a reasonable expectation of solitude or privacy exists.[106] When the surprise interview is a place of business, as is often the case, the court may

---

[101] Green Valley School, Inc. v. Cowles Florida Broadcasting, Inc., 327 So. 2d 810 (Fla. App. 1976).

[102] *See* Holman v. Central Arkansas Broadcasting, 610 F.2d 542 (8th Cir. 1979); Rifkin v. Esquire, 8 Med. L. Rep. (BNA) 1384 (C.D. Cal. 1982); Jenkins v. Winchester Star, 8 Med. L. Rep. 1403 (W.D. Va. 1981). *But see* Smith v. Fairman, 98 F.R.D. 445 (E.D. Ill. 1982).

[103] Cassidy v. ABC, 60 Ill. App. 3d 831, 377 N.E.2d 126 (1978).

[104] *See* Estate of Berthiaume v. Pratt, M.D., 365 A.2d 792 (Me. 1976); Barber v. Time, Inc., 348 Mo. 1199, 159 S.W.2d 291 (1942); Clayman v. Bernstein, 38 Pa. D. & C. 543 (1940).

[105] *See, e.g.*, Rafferty v. Hartford Courant, 36 Conn. Sup. 239, 416 A.2d 1215 (1980) (intrusion claim presented question for jury when existence and terms of purported consent to reporter and photographer disputed); Belluamo v. KAKE-TV & Radio, Inc., 3 Kan. App. 2d 461, 596 P.2d 932 (1979) (jury question presented on whether consent by partner prior to television broadcast); Barber v. Time, Inc., 348 Mo. 1199, 159 S.W.2d 291 (1942) (hospital patient granted interview but not permission to use name and photograph; consent was exceeded and intrusion claim actionable).

[106] *See supra* § 10.03[4][a] and nn. 98-104.

approach the matter in terms of the scope of "consent," express or implied. In one case reporters and a camera crew from CBS entered an exclusive restaurant with the cameras rolling in response to an alleged health violation by the restaurant. A motion to dismiss a trespass claim on the ground that the restaurant was open to the public was denied, on the theory that the consent to the public to enter was limited to entry for the purchase of the restaurant's food and services; no consent to enter for the purposes of a telecast had been granted.[107]

§ 10.04 Publication of Private Facts

[1] The Common Law Elements

Whereas defamation and false light invasion of privacy both are triggered by the publication of *false* statements, the privacy tort known as "publication of private facts" (or publication of "embarrassing" facts) involves publication of *true facts* that the common law regards as private, and essentially nobody else's business.

For this tort to be actionable, three basic elements must be met under common law. The three are discussed below.

[a] There Must Be a Public Disclosure

Unlike defamation, which defines "publication" to encompass any communication of the defamatory statement to someone other than the plaintiff, the publication required for the tort of publication of private facts is broader—there must be sufficient publicity given to the facts so that they may be considered disclosed to the public at large, or to so many persons that the matter is likely to become one of public knowledge.[108] As a practical matter, of course, any publication by a media defendant would be likely to satisfy the public disclosure requirement.

---

107 LeMistral, Inc. v. Columbia Broadcasting System, 61 A.D.2d 491, 402 N.Y.S.2d 815 (1st Dept. 1978).

108 *See* Santieteban v. Goodyear Tire & Rubber Co., 306 F.2d 9 (5th Cir. 1962); Kinsey v. Macur, 107 Cal. App. 3d 265, 165 Cal Rptr. 608 (1980); Restatement (Second) of Torts § 652D comment a (1977).

[b] Facts Must Be Private

[i] In General

The essence of the tort is letting the cat out of the bag; there is no cause of action when the facts are already known to the public,[109] or when the facts are not of a "private" nature.[110] Truly intimate or private matters, however, such as one's private sexual affairs[111] or intimate details about the health of one's self or one's family,[112] may quite legitimately be regarded as no one else's concern, and therefore subject to the common law's protection.

In *Sipple v. Chronicle Publishing Co.*,[113] plaintiff Oliver Sipple had grabbed the arm of Sara Jane Moore as she was about to fire a gun and shoot President Gerald Ford. Considered a hero for his selfless action, Sipple received substantial media attention. A number of articles mentioned the fact that Sipple was a prominent member of the gay community in San Francisco. Sipple brought suit against a number of newspapers, claiming that the public disclosure of his homosexuality was an invasion of his privacy through publication of a private fact. In holding against Sipple, the court noted that his homosexuality was not a private matter in his case, because he was well known in the gay community in San Francisco and a number of other cities as a gay leader.

[ii] Breach of Confidential Relationship

A factor that may be influential in determining whether a "private" fact is disclosed is whether the breach of a confidential relationship is involved, such as disclosures by a doctor[114] or psychiatrist.[115] In such instances the cause of action might be analyzed either as a pure invasion of privacy ("private facts") claim or as a claim resting on the breach of confidentiality itself.

---

[109] Wolf v. Regardie, 533 A.2d 1213 (D.C. 1989); Sipple v. Chronicle Publishing Co., 154 Cal. App. 3d 1040, 201 Cal. Rptr. 655 (1984); Werner v. Times-Mirror Co., 193 Cal. App. 2d 111, 117 (1961); Restatement (Second) of Torts § 652D comment b (1977).

[110] *See* Gill v. Hearst Publishing Co., 40 Cal. 2d 224, 253 P.2d 441 (1953); Humiston v. Universal Film Mfg. Co., 189 A.D. 467, 178 N.Y.S. 752 (1919).

[111] Garner v. Triangle Publications, 97 F. Supp. 546 (S.D.N.Y. 1951).

[112] Bazemore v. Savannah Hospital, 171 Ga. 257, 155 S.E. 194 (1930).

[113] 154 Cal. App. 3d 1040, 201 Cal. Rptr. 655 (1984).

[114] *See* Horne v. Patton, 291 Ala. 701, 287 So. 2d 824 (1973).

[115] Doe v. Roe, 93 Misc. 2d 201, 400 N.Y.S.2d 668 (1977).

[iii] Breach of Promise by Reporter

Most efforts to establish a private facts claim based on alleged breach of promise by a reporter to keep information confidential have failed.[116] Theoretically, however, such a claim might in appropriate factual circumstances be valid. The plaintiff in such a case must demonstrate that his consent to publish the confidential material was exceeded, or he must establish a breach of contract. A plaintiff might prevail under these circumstances by establishing, for example, the breach of an agreement to give an "exclusive" interview granted on the condition that it be used in only one specified publication.[117]

[c] Disclosure Offensive to a Reasonable Person

The common law's principal safeguard against frivolous invocation of the private facts tort is the requirement that the disclosure be highly offensive to a reasonable person of ordinary sensibilities.[118] The classic explication of the standard is in *Sidis v. F-R Publishing Corp.*,[119] in which the court held nonactionable a magazine's disclosure of the present activities of a child mathematics prodigy, on the ground that none of the revelations would be objectionable to a reasonable person.

[2] Constitutional Law Restrictions

[a] Public Records

[i] *Cox Broadcasting Corp. v. Cohn*

In *Cox Broadcasting Corp. v. Cohn*,[120] the father of a deceased rape victim sued under a private facts invasion of privacy theory for the pub-

---

116 *See* Doe v. American Broadcasting Cos., 543 N.Y.S.2d 455, A.2d (1989) (claim of breach of contract and negligent and intentional infliction of emotional distress was dismissed when defendant aired documentary on rape victims and plaintiff was identifiable after she was told she would not be); Poteet v. Roswell Daily Journal, 92 N.M. 170, 584 P.2d 1310 (1979).

117 *See* Cher v. Forum International, 692 F.2d 634 (9th Cir. 1982), *cert. denied*, 462 U.S. 1120 (1983) (actress granted interview, allegedly under contract that it be published only in *US* magazine. District Court victory for Cher reversed because contract not established); Falwell v. Penthouse International, Ltd., 521 F. Supp. 1204 (W.D. Va. 1981) (Rev. Jerry Falwell's claims arising from publication by *Penthouse* of interview with free-lance reporters dismissed, though claim against reporters themselves for breach of contract could be actionable).

118 *See* Virgil v. Time, Inc., 527 F.2d 1122 (9th Cir. 1975), *cert. denied*, 425 U.S. 998 (1976). Restatement (Second) of Torts § 652D comment c (1977).

119 113 F2d 806 (2d Cir. 1940).

120 420 U.S. 469 (1975).

lication of his daughter's name. Six youths were indicted for the murder and rape, and the crime and subsequent proceedings received substantial press coverage. The victim's name had not appeared in the press; a Georgia statute, in fact, made it a misdemeanor to publish or broadcast the name of a rape victim.[121] A reporter learned of the victim's name by examining copies of the indictments, which were available for his inspection in the courtroom. The Georgia Supreme Court held that a common law cause of action for public disclosure of private facts had been stated.[122] Even though it was the daughter's privacy that had been most directly invaded, the Georgia court held that the father had a valid claim in his own right because of the publication of his daughter's name.

The U.S. Supreme Court reversed. Without reaching the question of whether the first amendment always prohibits the imposition of liability for the publication of truthful facts, the Court held that the first amendment at least prohibits the creation of tort liability for the publication of facts "obtained from public records—more specifically, from judicial records which are maintained in connection with a public prosecution which themselves are open to public inspection."

[ii] After *Cox*—The Access Cases

In *Smith v. Daily Mail Publishing Co.*,[123] the Court struck down a West Virginia law making it a crime to publish the name of a child prosecuted in criminal proceedings. In *Globe Newspaper Co. v. Superior Court*,[124] the Supreme Court struck down a Massachusetts statute absolutely barring press access to rape trials in which the victims are minors. The Court in the *Globe Newspaper* case stated that "[w]here . . . the State attempts to deny the right of access in order to inhibit the disclosure of sensitive information, it must be shown that the denial is necessitated by a compelling governmental interest, and is narrowly tailored to serve that interest."[125]

In *Press-Enterprise Co. v. Riverside County Superior Court*,[126] the Court held that a trial judge erred in ordering closure of jury voir dire proceedings in a criminal trial for six weeks, emphasizing that the courts must make specific findings to overcome the presumption of

121 *See id.* (citing Ga. Code Ann. § 26-9001).
122 231 Ga. 60, 200 S.E.2d 127 (1973).
123 443 U.S. 97 (1979).
124 457 U.S. 596 (1982).
125 *Id.* at 606-07.
126 104 S. Ct. 819 (1984).

openness established in the *Globe* case, including the exploration of adequate alternate choices to closure.

More recently, in *Florida Star v. B.J.F.*,[126.1] the Supreme Court struck down a Florida statute making it unlawful to print, publish, or broadcast in any instrument of mass communication the name, address, or other identifying fact of a victim of a sexual offense.[126.2]

After appellee, B.J.F., reported to the local sheriff she was a victim of a robbery and rape, the police department prepared a report that identified the appellee by her full name and then placed the report in its press room, where full access is available to the press. Appellant published this information verbatim, including appellee's full name, in its publication.[126.3]

The Court relied on the *Daily Mail* principle that "if a newspaper lawfully obtains truthful information about a matter of public significance, then state officials may not constitutionally punish publication of the information, absent a need to further a state interest of the highest order."[126.4]

The Court concluded that although the state's interests are highly significant, they are not enough to limit the publishing of the information, because of the manner the newspaper obtained the information. There are more limited means available to protect the victim and it was the government, not the defendant, who failed in its duty to the victim.[126.5]

[iii] Definition of Public Record

Police records,[127] records generated at preliminary trial stages,[128] and medical records in state facilities[129] have all been held to be public

---

126.1 57 U.S.L.W. 4816 (1989).

126.2 *Id.* at 4816.

126.3 *Id.* at 4817.

126.4 *Id.* at 4818 (The Court also emphasized that the *Daily Mail* principle did not settle whether the government may punish a newspaper for publishing information unlawfully acquired. *Id.* at 4819.).

126.5 *Id.* at 4819-20.

127 Ayers v. Lee Enterprises, Inc., 227 Or. 527, 561 P.2d 998 (1977).

128 Poteet v. Roswell Daily Record, 92 N.M. App. 170, 584 P.2d 1310 (1978).

129 *See* Boyles v. Mid-Florida Television Corp., 431 So. 2d 627 (Fla. App. 1983) (state health department report into death of mentally retarded child held to be public record); Howard v. Des Moines Register, 283 N.W.2d 289 (Iowa 1980), *cert. denied*, 445 U.S. 904 (1980) (record of 18-year-old woman sterilized at a county home which had been forwarded to Governor's office in connection with complaints concerning the home held to be a public record).

records immune from liability when disclosed under the *Cox* principle. A state may, however, maintain some records on a confidential basis, and when it does, the *Cox* principle may be held inapplicable.[130]

[b] The Newsworthiness Privilege

[i] In General

The most significant defense to the publication of private facts tort is the "newsworthiness privilege" (or "general interest" privilege), a defense that is now usually articulated as an outgrowth of first amendment doctrine, but that actually has antecedents in common law doctrine pre-dating *New York Times Co. v. Sullivan.* This "privilege" is sometimes not truly a defense but merely shorthand for the conclusion that one of the elements of the prima facie case—the requirement that the facts disclosed be private—is not satisfied. Courts will thus sometimes treat the absence of "private facts" and the newsworthiness privilege as alternative articulations for what is essentially the same rationale.[131] The *Restatement (Second)* expresses the privilege in terms of the prima facie case, stating that to be actionable the disclosure must not be "of legitimate concern to the public."[132]

(*Text continued on page 10-27*)

---

[130] *See* Industrial Foundation of the South v. Texas Industrial Accident Bd., 540 S.W.2d 668 (Tex. 1976), *cert. denied,* 430 U.S. 931 (1977).

[131] In Sipple v. Chronicle Publishing Co., 154 Cal. App. 3d 1040, 201 Cal. Rptr. 655 (1984), discussed at text accompanying note 94, *supra,* the court denied the private facts claim of the person who disrupted an assassination attempt on President Ford's life, on the ground that the private fact disclosed—the plaintiff's homosexuality—was not truly private, and was newsworthy.

[132] Restatement (Second) of Torts § 652D (1977). *See also* McNally v. Pulitzer Publishing Co., 532 F.2d 69 (8th Cir. 1976), *cert. denied,* 429 U.S. 855 (1977); Thompson v. Curtis Publishing Co., 193 F.2d 953 (3d Cir. 1952); Kapelas v. Koffman, 1 Cal. 3d 20, 81 Cal. Rptr. 360, 459 P.2d 912 (1969); Baker v. Burlington Northern, Inc., 99 Idaho 688, 587 P.2d 829 (1978); Winegard v. Larsen, 260 N.W.2d 816 (Iowa 1977).

[ii] The Privilege Is Broadly Defined

The privilege is "[n]ot merely limited to the dissemination of news either in the sense of current events or commentary on public affairs. Rather, the privilege extends to information concerning *interesting phases of human activity* and embraces all issues about which information is needed or appropriate so that individuals may cope with the exigencies of their period."[133] The scope of the newsworthiness privilege is broader than any comparable defamation privileges emanating from *New York Times,* precisely because, as the Court recognized in *Cox,* the conflict between the first amendment and the private facts tort is particularly acute. Thus "[a] factually accurate public disclosure is not tortious when connected with a newsworthy event even though offensive to ordinary sensibilities."[134] The concept of newsworthiness is so broad, in fact, that it has swallowed up much of the tort,[135] emcompassing matters as diverse as diseases,[136] accidents,[137] births,[138] marriages,[139] divorces,[140] murders,[141] suicides and suicide attempts,[142] many sorts of crimes,[143] arrests,[144] personal tragedies,[145] the exploits of war heroes,[146] preventers of assassinations,[147] the adult life of child prodigies,[148] the

133 Campbell v. Seabury Press, 614 F.2d 395, 397 (5th Cir. 1980).

134 Neff v. Time, Inc., 406 F. Supp. 858, 861 (W.D. Pa. 1976).

135 *See* Hill, *Defamation and Privacy Under the First Amendment,* 76 Colum. L. Rev. 1205, 1253 (1976).

136 Barber v. Time, Inc., 348 Mo. 1199, 159 S.W.2d 291 (1942).

137 Kelly v. Post Publishing Co., 327 Mass. 275, 98 N.E.2d 286 (1951).

138 Meetze v. Associated Press, 230 S.C. 330, 95 S.E.2d 606 (1956).

139 Aquino v. Bulletin Co., 190 Pa. Super. 528, 154 A.2d 422 (1959).

140 Berg v. Minneapolis Star & Tribune Co., 79 F. Supp. 957 (D. Minn. 1948).

141 Leopold v. Levin, 45 Ill. 2d 434, 259 N.E.2d 250 (1970); Bremmer v. Journal-Tribune Co., 247 Iowa 817, 76 N.W.2d 762 (1956).

142 Samuel v. Curtis Publishing Co., 122 F. Supp. 327 (N.D. Cal. 1954); Metter v. Los Angeles Examiner, 35 Cal. App. 2d 304, 95 P.2d 491 (1939).

143 Elmhurst v. Pearson, 80 U.S. App. D.C. 372, 153 F.2d 467 (1946); Bernstein v. National Broadcasting Co., 129 F. Supp. 817 (D. D.C. 1955), *aff'd,* 98 U.S. App. D.C. 112, 232 F.2d 369, *cert. denied,* 352 U.S. 945 (1956).

144 Miller v. News Syndicate Co., 445 F.2d 356 (2d Cir. 1971); Firth v. Associated Press, 176 F. Supp. 671 (E.D.S.C. 1959); Penwell v. Taft Broadcasting Co., 13 Ohio App. 3d 382, 469 N.E.2d 1025 (1984).

145 Howard v. Des Moines Register, 283 N.W.2d 289 (Iowa 1979), *cert. denied,* 445 U.S. 904 (1980).

146 Stryker v. Republic Pictures Corp., 108 Cal. App. 2d 191, 238 P.2d 670 (1951).

147 Sipple v. Chronicle Publishing Co., 154 Cal. App. 3d 1040, 201 Cal. Rptr. 635 (1984).

148 Sidis v. F-R Publishing Corp., 113 F.2d 806 (2d Cir.), *cert. denied,* 311 U.S. 711 (1940).

activities of inventors,[149] actors and entertainers,[150] athletes,[151] and a magazine's statement that the plaintiff was one of America's 400 wealthiest individuals.[152] Not the case with the public controversy standard for defamation, [153] the press is largely able to bootstrap itself into the newsworthiness defense by turning the "public interest" test into virtually anything the public may be interested in.[154]

[iii] The Nexus Requirement

When a private figure plaintiff is involved, courts generally require some "nexus" between the plaintiff and the matter of legitimate public interest to qualify the defendant for the newsworthiness privilege.[155] The nexus requirement is construed very liberally, and is much broader than the definition for limited public figure status in defamation, which requires the plaintiff to voluntarily thrust himself into a public controversy.[156] Rather, the nexus requirement for the newsworthiness privilege in a private facts claim merely requires that a logical connection exist between the plaintiff and the newsworthy matter.[157]

[iv] Balancing Newsworthiness Against Intrusiveness

In determining whether the newsworthiness privilege applies, courts have long engaged in the practice of balancing the relative newsworthiness of the publication against its level of offensiveness and intrusiveness into private matters. In *Briscoe v. Reader's Digest Association, Inc.*,[158] the court held that the criteria for determining newsworthiness are: (1) the social value of the facts published; (2) the depth of

---

149 Corliss v. E.W. Walker Co., 64 F. 280 (D. Mass. 1894).

150 Chaplin v. National Broadcasting Co., 15 F.R.D. 134 (S.D.N.Y. 1953); Gavrilov v. Duell, Sloan & Pearce, 84 N.Y.S.2d 320, *aff'd*, 276 A.D. 826, 93 N.Y.S.2d 715 (1948).

151 Cohen v. Marx, 94 Cal. App. 704, 211 P.2d 320 (1950); Ruth v. Educational Films, 194 A.D. 893, 184 N.Y.S. 948 (1920).

152 Davis v. Forbes, 10 Med. L. Rep. (BNA) 1272 (N.D. Tex. 1983).

153 *See supra* § 2.10.

154 Prosser & Keeton, *supra* note 3, § 117, at 860.

155 *See, e.g.*, Gilbert v. Medical Economics, 665 F.2d 305 (10th Cir. 1981); Campbell v. Seabury Press, 614 F.2d 395 (5th Cir. 1980); Pierson v. News Group Publications, Inc., 549 F. Supp. 635 (S.D. Ga. 1982); Dresbach v. Doubleday, 518 F. Supp. 1285 (D. D.C. 1981); Friedan v. Friedan, 414 F. Supp. 77 (S.D.N.Y. 1977); Carlisle v. Fawcett Publications, Inc., 201 Cal. App. 2d 733, 20 Cal. Rptr. 405 (1962).

156 *See supra* § 2.13.

157 In Gilbert v. Medical Examiner, 665 F.2d 305 (10th Cir. 1981), for example, the court held that a sufficient nexus existed between disclosure of the name, photograph, psychiatric history, and marital problems of an anesthesiologist and a story of legitimate public interest concerning a medical malpractice claim involving the plaintiff.

158 4 Cal. 3d 529, 93 Cal. Rptr. 866, 483 P.2d 34 (1971).

the article's intrusion into ostensibly private affairs; and (3) the extent to which the individual voluntarily acceded to a position of fame or notoreity.[159] This balancing process merely introduces an element of flexibility that may be drawn upon in appropriate cases. Some stories will be so newsworthy that they will receive complete first amendment immunity no matter how offensive. One of the lessons of *Cox*, albeit a "public records" case, is that first amendment protection extends even to something as emotionally wrenching and scarring as a murder-rape.[160] By the same token, when the offensiveness of the revelation is extreme, it will take a relatively substantial assertion of newsworthiness to justify it; a mere colorable claim to newsworthiness will not talismanically insulate the defendant in such cases.[161]

[v] The Effect of the Passage of Time

Paralleling a related problem in the law of defamation concerning the "fading" public figure[162] is the issue presented by a number of publication of private facts invasion of privacy cases: how the passage of time between the original newsworthy event and the publication of the story is to be treated. Perhaps the classic case permitting recovery because of a lapse of time is *Melvin v. Reid*,[163] where the plaintiff was Gabrielle Darley, a former prostitute who had been tried and acquitted in a famous murder case. She later married, left the state, and "lived an exemplary, virtuous, honorable, and righteous life." Seven years after the murder trial the defendants produced a movie based on her story. Entitled "The Red Kimono," the film used Darley's maiden name and was promoted as a "true story." In a carefully limited holding, the court held that the *facts* of Darley's life were public, but the use of her name, in light of the passage of time, was actionable. Since Darley's name was a matter of public judicial record, however, it seems highly doubtful that the result in the case survives the *Cox Broadcasting* decision.[164]

---

159 4 Cal. 3d at 541. *See also* Sipple v. Chronicle Publishing Co., 154 Cal. App. 3d 1040, 201 Cal. Rptr. 635 (1984); Forsher v. Bugliosi, 26 Cal. 3d 792, 811-12, 163 Cal. Rptr. 628, 608 P.2d 716 (1980).

160 *See supra* § 2.04[2][a][i].

161 *See* Sidis v. F-R Publishing Co., 113 F.2d 806, 809 (2d Cir.), *cert. denied*, 311 U.S. 711 (1940); McCabe v. Village Voice, 550 F. Supp. 525 (E.D. Pa. 1982).

162 *See supra* § 2.19.

163 112 Cal. App. 285, 297 P. 91 (1931).

164 Cox Broadcasting Corp. v. Cohn, 420 U.S. 469 (1975). *See supra* § 2.04[2][a][i].

Similarly, in *Briscoe v. Reader's Digest Association, Inc.*,[165] the court held actionable a report concerning the plaintiff's involvement in a hijacking attempt 11 years prior to the story, relying on the passage of time. It appears that *Briscoe* is also undermined by *Cox*.

As in the defamation area,[166] the "passage of time" argument has not, for the most part, been successful, particularly when past criminal activity is involved.[167] Nevertheless, it is not inconceivable that the social interest in facilitating the criminal's rehabilitation, the offensiveness of the publication, and the lack of any apparent independent reason for dredging up the story might, when a substantial passage of time is involved, permit recovery, at least with regard to facts *not* falling within the apparently absolute protection of public records in *Cox.*[168] If the prior criminal record has been sealed or expunged, for example, *Cox* might be distinguishable.[169] On balance, however, passage of time simply does not appear to be a "high return" plaintiff's argument.

---

165 4 Cal. 3d 529, 93 Cal. Rptr. 866, 483 P.2d 34 (1971).

166 *See supra* § 2.19. The more elaborate analysis contained in the defamation materials is essentially interchangeable with the analysis for privacy-based claims.

167 *See, e.g.*, Perry v. Columbia Broadcasting Systems, Inc., 499 F.2d 797 (7th Cir.), *cert. denied*, 419 U.S. 884 (1974) (four decades of lapsed time does not vitiate newsworthiness of facts concerning entertainer); Westphal v. Lakeland Register Publishing Co., 2 Med. L. Rep. (BNA) 2262 (Fla. Cir. Ct. 1977), *aff'd*, 4 Med. L. Rep. (BNA) 1336 (Fla. App. 1978) (facts over 20 years old not actionable because matters of public record); Leopold v. Levin, 45 Ill. 2d 434, 259 N.E.2d 250 (1970) (Leopold and Loeb murder case newsworthy despite passage of time); Montesano v. Las Vegas Review Journal, 9 Med. L. Rep. (BNA) 2267 (Nev. Sup. 1983) (20-year-old juvenile offense remains newsworthy); McCormick v. Oklahoma Publishing, 613 P.2d 737 (Okla. 1980) (no claim permitted for publication of fact that plaintiff's name had appeared 20 years earlier on an official list of organized crime suspects).

168 These factors are suggested by Norris v. King, 355 So. 2d 21 (La. App. 1978), *cert. denied*, 439 U.S. 995 (1978).

169 *But see* Shifflet v. Thomson Newspapers, 8 Med. L. Rep. (BNA) 1199 (Ohio Sup. Ct. 1982) (reference to expunged conviction over 18 years old not actionable).

CHAPTER 11

Emotional Distress, Injurious Falsehood, and Negligent Publication

§ 11.01 Emotional Distress

[1] Overview

The torts of intentional infliction of emotional distress (or "outrage") and negligent infliction of emotional distress have become increasingly popular causes of action against the media in recent years. The emotional distress torts are not limited in any sense to media activity, they may involve virtually any aspect of life, but for the purposes of this book they are primarily examined in the context of their relationship to defamation and invasion of privacy. Plaintiffs appear to be making growing use of emotional distress causes of action as adjuncts to more traditional defamation and privacy claims against the media, and at times as the sole alleged basis of liability.

Looking at the emotional distress torts from the broader historical perspective of the evolution of tort law, the trend toward increasing judicial receptivity permitting recovery for emotional distress is unmistakable. Professor Magruder, in a famous essay, wrote: "Against a large part of the frictions and irritations and clashings of temperaments inci-

(*Text continued on page 11-3*)

dent to participation in community life, a certain toughening of the mental hide is a better protection than the law could ever be. . . . No pressing social need requires that every abusive outburst be converted into a tort; upon the contrary, it would be unfortunate if the law closed all the safety valves through which irascible tempers might legally blow off steam."[1]

The long-term evolution of the law of torts, however, has been to gradually discard this tough-minded common law hostility to recovery for emotional distress. Media defendants must anticipate that this evolution will continue, and that the emotional distress torts will gradually become yet another significant liability risk to which they will be exposed.[2]

[2] Intentional Infliction of Emotional Distress, or "Outrage"

[a] The Elements

The tort of intentional infliction of emotional distress (which in some states goes by the name of the tort of "outrage"[3]) requires four elements to state a prima facie case.

[i] Intentional or Reckless Conduct

This action is in the family of intentional torts, and intentional or reckless conduct is required to support the action.[4]

[ii] Extreme and Outrageous Conduct

At the heart of the emotional distress tort lies the requirement of extreme and outrageous conduct. The conduct must be beyond all bounds of normal human decency, and regarded as atrocious and intolerable

---

[1] Magruder, *Mental and Emotional Disturbance in the Law of Torts,* 49 Harv. L. Rev. 1033, 1035, 1053 (1936).

[2] For an excellent recent theoretical treatment of this whole field of tort recovery, *see* Ingber, *Rethinking Intangible Injuries: A Focus on Remedy,* 73 Cal. L. Rev. 772 (1985).

[3] In Arkansas, for example, the Arkansas Supreme Court in 1980 gave recognition to a cause of action it labeled "intentional infliction of emotional distress." *See* M.B.M. Corp., Inc. v. Counce, 268 Ark. 269, 596 S.W.2d 681 (1980). In a subsequent decision, without changing the elements of the action, the court adopted the more compact terminology "outrage" to describe the tort. *See* Tandy Corp. v. Bone, 283 Ark. 399, 678 S.W.2d 312 (1984); Givens v. Hixson, 275 Ark. 370, 631 S.W.2d 263 (1982).

[4] *See, e.g.,* Pierson v. News Group Publications, Inc., 549 F. Supp. 635 (S.D. Ga. 1982); Harris v. Jones, 281 Md. 560, 380 A.2d 611 (Ct. App. 1977); Restatement (Second) of Torts § 46(1) (1977).

in a civilized society.[5] This very high standard of culpability exists to screen out claims amounting to "mere insults, indignities, threats, annoyances, petty oppressions, or other trivialities"[6] that simply must be endured as part of life.

[iii] Severe Emotional Distress

The distress must be severe, to the extent that no reasonable person could be expected to endure it.[7]

[iv] Causation

Causation is a prerequisite to all tort recovery, of course, but it is usually given special emphasis in the emotional distress area, so as to keep within reasonable bounds the potential expansiveness of the tort.

[b] Application to Media Cases

The threat to media defendants posed by the intentional infliction of emotional distress tort is that courts may be less willing to recognize first amendment protection in this area than in the defamation and privacy areas, since first amendment jurisprudence in the defamation and privacy fields is so much more fully developed. Fortunately, the common law elements of the tort provide reasonably strong protection. Applied conscientiously, in fact, the tort has built-in safeguards that are essentially equivalent to the protections under *New York Times*[8] and *Gertz.*[9] Since intentional or reckless conduct of an extreme and outrageous nature creating severe distress is required, *in theory* a defendant has roughly the same quantum of protection from emotional distress liability as in public figure defamation or privacy actions. Courts should be alert, however, not to permit causes of action that are in truth actions for defamation or invasion of privacy to be renamed "infliction of emo-

---

[5] *See, e.g.,* M.B.M. Corp., Inc. v. Counce, 268 Ark. 269, 596 S.W.2d 681 (1980); State Rubbish Collectors Ass'n v. Siliznoff, 38 Cal. 2d 330, 240 P.2d 282 (1952); Paris v. Division of State Compensation Ins. Funds, 517 P.2d 1353 (Colo. App. 1973); Slocum v. Food Fair Stores of Florida, 100 So. 2d 396 (Fla. 1958); Harris v. Jones, 281 Md. 560, 380 A.2d 611 (1977); Prosser, *Intentional Infliction of Mental Suffering: A New Tort,* 37 Mich. L. Rev. 874, 887 (1939).

[6] Restatement (Second) of Torts § 46 comment d (1977).

[7] *See* M.B.M. Corp., Inc. v. Counce, 268 Ark. 269, 596 S.W.2d 681 (1980); Savage v. Boies, 77 Ariz. 355, 272 P.2d 349 (1954); State Rubbish Collectors Ass'n v. Siliznoff, 38 Cal. 2d 330, 240 P.2d 282 (1952); Delta Finance Co. v. Ganakas, 93 Ga. App. 297, 91 S.E.2d 383 (1956).

[8] New York Times Co. v. Sullivan, 376 U.S. 254 (1964).

[9] Gertz v. Robert Welch, Inc., 418 U.S. 323 (1974).

tional distress" so as to end-run the common law and first amendment checks and balances that have come to surround the defamation and privacy torts.[10]

[c] The *Hustler v. Falwell* Litigation

[i] The Lower Court Decisions

In *Falwell v. Flynt,*[11] Larry Flynt and *Hustler* magazine ran an "ad parody" in which Jerry Falwell was depicted as endorsing Campari liqueur. Campari had run a series of ads in which celebrities talked about their "first time." In the *Hustler* parody Falwell was the celebrity. He described the first time he had sex with his mother in an outhouse in Lynchburg, Va. Falwell and his mother were made out to be drunken, incestuous hypocrites. The ad was labeled "ad-parody—not to be taken seriously," and was indexed in the table of contents as "Fiction—Ad and Personality Parody."

Falwell sued Flynt in federal district court in Virginia, on three theories: defamation, appropriation of his name or likeness, and intentional infliction of emotional distress. Exercising his own first amendment prerogatives, Reverend Falwell also launched an impressive counterattack against Flynt and *Hustler* magazine. Reverend Falwell's Moral Majority, Inc. sent out two mailings over Falwell's signature. One was a mailing to 500,000 "rank-and-file" members, which described the *Hustler* parody and asked for contributions to help Falwell "defend his mother's memory." A second mailing to 26,900 "major donors" included a copy of the parody with eight of the most offensive words blacked out. A third mailing, signed by Falwell, under the auspices of his show, the "Old Time Gospel Hour," was sent to 750,000 persons. Falwell also used his television program to discuss the parody and to counterattack Flynt, displaying the ad on national television. Within 30 days of the mailings, Moral Majority received $45,000, and the "Old Time Gospel Hour" received $672,000. Falwell used his access to the media to attack Flynt with specific reference to the parody, and for a more generalized attack on pornography. These attacks did not mince words. Falwell wrote, for example:

---

[10] *See* Pring v. Penthouse International, Ltd., 695 F.2d 438 (10th Cir. 1982), *cert. denied,* 462 U.S. 1132, 103 S. Ct. 3112 (1983)(applying same first amendment protections to intentional infliction of emotional distress claim as to defamation claims).

[11] 797 F.2d 1270 (4th Cir. 1986), *rehearing en banc denied,* 805 F.2d 484, *rev'd,* Hustler Magazine v. Falwell, 108 S. Ct. 876 (1988). Judge J. Harvie Wilkinson authored a stirring dissent from the denial of rehearing en banc. *See* 805 F.2d at 484.

> Now pornography has thrust its ugly head into our everyday lives and is multiplying like a filthy plague. . . . And there, in my opinion, is clear proof that the billion dollar sex industry, of which Larry Flynt is a self-declared leader, is preying on innocent, impressionable children to feed the lusts of depraved adults. For those porno peddlers, it appears that lust and greed have replaced decency and morality.[12]

Falwell lost his defamation claim; the jury correctly found that no reasonable person could have understood the ad as meant to describe actual facts about Reverend Falwell. The appropriation claim also failed, because Falwell's name and likeness had not been used for purposes of trade, a requirement under Virginia law. The jury did find, however, that Falwell had met the burden of establishing intentional infliction of emotional distress, and it awarded Falwell $100,000 in compensatory damages and $100,000 in punitive damages. A panel of the Fourth Circuit affirmed. The Fourth Circuit voted by a narrow margin, 6-5, to deny rehearing en banc.

[ii] An Analysis of the Fourth Circuit Holding

The essential elements of infliction of emotional distress in Virginia are that the wrongdoer's conduct (1) is intentional or reckless; (2) offends generally accepted standards of decency or morality; (3) is causally connected with the plaintiff's emotional distress; and (4) caused emotional distress that was severe.[13]

There has been, of course, much talk about the capacity of the emotional distress tort to "swallow up" the torts of defamation and invasion of privacy.[14] A novel and extremely significant constitutional question, however, is posed by the *Falwell* case. The basic truth is that the jury in the suit was permitted to assess $100,000 in compensatory damages and $100,000 in punitive damages against the defendants for telling a bad, dirty joke. The pressing constitutional question is whether permitting tort recovery for "outrageous" speech which is calculated to cause emotional distress runs afoul of the first amendment because it permits a jury to punish speech that is not obscene, false, commercially fraudulent, or imminently fraught with violence but is merely offensive to "generally accepted standards of decency or morality."

---

12 *See* Hustler Magazine, Inc. v. Moral Majority, Inc., 796 F.2d 1148, 1150 (9th Cir. 1986). This suit was commenced by *Hustler* against Falwell's group, Moral Majority, Inc., for alleged violation of *Hustler*'s copyright in the ad parody when Falwell distributed copies of the parody. The Ninth Circuit held that the use of the ad by Falwell to counterattack Flynt and *Hustler* was a "fair use" that did not violate *Hustler*'s copyright.

13 Womack v. Eldridge, 215 Va. 338, 342, 210 S.E.2d 145, 148 (1974).

14 *See supra* §§ 10.01-10.03.

From the first amendment perspective, it is not the other torts that are in danger of being "swallowed up," it is decades of well-developed doctrines spanning a wide spectrum of first amendment concerns, including decisions involving obscenity,[15] "fighting words,"[16] incitement to violence,[17] symbolic speech,[18] commercial speech,[19] invasion of privacy,[20] and defamation.[21] The Supreme Court, in holdings that encompass the entire landscape of first amendment decisions, has consistently refused to permit the abridgement of speech merely because the speech is emotionally disturbing or offensive to the recipient's sensibilities.[22] The Court has always required that the regulation of speech be predicated on a connection to some more palpable social harm.[23] Constitutional protections that have evolved to prohibit the penalizing of speech merely because it is rough-edged, indecorous, or outside of mainstream sensibilities will be sabotaged by artful, ingenious resort to the emerging tort theories which permit such speech to be curtailed solely on the basis of its capacity to generate emotional disturbance.

The Court of Appeals in *Falwell* reasoned that because the cause of action for intentional infliction of emotional distress under Virginia law contains a requirement of intentional or reckless misconduct, it already

15 *See* Miller v. California, 413 U.S. 15 (1973).

16 *See* Cohen v. California, 403 U.S. 15, 20 (1970); Caplinsky v. New Hampshire, 315 U.S. 568 (1942).

17 *See* Hess v. Indiana, 414 U.S. 105 (1973); Brandenburg v. Ohio, 395 U.S. 444 (1969).

18 *See* Street v. New York, 394 U.S. 576, 592 (1969).

19 *See* Dun & Bradstreet, Inc. v. Greenmoss Builders, Inc., 472 U.S. 749 (1985).

20 *See* Cox Broadcasting v. Cohn, 420 U.S. 469 (1975).

21 *See* Gertz v. Robert Welch, Inc., 418 U.S. 323 (1974); New York Times Co. v. Sullivan, 376 U.S. 254 (1964).

22 *See, e.g.,* NAACP v. Clairborne Hardware Co., 458 U.S. 886, 910 (1982) ("Speech does not lose its protected character . . . simply because it may embarrass others."); Cohen v. California, 403 U.S. 15, 25 (1971) ("For, while the particular four-letter word being litigated here is perhaps more distasteful than most others of its genre, it is nevertheless often true that one man's vulgarity is another's lyric."); Street v. New York, 394 U.S. 576, 592 (1969) ("Any shock effect of appellant's speech must be attributed to the content of the ideas expressed. It is firmly settled that under our Constitution the public expression of ideas may not be prohibited merely because the ideas themselves are offensive to some of their hearers."); Terminiello v. Chicago, 337 U.S. 1, 4 (1949) ("A function of free speech under our system is to invite dispute. . . .That is why freedom of speech . . . is nevertheless protected against censorship and punishment, unless shown likely to produce a clear and present danger of a serious substantive evil that rises far above public inconvenience, annoyance, or unrest.").

23 *See, e.g.,* Brandenburg v. Ohio, 395 U.S. 444 (1969); Terminiello v. Chicago, 337 U.S. 1 (1949).

has "built in" a level of fault equivalent to the "actual malice" standard required in the defamation context.[24]

The analysis of the Court of Appeals is seductive, if superficial. The imposition of the actual malice standard in public figure defamation cases, the court argued, does not change the essence of the defamation tort, it merely raises the minimum threshold of fault.[25] So, too, the court reasoned, the first amendment should not be employed to alter the essential elements of the emotional distress tort, but rather should merely require the minimum threshold of fault equivalent to that required in the defamation context. The court held that the record supported the conclusion that the publisher Flynt acted intentionally or recklessly to inflict emotional distress upon Reverend Falwell in publishing the ad parody. This intent to inflict emotional distress, the court held, was fault sufficient to satisfy first amendment requirements.[26]

The fallacy of the Court of Appeals's logic is the assumption that intent to cause emotional distress is the constitutional equivalent to intent to make a defamatory misstatement of fact. It has long been recognized, however—indeed, it is axiomatic—that intent to cause emotional distress is not the equivalent of actual malice in a defamation suit. That speech is published with common law malice, out of hatred, ill will, or spite, is not enough to satisfy the *New York Times* standard in a defamation action.[27]

The difficult and novel question posed by the *Falwell* case is whether intent to cause emotional distress satisfies first amendment fault requirements when the essence of the tort is not a factual misstatement but the infliction of the distress itself. To resolve that issue it is not enough to simply lift the terms "intentional" or "reckless" out of the *New York Times* case and plug them into the elements of the emotional distress tort, and assume they mean the same thing.

Terms describing levels of fault have no meaning in the abstract. The terms "intentional," "reckless," and "negligent" are always relational;

---

[24] Falwell v. Flynt, 797 F.2d 1270, 1274-76 (4th Cir. 1986), *rev'd,* Hustler Magazine v. Falwell, 108 S. Ct. 876 (1988).

[25] *Id.* This line of argument was recently rejected by the California Supreme Court. *See* Blatty v. New York Times Co., 42 Cal. 3d 1033, 232 Cal. Rptr. 542, 728 P.2d 1177 (1986), *pet. for cert. filed* May 1987.

[26] Falwell v. Flynt, 797 F.2d 1270, 1274-76 (4th Cir. 1986), *rev'd,* Hustler Magazine v. Falwell, 108 S. Ct. 876 (1988).

[27] *See, e.g.,* Dun & Bradstreet, Inc. v. Greenmoss Builders, Inc., 472 U.S. 749, 754 (1985); Greenbelt Cooperative Publishing Ass'n v. Bresler, 398 U.S. 6, 10, n.3 (1970); Garrison v. Louisiana, 379 U.S. 64, 78 (1964). *See also supra* §§ 3.15-3.16.

they make sense only as descriptions of relations between an actor's conduct and specific risks. In Judge Cardozo's famous explication of the terms "negligence" and "proximate cause" in *Palsgraf v. Long Island Railroad Co.*,[28] he emphasized that there is no such thing as "negligence in the air," and that it is impossible to even think of negligence except in relational terms. The same is true for "intentional" or "reckless" conduct.

When the Supreme Court "constitutionalized" part of the law of defamation in *New York Times Co. v. Sullivan*, it established a relational connection between the publisher's conduct and a specific risk: the risk of publication of a defamatory false statement of fact. It is logically impossible to simply lift the *New York Times* formulation out of the context of defamation and apply it literally to the tort of infliction of emotional distress because the relationship between the publisher's conduct and the risk encompassed by the emotional distress tort is different in kind from the relationship between conduct and the risk at stake in defamation.

The term "actual malice" as used in *New York Times* is nonsensical when applied mechanically to the emotional distress claim in *Falwell*. One cannot speak meaningfully about the publisher's subjective doubt as to truth or falsity when neither the initial decision making process of the publisher nor the subsequent injury to the plaintiff has anything to do with the truth or falsity of the communication, or with its capacity to inflict reputational damage.

The terms "intentional" and "reckless" are meaningful in this case only in their relation to a very different risk: the risk that the publisher's conduct would proximately cause severe emotional distress. It is confusing even to ask, "How should the standard of *New York Times Co. v. Sullivan* apply to this case?" For the "standard" in the *Times* decision was crafted for a different relationship between an actor's conduct and risk of social harm. The proper question to ask is, "How should the first amendment be applied to restrict a state's decision to impose penalties for this sort of conduct in relation to this sort of risk?" When conceived in those terms, the first amendment issue posed is both profound and stark: May compensatory and punitive damages be awarded in a tort suit when a publisher acts intentionally or recklessly in relation to the risk that his publication will inflict severe emotional distress on another?

---

[28] 248 N.Y. 339, 162 N.E. 99 (1928).

The fact that the *New York Times* standard cannot be mechanically plugged into the emotional distress tort does not make the *Times* holding irrelevant. Rather, the *Times* case remains useful as part of the broader universe of first amendment cases that are instructive as to the relative weights of the competing interests posed in the emotional distress context. What is revealed by *New York Times* and its progeny, and first amendment cases in many other contexts, is this cardinal principle: the power of speech to generate severe emotional disturbance is *never* enough, standing alone, to justify abridgement of that speech, even when the infliction of emotional disturbance is intentional. Speech may be curtailed by the government only when it produces some other, more palpable species of social harm which the government may seek to prevent.[29]

In defamation and false light invasion of privacy actions, the causes of action concern more than the protection of reputation and emotional tranquility; they also serve the state interest deterring the publication of damaging false information. Because there is "no constitutional value in false statements of fact,"[30] a state may provide remedies for the emotional injuries arising from such false statements. So, too, states may legitimately ban obscene publications, after meeting the relatively rigorous definitional requirements of obscenity, because constitutionally obscene material has been declared by the Court to be utterly devoid of first amendment value.[31] In the special first amendment context of broadcast regulation, with the unique social interests at stake in the regulation of the broadcast spectrum, the government also possesses a narrow power to regulate vulgar speech that does not rise to the level of the legally obscene.[32] Never, however, has the Court permitted speech to be abridged because of its emotional impact alone.

Two central rationales supporting the Court's current defamation rules apply well to emotional distress suits predicated on satiric attacks upon public figures. The first is the assumption of risk rationale. In *Gertz* the Court held that one who enters the public arena must accept an increased exposure to defamation as part of the price of fame and influence.[33] This aspect of *Gertz* largely reflects the common sense dictum that he who enters the kitchen must accept the heat. If this first

---

29 *See* authorities cited in note 114, *infra*.

30 Gertz v. Robert Welch, Inc., 418 U.S. 323, 339 (1974).

31 *See* Miller v. California, 413 U.S. 15 (1973).

32 *See* FCC v. Pacifica Foundation, 438 U.S. 726 (1978).

33 Gertz v. Robert Welch, Inc., 418 U.S. 323, 345 (1974). *See also supra* § 2.06.

amendment principle requires that public figures assume some enhanced risks of being lied about, then surely it also applies with even more force to the increased risk of being subjected to emotional distress.

In a pluralistic culture, a culture diverse enough to count both Jerry Falwell and Larry Flynt within its constellation of influential public figures, it is inevitable that prominent individuals will occasionally be subjected to unwanted and severe emotional distress. In all candor, Larry Flynt and Jerry Falwell occupy positions in the spectrum of American life that are likely to evoke deep feelings of loyalty and affection from some quarters, disgust and revulsion from others. To be attacked is never pleasant, but it is part of the risk that the first amendment requires Reverend Falwell to assume as part of the price of his political and religious ministry. As Professor Magruder noted long ago, "Against a large part of the frictions and irritations and clashing of temperaments incident to participation in community life, a certain toughening of the mental hide is a better protection than the law could ever be . . .; upon the contrary, it would be unfortunate if the law closed all safety valves through which irascible tempers might legally blow off steam."[34] Professor Magruder was writing about the sound management of the tort system, but 50 years later his words have taken on a constitutional dimension. *Gertz* teaches that there is an assumption of risk component to the first amendment. This assumption of risk is an essential element to a pluralistic, robust, and open culture. In the words of Cardozo, "The timorous may stay at home."[35]

The second rationale articulated in *Gertz* was the counterspeech principle. Public officials and public figures, the Court reasoned, are more likely to have effective opportunities for self-help when they are defamed; their very prominence insures some degree of access to the media, permitting them to correct the lie with counterspeech.[36] Once again, if access to the media as a means of self-help justifies substantial first amendment protection for defamatory speech, it is all the more a justification for constitutional protection of speech that has merely inflicted emotional injury. No matter what the technical name given to the cause of action, the common law has always been extraordinarily wary of permitting recovery for name-calling, insults, epithets, and ver-

[34] Magruder, *Mental and Emotional Disturbance in the Law of Torts,* 49 Harv. L. Rev. 1033, 1035, 1053 (1936).

[35] Murphy v. Steeplechase Amusement Co., 250 N.Y. 479, 166 N.E. 173, 174 (1929).

[36] Gertz v. Robert Welch, Inc., 418 U.S. 323, 344 (1974). *See also supra* § 2.05.

bal abuse, not merely because of the assumption of risk principle but on the secondary rationale that such language reflects as negatively on the speaker as on the victim.[37] The modern first amendment counterpart to this wisdom is that a public figure subjected to an outrageous satiric attack may be very well able to turn the tables on his attacker by using his own access to the media to display his outrage.

The counterattack by Reverend Falwell was precisely the sort of self-help remedy the Court contemplated in *Gertz.* Rather than use the media to "counter the lie," of course, Falwell used it to "counter the distress," by bluntly and colorfully attacking Flynt. That attack was financially lucrative for Falwell, and it served as a useful device for combining his own emotive and cognitive use of language to further his own ideological positions. This is exactly the sort of response the first amendment is intended to encourage. The salvos between Flynt and Falwell give true meaning to the ideal of wide-open and robust speech. Nothing could be more antithetical to first amendment values, however, than to give to either side the option of invoking the heavy machinery of the state tort system to exact compensation and punitive damages for the hurt feelings that may inevitably accompany these rough exchanges.

An outrageous opinion directed against a public figure will virtually by definition be intentionally or recklessly designed to generate severe emotional distress. Opinions are always "intentional"; they are meant to have an effect. As Holmes instructed, "Every idea is an incitement."[38]

The use of the Virginia cause of action for emotional distress to punish Larry Flynt for speech that the jury found not to be understood as factual is nothing more than the resuscitation of a cause of action for outrageous opinion.[39] The second element of the cause of action, the requirement that the conduct "offends generally accepted standards of decency or morality,"[40] requires that the judge and jury do what the first amendment forbids, examine their consciences to determine if Flynt's opinion was "indecent" or "immoral."

---

37 *See supra* § 4.03.

38 Gitlow v. New York, 268 U.S. 652, 673 (1975) (Holmes, J., dissenting).

39 *See supra* § 6.02[3].

40 *See* Womack v. Eldridge, 215 Va. 338, 342, 210 S.E.2d 145, 148 (1974).

[iii] The Supreme Court's Decision

The Supreme Court reversed the Fourth Circuit in an 8–0 ruling.[41] Chief Justice Rehnquist began his opinion for the Court by reviewing the history of the case, including the jury's verdict and the decision of the Fourth Circuit Court of Appeals affirming the $200,000 jury award. He then summarized the issues facing the Supreme Court. "This case," wrote Rehnquist, "presents us with a novel question involving First Amendment limitations upon a State's authority to protect its citizens from the intentional infliction of emotional distress."[42] Chief Justice Rehnquist then described the Campari ad parody as offensive to Jerry Falwell, and "doubtless gross and repugnant in the eyes of most."[43]

The Chief Justice began his analysis with an essay on the purposes of the first amendment. "At the heart of the First Amendment," he wrote, "is the recognition of the fundamental importance of the free flow of ideas and opinions on matters of public interest and concern."[44] He noted that " 'the freedom to speak one's mind is not only an aspect of individual liberty—and thus a good unto itself—but also is essential to the common quest for truth and the vitality of society as a whole.' "[45] The Court has been particularly vigilant, he observed, to ensure that ideas remain free from governmentally imposed sanctions, because the "First Amendment recognizes no such thing as a 'false' idea."[46]

This does not mean, cautioned the Chief Justice, "that *any* speech about a public figure is immune from sanction in the form of damages."[47] Speech that is libelous in the conventional sense—speech that contains genuine misstatements of fact and that injures reputation—may be penalized in some circumstances. But even here, Chief Justice Rehnquist admonished, the Constitution requires that the rules of libel be fashioned to provide sufficient breathing space for free speech. Chief Justice Rehnquist then proceeded to wholeheartedly endorse *New York Times Co. v. Sullivan* and its progeny. For public figures and public offi-

---

[41] Hustler Magazine v. Falwell, 108 S. Ct. 876 (1988).

[42] *Id.* at 879.

[43] *Id.*

[44] *Id.*

[45] *Id.*, quoting Bose Corp. v. Consumers Union of United States, Inc., 466 U.S. 485, 503-04 (1984).

[46] 108 S. Ct. at 879, citing Gertz v. Robert Welch, Inc., 418 U.S. 323, 339 (1974).

[47] 108 S. Ct. at 880 (emphasis in original).

cials, it was critical that they prove that the offending statement was *both* false and made with actual malice.[48]

The argument of the Fourth Circuit, however, was that the rules emanating from *New York Times* did not apply to the emotional distress tort, and that the state's interest in protecting its citizens from emotional distress far outweighed any interest the speaker may have in propagating vulgar and shocking speech. It should adequately protect first amendment interests, the Fourth Circuit had argued, to require that the plaintiff prove intent to inflict the distress and to prove that the speech is offensive and outrageous.

But in the world of debate over public affairs, Chief Justice Rehnquist pointed out, many things are done with motives that are less than admirable, and they do not for that reason alone forfeit first amendment protection. That an utterance is spoken out of hatred does not mean it is false. The Chief Justice thus wrote that "while such a bad motive may be deemed controlling for purposes of tort liability in other areas of the law, we think the First Amendment prohibits such a result in the area of public debate about public figures."[49]

This conclusion, the Chief Justice argued, was necessary to avoid censoring the work of political cartoonists and satirists. The art of caricature, he argued, is based on deliberate distortion or exaggeration for satirical effect. The cartoonist's method is often not reasoned or evenhanded, but slashing and one-sided, full of black scorn and ridicule. Chief Justice Rehnquist engaged in a moving tribute to the great American tradition of spirited satire and parody of public figures. He described the cartoons of Thomas Nast, who published in *Harper's Weekly* in the post-Civil War era. Nast engaged in a graphic vendetta against William M. "Boss" Tweed and his corrupt "Tweed Ring" in New York City. Nast was effective because he constantly went beyond the bounds of good manners and taste. The Chief Justice recalled caricatures of George Washington, James G. Blaine, and Abraham Lincoln, and cartoonists' renditions of "Teddy Roosevelt's glasses and teeth, and Franklin D. Roosevelt's jutting jaw and cigarette holder."[50] From the viewpoint of history, he argued, "it is clear that our political discourse would have been considerably poorer without them."[51]

---

48 *Id.*

49 *Id.* at 881.

50 *Id.*

51 *Id.*

But could not these famous caricatures in political cartoons be distinguished from the coarse *Hustler* parody? Chief Justice Rehnquist conceded that the *Hustler* parody was at best a distant cousin of the conventional political cartoon, "and a rather poor relation at that."[52] In what may have been the single most important analytic step in his opinion, however, the Chief Justice argued that there was simply no way to draw a principled distinction between the *Hustler* parody and other satiric efforts. "If it were possible," stated Rehnquist, "by laying down a principled standard to separate the one from the other, public discourse would probably suffer little or no harm."[53] But the Supreme Court was doubtful, he explained, that any reasonably concrete standard could ever be articulated. One thing was certainly clear: the amorphous pejorative "outrageous" was too subjective to withstand first amendment requirements. To permit a jury to impose liability for mere "outrageousness" would invite jurors to base liability on the basis of their tastes and prejudices.[54]

Chief Justice Rehnquist then made it clear that the mere capacity of speech to embarrass or offend did not strip it of its protected character. In citing the holdings in *FCC v. Pacifica Foundation,*[55] the George Carlin "seven dirty words" case, and *Chaplinsky v. New Hampshire,*[56] the "fighting words" case, the Chief Justice emphasized that those holdings represented narrow exceptions to the general first amendment rule that the government must remain neutral in the marketplace of ideas. While the Court had recognized that all speech is not of equal first amendment importance, Chief Justice Rehnquist explained, the speech in this case simply did not fit into the precisely drawn categories in which lower levels of protection had been permitted.[57] "We conclude," wrote Chief Justice Rehnquist, "that public figures and public officials may not recover for the tort of intentional infliction of emotional distress by reason of publications such as the one here at issue without showing in addition that the publication contains a false statement of fact which was made with 'actual malice,' i.e., with knowledge that the statement was false or with reckless disregard as to whether it was

[52] *Id.*
[53] *Id.*
[54] *Id.*
[55] 438 U.S. 726 (1978).
[56] 315 U.S. 568 (1941).
[57] 108 S. Ct. at 881.

true."[58] Here, the jury had explicitly found that the statement was not factual. In the absence of a misstatement of fact, Falwell could not, the Chief Justice explained, recover for the mere intentional infliction of emotional distress. Only Justice Byron White failed to join the Rehnquist opinion, instead filing a brief, two-sentence separate concurring opinion. "As I see it, the decision in *New York Times v. Sullivan,* has little to do with this case, for here the jury found that the ad contained no assertion of fact,"[59] wrote Justice White. "But I agree with the Court that the judgment below, which penalized the publication of the parody, cannot be squared with the First Amendment."[60]

[3] The Future of the Intentional Infliction of Emotional Distress Tort

[a] Overview

If first amendment doctrines are potent enough to destroy Falwell's claim, are they *too* potent? Does disqualifying the Reverend Falwell from recovery necessarily interfere with the tort of infliction of emotional distress in *all* situations in which speech is a component of the distress-inflicting conduct? When the speech is an element of some other oppressive, coercive, or harassing activity, might it not, in combination with that other activity, create a cause of action that would raise less serious first amendment objections? Infliction of emotional distress by an oppressive bill collector, or through sexual harassment on the job, may be effectuated by "speech." But the gravamen of the tortious activity in such cases is arguably the proscription of underlying nonspeech conduct, such as an oppressive commercial tactic, or antisocial behavior in the workplace. The penalty exacted on speech in such cases appears incidental to the governmental purpose of regulating the purely expressive component of the conduct.[61]

The interrelationships between the torts of libel, slander, false light invasion of privacy, intrusion, publication of embarrassing facts, appropriation of likeness, and infliction of emotional distress are volatile and constantly changing. In a strict sense, however, these issues pose no federal constitutional questions, but are rather problems for the sound ad-

---

58 *Id.*

59 108 S. Ct. at 883 (White, J., concurring).

60 *Id.*

61 Smolla, *Emotional Distress and the First Amendment: An Analysis of* Hustler v. Falwell, 20 Ariz. St. L.J. 423 (1988).

ministration of state tort systems. As far as the Constitution is concerned, a state should be free to combine or separate these torts as it pleases, with as much or as little overlap in elements or functions as it deems wise. Nothing in the first amendment, for example, necessarily dictates a rule that when a defamation claim fails, an emotional distress claim arising from the same facts also fails.[62]

Fear that the tort of emotional distress could destroy core first amendment values must thus be balanced against a countervailing fear that will certainly drive many to attack the Supreme Court's ruling in *Hustler*—the fear that the first amendment ruling in favor of Flynt will effectively eliminate all future claims for emotional distress. For if the first amendment does bar Reverend Falwell's recovery against *Hustler* and Flynt, what is left of tort recovery for emotional distress? Assuming that Falwell's distress was indeed "severe," that Flynt's inducement of that distress was "intentional," and that the means used offended "generally accepted standards of decency or morality," is there any type of infliction of emotional distress that survives the Supreme Court's decision? If what *Hustler* published failed to pierce the shield of the first amendment, what would?

[b] Nonspeech Cases

[i] The Problems of a Simplistic Division

One simple answer is that tort law may continue to permit recovery for infliction of emotional distress, without running afoul of the first amendment, when the tortious activity does not involve speech. This answer, however, is easily discredited because it is surely underinclusive. There are too many examples of activity involving communication, verbal or symbolic, that strike one intuitively as beyond first amendment protection. The challenge, therefore, is to articulate some first amendment principle to guide that intuition.

[ii] Nonspeech Masquerading as Speech

In certain cases, one may avoid first amendment concerns by unmasking that which purports to be communicative activity to reveal nonspeech masquerading as speech. In *Johnson v. Woman's Hospital*,[63] for example, the court allowed an action for infliction of emotional distress when the defendant displayed a dead newborn child in a formal-

---

[62] *Id.* at 461.

[63] 527 S.W.2d 133 (Tenn. Ct. App. 1975).

dehyde jar to the plaintiff. The mere one sentence restatement of the facts in *Johnson* is nauseating; little imagination is required to conjure the overwhelming emotional shock that must have consumed the plaintiff upon actually seeing the dead baby in a jar of formaldehyde. The distress, however, comes from what was seen. If recovery was legitimate in *Johnson,* it must be distinguished from the distress that results from seeing, on a magazine page, one's depiction as having had sexual intercourse with one's mother in an outhouse.

Emotional distress cases involving visceral shock at simply observing activity are now well established in the tort tradition. Courts have permitted recovery for the mutilation of a spouse's dead body,[64] for witnessing a scene in which one's child is violently killed,[65] and even against an estate, for the decedent's act of committing suicide in the plaintiff's kitchen.[66] The medium through which harm is transmitted in these cases is "communicative" in the literal sense that the emotional injury is caused by what one absorbs by the senses in sight and sound. The famous line of cases emanating from *Dillon v. Legg,*[67] indeed, require direct sensory observance as an element of the cause of action.[68]

One might argue, however, that these emotional distress cases do not truly involve "speech," because they are all examples of the antithesis of Marshall McLuhen's statement that the "medium is the message." In these cases there is medium but there is no message. It is not the idea of a dead baby in a formaldehyde jar, a mutilated corpse, or a suicide discovered in one's kitchen that is communicated; rather it is the reality of those events and actions that is observed. If it is speech at all, it is speech without a speaker. When one cannot plausibly argue that either the free trade of ideas or the self-fulfillment of a speaker is implicated, no first amendment concerns exist.[69]

[c] Emotional Distress for the Content of Speech

[i] The Problem

The pseudo-speech cases discussed above do not cover the entire spectrum of situations in which emotional distress is inflicted through

---

64 Alderman v. Ford, 146 Kan. 698, 72 P.2d 981 (1981).

65 Dillon v. Legg, 68 Cal. 2d 728, 441 P.2d 981 (1981).

66 Blakeley v. Chortal's Estate, 236 Iowa 787, 20 N.W.2d 28 (1945).

67 68 Cal. 2d 728, 441 P.2d 981 (1981).

68 *See* Ochoa v. Superior Court of Santa Clara County, 39 Cal. 3d 159, 216 Cal. Rptr. 661, 703 P.2d 1 (1985); Justus v. Atchison, 19 Cal. 3d 564, 139 Cal. Rptr. 97, 565 P.2d 122 (1977); Campbell v. Animal Quarantine Station, 63 Hawaii 577, 632 P.2d 1066 (1981).

69 Smolla, *supra* note 61, at 463.

apparently communicative conduct. Tort law has become increasingly hospitable to causes of action in which "real speech" is the primary vehicle through which the defendant induces distress—cases in which a speaker and a message clearly exists, and the distress is caused by the content of the message.[70]

Although this species of recovery has gained accelerated momentum in recent years, it has an old and venerable pedigree. In *Wilkinson v. Downton,*[71] the losing defendant was a practical joker who told a woman that her husband had been severely injured in an accident. The defendant could not interpose the comeback "can't you take a joke?" as a defense in *Wilkinson;* the court ruled that statements about the death or personal injury of loved ones were simply not joking matters in civilized life. Later, in fact, an entire class of cases developed in which courts imposed liability for erroneous messages announcing a relative's death.[72]

[ii] Modern Examples

An intriguing modern manifestation of this issue is posed by *Molien v. Kaiser Foundation Hospital,*[73] in which a doctor erroneously told a patient that she had a venereal disease, and the patient repeated the information to her husband. The marital friction caused by the false diagnosis led to a divorce. The California Supreme Court permitted the husband to recover for the emotional distress caused by the false medical information given to his ex-wife.[74]

Recovery for emotional distress is indeed routinely predicated upon expressive activity in which the distress is undeniably linked to the content of the message. Debt collection cases, for example, are among the most common fact patterns for emotional distress recovery.[75] Courts have held defendants liable for the distress created in attempting to recover debts even when the speech of the debt collector is directed only to the debtor, and not communicated to third persons.[76] The emotional distress tort is also a recurring vehicle for recovery when persons

---

70 *Id.*

71 2 Q.B. 57 (1897).

72 *See, e.g.,* Kaufman v. Western Union Tel. Co., 224 F.2d 723 (5th Cir.), *cert. denied,* 350 U.S. 947 (1955); Johnson v. State, 37 N.Y.2d 378, 372 N.Y.S.2d 638, 334 N.E.2d 590 (1975).

73 27 Cal. 3d 916, 167 Cal. Rptr. 831, 616 P.2d 813 (1980).

74 *Id.* at 931, 167 Cal. Rptr. at 839, 616 P.2d at 821.

75 Smolla, *supra* note 61, at 464.

76 *Id.*

are falsely accused of shoplifting,[77] or of stealing from the employer's cash drawer.[78] Courts have also ruled that repeated sexual advances are sufficient grounds for recovery based on infliction of emotional distress.[79]

[iii] Use of Other Torts

In other contexts, courts permit recovery for the outrage of *what is said* under the rubric of some recognized tort other than infliction of emotional distress, even though the only compensable injury is emotional disturbance. In *Fisher v. Carrousel Motor Hotel, Inc.*,[80] for example, the plaintiff was a black customer attending a luncheon at a restaurant club. As he picked up his plate to go through the line, an employee of the cafeteria grabbed the plate from him and said that blacks could not be served in the club.[81] A recovery of compensatory and punitive damages for battery was upheld. Although the case has been used as an example of an arcane common law rule in the law of battery—that a battery may be consummated by an offensive touching of not only the person of the plaintiff, but an "appurtenance," such as an umbrella or plate—the case is really a powerful example of recovery for emotional distress for the offensiveness of that which was communicated. The case had no relationship to the law of battery other than its demonstration of the quicksilver ingenuity with which a clever plaintiff's lawyer may press an old tort to do new tricks. The damages awarded under the Texas tort system expressed the community's outrage at the offensiveness of the race hate and insult to human dignity embodied in a vicious slur such as "we don't serve niggers here."[82]

[iv] Sexual Harassment

Courts have permitted a parallel form of recovery in battery or assault cases involving sexual harassment, in which the physical touching is fleeting or nonexistent, and but for its verbal accompaniment, innocuous. In *Western Union Telegraph Co. v. Hill*,[83] for example, the defendant's employee leaned across the counter to touch a woman's hand, although he never made contact. He said to her, "If you will come back

---

77 *Id.*

78 *Id.*

79 *Id.*

80 424 S.W.2d 627 (Tex. 1967).

81 *Id.* at 628-29.

82 Smolla, *supra* note 61, at 464.

83 25 Ala. App. 540, 150 So. 709 (1933).

here and let me love you and pet you, I will fix your clock."[84] Although the court analyzed the matter in terms of whether the counter was sufficiently narrow to allow the man's arm to reach the plaintiff, it was not the attempted touching but the sexual advance that really formed the heart of the case, and it was what the defendant said that "consummated" the sexual advance.

After *Hustler*, do the rulings in these cases violate the first amendment? How will a court distinguish the insult to human dignity wrapped up in the epithet "nigger" or in the uninvited sexual come-on from the insult of being portrayed as one who has sex with one's mother?

[v] The *Firestone* Case Example

To strike the iron where it is even hotter in first amendment terms, consider that the Supreme Court has upheld recovery under the law of defamation when the only injury for which the plaintiff seeks compensation is the emotional distress induced by the demafatory statement. In *Time, Inc. v. Firestone*,[85] Mary Alice Firestone, ex-wife of Russell Firestone, a scion of the wealthy Firestone family, sued for defamation arising from a brief "milestones" blurb in *Time* magazine announcing her divorce judgment. *Time* had summarized the grounds for the divorce in terms that made Firestone appear to have a wide-open, robust, and uninhibited sex life with men other than her husband. Although her suit was for defamation, she dropped all claims for reputational injury and predicated her entire recovery on the emotional anguish caused by *Time*'s characterization.[86] The Supreme Court upheld Firestone's jury verdict of $100,000, holding that the first amendment's requirement of "actual injury" for private defamation cases could be satisfied by proving subjective emotional harm—no external injury to reputation was constitutionally mandated.[87] If the first amendment permits recovery for emotional distress in a defamation case in which no reputational damage is claimed, why should it not also permit recovery when the pretense of the defamation action is dropped, and a spade is called a spade? Would Mary Alice Firestone have lost in the Supreme Court (assuming she could surmount any obstacles posed by Florida law), if she had chosen to style her claim as one for infliction of emotional distress?

---

84 *Id.* at 542, 150 So. at 710.

85 424 U.S. 448 (1976).

86 *See supra* § 9.06[5].

87 *Id.*

[d] A Multitiered Solution for the Future

These questions concerning the implications of the Supreme Court's decision in *Hustler* must be addressed in light of the two most important "clues" dropped in Chief Justice Rehnquist's opinion. The first clue is the explicit limitation of the holding to public officials and public figures.[88] The second clue is the insistence in the opinion that "not all speech is of equal First Amendment importance."[89] Against the backdrop of these two themes in the opinion, a multitiered solution to the questions left unanswered by the *Hustler* decision may be constructed.

[i] A Scale of Liability Factors

The universe of tort recovery for emotional distress may be schematically arranged according to five variables: (1) whether the underlying tortious conduct is expressive or nonexpressive; (2) whether, if the conduct is expressive, the plaintiff is a public figure or public official, or a private figure; (3) whether, if the conduct is expressive, the communication involves matters of public interest; (4) whether the victim's emotional distress is coupled with injury other than emotional distress; and (5) whether the actor's conduct may be fairly characterized as satisfying all of the elements of some tort other than emotional distress, or instead must be challenged exclusively under the rubric of emotional distress.[90]

All nonexpressive tortious conduct is outside of first amendment concern. Whether to permit recovery for expressive conduct causing emotional distress, however, involves an intricate balance of the remaining variables. A proper accommodation of first amendment values and the plaintiff's interest in emotional distress cases would apply the five variables listed above according to the following rules:

(1) When the conduct is nonexpressive, the plaintiff may recover if the state law elements of the tort are satisfied, because no first amendment interests are at stake.

(2) When the conduct is expressive, the plaintiff is absolutely barred from recovery when: (a) the plaintiff is a public official or public figure; (b) the speech involves a matter of public concern; (c) no injury other than emotional distress exists; and (d) no tort other than infliction of emotional distress has been committed. (Reverend Falwell's case falls

---

[88] 108 S. Ct. at 882.

[89] *Id.*, quoting Dun & Bradstreet, Inc. v. Greenmoss Builders, Inc., 472 U.S. 749, 758 (1985).

[90] Smolla, *supra* note 61, at 467.

into this category and thus, as the Supreme Court held, is absolutely barred.)

(3) When the conduct is expressive, and there is either injury suffered other than emotional distress, or a tort committed other than intentional infliction of emotional distress, the plaintiff may recover subject to these restrictions:

(a) When the plaintiff is a public figure or official, and the speech concerns matters of public interest, one may recover for emotional distress only when: (i) the challenged conduct is reckless or intentional with regard to the risk of the *nonemotional distress* component of the injury; or (ii) when the defendant commits a tort other than intentional infliction of emotional distress and the conduct is intentional or reckless with regard to the legal interest protected by that tort. In addition to these requirements, all other currently existing first amendment restraints upon recovery for that tort, including absolute protection for opinion, must be satisfied.

(b) When the plaintiff is a public figure or official, but the speech does not involve matters of public concern, the same rules apply as in (a) above, but the minimum constitutional fault threshold is dropped to negligence.

(c) When the plaintiff is a private figure, but the speech involves issues of public concern, the same rules apply as in (a) above, but the minimum constitutional fault threshold is dropped to negligence.

(d) When the plaintiff is a private figure and the speech does not involve any issue of public concern, the case is treated for first amendment purposes as if it were nonexpressive conduct, and no first amendment restrictions will apply, relegating the defendant's protection solely to that available under applicable common law rules.[91]

[ii] The Logic of the Scale

The matrix of rules outlined above tracks, in its analytic structure, the multitiered constitutional fault structure in defamation created by combining *New York Times Co. v. Sullivan, Gertz v. Robert Welch, Inc.,* and *Dun & Bradstreet, Inc. v. Greenmoss Builders, Inc.*[92] It does not, however, simply restate the current rules for defamation, substituting for "defamation" the term "emotional distress"; such an approach would fall into the trap set by the Fourth Circuit's enticing but flawed

[91] *Id.*

[92] *See supra* §§ 3.01-3.05.

analysis in the *Hustler* case.[93] Instead, the appropriate analysis readjusts the first amendment matrix governing defamation to reflect the different balance of social interests posed by emotional distress cases. That balance requires absolute immunity at the "high end" of the scale, when public plaintiffs sue to recover for injuries caused by expressive conduct involving issues of public concern, and the only actual injury or legal interest implicated is emotional distress. When public plaintiffs sue to recover for injuries caused by public speech, the capacity of the speech to cause emotional disturbance is simply never enough, standing alone, to justify its abridgement.[94]

No absolute immunity is mandated, however, when the case implicates some interest of the plaintiff other than the disturbing quality of the speech; in such cases, the regulation of speech is incidental to the protection of some palpable social interest distinct from the capacity of the speech to disturb. The test for whether speech is being restricted because of a state interest other than the disturbance quality of the speech is whether one can identify, either factually or legally, some nonemotional injury to the plaintiff. Thus, the fact that the plaintiff can prove nonemotional injury, or that the plaintiff can point to some independently cognizable nonemotional distress tort, such as assault, battery, defamation, or invasion of privacy, is evidence that such a palpable state interest exists.[95] Even in such cases, however, the sacrifice of first amendment freedom must be meticulously balanced against the strength of the state interest, according to the sliding scale in the rules above. When the plaintiff and the speech are both public, the first amendment interest is at its highest level. Abridgement of that interest through tort liability is thus permitted only when there is intentional or reckless conduct with regard to a risk other than the distress-inducing potential of the speech. It is critical that the intentional or reckless conduct be in relation to the other palpable interest being protected, and not simply to the risk of causing distress; if the risk is only related to distress, the case must fall within category (2) above, in which the expressive conduct is absolutely protected.[96]

This rationale remains applicable as one moves down the scale to speech that involves public figures but no public issues, or public issues but no public figures. Because first amendment concerns for penalizing

---

93 *See supra* § 11.01[2][b][ii].

94 Smolla, *supra* note 61, at 468.

95 *Id.*

96 *Id.*

speech for its disturbance potential alone still exist in these cases, it remains essential that the fault standard applied be in relation to risks other than the emotional distress evoked by the speech. On the other hand, because *Gertz* informs us that private figures are in greater need and more deserving of tort remedies for injurious speech than public figures,[97] and because speech concerning private matters and public figures is of less first amendment significance than speech linked to a plaintiff's public figure status,[98] the balance in these suits swings towards negligence rather than reckless or intentional conduct. The defendant must thus show both the public status of the plaintiff and the public status of the speech to receive the benefit of the "knowing or reckless" test. Showing only one of the two drops the minimum first amendment standard to negligence. In all of these cases, however, the first amendment requires that the risk be in relation to something other than the emotional content of the speech.[99]

[iii] Applying the Scale

One should have no illusions, of course, that the process of separating these interests will always be easy. That does not mean, however, that such separation is impossible.

One of the most difficult cases that illustrates the problem of separating the emotive quality of speech from the invasion of other, more palpable interest is *Vietnamese Fishermen's Association v. Knights of Ku Klux Klan.*[100] In that case, hooded and robed Ku Klux Klansmen rode past boats containing Vietnamese fishermen. The Klansmen carried guns, and were in a boat that contained a cannon and a figure hung in effigy. The Klansmen fired a cannon towards the Vietnamese fishermen's boat.

The court held that in such circumstances Texas law might support an action against the Klan members for intentional infliction of emotional distress.[101] Apparently, no first amendment defense was raised. But if a first amendment defense had been vigorously pressed, what would the correct result have been? Under the analysis here, the case turns on the guns and the firing of the cannon. As the district court recognized, brandishing the weaponry may have been sufficiently threat-

97 *See supra* §§ 2.05-2.06.
98 *See* Dun & Bradstreet, Inc., v. Greenmoss Builders, Inc. 472 U.S. 749, 758 (1985).
99 Smolla, *supra* note 61, at 469.
100 518 F. Supp. 993 (S.D. Tex. 1981).
101 *Id.* at 1013.

ening to constitute assault.[102] Although the outrage one feels at the actions of the Klan is fed primarily by the repugnance of the race hate displayed against the Vietnamese fishermen, in a free society the abominable speech of racists must be tolerated unless it threatens to ripen into more palpable harm. Had the Klansmen merely boated past the Vietnamese fishermen with sheets and shotguns and figures hung in effigy, shouting "gooks go home" the first amendment should bar recovery. In such circumstances, the repugnance of the conduct would be in the message conveyed, a message driven home by the combination of the racial slur, and the symbols of the sheets, guns, and hanging effigy. But the harm would still be *only* in the disturbing quality of this message.

Once this speech escalates to threats of violence, however, an interest other than the emotional disturbance caused by the content of the speech is implicated. The brandishing of firearms and shooting of the cannon combine to satisfy the common law definition of assault, by creating a reasonable apprehension of bodily harm. No reasonable person in the position of the Vietnamese fishermen could fail to be fearful of an hysterical physical attack in such circumstances. The Klansmen were at least negligent with regard to the threat of physical harm—indeed, they were almost certainly intentionally seeking to intimidate through physical threats; therefore, imposing liability for infliction of emotional distress does not offend the first amendment.

Similarly, in *Chuy v. Philadelphia Eagles Football Club,*[103] the Philadelphia Eagles' staff physician erroneously informed a newspaper that Chuy, one of the Eagles' players, had a fatal illness. Arguably, only the emotional impact of the speech formed the predicate for liability. On closer examination, however, *Chuy* is more subtle, and actually involves the intentional invasion of a more concrete interest of the plaintiff. *Chuy* involved an intentional lie—the doctor deliberately spread a false statement of fact about Chuy's physical condition. The only reason the statement was not libelous was that under Pennsylvania law the imputation of serious disease is deemed defamatory only if it is a stigmatizing illness, such as venereal disease.[104] But as *Firestone* instructs, spreading a false statement of fact is a palpable harm which a state may use as

---

102 *Id.* at 1012.

103 595 F.2d 1265 (3d Cir. 1979) (en banc).

104 *Id.* at 1281.

the basis for tort liability even when no reputational damage ensues.[105] The false statement in *Chuy* was verbal assault in a literal sense. The power of the statement was indistinguishable from the power of a bullet zipping past one's ear—Chuy thought he was going to die. The fact that the speech failed to meet all the technical requirements for defamation did not alter the fact that the harmful quality of the speech was not solely its emotional offensiveness, but its factual error—a factual error deliberately made by a doctor in a doctor/patient relationship and calculated to mislead the patient about his own health.

[iv] The Lax Standard for Private Figure/Private Speech Cases

When the plaintiff is a private figure, and the speech at issue does not address any issue of public concern, first amendment restrictions on emotional distress recovery will be completely eliminated under this proposed scale. Under the logic of *Dun & Bradstreet,*[106] the first amendment value of this species of speech is so low that the unvarnished rules of the common law are sufficient to protect it, and no independent first amendment rules will apply.[107] The oppressive bill collector's speech, for example, involves a private figure plaintiff, and speech that falls squarely within the type of commercial speech stripped of special first amendment protection in *Dun & Bradstreet.* Just as common law defamation rules operated without first amendment interference in the commercial defamation context, they would operate untrammeled in the context of commercial emotional distress. An act of sexual harassment in the workplace presents exactly the same first amendment balance; the plaintiff is a private figure and the speech concerns private matters.

In both examples, our confidence that no special first amendment rules should be imposed comes largely from the intuition that the speech is inextricably wrapped up in the invasion of interests of the plaintiff other than the content of the speech itself. The speech is part of some other nonspeech business, such as a proposal to engage in a commercial or a sexual transaction. The decision to treat the conduct as tortious is really aimed at the transaction itself.

This analysis will accommodate equitably the vast run of cases. Like any scheme of legal rules, however, it will inevitably have some rough edges. One might ask, for example, whether cases falling into the pri-

---

105 Smolla, *supra* note 61, at 471.

106 Dun & Bradstreet, Inc., v. Greenmoss Builders, Inc., 474 U.S. 749 (1985).

107 Smolla, *supra* note 61, at 471-74.

vate figure/private speech category are genuinely different in kind from cases in which the plaintiff is public but the speech is private. Does it make sense to treat a public figure victimized by an oppressive bill collector, or by verbal sexual aggression, differently from a private figure so victimized? Even if the first amendment interferes with Jerry Falwell's right to recover from Larry Flynt for emotional distress, should it also interfere with his right to sue the abusive collection agency? One might pose the same problem in reverse: if the decision is made that fault in relation to a risk other than distress is required when the speech or the plaintiff is public, why shouldn't fault in relation to some nonemotional distress interest also be required in the private figure/private speech situation? After all, the rationale for excusing this latter category from first amendment protection is that cases in this category usually involve some palpable nonspeech interest. Some private figure/private speech verbal inflictions of emotional distress will not involve any other nonspeech "transactions." Suppose a capricious, malicious defendant walks up to a stranger on the street and screams an abusive insult. Does the first amendment permit whatever recovery the common law provides, even though this speech does not fit comfortably into the supposition that some other "transaction" is involved? In short, why not treat all of these cases alike, and either require first amendment protection for all of them or none of them?[108]

And if one must choose between all or none, surely the choice must be all. When the private figure, viciously assaulted with a torrent of gratuitous vulgarity on the street, sues for emotional distress, should not the first amendment impose the same sort of restrictions that have evolved in the criminal context in the "fighting words" cases—a showing of risk of imminent harm other than the smarting of the words themselves? Why shouldn't the plaintiff bear the burden in *every* case to demonstrate the defendant's fault in relation to some risk other than the capacity of the speech to cause emotional disturbance?

The answer to these objections involves three observations. First, the descending scale proposed here is, like the analogous scale in the first amendment rules for defamation, based on the large run of cases, and the paradigms one expects to find in each category. The notion in *Gertz* that public figures assume greater risks and have greater access to channels of counterspeech will not be true in all cases; the soundness of the rule turns on how well the probabilities for most cases have been as-

[108] *Id.*

sessed. Second, downside risks to a uniform rule exist regardless of the direction in which the rule is bent. A single standard applied across the board will either provide too much or too little first amendment protection. A graduated scale helps prevent fewer improperly balanced cases from escaping. Third, there is a federal benefit to keeping the intrusion of constitutional rules upon the law of torts confined to bright line factors. If a first amendment calculus were made an explicit requirement in every emotional distress case the tort would indeed be swallowed up by the federal Constitution.[109]

[v] Conclusion

Tort law must be trusted to do some of its own work. Whatever fears we may have that occasionally in a private figure/private speech case there will be no social interest at stake other than the capacity of the speech to disturb should be alleviated by trust in the internal gyroscope of the law of torts. Tort law will, in its own wisdom, tend to screen out most emotional distress claims in which no interest or harm other than the emotive quality of the speech is implicated. It has long been hard legal doctrine that mere verbal abuse, standing alone, is not actionable.[110] Under standard defamation, privacy, and emotional distress rules, plaintiffs are told that the door of tort recovery is not open for the routine slings and arrows of outrageous fortune.

If tort law may be trusted in cases involving private figures and private speech, the flip side is that we cannot trust it to be sufficiently sensitive to first amendment values in public figure or public speech cases. Preoccupation with common law elements of infliction of emotional distress will distract attention from the possibility that a plaintiff is seeking recovery only because of the emotional content of the speech at issue. Because the probabilities of improperly penalizing protected speech in public figure or public speech cases run higher than in private figure/private speech cases, the first amendment now requires that the plaintiff actually perform the task of separating the interest involved. Unless the plaintiff can articulate some interest other than emotional disturbance, and can demonstrate at least negligence in relation to that interest, the first amendment should bar recovery. When both public figures and private speech are involved, the fear that tort liability is being imposed solely because of the disturbing quality of the speech

---

109 *Id.*

110 *See supra* §§ 4.03, 6.12[10].

is now at its highest, and the probability that that speech is within the core of the first amendment is at its highest as well. The threat of self-censorship is now so intense that only intentional or reckless misconduct in relation to some risk independent of emotional distress will justify liability. In these cases, the plaintiff is being forced to demonstrate the separation of emotional distress interests from more palpable interests that we were willing to simply assume existed in the private figure/private speech cases. When the *only* harm caused by such public speech about public figures is emotional distress, however, the first amendment compels absolute protection.[111]

[4] Negligent Infliction of Emotional Distress

[a] Recovery for Mental Disturbance

Negligent misconduct of almost any nature may give rise only to mental or emotional injuries. The traditional common law position was to deny recovery in such cases, unless some sort of "physical impact" upon the body of the plaintiff triggered the distress.[112]

[b] The Physical Manifestation Position

Gradually this view gave way to the "physical manifestation rule"—the position that negligence causing emotional or mental distress which ripened into a physical illness or injury was actionable.[113]

[c] Emergence of "Pure" Emotional Distress Recovery

The most modern stage in the evolutionary process abandons requirements of physical manifestation altogether, permitting a "pure" action for negligent infliction of emotional distress.[114]

---

111 Smolla, *supra* note 61, at 471-74.

112 *See* Mitchell v. Rochester Ry., 151 N.Y. 107, 45 N.E. 354 (1896); W. Prosser, W. Keeton, D. Dobbs, R. Keeton, & D. Owen, Prosser and Keeton on Torts § 54, at 363 (5th ed. 1984).

113 *See, e.g.*, Towns v. Anderson, 579 P.2d 1163, 1165 (Colo. 1978); Vicnire v. Ford Motor Credit Co., 401 A.2d 148, 155 (Me. 1979); Payton v. Abbott Labs, 386 Mass. 540, 437 N.E.2d 171, 181 (1982); Sears, Roebuck & Co. v. Young, 384 So. 2d 69, 71 (Miss. 1980); Fournell v. Usher Pest Control Co., 208 Neb. 684, 305 N.W.2d 605 (1981); Wyatt v. Gilmore, 290 S.E.2d 790 (N.C. App. 1982).

114 *See, e.g.*, Molien v. Kaiser Foundation Hospitals, 27 Cal. 3d 916, 167 Cal. Rptr. 831, 616 P.2d 813 (1980); Rodrigues v. State, 52 Hawaii 156, 472 P.2d 509 (1970); Bass v. Nooney Co., 646 S.W.2d 765 (Mo. 1983); Miller, *The Scope of Liability for Negligent Infliction of Emotional Distress: Making "The Punishment Fit the Crime,"* 1 U. Hawaii L.

[d] Applicability to Media

Recovery for negligent infliction of emotional distress would completely overwhelm the whole matrix of defamation and privacy torts if it became an all purpose workhorse for redress of psychic injury. No such role is appropriate for the tort, and thus far its use in the context of published speech has been limited to specialized situations in which liability is appropriate but no other publication related tort is available, e.g., the incorrect notice of a loved one's death,[115] or a false report of serious illness.[116]

In a recent well-reasoned opinion, Justice Greenfield in a New York decision applied first amendment principles to bar a claim for negligent infliction of emotional distress against a media defendant. In *Rubinstein v. New York Post Corp.,*[117] the *New York Post* and *New York Daily News* published obituary notices for the plaintiff, who was in fact alive and well. The mistake was apparently the result of a third person's "malice . . . or warped sense of humor."[118] The court recognized that the plaintiff was probably attempting to use the emotional distress theory to avoid the strictures attendant to a libel action: "Possibly to avoid the rigorous limitations which are to be applied in libel suits, plaintiff alleged that the newspaper 'negligently and carelessly published false information, and failed to publish a timely retraction.' "[119]

The court quite alertly foreclosed this end-run effort, citing *Gertz*[120] and *New York Times*[121] and stating, "The Supreme Court has imposed burdens on a party suing a publication in order to protect First Amendment rights of free speech. A plaintiff cannot avoid the constitutional protections afforded to publications by alleging as an alternative theory 'the negligent infliction of emotional harm.' "[122] Given the rarity of such pranks and the burdens of independently verifying the fact of death

---

Rev. 1 (1979); Nolan & Ursin, *Negligent Infliction of Emotional Distress: Coherence Emerging from Chaos,* 33 Hastings L.J. 583 (1982).

[115] This is the so-called death telegram rule. *See, e.g.,* Kaufman v. Western Union Tel. Co., 224 F.2d 723 (5th Cir.), *cert. denied,* 350 U.S. 947 (1955); Johnson v. State, 37 N.Y.2d 378, 372 N.Y.S.2d 638, 334 N.E.2d 590 (1975).

[116] Ferrara v. Galluchio, 5 N.Y.2d 16, 176 N.Y.S.2d 996 (1958)(false report of cancer).

[117] 11 Med. L. Rep. (BNA) 1329 (N.Y. Sup. 1985).

[118] *Id.* at 1330.

[119] *Id.*

[120] 418 U.S. 323 (1974).

[121] 376 U.S. 254 (1964).

[122] 11 Med. L. Rep. (BNA) at 1330.

when obituary notices are phoned in to a publisher, the court dismissed the actions.[123]

§ 11.02 Injurious Falsehood

[1] Overview

In the modern law the tort of "injurious falsehood" is the general umbrella term for a collection of torts such as "slander of title," "product disparagement," or "trade libel" that share as a common component injury to business or commercial interests caused by the publication of false information.[124]

The tort has quite ancient origins. "Slander of title" cases involving the casting of aspersions upon another's interest in land date back before the year 1600.[125] The related tort concepts known variously as "product disparagement," "disparagement of quality," or "trade libel" cover more generalized business injuries not necessarily tied to an interest in property.[126]

[2] Elements of the Cause of Action

[a] Falsity

[i] In General

As in an action for defamation, liability for injurious falsehood is predicated on falsity.[127]

[ii] Burden of Proof

The plaintiff bears the burden of proving the disparaging statement is false.[128]

[iii] Opinion Not Actionable

Mere opinion is not actionable. Thus, "to say that the plaintiff's product is not as good as defendant's is not a tort at all."[129]

---

123 *Id.* at 1330-31

124 *See generally* Prosser and Keeton, *supra* note 112, § 128.

125 *Id.*, § 128, at 962 (citing Gerrard v. Dickenson, 78 Eng. Rep. 452 (1588)).

126 Prosser and Keeton, *supra* note 112, § 128, at 967.

127 *See, e.g.*, Kirsch v. Barnes, 153 F. Supp. 260 (N.D. Cal. 1957).

128 Prosser and Keeton, *supra* note 112, § 128, at 967.

129 *Id.*, § 128, at 967-68. Reference should be made to the richly developed body of law on the fact/opinion distinction in defamation cases. *See* Chapter 6, *supra*.

[b] Injury to Pecuniary Interests

The gravamen of the tort is injury to interests of pecuniary value, such as interests in property, products, or business.[130]

[c] Publication

As with defamation, injurious falsehood requires publication to a third person.[131]

[d] Special Harm

In keeping with the commercial nature of the interests protected, special harm in the form of actual pecuniary loss is essential to the cause of action.[132]

[e] Intent, Malice, or Fault

There appears to be a consensus that injurious falsehood is not a strict liability tort.[133] Unfortunately, there is very little consensus as to what sort of intent, malice, or fault is required to support the tort. Decisions frequently require "malice,"[134] but it is not completely clear what is meant by the term.[135] Three types of "malice" appear to dominate modern formulations of the tort:

(1) intent to cause harm;
(2) recklessness; and
(3) spite or ill will.[136]

---

130 *See* Jetco Electronic Indus. v. Gardiner, 325 F. Supp. 80 (S.D. Tex. 1971); Chrysler Credit Corp. v. Ostly, 42 Cal. App. 3d 663, 117 Cal. Rptr. 167 (1974); Continental Development Corp. v. Duval Title & Abstract Co., 356 So. 2d 925 (Fla. App. 1978); Horning v. Hardy, 36 Md. App. 419, 373 A.2d 1273 (1977); Mink Hollow Development Corp. v. State, 87 Misc. 2d 61, 384 N.Y.S.2d 373 (1976); Restatement (Second) of Torts § 623A (1977).

131 *See, e.g.,* Womack v. McDonald, 219 Ala. 75, 121 So. 57 (1929); Arnold v. Producer's Oil Co., 196 S.W. 735 (Tex. Civ. App. 1917).

132 Restatement (Second) of Torts § 623A (1977).

133 *See generally* Prosser, *Injurious Falsehood: The Basis of Liability,* 59 Colum. L. Rev. 425 (1959).

134 *See, e.g.,* Systems Operations, Inc. v. Scientific Games Development Corp., 555 F.2d 1131 (3d Cir. 1977); Gehrke v. Janowitz, 55 Mich. App. 643, 223 N.W.2d 107 (1974).

135 Prosser and Keeton, *supra* note 112, § 128, at 968-69.

136 *See id.,* § 128, at 969-70.

[3] Privileges

[a] Common Law Privileges

[i] Product and Business Comparisons

It is well established that in the interest of robust economic competition there is a conditional common law privilege to compare a competitor's product or business unfavorably with one's own.[137] The publisher must honestly believe in his statement,[138] but the belief need not be a reasonable one.[139]

[ii] Applicability of Defamation Privileges

All absolute and conditional privileges that apply to defamation actions are transferable to actions for injurious falsehood.[140]

[b] Constitutional Privileges

[i] Pre-*Dun & Bradstreet* Trends

Prior to 1985, there appeared to be a growing recognition that the constitutional principles emanating from *New York Times* and *Gertz* ought to apply, at least to some degree, to injurious falsehood cases. The *Restatement (Second),* for example, took the position that although it was impossible to predict the extent to which first amendment principles developed in defamation cases would be transferred to the injurious falsehood tort, some importation of constitutional protections seemed likely.[141]

[ii] The Impact of *Dun & Bradstreet*

As discussed at length in Chapter 3,[142] the Supreme Court in *Dun & Bradstreet, Inc. v. Greenmoss Builders, Inc.,*[143] substantially degraded the level of first amendment protection covering defamatory speech involving an erroneous credit report. Commercial speech, the Supreme Court held, did not deserve the enhanced protection from defamation liability emanating from the *New York Times* and *Gertz* line of cases.

---

137 *See, e.g.,* Frankfort Oil Co. v. Snakard, 279 F.2d 436 (10th Cir.), *cert. denied,* 364 U.S. 920 (1960); Leslie v. Western Steel Co., 202 F. Supp. 27 (S.D. Tex. 1962); Restatement (Second) of Torts § 647 (1977).

138 *See, e.g.,* Rogers Carl Corp. v. Moran, 103 N.J. Super. 163, 246 A.2d 750 (1968).

139 *See, e.g.,* Williams v. Phillips Petroleum Co., 453 F. Supp. 967 (S.D. Ala. 1978).

140 Restatement (Second) of Torts §§ 635, 646A (1977).

141 *Id.,* § 623A comment c.

142 *See supra* §§ 3.02-3.05.

143 472 U.S. 749, 105 S. Ct. 2939 (1985).

Although it is still too early to assess the full impact of *Dun & Bradstreet*, that case would seem to pave the way for a general relaxation of first amendment restrictions on injurious falsehood actions, since such actions tend by definition to involve the sort of commercial speech elements at issue in *Dun & Bradstreet.* As a practical matter, therefore, common law doctrines may bear most of the weight of defenses to such actions in the future.

[4] Relationship Between Defamation and Injurious Falsehood

Injurious falsehood and defamation are similar in many respects.[144] The overlap between the two torts means that the same speech may in appropriate circumstances give rise to both causes of action. In such instances, however, only one recovery is permitted; damages may not be duplicated.[145]

The two torts do have different origins, elements, and missions, however. Defamation actions exist to redress individual interests in reputation, whereas injurious falsehood has always been a commercial and business oriented tort designed to protect economic interests.[146]

[5] Remedies

[a] Damages for Pecuniary Loss

Damages for injurious falsehood are by the very defining elements of the tort limited to pecuniary losses. Traditionally these losses must be established with substantial specificity, such as a demonstrable loss of sales, customers, or contracts.[147]

[b] Punitive Damages

Once special damages are established, punitive damages are also permitted if the requisite level of malice is established.[148]

---

144 *See generally* El Meson Espanol v. NYM Corp., 521 F.2d 737 (2d Cir. 1975); Midwest Glass Co. v. Stanford Development Co., 34 Ill. App. 3d 130, 339 N.E.2d 274 (1975).

145 Restatement (Second) of Torts § 623A comment g (1977).

146 *Id.*

147 Prosser and Keeton, *supra* note 112, § 128, at 970-73.

148 *See, e.g.*, Diapulse Corp. of America v. Birtcher Corp., 362 F.2d 736 (2d Cir. 1966).

[c] Availability of Injunctive Relief

In contrast to their rulings on the law of defamation, which have followed the axiom that "equity will not enjoin a libel,"[149] courts are far more willing to grant injunctive relief in injurious falsehood cases.[150] However, "[e]ven commercial disparagement may carry with it important political or social comment of the sort especially important to free speech interests."[151] Injuries to commercial interests may in fact be easily quantifiable, creating an adequate remedy at law and obviating the need for equitable relief. Although injunctive relief is not absolutely barred, therefore, it remains the exception and not the rule in injurious falsehood cases.[152]

§ 11.03 Negligent Publication

[1] Overview

One of the more significant recent developments in media practice has been the emergence of suits brought for physical injuries allegedly traceable to the content of published material. The lyrics of a rock song may be alleged to induce teenagers to act in self-destructive ways, the recipe in a cookbook may explode when the directions are followed, or an advertisement in a magazine may involve the solicitation of criminal activity. Plaintiffs in these situations do not sue for libel or invasion of privacy or infliction of emotional distress, but for the physical consequences of the speech. They attempt to treat their injuries as essentially indistinguishable from any routine negligence or products liability case.

Even within the contours of traditional tort theory, these suits pose difficult problems of proximate cause, foreseeability, and intervening and superceding cause. The issues become even more difficult when first amendment considerations are factored in.

---

149 *See supra* § 9.12[1][a].

150 *See generally* D. Dobbs, Handbook on the Law of Remedies § 6.7, at 507-08, § 6.8, at 524. *See also* discussion and authorities in § 9.01[1][d], *supra.*

151 Dobbs, *supra* note 150, § 6.07, at 506. *But see* Dun & Bradstreet, Inc. v. Greenmoss Builders, Inc., 105 S. Ct. 2939 (1985).

152 *See, e.g.,* Girl Scouts of America v. Personality Posters Mfg., 304 F. Supp. 1228 (S.D.N.Y. 1969); Krebiozen Research Foundation v. Beacon Press, 334 Mass. 86, 134 N.E.2d 1, *cert. denied,* 352 U.S. 848 (1956); Dobbs, *supra* note 150, § 6.7, at 506; Prosser and Keeton, *supra* note 112, § 128, at 976-77.

[2] Faulty Instructions and Misinformation

A number of courts have applied theories of strict liability in cases involving faulty information on published maps or navigational charts.[153] The underlying theory of these cases is that nautical charts or airline charts are instruments of navigation essentially indistinguishable from a compass or radar equipment. Even though the map or chart conveys information and is, in one sense, "speech," these cases have been treated as products liability actions in which the manufacturer is held liable just as if it had defectively manufactured any other type of product. No first amendment concerns have been superimposed on the analysis in such cases, for they seem to be near-cousins to the kinds of routine products liability cases that are predicated on defective warnings or instructions accompanying a product—cases that also technically involve "speech."

Attempts have also been made to apply this type of tort theory to the content of books, magazines, newspapers, and other publications that are not *intrinsically* instruments for performing physical activities, in the way that a navigational chart or the instructions that are appended to a product are inextricably intertwined with physical activity. In these sorts of cases, courts have recognized that first amendment concerns do exist, and they have engrafted fault or causation rules upon these causes of action designed to protect first amendment values.

In *Jones v. J.B. Lippincott Co.*[154] a nursing student consulted a medical textbook, and pursuant to instructions in the book, gave herself a hydrogen peroxide enema for constipation that caused her personal injury. She sued the author for negligence and the publisher under theories of negligence and strict liability. The court had before it the motion for summary judgment of the publisher. The court held that the publisher had not been involved in the content of the section in the textbook that gave rise to the injury, had no duty of care to the plaintiff, and had not made any warranty as to the book's contents. Specifically addressing the claim of strict liability, the court held that to extend strict products liability rules to the content of books or other published material "could chill expression and publication which is inconsistent with fundamental free speech principles."[155]

---

[153] *See* Brocklesby v. United States, 767 F.2d 1288 (9th Cir. 1985); Saloomey v. Jeppesen & Co., 707 F.2d 671 (2d Cir. 1983).

[154] 15 Med. L. Rep. (BNA) 2155 (D. Md. 1988).

[155] 15 Med. L. Rep. (BNA) at 2156, *citing* Gertz v. Robert Welch, Inc., 418 U.S. 323 (1974).

In *Libertelli v. Hoffman-LaRoche, Inc.*[156] the court refused to permit liability in a case in which the plaintiff alleged that she had become addicted to valium because the defendant's book, *Physician's Desk Reference,* had negligently omitted certain information concerning the drug. The court held that "the applicable First Amendment standard for imposing liability on publishers for erroneous informational articles is substantively indistinguishable from the tort standard for false advertising," and that a " 'newspaper is only liable if it publishes a false advertisement maliciously or with intent to harm another or acts with total reckless abandon.' "[157]

This stringent standard was recently applied to allegedly faulty financial information published by Standard & Poor's. In *First Equity Corporation of Florida v. Standard & Poor's Corp.*[158] the court imposed the actual malice standard upon a claim brought by a Florida broker and investment advisor for allegedly erroneous information published by Standard & Poor's concerning convertible bonds of Pan American Airways. The court granted summary judgment for the defendants because the plaintiffs were unable to demonstrate a triable issue of fact on Standard & Poor's knowledge of falsity or reckless disregard for truth or falsity. While the court took note of the parallels between the actual malice standard it was imposing upon the defendants and the first amendment actual malice standard, the court treated its invocation of the actual malice requirement as a rule of tort law, not constitutional law.

In *Keenum v. Remmington Arms Co.*[159] the plaintiff alleged that he was injured in a rifle accident caused by the modifications he made in a rifle, following the directions in an article published in the magazine *Guns & Ammo.* The plaintiff sued the gun manufacturer, the magazine publisher, and the author of the magazine, under theories of product liability, negligence, and breach of warranty. Summary judgment was granted for all defendants because the plaintiff had not produced any evidence of a causal connection between the modifications and his accident.

---

[156] 7 Med. L. Rep. (BNA) 1734 (S.D.N.Y. 1981).

[157] *Id.* at 1736, *citing* New York Times Co. v. Sullivan, 376 U.S. 254 (1964).

[158] 869 F.2d 174 (2d Cir. 1989), *affirming* 690 F. Supp. 256 (S.D.N.Y. 1988).

[159] 15 Med. L. Rep. (BNA) 1447 (W.D. Okla. 1988).

[3] Inducement of Self-Destructive Behavior

Plaintiffs have recently commenced wrongful death and personal injury actions against rock musicians and record companies for suicides and injuries allegedly caused by the lyrics of rock songs. In *Judas Priest v. Nevada District Court,*[160] for example, the Nevada Supreme Court upheld the assertion of long-arm jurisdiction in Nevada against the rock musicians in Judas Priest, a British rock group. The plaintiffs asserted recovery for the wrongful death of one youth and the gunshot wounds of a second youth, who allegedly engaged in their self-destructive actions as a result of the lyrics on a Judas Priest album entitled "Stained Glass."

A similar cause of action, brought against rock musician Ozzy Osbourne and his record company, was held barred by the first amendment in *McCollum v. CBS, Inc.*[161] The court held that an accusation that lyrics in Osbourne's songs caused a nineteen-year-old boy to shoot and kill himself had to be tested against the first amendment test for incitement to violence established in such Supreme Court decisions as *Brandenburg v. Ohio*[162] and *Hess v. Indiana.*[163] Under that test liability can be imposed only when the speech is directed to inciting imminent lawless action and is likely to incite or produce such action.[164] The court in *McCollum* held that plaintiff's had not demonstrated that Osbourne's music was *directed and intended* toward the goal of bringing about the imminent suicide of his listener's, nor that it was *likely* to produce that result.

There is no question that *McCollum* was correctly decided. One of the most powerful themes in modern first amendment jurisprudence—a theme emanating forcefully from cases such as *Brandenburg* and *Hess*—is that the causal nexus between speech and violence must be extremely tight and compellingly obvious before liability for the speech may be imposed. It is never enough to show that speech in some vague way contributes to an atmosphere of violence, or has some general tendency to promote lawless action. Particularly when the speech is artistic expression, attempts to impose liability under the *Brandenburg* test should be doomed to failure, virtually without exception.

---

160 760 P.2d 137 (Nev. 1988).

161 202 Cal. App. 3d 989, 249 Cal. Rptr. 187 (1988).

162 395 U.S. 444 (1969).

163 414 U.S. 105 (1973).

164 Brandenburg v. Ohio, 395 U.S. 444, 447 (1969).

[4] Liability for Publication of Criminal Solicitations

In *Eimann v. Soldier of Fortune Magazine, Inc.*[165] the magazine *Soldier of Fortune,* a publication focusing on mercenary activities and military affairs, was sued for having published a classified advertisement for personal services that led to the hiring of an assassin by a husband to shoot and kill his wife. The incident involved a man named John Wayne Hearn, who was hired by Robert Black to shoot and kill his wife Sandra, for $10,000. Black located Hearn through an advertisement that ran in the classified advertisements of *Soldier of Fortune,* which read:

> EX-MARINES—67-69 'Nam Vets, Ex-DI, weapons specialist—jungle warfare, pilot, M.E., high risk assignments, U.S. or overseas. (404) 991-2684.

Through the advertisement, Hearn and Black eventually contracted for the murder of Sandra Black, and Hearn shot and killed Sandra.

Sandra Black's son and mother brought a wrongful death suit against *Soldier of Fortune* and won a jury verdict against the magazine of $9.4 million. The United States Court of Appeals for the Fifth Circuit reversed the award. The defendants and *amici curiae* had urged the court of appeals to apply first amendment standards in its review, but the court determined that it did not need to do so, instead resolving the case under Texas tort law. The court did, however, utilize the limited first amendment protection applied to commercial speech in assessing the appropriate balance of risk and utility required for it to render a decision under Texas tort principles.[166]

The court of appeals held that the magazine did owe a duty of care to the general public, but that the contours of that duty were shaped through risk-benefit analysis. Applying the famous algebraic formula of Judge Learned Hand, the court held that liability turns "on whether the burden of adequate precautions, B, is less than the probability of harm, P, multiplied by the gravity of the resulting injury, L."[167] In judg-

---

165 16 Med. L. Rep. (BNA) 2148 (5th Cir. 1989).

166 *Id.* at 2153. ("While we do not reach SOF's first amendment arguments, the Supreme Court's recognition of limited first amendment protection for commercial speech nonetheless highlights the important role of such communication for purposes of risk-benefit analysis.")

167 *Id.* at 2152, *citing* United States v. Carroll Towing, 159 F.2d 169, 173 (2d Cir. 1947) (Hand, J.).

ing whether, in the *Soldier of Fortune* case, "B is less than PL,"[168] the court noted that the gravity of harm was very serious—murder for hire—but the risk level was relatively remote. The court was heavily influenced by the fact that the advertisement was facially innocuous, using such terms as "weapons specialist" and "high risk assignments." Despite the efforts of the plaintiffs to bolster their case on foreseeability by introducing evidence concerning the "context" of the advertisement, such as the nature of the stories the magazine published, and other classified advertisements that offered such services as "Mercenary for Hire," "bounty hunter," and "mechanic," the court found the risk of serious harm too small to constitute a breach of duty by the magazine.

---

[168] *Id.*

PART III

Litigation, Counseling, and Strategy

CHAPTER 12

Litigation

§ 12.01 Subject Matter Jurisdiction

[1] Definition

[a] In General

In choosing the proper forum in which to litigate a defamation or privacy action a court competent to hear such types of cases must be chosen. Jurisdictional rules relating to the type of lawsuit a court may adjudicate define a court's "subject matter" jurisdiction.[1]

[b] State Courts

In state court systems the subject matter limitations on jurisdiction are relatively few, and generally involve only minimum and maximum

[1] *See* F. James & G. Hazard, Civil Procedure § 12.2, at 604-05 (2d ed. 1977).

amounts in controversy, or provisions for specialized courts for such matters as probate or domestic relations disputes. Most state court systems have trial courts of relatively comprehensive jurisdiction at the county or municipal level, usually referred to as state courts of "general" subject matter jurisdiction, which are competent to entertain any tort action other than small claims. Suits for defamation and invasion of privacy in state court are typically brought in these "workhorse" courts of the state judicial system.

[2] Federal Court Limitations

All federal courts are courts of "limited jurisdiction,"[2] empowered to adjudicate only two types of subject matter:

(1) Cases "arising under" the Constitution, treaties, and laws of the United States;[3] and

(2) Cases "between Citizens of different states . . . and between a State, or the Citizens thereof, and foreign States, Citizens or Subjects."[4]

[3] Federal Court Subject Matter Jurisdiction over Defamation and Privacy Cases

[a] In General

[i] Normally No Federal Question

Defamation and invasion of privacy actions are creatures of state tort law. They normally do not "arise under" federal law, and confer no "federal question" subject matter jurisdiction on federal courts.

Although defendants frequently rely on the first amendment as a *defense* in defamation and privacy cases, it is axiomatic that it does not suffice for federal question jurisdiction that the answer raises a federal question as a defense.[5]

---

[2] *See generally* C. Wright, Law of Federal Courts § 7, at 22 (4th ed. 1983).

[3] U.S. Const. art. III, § 2, cl.1.

[4] *Id.*

[5] The classic case is Louisville & N.R. Co. v. Mottley, 219 U.S. 467 (1911).

[ii] Diversity of Citizenship—Nonmedia Cases

To obtain subject matter jurisdiction in federal court over a defamation or invasion of privacy action, diversity of citizenship is normally required.[6] Since many acts of defamation or invasion of privacy involving private nonmedia defendants will concern citizens of the same state, diversity frequently will not exist in nonmedia cases.

[iii] Diversity of Citizenship—Media Cases

Media defendants are almost always corporate defendants. A corporation is deemed a citizen of any state in which it has been incorporated and the state in which it has its principal place of business.[7] Since media outlets, particularly those of a national nature, often are incorporated and have their principal place of business in states other than the plaintiff's state, diversity in media cases is more common.

[iv] The Rule of Complete Diversity

Complete diversity between the real parties in interest is required.[8] Suppose a citizen of Kansas is allegedly defamed by a newspaper incorporated in Delaware and having its principal place of business in Missouri. The reporter who authored the story is also a citizen of Kansas. If the plaintiff chose to sue only the newspaper, complete diversity would exist, since the plaintiff, a citizen of Kansas, would be suing a paper deemed a citizen of Delaware and Missouri. Should the reporter also be joined as a defendant, however, complete diversity would not exist, since both the plaintiff and one of the defendants would be Kansas

---

[6] The only exception to this rule would involve the rare situation in which the action is brought under the rubric of a deprivation of civil rights, creating federal question jurisdiction. Some invasions of privacy by state or federal officials, for example, clearly "arise under" the Constitution. *See, e.g.*, Bivens v. Six Unknown Named Agents, 403 U.S. 388 (1971). These sorts of suits are essentially civil rights actions, however, and are distinct from the conventional private tort actions that form the subject matter of this book. In Paul v. Davis, 424 U.S. 693 (1976), the Supreme Court held that a reputational invasion by a state official did not give rise to an action for deprivation of life, liberty, or property under the due process clause. *See generally* Smolla, *The Displacement of Federal Due Process Claims by State Tort Remedies:* Paratt v. Taylor *and* Logan v. Zimmerman Brush Company, 1982 U. Ill. L. Rev. 831. As a practical matter, therefore, the sorts of tort law defamation and privacy actions that fall within the coverage of this book do not involve federal question jurisdiction. *See* May v. Michigan, 10 Med. L. Rep. (BNA) 2454 (E.D. Mich 1984).

[7] 28 U.S.C.A. § 1332(c) (1958). Although the usual basis for diversity involves citizens of different states, diversity may also exist between citizens of a state and a foreign country. Such was the basis of federal jurisdiction, for example, in Israeli Minister Ariel Sharon's suit against *Time*. Sharon v. Time, Inc., 599 F. Supp. 538 (S.D.N.Y. 1984).

[8] Strawbridge v. Curtiss, 7 U.S. (3 Cranch) 267 (1806).

citizens, and the action could not be maintained in federal court.[9]

[b] Attempts to Manufacture Diversity

Parties may never confer subject matter jurisdiction on federal courts, such as by consent or waiver,[10] or by "manufacturing" diversity of citizenship.[11]

§ 12.02 *In Personam* Jurisdiction

[1] Definition

In personam jurisdiction (or "personal jurisdiction," or "jurisdiction over the person") does not refer to the content or subject matter of the suit but rather to the territorial limitations on the court's power to exercise jurisdiction over the person of the defendant and issue a binding judgment against him.[12]

[2] Lack of Jurisdiction

Unlike subject matter jurisdiction,[13] defects in a court's *in personam* jurisdiction may be waived, and the failure to raise an objection by timely motion or pleading as appropriate under the rules of the jurisdiction will be deemed a waiver.[14]

[3] Due Process Limitations

[a] The Minimum Contacts Requirement

[i] Physical Presence

In the nineteenth century the jurisdiction of state courts was conceptualized in terms of physical power tied to territorial boundaries. Under the due process clause states could exercise jurisdiction over persons and property physically present within the territorial boundaries of the

---

[9] *See* Wright, *supra* note 2, § 24, at 140-41.

[10] *See* Sonsa v. Iowa, 419 U.S. 393, 398 (1975); Reale International, Inc. v. Republic of Nigeria, 647 F.2d 330, 331-32 (2d Cir. 1981).

[11] Kramer v. Caribbean Mills, Inc., 394 U.S. 823 (1969); McSparran v. West, 402 F.2d 867 (3d Cir. 1968), *cert. denied*, 395 U.S. 903 (1969).

[12] Wright, *supra* note 2, § 64, at 416-19.

[13] *See supra* note 10.

[14] *See generally* Wright, *supra* note 2, § 66, at 434-35.

state, but not over defendants outside the state's borders.[15] Physical presence is still a sufficient basis for the exercise of jurisdiction over a defendant, but, since 1945, it is no longer required.

[ii] *International Shoe* and Its Progeny

In the landmark decision *International Shoe Company v. Washington,*[16] the Supreme Court discarded physical presence as the touchstone for analysis of due process limitations on *in personam* jurisdiction, in favor of a more flexible "minimum contacts" test. Under *International Shoe* a state may exercise jurisdiction over a nonresident defendant if the defendant has had such "minimum contacts" with the forum state "that the maintenance of the suit does not offend 'traditional notions of fair play and substantial justice.' "[17]

In the years since *International Shoe* the minimum contacts standard has been gradually refined. In judging whether sufficient minimum contacts exist, the focus is on "the relationship among the defendant, the forum, and the litigation."[18] The inquiry is into the quality and nature of the defendant's contacts;[19] the test is not "mechanical or quantitative."[20] In an important elaboration on *International Shoe,* the Court in *Hanson v. Denckla*[21] held that there must "be some act by which the defendant purposefully avails itself of the privilege of conducting activities within the forum State, thus invoking the benefits and protections of its laws."[22]

[iii] The *World-Wide Volkswagen* Formulation

The Supreme Court's most detailed explication of the minimum contacts standard came in 1980 in *World-Wide Volkswagen Corp. v.*

---

[15] *See* Pennoyer v. Neff, 95 U.S. 714, 722 (1878).

[16] 326 U.S. 310 (1945).

[17] *Id.* at 316 (quoting Milliken v. Meyer, 311 U.S. 457, 463 (1940)).

[18] Shaffer v. Heitner, 433 U.S. 186, 204 (1977). *See also* Calder v. Jones, 104 S. Ct. 1482, 1486 (1984); Rush v. Savchuk, 444 U.S. 320, 332 (1980).

[19] Mississippi Interstate Express, Inc. v. Transpo, Inc., 681 F.2d 1003, 1006 (5th Cir. 1982).

[20] International Shoe Co. v. Washington, 326 U.S. 310 319 (1945); Olsen v. Government of Mexico, 729 F.2d 641, 649 (9th Cir. 1984). In McGee v. International Life Insurance Co., 355 U.S. 220 (1957), the Court upheld an assertion of jurisdiction by California against a Texas insurance company in a case concerning a life insurance policy on a California resident, though the company had no agents or offices in California and, but for the policy in suit, had not solicited or conducted business in California.

[21] 357 U.S. 235 (1958).

[22] *Id.* at 253 (citing International Shoe Co. v. Washington, 326 U.S. 310, 319 (1945)).

Woodson.[23] The owners of a car purchased in New York brought suit against the dealer and wholesaler of the car in Oklahoma, in a case arising from an accident within Oklahoma. The Supreme Court held that Oklahoma courts could not exercise *in personam* jurisdiction over the defendants. The Court noted that the minimun contacts requirement serves twin functions: protecting defendants from the burdens of litigation in a distant and inconvenient forum and insuring that states "do not reach out beyond the limits imposed on them by their status as coequal sovereigns in a federal system."[24] The Court listed six factors relevant to the minimun contacts inquiry:

(1) the burden on the defendant;
(2) the interests of the forum state in the lawsuit;
(3) the interests of the plaintiff;
(4) the interests of the interstate judicial system in efficiency;
(5) the interests of the various states in advancing fundamental social policies; and
(6) the foreseeability from the defendant's perspective that a suit might appropriately be brought in the forum state.[25]

[b] Relevance of the First Amendment

[i] The Pre-1984 Split of Authority

Prior to 1984, courts were split as to whether first amendment considerations were relevant to jurisdictional analysis. A number of decisions took the position that the potential chill on free expression posed by the possibility of suit in distant forums where only a relatively small number of copies of a publication were circulated required a stronger showing of "minimum contacts" against media defendants.[26] Other

---

23 444 U.S. 286 (1980).

24 *Id.* at 291-92.

25 *Id.* at 292-97. The Court, in discussing the foreseeability element, stated that "the foreseeability that is critical to due process analysis is not the mere likelihood that a product will find its way into the forum state. Rather, it is that the defendant's conduct and connection with the forum state are such that he should reasonably anticipate being haled into court there." *Id.* at 297.

26 *See, e.g.,* Cox Enterprises v. Holt, 678 F.2d 936 (11th Cir.), *rehearing granted,* 691 F.2d 989 (11th Cir. 1982); Edwards v. Associated Press, 512 F.2d 258, 268 n.39 (5th Cir. 1975); Talcott v. Midnight Publishing Corp., 427 F.2d 1277 (5th Cir. 1970); New York Times Co. v. Connor, 365 F.2d 567, 572 (5th Cir. 1966); McCabe v. Kevin Jenkins & Assocs., 531 F. Supp. 648 (E.D. Pa. 1982); Margoles v. Johns, 333 F. Supp. 942 (D.D.C. 1971), *aff'd,* 483 F.2d 1212 (D.C. Cir. 1973). Some decisions held that first amendment considerations should at least influence transfer or change of venue motions. *See* Buckley

decisions took an opposite view, holding that the first amendment was irrelevant to the minimum contacts assessment.[27]

[ii] The Supreme Court's Resolution in *Calder v. Jones* and *Keeton v. Hustler Magazine, Inc.*

In 1984, the Supreme Court resolved the lower court split by holding that first amendment considerations should not play a role in minimum contacts analysis.[28] In *Calder v. Jones*,[29] actress Shirley Jones, a California resident, brought suit for libel, invasion of privacy, and intentional infliction of emotional distress against the *National Enquirer*, its local distributing company, Ian Calder, its president and editor, and John South, the writer of the allegedly offensive article. The suit was filed in a California court. The *Enquirer's* circulation in California is over 600,000 and neither it nor its distributing company objected to jurisdiction in California. The editor and president, Calder, was a Florida resident who had been to California only twice in his life, once on a pleasure trip and once as a witness in an unrelated trial. Calder had reviewed, edited, and approved the article. The reporter South, a Florida resident, had written most of the story from Florida, relying on telephone calls to contacts in California. South frequently traveled to California on business.[30]

The Supreme Court rejected "the suggestion that First Amendment concerns enter into the jurisdictional analysis,"[31] taking the position that the "infusion of such considerations would needlessly complicate an already imprecise inquiry."[32] Whatever chill to protected first amendment activity is presented by defamation actions is already taken into account, the Court held, in the substantive rules set forth in *New*

---

v. New York Post Corp., 373 F.2d 175 (2d Cir. 1967); Cordell v. Detective Publications, Inc., 307 F. Supp. 1212 (E.D. Tenn. 1968), *aff'd*, 419 F.2d 989 (6th Cir. 1969).

[27] *See* Church of Scientology v. Adams, 584 F.2d 893, 899 (9th Cir. 1978); Anselmi v. Denver Post, Inc., 552 F.2d 316 (10th Cir.), *cert. denied sub. nom.* Times Mirror Co. v. Anselmi, 432 U.S. 911 (1977); David v. National Lampoon, Inc., 432 F. Supp. 1097 (D.S.C. 1977); Roy v. North American Newspaper Alliance, Inc., 106 N.H. 92, 205 A.2d 844 (1964). The issue generated, if nothing else, one of the better law review titles in the area. *See* Comment, *Long Arm Jurisdiction Over Publishers: To Chill a Mocking Word*, 67 Colum. L. Rev. 342 (1967).

[28] *See generally* Note, *Personal Jurisdiction Over Publishers In Defamation Actions: A Current Assessment*, 30 Vill. L. Rev. 193 (1985).

[29] 104 S. Ct. 1482 (1984).

[30] *Id.* at 1485.

[31] *Id.* at 1487.

[32] *Id.* (citing Estin v. Estin, 334 U.S. 541 (1948)).

York Times and *Gertz*.[33] "To reintroduce those concerns at the jurisdictional stage would be a form of double counting."[34] The Court unanimously upheld the assertion of jurisdiction in California.[35]

Similarly, in *Keeton v. Hustler Magazine, Inc.*,[36] the Court unanimously held that jurisdiction in a libel action could be sustained in New Hampshire, in a suit brought by Kathy Keeton, a New York resident, against *Hustler* magazine, an Ohio corporation with its principal place of business in California. New Hampshire, with its unusual six year statute of limitations for libel, was the only state in which the limitations period on Keeton's action had not run. Less than one percent of *Hustler*'s circulation was in New Hampshire, with a monthly circulation in the state estimated at somewhere between 10,000 to 15,000 copies.[37] Once again the Court refused to let first amendment considerations influence the jurisdictional issue, stating that "we reject categorically the suggestion that invisible radiations from the First Amendment may defeat jurisdiction otherwise proper under the Due Process Clause."[38]

[c] Factors that Influence *In Personam* Jurisdiction Determinations

[i] Circulation Level

Prior to *Keeton* and *Calder* there was substantial authority for the proposition that relatively small levels of circulation within a state are normally insufficient minimum contacts to support jurisdiction.[39]

Keeton and *Calder* cast doubt on the continued vitality of many of these holdings, by essentially equating sales of published materials to sales of any other manufactured product. Certainly, *Keeton* stands for

---

33 104 S. Ct. at 488 (citing New York Times Co. v. Sullivan, 376 U.S. 254 (1964); Gertz v. Robert Welch, Inc., 418 U.S. 323 (1974)).

34 104 S. Ct. at 1488.

35 The factors assessed by the Court in sustaining jurisdiction are discussed in § 12.02[3][c], *supra*.

36 104 S. Ct. 1473 (1984).

37 *Id.* at 1477.

38 *Id.* at 1481 n.12.

39 *See, e.g.*, Church of Scientology v. Adams, 584 F.2d 893 (9th Cir. 1978); Buckley v. New York Times Co., 338 F.2d 470, 474 (5th Cir. 1964); Walker v. Field Enterprises, Inc., 332 F.2d 632 (10th Cir. 1964); Tate v. New York Post Corp., 11 Med. L. Rep. (BNA) 1151 (E.D. Tenn. 1984); Kersh v. Angelosante, 8 Med. L. Rep. (BNA) 1282 (N.D. Tex. 1982); Gonzalez v. Atlanta Constitution, 4 Med. L. Rep. (BNA) 2146 (N.D. Ill. 1979); McBride v. Owens, 454 F. Supp. 731 (S.D. Tex. 1978); Sipple v. Des Moines Register & Tribune Co., 82 Cal. App. 3d 143, 147 Cal. Rptr. 59 (1978).

the proposition that to defeat *in personam* jurisdiction it is not enough that only a miniscule portion of the defendant's magazine sales took place in the forum state.

Applying *Keeton*, one district court has held that the sale of 275 copies of a magazine in the Virgin Islands, though this figure was miniscule in comparison to total circulation, was, given the limited population of the forum jurisdiction, sufficient to support jurisdiction.[40] The Eleventh Circuit, in interpreting *Keeton* and *Calder*, similarly sustained jurisdiction in Alabama over a Washington-based weekly newspaper with 2 percent of its circulation in Alabama, where Alabama was a "significant market" for the defendant.[41]

[ii] Nexus Between the Story and the Forum State

Under *World-Wide Volkswagen*,[42] the forum state's interest in the subject matter of the litigation is a factor to be considered in weighing minimum contacts. When the allegedly defamatory publication involves significant events within the forum state,[43] or is purposefully aimed or targeted at an audience[44] within the forum state, jurisdiction is more likely to be sustained.[45] This factor was expressly emphasized in *Calder v. Jones*;[46] the court noted that the editor and publisher "knew that the brunt of that inquiry would be felt by respondent in the State in which she lives and works and in which the *National Enquirer* has its largest circulation."[47]

[iii] Plaintiff's Residence and Contacts in Forum

Keeton squarely holds that the plaintiff's lack of residence or significant contacts in the forum state does not preclude the assertion of

---

40 Samad v. High Society Magazine, 10 Med. L. Rep. (BNA) 1930 (D.V.I. 1984).

41 Army Times Publishing Co. v. Watts, 730 F.2d 1398 (11th Cir. 1984). *See also* Akbar v. New York Magazine Co., 490 F. Supp. 60 (D.D.C. 1980).

42 World-Wide Volkswagen Corp. v. Woodson, 444 U.S. 286, 292 (1980). *See supra* § 12.02[3][a][iii].

43 *See* Keeton v. Hustler Magazine, Inc., 104 S. Ct. 1473, 1481 (1984)(forum "may be the focus of the activities of the defendant out of which the suit arises"); Anselmi v. Denver Post, Inc., 552 F.2d 316 (10th Cir.), *cert. denied sub nom.* Times Mirror Co. v. Anselmi, 432 U.S. 911 (1977).

44 *See* Edwards v. Associated Press, 512 F.2d 258 (5th Cir. 1975); Casano v. WDSU-TV, Inc., 313 F. Supp. 1130, 1142-43 (S.D. Miss 1970), *aff'd*, 464 F.2d 3 (5th Cir. 1972).

45 When the events in the offending publication bear no relation to the forum state, on the other hand, that is a factor to be weighed against jurisdiction. *See* Church of Scientology v. Adams, 584 F.2d 893, 898 (9th Cir. 1978).

46 104 S. Ct. 1482 (1984).

47 *Id.* at 1487.

jurisdiction.[48] At the same time, however, *Keeton* acknowledged that "[t]he plaintiff's residence is not, of course, completely irrelevant to the jurisdictional inquiry."[49] The "[p]laintiff's residence may well play an important role in determining the propriety of entertaining a suit against the defendant in the forum."[50] Given that the plaintiff in *Keeton* had virtually no relationship with the forum state, however, and was quite transparently shopping in the only forum in which the statute of limitations had not expired, it appears that the plaintiff's residence is a one way street in judging minimum contacts: "[P]laintiff's residence in the forum may . . . *enhance* defendant's contacts with the forum,"[51] but it is "not a separate requirement, and lack of residence will not defeat jurisdiction established on the basis of defendant's contacts."[52]

[iv] News Gathering

News gathering may be a factor in weighing whether minimun contacts exist,[53] but it is generally held that mere sporadic or isolated news gathering efforts in a state will not without more be sufficient to sustain jurisdiction.[54]

[v] Advertising and Solicitation Efforts

Prior to *Keeton* and *Calder,* decisions appeared to discount advertising and solicitation of advertising efforts within the forum as significant factors favoring the exercise of jurisdiction.[55]

The overall tenor of the *Calder* and *Keeton* decisions, however, is to equate analysis of long arm jurisdiction over media defendants with that of any other business enterprise. The deliberate exploitation of a market is generally an important factor in minimum contacts analysis[56] and it would appear likely that advertising and solicitation efforts

---

48 104 S. Ct. at 1479-81.

49 *Id.* at 1481.

50 *Id.*

51 *Id.* (emphasis added).

52 *Id.*

53 *See* McGuire v. Brightman, 79 Cal. App. 3d 776, 145 Cal. Rptr. 256 (1978).

54 *See* New York Times Co. v. Connor, 365 F.2d 567 (5th Cir. 1966); Buckley v. New York Times Co., 338 F.2d 470, 474 (5th Cir. 1964); Akbar v. New York Magazine Co., 490 F. Supp. 60 (D.D.C. 1980); Margoles v. Johns, 333 F. Supp. 942 (D.D.C. 1971), *aff'd,* 483 F.2d 1212 (D.C. Cir. 1973).

55 *See* Church of Scientology v. Adams, 584 F.2d 893 (9th Cir. 1978); Buckley v. New York Times Co., 338 F.2d 470 (5th Cir. 1964); Riverhouse Publishing Co. v. Porter, 278 F. Supp. 1, 8 (D.R.I. 1968); Sipple v. Des Moines Register & Tribune Co., 82 Cal. App. 3d 143, 147 Cal. Rptr. 59 (1978).

56 *See* Keeton v. Hustler Magazine, Inc., 104 S. Ct. 1473, 1481 (1984).

within the forum will in future decisions emerge as factors militating in favor of the maintenance of jurisdiction.

[4] Long Arm Statutes

In the aftermath of *International Shoe*[57] most states enacted "long arm" statutes to permit their courts to assert jurisdiction over nonresidents.[58] As a practical matter, most long arm statutes today are interpreted quite liberally, permitting the exercise of jurisdiction to the full extent permitted by the due process clause.[59] Nevertheless, to assert jurisdiction over a nonresident defendant, both the long arm statute and due process requirements must be complied with. Since many long arm statutes specify particular contacts that create jurisdiction, such as the "transaction of business" or "commission of a tortious act" within a state, it is possible that in some instances long arm jurisdiction is not statutorily authorized even though no due process impediment to jurisdiction exists. The tendency, however, is to construe statutory long arm jurisdiction as expansively as the Constitution permits,[60] and there is very little practical chance of defeating jurisdiction over the defendant in a defamation or privacy case on a statutory basis if such jurisdiction would otherwise be permissible under due process minimum contacts analysis. A federal district court entertaining a diversity of citizenship case is limited to the assertion of *in personam* jurisdiction that would be permitted in the relevant state court.[61]

§ 12.03 Conflicts of Laws

[1] Overview

[a] Relationship to *In Personam* Jurisdiction

The mere fact that a state may exercise *in personam* jurisdiction over the defendant in a defamation or privacy case does not mean that it may

---

[57] International Shoe Co. v. Washington, 326 U.S. 310 (1945). *See supra* § 12.02[3][a][ii].

[58] *See* James and Hazard, *supra* note 1, § 12.14, at 632. *See also* Currie, *The Growth of Long Arm*, 1963 U. Ill. L. Forum 533.

[59] *See, e.g.*, Roy v. North American Newspaper Alliance, Inc., 106 N.H. 92, 95, 205 A.2d 844, 846 (1964); Cal. Code Civ. Pro. § 410.10; N.H. Rev. Stat. Ann. § 300:14.

[60] James & Hazard, *supra* note 1, § 12.14, at 633-34.

[61] *See* Arrowsmith v. United Press International, 320 F.2d 219 (2d Cir. 1963)(en banc).

or will choose to apply its own law to the litigation.[62] The forum state's conflicts rules will determine the body of law to be applied to the litigation, rules that will have both state law and federal constitutional law components.

[b] Forum Shopping

Throughout this volume it has been made quite evident that individual states may vary widely in the substantive law they apply to defamation and privacy cases. There are many variations, for example, in fault standards,[63] in interpretation of the fact/opinion distinction,[64] and in the application of the libel and slander per se and per quod rules.[65] In the privacy field, there are substantial differences in the degree to which states recognize and apply the various privacy torts;[66] and there are similar differences concerning the right of publicity.[67] Additionally, states may apply very different rules on the availability of damages (particularly punitive damages),[68] on statutes of limitations,[69] and on critical "procedural" matters such as the standards for summary judgment practice[70] or reporter's shield laws.[71] These differences create powerful incentives for plaintiffs to forum shop, seeking a jurisdiction in which the substantive (and sometimes, procedural) rules likely to be critical in the case are the most favorable.

[c] Vulnerability to Abusive Forum Shopping

[i] The Impact of *Calder* and *Keeton*

In combination, *Calder v. Jones*[72] and *Keeton v. Hustler Magazine,*

---

[62] *See, e.g.,* Keeton v. Hustler Magazine, Inc., 104 S. Ct. 1473, 1480 (1984)(Supreme Court expressly separated jurisdiction and choice of law inquiries, stating, "The issue is personal jurisdiction, not choice of law.")(quoting Hanson v. Denckla, 357 U.S. 235, 254 (1958)).

[63] *See* Chapters 2 and 3, *supra.*

[64] *See* Chapter 6, *supra.*

[65] *See* Chapter 7, *supra.*

[66] *See* Chapter 10, *supra.*

[67] *See supra* § 10.01[3].

[68] *See* Chapter 9, *supra.*

[69] *See infra* § 12.03[7][b] and note 116.

[70] *See infra* § 12.07.

[71] *See infra* § 12.06[2][b].

[72] 104 S. Ct. 1482 (1984).

Inc.[73] greatly expand the ability of plaintiffs to assert jurisdiction over media defendants in distant forums throughout the United States.[74] Since many media outlets engage in broadcast dissemination or publication circulation across the United States, and since tort standards for media-related cases often vary dramatically, as an industry the media is acutely vulnerable to potentially abusive forum shopping.[75]

[ii] Double Counting the First Amendment

That the media may be peculiarly vulnerable to forum shopping abuses does not mean that courts should necessarily take first amendment values into consideration in deciding conflicts questions. *Keeton* and *Calder* both rejected the importation of special first amendment standards when weighing minimum contacts for the purposes of *in personam* jurisdiction, taking the position that to apply the first amendment at both the substantive law and procedural law stages of the litigation "would be a form of double counting."[76] The Court has similarly rejected special first amendment standards for discovery in defamation cases,[77] and has intimated that no special standards should apply to summary judgment motions.[78] These holdings might well lead courts to conclude that no special first amendment considerations should apply to choice of law determinations in media cases. Nonetheless, choice of law questions are by their very nature different from other "procedural" issues such as *in personam* jurisdiction,[79] and must by their very nature reflect fairness considerations that are intertwined with the substantive interests embodied in the torts being litigated. In media-related torts those substantive interests invariably pose tradeoffs between reputational or privacy interests and free speech interests. It is one thing not to "double count" speech interests, and another not to count them at all. Given the peculiar vulnerability of media defen-

---

[73] 104 S. Ct. 1473 (1984).

[74] *See* analysis in § 12.02[3][b][ii], *supra.*

[75] For an outstanding recent explication of these issues, *see* Pielemeier, *Constitutional Limitations on Choice of Law: The Special Case of Multi-State Defamation*, 133 U. Pa. L. Rev. 381 (1985). The author is greatly indebted to Professor Pielemeier's excellent scholarship for the conflicts materials contained in this section, and would strongly recommend the article cited above to anyone expecting conflicts issues to occupy a significant role in a suit.

[76] Calder v. Jones, 104 S. Ct. 1482, 1488 (1984). *See also* Keeton v. Hustler Magazine, Inc., 104 S. Ct. 1473, 1481 n.12 (1984).

[77] Herbert v. Lando, 441 U.S. 153 (1979). *See infra* § 13.06.

[78] *See* Hutchinson v. Proxmire, 443 U.S. 111, 120 n.9 (1979).

[79] *Keeton*, of course, explicitly recognizes this point. *See supra* note 62.

dants to forum shopping, courts should quite legitimately remain sensitive to first amendment considerations as factors in the mix when making choice of law judgments.

[d] Approaches to Conflicts Problems

It has long been recognized that chaos dominates the choice of law determinations in defamation cases; at times it seems as if there are as many approaches as there are states.[80] In recent years the confusion has grown, largely because the entire field of conflicts of laws has been characterized by an increasing use of new systems of choice of law by various states.[81] The principal conflicts systems discussed below are the traditional territorial approach, the most significant relationship approach, Robert Leflar's better rule approach, the interest analysis approach, and the forum law approach. It may well be worth remembering, however, the typically colorful words of William Prosser, words that still haunt the field: "Choice of law in defamation cases is a dismal swamp, filled with quaking quagmires, and inhabited by learned but eccentric professors who theorize about mysterious matters in a strange and incomprehensible jargon."[82]

[2] Territorialist Approaches

[a] Place of the Wrong

A respectable minority of jurisdictions[83] continue to follow the traditional *lex locus delicti* approach to conflicts of laws, under which the law governing tort liability is determined by the "place of the wrong."[84] "Substantive" issues are governed by the place of the wrong; "procedural" issues are governed by the forum's law.[85] The place of the wrong is the place where the "last event necessary to make the actor liable for

---

80 *See generally* Palmiso v. News Syndicate Co., 130 F. Supp. 17 (S.D.N.Y. 1955). *See also* Pielemeier, *supra* note 75; Rose, *Interstate Libel and Choice of Law: Proposals for the Future,* 30 Hastings L.J. 1515 (1979).

81 *See generally* E. Scoles & D. Hay, Conflicts of Laws 16-41 (1982).

82 Prosser, *Interstate Publications,* 51 Mich. L. Rev. 959, 971 (1953).

83 Professor Pielemeier counts 17 states that follow the traditional territorialist approach. Pielemeier, *supra* note 75, at n.75.

84 *See* Restatement of Conflict of Laws § 378 (1934).

85 *See, e.g.,* Levy v. Steiger, 233 Mass. 600, 601, 124 N.E. 477, 477 (1919).

an alleged tort takes place."[86] In a defamation suit this last event is the place where the defamatory statement is heard by others.[87]

[b] Relation to Single Publication Rule

A literal application of the "place of the wrong" rule leads to the bizarre result that a multistate publication of a defamatory statement gives rise to a separate tort in each state in which publication occurs, and is governed by the law of each such state.[88] As previously discussed,[89] this has generally been regarded as untenable for modern American society, as it would unreasonably burden nationwide media outlets. Most states today have thus adopted the "single publication rule," pursuant to which only one action for damages suffered in all jurisdictions may be maintained.[90]

[c] Practical Result of Territorialist Approach

Courts following the territorialist approach have not been completely consistent, but the most common result in cases in which the forum state is one of the states in which the publication of the defamatory statement took place is to simply apply forum law.[91] Since dissemination of the defamatory statement usually does take place, at least to some degree, in the forum state (note that this is often the basis for asserting long arm jurisdiction[92]), as a practical matter the law most likely to be applied by territorialist states is the law of the forum.

[3] The Most Significant Relationship Approach

The "most significant relationship" approach to conflicts problems, adopted by the *Restatement (Second) of Conflicts,* bases choice of law

---

[86] Restatement of Conflicts of Laws § 377.

[87] *Id.*, § 377, Illustration 7.

[88] *See* Hartman v. Time, Inc., 166 F.2d 127, 133-36 (3d Cir.), *cert. denied,* 334 U.S. 838 (1948); O'Reilly v. Curtis Publishing Co., 31 F. Supp. 364, 365 (D. Mass. 1940); Restatement of Conflict of Laws § 384(1) (1934).

[89] *See supra* § 4.13[4].

[90] *See* Keeton v. Hustler Magazine, Inc., 104 S. Ct. 1473, 1477 and n.2 (1984); Restatement (Second) of Torts § 577A(4) (1977). The single publication rule is discussed further in § 4.13[4], *supra.* There are still isolated decisions rejecting the single publication rule. *See* Lewis v. Reader's Digest Ass'n, 162 Mont. 401, 406, 512 P.2d 702, 704 (1973).

[91] *See* Leflar, *Choice of Law: Torts: Current Trends,* 6 Vand. L. Rev. 447, 454-56 (1953); Prosser, *supra* note 82, at 971-78; Pielemeier, *supra* note 75, at nn. 84-86.

[92] *See supra* § 12.02[3][c][i].

on the state with the most significant relationship to the cause of action.[93] In a defamation or invasion of privacy action the *Restatement (Second)* specifically provides that the state with the most significant relation is usually the plaintiff's domicile (if a natural person)[94] or principal place of business (if a corporation).[95] The rationale for the plaintiff's domicile position is that the plaintiff normally will suffer the most damage in his or her home state, where he or she is likely to be well known.[96] Although the most significant relationship approach to conflicts is designed to permit a degree of case-by-case flexibility, courts following the *Restatement (Second)* in defamation and privacy cases appear strongly inclined to apply the law of the plaintiff's domicile.[97]

[4] The Better Rule Approach

The "better rule" approach, developed through the scholarship of Dr. Robert A. Leflar,[98] approaches conflicts resolutions through five choice-influencing considerations:

(1) predictability of results;
(2) maintenance of interstate and international order;
(3) simplification of the judicial task;
(4) advancement of the forum's governmental interests;
(5) application of the better rule of law.[99]

As a practical matter courts that follow Dr. Leflar's conflicts jurisprudence in torts cases tend to concentrate on the forum's governmental interests and the better rule of law, usually resulting in application of

---

93 Restatement (Second) of Conflict of Laws §§ 6, 150 (1971).

94 *Id.*, § 150(2). *See also id.*, § 552 comment d.

95 *Id.*, § 150(3).

96 *Id.*, § 150 comments e & f. *See also* Hanley v. Tribune Co., 527 F.2d 68, 70 (9th Cir. 1975).

97 *See, e.g.*, Reeves v. American Broadcasting Companies, 719 F.2d 602 (2d Cir. 1983); Fleury v. Harper & Row Publishers, Inc., 698 F.2d 1022 (9th Cir.), *cert. denied*, 104 S. Ct. 149 (1983); System Operations, Inc. v. Scientific Games Development Corp., 555 F.2d 1131, 1136-39 (3d Cir. 1977); Hanley v. Tribune Publishing Co., 527 F.2d 68, 69-70 (9th Cir. 1975); Dowd v. Calabrese, 589 F. Supp. 1206, 1210 (D.D.C. 1984); Machleder v. Diaz, 538 F. Supp. 1364, 1369-70 (S.D.N.Y. 1982); Fitzpatrick v. Milky Way Products, Inc., 537 F. Supp. 165, 171 and n.16 (E.D. Pa. 1982); Velle Transcendental Research Ass'n, Inc. v. Esquire, 41 Ill. App. 3d 799, 354 N.E.2d 622, 625 (1976).

98 *See generally* R. Leflar, American Conflicts Law (3d ed. 1977); Leflar, *Conflicts Law: More on Choice-Influencing Considerations*, 54 Calif. L. Rev. 1584 (1966).

99 Leflar, *More on Choice-Influencing Considerations*, *supra* note 98, at 1586-88.

the law of the forum.[100] Exceptions exist, however. In *Gravina v. Brunswick Corp.*,[101] the law of the forum state (and state of plaintiff's domicile) was not applied when the forum did not recognize an invasion of privacy action for unauthorized use of a photograph. Instead, the law of Illinois, the defendant's domicile, was followed, on the theory that Illinois adhered to the better rule of law, reflecting "the steady trend toward recognition of the right or privacy . . . across the country."[102]

[5] Governmental Interests Analysis

Under governmental interests analysis, created by the scholarship of Professor Brainerd Currie, the court first identifies the governmental policy interests served by the laws of the states involved. If policies of one state are advanced by application of its law, and policies of the other state are not actually affected, there is no "true conflict," and the policy of the state served by the application of its law governs. When policies of more than one state are affected by the choice of law and they are in unavoidable conflict, a "true conflict" exists which is generally to be resolved by favoring forum law.[103] The California Supreme Court has applied a "comparative impairment" approach to governmental interests analysis, "applying the law of the State whose interests would be the more impaired if its law were not applied."[104] Again, there are inconsistencies, but as a practical matter courts engaging in interest analysis usually end up applying forum law.[105]

[6] The Forum Law Approach

There is authority in some jurisdictions for the proposition that the whole confusing matrix of conflicts rules should essentially be abandoned in favor of consistent application of forum law, unless the ap-

---

[100] *See* Milkovich v. Saari, 295 Minn. 155, 170, 203 N.W.2d 408, 416-17 (1973); Clark v. Clark, 107 N.H. 351, 356-57, 222 A.2d 205, 209-10 (1966).

[101] 338 F. Supp. 1 (D.R.I. 1972).

[102] *Id.* at 6-7.

[103] *See generally* B. Currie, *Selected Essays on the Conflicts of Laws* (1963); Currie, *Notes on Methods and Objectives in the Conflicts of Laws*, 159 Duke L.J. 171, 178).

[104] Bernhard v. Harrah's Club, 16 Cal. 3d 313, 320, 546 P.2d 719, 723, 128 Cal. Rptr. 215, 219, *cert. denied*, 429 U.S. 859 (1976).

[105] *See* Pielemeier, *supra* note 75, at n.107 (quoting Juenger, *Conflict of Laws: A Critique of Interest Analysis*, 32 Am. J. Comp. L. 1, 43 (1984)("In almost every case in which courts have resorted to interest analysis they ended up applying forum law.")).

plication of forum law is constitutionally forbidden.[106]

[7] Constitutional Limitations on Choice of Law Decisions

[a] Generally

The due process and full faith and credit clauses of the United States Constitution place outer limits on the extent to which the forum state may apply its own law to causes of action having relationships to other states, and occasionally the Supreme Court will strike down the forum's application of its own law.[107] These occasions are extremely rare, however. In the leading modern case, *Allstate Insurance Co. v. Hague,*[108] the Supreme Court upheld Minnesota's application of its own law despite the fact that the accident involved occurred in Wisconsin, all persons involved in the accident were at the time Wisconsin residents, and the insurance policy in suit was purchased and delivered in Wisconsin and applied to Wisconsin automobiles. The wife of the deceased had become a Minnesota resident prior to instituting litigation; her husband had worked in Minnesota and commuted there daily. The Supreme Court in *Hague* announced an extremely permissive constitutional choice of law rule: A "[s]tate must have a significant contact or significant aggregation of contacts, creating state interests, such that choice of its law is neither arbitrary nor fundamentally unfair."[109]

Given the relatively miniscule contacts possessed by Minnesota in *Hague,* the actual standard may be even more lenient than the verbal standard announced by the Court.[110] Virtually any significant contact will apparently permit application of forum law if the forum so chooses.

[b] The Impact of *Keeton*

The Supreme Court in *Keeton v. Hustler Magazine, Inc.*[111] explicitly

---

106 *See* Foster v. Leggett, 484 S.W.2d 827, 829 (Ky. 1972)("[I]f there are significant contacts—not necessarily the most significant contacts—with Kentucky, the Kentucky law should be applied.").

107 *See* Order of United Commercial Travelers v. Wolfe, 331 U.S. 586 (1947).

108 449 U.S. 302 (1981).

109 *Id.* at 312-13.

110 *See generally* Hay, *Reflections on Conflict-of-Laws Methodology,* 32 Hastings L.J. 1644, 1659 (1981).

111 104 S. Ct. 1473 (1984).

disclaimed any intent to reach choice of law questions in the case.[112] Nevertheless, if one superimposes the reasoning of *Keeton* on the highly permissive constitutional choice of law limitations emanating from *Hague*, the conclusion is that New Hampshire could constitutionally apply its substantive law to the case. The Court wrote, for example, that New Hampshire had a significant "interest in redressing injuries that occur within the State and its interest in cooperating with other States in the application of the single publication rule demonstrates the propriety of requiring respondent to answer a multistate libel action in New Hampshire."[113] However, New Hampshire also had an interest *"in safeguarding its populace from falsehoods."*[114] In a particularly dramatic passage, the Court remarked that "[f]alse statements of fact harm both the subject of the falsehood *and* the readers of the statement. New Hampshire may rightly employ its libel laws to discourage the deception of its citizens."[115]

These New Hampshire interests were articulated by the Court in reference to jurisdictional analysis, but they would appear perfectly transferable to the sort of extremely permissive relationship requirements for choice of law established in *Hague*. Putting *Hague* and *Keeton* together, in short, creates a chilling prospect for media defendants: In any state in which some appreciable (but in relative terms, quite small) level of circulation occurs, sufficient minimum contacts for both jurisdiction and choice of law will exist. The Constitution would appear to impose no meaningful restraints on forum shopping.[116]

---

[112] *Id.* at 1480.

[113] *Id.*

[114] *Id.* at 1479 (emphasis added).

[115] *Id.* (emphasis in original).

[116] By far the most important forum-shopping element in *Keeton* was the fact that New Hampshire, because of its unusually long limitations period (six years), was the only state in which the plaintiff's cause of action remained alive. The Supreme Court noted that procedural issues are generally governed by the forum state's law, and that New Hampshire treats statutes of limitations as procedural. *Id.* at 1480 n.10 (citing Gordon v. Gordon, 118 N.H. 356, 360, 387 A.2d 339, 342 (1978); Barrett v. Boston & Maine R.R., 104 N.H. 70, 178 A.2d 291 (1962)). The Court further noted that there has been substantial academic criticism of the rule that permits the forum to apply its own limitations period regardless of the contacts between the forum state and the litigation. 104 S. Ct. at 1480 n.10 (citing Weintraub, Commentary on the Conflict of Laws § 9.2B, at 517 (2d ed. 1980; Martin, *Constitutional Limitations on Choice of Law*, 61 Cornell L. Rev. 185, 221 (1976); Lorenzen, *The Statute of Limitations and the Conflict of Laws*, 28 Yale L.J. 492, 496-97 (1919)). "But we find it unnecessary," the Court stated, "to express an opinion at this time as to whether any arguable unfairness rises to the level of a due process violation." 104 S. Ct. at 1480 n.10.

§ 12.04 Removal, Transfer, and *Forum Non Conveniens*

[1] Removal from State Court to Federal Court

A nonresident defendant may remove from state court to federal court any action that would originally have been cognizable in federal court under diversity jurisdiction.[117] Further, "whenever a separate and independent claim or cause of action, which would be removable if sued upon alone, is joined with one or more otherwise non-removable claims or causes of action, the entire case may be removed and the district court may determine all issues therein, or, in its discretion, may remand all matters not otherwise within its original jurisdiction."[118] Thus, if a California resident sues a New York media defendant and a California reporter in state court, the New York defendant may have the entire case removed to California federal district court if the claim satisfies the "separate and independent standard."[119] Removal may be particularly apt when the joinder of the in-state defendant was a device to defeat removal.[120]

Once the petition for removal is filed with the state court, the state court is prohibited from proceeding with the case.[121] To challenge the removal, remand must be sought in federal court, on the grounds that "the case was removed improvidently and without jurisdiction."[122]

[2] Transfer

Transfer of a cause of action from one federal district court to another is authorized by the liberal language of Section 1404(a) of the judicial code: "For the convenience of parties and witnesses, in the interest of justice, a district court may transfer any civil action to any other district or division where it might have been brought."[123] The most celebrated recent use of the transfer device in a defamation case came in *Westmoreland v. CBS*,[124] in which CBS successfully managed to get General William Westmoreland's suit transferred from his home state of South

---

117 28 U.S.C.A. § 1441. *See generally* Wright, *supra* note 2, § 38, at 210. Federal question cases are also removable, without regard to the residency of the parties.

118 28 U.S.C.A. § 1441(c).

119 *See* Dodd v. Fawcett Publications, Inc., 329 F.2d 82, 85 (10th Cir. 1964).

120 *See* Lewis v. Time, Inc., 83 F.R.D. 455 (E.D. Cal. 1979).

121 28 U.S.C.A. § 1446.

122 *Id.* § 1447(c).

123 28 U.S.C.A. § 1404(a). *See also generally* Hoffman v. Blaski, 363 U.S. 335 (1960).

124 8 Med. L. Rep. (BNA) 2493 (D.S.C. 1982).

Carolina to the Southern District of New York. The district court approved the transfer because CBS and most of the other parties and witnesses were New York residents.

[3] *Forum Non Conveniens*

The doctrine of *forum non conveniens* is a discretionary judicial self-restraint device that permits a court to decline to exercise its rightful jurisdiction over a case when it appears the case would more appropriately be brought elsewhere.[125] In the federal system the doctrine has been largely superseded by the transfer provisions of Section 1404(a),[126] but it remains a significant component of state practice.[127] A court that dismisses an action on the grounds that it would more conveniently and economically be brought elsewhere may, and often will, condition dismissal on the defendant's agreeing to submit to jurisdiction in the more convenient forum, and to waive imperfections such as the running of the statute of limitations.[128]

[4] First Amendment Considerations

Recognizing that first amendment rights may be chilled by the prospect of litigating defamation or privacy claims in distant forums, a number of courts have stated that free speech values should be taken into account when a nonresident defendant moves for removal, transfer, or change of venue.[129]

After *Keeton* and *Calder*, there is the worry that *any* specialized procedural treatment of defendants on first amendment grounds might be disfavored as "double counting."[130] The double counting rationale, however, has less force when the accomodation of free speech interests that takes place in transfer to a more convenient and appropriate forum does no more than return the litigation to a more neutral procedural

---

125 *See, e.g.*, Gulf Oil Corp. v. Gilbert, 330 U.S. 501 (1947).

126 *See supra* § 12.04[2].

127 *See, e.g.*, Price v. Anderson, T. & S.F. R.R., 42 Cal. 2d 577, 268 P.2d 457 (1954); Silver v. Great American Insurance Co., 29 N.Y.2d 356, 328 N.Y.S.2d 398, 278 N.E.2d 619 (1972); Barret, *The Doctrine of Forum Non Conveniens*, 35 Cal. L. Rev. 380 (1947).

128 *See* James & Hazard, *supra* note 1, §§ 12.29, at 685.

129 *See, e.g.*, Buckley v. New York Post Corp., 373 F.2d 175 (2d Cir. 1967); Westmoreland v. CBS, Inc., 8 Med. L. Rep. (BNA) 2493, 2496-97 (D.S.C. 1982); Lewis v. Time, Inc., 83 F.R.D. 455 (E.D. Cal. 1979); Cordell v. Detective Publications, Inc., 307 F. Supp. 1212 (E.D. Tenn. 1968), *aff'd*, 419 F.2d 989 (6th Cir. 1969).

130 *See supra* § 12.02[3][b][ii]

posture, that is, away from a jurisdiction chosen because it offers the opportunity to exploit the media's special vulnerability to forum shopping. One would hope, therefore, that courts will continue to entertain such motions in media cases with a degree of liberality.

§ 12.05 Pleading Considerations

[1] Defamatory Words

Despite the trend in civil litigation toward "notice" pleading rather than "fact" pleading, the tradition in defamation actions is to require that the specific defamatory language be pleaded;[131] this is a widely followed practice even when not strictly required under local pleading rules.

[2] Defamatory Meaning and the "Of and Concerning" Requirement

The complaint must sufficiently state the defamatory meaning (express or implied) upon which the cause of action is based, as well as the aspects of the communication that are "of and concerning" the plaintiff.[132]

[3] Required Fault Level

The pleading must allege the level of fault—actual malice, gross negligence, or negligence, as the case may be—that is required under state and federal rules given the status of the plaintiff and the speech.[133]

[4] Special Damages

As dictated by the requirements of the jurisdiction involving special damages and the libel and slander per se and per quod distinctions, special damages must be alleged with more than conclusory specificity.[134]

---

131 *See, e.g.*, Haub v. Friermuth, 1 Cal. App. 556, 82 Pac. 571 (1905).

132 *See supra* §§ 4.05[2], 4.09.

133 *See supra* §§ 3.01-3.05.

134 *See* Chapter 7, *supra*.

[5] Other Considerations

In other respects, pleading requirements and strategy in defamation and privacy litigation tend to resemble other tort litigation. If general observations are possible, the primary distinguishing characteristic is a tradition of greater factual detail and specificity with regard to most elements of the complaint than might otherwise be true in civil actions.

§ 12.06 Special Discovery Issues

[1] Inquiry into Editorial Process

[a] Function of the Inquiry

As previously discussed at length,[135] the editorial decision-making process plays a critical role in the plaintiff's effort to establish the requisite level of fault—actual malice, gross irresponsibility, or negligence—as well as the existence of ill-will malice,[136] which may be necessary to obtain punitive damages or defeat a common law privilege.[137] In modern defamation or privacy cases, the defendant's state of mind is often the very heart of the case, and to discern that state it is often necessary to reconstruct the process of composing and editing the defamatory communication.

[b] Scope of the Inquiry

In *Herbert v. Lando*,[138] the public figure plaintiff sued CBS, producer Barry Lando, and reporter Mike Wallace for defamation allegedly arising from a segment on "60 Minutes." During his deposition Lando answered most of the questions posed, but he declined to answer questions concerning such issues as his conclusions about the veracity of certain CBS witnesses, his investigation of some matters but not others, and the substance of his conversations with Mike Wallace in the preparation of the program. Lando maintained that the first amendment protected him from disclosing these internal editorial thought processes and discussions.

Justice White, writing for a 6-3 majority, held that the information

135 *See supra* §§ 3.13-3.20.

136 *See supra* § 9.08[3][b].

137 *See supra* § 9.08.

138 441 U.S. 153 (1979).

sought was discoverable and not protected by any special first amendment privilege. Justice White reasoned that *New York Times* requires the plaintiff to establish the subjective state of mind of the defendant, and to accept Lando's argument would erect an "impenetrable barrier" to recovery.[139]

[c] Relationship to Confidential Source Privilege

The recognition in *Herbert* that editorial thought and decision-making processes are subject to discovery should not be confused with the confidential source privilege, which protects a reporter in certain circumstances from revealing a confidential source. A reporter may thus be forced to discuss his thought processes but be privileged from revealing his sources.[140]

[2] Confidential Sources

[a] Qualified First Amendment Privilege

[i] *Branzburg v. Hayes*

In *Branzburg v. Hayes*,[141] a very narrowly divided Supreme Court held 5-4 that the first amendment does not provide an absolute privilege for a reporter to refuse to reveal confidential sources. Justice Powell cast the swing fifth vote; his opinion adopted a qualified privilege under which "[t]he asserted claim to privilege should be judged on its facts by the striking of a proper balance between freedom of the press and the obligation of all citizens to give relevant testimony. . . ."[142] Justice Powell took the position that the "balance of these vital constitutional and societal interests on a case-by-case basis accords with the tried and traditional way of adjudicating such questions."[143]

[ii] Lower Court Interpretations of *Branzburg*

Justice Stewart has observed that given the alignment in *Branzburg* and Justice Powell's concurring opinion, the case was decided "by a

139 *Id.* at 170.

140 *See, e.g.*, Greenleigh Associates v. New York Post, 6 Med. L. Rep. (BNA) 2423 (N.Y. App. Div. 1980).

141 408 U.S. 665 (1972).

142 *Id.* at 710 (Powell, J., concurring).

143 *Id.* at 710-11 (Powell, J., concurring).

vote of four and a half to four and a half."[144] The consensus of lower court interpretations of *Branzburg* has been to regard Justice Powell's vote as controlling and to adopt a qualified privilege for reporters for the revelation of confidential sources.[145]

[iii] The Balancing Test

In defining the elements of the qualified privilege not to reveal confidential sources, an influential opinion has been that of Justice Stewart, written 14 years prior to *Branzburg* while Justice Stewart was still a court of appeals judge, in *Garland v. Torre.*[146] The *Garland* case arose out of a suit by Judy Garland against a columnist, who refused to reveal the source of a quote attributed to Garland. Justice Stewart adopted a balancing test to analyze the claim of privilege.

In *Miller v. Transamerican Press, Inc.,*[147] the Fifth Circuit, borrowing from *Garland,* established the elements of the balancing test that have been adopted with occasional minor variations by most of the courts that have considered the matter. The test is:

(1) Is the information relevant?
(2) Can the information be obtained by alternate means? and
(3) Is there a compelling interest in the information?[148]

In elaborating on this formulation, the court later stated that:

> We do not mean to intimate that a plaintiff will be entitled to know the identity of the informant merely by pleading that he was injured by an untrue statement. Before receipt of such information the plaintiff must

---

[144] Stewart, *Or Of the Press,* 26 Hastings L.J. 631, 635 (1975). *See also* Goodale, Branzburg v. Hayes *and the Developing Qualified Privilege for Newsmen,* 26 Hastings L.J. 709, 715-19 (1975).

[145] *See, e.g.,* Bruno & Stillman v. Globe Newspaper, 633 F.2d 583, 598 (1st Cir. 1980); Miller v. Transamerican Press, Inc., 621 F.2d 721, 725 (5th Cir.), *modified and rehearing denied,* 628 F.2d 932 (1980), *cert. denied,* 450 U.S. 1041 (1981); Carey v. Home, 492 F.2d 631 (D.C. Cir.), *cert. dismissed,* 417 U.S. 938 (1974); Continental Cablevision, Inc. v. Storer Broadcasting Co., 583 F. Supp. 427, 436 (E.D. Mo. 1984); Mize v. McGraw-Hill, Inc., 82 F.R.D. 475 (S.D. Tex. 1979), *on rehearing,* 86 F.R.D. 1 (1980); Gadsden County Times v. Horne, 426 So. 2d 1234 (Fla. Ct. App. 1983); New Hampshire v. Siel, 122 N.H. 254, 444 A.2d 499 (1982); Austin v. Memphis Publishing, 655 S.W.2d 146 (Tenn. 1983); Clampitt v. Thurston County, 98 Wash. 2d 638, 658 P.2d 641 (1983).

[146] 259 F.2d 545, 549-50 (2d Cir.), *cert. denied,* 358 U.S. 910 (1958).

[147] 621 F.2d 721 (5th Cir.), *modified and rehearing denied,* 628 F.2d 932 (1980), *cert. denied,* 450 U.S. 1041 (1981).

[148] 621 F.2d at 726. *See also, e.g.,* Carey v. Hume, 492 F.2d 631 (D.C. Cir.), *cert. dismissed,* 417 U.S. 938 (1974); Gadsden County Times v. Horne, 426 So. 2d 1234 (Fla. Ct. App. 1983).

show substantial evidence that the challenged statement was published and is both factually untrue and defamatory; that reasonable efforts to discover the information from alternate sources have been made and that no other reasonable source is available; and that knowledge of the identity of the informant is necessary to proper preparation and presentation of the case.[149]

Other courts have been similarly strict in articulating the privilege, stating the test in terms that put a substantial burden on the party seeking disclosure before it is compelled.[150]

[b] State Shield Laws

Over half the states have enacted reporter's shield laws that provide some degree of protection from the compelled disclosure of sources. These laws vary significantly in scope and effect. Some are essentially equivalent to the qualified privilege recognized under the first amendment after *Branzburg*. Many of them, however, provide privileges against disclosure stronger than those recognized in *Branzburg* and its progeny. A federal court sitting in a diversity case will apply the state shield law of the state if it is articulated in terms of a witness's privilege.[151] Some shield laws merely direct limitations on the sanctions permissible when disclosure is not made, such as immunity from contempt.[152] In such instances the Federal Rules of Evidence do not technically require that the federal court apply the shield law, but federal courts will nonetheless give authoritative deference to the state policies reflected in the shield statute.[153]

[i] Absolute Immunity

Several states have construed their shield laws as absolute. New Jersey, for example, treats its shield statute as creating an absolute privi-

---

[149] Miller v. Transamerican Press, Inc., 628 F.2d at 932 (per curiam opinion denying rehearing in *Miller* and elaborating on test established in original opinion).

[150] *See, e.g.*, Clampitt v. Thurston County, 98 Wash. 2d 638, 658 P.2d 641, 644-46 (1983)(courts should "do their utmost" to avoid forced disclosure, which should be considered "a last resort;" party seeking to overcome privilege must "do more than state a cause of action").

[151] *See* Mazzella v. Philadelphia Newspapers, Inc., 479 F. Supp. 523 (E.D.N.Y. 1979); Fed. R. Evid. 501.

[152] *See* KSDO v. Superior Court, 136 Cal. App. 3d 375, 383-84, 186 Cal. Rptr. 211 (1982).

[153] *See* Baker v. F & F Investment, 470 F.2d 778 (2d Cir. 1972), *cert. denied*, 411 U.S. 966 (1973).

lege against disclosure in civil cases,[154] though not in criminal cases.[155] Pennsylvania's statute is typical of the absolute protection approach, stating broadly that no person connected with the news media "shall be required to disclose the source of any information procured or obtained by such person, in any legal proceeding, trial or investigation before any government unit."[156] It has been interpreted as protecting "all sources of information—persons, documents, and recordings—with the exception of information for which the privilege was waived by actual publication or public disclosure."[157] The broad language of the Pennsylvania-type statute confers "blanket protection" from compelled disclosure.[158] At times courts interpreting statutes drafted broadly in the manner of the Pennsylvania law have upheld the invocation of the reporter's privilege on the facts before them without reaching the question of whether the privilege conferred by the law is absolute.[159]

New York amended its shield law in 1981 to create absolute protection for journalists,[160] though there is some split of authority as to whether the absolute protection embraces all sources or only those who supply information on a confidential basis.[161] In *Beach v. Shanley,*[162] the New York Court of Appeals gave the confidentiality policies underlying the New York shield law a ringing endorsement, stating that "[t]he inescapable conclusion is that the shield law provides a broad protection to journalists without any qualifying language. It does not distinguish between criminal and civil matters, nor does it except situations

---

154 *See* Maressa v. New Jersey Monthly, 89 N.J. 176, 445 A.2d 376, *cert. denied,* 459 U.S. 907 (1982). *See also* Resorts International v. NJM Associates, 89 N.J. 212, 445 A.2d 395, *cert. denied,* 459 U.S. 907 (1982).

155 Maressa v. New Jersey Monthly, 445 A.2d at 379; State v. Boiardo, 82 N.J. 446, 414 A.2d 14 (1980).

156 Pa. Stat. Ann. tit. 42, § 5942 (Purdon 1979).

157 Steaks Unlimited, Inc. v. Deaner, 623 F.2d 264, 278 (3d Cir. 1980)(the shield law was held to protect against disclosure of "outtakes").

158 Mazzella v. Philadelphia Newspapers, Inc., 479 F. Supp. 523 (E.D.N.Y. 1979). *See also* D'Alfonso v. Abell, 9 Med. L. Rep. (BNA) 1015, 1016 n.1 (D. Md. 1983).

159 *See* Saxton v. Arkansas Gazette Co., 264 Ark. 133, 569 S.W.2d 115 (1978); Jenoff v. Hearst Corp., 3 Med. L. Rep. (BNA) 1911 (D. Md. 1978).

160 N.Y. Civil Rights Law § 79-h (1981).

161 *Compare* People v. Iannaccone, 112 Misc. 2d 1057, 1058-62 (N.Y. Sup. 1982), *aff'd without opinion,* 96 A.D.2d 488 (1st Dept. 1982)(absolute privilege for both confidential and nonconfidential sources), *and* Lawless v. Clay, 9 Med. L. Rep. (BNA) 1223 (N.Y. Sup. 1982)(same), *with* People v. Bova, 118 Misc. 2d 14 (N.Y. Sup. 1983).

162 62 N.Y.2d 241, 415 N.E.2d 304, 476 N.Y.S.2d 765 (1984).

where the reporter observes a criminal act."[163]

A recent federal district court construction of Rhode Island's shield law has similarly construed it as absolute.[164]

[ii] Qualified Immunity

Some shield laws are less expansive in their coverage, subject to defeasance under certain statutorily prescribed circumstances,[165] or upon the satisfaction of a balancing test essentially equivalent to prevailing post-*Branzburg* first amendment standards.[166] The Oklahoma shield law, for example, has been construed as requiring that "the evidence be clear and convincing that the information sought is relevant to a significant issue" and that "the information could not with due diligence be obtained by alternate means."[167]

[c] Sanctions for Failure to Reveal Sources

[i] Contempt

Contempt is a sanction typically available under rules of civil procedure for failure to comply with a discovery order.[168] It is occasionally used against reporters in media cases.[169] Some shield laws, rather than conferring a true privilege against disclosure of confidential sources, operate merely to confer immunity from contempt, permitting the application of other sanctions.[170]

[ii] Striking of Pleadings and Entry of Default Judgment

The failure to comply with a proper disclosure order (one not barred by the first amendment or applicable shield law) may result in the striking of the nondisclosing party's pleadings and the entry of a default judgment against that party.[171] This remedy is strongly disfavored, how-

---

163 *Id.* at 251.

164 Fischer v. McGowan, 585 F. Supp. 978 (D.R.I. 1984).

165 Some shield statutes, for example, have little or no application in defamation actions. *See* Ill. Ann. Stat. ch. 51, § 111 (1978); Or. Rev. Stat. § 44.530 (1977); Tenn. Code Ann. § 24-114 (1978).

166 *See* Cal. Const. art. I, § 2(b) (1980); Okla. Stat. Ann. tit. 12, § 2506 (1980).

167 Taylor v. Miskovsky, 7 Med. L. Rep. (BNA) 2408, 2410 (Okla. 1981).

168 *See* F.R.C.P. 37(b).

169 *See* Caldero v. Tribune Publishing Co., 98 Idaho 288, 562 P.2d 791, *cert. denied,* 434 U.S. 930 (1977).

170 *See* KSDO v. Superior Court, 136 Cal. App. 3d 375, 186 Cal. Rptr. 211 (1982); Oak Beach Inn Corp. v. Babylon Beacon, 62 N.Y.2d 158, 476 N.Y.S.2d 269 (1984).

171 *See* Rancho La Costa v. Penthouse, 6 Med. L. Rep. (BNA) 1540 (Cal. Super. 1980); F.R.C.D. 37(b).

ever, and is usually treated as a penalty disproportionate to the offense. In *Oak Beach Inn Corp. v. Babylon,*[172] for example, the New York Court of Appeals held that New York's shield law, while conferring absolute immunity from contempt for nondisclosure, leaves other discovery sanctions still intact. The court held, however, that the sanction of totally stripping a newspaper of its entire defense was too harsh. Relief, the court held, "should adequately protect the plaintiff's interest without intolerably burdening the newspaper."[173] More limited sanctions, such as precluding reliance on information from the source in defending against the allegation of malice, forcing the paper to rely on proof of its own independent investigation, would have been sufficient. "A newspaper," the court stated, "should not be required to accept substantial financial loss as the price for continuing to honor a commitment to maintain the confidentiality of one of its sources."[174]

Similarly, in *Sierra Life v. Magic Valley Newspapers,*[175] the Idaho Supreme Court reversed a $1.9 million default judgment entered for failure to disclose sources, holding that while "mindful that a defendant ought not profit from his own refusal to make discovery, . . . such recalcitrance should not take away those defenses which are not affected by his refusal to disclose."[176]

[iii] Preclusion of Reliance on Source or Presumption that No Source Existed

The most appropriate and narrowly tailored sanctions available in cases of unprivileged nondisclosure involve more surgical elimination of the nondisclosing party's right to rely on certain evidence, or oppose certain allegations, or the existence of certain facts. For example, the court may impose a presumption that no source existed.[177] Alternatively, the court may preclude proof of reliance on the source, forcing the defendant to resort to other evidence to defend against allegations of actual malice.[178]

---

[172] 62 N.Y.2d 158, 476 N.Y.S.2d 269 (1984).

[173] *Id.* at 166-67.

[174] *Id.*

[175] 101 Idaho 795, 623 P.2d 103 (1980).

[176] 623 P.2d at 107.

[177] DeRoburt v. Gannett, 507 F. Supp. 880 (D. Hawaii 1981); Downing v. Monitor Publishing Co., 415 A.2d 683 (N.H. 1980).

[178] Oak Beach Inn Corp. v. Babylon Beacon, 62 N.Y.2d 158, 476 N.Y.S.2d 269 (1984); Greenberg v. CBS, Inc., 69 A.D.2d 693, 419 N.Y.S.2d 988 (1979).

[3] Breach of Contract for Revealing Sources

May a news organization be held liable for breach of contract when it reveals the identity of a source after it has promised to keep the source's identity confidential? In *Cohen v. Cowles Company*[178.1] the court held that such liability could exist. The case arose from events surrounding a story provided to the *Minneapolis Star and Tribune* and other organizations by the plaintiff Dan Cohen. Cohen contacted reporters at four news organizations, offering to provide information concerning a prior misdemeanor conviction of a candidate for statewide office, information not then publicly known. Cohen offered to provide this information on the explicit condition that his identity not be disclosed by the news organizations. The reporters agreed to these terms, promising not to reveal Cohen's name. Editors of the *St. Paul Pioneer Press* and the *Minneapolis Star and Tribune* later decided to override the commitment made by the reporters, and to name Cohen as the source for the story. Cohen then brought suit for breach of contract and fraudulent misrepresentation.

The court upheld a jury verdict in favor of the plaintiffs, treating the case as a straightforward contract action. The court refused to hold that the first amendment immunized the defendants from what would otherwise have been a clear-cut breach of contract. In addressing the defendants' first amendment arguments, the court reasoned that newspapers have no special immunity from the application of general laws, such as the law of contracts. Even those first amendment protections that do specially protect the press, the court reasoned, do not immunize it from deliberate misconduct. The editors in the *Cohen* case, the court ruled, engaged in a deliberate corporate decision to breach their agreement, and should be liable for the damages that ensued.

§ 12.07 Summary Judgment Practice

[1] Overview

[a] The Traditional Skepticism

The story is told about a judge in New Orleans with a sign in his courtroom: "No Drinking, No Smoking, No Summary Judgments." Traditionally, summary judgment is a disfavored procedural device because it

178.1 15 Med. L. Rep. (BNA) 2288 (Minn. Dist. Ct., 4th Dist. 1988).

deprives a party of his "day in court" before a jury.[179] "State of mind" has usually been conceptualized as a jury question not readily susceptible to summary judgment determination.[180]

[b] Competing First Amendment Tensions

Suits against the media often chill first amendment freedoms because of the huge costs attendant to carrying a defense through trial. In response to the concern that the costs of defending against unmeritorious claims may induce self-censorship on the part of media defendants, courts in the years after *New York Times* evolved the principle that summary judgment was a *favored* procedural device in defamation cases subject to *New York Times* protection. The Fifth Circuit thus stated that "where a publication is protected by the *New York Times* immunity rule, summary judgment, rather than trial on the merits, is the proper vehicle for affording constitutional protection in the proper case."[181] Summary judgment was thought of as a screening device particularly useful in first amendment cases as a tool for "shielding the press from harassment."[182] Prior to 1979, a consensus appeared to be emerging that summary judgment was "favored" in defamation cases.[183]

(*Text continued on page 12-33*)

179 *See generally* C. Wright & A. Miller, 10 Federal Practice and Procedure §§ 2711 *et seq.* (1973).

180 *Id.* § 2730, at 590-92.

181 Bon Air Hotel v. Time, 426 F.2d 858, 864-65 (5th Cir. 1980).

182 Martin Marietta Corp. v. Evening Star Newspaper Co., 417 F. Supp 947, 954 (D.D.C. 1976).

183 *See, e.g.,* Southard v. Forbes, 588 F.2d 140, 145-46 (5th Cir. 1979), *cert. denied,* 444 U.S. 932 (1979); Carson v. Allied News Co., 529 F.2d 206, 210 (7th Cir. 1976); Time, Inc. v. McLaney, 406 F.2d 565, 922 (1969); Washington Post Co. v. Keogh, 365 F.2d 965, 968 (D.C. Cir. 1966), *cert. denied,* 385 U.S. 1011 (1967); Reliance Insurance Co. v. Barron's, 442 F. Supp. 1341, 1343-44 (S.D.N.Y. 1977); Fram v. Yellow Cab Co., 380 F. Supp. 1314, 1335 (W.D. Pa. 1974); Spern v. Time, Inc., 324 F. Supp. 1201, 1204 (W.D. Pa. 1971); Rinaldi v. Holt, Rinehart & Winston, 42 N.Y.2d 369, 336 N.E.2d 1299 (1977).

[c] The Burger Footnote in *Hutchinson v. Proxmire*

The march of precedent favoring summary judgment in defamation cases was brought to an abrupt halt—at least, the marchers were scattered considerably—by a famous (or infamous, as the case may be) footnote by Chief Justice Burger, writing for the Court in *Hutchinson v. Proxmire.*[184] In unabashed dicta, the Chief Justice stated in the fateful "footnote nine": "Considering the nuances of the issues raised here, we are constrained to express some doubt about the so-called 'rule.' The proof of 'actual malice' calls defendant's state of mind into question . . . and does not readily lend itself to summary disposition."[185]

[2] The Post-*Hutchinson* Split

[a] The Neutrality Principle

[i] In General

In the aftermath of *Hutchinson,* a number of courts have retreated to neutral territory, adopting the view that summary judgment in defamation cases are to be treated "neutrally," just as they would be handled in any other civil litigation: neither specially favored nor disfavored within the parameters of the usual civil procedure and substantive law rules. The Second Circuit, for example, has stated that "neither grant nor denial of a motion is to be preferred."[186] Under this view, which has gained a substantial number of adherents, defamation actions are procedurally no different from any other actions; "any 'chilling effect' caused by the defense of a lawsuit itself is simply to be disregarded, to have no force and effect."[187]

[ii] The Analogy to *Calder* and *Keeton*

The Supreme Court's jurisdictional holdings in *Calder v. Jones*[188] and

---

[184] 443 U.S. 111 (1979).

[185] *Id.* at 120 n.9. The Chief Justice, though making his position on the issue clear, also stated that "[i]n the present posture of the case however, the propriety of dealing with such complex issues by summary judgment is not before us." *Id.*

[186] Yiamouyiannis v. Consumers Union of the United States, Inc. 619 F.2d 932, 939-40 (2d Cir.), *cert. denied,* 449 U.S. 839 (1980).

[187] *Id. See also, e.g.,* Schultz v. Newsweek, 668 F.2d 911, 917 (6th Cir. 1982); Pep v. Newsweek, 553 F. Supp 1000, 1001 (S.D.N.Y. 1983); National Nutritional Foods Ass'n v. Whelan, 492 F. Supp. 374, 379 (S.D.N.Y. 1979); Gray v. WALA-TV, 384 So. 2d 1062 (Ala. 1980); Bruno v. New York News, 89 A.D.2d 260, 266 (3d Dept. 1982); Braig v. Field Communications, 456 A.2d 1366, 1377 (Pa. Super. 1983).

[188] 104 S. Ct. 1482 (1984).

Keeton v. Hustler Magazine, Inc.[189] would appear to support the neutrality approach in the sense that they evince a general hostility toward the importation of first amendment concerns into the procedural side of a defamation case, on the theory that such concerns are already reflected in substantive law standards.[190]

[b] The Continuation of Summary Judgment

Hutchinson's footnote nine many have spurned more hostility than acceptance. The majority position continues to be that summary judgment is a favored remedy in defamation cases, because of the threat posed to the first amendment by protracted litigation.[191]

[3] Defeating a Summary Judgment Motion in Public Figure Cases

[a] The Actual Malice Obstacle

Whether the jurisdiction treats summary judgment as favored, disfavored, or neutral in procedural terms, the actual malice standard is sufficiently difficult to meet to make summary judgment in favor of defendants relatively common in public figure cases, simply as a matter of substantive law.[192]

---

189 104 S. Ct. 1473 (1984).

190 *See supra* § 12.02[3][b][ii].

191 *See, e.g.*, Brown v. Herald Co., 698 F.2d 949, 951 (8th Cir. 1983); Lawrence v. Moss, 639 F.2d 634 (10th Cir. 1981); Schuster v. U.S. News & World Report, Inc., 602 F.2d 850 (8th Cir. 1979); Stuart v. Gambling Times, 534 F. Supp. 170, 172 (D.N.J. 1982); Church of Scientology of California v. Siegelman, 481 F. Supp. 866, 867 (S.D.N.Y. 1979); Reader's Digest v. Marin County Superior Court, 37 Cal. 3d 244, 208 Cal. Rptr. 137, 690 P.2d 610 (1984); Rood v. Finney, 418 So. 2d 1, 3 (La. App.), *cert. denied*, 420 So. 2d 979 (La. 1982), *cert. denied*, 460 U.S. 1013 (1983); Lins v. Evening News Ass'n, 129 Mich. App. 419, 342 N.W.2d 573, 577 (1983). *See also* Karaduman v. Newsday, Inc., 435 N.Y.S.2d 556, 562, 416 N.E.2d 557, 563 (1980)(distinguishing *Hutchinson* as relating to federal procedural standards and constitutional malice rather than state-defined fault and procedural standards).

192 *See, e.g.*, Steaks Unlimited, Inc. v. Deaner, 623 F.2d 264, 275-76 (3d Cir. 1980); Yiamouyiannis v. Consumers Union of the United States, Inc., 619 F.2d 932, 940-42 (2d Cir.), *cert. denied*, 449 U.S. 839 (1980); Roberts v. Dover, 525 F. Supp. 987, 991 (M.D. Tenn. 1981); Loeb v. New Times Communications Corp., 497 F. Supp. 85, 94 (S.D.N.Y. 1980).

[b] The Convincing Clarity Issue

It is axiomatic that, *at trial,* proof of actual malice must be established "with convincing clarity."[193] Prior to 1986, there had been a split of authority as to whether the clear and convincing standard also applied with regard to the proof a plaintiff must present to defeat a defense motion for summary judgment. The majority position was to require clear and convincing evidence,[194] but the cases were not uniform.[195] In *Anderson v. Liberty Lobby, Inc.,*[196] the Court was presented with the question of whether the standard in *New York Times Co. v. Sullivan*[196.1] requiring a plaintiff to demonstrate actual malice with "clear and convincing"[196.2] evidence must be considered by a court in ruling on a motion for summary judgment under the Federal Rules of Civil Procedure.[196.3] The Court ruled, in a 6-3 decision, that when determining if a genuine factual issue as to actual malice exists in a libel suit brought by a public figure, a trial judge must bear in mind "the quantum and quality of proof necessary to support liability under *New York Times.*"[196.4] The Court held that there is no genuine issue if the evidence brought forward in the opposing affidavits is "of insufficient caliber or quantity to allow a rational finder of fact to find actual malice by clear and convincing evidence."[196.5]

Liberty Lobby was an important press victory because aggressive summary practice has long been integral to media defensive strategy

---

193 *See* Gertz v. Robert Welch, Inc., 418 U.S. 323, 342 (1974); New York Times Co. v. Sullivan, 376 U.S. 254, 285-86 (1964). *See also supra* § 3.07.

194 *See, e.g.,* Yiamouyiannis v. Consumers Union of the United States, Inc., 619 F.2d 932 (2d Cir.), *cert denied,* 449 U.S. 839 (1980); United Medical Labs v. CBS, 404 F.2d 706, 713 (9th Cir. 1968); Hoffman v. Washington Post Co., 433 F. Supp. 600, 604-05 (D.D.C. 1977), *aff'd,* 578 F.2d 442 (1978); Trans World Accounts, Inc. v. Associated Press, 425 F. Supp. 814, 822 (N.D. Cal. 1977); Reader's Digest v. Marin County Superior Court, 37 Cal. 3d 244, 208 Cal. Rptr. 137, 690 P.2d 610 (1984); Bandelin v. Pietsch, 98 Idaho 337, 563 P.2d 399, 398, *cert. denied,* 434 U.S. 891 (1977); Sims v. KIRO, 580 P.2d 642 (Wash. App. 1978), *cert. denied,* 441 U.S. 945 (1979).

195 *See* Wilkins v. Record Publishing Co., 4 Med. L. Rep. (BNA) 1605, 1607-08 (N.D. Ohio 1978); Ammerman v. Hubbard Broadcasting, 91 N.M. 250, 572 P.2d 1258 (Ct. App. 1977).

196 106 S. Ct. 2505 (1986).

196.1 376 U.S. 254 (1964).

196.2 *Id.* at 285-86. *See also* Gertz v. Robert Welch, Inc., 418 U.S. 323, 342 (1974).

196.3 *See* Fed. R. Civ. P. 56.

196.4 106 S. Ct. at 2513.

196.5 *Id.*

in libel litigation.[196.6] *Liberty Lobby* was cast by the Court essentially as a civil procedure ruling, however, and not as a first amendment case.[196.7] The Court went out of its way, in fact, to avoid importing first amendment values into its procedural analysis—a trend visible in a number of recent procedural decisions involving defamation.[196.8] As previously discussed, this trend toward "procedural neutrality" may often be as much a detriment as a benefit to defense interests.[196.9]

The three dissenters in *Liberty Lobby,* it should be pointed out, consisted of the improbable coalition of Justice Brennan, Justice Rehnquist, and Chief Justice Burger.[196.10] This alignment betrays the larger significance of *Liberty Lobby:* the Court conceptualized this case not as a first amendment decision but as a civil procedure ruling. The case turned on a subtle procedural problem—the extent to which a substantive law evidentiary standard concerning the quality of evidence necessary to state a prima facie case must be factored into the judgmental decision as to whether a genuine issue of material fact exists on a summary judgment motion.[196.11] The first amendment as such played no role in the analysis of any of the Justices who authored opinions, other than the incidental fact that the first amendment happened to be the source of the particular substantive evidentiary rule at stake in the case.

Liberty Lobby is thus an interesting mixed bag from the perspective of the media. On the one hand it is a resounding victory on an issue of critical pragmatic importance—it resolves a conflict among lower courts in exactly the way the media bar hoped it would, making it easier for defendants to prevail on motions for summary judgment. Summary judgment practice is more important today than ever, as rising litigation expenses in defamation cases make the effective preemptive strike through summary judgment a vital element in reducing the chilling effect on free speech that litigation itself poses.[196.12]

On the other hand, *Liberty Lobby* also stands for a proposition less

---

196.6 *See* Washington Post Co. v. Keogh, 365 F.2d 965 (D.C. Cir. 1966), *cert denied,* 385 U.S. 1011 (1967). *See also supra* § 12.07[1].

196.7 See *infra* notes 196.10-196.15, and accompanying text.

196.8 *See* Calder v. Jones, 465 U.S. 783, 790-91 (1984); Keeton v. Hustler, 465 U.S. 770 (1984); Hutchinson v. Proxmire, 443 U.S. 111, 120 N.9 (1979); Herbert v. Lando, 441 U.S. 153 (1979).

196.9 *See supra* § 12.03[1][c][ii].

196.10 106 S. Ct. at 2515 (Brennan, J., dissenting); *Id.* at 2520 (Rehnquist, J. (joined by Burger, C.J.), dissenting).

196.11 *Id.* at 2510-14.

196.12 *See supra* § 12.07[1][b].

warmly consoling to media interests, a proposition that has been emerging in a number of recent cases in which first amendment principles and procedural rules intersect. That principle is one of "procedural neutrality": litigation rules in defamation cases are to be applied "neutrally"—that is, they are to be applied just as they would in any other form of litigation, *and first amendment values are not to be factored in to give defendants any special advantages.*

To live by the sword is to die by the sword, and neutrality is a sword that is quite sharply double-edged. The Court stated in *Liberty Lobby,* for example, that its holding was not meant to denigrate the role of the jury, or authorize trial on affidavits.[196.13] Credibility determinations, the weighing of evidence, and the drawing of legitimate inferences remain the functions of the jury, not the judge on summary judgment motion, and the "evidence of the non-movant is to be believed, and all justifiable inferences are to be drawn in his favor."[196.14] The Court further seemed to admonish trial judges to err on the side of denying summary judgment "where there is reason to believe that the better course would be to proceed to a full trial."[196.15]

[4] Negligence Standard Cases

[a] In General

Summary judgment motions in cases tried under a negligence standard have generated dramatically fewer published opinions than actual malice cases; defendants are apparently more restrained in attempting to dispose of negligence cases at the summary judgment stage. This phenomenon reflects three realities:

(1) Negligence is a significantly lower fault standard than actual malice and thus it is easier for a plaintiff to put forward evidence establishing a genuine issue of material fact.

(2) Negligence cases are governed by a mere preponderance of the evidence test, not the clear and convincing clarity standard.[197]

(3) There is a powerful tradition in tort litigation reflecting both the "common sense" of the community notions built into the

---

196.13 106 S. Ct. at 2513.

196.14 *Id.* (citing Adickes v. S.H. Kress & Co., 398 U.S. 144 (1970)).

196.15 106 S. Ct. at 2514 (citing Kennedy v. Silas Mason Co., 334 U.S. 249 (1948)).

197 *See supra* § 3.08.

"ordinary reasonable person" test, and civil procedure traditions which say that negligence issues are quintessentially matters for the jury.[198]

[b] The Impact of *Dun & Bradstreet*

Negligence cases after *Dun & Bradstreet, Inc. v. Greenmoss Builders, Inc.*,[199] will, to the extent the negligence standard is mandated by the Constitution, involve issues of public concern.[200] One of the few potential benefits of *Dun & Bradstreet*, from a media perspective, is that defendants may legitimately argue that summary judgment is as important a first amendment screening device in constitutional negligence cases as in constitutional actual malice cases, since the *speech* in both types of cases will involve issues of public concern.[201]

§ 12.08 Directed Verdicts and J.N.O.V.'s

[1] As Devices for Jury Control

Directed verdicts, and their more common post-verdict cousins, judgments notwithstanding the verdict (j.n.o.v), are the primary devices through which trial judges control the actions of juries in defamation and privacy cases. There is impressive evidence that juries frequently apply their own versions of justice in defamation cases, versions not necessarily consistent with the standards of the first amendment or the common law.[202] A recent Libel Defense Resource Center study indicated that j.n.o.v.'s are enormously important devices for jury control; in the LDRC's 1984 study j.n.o.v.'s were granted in 55 percent

---

198 *See* Wright & Miller, *supra* note 179, § 2729, at 560-61 (1973).

199 105 S. Ct. 2939 (1985).

200 *See supra* §§ 3.02-3.05.

201 *See* Lake Havasu Estates, Inc. v. Reader's Digest Ass'n, Inc., 441 F. Supp. 489, 492 (S.D.N.Y. 1977) (negligence case; summary judgment held to be preferred procedure) (quoting Meeropol v. Nizer, 381 F. Supp. 29 (S.D.N.Y. 1974), *aff'd*, 560 F.2d 1061 (2d Cir. 1977), *cert. denied*, 434 U.S. 1013 (1978)("Summary judgment is particularly appropriate at an early stage in cases where claims of libel or invasion of privacy are made against publications dealing with matters of public interest or concern")).

202 *See generally* Smolla, *The Rejuvenation of the American Law of Libel*, 132 U. Pa. L. Rev. 1 (1983).

of all cases in which the motion was made, up from 23 percent in a 1982 study.[203]

[2] General Standards

Directed verdicts and j.n.o.v.'s are governed by identical standards.[204] Under the Federal Rules of Civil Procedure a motion for j.n.o.v. is essentially a motion for directed verdict deferred until after the jury has returned its verdict.[205] Traditionally, the procedural standard for directed verdicts and j.n.o.v.'s is quite strict: "Unless the evidence, along with all inferences reasonably to be drawn therefrom, when viewed in the light most favorable to the plaintiff, is such that reasonable jurors in fair and impartial exercise of their judgment could not reasonably disagree in finding for the defendant, the motion is denied."[206]

[3] Applying the Standards

[a] First Amendment Concerns Applied to Summary Judgment Motions

In *Tavoulareas v. Washington Post Co.*,[207] the court argued that the first amendment concerns applicable to summary judgment motions should not be equated with motions for directed verdicts or j.n.o.v.'s:

> Whatever value *summary judgment* has in sparing defamation defendants the expense of actually going to trial, there is no such value in *judgments n.o.v.*, for they come into being *after* the trial is over and virtually all of the expense had been incurred. Strictly in terms of court costs and legal fees, the "chill" is the same whether judgment after trial is based on a jury verdict or a judgment n.o.v.[208]

[b] Relationship to Independent Review Doctrine

This observation in *Tavoulareas* is sensible, as far as it goes. A motion for summary judgment is a sort of first amendment "preemptive

---

203 Goodale, "Survey of Recent Media Verdicts, Their Disposition on Appeal and Media Defense Costs," in Media Insurance and Risk Management 1985 (J. Lankenau, ed.) (PLI 1985), at 69, 81.

204 *See* Vander Zee v. Karabatos, 589 F.2d 723, 726 (D.C. Cir. 1978), *cert. denied,* 441 U.S. 962 (1979).

205 Fed. R. Civ. P. 50(b).

206 Alden v. Providence Hospital, 382 F.2d 163, 165 (D.C. Cir. 1967).

207 759 F.2d 90, *rehearing en banc granted,* 763 F.2d 1472 (D.C. Cir. 1985).

208 *Id.* at 104 (emphasis in original).

strike." Directed verdicts and j.n.o.v.'s, however, come after the legal costs have already mounted, whether or not the defendant ultimately prevails. The *Tavoulareas* position may nonetheless ignore a *different* first amendment value that is more important at the post-verdict stage than prior to trial: the role of judges as independent evaluators of the facts that comprise first amendment litigation judgments. The trial judge's proper approach to a directed verdict or j.n.o.v. motion, therefore, is inextricably intertwined with the issue discussed in the next section, independent review.

§ 12.09 Appeals and the Doctrine of Independent Judicial Review

[1] History of the Doctrine

The Supreme Court has long recognized that constitutional guarantees are meaningless protections if they may be freely subverted through the disingenuous manipulation of facts. To prevent first amendment freedoms from being lost in the process of the application of law to fact the Court has held that appellate courts have the duty to "make an independent examination of the whole record" in order to make sure "that the judgment does not constitute a forbidden intrusion on the field of free expression."[209]

[2] Reaffirmation of the Doctrine in *Bose v. Consumers Union*

The Supreme Court reaffirmed the independent appellate review doctrine in *Bose Corp. v. Consumers Union of United States, Inc.*[210] *Bose* presented an apparent conflict between Rule 52(a) of the Federal Rules of Civil Procedure, which establishes the deferential "clearly erroneous" standard of review of trial judge findings of fact, and the independent appellate review principle. The Court, after carefully reviewing the independent appellate review doctrine, concluded in quite eloquent language that the rule remained a cornerstone of first amendment jurisprudence:

> The requirement of independent appellate review reiterated in *New*

[209] New York Times Co. v. Sullivan, 376 U.S. 254, 284-86 (1964). *See also* NAACP v. Claiborne Hardward, 458 U.S. 886, 933-34 (1983); Greenbelt Cooperative Publishing Ass'n v. Bressler, 398 U.S. 6 (1970); St. Amant v. Thompson, 390 U.S. 727, 732-33 (1968).

[210] 104 S. Ct. 1949 (1984).

> *York Times v. Sullivan* is a rule of federal constitutional law. It emerged from the exigency of deciding concrete cases; it is law in its purest form under our common law heritage. It reflects a deeply held conviction that judges—and particularly members of this Court—must exercise such review in order to preserve the precious liberties established and ordained by the Constitution. The question whether the evidence in the record in a defamation case is of the convincing clarity required to strip the utterance of First Amendment protection is not merely a question for the trier of fact. Judges, as expositors of the Constitution, must independently decide whether the evidence in the record is sufficient to cross the constitutional threshold that bars entry of any judgment that is not supported by clear and convincing proof of "actual malice."[211]

[3] Does *Bose* Swing "Both Ways?"

Does the independent appellate review doctrine apply only to factual determinations unfavorable to the speaker, or does it operate both ways, allowing the appellate court to independently examine the record to reverse a factual finding that went against the plaintiff? In the *Falwell* case,[211.1] the critical jury finding was that the ad parody could not be understood as factual. During oral argument, a number of Justices asked questions concerning the status of that finding under *Bose.*

Chief Justice Rehnquist asked *Hustler's* lawyer, Alan Isaacman, "You think *Bose* is a one-way street?" Isaacman answered that it was one-way, designed only to protect the speaker. Justice O'Connor later returned to the issue in an interesting exchange:

Justice O'Connor: Well, that gets us back to *Bose* and whether we have to reexamine this statement for ourselves to determine whether it's a factual statement.

Mr. Isaacman: Well, that brings me back to my response, Justice O'Connor, that if there were an adverse determination to the speaker, this court would have an independent obligation to examine.

Justice O'Connor: I don't think *Bose* spelled it out that way. I don't read that necessarily into *Bose.* So you may be asking us to move on to another step beyond that case.

Mr. Isaacman: Well, the only thing I would say is the only case I saw that dealt with that is *Brown v. KNB Corporation,* a Connecticut Supreme Court case decided August 18, 1987. And my reading of that is that the independent review goes one way and it goes to review the

---

[211] *Id.* at 1965.

[211.1] Hustler Magazine v. Falwell, 108 S. Ct. 876 (1988).

adverse determination against the speaker. It doesn't go to review a finding that there was—

Justice O'Connor: I suppose that Connecticut case isn't binding on us.

As it turned out, the Supreme Court *did* accept the jury's finding in *Falwell,* but Chief Justice Rehnquist's opinion did not mention the *Bose* one-way street issue. As this issue continues to be thrashed out, certainly the Supreme Court's *implicit* acceptance of the jury's finding in *Falwell* as controlling will provide at least modest additional persuasive authority for the position that *Bose* is a one-way street.[211.2]

In an interesting development on March 28, 1988, Justice White wrote an opinion dissenting from a denial of *certiorari* in a nonlibel first amendment decision, *Don's Porta Signs, Inc. v. Clearwater, Florida,*[211.3] which posed the *Bose* one-way street issue. The case involved the application of first amendment commercial speech rules to an ordinance banning portable signs. The district court struck down the city ordinance. That decision, however, was reversed by the Eleventh Circuit, which held that *Bose* mandated it to independently review the record when the trial court has found a first amendment violation, as well as when it has rejected a first amendment claim.[211.4] Citing a split in authority among the circuits,[211.5] Justice White wrote that he would have granted *certiorari* to resolve this conflict "as to the standard of review to be applied to trial courts' findings of fact in cases holding that the First Amendment has been violated."

[4] "Preliminary" Facts vs. "Ultimate" Facts

The vitality of the actual malice standard and the doctrine of independent appellate review is substantially bound up in how one views the impact of *Bose* on the traditional standard governing jury verdicts. Although the precise verbal formulation tends to vary from jurisdiction to jurisdiction, the general approach is traditionally the same every-

---

211.2 *See* R. Smolla, Jerry Falwell v. Larry Flynt: The First Amendment on Trial 266-68 (1988).

211.3 No. 87-1176, 56 U.S.L.W. 3665 (March 28, 1988) (White, J., dissenting).

211.4 829 F.2d 1051 (11th Cir. 1987), *cert. denied,* 56 U.S.L.W. 3665 (March 28, 1988).

211.5 In addition to the Eleventh Circuit's decision in *Don's Porta Signs,* Justice White listed the Fifth Circuit as adhering to the "two-way" interpretation on *Bose,* citing Lindsay v. City of San Antonio, 821 F.2d 1103, 1107 (5th Cir. 1987). He cited the Seventh and Ninth Circuits as adopting the "one-way" view of *Bose,* citing Daily Herald Co. v. Munro, 838 F.2d 380 (9th Cir. 1988) and Planned Parenthood Ass'n v. Chicago Transit Auth., 767 F.2d 1225 (7th Cir. 1985).

where: a court may overturn the verdict of the jury only when the evidence, together with all inferences that can reasonably be drawn therefrom, is so one-sided in favor of the moving party that reasonable persons could not disagree on the verdict.[212] This is usually translated into the shorthand of considering all evidence and inferences in the light most favorable to the verdict and abstaining from assessing credibility or weighing evidence.[213]

An intense debate has begun to develop over how the traditional deference owed to jury verdicts is to be meshed with the more searching independent review mandated by *Bose.* The debate surfaced in two of the more prominent libel decisions in 1987, *Tavoulareas v. Washington Post Co.*[214] and *Brown & Williamson Tobacco Corporation v. Jacobson,*[215] and promises to continue to be one of the most critical emerging issues in libel litigation.

The narrow, pro-plaintiff view is that *Bose* does not alter the traditional rule governing review of jury verdicts, and that judicial deference must be given to presumed jury findings on underlying facts, evaluations of credibility, and the drawing of inferences.[216] An example of the narrow approach to *Bose* is provided by a 2-to-1 decision by a panel of the United States Court of Appeals for the Sixth Circuit in *Connaughton v. Harte-Hanks Communications.*[216.1] The court limited the *Bose* de novo review to "preliminary, operative, or subsidiary factual determinations anchored in credibility determinations." The *Connaughton* court expressly criticized the approach taken by the *Tavoulareas* en banc majority—and by implication the *Bose* decision itself—as "impinging a plaintiff's constitutional right to a jury trial."

The Supreme Court granted *certiorari* in the *Connaughton* case, and recently rendered an opinion that has thrown the current status of the *Bose* doctrine into an even greater state of confusion. While the Supreme Court's decision in *Harte-Hanks Communications, Inc. v. Con-*

---

212 *See, e.g.,* Tavoulareas v. Washington Post Co., 817 F.2d 762, 776 (D.C. Cir.) (en banc), *cert. denied,* 108 S. Ct. 200 (1987); Vander Zee v. Karabatsos, 589 F.2d 723, 726 (D.C. Cir. 1978), *cert. denied,* 441 U.S. 962 (1979). *See generally* C. Wright, *Law of Federal Courts* § 95, at 468-69 (3d ed. 1976).

213 *See* Tavoulareas v. Washington Post Co., 817 F.2d 762, 776 (D.C. Cir.) (en banc), *cert. denied,* 108 S. Ct. 200 (1987)

214 *Id.*

215 Slip. op. Nos. 86-2474 and 86-2475 (7th Cir. Aug. 12, 1987).

216 The earlier panel decision in *Tavoulareas* appeared to approach this view. *See* 759 F.2d 90 (D.C. Cir. 1985).

216.1 842 F.2d 825 (6th Cir. 1988).

naughton[216.2] reaffirmed the continuing vitality of the actual malice standard and the *Bose* rule of independent appellate review, it did little to clarify the scope of the *Bose* standard.

The *Connaughton* case involved a candidate for the position of Municipal Judge in Hamilton, Ohio, Daniel Connaughton. The local newspaper, the *Journal News,* supported the reelection of Connaughton's opponent, the incumbent judge. A month before the election Connaughton had the good fortune to see his opponent's Director of Court Services arrested on bribery charges. On the day of the arrest, however, Connaughton had the bad fortune of seeing the *Journal News* publish a front-page story quoting a grand jury witness named Alice Thompson as stating that Connaughton had used "dirty tricks" and offered her and her sister jobs and a trip to Florida "in appreciation" for their help in the grand jury investigation of bribery in his opponent's administration. Connaughton sued the paper for libel and won a jury verdict of $5,000 in compensatory damages and $195,000 in punitive damages.

The United States Court of Appeals for the Sixth Circuit affirmed the verdict, following the narrow approach to *Bose.* The court of appeals identified eleven "subsidiary" facts that the jury *could have* found and held that they were not clearly erroneous, and that cumulatively, they provided clear and convincing evidence of actual malice. The court of appeals did not attempt to make an independent assessment of the credibility of conflicting oral testimony.

The Sixth Circuit's approach implicated two related questions concerning the *Bose* standard. Under the narrow view of *Bose,* which the court of appeals followed, appellate judges must make their own "independent" assessment of the facts allegedly establishing actual malice *but* must assume that all facts that *could* reasonably be found in favor of the plaintiff *were* found in favor of the plaintiff. This view preserves the traditional appellate deference to underlying facts, evaluations of credibility, and the drawing of inferences on all issues that could have supported the verdict. Under the broad view, by contrast, "independent" truly means independent, with the appellate court reviewing *de novo* all facts in the record bearing on actual malice.

Closely related to this conflict was a question of "accumulation." Must there be facts in the record which, standing alone, would support a finding of actual malice, or is it enough that several factors, none of which standing alone would constitute actual malice, produce an over-

---

216.2 109 S. Ct. 2678 (1989).

all judgment, when accumulated, that actual malice existed? These questions are of portentous practical significance, because plaintiffs tend to fare extremely well before juries in defamation cases, and defendants have counted on a high reversal rate by appellate courts as their primary source of first amendment protection.

The United States Supreme Court affirmed the *Connaughton* verdict. The Supreme Court's decision, however, failed to adopt either the broad or narrow view of *Bose,* but instead followed a confusing middle course. While the jury *may* have found in favor of the plaintiff on each of the eleven subsidiary facts identified by the court of appeals, the Supreme Court held, the case should have been reviewed on less speculative grounds. In engaging in its own independent review of the record, the Court held, it would confine itself to only those issues that the jury *must* have found in order for it to return a verdict. When those findings are considered along with the undisputed evidence, the Court held, the conclusion that actual malice existed was supported by clear and convincing evidence.

The Court noted that the key figure in the case was Patsy Stephens, the sister of Alice Thompson—for it was Stephens who Connaughton allegedly attempted to influence. Yet the newspaper failed to interview Stephens, and also failed to view videotapes of Connaughton's interview with Stephens. Connaughton had denied the charges against him in an interview with the paper's reporters, and five other witnesses interviewed by the paper had corroborated Connaughton's story. While the mere failure to fully investigate a story is not actual malice (that would be to confuse actual malice with mere negligence), the deliberate avoidance of the truth is—and here it appeared that the paper deliberately shut its eyes to anything that would have cast doubt on Thompson's allegations.

The *Connaughton* case raises more questions than it answers. The critical issue of whether the narrow or broad view of *Bose* should govern was ducked, and the Court adopted a complicated and awkward middle position on the question of accumulation. How, for example, is an appellate court to determine which of the facts supporting actual malice that the jury *could* have found were facts that it *must* have found?

Adding to the confusion, five Justices filed or joined concurring opinions, each exerting a bit of "spin control" on what exactly the majority opinion meant. Justice Scalia filed the most candid concurrence; he would simply have adopted the narrow view of *Bose* and adopted the analysis of the Sixth Circuit.[216.3] Justice Kennedy apparently agreed with Justice Scalia, though he did not join Scalia's opinion, but instead wrote a one-sentence concurrence of his own, stating: "I join the opinion of the Court, for in my view it is not inconsistent with the analysis set out in Justice Scalia's separate concurrence."[216.4] This is, to say the least, a curious position, since obviously Justice Scalia thought his opinion differed markedly from that of the majority. Justice Kennedy seemed to want to join both opinions, notwithstanding their professed inconsistency. Justice White, in an opinion joined by Chief Justice Rehnquist, concurred on grounds that were even more pro-plaintiff than the Sixth Circuit's and the approach of Justice Scalia. Justice White stated that "in cases like this the historical facts—*e.g.*, who did what to whom and when—are reviewable only under the clearly erroneous standard mandated by Rule 52. Credibility determinations fall in this category, as does the issue of knowledge of falsity."[216.5] Justice White, who dissented in *Bose*, would thus be content to do away with the standard of independent appellate review altogether, with the exception of the limited issue of whether, *given* the "historical facts" as found by the trier-of-facts, they would constitute "actual malice." The fifth concurring opinion in *Connaughton* was filed by Justice Blackmun. Unlike the other four Justices who concurred, Justice Blackmun sought to broaden the scope of independent appellate review, and he wrote to express his adherence to truly independent review of the actual malice standard by appellate courts.[216.6]

In the end, plaintiffs could take solace in the fact that a substantial jury verdict had been upheld by the Supreme Court in a libel case—an exceedingly rare event. The *Connaughton* decision marked the only jury verdict to be affirmed by the Supreme Court in a full opinion in a libel case for twenty-two years, going as far back as the judgment in *Curtis Publishing Co. v. Butts.*[216.7] Plaintiffs could also see encouragement in the fact that the narrow view of *Bose* had not been rejected, and much in the Court's opinion seemed to authorize the cumulative "whole is greater than the parts" approach to appellate review of the actual malice finding. Further, several of the concurring Justices appeared to voice support for a relatively restrictive view of *Bose.*

216.3 *Id.* at 2700-01 (Scalia, J., concurring in the judgment).

216.4 *Id.* at 2700 (Kennedy, J., concurring).

216.5 *Id.* at 2699 (White, J., concurring.

216.6 *Id.* at 2699-700 (Blackmun, J., concurring).

216.7 388 U.S. 130 (1967).

Defendants, on the other hand, could find comfort in the fact that the narrow view of *Bose* had not been explicitly adopted, and that the Court took pains to affirm its allegiance to the theory of independent review. On the whole, one must conclude that the Court did media law practice a disservice in *Connaughton* for failing to face up to the underlying conflicts it posed and clearly resolve them. What the Court instead did was insure that there will be as many inconsistent permutations of *Connaughton* among the lower courts as there had been of *Bose.*

As lower courts parse the meaning of *Connaughton,* it is to be hoped that they will perceive the critical significance of the broader view of *Bose* to the preservation of first amendment principles.

The broad, pro-defense view is that the *Bose* requirement of de novo review means that no deference at all is to be paid to the jury's presumed findings, and that independent appellate review means exactly what it says—review independent of the jury.[217]

The broad view of *Bose* is certainly the correct view, and the very best proof of that may be found in the *Bose* opinion itself. *Bose* is filled with statements indicating that the de novo review principle is not restricted merely to so-called ultimate facts but rather directs the Court to get into the nitty-gritty of the preliminary factual findings upon which the ultimate facts are based.[218] Not only does the *Bose* opinion contain many verbal clues that this is what the Court had in mind, even more important, this is precisely what the Supreme Court did in *Bose:* it examined closely the trial court's credibility choices and factual inferences, en route to overruling the Court's ultimate finding of actual malice.[219]

This critical issue has been placed in particularly sharp relief in the *Tavoulareas v. Washington Post*[220] litigation. In March, the District of Columbia Court of Appeals, in an en banc decision, vacated a prior panel decision and overturned the jury verdict which Tavoulareas had won.[221] The Court refused to adopt either the narrow or the broad view of *Bose,* stating that even under the narrow view the plaintiff had failed to meet his burden of establishing actual malice by clear and convincing

---

217 *See* Tavoulareas v. Washington Post Co., 817 F.2d 762, 777 (D.C. Cir.) (en banc), *cert. denied,* 108 S. Ct. 200 (1987) (citing Supplemental Brief of Appellees at 6-16).

218 The Court in *Bose* noted, for example, that "the rule of independent review assigns to judges a constitutional responsibility that cannot be performed in the particular case by a jury or by a trial judge." Bose Corp. v. Consumers Union, 466 U.S. 485, 501 (1984).

219 *See id.* at 511-14.

220 817 F.2d 762 (D.C. Cir.) (en banc), *cert. denied,* 108 S. Ct. 200 (1987).

221 *See* 759 F.2d 90 (D.C. Cir. 1985).

evidence.[222] Note that the Court also held that the plaintiff failed to meet the burden of proving that the principal defamatory charge in the litigation, that Tavoulareas had set up his son in business, was false.[223]

Although the *Tavoulareas* court purported to avoid reaching the question as to the scope of the *Bose* standard, it is worth examining to some degree the manner in which the court actually set out to apply the standard, because the court's opinion is very instructive in pointing out the way in which the broader *Bose* interpretation may successfully be pressed upon courts in the future. Before doing that, however, *Tavoulareas* and the *Bose* debate must first be placed in a larger context. In the last twenty years a pattern has emerged in the application of the actual malice standard. Courts permit a wide range of factors to be considered as evidence probative of the existence of actual malice. At the same time, however, courts repeatedly emphasize that no one of these factors will, standing alone, constitute actual malice.[224] Consider for a moment the list of factors that may be probative, but generally not dispositive, of actual malice: common law ill will malice is never dispositive, but may be probative;[225] mere failure to further investigate, fact-check, or corroborate is never dispositive, but such a failure, if glaring and obvious, may be probative of a deliberate decision to avoid finding the truth;[226] mere reliance on a biased source is not dispositive, but such reliance, with other factors, may be probative;[227] mere reliance on anonymous sources is not dispositive, but may be probative;[228] and editorial point of view, lack of balance, consistent resolution of all conflicts against the plaintiff, disingenuous editing, preconceived story line biases, or the ignoring of expressions of doubt by others within the news organization may be probative, though usually not dispositive.[229]

The factors just listed, along with others, are the practical issues routinely litigated under the actual malice determination. Clearly, courts permit this sort of evidence to be admitted as probative of actual malice. It is thus inevitable that the integrity of the actual malice standard as a meaningful defense will ultimately come down to such razor thin

---

222 817 F.2d at 777.

223 *Id.* at 778-88.

224 *See supra* §§ 3.13-3.23.

225 *See supra* §§ 3.15-3.16.

226 *See supra* §§ 3.17-3.18.

227 *See supra* §3.19.

228 *See supra* § 3.19[3].

229 *See supra* § 3.20.

questions as the extent to which these various factors may be aggregated by the jury. Should the jury be permitted to produce a whole greater than the sum of its parts? Once the jury has spoken with a verdict for the plaintiff, must the reviewing court take the position that because of the traditional deference to jury verdicts, all the evidence that was admitted as merely probative must now be treated on review as dispositive, since every inference and credibility judgment must be assessed in the light most favorable to the verdict?

Although the *Tavoulareas* court claimed that it did not reach this issue, in fact the Court's opinion was a classic exercise of conscientious and aggressive independent appellate review in which the record was reexamined in painstaking detail. One may find in that examination an extremely important pattern. The court deferred to the jury's verdict (by assessing facts in a light most favorable to that verdict) only at a very rudimentary level. The court was deferential only with regard to basic preliminary facts, and only with regard to purely factual inferences—inferences, for example, as to what particular actions or statements establish concerning basic motives. The court refused, however, to give any deference to the mixed factual and legal inferences that could be drawn from these facts.

For example, after crediting all of the evidence which the jury could have believed established that the *Post*'s principal source for the story was personally biased against the Tavoulareas family, the court nevertheless used its independent judgment to hold that that evidence of bias—in light of all the other corroborative evidence gathered by the *Post*'s reporter, and in light of other evidence favoring the source's credibility—was insufficient to establish actual malice.[230]

Similarly, in dealing with an internal memorandum written by a copy editor at the *Post* that was critical of the story, the court credited all inferences most favorable to Tavoulareas from the memorandum, and then went on to hold that any disbelief by the editor expressed in the memorandum was unconnected to any false defamatory statement, and thus could not support an actual malice finding.[231]

Perhaps the most far-reaching aspects of the Court's actual malice analysis, however, concerned evidence relating to the *Post*'s alleged ill will, bad motives, and aggressive, adversarial journalistic style. A *Post* reporter had said that "it is not every day that you knock off one of the seven sisters," that he had written "a case against Tavoulareas," that

---

230 817 F.2d at 790-93.

231 *Id.* at 793-94.

he "blew Tavoulareas out of the water" and sent him home with his "tail between his legs."[232] The court took the position that as to actual malice these statements were utterly lacking in probative value. It noted that this was very similar to the vernacular of courtroom litigators and that it merely demonstrated an adversarial stance between the reporter and the plaintiff. The court noted that the journalistic profession, like the legal profession, is grounded in the belief that the adversarial process is an engine of truth and that it was fully consistent with sound investigative reporting to be adversarial.[233] The court did chide the *Post* reporter for a fourth statement in which he asked whether there was a family member who could rifle Tavoulareas's safe and photocopy documents. The court said that even if this reference to rifling the files was a joke, it was "beyond the pale."[234] But then, in an extremely important sentence, the court said: "We do not sit as some kind of journalism review seminar, offering our observations on contemporary journalism and journalists." And in a critical next remark the court stated: *"Neither do juries."*[235] The court noted that at most the statement about rifling the safe expressed a willingness to get evidence by improper means, but it was not at all probative of a willingness to publish unsupported allegations.[236]

Finally, in an extremely significant analysis, the court gave full credit to evidence indicating pressure within the *Post* to produce high impact stories of wrongdoing, stories that editor Bob Woodward quite succinctly testified he had come to call "holy shit stories."[237] To its great credit the court in *Tavoulareas* emphasized that far from being evidence of actual malice, such pressure is in fact designed to spur reporters to engage in "one of the highest functions of the press in our society."[238] The crucial analytical point was that pressure to produce high impact stories is not equivalent to pressure to produce high impact stories with little or no regard for their accuracy. Only the second type of pressure, which did not exist at the *Post*, would have been legitimately probative of actual malice.[239]

---

232 *Id.* at 795.
233 *Id.*
234 *Id.* at 796.
235 *Id.* (emphasis added).
236 *Id.*
237 *Id.* at n.48.
238 *Id.*
239 *Id.* at 797.

The discussion of *Bose* in *Tavoulareas* was picked up by the Seventh Circuit Court of Appeals in *Brown & Williamson Tobacco Corporation v. Jacobsen.*[240] Like the *Tavoulareas* court, the *Jacobson* court refused to explicitly adopt either the broad or the narrow view of *Bose.* The court in *Jacobson* instead posited that for the sake of the case before it, it would assume that the broad, pro-defense view of *Bose* applied.[241] Unfortunately for the defendants, Jacobson and CBS, the court then went on to affirm the jury verdict for the plaintiff, even though the court purported to follow the more liberal *Bose* formulation.

The current state of this fluid issue may best be encapsulated in a December 1986 decision by the Illinois Supreme Court on the *Bose* problem. The court in *Wanless v. Rothballer*[242] overturned a $500,000 jury verdict, stating that while it would defer to the jury on discrete facts, which it defined as "what was done or said by the parties," the "accuracy of the news accounts," and the "credibility of witnesses," the court should nevertheless, under *Bose,* review de novo the application of those discrete facts to the actual malice standard. The court then went on to engage in a law-to-fact analysis quite similar to that which was to take place in *Tavoulareas.* Now, in the very best of all possible worlds, one might hope for a clear and unequivocal judicial consensus that the broad reading of *Bose* is the proper reading. As of this writing, the plaintiff in *Tavoulareas* has petitioned for certiorari, inviting the Supreme Court to abandon the entire public figure doctrine, or at least to overrule the en banc Court of Appeals's application of *Bose.* It is possible, therefore, that the Supreme Court will itself resolve the *Bose* problem. Even in the absence of a clean kill of the restrictive view of *Bose,* however, cases such as *Tavoulareas* and *Rothballer* point the way to an intermediate approach that may be developed to the defendant's advantage, driving a wedge between preliminary facts and inferences at a very rudimentary level and the mixed law and fact evaluations upon which the actual malice standard really rests. This intermediate position, which essentially was what was applied in *Tavoulareas,* is not, however, a completely secure one—indeed the earlier panel decision claimed to be using this sort of method when it affirmed the jury verdict

---

240 Slip. op. Nos. 86-2474 and 86-2475 (7th Cir. Aug. 12, 1987).

241 Slip. op. at 16-17.

242 13 Med. L. Rep. (BNA) 1849 (Ill. Sup. Ct. 1986).

in *Tavoulareas*[243]—ultimately, therefore, the only real security will come from a firm judicial acceptance of the idea of complete independent review.

The point of *Bose* is that first amendment cases are in some respects different from ordinary civil litigation. *The Constitution may be just as easily subverted by manipulation of the "preliminary" facts in the record as by manipulation of the ultimate conclusions.* The buffer zone for free speech created by *New York Times* requires meaningful review of the actual malice and convincing clarity standards, review that is rendered impotent if all reasonable inferences must be given in favor of the jury's finding.

The theme emerging from many recent cases is that no special first amendment considerations should permeate procedural rules in defamation cases, for that would be a form of "double counting."[244] The mistake in this analysis in the context of *Bose* is that the independent appellate review doctrine is *not procedural.* Rather, as the Supreme Court in *Bose* resoundingly emphasized, the doctrine goes to the very heart of the substantive rule of actual malice established in *New York Times.* The Court in *Bose* characterized it as "a rule of federal constitutional law"[245] the application of which "is not merely a question for the trier of fact."[246] The principle of independent review does not exist to give first amendment values an *extra* counting but rather to insure that they have been given *sufficient* counting.

---

243 *See* 759 F.2d 90 (D.C. Cir. 1985), *vacated,* 817 F.2d 762 (D.C. Cir.) (en banc), *cert. denied,* 108 S. Ct. 200 (1987).

244 *See, e.g.,* Calder v. Jones, 465 U.S. 783 (1984). *See supra* § 12.03[1][c][ii].

245 466 U.S. 485, 510 (1984).

246 *Id.* at 511.

CHAPTER 13

Counseling and Strategy

§ 13.01 Counseling Media Clients

[1] Bad Image of the Press

General public esteem for the mainstream press is at a relatively low level today, judging by public opinion polls. Gallup Polls taken in 1984, 1983, and 1981, for example, expressed a general "confidence rating" for television of approximately 25%, placing it last on a list that includes churches, the military, banks, the Supreme Court, public schools, Congress, big business, and organized labor.[1] Newspapers fare marginally better, with a confidence rating of 34%, but that still places the press well below many of the other major institutions in American life.[2] In the 1980s the print and broadcast press finds itself virtually under siege with libel and invasion of privacy litigation,[3] and the responses of juries appear to parallel the negative picture of the press that the opinion polls reveal.[4]

[2] The Good News and Bad News in the Statistics

As previously discussed, study efforts by Professor Marc Franklin and the Libel Defense Resource Center indicate that juries are overwhelmingly favorable to plaintiffs, while the overall success rate for plaintiffs after all appeals remains low.[5]

---

1 *See The Media in the Dock,* Newsweek, October 22, 1984, at 66-72.

2 *Id.*

3 *See generally* Smolla, "Why Has the Media Become a Litigation Target and What's to Be Done?" in Media Insurance and Risk Management 1985 (J. Lankenau, ed.)(PLI 1985).

4 *See* Smolla, *Let the Author Beware: The Rejuvenation of the American Law of Libel,* 132 U. Pa. L. Rev. 1 (1983).

5 *See* the statistics cited in § 9.13, *supra.*

§ 13.02 The Dominant Problems of Media Litigation

[1] The High Costs of Defense

The encouraging fact that the average jury award may very well be reduced or eliminated on appeal is tempered by the long and expensive road the defendant may be forced to travel. No exact information on litigation defense costs is available, but what information does exist is intimidating. One insurer has estimated that litigation defense costs consume in the range of 80 percent of all out-of-pocket expenses in media litigation, dwarfing what is spent on actual payments of awards and settlements. In blockbuster suits, the defense costs can be in multiple millions of dollars.[6] The defense costs in the *Westmoreland v. CBS* litigation have been estimated at between $6 million and $10 million, in *Sharon v. Time, Inc.* in the range of $1.5 million.[7] Fees of $200,000 to $300,000 are not uncommon.[8] (Legal fees in major market areas such as New York, Washington, and San Francisco are likely to run in the range of $200 to $250 per hour, and in less populous markets, from $80 to $125 per hour.[9]) One result of this phenomenon has been a sudden and drastic increase in insurance premium rates, often with less expansive coverage.[10]

[2] The Chilling Effect on Free Speech

There is a direct economic equation between the costs of defense in media cases and the exercise of free speech rights by media outlets. The most infamous example is the *Alton Telegraph* case, in which a small newspaper in Alton, Illinois, was forced into bankruptcy because of its financial inability to post an appeals bond from a judgment of $6.7 million compensatory damages and $2.5 million punitive damages.[11] Such dramatic examples, however, are perhaps less worrisome than the gradual erosion of editorial independence that may take place over

---

6 *See* Smolla, *supra* note 4, at 12-14.

7 *See* Goodale, "Study of Recent Media Verdicts, Their Disposition on Appeal, and Media Costs" 69, 86-87, in Media Insurance and Risk Management 1985 (J. Lankenau, ed.)(PLI 1985).

8 *Id.* at 87.

9 *Id.*

10 *See* Chapter 14, *infra.*

11 *See* Green v. Alton Telegraph Co., 107 Ill. App. 3d 755, 438 N.E.2d 203 (1982); Smolla, *supra* note 4, at 12-13, and nn.72-74.

time as media outlets of all sorts find their litigation and legal costs rising.

§ 13.03 Preventative Counseling

[1] Legal Advice vs. Journalistic or Artistic Judgment

One of the great temptations for the attorney who regularly counsels a media outlet, whether it be a major national publication or a small local radio station, is to resolve in advance all potentially dangerous story problems against the client, and to counsel the client not to run the story. Preventative counseling is obviously one of the most important functions of the media lawyer, but in engaging in that counseling the attorney ought to be sensitive to the sometimes murky line between legal advice and journalistic or artistic judgment. The " chilling effect" that libel litigation can have on investigative reporting, for example, ought not be encouraged by a newspaper's own legal counsel. The lawyer's function should instead be to state the range of risks posed by a particular story as precisely and accurately as the lawyer's skill and judgment permit, and to suggest an alternative, when appropriate, but the lawyer should allow the client to decide the levels of risk it is willing to assume.

[2] The Special Role of Regular Counsel

Obviously a lawyer who routinely works with his or her journalistic clients will never be able to maintain complete separation between legal and editorial judgment, and indeed the client may wish for the lawyer to breach the wall, just as clients quite legitimately want both legal and business advice from their regular counsel. The point is that the media lawyer ought never disguise what is in fact a judgment on editorial or business policy as a statement of the client's legal situation.

If, for example, the media attorney is asked whether a particular story ought to be published—a story that is supported by a detailed account from one source, but unverified by documents or other corroborating evidence—the attorney has to distinguish between making an assessment of the defamation risks, on the one hand, and making an editorial assessment of the newsworthiness of the story and the investigative abilities of the journalist, on the other hand. The attorney might thus advise the editor that since the story involves a public official, there is no exposure to liability if the newspaper runs it without knowledge of falsity or reckless disregard of the truth. It may be "reckless" to run the story in the absence of some verification if the source's information is so highly improbable that instant subjective doubts are raised as to its truth,[12] and the client deserves this advice from the attorney. But the source's information may not be at all improbable; the identity and position of the source, the detail with which the information is communicated, and the inherent plausibility of the story all may be factors weighing toward publishing it. The client deserves to be given this information as well, so that the real decision makers can bring their own journalistic and business judgment to bear on whether the story ought to be printed. The client may seek the lawyer's input on these judgments also, but the important thing is that the client not be misled by either overly cautious or overly cavalier legal advice.

Of course, some media clients are often frustrated by what appears to be an unwillingness on the part of their attorneys, given the ambiguity and the fluidity of much of the modern law of privacy and defamation, to take a firm stance even as to supposedly "black letter" law. The lawyer who too often hides behind these ambiguities is not very useful as a preventative counselor. The able media lawyer, if called upon in advance (more often than not, the attorney is called in only after the fact) ought to be able to give a reasonably firm judgment in most situations. The "art" comes in developing the instinct for when the client is best served by simple firm advice, and when the client is best served by a much more equivocal explanation.

§ 13.04 Cost Reduction in Litigation

[1] The Assertion of More Stringent Control by In-House Counsel

The high costs of media defense litigation has evoked a quite natural and appropriate "market response" from in-house counsel responsible for supervising litigation against media outlets: a new assertiveness in the attempt to keep litigation costs down. This often means exercising

[12] *See supra* § 3.18.

tighter control over the decisions and fees of outside counsel retained to handle litigation matters.[13]

[2] Some Cost Control Devices

Among the sorts of devices that may be useful in controlling defense costs are the following:

[a] Budget Reports

A budget (usually regarded as only a guideline) detailing anticipated litigation steps and their costs tend to keep billing more realistic.

[b] Periodic Strategy Assessments

Not every libel suit is a blockbuster; not every plaintiff is serious in prosecuting the case; not every case deserves a full custom treatment. Realistic strategy assessment on a periodic basis as to whether to take an aggressive or low profile "wait and see" defense posture, in consultations between in-house and outside counsel, can reduce costs.

[c] Holding Back on Aggressive Early Discovery

An issue related to strategy assessment involves timing of defense efforts. Experience indicates that some libel and privacy suits just wither away and die—plaintiffs lose interest or become intimidated by the expense of litigation, or they may have filed the suit primarily for its instant news value, for catharsis, or to restore self-image, but were never really serious about seeing it to the bitter end. It is not always necessary to depose the plaintiff in the first months after filing, or to spend $10,000 preparing a motion for summary judgment. At times, the best judgment is to go slowly at first, and it also saves money.

[d] Sharing and "Cross-Fertilization" of Legal Research

A media outlet that is sued with relative frequency can build its own impressive library of briefs, memoranda, sample pleadings, motions, and interrogatories, eliminating the need to constantly reinvent the

---

13 *See* Lucan, "Controlling Litigation Costs," 167, 173-81, and "The New York Times Company Guidelines for Controlling Costs of Legal Services," at 189, in Media Insurance and Risk Management 1985 (J. Lankeneau, ed.)(PLI 1985).

wheel. The key is to develop a system of indexing that makes such previous efforts readily identifiable and retrievable.

§ 13.05 Media Counterclaims Against Plaintiffs

One newly emerging technique for "raising the ante" in antimedia litigation is to file a counterclaim against the plaintiff. In *LaRouche v. NBC*,[14] NBC successfully counterclaimed in a libel suit brought against it by Lyndon LaRouche; a jury award of $3 million in punitive damages in favor of NBC was reduced to $200,000, through remittur. The theory of NBC's counterclaim, sustained by the court, was the tort of "interference with business relations."[15]

§ 13.06 Should Reporters Destroy Notes, Records, Tapes, or Files?

Lawyers who represent media clients must at times decide whether to advise clients to get rid of notes, records, tapes, files, or other "hard" evidence that might be embarrassing or incriminating in later litigation. One theory favors destruction, on the obvious rationale that if litigation arises such material will later be discoverable, and often will in hindsight be given a more sinister interpretation that it deserves. An opposing viewpoint is that such material should always be retained, particularly for controversial stories, on the theory that it is far more likely in the long run to be exonerating than incriminating, and destroying it only raises adverse suspicions.

Perhaps the soundest position is to advise clients to follow whatever storage or destruction procedures would normally be undertaken in the ordinary course of business. If video tapes are routinely erased and reused, for example, or disused files destroyed, these practices can continue. As a "standing order," however, it does not make sense to encourage reporters or editors to destroy notes or files that may be useful for future stories, or, conversely, to retain such material beyond its useful life, merely because of the threat of litigation.

The nature of the debate over how best to advise journalists regarding the destruction of their notes and other records was altered drastically by the recent opinion of the Seventh Circuit in *Brown &*

---

[14] 11 Med. L. Rep. (BNA) 1655 (E.D. Va. 1985).

[15] *Id.* at 1656-58.

Williamson Tobacco Corp. v. Jacobson.[15.1] That decision affirmed an extremely high damages award against CBS and correspondent Walter Jacobson, for allegedly defamatory statements made by Jacobson during a "Perspective" commentary on the marketing tactics of cigarette advertisers.[15.2] The text of Jacobson's broadcast was highly critical of the marketing strategies of the manufacturers of Viceroy cigarettes. An earlier script had apparently been more balanced, including material telling the manufacturer's side of the story. CBS and Jacobson initially managed to get the case dismissed by the federal district court in Chicago. Upon learning of the dismissal, a CBS employee, somewhat suspiciously, located and destroyed crucial parts of the earlier, more balanced script. The Court of Appeals, meanwhile, reversed the distirict court's dismissal, ordering the case to proceed. During the subsequent discovery period, it was found that the earlier script, along with other material pertinent to the broadcast, had been partially destroyed and no copies were to be found.[15.3] This became one of the single most important episodes in the litigation, for in reviewing the record to determine whether the jury's verdict was supported by clear and convincing evidence of actual malice, the Court of Appeals very heavily emphasized the destruction of the script as evidence of actual malice. The court's train of reasoning appeared to be that an editorial decision to eschew an "evenhanded" broadcast in favor of a less balanced, more hard-hitting script could be probative of knowing or reckless disregard for the truth. The deliberate destruction of the prior script could therefore be used as an inference that the script would have tended to establish such subjective fault, and therefore could legitimately be used to support the actual malice finding.[15.4]

The *Jacobson* case raises at least two significant points. First, the

---

15.1 Slip. op. Nos. 86-2474 and 86-2475 (7th Cir. Aug. 12, 1987).

15.2 The Court of Appeals affirmed $2,050,000 in punitive damages and $1,000,000 in compensatory damages.

15.3 The material was destroyed by Jacobson's researcher. It included an 18 page sample script, an annotated copy of an FTC report from which much of the story was drawn, and various interview notes. Only the parts of the documents that would have been relevant to the litigation were destroyed.

15.4 The court stated that a "court and a jury are entitled to presume that documents destroyed in bad faith while litigation is pending would be unfavorable to the party that has destroyed the documents." Slip op. at 28 (citing Coates v. Johnson & Johnson, 756 F.2d 524, 551 (7th Cir. 1985); S.C. Johnson & Son v. Louisville & Nashville R.R., 695 F.2d 253, 258-59 (7th Cir. 1982); Nation-Wide Check v. Forest Hills Distributors, 692 F.2d 214, 217-19 (1st Cir. 1982)).

Court of Appeals's technique triggers a troubling question: To what extent should journalistic conduct after a story has run—indeed, after litigation has commenced—be admitted as probative of actual malice? The traditional position is that the actual malice determination is to be made primarily upon the behavior leading up to publication.[15.5] The willful destruction of evidence, of course, is a direct assault on the integrity of the judicial process. If *Jacobson* is understood as essentially an abuse of discovery ruling, then it may be tolerable on those narrow grounds. But the Court of Appeals did not analyze the case in terms of disciplinary sanctions for destroying evidence; rather, the court undertook a more "routine" review of the record for evidence of actual malice. Viewed in those terms, the affirmance of a very substantial damages award largely on the relatively thin reed of a partially destroyed script does appear quite out of line with prior cases. One hopes that *Jacobson* will not be extended to place journalists at their peril for any arguably suspicious behavior well after the story has run.

The second lesson to be garnered from *Jacobson* is the blunt preventative homily: don't lose or destroy anything once a story has become a target of controversy. This admonition is nothing new to lawyers—indeed, the CBS legal department has a standing rule (in place at the time of the Jacobson matter) against any such destruction without the permission of the legal department. The problem, of course, is to get the message across to journalists, who may not always realize how well the plaintiff's attorney may be able to ferret out such destruction. The power of civil discovery makes pretty good "investigative reporters" of us all. Destruction of potential evidence surrounding a story that has drawn fire and may lead to litigation is both ethically untenable journalistic behavior and possible legal suicide. Counsel who regularly brief journalists may wish to use the *Jacobson* example as a way of driving home that message.

§ 13.07 When the Press Sues the Press

Reporters, editors, publishers, and media outlets have in recent years been increasingly active as plaintiffs against other media outlets.[16]

15.5 *See supra* § 3.22[1].

16 *See, e.g.*, Keeton v. Hustler Magazine, Inc., 104 S. Ct. 1473 (1984); Loeb v. New Times Communications Corp., 497 F. Supp. 85 (S.D.N.Y. 1980); Loeb v. Globe Newspaper Co., 489 F. Supp. 481 (D. Mass. 1980); Guccione v. Hustler, 7 Med. L. Rep. (BNA) 2077 (Ohio Ct. App. Franklin City 1981).

These internecine battles take their toll on the general first amendment freedoms enjoyed by all media outlets. Members of the press of course have the same rights as anyone to pursue civil litigation. Self-restraint in this area, however, would seem to be to everyone's collective advantage. Victories that a publisher may notch in one suit may come back to haunt that publisher in the next. To the extent that the media is committed to the ideals embodied in the *New York Times* case, the best cure for offending speech is counterspeech, not litigation.

§ 13.08 Role of the Plaintiff's Lawyer

[1] Realism About Litigation

Under modern constitutional rules in defamation actions, plaintiffs often have the burden of proving that what was said about them was false.[17] In every defamation case, the truth or falsity of the defamatory statement is potentially the focal point of the litigation. Furthermore, even if the defamatory statement is proven to be false, evidence that the plaintiff already has a bad reputation is admissible in mitigation of damages.[18] This means that in a hotly contested defamation action the plaintiff's life and character may well be under a high powered litigation microscope.[19] If the defendant chooses to be aggressive in its pursuit of discovery (and in many cases the defendant most surely will), the plaintiff's life may become an open book.

From the perspective of the plaintiff's lawyer, two practical consequences are presented by the operation of this combination of substantive law and the rules of discovery. First, there may be some battles over the "truth" of a charge that are virtually impossible to resolve. After a long and bitter discovery period and trial, the truth may be no clearer

(*Text continued on page 13-9*)

---

17 *See supra* § 5.05.

18 *See supra* § 9.10[4].

19 In Sharon v. Time, Inc., 599 F. Supp. 538 (S.D.N.Y. 1984), Ariel Sharon's entire life, going back to his boyhood, became part of the litigation.

than it was when the client first stepped into the lawyer's office. In many situations, as just stated, the burden of proof is on the plaintiff to prove falsity.[20] Given the overwhelming statistical inclination of juries to side with plaintiffs, of course, many prudent plaintiffs may well be willing to gamble on the truth issue, even when definitive proof is difficult to garner. But in view of the very low incidence of plaintiff's success on appeal, a realistic plaintiff's attorney should acknowledge that the sense of vindication that comes from the plaintiff's victory at trial will often, the statistics tell us, be diminished on appeal. The competent attorney does not sugarcoat the uphill battle that often lies before his or her client.

[2] Skeletons in the Closet

[a] In General

The second practical consequence of the defamation litigation process is that—as awkward as it may be to discuss with one's client—the discovery process may uncover skeletons in the client's closet. The most infamous example is that of Oscar Wilde, who was accused of being homosexual by the Marquis of Queensberry, the father of Wilde's close companion Lord Alfred Douglas. Wilde sued the Marquis of Queensberry for libel, lying to his own attorneys by insisting that he was not homosexual. The trial revealed that the charges were in fact true. Wilde not only lost his libel suit, he was indicted and convicted of illegal homosexual conduct and spent two years in prison.

[b] Substantial Truth

Even if the precise defamatory statement made about the would-be plaintiff is false, the client should be warned that picayune and technical deviations from the truth are not enough to establish falsity,[21] so that if the gist or sting of the charge is accurate, litigation should not be pursued. Similarly, since other bad acts or proof of bad reputation is admissible in mitigation of damages, the client should be warned that the "skeletons in the closet" need not be the precise ones at issue in the defamatory statement, and the plaintiff's Pyrrhic victory on the charge

---

20 *See supra* § 5.05.

21 *See supra* §§ 5.08-5.09.

at issue may leave the plaintiff with little recompense in damages and a worse reputation than he or she started with.

[3] Invasion of Privacy Suits

A parallel problem may exist in invasion of privacy suits. A media story improperly revealing private facts may create a cause of action in favor of one's client, but if the publication was not widely disseminated, the publicity that the litigation itself could spawn might constitute a worse invasion of privacy and more personal embarrassment than the original tort itself.

[4] The Advantage of Prudent Disclosures

These "truth in libel and privacy litigation" disclosures will not and should not deter the honest litigant who has genuinely been injured; but they are disclosures that the prudent plaintiff's counsel should probably make as a matter of course. It is always in the best interests of one's client to be realistic in assessing costs and benefits to the client prior to launching litigation.

§ 13.09 Litigation Strategy in a Federal System

[1] The Interplay of Evolving Constitutional and Common Law Rules

For a few years after the *New York Times* decision it appeared that first amendment principles would render common law rules governing defamation and privacy virtually obsolete. The changes worked on the defamation and privacy torts by the progeny of *New York Times* seemed to be totally displacing common law rules with evolving first amendment principles. Had first amendment doctrines managed to obviate common law rules completely, the defamation and privacy fields would probably be far less complex today. But since the mid-1970s, the Supreme Court has dramatically slowed down the imposition of first amendment constraints on state defamation and privacy law, and state created law and rules have reemerged with new importance.[22] The able attorney handling a defamation or privacy suit today

---

[22] *See, e.g.*, Dun & Bradstreet, Inc. v. Greenmoss Builders, Inc., 105 S. Ct. 2939 (1985). *See supra* §§ 3.02-3.05.

must pay as much attention to common law issues as constitutional questions, as more and more defamation and privacy suits are won or lost on state rather than federal grounds. First amendment considerations, of course, remain enormously important, and even dominant, in many cases. But defamation and privacy laws have not been, and clearly will not be (at least in the foreseeable future), totally constitutionalized.

[2] The Freedom of States Within the Constitutional Framework

Constitutional doctrine has not totally overwhelmed state tort rules in the defamation and privacy fields; a by-product of this is the states' freedom to experiment, as long as they do not violate the contours of the Constitution.[23] The constitutional rules merely set minimum floors of protection for defendants. States remain free to give defendants substantially more protection than the first amendment requires. There is, in fact, no constitutional requirement that a state recognize a particular tort as existing at all. A state may choose, for example, to severly restrict or entirely eliminate the torts of infliction of emotional distress and public disclosure of private facts. Such a complete elimination recently took place when the Supreme Court of North Carolina decided that in North Carolina no cause of action exists at all for placing a person in a false light in the public eye.[24]

[3] Some Practical Strategic Considerations Arising from the Interplay of Constitutional and Common Law Rules

[a] In General

Compared to the vast number of lower court decisions in the last two decades, the Supreme Court has heard only a small number of significant defamation and privacy cases since 1964. Many traditional common law defamation and privacy rules are *theoretically* subject to constitutional attack, but definitive Supreme Court pronouncements have yet to be made on many of them. This means in essence that, until the Court sets the standard, states are not merely free to be "ahead" of the Supreme Court in protecting defendants, they are just as free to "lag behind." Further, the meshing of common law principles and

---

23 *See supra* §§ 3.09-3.12.

24 Renwick v. News and Observer Publishing Co., 310 N.C. 312, 312 S.E.2d 405 (1984). *See supra* § 10.02[7].

constitutional law principles is often very confusing, and the states are frequently divided on how to interpret even those first amendment principles the Supreme Court has supposedly already made clear.[25]

[b] Forum Shopping

From the perspective of the plaintiff's attorney, the interests of the client may often be valuably served by forum shopping. Recent developments have expanded the jurisdictional and venue opportunities in many defamation and privacy cases.[26] Careful attention to differences in substantive law (both state common law *and* prevailing state *interpretation* of first amendment requirements) and in conflicts of law principles[27] may very well affect the ultimate outcome of the litigation.

[c] Defense Considerations

From the perspective of defense counsel, the interplay between common law and constitutional law doctrines contains both a valuable opportunity and a potentially dangerous trap. The valuable opportunity is simple: It is always open to the defense to argue vigorously for the adoption of state rules that give defendants more protection than the Supreme Court requires. This is no defense lawyer's pipedream; a surprising number of states have developed rules of fault,[28] construction,[29] damages,[30] or confidential privilege[31] that in one way or another place defendants in litigation positions superior to first amendment minimums.

The ironic consequence is that at times defendants may be better off in state court than in federal court, because federal judges, bound by *Erie*[32] to apply state law in diversity cases, may be more reluctant than their state counterparts to fashion innovative defenses based on state law. Obviously, defendants will often not have any choice over the

---

25 *See, for example,* the many different formulations currently extant with regard to the fact/opinion distinction, reviewed in Chapter 6, *supra.*

26 *See supra* §§ 12.02-12.03.

27 *See supra* § 12.02.

28 *See supra* § 12.11.

29 *See supra* § 4.02[2].

30 *See* Chapter 9, *supra*

31 *See supra* § 12.06[2][b].

32 Erie R.R. v. Tompkins, 304 U.S. 64 (1938). LDRC statistics, however, continue to indicate that success rates for the media are significantly higher in federal than in state court. *See* Goddale, *supra* note 7, at 69-87.

forum, and there will frequently be considerations other than the *Erie Railroad* problem that tip the strategic balance back toward a particular federal district court. But in those cases initially filed by plaintiffs in state court in which removal to federal court would be available, defense counsel should avoid any reflexive assumption that removal is the preferable course of action.

[4] Independent and Adequate State Grounds

In litigation involving the simultaneous use of common law and constitutional law defenses and privileges by the defendant, it will at times be very important for defense counsel to urge the lower state or federal court to clearly delineate and separate state and federal grounds for decison in its opinion, so as to insulate the decision from reversal by the United States Supreme Court. Decisions in state supreme courts, for example, frequently so intertwine first amendment and state common law doctrines that it is impossible to tell whether the decision rests on state or federal grounds.[33] This may occur because the lower court thinks that *the policies* in federal first amendment decisions should also inform the evolution of state common law doctrine.[34] In borrowing from first amendment theory, however, the lower court (the state supreme court, for example) should make it clear that it is acting solely in its capacity as an arbiter of the common law of the state and not resting its decision on the dictates of federal constitutional law. The significance of this state law basis is that if the decision is regarded by the United States Supreme Court as a decision compelled by the federal Constitution and grounded in the requirements of the first amendment, and if the decision proves to be based on erroneous reading of the Constitution, it may be reversed by the United States Supreme Court. If, however, the case merely is grounded in theory borrowed from the first amendment in an attempt to interpret state law, it is insulated from reversal, and it is also protected from evisceration by subsequent United States Supreme Court decisions. The reliance on state grounds, however, must be clear and explicit; the governing stan-

---

[33] *See, e.g.*, Colson v. Stieg, 89 Ill. 2d 205, 433 N.E.2d 246 (1982).

[34] *See* Smolla and Malone, *The Future of Defamation in Illinois After* Colson v. Stieg *and* Chapski v. Copley Press, Inc., 32 De Paul L. Rev. 219, 224-28 (1983).

dard employed by the Supreme Court was recently stated in *Michigan v. Long:*[35]

> Accordingly, when, as in this case, a state court decision fairly appears to rest primarily on federal law, or to be interwoven with the federal law, and when the adequacy and independence of any possible state law ground is not clear from the fact of the opinion, we will accept as the most reasonable explanation that the state court decided the case the way it did because it believed that federal law required it to do so. If a state court chooses merely to rely on federal precedents as it would on the precedents of all other jurisdictions, then it need only make clear by a plain statement in its judgment or opinion that the federal cases are being used only for the purpose of guidance, and do not themselves compel the result that the court has reached. In this way, both justice and judicial administration will be greatly improved. If the state court decision indicates clearly and expressly that it is alternatively based on bona fide separate, adequate, and independent grounds, we, of course, will not undertake to review the decision.[36]

The most significant recent example of the perils of confusing state common law and federal constitutional law in the context of *New York Times* and its progeny came in the "human cannonball case," *Zacchini v. Scripps-Howard Broadcasting Co.*[37] The case involved an entertainment act in which Hugo Zacchini was shot from a cannon into a net 200 feet away. A free-lance reporter filmed the act after Zacchini had explicitly asked him not to do so. The film clip, lasting 15 seconds and including a favorable commentary, was broadcast that evening on the local 11 o'clock news. The Ohio Supreme Court held that Ohio state tort law recognized a "right of publicity" that protected the commercial value of Zacchini's performance. This state-created tort gave Zacchini the right to prevent his name, likeness, or performance from being appropriated without his consent.[38]

The Ohio court's holding intertwined first amendment and common law concepts. The Ohio court placed its principal reliance on United States Supreme Court opinions after *New York Times*, primarily *Time, Inc. v. Hill.*[39] The Ohio court stated:

> [S]ince the gravamen of the issue in this case is not whether the degree of intrusion is reasonable, but whether First Amendment principles require that the right of privacy give way to the right to be informed of

[35] 103 S. Ct. 3469 (1983).

[36] *Id.* at 3476.

[37] 433 U.S. 562 (1977).

[38] *See supra* § 10.01[3].

[39] 385 U.S. 374 (1967).

> matters of public interest and concern, the concept of privilege seems the more useful and appropriate one.[40]

Moreover, the Ohio Supreme Court held that there is "a privilege to report matters of legitimate public interest even though such reports might intrude on matters otherwise private."[41] The United States Supreme Court granted certiorari and reversed.

Had the Ohio Supreme Court rested its decision explicitly on *both* state and federal grounds, *either of which* would have been dispositive, the United States Supreme Court would have had no jurisdiction to review the decision. The "independent and adequate state ground" doctrine precludes Supreme Court review of a state court judgment, even if that state court judgment erroneously interprets federal law, whenever the significance of the error concerning federal law is obviated by a state law precept which independently supports the judgment.[42] This lack of federal jurisdiction when an independent and adequate state ground exists stems from the Article III principle that federal courts may not render "advisory opinions"; if "the same judgment would be rendered by the state court after [the Supreme Court] corrected its views of federal laws, [the] review could amount to nothing more than an advisory opinion."[43]

In reviewing the Ohio court decision, the United States Supreme Court discussed the independent and adequate state ground issue and conceded that there was "no doubt that petitioner's complaint was grounded in state law and that the right of publicity which petitioner was held to possess was a right arising under Ohio law."[44] The Court further admitted that the "source of [the] privilege [on which the Ohio court relied] was not identified."[45] Nevertheless, the Supreme Court was convinced that a careful reading of the state supreme court's opinion indicated that the decision rested on the Ohio court's view of first amendment principles. The Ohio court's opinion was phrased in terms of first amendment doctrines, cited first amendment cases, and failed

---

[40] 47 Ohio St. 2d 224, 234 N.5, 351 N.E.2d 454, 461 n.5 (1976).

[41] *Id.* at 234, 35 N.E.2d at 461.

[42] *See generally* Michigan v. Long, 103 S. Ct. 3469 (1983).

[43] Zacchini v. Scripps-Howard Broadcasting Co., 433 U.S. 562, 566 (1977).

[44] *Id.*

[45] *Id.* at 568.

to mention the Ohio Constitution.[46] Far more critical to a media defense attorney, however, is the following statement made in *Zacchini:*

> Even if the judgment in favor of respondent must nevertheless be understood as ultimately resting on Ohio law, it appears that at the very least the Ohio court felt compelled by what it understood to be federal constitutional considerations to construe and apply its own law in the manner it did.[47]

It is prudent in light of *Zacchini* that defense counsel who believe that they will persuade the state court to adopt defenses more liberal than those required by the first amendment, and who feel there is some risk of Supreme Court review, also make efforts to convince the state court to clearly demark the independent and adequate state ground upon which the decision exclusively or alternatively rests.

§ 13.10 Publicity Surrounding Media Trials

[1] "Trying the Case in the Newspapers"

One or both sides of a defamation action may find it as important to influence public opinion as to win the litigation. In both the *Westmoreland* and *Sharon* cases the litigants were always conscious of media coverage and made what efforts they could to put their various positions in a favorable light.

[2] Discovery and Protective Orders

In *Seattle Times Co. v. Rhinehart*[48] the Supreme Court upheld a protective order barring disclosure by the defendant newspaper of information obtained by the newspaper during the course of extensive discovery, as part of a libel suit brought against the paper by a religious group. The court held that the order was not a prior restraint, and that the pretrial discovery process was not comparable to the rights of access that attach to a public trial. The Court found the order reasonable in light of the countervailing interests in free exercise of religion, which might have been adversely affected by the newspaper's dissemination of the information revealed in discovery.

Rhinehart thus to some degree lowers the leverage of defendants

---

[46] *Id.*
[47] *Id.*
[48] 104 S. Ct. 2199 (1984).

trying to use discovery as a tool for embarrassing the plaintiff through the publication of further stories, by opening up to plaintiffs the avenue of seeking protective orders.[49]

---

[49] *See generally* Tavoulareas v. Washington Post Co., 737 F2d 1170 (D.C. Cir. 1984) (opinion on protective order).

CHAPTER 14

Insurance

§ 14.01 Availability and Basic Terms

[1] Availability in General

Media insurance was once readily available at relatively modest cost.[1] This picture has changed. Economic factors within the insurance industry, the general increase in media litigation, and the escalation of media litigation defense costs have reduced the availability of media insurance, increased the cost of that insurance which is available, and restricted the scope of coverage. The number of domestic companies issuing media insurance is quite small. Among the companies issuing such insurance are Employer's Reinsurance Corporation, Media/Professional Insurance, Inc., and the Mutual Insurance Company Ltd. (insurance available only to members of the American Newspaper Pub-

---

[1] The information contained in this chapter is a brief synopsis of materials in Media Insurance and Risk Management 1985 (J. Lankeneau, ed.)(PLI) and information gathered by the author as a speaker and participant in the PLI conference from which the volume cited was published. The author gratefully acknowledges the insights gained from other participants and Chairman John Lankenau, and would strongly recommend the PLI publication from the conference to attorneys charged with negotiating coverage or handling claims on an ongoing basis.

lishers Association). Fireman's Fund, Chubb, and the Seaboard Companies also issue certain types of media insurance. The prospective purchaser in today's market is well advised to obtain the services of a qualified insurance broker.

[2] "Occurrence" vs. "Claims Made" Policies

Traditionally, the policies have been so-called occurrence policies, policies that provide insurance coverage for losses arising from events that take place during the specified coverage period, without regard to when the claim is asserted. There are indications, however, that media insurance may increasingly become available only on a "claims made" policy basis. A claims made policy essentially covers claims asserted during the specified policy period, without regard to when the events giving rise to the claim took place.

[3] Torts Covered

The available policies differ somewhat in their coverage of media related torts. The policy may be written in terms of "libel or slander or other defamation or disparaging material," or the policy may explicitly list other "satellite" causes of action such as intrusion, false light invasion of privacy, publication of embarrassing private facts, invasion of right of publicity, product disparagement, trade libel, infliction of emotional distress, or outrage. The purchaser of media insurance should be extremely careful in negotiating the specific inclusion of a wide range of torts covered, or sufficiently broad umbrella language, keeping in mind the nature of the media outlet's output.

§ 14.02 Factors in Setting Policy Provisions

Corresponding to the general deterioration of the media insurance market, media outlets no longer have the luxury of selecting their own levels of deductibles and coverage limits. Today the size of the deductible is often dictated by the insurance underwriter, and high limits on coverage may be prohibitively expensive. As one would expect, the factors weighed by the carrier in determining whether to accept an application for insurance and, if accepted, in determining the policy provisions, are directly related to the level of risk posed by the media outlet's operations. The list of factors below is suggested by the published remarks of Larry Worrall, President and General Counsel of Media/Professional Insurance, Inc.,[2] one of the principal issuers of media insurance:

[1] In-House Counsel

When an applicant has in-house counsel, particularly counsel of high quality and experience, that is a favorable factor.

[2] The Jurisdiction

Variations in state law and in the behavior patterns of juries within different states make the jurisdiction in which the outlet is most likely to be sued a significant factor.

[3] Reputation of Outside Counsel

The reputation, caliber, and expense of the outside law firms likely to represent an applicant in the event of litigation are, when known, factors considered.

[4] The Type of Media Outlet

The genre and style of the media outlet are significant factors. Risks vary considerably between book publishers, authors, television broadcasts, radio broadcasts, magazines, and newspapers.

[5] Degree of Investigative or Controversial Reporting

Tendencies to engage in hard-hitting investigative reporting, or to engage in publishing or reporting controversial stories, weigh against an applicant. (This is a prime example of the potential chilling effect of antimedia litigation on first amendment freedoms, for the high first amendment value in investigative reporting and coverage of controversial issues may be sacrificed when a media outlet or book publisher or author simply cannot obtain insurance coverage.) No matter how well documented and well written, some books may never be published because the risks posed make insurance prohibitive.

---

[2] *Id.*

[6] Publications or Broadcast Outlets of a Sexually Oriented Nature

Magazines and other media oriented toward sexual activity and nudity may be perceived by some insurance carriers as adverse risks, because of the fear that juries are apt to punish such outlets when they become embroiled in litigation. The same investigative story published in a "mainstream magazine" and in a "men's magazine" may fare drastically differently in the jury room, and insurance carriers are sensitive to this problem.

[7] Tendency to Sue Other Media Outlets

Although not technically related to an applicant's actual risk history, some insurance carriers may tend to look askance at media outlets that routinely engage in antimedia litigation against other media outlets, on the theory that "playing both sides of the first amendment fence" has a tendency to raise media litigation costs generally, create "bad" media law, and undercut public perceptions about the press.

CHAPTER 15

Defamation in the Workplace

§ 15.01 The Growing Significance of Employee/Employer Defamation Suits

[1] The Increasing Prevalence

Employers across the nation are facing an upsurge in defamation suits brought by discharged employees.[1] Defamation has become a commonplace in employee termination litigation. The defamation claim may be joined with other causes of action, such as wrongful discharge, or it may stand alone as the only theory of recovery. The *Wall Street Journal* has reported that approximately one-third of all defamation actions reported today are suits filed by fired employees against their former employers.[2] A prominent plaintiff's employment lawyer recently put the matter succintly: "Spread the word. Every wrongful discharge must be looked at as a defamation case."[3] A number of these suits, such as the case brought against singer Diana Ross, have had particularly high visibility,[4] and others have ended in substantial jury awards[5]—all of which tends to further fuel the surge in this type of litigation.

---

[1] *See* Middleton, *Employers Face Upsurge in Suits Over Defamation,* National L.J., May 4, 1987, at 1; Stricharchuk, *Fired Employees Turn the Reason for Dismissal into a Legal Weapon,* Wall St. J., Oct. 2, 1986, at 33.

See McCandless & Lofholm, *False & Defamatory,* The Brief (publication of the ABA Tort and Insurance Practice Section), vol. 16, no. 4, summer 1987, at 12; an article taken largely from a paper delivered by Ms. Sandra R. McCandless, of Graham & James, San Francisco, at the ABA Tort and Insurance Practice Section Spring Conference in Washington, D.C., in May 1987. The author wishes to express his sincere appreciation for the insights and expertise of Ms. McCandless and her co-author Mr. Lofholm, for Ms. McCandless's remarks at the conference and for the article cited above, which have been drawn upon throughout this chapter.

[2] Stricharchuk, *supra* note 1, at 33.

[3] Middleton, *supra* note 1, at 30 (quoting remarks of Paul H. Tobias, of Tobias & Kraus, Cincinnati, founder of Plaintiff Employment Lawyers Association).

[4] Davis v. Ross, 754 F.2d 80 (2d Cir. 1985). Diana Ross's case was a principal focus of a *Newsweek* article focusing on workplace defamation. *See The Revenge of the Fired,* Newsweek, Feb. 16, 1987, at 46-47.

[5] *See, e.g.,* Frank B. Hall & Co. v. Buck, 678 S.W.2d 612 (Tex. App. 1984), *cert. denied,* 472 U.S. 1009 (1985) ($1.9 million).

[2] Typical Situations Giving Rise to Suits

[a] Reference Letters and Other Communications to Third Parties

Traditionally, defamation suits brought against former employers by disgruntled employees arise in the context of unfavorable reference letters or other communications to third parties concerning the employee's job performance, or the circumstances surrounding the employee's termination.[6] Such suits have also arisen from communications to persons other than prospective new employers, such as reporters or customers.[7]

[b] Communications Within the Company

More recently, a second type of communication has begun to trigger defamation actions: communications completely internal to the company. Statements made to co-workers within the corporation concerning the reasons for an employee's discharge,[8] statements made in internal performance evaluations,[9] statements made during corporate office meetings,[10] in internal correspondence and memoranda,[11] and in internal security reports[12] have all been the basis for defamation actions. A variation on this theme involves communication by corporate person-

---

[6] *See, e.g.*, Davis v. Ross, 754 F.2d 80 (2d Cir. 1985); Marshall v. Brown, 141 Cal. App. 3d 408, 190 Cal. Rptr. 392 (1983); Frank B. Hall & Co., Inc. v. Buck, 678 S.W.2d 612 (Tex. App. 1984), *cert. denied*, 472 U.S. 1009 (1985).

[7] *See* Pittman v. Larson Distributing Co., 724 P.2d 1379 (Colo. App. 1986) (customer); Carney v. Memorial Hosp. & Nursing Home of Greene County, 64 N.Y.2d 770, 485 N.Y.S.2d 984, 475 N.E.2d 451 (1985) (reporter).

[8] Jones v. J.C. Penney Co., 164 Ga. App. 432, 297 S.E.2d 339 (1982).

[9] McCone v. New England Tel. & Tel. 393 Mass. 231, 471 N.E.2d 47 (1984).

[10] Loughry v. Lincoln First Bank, 67 N.Y.2d 369, 502 N.Y.S.2d 965, 494 N.E.2d 70 (Ct. App. 1986); Stukuls v. State, 42 N.Y.2d 272, 366 N.E.2d 829 (1977); Worley v. OPS, 686 P.2d 404 (Or. App. 1984); Benassi v. Georgia Pacific, 62 Or. App. 698, 662 P.2d 760, *as modified by* 63 Or. App. 672, 667 P.2d 532 (1983); Banas v. Matthews International Corp., 348 Pa. Super. 464, 502 A.2d 637 (1985); Bolling v. Baker, 671 S.W.2d 559 (Tex. App. 1984).

[11] Cashio v. Holt, 425 So. 2d 820 (La. App. 1983) (discharge letter); Franksom v. Design Space Int'l, 380 N.W.2d 560 (Minn. App. 1986) (internal memorandum); Bush v. Mullen, 478 So. 2d 313 (Miss. 1985) (intraoffice petition); Agriss v. Roadway Express, Inc., 483 A.2d 456 (Pa. Super. 1984) (warning letter); Gordon v. St. Joseph's Hosp., 496 A.2d 132 (R.I. 1985) (internal memorandum).

[12] Sturdivant v. Seabound Systems, 459 A.2d 1058 (D.C. App. 1983).

nel solely to the employee being fired, who then repeats the defamatory statements to prospective new employers when they question the applicant about the reasons for his or her termination from the prior job.[13] As discussed below,[14] these various forms of intracorporate communication have created increasing defamation litigation, as courts have steadily relaxed traditional restrictions concerning the definition of "publication" of the defamation to third parties.

[3] An Overview of Special Problems for Workplace Defamation

Theoretically, defamation cases arising in the workplace are governed by the same common law and constitutional law rules applicable to defamation suits generally. Workplace defamation suits, however, do have a special character of their own, first because they pose a number of unique doctrinal problems, and second because the practical dynamics of these suits are heavily colored by the broader issues of employer-employee relations law. Although the law of defamation generates the technical rules governing the employee's suit, those rules often take on a unique complexion in employee litigation, precisely because they are now being put to the service of regulating the employer's conduct, and thus cannot be separated from the larger picture of employer-employee relations.

The practical and philosophical significance of this importation of defamation as a new weapon in the plaintiff's arsenal in termination litigation is discussed later in this Chapter.[15] What follows first, however, is a series of sections discussing special problem areas in the implementation of traditional defamation rules in the context of employee suits. The reader should refer to the other chapters of this treatise for more complete discussion of these topics, as well as for discussion of those aspects of defamation litigation not singled out for special concern in the employee-employer context. The sections below merely emphasize those areas that appear to generate recurring difficulty in workplace defamation actions.

---

13 *See* Lewis v. Equitable Life Assur. Soc'y, 389 N.W.2d 876 (Minn. 1986).

14 *See infra* § 15.02.

15 *See infra* § 15.07.

§ 15.02 Publication

[1] Overview: Internal, External, and Compelled Self-Publication

"Publication" is an essential element of the cause of action for defamation; it is a term of art defined as communication to a "third person," someone other than the originator and the person defamed.[16] In the employee-employer context, any "external" communication of defamatory information to someone other than the employee will automatically satisfy the publication requirement. Difficulties begin to arise, however, with regard to "internal" communications—statements made by one member of the corporation to another.[17] A third, hybrid situation involves "compelled self-publication" in which the defamatory information is communicated by the corporation only to the discharged employee, who then repeats that information to a third party.[18] This is the most problematic publication issue of all, posing sharply competing policy considerations.

[2] Internal Communications

[a] The Minority No-Publication Position

The minority position is that purely intracorporate communications do not constitute publication to a third party.[19] The roots of this position may be traced to early cases involving stenographers. The seminal case, *Owen v. Ogilvie Publishing Co.,*[20] took the position that no publication took place when a general manager dictated a letter to one of the corporation's stenographers, a letter that expressed suspicion that the plaintiff had stolen money from the cash drawer. "It was a part of the manager's duty," the court stated, "to write letters for the corporation, and it was the duty of the stenographer to take such letter in shorthand."[21] The court then reasoned that the dictation of the letter was merely the corporation speaking to itself. "The manager could not write and publish a libel alone," the court noted, and thus "he could not charge the corporation with the consequences of this act, where the

---

16 *See supra* § 4.12[1].

17 *See infra* § 15.02[2].

18 *See infra* § 15.02[3].

19 *See generally* Lowhurst, *Intra-Corporate Communications: Sufficient for Defamation or Mere Corporate Babbling?* 7 Comm/Ent, L.J. 647 (1985).

20 32 A.D. 465, 53 N.Y.S. 1033 (1898).

21 *Id.* at 466; 53 N.Y.S. at 1034.

corporation, in the ordinary conduct of its business, required the action of the manager and the stenographer."[22]

A significant number of courts have found the no-publication position persuasive, at least in the narrow context of dictation, on the grounds that such dictation is a practical business necessity, in effect a mere mechanical extension of the speaker's own writing process.[23] As a Tennessee court put it, "the stenographer, if a coemployee in a corporation, has no distinct third party identity, and if an employee of an individual, is a confidential instrumentality only of the libelant, not recognized, when engaged in the performance of this mainly mechanical duty, as possessing an independent third party personality."[24]

Out of these stenographer decisions a handful of courts evolved a broader no-publication position, holding that no communication from one corporate employee to another was ever a publication.[25] The most famous statement of this position came in *Prins v. Holland-North American Mortgage Co.*,[26] involving an allegedly defamatory letter sent from a corporate headquarters to another corporate office. "For a corporation," the court held, "acting through one of its agents or representatives to send a libelous communication to another of its representatives cannot be a publication of the libel or the part of the corporation. It is but communicating with itself."[27]

This position continues to have adherents. In *K-Mart Corporation, Inc. v. Pendergrass*,[28] for example, the court held that no publication occurred when a report accusing an employee of theft was seen by no one other than corporate managers or employees of K-Mart. Similar results have been reached in a significant number of cases.[29]

---

22 *Id.* at 466-67; 53 N.Y.S. at 1034.

23 *See* Mims v. Metropolitan Life Ins. Co., 200 F.2d 800, 802 (5th Cir.), *cert. denied*, 345 U.S. 940 (1953); Burney v. Southern Ry., 276 Ala. 637, 641-42, 165 So. 2d 726, 730-31 (1964); Central of Ga. Ry. v. Jones, 18 Ga. App. 414, 89 S.E. 429 (1916); Satterfield v. McLellan Stores, 215 N.C. 582, 585-86, 2 S.E.2d 709, 711 (1939); Chalkley v. Atlantic Coast Line Ry., 150 Va. 301, 331-35, 143 S.E. 631, 639-40 (1928); Montgomery Ward & Co. v. Nance, 165 Va. 363, 380-81, 182 S.E. 264, 270-71 (1935).

24 Freeman v. Dayton Scale Co., 159 Tenn. 413, 421, 19 S.W.2d 255, 258 (1929).

25 *See* Lowhurst, *supra* note 19, at 657-61.

26 107 Wash. 206, 181 P. 680 (1919).

27 *Id.* at 208-09, 181 P. at 80-81.

28 494 So. 2d 600 (Ala. 1986).

29 *See* Western Union Tel. Co. v. Lesesne, 198 F.2d 154, 157-58 (4th Cir.), *cert. denied*, 344 U.S. 896 (1952); Halsell v. Kimberly-Clark Corp., 683 F.2d 285, 289 (8th Cir. 1982), *cert. denied*, 459 U.S. 1205 (1983); United States Steel Corp. v. Darby, 516 F.2d 961 (5th Cir. 1976); LuAllen v. Home Mission Bd. of Southern Baptist Convention, 125 Ga. App.

[b] The Majority Publication Position

A growing number of decisions have rejected the rationales of the no-publication rule.[30] In the dictation context, these decisions adopt the view that speaking to one's secretary or to a stenographer is not equivalent to speaking into an inanimate machine such as a tape recorder or using a personal computer but is, rather, a communication to another human being, who may well have diminished esteem for the person being defamed.[31] As one court put it, the "evil effect is in the loss of esteem by the stenographer in person, and not in any relation to the chief agent nor the common employer."[32]

If this rationale is persuasive in the narrow dictation context, it is even more compelling when more general forms of intracorporate communication are involved. For if dictation to a secretary may cause reputational damage, surely dissemination to other corporate managers or co-workers carries a substantially greater capacity to cause reputational harm. Cases have thus held that statements in discharge letters to the employee,[33] office petitions,[34] and internal security reports,[35] statements to co-workers,[36] warning letters,[37] statements in management or employee meetings,[38] performance evaluations,[39] and internal

---

456, 459, 188 S.E.2d 138, 140 (1972); Wyant v. S.C.M. Corp., 692 S.W.2d 814 (Ky. App. 1985); Ellis v. Jewish Hosp. of St. Louis, 581 S.W.2d 850 (Mo. App. 1979); Helleson v. Knaus Truck Lines, Inc., 370 S.W.2d 341, 344 (Mo. 1963); Jones v. Golden Spike Corp., 97 Nev. 24, 26-27, 623 P.2d 970-71 (1981); Magnolia Petroleum Co. v. Davidson, 194 Okla. 115, 119, 148 P.2d 468, 471 (1944); Flynn v. Reinke, 199 Wis. 124, 129-31, 225 N.W. 742, 744 (1929).

30 *See* Lowhurst, *supra* note 19, at 662.

31 *See, e.g.*, Globe Furniture Co. v. Wright, 265 F. 873 (D.C. Cir. 1920); Gambrill v. Schooley, 93 Md. 48, 48 A. 730 (1901); Ostrowe v. Lee, 256 N.Y. 36, 175 N.E. 505 (1931); Sun Life Assurrance Co. v. Bailey, 101 Va. 443, 445-46, 44 S.E. 692, 693 (1903).

32 Berry v. City of New York Ins. Co., 210 Ala. 369, 371, 98 So. 290, 292 (1923).

33 Cashio v. Holt, 425 So. 2d 820 (La. App. 1983).

34 Bush v. Mullen, 478 So. 2d 313 (Miss. 1985).

35 Sturdivant v. Seaboard Systems, 459 A.2d 1058 (D.C. App. 1983).

36 Jones v. J.C. Penney Co., 164 Ga. App. 432, 297 S.E.2d 339 (1982).

37 Agriss v. Roadway Express, Inc., 483 A.2d 456 (Pa. Super. 1984).

38 Loughry v. Lincoln First Bank, 67 N.Y.2d 369, 502 N.Y.S.2d 965, 494 N.E.2d 70 (1986); Worley v. OPS, 686 P.2d 404 (Or. App. 1984); Benassi v. Georgia Pacific, 62 Or. App. 698, 662 P.2d 760, *as modified by* 63 Or. App. 672, 667 P.2d 532 (Or. App. 1983); Banas v. Matthews International Corp., 502 A.2d 637 (Pa. Super. 1985); Bolling v. Baker, 671 S.W.2d 559 (Tex. App. 1984).

39 McCone v. New England Tel. & Tel., 393 Mass. 231, 471 N.E.2d 47 (1984).

memoranda or correspondence of all kinds[40] may constitute publication.

This now appears to be the majority position[41] and is gaining momentum. Those jurisdictions adopting this expansive view of internal publication effectively eliminate no-publication as a meaningful defense in workplace defamation cases, for it is hard to imagine defamatory statements concerning an employee that do not involve *some* contact with a third party, i.e., an employee other than the person defamed. The only sort of statement that would not quality as defamatory intracorporate defamation in such jurisdictions would be a simple one-on-one confrontation between the corporate employee speaking the defamation and the employee being defamed, with no one else listening, no further repetition to others, and no written version of the defamation even seen by anyone else. Except for this relatively rare scenario, publication will exist and the corporation will be forced to defend itself on some other ground, such as truth, opinion, or privilege.

[3] Compelled Self-Publication

[a] Overview

The most far-reaching relaxation of the publication requirement in workplace defamation cases has been the novel doctrine of "compelled self-publication." The traditional rule governing publication was that communication *only* to the person defamed was not publication, because no third party received the statement. Further, the repetition of the defamatory statement to a third party by the person defamed was not deemed publication by the originator—the logic being that the repetition was the victim's own doing and not the fault of the originator.[42] There was, however, an established exception to this rule: when the originator knew or should have known that communication to a third person was foreseeable, the originator would be charged with publication to that third party.[43] These cases, however, tended to involve repetition that was virtually inevitable, such as the reading of

---

[40] *See* Franksom v. Design Space Int'l, 380 N.W.2d 560 (Minn. App. 1986); Gordon v. St. Joseph's Hosp., 496 A.2d 132 (R.I. 1985).

[41] *See* Lowhurst, *supra* note 19, at 671; McCandless, *supra* note 1, at 14. *See also* Annot., *Libel and Slander: Dictation to Defendant's Secretary, Typist or Stenographer as Publication,* 62 A.L.R. 3d 1207 (1975).

[42] *See supra* § 4.12[4].

[43] *See id.*

letters by other family members, or by a third person reading the letter to a blind or illiterate recipient.[44]

The doctrine of compelled self-publication in the context of discharged employees widens this exception to completely swallow the rule. In jurisdictions accepting the doctrine, when defamatory statements are communicated directly to employees upon their discharge and those employees are then compelled to reveal to prospective new employers why they left their previous employment, such repetition of the defamatory statement will constitute publication by the first employer.

[b] Authority Supporting the Doctrine

[i] Early Authority

One of the first cases to involve compelled self-publication was *Colonial Stores, Inc. v. Barrett.*[45] During World War II, the War Manpower Commission required persons seeking employment to present a "certificate of availability" to prospective employers. The defendant, the former employer, actually wrote on this certificate the reasons for the plaintiff's discharge. The Georgia court held that publication by the original employer took place when the employee presented the certificate to the prospective new employee. It is worth noting that *Colonial Stores* represented only a modest advance on the traditional exception embodying foreseeable repetition to third persons, since the defamatory statement was written on a document which *by law* was required to be shown to future employers.

A significant jump occurred in *Grist v. Upjohn Co.,*[46] in which the allegedly false and defamatory statements were made orally, only to the plaintiff. The court held that publication could take place when the plaintiff repeated the communication to prospective employers. Similarly, in *McKinney v. County of Santa Clara,*[47] the doctrine was recognized in a suit by a discharged deputy sheriff against his former employer. The court stated that publication would be attributed to the

[44] *See* Roberts v. English Mfg. Co., 155 Ala. 414, 46 So. 752 (1908); Rummey v. Worthley, 186 Mass. 144, 71 N.E. 316 (1904); Thomson v. Cash, 119 N.H. 371, 402 A.2d 651, 653-54 (1979); Hedgpeth v. Coleman, 183 N.C. 309, 11 S.E. 517 (1922). *See also supra* § 4.12[2], [4].

[45] 73 Ga. App. 839, 38 S.E.2d 306 (1946).

[46] 16 Mich. App. 452, 168 N.W.2d 389 (1969).

[47] 110 Cal. App. 3d 787, 168 Cal. Rptr. 89 (1980).

originator of the defamation when the person defamed is "operating under a strong compulsion to republish the defamatory statement and the circumstances which create the strong compulsion are known to the originator of the defamatory statement at the time he communicates it to the person defamed."[48]

[ii] The *Lewis v. Equitable Life* Decision

The most significant recent decision supporting the theory of compelled self-publication is *Lewis v. Equitable Life Assurance Society,*[49] a case that may very well have turned heavily on its own somewhat egregious facts. The plaintiffs in *Lewis* were four women sent by the company, Equitable, from Minnesota to its Pittsburgh office to provide assistance for two weeks as dental claim approvers. None of the plaintiffs had ever traveled on business for Equitable before. They were briefed on expenses but not given a copy of the company expense guidelines. They were given travel allowances of $1,400. When they returned from their trips they were commended on the substantive work they had done in Pittsburgh. They were also told for the first time that they must submit expense reports. They prepared reports that accurately reflected their expenses. Equitable nevertheless asked the plaintiffs to modify the reports, because certain minor claimed expenses were not consistent with company policy. The employees made these changes. Equitable next, however, asked for further, more significant modifications; attempting to recoup approximately $200 from each plaintiff. The plaintiffs refused to make these changes, on the grounds that the claimed expenses were honestly incurred and were consistent with the oral instructions they had received prior to leaving for Pittsburgh. The company never disputed that in fact all of the claimed expenses were bona fide and honestly incurred. The company would not alter its demands, however, and the employees were first put on probation, and finally terminated for refusing to change their reports. The official reason for termination cited by the company was "gross insubordination." Because they were fired for gross insubordination, they received no severance pay.

In seeking new employment, the plaintiffs were asked by prospective employers to disclose the reasons for leaving Equitable. Each stated that she had been terminated for "gross insubordination" and attempt-

[48] *Id.* at 798-99; 168 Cal. Rptr. at 94.

[49] 389 N.W.2d 876 (Minn. 1986).

ed to explain the circumstances. Equitable never published in writing or stated orally the reasons for the discharge; its policy was to supply only the dates of employment and final job title of a former employee.

The four plaintiffs experienced varying difficulty in seeking subsequent employment; one was successful after disclosing the full story, another obtained employment only by lying on an initial job application and then explaining the truth in an interview; a third obtained a job only by leaving blank the application question concerning reasons for leaving her last job; a fourth never managed to get reemployed. All claimed to suffer emotional and financial hardship as a result of this sequence of events.

The Minnesota Supreme Court held that in these circumstances the repetition by the plaintiffs of the charges of "gross insubordination" to prospective new employers would constitute publication by Equitable. The concept of compelled self-publication, the court held, "does no more than hold the originator of the defamatory statement liable for damages caused by the statement where the originator knows, or should know, of circumstances whereby the defamed person has no reasonable means of avoiding publication of the statement or avoiding the resulting damages; in other words, in cases where the defamed person was compelled to publish the statement."[50]

[c] The Competing Interests

The doctrine of compelled self-publication has far-reaching implications. Although the expansion of the term "publication" to include purely intracorporate communication has already, in many jurisdictions, substantially broadened exposure to defamation liability from discharged employees,[51] the doctrine of compelled self-publication erases the last vestige of shelter. Under the doctrine, even a private, one-on-one confrontation between the "discharger" and the "dischargee" will result in publication when the dischargee repeats the statement to prospective new employers. For despite attempts to verbally circumscribe the doctrine with such limiting terminology as "strong compulsion to republish," cases such as *McKinney*[52] and *Lewis*[53] treat

50 *Id.* at 888.

51 *See supra* § 15.02[2].

52 McKinney v. County of Santa Clara, 110 Cal. App. 3d 787, 168 Cal. Rptr. 89 (1980). *See supra* § 15.02[3][b].

53 Lewis v. Equitable Life Assur. Soc'y., 389 N.W.2d 876 (Minn. 1986). *See supra* § 15.02[3][b].

subsequent job applications and interviews as sufficiently compelling to qualify.

From the employee's perspective, this compulsion is indeed quite real. Confronted with questions concerning the last job, the employee has only a limited range of options. He or she may be completely forthright, explaining the entire story and hoping that the person listening will be fair-minded. Alternatively, the applicant may lie, enduring the guilt of dishonest behavior and running the risk of being caught in the deception, an eventuality likely to be perceived as an incriminating admission that the applicant indeed had something to hide. A third option is to attempt to avoid the dilemma entirely by leaving questionnaires blank or answering evasively and hoping for the best.

The law of defamation certainly cannot put a premium on lying or evasiveness. Public policy appears to require that employees be encouraged to speak the truth about the circumstances surrounding their prior terminations. If that policy is accepted, the concept of compelled self-publication no longer seems as radical a departure from conventional rules governing publication as it once did. Honest, candid people *will* in fact be compelled to repeat the defamatory statements, and that repetition is well within the bounds of foreseeability traditionally required by the law of torts.

There are also, however, powerful competing interests. Public policy should encourage honesty and candor on the part of employers as well as employees; it will not do for the law of defamation to create rules that unreasonably discourage employers from "telling it like it is" to employees whom they are terminating. It seems bizarre, at best, to create legal incentives for the dissatisfied employer to say, "Employee, you are fired, but I cannot tell you why, for fear that you will be compelled to repeat the charge and then sue me for defamation."

The doctrine of compelled self-publication also carries a second set of baggage—the suspicion that it is simply the device through which liability for wrongful discharge may be recast under the rubric of defamation, opening the door to liability in those states that either do not recognize the wrongful discharge action or severely limit its availability.

Defendants are likely to perceive defamation claims brought by former employees as suits brought primarily for their nuisance value, with the high costs of defending the cases increasing the discharged employee's settlement leverage. Plaintiffs, on the other hand, are likely to perceive defamation actions as one of the few plausible legal avenues for redress of wrongful behavior by the employer, particularly in those states where the legal rules governing at-will employment remain harshly stacked against the employee.

The publication element of the tort of defamation is *not* the best legal vehicle for resolving these competing interests. There is no flexibility or subtlety to the element of publication: the defamatory speech is either published or it is not. Perhaps the best legal solution is to accept the doctrine of compelled self-publication in those instances in which the repetition of the defamatory statement by the discharged employee is essential if the employee is to avoid having to lie to the subsequent employee. At the same time that an expansive view of publication is recognized, however, courts should also take an expansive view of those defenses which more aptly embody the legitimate competing interests of the employer,[54] such as lack of defamatory meaning, opinion, and the related privilege and fault standards. Those defenses, unlike the publication element, are not mechanical all-or-nothing doctrines, they are, rather, flexible defenses that may be applied so as to rationally accommodate the competing interests. Defamation actions should not be a surrogate for wrongful discharge suits. If that is to be avoided, however, it should not be through a niggardly construction of "publication" but through a liberal construction of other defenses.

§ 15.03 Defamatory Meaning and Opinion

[1] Special Problems in Employee Evaluations

Employee evaluations pose special problems in determining the related issues of defamatory meaning and the fact/opinion distinction. Evaluations may be vague or evasive, they may carry innuendo understood by the recipient though not apparent on the face of the statement, and they may be nonactionable opinions rather than misstatements of facts. To insure the breathing space necessary for candid employee evaluations, courts should be specially sensitive to the possibility that the allegedly defamatory language is simply not actionable at all.

---

[54] *See infra* §§ 15.03, 15.05, 15.07.

[2] Defamatory Meaning

Many negative statements concerning an employee's work performance will easily satisfy the requirement of defamatory meaning.[55] Statements alleging fraud or dishonesty, sexual misconduct, alcohol or drug abuse, or simple incompetence will usually qualify.[56] The statements need not be sharply specific; in a recent California case, for example, liability was established by statements describing the employee as "erratic in work hours," as bringing "her personal problems to the office," and as causing her husband, a co-employee, "to have a mental breakdown."[57]

Courts should nevertheless be alert to the fact that many evaluations are simply too watered down and amorphous to qualify as carrying defamatory meaning. Typical statements such as "he no longer fit in with our plans," or "we felt we needed a change of direction," or we were "looking for new ideas" or a "fresh approach," or we "didn't like the way things were working out" should normally be dismissed as nondefamatory. The plaintiff may perceive these statements as mere euphemisms for more damning sentiments that the employer has left unsaid, and the plaintiff may very well feel that the stated grounds are irrational or unfair. But the law of defamation must be grounded in what is actually communicated; it is not a forum for trying causes of action based on unfair or arbitrary terminations. When the employer does not say anything negative to the employee, or to anyone else, beyond the sort of vague and neutral type of statement described above, the defamation count should be dismissed.

[3] The Fact/Opinion Distinction

In the employee evaluation context it is critical to remember that defamation must be predicated on false *statements of fact.* In the Supreme Court's *Gertz*[58] decision the Court stated that under the first

---

[55] *See generally supra* §§ 4.01-4.08.

[56] *See, e.g.,* Marshall v. Brown, 141 Cal. App. 3d 408, 190 Cal. Rptr. 392 (1983); Four Star Stage Lighting v. Merrick, 56 A.D.2d 767, 392 N.Y.S.2d 297 (1st Dept. 1977); Amelkin v. Commercial Trading Co., 23 A.D.2d 830, 259 N.Y.S.2d 396 (1st Dept. 1965), *aff'd,* 17 N.Y.2d 500, 214 N.E.2d 379, 267 N.Y.S.2d 218 (1966); Frank B. Hall & Co. v. Buck, 678 S.W.2d 612 (Tex. App. 1984). *cert. denied,* 472 U.S. 1009 (1985).

[57] Marshall v. Brown, 141 Cal. App. 3d 408, 190 Cal. Rptr. 392 (1983).

[58] Gertz v. Robert Welch, Inc., 418 U.S. 323 (1974). *See supra* § 6.03[3].

amendment "there is no such thing as a false idea,"[59] a statement that has generally come to be accepted as an absolute constitutional prohibition on liability for opinion.[60] The problem, of course, is to separate opinion from fact—a problem so thorny that an entire chapter of this treatise is devoted to the issue.[61]

In the context of employee evaluations, many statements have elements of factual content and subjective judgment intertwined, and fall into linguistic gray areas. Perhaps the most celebrated example involved entertainer Diana Ross, who circulated a reference letter stating with regard to seven former employees: "If I let an employee go, it's because either their work or their personal habits are not acceptable to me. I do not recommend these people."[62] The Second Circuit held that the letter was not a mere expression of opinion; rather it created a triable jury issue as to whether it carried defamatory factual meaning. After the decision Ross and the plaintiffs reached an undisclosed settlement, avoiding trial.[63]

A wide variety of tests have emerged under the fact/opinion distinction.[64] In applying those tests in the context of defamation in the workplace, courts should be particularly vigilant in not permitting the discredited doctrine of "unfair opinion" or "unreasonable opinion" to creep into the litigation.[65] If the statement is opinion, it is simply not actionable, even if it is unfair, unreasonable, capricious, or outrageous. It must be remembered that opinions may be damaging and yet not be actionable. An unfair opinion about an employee may very well harm that employee, but as long as it is mere opinion, the law of defamation cannot be asked to charge to the employee's rescue.[66]

Without intending to preempt the extended discussion of the fact/opinion dichotomy in other parts of this treatise, suffice it to say by way of summary that courts should be sensitive to such factors as the functional context of the communication,[67] the degree of subjectivity in tone

---

59 418 U.S. at 339.

60 *See supra* § 6.03[3].

61 *See* Chapter 6.

62 Davis v. Ross, 754 F.2d 80, 81 (2d Cir. 1985).

63 *See* Newsweek, *supra* § 15.01, note 4.

64 *See supra* §§ 6.04-6.08.

65 *See supra* § 6.02[3].

66 *See supra* § 6.09[2].

67 *See, e.g.*, Ollman v. Evans, 750 F.2d 970, 982-83 (D.C. Cir. 1983); Information Control Corp. v. Genesis One Computer Corp., 611 F.2d 781 (9th Cir. 1980). *See also supra* § 6.08[3][c].

and style of the evaluation,[68] the extent to which rhetorical hyperbole and figures of speech meant to convey subjective impressions are present,[69] the extent to which the statement involves judgments without objective verifiability,[70] and the extent to which the statement sets forth the factual predicate for the evaluation,[71] thus tipping off the recipient that the negative evaluation is merely the speaker's subjective assessment of the conclusions to be drawn from those facts.[72]

§ 15.04 The Per Se and Per Quod Special Harm Rules

Defamatory statements about employees may be either written "libels" or oral "slanders." In modern defamation law the significance of the libel/slander dichotomy rests in the relevance of that dichotomy to one issue: the sometimes-imposed requirement that a plaintiff plead and prove "special damages" or "special harm."[73] Special harm is a term of art in defamation that refers to actual pecuniary loss.[74] In a nutshell, the prevailing common law position (as discussed in detail in Chapter 7, there are a number of confusing variations among the states[75]) is that the plaintiff in an action for slander must prove special damages, unless the defamation falls within one of four special categories of "slander per se": (1) imputation of a serious crime involving moral turpitude; (2) possession of a loathsome disease; (3) an attack on the plaintiff's competency in his business, trade, or profession; or (4) unchastity in a woman.[76] Slanders not falling within these four categories (slanders "per quod")

---

[68] *See* Buckley v. Littell, 539 F.2d 882 (2d Cir. 1976), *cert. denied,* 429 U.S. 1062 (1977). *See also supra* § 6.12[5].

[69] *See, e.g.*, Old Dominion Branch No. 496, National Ass'n of Letter Carriers v. Austin, 418 U.S. 264 (1974); Greenbelt Cooperative Publishing Ass'n v. Bresler, 398 U.S. 6 (1970). "Rhetorical hyperbole" may be conceptualized as a defense going to the lack of defamatory meaning, or as an element in judging the statement to be opinion, or both. *See also supra* § 4.04[1].

[70] *See supra* § 6.07.

[71] *See* Lewis v. Time, Inc., 710 F.2d 549, 555-56 (9th Cir. 1983); Restatement (Second) of Torts § 566 (1977). *See also supra* § 6.04.

[72] *See* Burns v. Denver Post, Inc., 43 Colo. App. 325, 606 P.2d 1310, 1311 (1979). *See also supra* § 6.04[1].

[73] *See supra* § 7.01.

[74] Restatement (Second) of Torts § 575, comment b (1977).

[75] *See supra* §§ 7.04-7.07.

[76] *See supra* § 7.05. For a criticism of the sexism inherent in limiting the unchastity category to women only, with a suggestion that such a tort rule is inconsistent with modern equal protection clause jurisprudence, *see supra* § 7.05[5].

require special damages. Originally all libels were actionable without proof of special harm, but gradually the rule developed that libels in which the defamatory meaning was clear from the face of the words were actionable "per se" without proof of special damages, while libels requiring proof of extrinsic facts to support their defamatory meaning were considered "per quod" and did require special damages.[77]

In the context of defamation in the workplace, the defamatory statement will almost always, if oral, fall into the category of slander per se, since it will qualify as an attack on the plaintiff's competency in his or her business, trade, or profession. If the defamation is written, most libels involving defamation in the workplace will be sufficiently clear on their face to qualify as "libel per se." If the statement is sufficiently ambiguous to require proof of extrinsic facts to support its defamatory meaning, in many states special harm will need to be established.[78]

§ 15.05 Truth

[1] Substantial Truth

In the context of defamation in the workplace, the vital issues governing truth are the "substantial truth" doctrine and the question of who has the burden of proof. With regard to the substantial truth test, it is extremely important to keep in mind that the truth defense will protect the defendant from liability even if the precise literal truth of the defamatory statement cannot be established.[79] Minor inaccuracies in terminology or detail should not prevent a statement from being held "substantially true," as long as the "gist" or "sting" of the defamation is true.[80]

[2] Burden of Proof

The original common law position was that the defendant bore the burden of proving that the defamatory statements were true.[81] In

---

77 *See supra* § 7.06.

78 *See supra* § 7.06[3].

79 *See, e.g.*, Wehling v. CBS, 721 F.2d 506 (5th Cir. 1983); Alioto v. Cowles Communications, Inc., 623 F.2d 616 (9th Cir. 1980), *cert. denied*, 449 U.S. 1102 (1981). *See also supra* § 5.08.

80 *See supra* § 5.08[3].

81 *See* Restatement of Torts § 613(2)(a) (1938).

Philadelphia Newspapers, Inc. v. Hepps, [82] the Supreme Court held that the first amendment requires that the burden of proof be placed on the plaintiff to show that the defamatory statements are false, at least where the speech is on matters of public concern and there is a media defendant.

Hepps leaves open the question of where the burden of proof should lie in nonmedia cases involving private figures and issues of private concern—the prototypical pattern in an employee defamation suit. For the reasons stated at length in the analysis of the implications of *Hepps* in Chapter 5,[83] the better position is that plaintiffs should *always* bear the burden of proving truth in defamation cases, without regard to the public or private status of the plaintiff or the speech, and without regard to the media or nonmedia status of the defendant.

This is true particularly in the context of defamation in the workplace, where any other position is likely to have a highly stultifying effect on the marketplace. Since it is the employee invoking the cumbersome and costly machinery of defamation litigation, the employee should not have the luxury of simply filing suit and forcing the employer to establish that the stated reasons for the discharge were accurate. Under that rule every termination accompanied by negative reasons would be at the employer's peril. Those employees who have been lied about should generally be able to meet their burden of proof. The burden comes into play only when the evidence is in equipoise, when the trier-of-fact simply cannot tell where the truth lies. In those situations the better balance of competing social interests is for the employer to prevail. Placing the burden on the employee assists in providing breathing space for candid evaluations, and it tends to offset to some degree the threat of frivolous litigation filed only for its nuisance settlement value.

§ 15.06 Vicarious Liability

[1] Direct Liability

Vicarious liability is not an issue in employee defamation actions in those instances in which the person generating the defamatory statement holds a substantial ownership interest in the enterprise, or holds

82 106 S. Ct. 1558 (1986).

83 *See supra* § 5.07.

such high managerial or other corporate authority that the remarks are simply deemed to come directly from the corporation.[84]

[2] Vicarious Liability *(Respondeat Superior)*

[a] Overview

The doctrines of vicarious liability for the most part apply to defamation actions just as they would apply to tort law generally.[85] Defamation by an employee will be attributed to the employer if it takes place "within the scope of employment."[86] To be within the scope of employment, the conduct must be of the "same general nature as that authorized, or incidential to the conduct authorized."[87] Even when the conduct is *forbidden* by the employer, however, it will often still be deemed to be in the scope of employment.[88] Thus, if "an agent is guilty of defamation, the principal is liable so long as the agent was *apparently* authorized to make the defamatory statement."[89]

In *Frank B. Hall & Co., Inc. v. Buck,*[90] an investigator posing as a prospective employer interviewed (and tape recorded) the dismissed employee's ex-supervisor, who described the plaintiff as lacking in scruples, "a Jekyll and Hyde," a "classical sociopath"; the list went on. The court found that the company was vicariously liable for the supervisor's statements, upholding awards of $605,000 in compensatory damages and $1,300,000 in punitive damages. The supervisor, in his capacity as vice-president and office manager, was apparently authorized to furnish the information, and was furthering his employer's business interests.

Even employees not high in the chain of command may be held to be acting in the scope of employment, despite the fact that giving out information is contrary to company policy. In *Carter v. Willert Home*

---

84 *See* McCandless, *supra* § 15.01, note 1, at 9-10.

85 *See supra* § 3.36.

86 *See generally* Cantrell v. Forest City Publishing Co., 419 U.S. 245 (1974); Manale v. City of New Orleans, 673 F.2d 122 (5th Cir. 1982); Brewer v. American National Ins. Co., 636 F.2d 150 (6th Cir. 1980).

87 Restatement (Second) of Agency § 229(1).

88 American Soc'y of Mechanical Engineers v. Hydrolevel Corp., 456 U.S. 556 (1982); Michelson v. Exxon Research and Engineering, 629 F. Supp. 418 (W.D. Pa. 1986); Restatement (Second) of Agency §§ 230, 231.

89 American Society of Mechanical Engineers v. Hydrolevel Corp., 456 U.S. 556, 566 (1982) (emphasis added).

90 678 S.W.2d 612 (Tex. App. 1984), *cert. denied,* 472 U.S. 1009 (1985).

Products, Inc.,[91] a secretary in a corporation told a finance company conducting a credit check on another employee that the employee, who had applied for a loan, was on "disciplinary lay-off," "would probably be fired," and had "credit complaints" against her as well as "judgments and garnishments." The secretary worked in the corporation's personnel department and was responsible for answering employment verification inquiries, but she was not authorized to provide any information other than verification of employment. Nonetheless, the court held that a factual question existed as to whether the defamatory statements were "incidental to" or "in furtherance of" her assigned tasks, or whether they bespoke "personal feelings of antipathy" toward the employee.[92]

[b] The Libel/Slander Distinction

Libels are held subject to normal vicarious liability principles in all jurisdictions. Most states apply exactly the same *respondeat superior* rules to slander. A small minority of jurisdictions, however, follow the rule that the doctrine of *respondeat superior* does not apply to slander unless the employer expressly ordered or directed the subordinate to speak the words.[93] The logic of the minority position is apparently that slander is presumptively a verbal "frolic and detour" of sorts, an employee "popping off" on his own, carried away by passions or excitements that ought not be attributed to the employer.

[c] Punitive Damages

The states are divided as to whether normal vicarious liability rules apply to punitive damages.[94] Approximately 18 states make no distinction between compensatory damages and punitive damages for the purposes of *respondeat superior* analysis.[95] Approximately 24 states,[96]

---

[91] 714 S.W.2d 506 (Mo. 1986).

[92] *Id.* at 512.

[93] *See* Sires v. Luke, 544 F. Supp. 1155, 1159 (S.D. Ga. 1982); Republic Iron & Steel Co. v. Self, 68 S. 328 (Ala. 1915); Nelson v. M & M Prods., 168 Ga. App. 280, 308 S.E.2d 607 (1983); Georgia Power Co. v. Busbin, 242 Ga. 612, 250 S.E.2d 442 (1978).

[94] *See* Ghiandi & Kircher, Punitive Damages Law and Practice ch. 24, Table 24-1 (1986). *See generally* Parlee, *Vicarious Liability for Punitive Damages: Suggested Changes in the Law Through Policy Analysis*, 68 Marq. L. Rev. 27, 31-32 (1984); Note, *Corporate Vicarious Liability for Punitive Damages*, 1985 B.Y.U. L. Rev. 317.

[95] Ghiandi & Kircher, *supra* note 94, at Table 24-4.

[96] *Id.*

however, follow the *Restatement (Second) of Agency* position under which vicarious liability is not imposed for punitive damages unless there is complicity between the master and servant, e.g., authorization, participation, consent, or ratification of the employee's conduct.[97]

In *Loughry v. Lincoln First Bank*,[98] for example, a former employee of a bank alleged that he was defamed by the bank when a bank officer and another bank employee accused him of misappropriating bank property and dealing in illegal drugs. The court found vicarious liability for compensatory damages, but applying the New York complicity requirement for punitive damages, held that the employer could be liable "only when a superior officer in the course of employment orders, participates in, or ratifies outrageous conduct."[99] In a highly instructive analysis, the court held that on the facts before it, no such complicity existed. Although the bank officer involved was a vice-president and manager of the real estate department, the bank had as many as 150 such officers, and the bank officer who made the statement had no significant managerial role with regard to overall bank operations. To be a "superior officer," the court stated, does not require the individuals to be "in the executive suite or topmost reaches of corporate government,"[100] but it does require that "the agent's level of responsibility within the entity should be sufficiently high that his participation in the wrongdoing renders the employer blameworthy and arouses the 'institutional conscience' for corrective action, . . . thus serving both the punishment and deterrence goals of punitive damages."[101]

§ 15.07 Fault Considerations

[1] Constitutional Requirements

The elaborate discussion of constitutional fault rules set forth in Chapters 3 and 4 of this treatise is in theory fully applicable to employee defamation suits, but in practice such suits will tend to fall within a small

[97] Restatement (Second) of Agency § 217(c). *See also* Smith-Johnson Motor Corp. v. Hoffman Motors Corp., 411 F. Supp. 670 (E.D. Va. 1975); Hartman v. Shell Oil Co., 68 Cal. App. 3d 240, 137 Cal. Rptr. 244 (4th Dist. 1977); Remeikis v. Boss & Phelps, Inc., 419 A.2d 986 (D.C. App. 1980); Loughry v. Lincoln First Bank, 67 N.Y.2d 369, 502 N.Y.S.2d 965, 494 N.E.2d 70 (1986).

[98] 67 N.Y.2d 369, 502 N.Y.S.2d 965, 494 N.E.2d 70 (1986).

[99] 494 N.E.2d at 75.

[100] *Id.* at 76.

[101] *Id.* (citations omitted).

range of the constitutional spectrum: suits in which the plaintiffs are private figures, the defamation is published in a nonmedia context, and the subject matter does not involve an issue of public concern.[102]

It is possible, of course, for an employee defamation suit to implicate any combination of public or private plaintiffs, public or private subject matter, and media or nonmedia defendants. If CBS were to fire Dan Rather on the grounds that he took a bribe to cover up a political scandal, announcing its reasons to the world on the *CBS Evening News*, Rather's defamation suit would be governed by the actual malice standard, since he is clearly a public figure, the issue is one of public concern, and the speech was broadcast through a media outlet.[103] Alternatively, a private figure fired by an employer for allegedly having sex with other employees while carrying the AIDS virus would probably be constitutionally required, under *Gertz*, to prove negligence, since the defamatory statement involved an issue of public concern.[104]

These will be relatively rare cases, however; most suits by employees will be "garden variety" defamation actions brought by private figures involving issues relevant only to the employer/employee relationship, and likely to be classified as matters of mere private concern.[105]

As explained at length in Chapter 3, it is not at all clear whether any constitutional fault requirements are any longer applicable to private figure cases involving issues of private concern and a nonmedia defendant.[106] In theory, the *Dun & Bradstreet*[107] case might thus be construed to permit states to apply the original common law rule of strict liability in defamation actions by private figure employees against employers for defamation not involving public issues.[108]

Many states, of course, may very well choose not to attempt to "exploit" *Dun & Bradstreet* in this manner, opting instead to treat all private figure defamation cases the same way, imposing at minimum a negligence standard for all cases.

---

102 *See generally supra* § 3.05, Figure 3.1.

103 *See generally supra* § 2.02.

104 *See supra* § 3.03.

105 *See* Dun & Bradstreet, Inc. v. Greenmoss Builders, Inc., 472 U.S. 749 (1985). *See also supra* § 3.03.

106 *See supra* § 3.02[3].

107 Dun & Bradstreet, Inc. v. Greenmoss Builders, Inc., 472 U.S. 749 (1985).

108 *See supra* § 3.02[3].

[2] Common Law Requirements

[a] Common Law Privileges

In light of the diminished importance of first amendment protections for defendants in employee defamation suits, the traditional common law defamation privileges have become extremely important in such actions, carrying the load usually borne by first amendment defenses in other contexts.

[i] Absolute Privileges

Although the various absolute common law privileges[109] will usually be inapplicable in employee suits, there is some authority for treating grievance proceedings conducted under collective bargaining agreements as absolutely privileged.[110] Defamation against an employee will at times take place in quasi-judicial administrative proceedings, such as proceedings before a state unemployment agency or equal employment opportunity commission. States that extend an absolute privilege to quasi-judicial proceedings will thus absolutely shelter the employer for statements made in such hearings.[111]

[ii] Conditional Privileges

Several related common law conditional privileges are based on the defendant's acting to further his self-interest, the interest of others, or a "common" interest. One or more of these privileges will usually attach to evaluations of former employees.[112] A conditional privilege extends to such evaluations, whether they are from a present or past employer to a prospective employer[113] or "within the chain of com-

---

[109] *See supra* §§ 8.02-8.06.

[110] *See, e.g.*, General Motors Corp. v. Mendicki, 367 F.2d 66 (10th Cir. 1966); Jaftes v. Kaufman, 324 F. Supp. 660 (D.D.C. 1971).

[111] *See supra* § 8.03[a].

[112] *See supra* § 8.08.

[113] Molinar v. Western Electric Co., 525 F.2d 521, 532 (1st Cir. 1975), *cert. denied*, 424 U.S. 978 (1976); Arsenault v. Allegheny Airlines, Inc., 485 F. Supp. 1373, 1379 (D. Mass.), *aff'd mem.*, 636 F.2d 1199 (1st Cir. 1980), *cert. denied*, 454 U.S. 821 (1981); Zuschek v. Whitmoyer Laboratories, 430 F. Supp. 1163, 1166 (E.D. Pa. 1977), *aff'd without opinion*, 571 F.2d 573 (3d Cir. 1978); Weenig v. Wood, 169 Ind. App. 413, 349 N.E.2d 235, 248 (1986); Sindorf v. Jacron Sales Co., 27 Md. App. 53, 341 A.2d 856, 865-66 (Md. Spec. App. 1975), *aff'd*, 276 Md. 580, 350 A.2d 688 (1976); Bratt v. International Business Machines Corp., 392 Mass. 508, 467 N.E.2d 126, 129 (1984); Lewis v. Equitable Life Assur. Soc'y, 389 N.W.2d 876, 889 (Minn. 1986); Gengler v. Phelps, 92 N.M. 465, 589 P.2d 1056, 1058-59 (Ct. App. 1978); Cribbs v. Montgomery Ward & Co., 202 Or. 8, 272 P.2d 978, 981 (1954); Swanson v. Speidel Corp., 110 R.I. 335, 293 A.2d 307, 310 (1972); Frank B.

mand" by one employee charged with evaluating a fellow employee and reporting to a superior.[114]

Very few defamatory statements carry more potential for devastating harm to the victim than false and defamatory employee evaluations, and courts are thus faced with a powerful conflict between protecting the substantial social interest in candid and honest appraisals of an employee's competence and the equally substantial interest in safeguarding the employee from undeserved injury. The conditional privilege to publish such evaluations is thus well established, but by the same token courts are alert to potential abuses of the privilege, such as circulation of unfavorable evaluations to those with no need to see them, particularly when the charges involved are serious.[115] The privilege has been extended to others who make employee evaluations, for instance physicians[116] and private investigation agencies.[117]

As noted in Chapter 8, a wide variety of standards govern defeasance of a conditional privilege, or so-called abuse of privilege.[118] The conditional privilege may be abused, and lost, through excessive publication, for publishing for reasons other than the protection of the interest giving rise to the privilege, for common law ("ill will") malice, for negligence, or for constitutional "actual malice" (knowledge of falsity or reckless disregard for truth or falsity).[119]

Since a conditional privilege will virtually always attach, as an initial matter, to statements made about employees, the single most critical determinant of the fault level governing the litigation will be the inter-

---

Hall Co. v. Buck, 678 S.W.2d 612 (Tex. App. 1984), *cert. denied*, 472 U.S. 1009 (1985). Duncantell v. Universal Life Ins. Co., 446 S.W.2d 934, 937 (Tex. Civ. App. 1969).

114 Dillard Department Stores, v. Felton, 276 Ark. 304, 634 S.W.2d 135, 136 (1982); Dobbyn v. Nelson, 2 Kan. App. 2d 358, 579 P.2d 721, *aff'd*, 225 Kan. 56, 587 P.2d 315 (1978); Berger v. Gilbert, 65 A.D.2d 882, 410 N.Y.S.2d 427 (1978); Stukuls v. State, 42 N.Y.2d 272, 397 N.Y.S.2d 740, 366 N.E.2d 829 (1977). *See also* Gaines v. Cuna Mutual Ins. Soc'y, 681 F.2d 982, 987 (5th Cir. 1982).

115 *See* Dillard Department Stores, Inc. v. Felton, 276 Ark. 304, 634 S.W.2d 135, 136 (1982); Weenig v. Wood, 169 Ind. App. 413, 349 N.E.2d 235, 248-49 (1976); Stukuls v. State, 42 N.Y.2d 272, 397 N.Y.S.2d 740, 366 N.E.2d 829 (1977).

116 Hoesl v. United States, 451 F. Supp. 1170 (N.D. Cal. 1978), *aff'd*, 629 F.2d 586 (9th Cir. 1980).

117 Campbell v. Willmark Service System, 123 F.2d 204 (3d Cir. 1941); Roscoe v. Schoolitz, 105 Ariz. 310, 464 P.2d 333 (1970); Freeman v. Mills, 97 Cal. App. 2d 161, 217 P.2d 687 (1950); Pierson v. Robert Griffin Investigations, Inc., 92 Nev. 605, 555 P.2d 843 (1976).

118 *See supra* § 8.09.

119 *See supra* § 8.09.

pretation of what is minimally required, under the law of the state, to defease the conditional privilege.

[b] The Argument for Actual Malice as the Governing Privilege Standard

In states treating strict liability as the "base" liability principle,[120] the common law conditional privilege governing employee evaluations will merely operate to raise the level of fault to negligence. Unfortunately, from a defense perspective, a negligence standard is very often of little use in a defamation case tried before a jury, owing to the powerful psychological inclination of juries *to infer negligence from the mere fact that the report was false.*

If the conditional privilege is interpreted as requiring common law malice such as spite or ill will to support it, the defense will enjoy modestly enhanced protection. Even common law malice, however, is often a porous defense, because the mutual friction and antipathy that frequently surround an employee's termination will frequently provide ample ammunition for the plaintiff.

As a practical matter, the only truly meaningful defense is actual malice. Even if juries disregard the tough "knowledge of falsity or reckless disregard" standard, appellate courts have consistently enforced the standard with rigor. Some courts have applied the actual malice standard to common law privileges,[121] and, significantly, the *Restatement (Second) of Torts*[122] takes that position. The case for the actual malice rule in the employer/employee context is buttressed by a number of policy arguments. First, at least some type of fault above negligence is required to give the common law privilege meaning if the "base level" of fault is negligence.[123] Although *Dun & Bradstreet* may

---

[120] This includes only those states that would interpret the *Dun & Bradstreet* decision as authorizing a strict liability standard in nonmedia cases involving private plaintiffs and private speech. *See supra* § 3.02[3].

[121] *See, e.g.,* Molinar v. Western Electric Co., 525 F.2d 521, 532 (1st Cir. 1975), *cert. denied,* 424 U.S. 978 (1976); Arsenault v. Allegheny Airlines, Inc., 485 F. Supp 1373, 1379 (D. Mass.), *aff'd mem.,* 636 F.2d 1199 (1st Cir. 1980), *cert. denied,* 454 U.S. 821 (1981); Hoesl v. United States, 451 F. Supp. 1170, 1179 (N.D. Cal. 1978); Roemer v. Retail Credit Co., 3 Cal. App. 3d 368, 83 Cal., Rptr. 540 (1970); Marchesi v. Franchino, 283 Md. 131, 387 A.2d 1129, 1131-33 (1978); Bratt v. International Business Machines Corp., 392 Mass. 508, 467 N.E.2d 126, 129 (1984).

[122] Restatement (Second) of Torts § 600 (1977).

[123] The analysis that follows in this subsection is taken in part from Smolla, Dun and Bradstreet, Hepps *and* Liberty Lobby: *A New Analytic Primer on the Future Course of Defamation,* 75 Geo. L.J., Issue 6 (1987, forthcoming).

in effect invite states to return to strict liability in private speech/private figure situations, there are powerful reasons for states to decline the invitation. The common law rule of strict liability for defamation was an anomaly within the overall structure of tort law even before the *New York Times* decision began to constitutionalize defamation. Scholars disagree as to whether the primary liability rule prior to the emergence of that coherent body of law we now call "torts" was strict liability or negligence. With the industrial revolution and the birth of the law of torts as an independent doctrinal system, however, the lines of demarcation became quite clear. The dominant liability rule in America was negligence.[124] The full intellectual weight of common law theorists from Holmes to Cardozo to Hand stood behind the proposition that the cumbersome machinery of the state should not be cranked up to transfer injury losses from the victim to the causer unless the victim could bear the burden of proof that the causer was at fault.[125]

The tort system did have limited areas in which the negligence principle was displaced by a rule of strict liability. Strict liability was reserved, however, for a relatively narrow band of conduct, principally for activity that could be classified as ultrahazardous or abnormally dangerous.[126] Tests for strict liability may have varied slightly in verbal formulation from state to state, but the essential requirements remained the same: the activity had to be uncommon, and it had to be the sort of activity in which a high risk of harm could not be eliminated even through the observance of utmost care.[127] This division of labor between negligence and strict liability dominated the analytic struc-

---

124 *See* Schwartz, *Tort Law and the Economy in Nineteenth Century America: A Reinterpretation,* 90 Yale L.J. 1117, 1720-27 (1981). Prior to the industrial revolution, there was little systematic treatment of injury cases; the body of law we now call torts had only dimly begun to take shape.

125 *See, e.g.,* United States v. Carroll Towing Co., 159 F.2d 169 (2d Cir. 1947) (Hand. J.); Palsgraf v. Long Island R.R., 248 N.Y. 339, 162 N.E. 99 (1928) (Cardozo, J.); Adams v. Bullock, 227 N.Y. 208, 125 N.E. 93 (1919) (Cardozo, J.); O. Holmes, The Common Law 94 (1881) ("The general principle of our law is that loss from accident must lie where it falls, and this principle is not affected by the fact that a human being is the instrument of misfortune.").

126 Even the notion of strict liability for ultrahazardous activity had a haphazard start. It was applied with inconsistency because the strength of the fault principle had taken an enormously strong hold on late nineteenth century judicial consciousness. *Compare* Sullivan v. Dunham, 161 N.Y. 290, 555 N.E. 923 (1900), *and* Hay v. Cohoes, 2 N.Y. 159 (1849), *with* Booth v. Rome, W & O. T. R.R., 140 N.Y. 267, 35 N.E. 592 (1893), *and* Losee v. Buchanan, 51 N.Y. 476 (1873).

127 *See, e.g.,* Luthringer v. Moore, 31 Cal. 2d 489, 190 P.2d 1 (1948).

ture of the law of torts and it resulted in negligence as the reigning liability rule in most circumstances. In this analytic structure, however, defamation stuck out like a sore thumb.[128] The strict liability standard for defamation remained purely out of the inertia of history; there in a sea of negligence was an island of strict liability. None of the traditional justifications for strict liability could be applied to defend the standard for defamation. Speech was not uncommon—it was as common as breathing, indistinguishable from the thousands of routine activities of social life to which the negligence rule applied.[129] Nor was speech by any measure abnormally dangerous or ultrahazardous in the graphic sense of other strict liability applications—no analogy to dynamite blasting, keeping ferocious animals, or building reservoirs was plausible.[130] Strict liability for defamation was never, in fact, defended by anyone on these grounds, and the attempt would have been futile.[131]

For the most part, no genuine analytic defense of strict liability for defamation was made; the practice among scholars and courts was to obediently follow history, at times noting that the history largely made no sense.[132] To the extent any effort was made, it was along predictable lines—assertions of the strong state interest in protecting one's good name. That justification, however, was fatally flawed: it could not be made to fit in with the liability rules for all the rest of the law of torts.[133] Elsewhere, the law of torts did not look at how badly the victim was hurt but at the nature of the risks surrounding the causer's activity, in determining the proper liability rule. People could be killed, maimed, or ruined for life, yet, unless the activity was ultrahazardous, the liability rule would still be at least negligence.[134] Singling out reputational injury for a special liability rule was thus lame and illogical, for strict liability was not the dominant rule for most of the injuries compensable through the tort system, no matter how catastrophic.[135]

Once negligence is accepted as the appropriate base standard in all defamation actions, the additional step of imposing the actual malice standard in contexts covered by common law privileges is logically

128 *See* Smolla, *supra* note 123.

129 *Id.*

130 *Id.*

131 *Id.*

132 *Id.*

133 *Id.*

134 *Id.*

135 *Id.*

compelling. Some additional barrier to the plaintiff's case must be imposed, or the privilege is illusory, for it would add nothing to the plaintiff's burden not already there. The true debate, then, is whether to select common law ill will malice, or the actual malice "knowing or reckless" approach.[136]

Actual malice is superior for three reasons. The first is simplicity. The law of defamation is already ridiculously complex and chaotic; when in doubt, we should simplify. Actual malice is the standard when constitutional privileges are applicable; in the interest of symmetry and simplicity that same standard should govern the common law. The second rationale for actual malice is that is has teeth. Given the emotionally charged atmosphere often surrounding an employee's dismissal, a standard that focuses on ill will often will not meaningfully separate those cases worthy of protection for the employer from those in which genuine abuse of the privilege exists.

The final rationale is by far the most important, for it goes to the heart of the purpose underlying the privilege. Although *Dun & Bradstreet* and other very recent Supreme Court cases[137] have generally degraded the first amendment value of commercial speech, that trend only frees the states to reach their own policy judgments. States are under no compunction to reflexively rebound toward harsh pro-plaintiff rules. The common law privilege surrounding employee evaluations serves the enormously important interest of encouraging the free flow of information needed for efficient, intelligent hiring decisions.

As is so often the case with the modern law of torts, the tort system's apparently increasing sympathy toward employee defamation suits tends to work at cross-purposes with a number of other legal developments. The tort system has shown a willingness to embrace a new theory of liability for "negligent hiring," in which employers are sued for failing to properly investigate a new hiree.[138] The threat of defamation suits against former employers of course creates a disincentive to supply information about employees, the precise opposite of the value at which the action for negligent hiring is aimed. As a more general matter, there is a powerful social interest in well-informed hiring deci-

---

[136] *Id.*

[137] *See, e.g.*, Posades de Puerto Rico Assocs. v. Tourism Co. of Puerto Rico, 106 S. Ct. 2968 (1986). *See also supra* § 2.24[3].

[138] *See* Di Cosala v. Boy Scouts of America, 450 A.2d 508 (N.J. 1982); Silver, *Negligent Hiring Claims Take Off*, ABA Journal, May 1, 1987, at 72.

sions. To the extent that the threat of defamation clogs the free flow of information about employees, it exacts a heavy social cost.

Defamation actions may also act, ironically, to diminish the rights of employees. American society has gradually and painfully come to accept the wisdom of treating employees as individuals who deserve at least a reasonable degree of self-determination and dignity in the performance of job tasks and the evaluation of that performance. The threat of defamation suits does more than block the flow of information "externally"—from one employer to another employer—it also chills candor "internally"—between employer and employee within the workplace. The ideal of fair procedural treatment of employees is largely wrapped up in frank evaluations, with some opportunity for the employee to present his or her "case" to an impartial party, and with an opportunity for the employee to correct past deficiencies before it's too late. Defamation actions may well encourage internal silence because of the fear that candor may later come back to haunt the employer, particularly in jurisdictions embracing the doctrine of compelled self-publication. The aggregate impact of a proliferation of defamation actions may thus be to encourage employers to treat employees with less procedural fairness.

Finally, the cause of action for defamation in the workplace is too often a surrogate for another cause of action—the action for "bad faith" dismissal or "wrongful termination." If the societal goal in a state is to effectively eliminate, or at least substantially modify the traditional status of the employee at will, then the appropriate legal response is to take that step openly, by explicitly embracing the cause of action for wrongful discharge. In those states that have rejected that doctrinal change, opting instead to retain the common law rules giving the employer essentially unfettered freedom to terminate employees at will, it is important that that policy decision not be undercut by the creation of what is essentially a wrongful termination suit through the back door of defamation.

Defamation actions do have a constructive role to play in the workplace, as a legal check against the deliberate or reckless maligning of an employee. The potential destruction of the employee's career that may be created by the deliberate or reckless smear requires a defamation remedy even for employees at will. To permit recovery for conduct less than actual malice, however, is to grant insufficient breathing space for information about employees, a vital species of commercial speech.

Table of Cases

References are to sections and footnotes

References are to sections and footnotes

References are to sections and footnotes

References are to sections and footnotes

B

References are to sections and footnotes

References are to sections and footnotes

References are to sections and footnotes

References are to sections and footnotes

References are to sections and footnotes

References are to sections and footnotes

References are to sections and footnotes

References are to sections and footnotes

References are to sections and footnotes

References are to sections and footnotes

References are to sections and footnotes

References are to sections and footnotes

D

References are to sections and footnotes

References are to sections and footnotes

References are to sections and footnotes

E

References are to sections and footnotes

F

References are to sections and footnotes

References are to sections and footnotes

References are to sections and footnotes

References are to sections and footnotes

References are to sections and footnotes

References are to sections and footnotes

References are to sections and footnotes

References are to sections and footnotes

H

References are to sections and footnotes

References are to sections and footnotes

References are to sections and footnotes

References are to sections and footnotes

References are to sections and footnotes

References are to sections and footnotes

References are to sections and footnotes

K

References are to sections and footnotes

References are to sections and footnotes

L

References are to sections and footnotes

References are to sections and footnotes

References are to sections and footnotes

Mc

References are to sections and footnotes

References are to sections and footnotes

References are to sections and footnotes

References are to sections and footnotes

References are to sections and footnotes

References are to sections and footnotes

References are to sections and footnotes

References are to sections and footnotes

References are to sections and footnotes

References are to sections and footnotes

References are to sections and footnotes

References are to sections and footnotes

References are to sections and footnotes

R

References are to sections and footnotes

References are to sections and footnotes

References are to sections and footnotes

References are to sections and footnotes

S

References are to sections and footnotes

References are to sections and footnotes

References are to sections and footnotes

References are to sections and footnotes

References are to sections and footnotes

References are to sections and footnotes

T

References are to sections and footnotes

References are to sections and footnotes

References are to sections and footnotes

U

References are to sections and footnotes

References are to sections and footnotes

W

References are to sections and footnotes

References are to sections and footnotes

References are to sections and footnotes

Y

Z

Index

References are to sections

References are to sections

References are to sections

References are to sections

References are to sections

References are to sections

References are to sections

References are to sections

References are to sections

References are to sections

References are to sections

References are to sections

References are to sections

References are to sections

References are to sections

References are to sections